Like a Tree Universally Spread

OXFORD STUDIES IN WESTERN ESOTERICISM

Series Editor
Henrik Bogdan, University of Gothenburg

Editorial Board
Jean-Pierre Brach, École Pratique des Hautes Études
Carole Cusack, University of Sydney
Christine Ferguson, University of Stirling
Olav Hammer, University of Southern Denmark
Wouter Hanegraaff, University of Amsterdam
Ronald Hutton, University of Bristol
Jeffrey Kripal, Rice University
James R. Lewis, University of Tromsø
Michael Stausberg, University of Bergen
Egil Asprem, University of Stockholm
Dylan Burns, Freie Universität Berlin
Gordon Djurdjevic, Siimon Fraser University
Peter Forshaw, University of Amsterdam
Jesper Aa. Petersen, Norwegian University of Science and Technology

INITIATING THE MILLENIUM
The Avignon Society and Illuminism in Europe
Robert Collis and Natalie Bayer

IMAGINING THE EAST
The Early Theosophical Society
Tim Rudbog and Erik Sand

MYSTIFYING KABBALAH
Academic Scholarship, National Theology, and New Age
Boaz Huss

SPIRITUAL ALCHEMY
From Jacob Boehme to Mary Anne Atwood
Mike A. Zuber

THE SUBTLE BODY
A Genealogy
Simon Cox

OCCULT IMPERIUM
Arturo Reghini, Roman Traditionalism, and the Anti-Modern Reaction in Fascist Italy
Christian Giudice

VESTIGES OF A PHILOSOPHY
Matter, the Meta-Spiritual, and the Forgotten Bergson
John Ó Maoilearca

LIKE A TREE UNIVERSALLY SPREAD
Sri Sabhapati Swami and Śivarājayoga
Keith Edward Cantú

Like a Tree Universally Spread

Sri Sabhapati Swami and Śivarājayoga

KEITH EDWARD CANTÚ

OXFORD
UNIVERSITY PRESS

OXFORD
UNIVERSITY PRESS

Oxford University Press is a department of the University of Oxford. It furthers the University's objective of excellence in research, scholarship, and education by publishing worldwide. Oxford is a registered trade mark of Oxford University Press in the UK and certain other countries.

Published in the United States of America by Oxford University Press
198 Madison Avenue, New York, NY 10016, United States of America.

Library of Congress Cataloging-in-Publication Data
Names: Cantú, Keith E., 1988– author.
Title: Like a tree universally spread : Sri Sabhapati Swami and Śivarājayoga / Dr. Keith Edward Cantú.
Description: 1. | New York : Oxford University Press, 2023. |
Series: Oxford studies in western esotericism |
Includes bibliographical references and index.
Identifiers: LCCN 2023006054 (print) | LCCN 2023006055 (ebook) |
ISBN 9780197665473 (hardback) | ISBN 9780197665497 (epub)
Subjects: LCSH: Śivarājayoga. | Capāpati Cuvāmikaḷ.
Classification: LCC BL1238.56.S45 .C36 2023 (print) |
LCC BL1238.56.S45 (ebook) | DDC 294.5/436—dc23/eng20230512
LC record available at https://lccn.loc.gov/2023006054
LC ebook record available at https://lccn.loc.gov/2023006055

DOI: 10.1093/oso/9780197665473.001.0001

Printed by Integrated Books International, United States of America

for Nasrin and Eddie,
who light up my life with love and liberty

Contents

List of Illustrations xi
Acknowledgments xvii
Abbreviations xxi

Introduction: Like a Tree Universally Spread 1
From Hidden Roots to Outer Blossoms 2
A Treelike "Translocalization" of Yoga 6
The Chapters and Methodology of This Book 11

1. Hagiographies and Old Diary Leaves 19
Extant Sources for Sabhapati's Life 20
Sabhapati's Childhood 23
A Search for Spiritual Truth 28
A Visionary Experience in Velachery 34
A Southbound Quest 39
Lectures and a Himalayan Flight 47
A Splash on the Lahore Scene 51
Shrish Chandra Basu and the Theosophical "Founders" 52
John Campbell Oman and "Sadhuism" 64
A Vision of Agastya Once in Fifty Years 66
Sabhapati in Bombay 71
Agastya and the Konnur Meditation Hall 72
South Indians to the Fore 76
Om Prakash Swamigal 77
Konnur Ramalinga Swamigal 84
Sabhapati Swami's Death and Disappearance 94

2. A Vast Forest of Printed Words 114
Textual Stemmata of Sabhapati's Works 116
The Alpha Stemma 117
Three Original Editions of VRY 117
CPSPS as Alpha Stemma 120
Detailed Contents of the Alpha Stemma 123
Bengali and German Translations 126
William Estep's *Esoteric Cosmic Yogi Science* 128
The Beta and Gamma Stemmata 129
Contextualizing Sabhapati's Vernacular Works 129

CPSPS as Beta and Gamma Stemmata 130
CTCSPV and the Gamma Stemma 132
RYB and the Beta Stemma 134
Pamphlets for Konnur Meditation Hall 138
Sabhapati's Literature in Telugu 143
Sabhapati's Tamil Work MCVTS 145

3. Seeds of a Cosmological Religion 154
Sabhapati's Two Gurus 157
Chidambara Swamigal and "Instructive Truth" 158
Shivajnana Bodha and the Tamil Siddhas 163
An Embodied Cosmos 167
Shiva as "Infinite Spirit" 168
A Cosmogonic Separation of "Faculties" 169
"Illustration by Examples" 171
The Tree Universally Spread 172
Emancipation and Transmigration 186
Household of the Body's Truth (*dehatattva*) 188
Connections with Tamil Śaiva Discourse 195
Views on Other Religions and Movements 201
Sabhapati and Buddhism 203
Sabhapati and Christianity 204
Sabhapati and Islam 207
Sabhapati and Zoroastrianism, or "Parsism" 208
Sabhapati and "Samajees" 211
Sabhapati and the "Theosophical Societies" 214
Sabhapati and Atheism 217

4. Breathing into Śivarājayoga 237
Three Branches of Yoga 238
Haṭha Yoga or "Yoga of Force" 240
Haṭha Rājayoga or "Royal Yoga of Force" 250
Śivarājayoga or "Royal Yoga for Shiva" 256
Śivarājayoga: From Purification to Nonbeing 260

5. Singing Mantras and Visualizing Flowers 279
Lyrical Compositions and Musical Poems 280
Incantation of Tones and Mantras 285
Sabhapati's Visual Diagrams 290
Changing Visual Representations 292
Svarūpa and Yoga 302

6. Dissecting the Nature of Śivarājayoga 313
Spiritual and Physical Phenomena 316
The Pure Ethers 323
A Naturalistic Cosmology of Yoga 329

7. Magical Fruits of Occult Yoga 356
Sabhapati and Theosophy 358
Franz Hartmann and Sabhapati in German Translation 360
Sabhapati and Thelemic "Magick" 362
William Estep and "Super Mind Science" 372

Epilogue: Parts of a Universal Tree 386

Appendix 1. A Translation of T2 *(in* MCVTS*)* 391
Excerpt of T2 (English Translation) 391
Excerpt of T2 (Original Tamil) 400
Appendix 2. Lexicon of Common Terms and Variants 409
Appendix 3. A Passage from VRY1 *on the "Pole" of Śivarājayoga* 413
References 429
Index 449

Illustrations

Figures

I.1. A schema to understand transitions between local, mesolocal, and translocal receptions of Sabhapati's literature as well as a phenomenon of "relocalization." 8

1.1. A map of several sites in South Asia associated with Sri Sabhapati Swami's life and works. Map created by the author. 24

1.2. C.S.I. Anderson Church on the Esplanade (today NSC Bose Road). Photo by the author. 27

1.3. An image of Vedashreni Chidambara Swamigal at his tumulus. Photo by the author. 30

1.4. A busy street around the Nagore Dargah. Photo by the author. 31

1.5. Dandeeswarar Vedashreni Temple as seen from the tank (Tam. *kuḷam*). Photo by the author. 37

1.6. An illustration from MCVTS depicting the southern Kailāsa mountain of Agastya's succession of gurus and students (Mpvl. *takṣaṇakailāca akastiyācalà parvata kurucişya pāramparaiya* [*sic*] *paṭam*). Photo by the author. 43

1.7. An illustration from CTCSPV depicting the "hermitage of the great rishi Agastya of the sacred Southern Kailāsa, the great Meru which is the Pothigai mountain" (Mpvl. *śrītakṣaṇakaiyilāsa mahāmēru potikācala akastiyamahāriṣi āsramam*). I am grateful to David Gordon White and Gudrun Bühnemann for respectively pointing out that a similar style of depicting yogis in pod-like caves was employed in at least one miniature by Purkhu of Kangra (ca. 1800–1815) and in a painting by Dakṣiṇāmūrti on Kailāsa (late eighteenth century, Tanjore style). Scan by the author. 44

1.8. The Basu brothers and some of their activities. Published in the Bengali journal *Prabāsī*, vol. 30, and photographed with permission at the Visva-Bharati University library (out of copyright). 54

1.9. The "Yogi's Admirers" (CPSPS, First Book, 24). Scan from copy of 1884 edition, courtesy of Bill Breeze. 69

1.10. A list of Sabhapati's new wave of Tamilian students who helped make MCVTS possible, published in MCVTS, 6. Photo by the author. 77

1.11. An undated (early twentieth-century) photograph of Om Prakash Swamigal on display at his hermitage and adorned with a garland. Photo by the author. 78

1.12. A woodblock portrait of Sabhapati as Guru Father Rishi from MCVTS. Photo by the author. 88

1.13. A painting of Konnur Ramalinga Swami now in the personal collection of the author. 89

1.14. An inscription showing the establishment of a *maṭam* in Murugambakkam by "Koṉṉūr Śrī Irāmaliṅkasvāmi" and the date of his *samādhi* or "composition" (i.e. death). Photo by the author. 90

1.15. A portion of the village survey map of "Konnur," "No. 71," traced "from the Original map of 1906" and obtained upon request at the Central Survey Office in Chepauk, Chennai. Sri Sabhapathy Lingeshwarar Koil is located in or near No. 343 with Sowmya Damodara Perumal Temple to the east with a still-extant temple tank (*kuḷam*), matching directions given in MCVTS. Photo by the author. 92

1.16. The *liṅga* traditionally associated with Sabhapati Swami's *jīva-samādhi* or tumulus at Sri Sabhapathy Lingeshwarar Koil. Photo by the author. 95

2.1. A chart depicting three principal textual stemmata of Sabhapati's works from 1880 to 1930 and their date of publication. Lines without arrows indicate parallel sources or intertextual references, while lines with arrows indicate a source relationship. 117

2.2. An advertisement found in the long edition of MCVTS that provides an example as to how CPSPS, not editions of VRY, was advertised among Sabhapati's works in three vernacular languages (Tamil, Hindi, and Telugu). Photo by the author. 125

2.3. An advertisement for CPSPS and CTCSPV found in the copy of RYB held at Om Prakash's *āśrama* in Kandal, near Ooty. Photo by the author. 131

2.4. A diagram of Sabhapati Swami given in CTCSPV, published in 1889. Photo by the author. 135

2.5. A diagram of Sabhapati Swami given in RYB, published in 1892. Photo by the author. 136

2.6. A handwritten dedication in a copy of RYB by Sabhapati's student Om Prakash Swamigal to one of his own disciples, Jashabhai Bhailal Bhai Patel of Gujarat. Photo by the author. 137

2.7. The title page of the copy of RYB dedicated to Jashabhai Bhailal Bhai Patel. Photo by the author. 139

2.8. Advertisements (*viḷamparaṅkaḷ*) from CĀT that show the pamphlets from the Konnur Meditation Hall and CPSPS. Photo by the author. 140

2.9. A photograph of the title page and/or cover page for MCVTS, from a laminated copy held by the Adyar Library. Photo by the author. 146

3.1. A page from Śrī Kumāratēvar, *Tiruvāymalarntaruḷiya cāstirakkōvai* that lists the names as part of a "history of the monastery" (*ātīṉavaralāṟu*). Photo by the author. 161

3.2. The tumulus of Mylapore Kuzhandaivel Swamigal (Mayilāppūr Kuḻandaivēl Cuvāmikaḷ), guru of Vedashreni Chidambara Swamigal (Vētacirēṇi Citampara Cuvāmikaḷ). Photo by the author. 162

3.3. An inscription at the tumulus of Mylapore Kuzhandaivel Swamigal that records his guru as Kumara Devar (Kumāratēvar) and another of his students as Muttaiya Swamigal (Muttaiyacuvāmikaḷ). Photo by the author. 163

3.4. The opening praise of MCVTS that mentions Sabhapati as a student of both Vedashreni Chidambara Swamigal (Vētacirēṇi Citampara Cuvāmikaḷ) in the *ātiṉam* of Kumara Devar (Kumāratēvar) as well as Shivajnana Bodha Rishi (Civanāṉabōta Ruṣi), the student of Agastya (Akasttiyar). Photo by the author. 164

3.5. Idols of some Tamil Siddha figures, including Tirumūlar and Irāmatēvar, in the tumulus of Vedashreni Chidambara Swamigal. Photo by the author. 165

3.6. A diagram of the "descent" or "emanations" of the Universal Spirit in the "thirty-two faculties," as outlined in editions of VRY and CPSPS. The idiosyncratic translations of "Prudence" for *kalā*, "Memory" for *nāda*, and so on are not direct translations but rather an attempt to communicate the embodied characteristics and qualities of each tattva or cakra in question. 173

3.7. A portion of the first main diagram in the First Book of CPSPS, between pages 24 and 25, entitled "The Posture of Brumha Gnyana Siva Raja Yoga Samadhi or Infinite Spiritual Communion." The letters (A through T) refer to the "Four Brightnesses" and the "Sixteen Rays," and the numbers 7 to 12 are the higher six of the twelve "Spiritual Lights" or cakras (see Figure 3.6 above). Scan from copy of 1884 edition, courtesy of Bill Breeze. 175

3.8. A diagram in CTCSPV containing "instruction on the mystery of the steadfast state of the yoga of gnosis, [namely] the states of mind, the states of knowledge, the states of the actions of the five causes, and the seven self-states of the eight inherent natures (*svarūpa*)" (*aṣṭa corupaṅkaḷiṉ maṉōpāva aṟivupāva pañcakāraṇakāriyapāva saptaham sapāva ñāṉayōka niṣṭaipāvarahasciya upatēcattiṟ kuṟiyapaṭam*), the cosmic *svarūpa*s being located along the central channel where one would expect to find cakras. Scan by the author. 177

3.9. Diagram Eight of CTCSPV that shows transmigrations in a "Snakes and Ladders" form. Scan by the author. 189

3.10. Chart from CTCSPV depicting the "truth of the body" (Mpvl. *tēkatattuvam*, = Skt. *dehatattva*). Scan by the author. 190

3.11. English translation of Figure 3.10 (original is in Tamil only), maintaining some of Sabhapati's own translations in his English works (such as "Finite Spirit" for *jīvātman*) for ease of comparison and contrast with the principles of VRY1 and CPSPS. 190

4.1. "Diagram Number Three, for the Description of Chapter Five / A diagram for the nine types of haṭha yoga and three types of *prāṇāyāma*" (Hi. *nakśā* (3) *tīn pañcam adhyāykā vivaraṇ / navavidh haṭayoga nimita aur trividh prāṇāyām nimitta nakśā*). This diagram is between pages 60 and 61 of RYB. Photo by the author of a copy held by the Adyar Library and Research Centre. 249

4.2. "Mysterious instruction on the four kinds of [temple] abodes" (*caturvita ālayaṅkaḷiṉ rakaciya upatēcam*), found in CTCSPV. Scan by the author. 259

4.3. "Diagram Number Five, for the Description of Chapter Seven / A diagram for the purposes of practicing all types of Śivarāja Jñāna Yoga" (Hi. *saptam adhyāy vivaraṇ—gintī (5) nakśā / sarvavidhi śivarāja jñānayoga abhyāske nimitt nakśā*). This diagram is between pages 88 and 89 of RYB, immediately preceding the seventh chapter. Photo by the author of a copy held by the Adyar Library and Research Centre. 267

4.4. "The Seventh Diagram, being an image of the ritual, practice, and experience of the steadfast absorption of the Royal Yoga for Shiva, which is the gnosis of the Infinite Spirit." From a copy of MCVTS held by Saraswathi Mahal Library in Thanjavur. 269

5.1. "Diagram on the students and community (Tam. *caṅkam*, < Skt. *saṅgha*) carrying out the instructions (< Skt. *upadeśa*) of the guru" (Tam. *ciṣyarkaḷ caṅkattōṭu kuru upatēcañ ceyyum paṭam*). This diagram was only preserved in two longer versions of MCVTS held at the Adyar Library and the Saraswathi Mahal Library in Thanjavur. Scan courtesy Siddhanai of the Tamil Digital Library, originally from the Saraswathi Mahal Library version (out of copyright). 282

5.2. A hand-painted replica by Sai Sampath, a local Chennai artist, of the original diagram in VRY (1880), with minor corrections in Photoshop by the author to make a few details match more closely. Original artwork in the author's personal collection. 293

5.3. The new version of the VRY1 diagram on the posture of samādhi, published in CPSPS, First Book (1884). Notice the addition of a legend at the bottom as well as the inclusion of new anatomical details, such as the brain and lungs, which were absent in the original diagram. Scan courtesy Bill Breeze (now in public domain). 295

5.4. A diagram in RYB (1892) entitled "Diagram Number Five, for the Description of Chapters One, Two, and Three / A diagram for the sixteen self-purifications of the mind, the knowledge of the principles, and meditation on the dissolution of the cakras (Hi. *nakśā* (1) *ek / pratham, dvitīya aur tṛtīya adhyāyoṅkā vivaraṇ / ṣoḍaśa mano ātmaśuddhi, tatvajñān aur dvādaś cakra layadhyānke nimitta nakśā*). Photo by the author. 297

5.5. A diagram in MCVTS (1913) that depicts similar content to Figures 5.2 through 5.4. Here the lotuses are numbered in more detail and the brain is also anatomically depicted as simple wavy lines. I am grateful to Scott Wilde for restoring this image from a distorted laminated version. Photo by the author at the Adyar Library and Research Centre. 298

5.6. A depiction in CTCSPV (1889) of Sabhapati Swami, his ritual implements, three of his students (including, notably for the time, a female student in the center), and a scribe. Scan by the author. 300

5.7. A depiction in CTCSPV (1889) of the landscapes of yoga, or different areas where *maṭālayam*s or what Sabhapati called "meditation halls" were to be located, and details on their construction. Scan by the author. 301

5.8. A depiction in CTCSPV (1889) of the training, meditative, and postural activity that would happen at these meditation halls, and a depiction of worship at a temple. Scan by the author. 302

5.9. A diagram published in CPSPS, Second Book (1890), entitled "No. 3 Diagram for Seven Spiritual States of God [*svarūpa*s] and for fifteen sorts of the Purifications of the Mind & Soul to get Godhead and Salvation." Photo by the author at the Adyar Library and Research Centre. 306

6.1. An excerpt from CTCSPV, page 27, that mentions oxygen and nitrogen in the context of what Sabhapati called "Phenomena." Scan by the author. 321

6.2. The title page of BRY, the Bengali translation of Sabhapati's lectures in which Ambikacharan's prologue appeared. Scan of an original copy consulted at the National Library of India (public domain). 330

7.1. "Zur Physiologie des Astralkörpers," published in the first edition of Franz Hartmann's work (FH1) and prompting a later note by Theosophical publishers to stress a distinction between the "etheric" and "astral" bodies. Scan by the author. 362

7.2. A portrait of Aleister Crowley published in *The Rites of Eleusis* (1910), likely depicting a YONI on account of Crowley being framed by a "vesica piscis," a shape he consciously employed and wrote about in his works. Photo by the author of a copy held in the Adyar Library and Research Centre. 363

7.3. A diagram from "Liber XIII" (1910) in *The Equinox* that includes the lower degrees of A.∴A.∴, which culminate in the "Knowledge and Conversation of the Holy Guardian Angel." One of two meditations related to Sabhapati's Śivarājayoga (*Liber HHH*, SSS) is part of the task of the Zelator, the *sefira* also attributed to haṭha yoga and the "Forging of the Magic Sword." Several of the other yoga categories appear to derive from Crowley's engagement with Swami Vivekananda's work. From a high-definition scan uploaded by Scott Wilde (used with permission, image in public domain). 365

7.4. An advertisement for *The Equinox* that includes the serialized essay "The Temple of Solomon the King" in which Sabhapati Swami's VRY1 is cited, and other instructions on ceremonial "Magick" specific to Crowley's order A.∴A.∴. Photo by the author of a copy held in the Adyar Library and Research Centre. 369

7.5. A portrait of Leila Waddell published in *The Rites of Eleusis* (1910). Her seated posture and A∴A∴ hood forms a notable contrast to Crowley's portrait in the same publication. Photo by the author of a copy held in the Adyar Library and Research Centre. 371

7.6. A portrait of William Estep in the frontispiece and the title page of his reprint of Sabhapati's work CPSPS (WE), published with its subtitle "Esoteric Cosmic Yogi Science." 373

Tables

3.1. A comparison of the cakras and assignment to places in the body from VRY1 (1880), CPSPS (1884/1890), RYB (1892), and MCVTS (1913). 179

3.2. A partial correlation of the "manservants" of CTCSPV with the lower six cakras and their locations in CPSPS and the three editions of VRY. 193

4.1. Sabhapati's attributions of the "wind of causation" (*kāraṇa vāyu*) in the three channels. 242

4.2. A list of Sabhapati's eleven *āsana*s in CPSPS and their likely correlates in ŚYP, the *Tirumantiram*, and the *Haṭhapradīpikā*. 247

4.3. The mantras and purifications associated with each of Sabhapati's twelve cakras, lotuses, or kingdoms. 265

5.1. The correspondence of musical syllables with cosmological inherent forms as found in CPSPS, Second Book, 156–57 (Mpvl. followed by Skt. in parentheses). 288

6.1. Each of the "Phenomena" compared with the principles from the "Other Religion," by which Sabhapati means materialistic philosophy as expressed in English, along with equivalents in Tamil and their associated *svarūpa*s suitable for meditative cultivation (*bhāvanā*) and yogic faculties in CPSPS. 320

Acknowledgments

There are countless people whom I could thank for this book, and I extend my gratitude to everyone, named and unnamed, who has facilitated this study of Sabhapati Swami and his method for Śivarājayoga. I would first like to offer my heartfelt thanks to my former adviser David Gordon White and my doctoral committee at the University of California, Santa Barbara, including Barbara Holdrege, Dwight Reynolds, Vesna Wallace, and Elaine Fisher of Stanford University. I offer special gratitude to Henrik Bogdan at the University of Gothenburg for his assistance in finding this book a suitable home in this series at Oxford University Press. I extend the utmost gratitude to Srilata Raman of the University of Toronto for lending her valuable time, expertise, and teaching, all of which continues to augment my research on this topic in incalculable ways. I also wish to thank Karl Baier of the University of Vienna for his recognition of the importance of this research from an early date. I also send my gratitude to Richard Salomon of the University of Washington, who first encouraged me to take seriously the study of Sanskrit and offered much mentorship. I am very grateful to scholars at both the Jagiellonian University in Kraków and the Center for Advanced Studies in the Humanities and Social Sciences Friedrich-Alexander-Universität Erlangen-Nürnberg who have supported this research at the postdoctoral level as it has transitioned from dissertation to a monograph, especially Cezary Galewicz, Ilona Kędzia, Piotr Borek, Andreas Nehring, and Bernd-Christian Otto—without their belief in my academic ability at crucial stages I would have been much less motivated to finish this task.

There are many people in South Asia to whom I owe gratitude for their assistance during my time in Tamil Nadu as an American Institute of Indian Studies Junior Fellow. I am eternally grateful to the entire staff of the Adyar Library and Research Centre, to Vinayagam Swamigal of the Sri Sabapathy Lingeshwar Koil in Villivakkam, Chennai, and his late father, Hariharan Swamigal; V. Suppiramaniya Chettiyar of Murugambakkam Village, Madurantagam Taluk for information on Konnur Ramalinga Swamigal; Sami Saravanan of the Om Prakash Swamigal Ashram in Kandal, Udhagamandalam; Selvamani Aiya, Padmanaban, and Natarajan of Chidambara Periya Swamigal's *jeeva-samadhi* in Velachery; E. Jegan Parthiban of the Tamil Nadu Archives Library; Chitthanai of the Tamil Virtual Academy, and Narayanan Raju, Sri Kumaran, and Kishore Babu of the Sri Sabapathy Lingeshwar Koil; Yuvaraj Sir, Uma Maheswari, and Balachand for their dedicated assistance during my research at the Tamil Nadu Archives; and S. Suriyakumar, Assistant Director of Drawing at the Central Survey Office in Chepauk, Chennai, for his gracious assistance in helping me to obtain unpublished village maps of Konnur, Villivakkam, and Velachery. I am grateful to Munish Kumar of Latent Light Culture in Delhi for sharing with me a typescript of one of Sabhapati's works, to my friends Sivasakthi, Valarmathi, Beulah, and Poorani for their assistance with Tamil interviews, and to Suveetha and Nagaraj for their assistance at various points with logistics. I extend my thanks to Saymon Zakaria and Idris Ali for tracking down Shrish Chandra Basu's native home in Bangladesh and for supporting publications on Sabhapati's Bengali-language translation. I also extend an infinite amount of gratitude to Priya Dharshini, Kartthik Sir, and all the teachers of Arise 'n' Shine preschool in Adyar, Chennai, for their nurturing support and childcare, without which fieldwork would have been impossible as a single parent in India.

On the esotericism side of this research, I am grateful to Bill Breeze, again Henrik Bogdan, Gordan Djurdjevic, Manon Hedenborg White, Richard Kaczynski, J. Daniel Gunther, Melissa Holm, Michael Kolson, Scott Wilde, Steve King, Hugh Urban, and many others for facilitating this research on Sabhapati Swami on behalf of their interest in and/or publications on Aleister Crowley, the author in whose books I first read Sabhapati's name in high school (see Chapter 7); Bill also graciously supplied me with materials on Franz Hartmann that assisted this research. I am also thankful to Scott for his scanning of two of the diagrams used in this book, and am grateful to Kurt Leland for sharing an original photographed edition of Sabhapati's work at an early date. I also thank Tim Boyd, president, and Jaishree Kannan, archivist, of the Theosophical Society (Adyar) for their generous permission to access the archives in Adyar and Blavatsky's and Olcott's personal papers.

I would also like to acknowledge several other scholars and researchers who have assisted with or supported this project at various points, directly or indirectly, including (in no particular order) Mriganka Mukhopadhyay, Julian Strube, Philip Deslippe, Magdalena Kraler, Marleen Thaler, Patrizia Ebner, Seth Powell, Daniela Bevilacqua, Mark Singleton, Jason Birch, Jacqueline Hargreaves, Jim Mallinson, Suzanne Newcombe, Dagmar

Wujastyk, Sravana Borkataky-Varma, Aaron Ullrey, Carola Erika Lorea, John Nemec, Isa Thompson, Julie Rocton, Eric Steinschneider, Dominic Goodall, Manasicha Akepiyapornchai, Jessica Bachman, Michael Ium, Anya Foxen, Jason Schwartz, Soundraakohila Madam, Nikola Rajić, Janani Mandayam Comar, Matthew Leveille, Nils Seiler, Ann Taves, Juan Campo, William Elison, Elliot Wolfson, Joseph Blankholm, Jens Schlieter, Wouter Hanegraaff, Jeff Kripal, Simon Cox, Charles Stang, Eva Wilden, Marina Alexandrova, Anya Foxen, Andreas Nehring, Bernd Christian Otto, Raquel Romberg, and Mariano Errichiello..

I also wish to thank Cynthia Read, Theo Calderara, Chelsea Hogue, Hemalatha Arumugam, Jamie Mortimer, and Richard Isomaki for their assistance with the contract, formatting, copyediting, and publishing of this book with Oxford University Press.

On a personal level, I wish to thank my wife Nasrin for her love and for believing in my *ajab gobeshona*, and my mother Gail, my sister Krista, my late father Eddie, my mother-in-law Sheuli, father-in-law Nasir Uddin, sister-in-law Nabila, and my son Eddie for their support and love.

Last but not least, I must also here acknowledge the memory of four cats in my life who brought me much calm and mental stability while up at all hours of the day or night writing: Bhairavi, Vellai Puli, Matangi, and Henry V.

Erlangen Bruck
April 2023 e.v.

Abbreviations

Primary Sources

ANB	G. Sabhapathi Yogi. *Aṭukkunilai pōtam*. Publisher unknown, 1894.
BRY	Śrīmat Sabhāpati Svāmī. *Bedāntadarśan o rājayog*. Kalikātā: Śrī Aghoranāth Barāṭ, 1885.
CĀT	Ñāṉakuru Capāpati Yōkīsvarar. *Cakalākama tiraṭṭu*. 4 extant parts. Madras: Printed by N. Kupusawmy Chettiar at the Duke of Edinburgh Press and the Hindu Theological Press, 1894.
CPSPS	The Mahathma Brumha Gnyana Mavuna Guru Sabhapathy Swamy Rishi Yogiswer. *Om: The Cosmic Psychological Spiritual Philosophy and Science of communion with and absorption in the Infinite Spirit, or Vedhantha Siva Raja Yoga Samadhi Brumha Gnyana Anubuthi, etc.* First Book, Madras: Hindu Press, 1884. Second Book, Bombay: Karnatak Press, 1890.
CTCSPV	Ñāṉakuruyōki Capāpati Cuvāmikaḷ. *Carvōpatēsa tatvañāṉa civarājayōka svayap pirammañāṉāṉupūti vētapōtam*. [Madras]: Empress of India Piras, 1889.
CU	Ñāṉakuru Yōkīsvara Capāpati Svāmikaḷ. *Cātaṉāppiyāsāṉupava upatēcam*. Vellore: Natasun & Co.–V.N. Press, 1898.
FH1	Franz Hartmann, trans. "Aus der Philosophie und Wissenschaft des Vedânta und Râja-Yoga, von Mahâtmâ Jñâna Guru Yogî Sabhapatti Svâmî." *Neue Lotusbluthen* 1, nos. 7–12 (July–December 1908).
FH2	Svami Sabhapatti. *Die Philosophie und Wissenschaft der Vedanta und Rāja-Yoga oder Das Eingehen in die Gottheit von Mahātma Jnāna Guru Yogi Sabhapatti Svāmī*. Trans. Franz Hartmann. Leipzig: Jaeger, 1909.
FH3	Svami Sabhapatti. *Die Philosophie und Wissenschaft der Vedānta und Rāja-Yoga oder das Eingehen in die Gottheit*. Trans. Franz Hartmann. Leipzig: Theosophisches Verlagshaus, 1926.
MCVTS	Capāpati Cuvāmikaḷ. *Carva māṉaca nittiya karmānuṣṭāṉa, carva tēvatātēvi māṉaca pūjāttiyāṉa, pirammakñāṉa rājayōka niṣṭai camāti, carva tīkṣākkramattiyāṉa, cātaṉā appiyāca kiramāṉucantāṉa, caṅkiraha vēta tiyāṉōpatēca smiruti*. Tiruccirāppaḷḷi: Ṣaṇmukavilās Piras, 1913.
RYB	Mahātmā Jñānaguruyogī Sabhāpati Svāmī. *Rājayoga brahmajñānānubhūti saṅgraha veda*. Bombay: Tattvavivecaka Chāpakhāne, 1892.

SVSAA	*Sarva vidha vicāraṇa sādhana abhyāsa anubhava, sarva tapa dhyāna upadēśa saṅgraha vidha [sic]*. Published in Telugu in the third quarter of 1890 (likely no longer extant).
ŚYP	*Śivayogapradīpikā*
T1	Tamil account prefaced to CTCSPV, published in 1889. English translation by Keith E. Cantú.
T2	Tamil account prefaced to MCVTS, published in 1913. English translation by Keith E. Cantú.
Ur-account	Account in English prefaced to *Om: A Treatise on Vedantic Raj Yoga Philosophy*, first published as "The Madras Yogi Sabhapaty Swami," in *The Theosophist* 1, no. 6 (March 1880): 145–47. Lahore, January 3, 1880.
VRY1	The Mahatma Giana Guroo Yogi Sabhapaty Swami. *Om: A Treatise on Vedantic Raj Yoga Philosophy*. Edited by Siris Chandra Basu. Lahore: "Civil and Military Gazette" Press, 1880.
VRY2	The Mahatma Jnana Guru Yogi Sabhapaty Swami Swami. *The Philosophy & Science of Vedanta and Raja Yoga*. 2nd ed. Lahore: R.C. Bary at the "Arya Press" by Ram Das, 1883. Reprinted in 1950.
VRY3	The Mahatma Jnana Guru Yogi Sabhapaty Swami. *Om: The Philosophy & Science of Vedanta and Raja Yoga*. 3rd ed. Edited by Srish Chandra Vasu. Lahore: R.C. Bary & Sons, 1895.
WE	Sabhapaty Swami and Wm. Estep. *Esoteric Cosmic Yogi Science, or, Works of the World Teacher*. Excelsior Springs, MO: Super Mind Science Publications, 1929.

Languages in Transliterations

Bng.	Bengali
Hnd.	Hindi
Mpvl.	Maṇipravāla (*maṇippiravāḷam*, or "Tamil-Sanskrit hybrid language")
Skt.	Sanskrit
Tam.	Tamil
Tam. Eng.	English words rendered in Tamil script
Tel.	Telugu

Introduction

Like a Tree Universally Spread

> You are like a tree universally spread. Your stem represents all the souls of all the creations, your larger branches are natural powers, your smaller branches are senses &c. Your leaves are intellect; conscience and ideas; your flowers are muse and memory, and your fruit is knowledge and wit, and your seed is wisdom. But in this spiritual state you will entirely forget what you are? Who you are? Whence you are? You will not have the least idea of the existence of your body and your twelve faculties.
>
> —Sabhapati Swami, VRY1, 26–27

This book is on a nineteenth- to early twentieth-century Tamil yogi named Sri Sabhapati Swami (Śrī Sabhāpati Svāmī, Capāpati Cuvāmikaḷ, Sabhapathy Swami, ca. 1828–1923/4) and particularly how his unique English and Sanskrit- and Tamil-based vernacular works on a system of yoga known as Śivarājayoga (Mpvl. *civarājayōkam*), the "royal yoga for Shiva" or even more literally "yoga of kings for Shiva," came to be entangled in historical and literary milieus across South Asia as well as modern occultism.[1] The title *Like a Tree Universally Spread* most directly refers to a metaphor of a cosmological tree that Sabhapati used in his work to describe a simultaneously all-pervading and self-dissolving experience of Śivarājayoga (see Chapter 4).[2] I find that this metaphor is also apt to describe the phenomenon of his literature and teachings on Śivarājayoga and how they spread outward across space and time. Traces of Sabhapati's literary "tree" are found in the far outer branches as well as the obscure, forgotten leaves of yesterday's pages but, when carefully analyzed, connect to a discernible trunk and root.

Sabhapati's literature had a significant impact on the development of what in this book for the sake of convenience could be called "Early Modern Yoga,"[3] although an analysis of his work challenges rigid periodizations of "premodern" and "modern" with regard to yoga. A growing number of authors have written about him over the past decades,[4] even if he remains largely

Like a Tree Universally Spread. Keith Edward Cantú, Oxford University Press. © Oxford University Press 2023.
DOI: 10.1093/oso/9780197665473.003.0001

forgotten today both in India and abroad. His works introduced elements of Tamil yogic practices to north India (especially former Punjab Province and Bengal), and he pioneered a yogic system that—on the surface—anticipates one later popularized by Swami Vivekananda (1863–1902), whose lectures on Râja Yoga, first published in 1896, are usually considered by scholars to mark the start of the modern period of yoga's history.[5] Yet Sabhapati, whose first work on Vedanta and raja yoga was published over fifteen years before Swami Vivekananda's lectures, was also a major figure in a larger movement to publish and disseminate editions of yogic texts in Indic vernacular languages as well as English in nineteenth-century India (see Chapter 2). Through his editor Shrish Chandra Basu he was known to the Indological pioneer Friedrich Max Müller (1823–1900),[6] and became a celebrated figure across India. In addition, he had close contacts with some of the founding members of the Theosophical Society, who later, however, severed ties with him. His practices also went on to find a home in the new religious movement Thelema via the literature of Aleister Crowley, discourses on magic and yoga via the German translation of Franz Hartmann, and American New Thought movements via William Estep (see Chapter 7). Given his publications, his relative prominence during his lifetime, and later influence, it is therefore remarkable that he is still scarcely mentioned at all in contemporary academic works on the historical development of Modern Yoga, or of Hinduism for that matter. This book therefore fills a major gap in scholarship by providing a meticulous examination of the contents of Sabhapati's teachings and publications in their local south Indian settings, across South Asia, and around the globe.

From Hidden Roots to Outer Blossoms

My examination of Sabhapati's teachings in terms of spatialized locality seeks to move research on colonial-era yoga beyond the web of what could be called the "discourse of authenticity," predicated on questions of culture.[7] I would argue that this discourse at present is salient to the growing academic fields of yoga studies and (Western) esotericism.[8] On the one hand, many scholars of yoga are presently engaged in the valuable process of excavating what in a recent book has been perhaps most aptly framed as the "roots of yoga," that is, source texts of haṭha yoga (Skt. *haṭhayoga*), rāja yoga (*rājayoga*),[9] and precursors to postural and meditative practice that are presented not just for philologically minded scholars but also for the interested public at large.[10] On the other hand, many equally valuable books published on Modern Yoga in the past decades show how yogis (< Skt. *yogī*, stem *yogin*) in their innovations often departed or reformulated the traditions of the past, and may be critical of the way the works of individual authors sometimes "blossomed" in their reception by new and enthusiastic audiences.[11] An unintended consequence is that yoga studies' dominant periodization of yoga into "premodern" (or "precolonial") roots and "modern" innovations often overlooks critical intersections between vernacular yoga traditions and actors on the margins of the colonial project during the early modern and post-Independence periods,[12] except perhaps to offer political or economic criticism predicated on late twentieth-century theoretical discourses on Orientalism (or Occidentalism, arguably its corollary).[13]

The expectation on scholars of "Modern Yoga" is to accordingly show how individual actors changed and modified teachings, often based on a combination of both Sanskrit and non-Indic texts and practices, to suit their contemporary audiences and social or economic concerns.[14] However, the contours of this premodern/modern dichotomy often marginalize or gloss over the blurry exchanges occurring within the colonial period itself, including the innovative contributions of South Asian religious authors and practitioners as well as their unique and idiosyncratic adaptations of regional vernacular and Sanskrit teachings on yoga.[15] These South Asian authors and practitioners felt compelled to adapt their teachings on yoga, often in vernacular languages or English, to the needs of their audiences, both pan-Indian and outside of India, for a wide variety of reasons. Sometimes this adaptation was in response to social or political pressure to conform with colonial-era norms and propriety, but these adaptations and representations of Indian teachings were also creatively reformulated according to their own volition and visionary agency, as Sabhapati's literature attests.[16] In other words, the impetus for the innovation and reformulation of yogic teachings was far from unidirectional from West to East, or a mere Orientalist or colonizing projection on a passive and receptive "East"; rather, colonial-era Indian authors actively participated in this innovation and reformulation.[17]

Tangible departures with yoga's past, such as the advent of Modern Postural Yoga (a typology coined by De Michelis) with its spandex, exercise balls, and global yoga studios, naturally and understandably lead to a scholarly and popular preoccupation with recovering a sense of premodern authenticity rooted in South Asian tradition. However, in the process contextual analyses of the interconnected histories of colonial-era religious practice are usually dispensed with in favor of delineating and sometimes protecting or preserving an image of "yoga" or "tantra," often Hindu, that is rooted in precolonial India. The full scope and stories of colonial-era yogis like Sabhapati that complicate this picture on all sides are often accordingly reduced to only considering their translocal engagements (for which see the following section). This book seeks to correct this reductive tendency by examining an example as to how local vernacular contexts also have informed these engagements, and that such contexts are also necessary to contextualize with reference to premodern South Asian social history and other Sanskrit and vernacular teachings on yoga.

Similar problems of reductive historicization have been addressed for decades in scholarship that treats of social aspects of vernacular Hindu responses to Christian missionary movements, and by extension responses to the spread of Islam in prior centuries.[18] In the scholarly wilderness of colonial-era yoga, however, many gaps in understanding these vernacular responses remain. For example, a more popular recent history of yoga by Alistair Shearer frames Sabhapati Swami principally as an "Indian Theosophist" and as "Christian missionary-educated," and then notes that his teachings on Śivarājayoga, which Shearer does not mention as such but understandably recognizes instead as a practice of tantra, form a "curious blend of Christianized asceticism and *chakra* meditation [that] was quite different from any authentically Tantric teaching of course, but it became acceptable to the [Theosophical] Society as an unobjectionable treatment of a foreign doctrine."[19] There are at least two major problems with Shearer's treatment. First, while Sabhapati Swami did receive his primary education at a missionary school, there is no record of his ever joining the Theosophical Society, and to some extent he was rejected by the society's founders.[20] Second, while Sabhapati certainly employs Christian terminology in his English works as translations of Sanskrit terms (e.g., "sin" for *pāpa*, lit. "vice"; "soul" or "spirit" for *ātman*, lit. "self," and so on), there is no concrete evidence that his instructions on canceling the cakras (< Skt. *cakra*, "chakra," lit. "wheel" or "disk") to attain the samādhi of Śivarājayoga can be described to any significant extent as "Christianised asceticism."[21] One need only examine Sabhapati's vernacular literature to see that Christian perspectives have no significant importance in his yogic system except when he or his editor Shrish Chandra is explicitly invoking outside points of view. The overarching problem with Shearer's portrayal of Sabhapati is that, like every other author writing on Sabhapati Swami to date, he has omitted any consideration of his vernacular (and especially Tamil) works that show different angles of his teachings. These vernacular works offer clear Indic referents and terminology for his yogic practices, however idiosyncratic they may be (see Chapter 4). Further complicating this picture is the fact that Sabhapati himself engaged Christianity as an alternative point of view (see Chapter 3), meaning that he was able to be self-reflexive about certain doctrinal differences, even if he himself only had a very limited view of Christianity from his childhood education. Although I am confident that Shearer meant well in the face of the embarrassing dearth of scholarship on this particular swami, this all points to the need to subject the vernacular contexts of Early Modern Yoga to the same rigorous analysis as Modern Yoga as well as its premodern forms.

Evaluating Sabhapati solely in the context of Christianity and Theosophy does raise an important point, however, namely that yogis in the colonial period were not embraced by Christian societies but instead were welcomed—albeit still often with reservations—by adherents to modern occultist movements, such as, for example, the early Theosophical Society founded by H. P. Blavatsky (1831–1891) and Henry Olcott (1832–1907) as well as to the Thelema of Aleister Crowley (1875–1947).[22] These occultists integrated, albeit in different ways, not only Hindu teachings but also ideas and rites from Buddhism, Daoism, Greco-Egyptian mythology, Jewish kabbalah, Christian mysticism, Sufism, and many other streams of thought into published occult literature and oral teachings.[23] Their movements also included many lesser-known personalities, including women and Black authors such as Paschal Beverly Randolph, who likewise were part of a broader trend in the nineteenth and early twentieth centuries to expand the contours of occultism to encompass teachings from a wide variety of sources outside of what is typically considered "Western."[24] Yet it is precisely where vernacular traditions of yoga and these actors of "Western" esotericism intersect—as in the case of Sabhapati Swami—that the argument for colonial-era inauthenticity becomes most salient. The works of De Michelis and Djurdjevic largely sidestep such a concern to focus on various historical actors and phenomenological comparisons, although Djurdjevic does briefly indicate the problems associated with an imbalanced scholarly focus on "the issue of legitimacy and the supremacy of origins."[25] Other prominent treatments on this intersection, however, as well as popular media, have more or less directly framed global interest in yoga—whether on the part of occultists or by practitioners of the "Modern Postural Yoga" of the for-profit studio—in the context of a commodification or exoticization of cultural traditions, which are distorted in the process.[26] To be sure, these modern occultists modified, appropriated, and adjusted traditional Hindu religious teachings to fit their own agendas, curricula, and worldviews, which is certainly a phenomenon fraught with economic and social implications and one deserving of just as much if not more critical appraisal.[27] However, a major finding of the research that led to this book is that early modern Indian authors also reformulated their own traditions to attract "foreign" audiences, and figures like Swami Vivekananda and the founders of the Theosophical Society were by no means the only actors in this reformulation; Sabhapati Swami was another node, although his recourse to the south Indian local cosmologies and religious practices of Śivarājayoga (see A Treelike "Translocalization" of Yoga and Chapters 3 and 4) appears to have been unique among such translocal figures.

Some scholars like De Michelis have analyzed yogis' engagement with colonial modernity and expressed it in terms of "modern re-elaborations."[28] Others like Karl Baier and Hugh Urban have used similar terminology such as "neo-hybrid," "syncretic," "innovative," and "Orientalist." In my view these are all fair ways of framing the encounter of yogis like Sabhapati with agents and authors negotiating with colonial power structures, and often use these adjectives in my own work. It may also understandably be the difficult task of the scholar to excavate what the premodern views really were, as unmediated as possible by the gloss of later changes on account of colonial encounters and education; such a task is obviously of great importance to history and should not be minimized.[29] However, to go a step further and neglect colonial re-elaborations on yoga as "inauthentic" or "less Indic" when compared to its precolonial forms is to also enter a discursive labyrinth of authenticity with competing claims of power structures and hegemonies, cultural and racial identity politics, and commercialization.[30] While the so-called pizza effect model of Agehananda Bharati is undoubtedly an important labyrinth to be studied and further understood in the context of the innumerable entanglements of modern history,[31] I find these discourses to also be inadequate when seeking to deliver a hermeneutical interpretation that encompasses both the deep roots and far-out branches of Sabhapati's literature and teachings on Śivarājayoga. If they had been adequate, much more would have undoubtedly been written on Sabhapati Swami by now.

A Treelike "Translocalization" of Yoga

In the previous section I showed that Sabhapati's near-total eclipse by other important figures in histories of Modern Yoga is at least partially due to a failure to fully appreciate the many different geographical contexts and vernacular audiences of his literature, contexts that spanned local Tamil, mesolocal pan-Indian, and translocal international levels; and which, with its relatively consistent Sanskrit linguistic base, was made accessible to new Indic vernacular (e.g., Hindi, Bengali, Telugu) and Anglophone audiences (see Chapter 2). One is reminded of the parable of the blind men and the elephant, with each aspect of his literature recognized as a single part while missing the whole. Throughout this book I have therefore located the local roots of Sabhapati's teachings in a regional Tamil form of Śivarājayoga, first taken up and promoted across India by a pan-Indian network of "Admirers," and later by new local networks of Tamil students (see Chapters 3 and 4). Anchoring my research in discourses around Śivarājayoga in Tamil modernity has been productive to a certain extent in allowing me to perceive how this discourse developed and changed over time. I have also engaged post-Orientalist critiques and questions of cultural property and appropriation, especially since Sabhapati's work concurrently reached international audiences on account of late nineteenth- and early twentieth-century Theosophists, Thelemites, and self-proclaimed American gurus (see Chapter 7). Yet this reception of his literature and teachings, which spans local, pan-Indian, and international audiences, has convinced me of the need for a wider set of theories and methods to analyze the philosophy, practice, and expansion of yoga in the Early Modern period.[32]

I have found that one way to more comprehensively and neutrally contextualize and examine the dissemination of Sabhapati's teachings on Śivarājayoga is by using Alejandra Ros's theoretical framing of "translocalization."[33] By this I specifically mean a framework that can analyze how Sabhapati's yogic literature and practices were translated and circulated through networks that gradually removed them from their original local religious (in this case Tamil) contexts, while at the same time never fully eliminating certain distinctive traces of their localized content.[34] This is a concept that is also actively used in translation enterprises today, such as when directors of media like films and video games make decisions on how to "regionalize" or "localize" the language or content to suit a given audience.[35]

While Ros only posits the existence of a local and translocal, I instead posit three main levels that assist with the analysis of his literature and the teachings that they contain (see also Figure I.1). This literature includes a wide variety of works in several languages that are surveyed in Chapter 2, with the acronyms and their full publication data given in the list of abbreviations: (1) *local* or

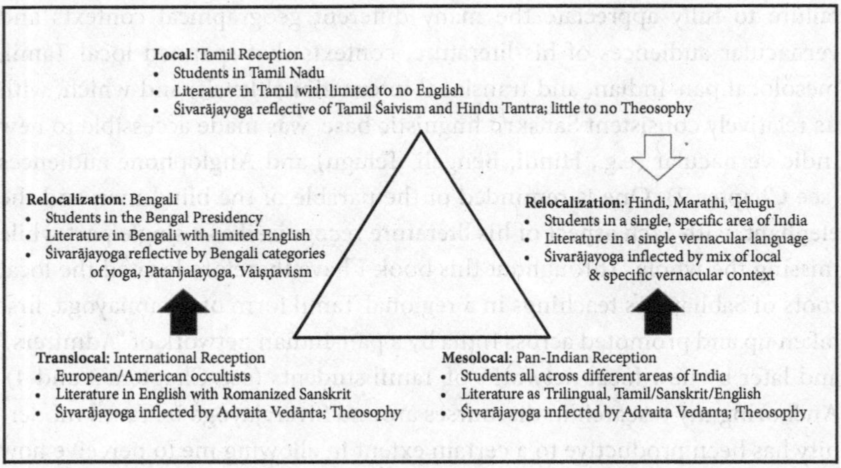

Figure I.1 A schema to understand transitions between local, mesolocal, and translocal receptions of Sabhapati's literature as well as a phenomenon of "relocalization."

Tamil contexts and their reception by his students in these regions (reflected by the Tamil works MCVTS, CTCSPV, ANB, CU, CĀT); (2) *mesolocal* or pan-Indian contexts and their reception by students across north and south India (reflected by the trilingual English, Sanskrit, and Tamil-language CPSPS); and (3) *translocal* or international contexts and their reception both by students across north and south India and in Europe and North America (e.g., the English-language works VRY1, VRY2, VRY3, FH, WE). To these may be added the phenomenon of "relocalization," or the way in which his literature was relocalized from points (2) or (3), that is, from the mesolocal or translocal contexts. As will be made clear in the analysis of the streams of his literature (see Chapter 2), some of Sabhapati's vernacular works (Hindi-language RYB, Telugu-language SVSAA, and a short portion of the Second Book of CPSPS in Marathi) could, in this schema, be understood as relocalized from a blend of local and mesolocal levels. Another work (the Bengali-language BRY), however, is a direct translation from VRY2, Sabhapati's most translocalized English work, and thus it uniquely reflects a relocalization from both mesolocal and translocal contexts; it also contains additional relocalized content, however, such as Bengali categories of yoga and a poem in which the Bengali Vaiṣṇava reformer Chaitanya Mahaprabhu (Caitānya Mahāprabhu) is mentioned in the prologue.

This categorization scheme should be considered a fluid heuristic for grasping the full "elephant" or "universal tree" of Sabhapati's work and influence. There is an especially significant overlap between the translocal and mesolocal levels, that is, the international and pan-Indian: this is due to the fact that these audiences were, to some degree, intertwined in colonial modernity as English gradually became a lingua franca in urban areas. There is accordingly evidence for the mesolocal moving to the translocal, as in the case of William Estep's translation of CPSPS (see Chapters 2 and 7). At the same time, translocal networks (e.g., the Theosophical Society, colonial-era education and publishing, traveling authors) expanded Sabhapati's teachings beyond even these English-language mesolocal or pan-Indian domains into other languages such as German and French. This notwithstanding, Sabhapati's local Tamil-language content (as well as its relocalized vernacular content in Bengali, Hindi, Telugu, and so on) has essentially remained forgotten in library archives until my present research into this book topic. Despite a vast geographical and cultural gulf between the local and translocal levels and their reception history, one finding of this book is that Sabhapati's instructions on Śivarājayoga are a connecting thread that ties together his English and Sanskritic vernacular literatures, and as a result I have made this the central topic in the chapters of this book.

The translocal level of engagement with Sabhapati's works is perhaps best exemplified by Sabhapati's archaic roman transliterations of Sanskrit, Tamil, and Hindi terms, unintentionally rendering his works, even those in English, obscure to many scholars and lay readers alike. However, in this book I examine the full range of Sabhapati's extant literature, including his vernacular works that provide recognizable Indic spellings and explanations of these terms for his Indian audiences who would have felt the need to read and understand their substantive content. In the process I argue that Sabhapati did not simply invent a new system of yoga, nor did he merely vocalize the Theosophical or Hindu reformist opinions of his day; there is no record of him ever joining modern societies like the Theosophical Society or Arya Samaj, for instance, despite some of his followers' involvement in these milieus (see Chapters 1 and 3).

A further argument for a localization-based approach is that Sabhapati's literature instead combined material from a wide variety of Indic textual sources and yogic practices that were circulating in religious milieus in the modern period, although this combination is not merely haphazard; there is a certain logic to this material that emerges when considering the specific contexts and vernacular audiences of a given work and its local religious milieus. Often there is a wide variety of material, not always relevant to yoga, that distinguishes his localized literature as well. Some examples of this include the following: only the Bengali translation makes reference to the Vaiṣṇava reformer Chaitanya, as already mentioned;[36] only the Hindi edition makes reference to Jwalaprasad Mishra, an important figure in the literary development of Hindi;[37] only the English works contain poems that translate Sanskrit terms into Christian terminology such as "sin" and "spirit"; the Tamil editions of his work make reference to Tamil-specific observances and religious rites not found in his works in other languages like English and Bengali, and so on.

While recognizing Sabhapati's clear engagement with translocal discourses and knowledge systems of colonial modernity in India, his vernacular works and translations, which as I mentioned earlier have not been previously considered in any published scholarship to date, also are deserving of their own contextualization. In this book I accordingly also situate Sabhapati's literature in the historical context of local south Indian milieus of texts and practices inspired by haṭha and rāja yoga that arose in the early modern period of yoga's history (ca. seventeenth to nineteenth centuries CE). While the compound Śivayoga (Mpvl. *civayōkam*) is variously used—and sometimes with different meanings—in both Vīraśaiva and Śaiva Saiddhāntika milieus, the use of the phrase Śivarājayoga (as *civarāja yōkam*, *civarāca yōkam*, or *civarāya yōkam* depending on how the Sanskrit phoneme *ja* is rendered) occurs in a Tamil context at least as early as the poetry of the circa eighteenth-century Tamil poet Thayumanavar (Tāyumāṉavar), where it is used in connection with the Tamil Siddhas (for this group see Chapters 3 and 4).[38]

Inspired by the scholarship of Jason Birch, Srilata Raman, Elaine Fisher, and Eric Steinschneider,[39] among others, I conclude that Sabhapati combines at least five Indic currents into his literature: (1) the Tamil Vīraśaiva synthesis of Śivayoga as evident by his explicit and traceable connection to the *paramparā* of the circa seventeenth-century author Kumara Devar (Kumāratēvar); (2) a Vedānta-based spirituality in this Vīraśaiva synthesis that reconciled a monistic idea of unity (Skt. *liṅgāṅgaikyabhāva*, lit. "being united as an auxiliary of [Shiva's] *liṅga*") with dualistic Śaiva Siddhānta and nondualist Advaita Vedānta; (3) haṭha yoga and rāja yoga texts composed in Sanskrit, which themselves are informed by Buddhist and Jaina ascetic as well as Śaiva and Buddhist Tantric traditions; (4) mythological material from Puranas, epics, and local Tamil lore, especially as pertains to the legend of Agastya; and (5) regional yogic and alchemical texts and traditions, such as those of the Tamil Siddhas (Tam. *cittarkaḷ*). Evidence suggests that these streams continued to coalesce and develop out of "Śivayoga," which had originated at least by the fifteenth century in Vīraśaiva milieus in other parts of India, especially Karnataka.[40] In subsequent centuries "Śivarājayoga" (Mpvl. *civarāja yōkam*) arose with its own distinctive features from Śivayoga, and it is this later development, Śivarājayoga, that is reflected in—but not exclusive to—Sabhapati's writing in the late nineteenth and early twentieth centuries (see Chapters 3 and 4).

The Chapters and Methodology of This Book

This book is divided into seven thematic chapters, each of which continues the metaphor of a tree and examines different levels and layers of Sabhapati Swami and his teachings on Śivarājayoga:

1. A biographical account of Sabhapati and his students as gleaned from his textual sources, library and archival records, and my ethnographic fieldwork at extant sites of relevance to Sabhapati's yoga, including an analysis and historiography of his web of relationships, with special attention to his collaboration with his Bengali editor Shrish Chandra Basu (S. C. Vasu)
2. A philological treatment of the three main textual "stemmata" of Sabhapati's literature, their terminology, and their translations, with special reference to his vernacular works
3. A comprehensive treatment of the Śaiva cosmology outlined in Sabhapati's literature, including an analysis of its sources in north and south Indian milieus, and his philosophical engagement with other religions, societies, and with atheism
4. A thorough analysis of Sabhapati's system of Śivarājayoga, including his framing of the other two branches of Haṭha Yoga and Haṭha Rājayoga, and an overview of the role that subtle physiology such as the Tantric cakras plays in his literature
5. An analysis of Sabhapati's aesthetic integration of music and mantric chanting, as well as an evaluation of his use of visual diagrams
6. An evaluation of the role of "science" in Sabhapati's literature, including his mention of oxygen and an analysis of a Bengali prologue by his

translator Ambikacharan Bandyopadhyay that engaged the Victorian naturalist worldview
7. The histories of several late nineteenth- to early twentieth-century occult authors who met with Sabhapati or published his work, such as Henry Olcott and Helena Blavatsky, Franz Hartmann, Aleister Crowley, and William Estep, and how Sabhapati's yoga was viewed as a kind of magic.

To these are appended an epilogue and a never-before-translated alternative account (T2) of Sabhapati's life found in his Tamil work MCVTS (Appendix 1); a lexicon of some of Sabhapati's main vocabulary in table form that enables scholars to make sense of some confusing archaic variants and roman transliterations of technical terms used in his work (Appendix 2); and an annotated passage that refers to Sabhapati's innovative technique of Śivarājayoga, which included visualizing the yogic central channel as a "pole," and which was subsequently translocalized in modern occult literature (Appendix 3). While I originally planned to publish more translations with this book, I have since acquired a contract to separately publish the collected works of Sabhapati Swami, critically edited, annotated, and translated (where applicable) in four volumes, and I have already submitted the manuscript for the first volume (an annotated reprint combining all three editions of VRY). These primary sources will be useful to scholars and lay readers interested in further exploration of the topics outlined in this book.

The methodology behind the chapters in this book is historical-critical and offers a solution to the problem of Sabhapati's neglect in scholarly literature by centering the discussion on Sabhapati himself and his own writings. At the same time, this topic spans various disciplines and academic fields of study in the humanities and social sciences, such as religious studies, South Asian studies and Indology, (Western) esotericism, subaltern studies, and many others, each of which sheds different light on Sabhapati's life and teachings. To bridge these fields I have centered the narrative on a specific "yogi" rather than "yoga" more generally, with the hypothesis that this historical method has the benefit of revealing what the practice of yoga meant to an actual nineteenth-century self-proclaimed practitioner of its spirituality.[41] My research methods are accordingly qualitative, and I construct my claims based on Sabhapati's primary texts, secondary academic literature, biographical accounts, archival data, my personal ethnographic fieldwork and recorded interviews, photographic evidence, nineteenth-century temple epigraphic inscriptions, colonial-era geography and cartography, religious art history, and other related sources.

The research for the book began when I was a doctoral candidate at the University of California, Santa Barbara, and fieldwork was carried out in India under the auspices of a named American Institute of Indian Studies (AIIS) junior fellowship (the Ludo and Rosane Rocher Research Fellowship in Sanskrit Studies), under which I was able to spend eight months researching full-time in Tamil Nadu and other relevant regions of India. Preliminary familiarity with the scope of this project was also obtained in prior years during my Tamil language training at the University of Wisconsin, Madison, at the AIIS Tamil school in Madurai, and independent visits to West Bengal, India, and Bangladesh. I was also awarded a Fulbright-Hays Doctoral Dissertation Research Abroad fellowship to conduct six months of further research into specific localized regions of Sabhapati's published literature (i.e., Mumbai, Kolkata), but this was indefinitely postponed due to the onset of the Covid-19 pandemic. It is my hope that the future will allow for many more opportunities to further research Sabhapati Swami's connection to these location-specific contexts. In the meantime this research was able to continue in my role as an assistant professor and postdoctoral researcher at the Jagiellonian University in Kraków, under the project "Cultures of Patronage" headed by Professor Cezary Galewicz, and subsequently at Friedrich-Alexander-Universität Erlangen-Nürnberg as part of the Center for Advanced Studies in the Humanities and Social Sciences project "Alternative Rationalities and Esoteric Practices from a Global Perspective." These projects have both offered support and insight for this research in its transformation into a book.

Notes

1. Part of the conversion of my doctoral dissertation into this book was carried out with assistance from a research project supported by the National Science Centre, Poland, research grant no. 2018/31/B/HS2/02328: UMO-2018/31/B/HS2/02328.
2. The metaphor is found in VRY1, 26–27, and CPSPS, First Book, 87.
3. I have elected to keep both Early Modern Yoga (which I generally date to the seventeenth to late nineteenth century) and Modern Yoga (following De Michelis, starting around 1896 with the publication of Vivekananda's *Yoga Philosophy*: *Râja Yoga*) capitalized since they define a specific trajectory of yoga's engagement in modernity. I have preferred to keep "yoga" lowercase when speaking about its practice in more general terms.

4. Most notable among these is Karl Baier, *Meditation und Moderne: Zur Genese eines Kernbereichs moderner Spiritualität in der Wechselwirkung zwischen Westeuropa, Nordamerika und Asien* (Würzburg: Königshausen & Neumann, 2009); Karl Baier, "Theosophical Orientalism and the Structures of Intercultural Transfer: Annotations on the Appropriations of the Cakras in Early Theosophy," in *Theosophical Appropriations: Esotericism, Kabbalah and the Transformation of Traditions*, ed. Julie Chajes and Boaz Huss (Beersheba, Israel: Ben-Gurion University of the Negev Press, 2016), 309–54; Henrik Bogdan, "Reception of Occultism in India: The Case of the Holy Order of Krishna," in *Occultism in a Global Perspective*, ed. Henrik Bogdan and Gordan Djurdjevic (London: Routledge, 2013), 177–203; Patrick D. Bowen, "'The Real Pure Yog': Yoga in the Early Theosophical Society and the Hermetic Brotherhood of Luxor," in *Imagining the East: The Early Theosophical Society*, ed. Tim Rudbøg and Erik Reenberg Sand (New York: Oxford University Press, 2020), 143–65. Among books not exclusively published for the academic market one will find treatment of Sabhapati Swami in Aleister Crowley et al., *Magick: Liber ABA, Book Four, Parts I–IV*, 2nd ed. (York Beach, ME: Samuel Weiser, 1997); Kurt Leland, *Rainbow Body: A History of the Western Chakra System from Blavatsky to Brennan* (Lake Worth, FL: Ibis Press, 2016); Aleister Crowley, David Curwen, and Henrik Bogdan, *Brother Curwen, Brother Crowley: A Correspondence* (York Beach, ME: Teitan Press, 2010); Phil Hine, *Wheels within Wheels: Chakras Come West* (London: Twisted Trunk, 2018); and Julian Strube, "Yoga and Meditation in Modern Esoteric Traditions," in *Routledge Handbook of Yoga and Meditation Studies*, ed. Suzanne Newcombe and Karen O'Brien-Kop (London: Routledge, 2021), 130–46.
5. Elizabeth De Michelis, *A History of Modern Yoga: Patañjali and Western Esotericism* (reprint, London: Continuum, 2008). For the broader history of rāja yoga in Sanskrit texts see Jason Birch, "Rājayoga: The Reincarnations of the King of All Yogas," *International Journal of Hindu Studies* 17, no. 3 (2013): 399–442; and Jason Birch, "The Amaraughaprabodha: New Evidence on the Manuscript Transmission of an Early Work on Haṭha- and Rājayoga," *Journal of Indian Philosophy* 47 (2019): 947–77.
6. F. Max Müller, *The Six Systems of Indian Philosophy* (London: Longmans, Green, 1899), 462–64.
7. For more on this discourse and for further examples see Keith Cantú, "'Don't Take Any Wooden Nickels': Western Esotericism, Yoga, and the Discourse of Authenticity," in *New Approaches to the Study of Esotericism*, ed. Egil Asprem and Julian Strube (Leiden: Brill, 2020), 109–26.
8. While there are earlier foundations for these fields, for the sake of simplicity I locate the beginning of Western esotericism or now often just "esotericism" (without the Western) in Antoine Faivre's *Access to Western Esotericism* (1994, a translation from two volumes in French published in 1986) and the beginning of yoga studies in Eliade's *Yoga: Immortality and Freedom* (1958).
9. The forms "haṭha yoga" (*haṭhayoga*, "yoga of force") and "rāja yoga" (*rājayoga*, "yoga of kings") are used in upright, non-italic form when used generally as in English. It should be kept in mind, however, that these forms of yoga are not fixed but have divergent meanings according to various authors, texts, and the time period in question, and also as specific categories of practice in the literature of Sri Sabhapati Swami.

10. James Mallinson and Mark Singleton, eds., *Roots of Yoga* (London: Penguin Books, 2017).
11. For some examples see De Michelis, *History of Modern Yoga*; Mark Singleton, *Yoga Body: The Origins of Modern Posture Practice* (New York: Oxford University Press, 2010); Suzanne Newcombe, *Yoga in Britain: Stretching Spirituality and Educating Yogis* (Bristol: Equinox Publishing, 2019); David Gordon White, *The Yoga Sutra of Patanjali: A Biography* (Princeton, NJ: Princeton University Press, 2014); Philip Deslippe, "From Maharaj to Mahan Tantric: The Construction of Yogi Bhajan's Kundalini Yoga," *Sikh Formations* 8, no. 3 (2012): 369–87; Magdalena Kraler, "Tracing Vivekananda's Prāṇa and Ākāśa: The Yogavāsiṣṭha and Rama Prasad's Occult Science of Breath," in *The Occult Nineteenth Century: Roots, Developments, and Impact on the Modern World*, ed. Lukas Pokorny and Franz Winter (London: Palgrave Macmillan, 2021), 373–99.
12. While a rigid periodization is complicated by a number of factors, in this book by "modern" period I mean from the year 1800, prior to India becoming a British colony, onward.
13. Edward W. Said, *Orientalism* (New York: Vintage Books, 1979); Saree Makdisi, *Making England Western: Occidentalism, Race, and Imperial Culture* (Chicago: University of Chicago Press, 2014). For more engagement with these perspectives in the context of yoga see Cantú, "Don't Take Any Wooden Nickels."
14. For recent examples see Mark Singleton and Ellen Goldberg, eds., *Gurus of Modern Yoga* (New York: Oxford University Press, 2014); Anya P. Foxen, *Biography of a Yogi: Paramahansa Yogananda and the Origins of Modern Yoga* (New York: Oxford University Press, 2017); Anya P. Foxen, *Inhaling Spirit: Harmonialism, Orientalism, and the Western Roots of Modern Yoga* (New York: Oxford University Press, 2020); Deslippe, "From Maharaj to Mahan Tantric."
15. This has started to change in recent years, for example with Baier, *Meditation und Moderne*; Kraler, "Tracing Vivekananda's Prāṇa and Ākāśa"; Dominic S. Zoehrer, "From Fluidum to Prāṇa: Reading Mesmerism through Orientalist Lenses," in *The Occult Nineteenth Century: Roots, Developments, and Impact on the Modern World*, ed. Lukas Pokorny and Franz Winter (New York: Palgrave Macmillan, 2021), 85–111.
16. For a survey of the tension between individual agency and social pressure in feminist contexts, also applicable to this context of subaltern dynamics, see Saba Mahmood, *Politics of Piety: The Islamic Revival and the Feminist Subject* (Princeton, NJ: Princeton University Press), 17–22.
17. For the alternate point of view, somewhat challenged by this reading of Sabhapati's literature, see Ronald B. Inden, *Imagining India* (Bloomington: Indiana University Press, 2000).
18. For the broader history of Christian and Islamic presence in south India see Susan Bayly, *Saints, Goddesses and Kings: Muslims and Christians in South Indian Society, 1700–1900* (Cambridge: Cambridge University Press, 1989); for the Bengal region see Asim Roy, *The Islamic Syncretistic Tradition in Bengal* (New Delhi: Sterling Publishers, 1983). For Islamic engagement with yoga see Carl Ernst, "Situating Sufism and Yoga," *Journal of the Royal Asiatic Society*, 3rd series 15, no. 1 (April 2005): 15–33.

19. Alistair Shearer, *The Story of Yoga from Ancient India to the Modern West* (London: C. Hurst, 2020), 118.
20. See Chapter One; Baier, "Theosophical Orientalism"; Keith Cantú, "Sri Sabhapati Swami: The Forgotten Yogi of Western Esotericism," in *The Occult Nineteenth Century: Roots, Developments, and Impact on the Modern World*, ed. Lukas Pokorny and Franz Winter (London: Palgrave Macmillan, 2021), 347–73.
21. One could understandably make a point, as Baier has, that his verbal refutations of the cakras (< Skt. *cakra*) resemble Islamic declarations, but there are also Indic antecedents for these kinds of guided rejections of aspects or principles (Skt. *tattva*) of the self as illusory; see Chapters 3 and 4. Sabhapati's terminology of the cakras as "kingdoms" is also reminiscent of Christian terminology, but then a wide variety of objects were known to be envisioned in the subtle body, not just lotuses, as attested by the art historical record; see Debra Diamond, ed., *Yoga: The Art of Transformation* (Washington, DC: Arthur M. Sackler Gallery, Smithsonian Institution, 2013).
22. For more on the contours of "occultism" see Wouter J. Hanegraaff, "Occult/Occultism," in *Dictionary of Gnosis & Western Esotericism*, ed. Wouter J. Hanegraaff (Leiden: Brill, 2006), 861–65. For bibliographic references on the Theosophical "founders" and Crowley see Chapter 7.
23. For examples of this in Theosophy see Erik Sand and Tim Rudbøg, eds., *Imagining the East: The Early Theosophical Society* (Oxford: Oxford University Press, 2019); Hans Martin Krämer and Julian Strube, eds., *Theosophy across Boundaries: Transcultural and Interdisciplinary Perspectives on a Modern Esoteric Movement* (Albany: SUNY Press, 2020); and for a more critical view see Christopher Partridge, "Lost Horizon: H.P. Blavatsky and Theosophical Orientalism," in *Handbook of the Theosophical Current*, ed. Olav Hammer and Mikael Rothstein (Boston: Brill, 2013), 309–33; for Thelema see Marco Pasi, *Aleister Crowley and the Temptation of Politics* (Durham, UK: Acumen, 2014); Gordan Djurdjevic, *India and the Occult: The Influence of South Asian Spirituality on Modern Western Occultism* (New York: Palgrave Macmillan, 2014); Henrik Bogdan and Gordan Djurdjevic, eds., *Occultism in a Global Perspective* (London: Routledge, 2013).
24. Manon Hedenborg White, *The Eloquent Blood: The Goddess Babalon and the Construction of Femininities in Western Esotericism* (New York: Oxford University Press, 2020); Hugh Urban, "The Yoga of Sex: Tantra, Orientalism, and Sex Magic in the Ordo Templi Orientis," in *Hidden Intercourse: Eros and Sexuality in the History of Western Esotericism*, ed. Wouter J. Hanegraaff and Jeffrey J. Kripal (Leiden: Brill, 2008), 401–43; John P. Deveney, *Paschal Beverly Randolph: A Nineteenth-Century Black American Spiritualist, Rosicrucian, and Sex Magician* (Albany: State University of New York Press, 1997).
25. Djurdjevic, *India and the Occult*, 12.
26. Hugh B. Urban, *Magia Sexualis: Sex, Magic, and Liberation in Modern Western Esotericism* (Berkeley: University of California Press, 2006); Partridge, "Lost Horizon"; Andrea R. Jain, *Selling Yoga: From Counterculture to Pop Culture* (New York: Oxford University Press, 2015).

27. For what is in my view a well-balanced step in this direction, see Baier, "Theosophical Orientalism."
28. De Michelis, *History of Modern Yoga*, 10.
29. For examples see Philipp Maas, "A Concise Historiography of Classical Yoga Philosophy," in *Periodization and Historiography of Indian Philosophy*, ed. Eli Franco (Vienna: Sammlung de Nobili, Institut für Südasien-, Tibet- und Buddhismuskunde der Universität Wien, 2013), 53–90; David Gordon White, *Kiss of the Yoginī: "Tantric Sex" in Its South Asian Contexts* (Chicago: University of Chicago Press, 2006); David Gordon White, *The Alchemical Body: Siddha Traditions in Medieval India* (Chicago: University of Chicago Press, 1996); David Gordon White, *Sinister Yogis* (Chicago: University of Chicago Press, 2009); James Mallinson, *The Khecarīvidyā of Ādinātha: A Critical Edition and Annotated Translation of an Early Text of Hathayoga* (New York: Routledge, 2007); Jason Birch, "Haṭhayoga's Floruit on the Eve of Colonialism," in *Śaivism and the Tantric Traditions: Essays in Honour of Alexis G.J.S. Sanderson*, ed. Dominic Goodall et al. (Leiden: Brill, 2020), 451–79; Seth Powell, "A Lamp on Śiva's Yoga: The Unification of Yoga, Ritual, and Devotion in the Fifteenth-Century Śivayogapradīpikā" (PhD dissertation, Harvard University, forthcoming); and many others.
30. For examples of these discourses see Foxen, *Inhaling Spirit*; Jain, *Selling Yoga*; Amanda J. Lucia, *White Utopias: The Religious Exoticism of Transformational Festivals* (Oakland: University of California Press, 2020); also Cantú, "Don't Take Any Wooden Nickels."
31. The "pizza effect" describes how "authentic" pizza from Italy traveled to the United States, and then Italians encountering that transformed pizza adjusted their own pizza to match the American pizza, making claims as to its authenticity. It was first mentioned in Agehananda Bharati, "The Hindu Renaissance and Its Apologetic Patterns," *Journal of Asian Studies* 29, no. 2 (February 1970): 267–87.
32. While I treat this in Chapter 7, further engagement can be found in Cantú, "Sri Sabhapati Swami"; and Cantú, "Don't Take Any Wooden Nickels."
33. While this is the terminology I use in this book, it is by no means the only one. For instance, Mriganka Mukhopadhyay has similarly applied the idea of "despatialization" and related concepts to great utility.
34. This is a slightly modified definition adapted from Alejandra Ros, "Translocalization," in *Encyclopedia of Global Religion*, ed. Mark Juergensmeyer and Wade Clark Roof (Thousand Oaks, CA: Sage Publications, 2012), 1301–02.
35. I am grateful to Mariana Carneiro, who at the time of writing works in the field of translation localization services for video games, for this insight.
36. For the significance of this figure in Bengal see Barbara A. Holdrege, *Bhakti and Embodiment: Fashioning Divine Bodies and Devotional Bodies in Kṛṣṇa Bhakti* (London: Routledge, 2015); Kṛṣṇadāsa Kavirāja, Edward Cameron Dimock, and Tony Kevin Stewart, *Caitanya Caritāmṛta of Kṛṣṇadāsa Kavirāja: A Translation and Commentary* (Cambridge, MA: Harvard University Press, 1999).
37. I am grateful to Jason Schwartz for pointing out the significance of this figure to me.

38. I am grateful to Srilata Raman for tracing this reference, which occurs in the sixth verse of his poetic composition “Cittarkaṇam.” A version of this poem has been published in Nā. Katiraivēr̲ Piḷḷai, *Tāyumāṉa Cuvāmi pāṭalkaḷ: mūlamum uraiyum* (Chennai: Cantiyā Patippakam, 2010), 149–63.
39. Examples include Birch, “The Amaraughaprabodha”; Srilata Raman, *The Transformation of Tamil Religion: Ramalinga Swamigal and Modern Dravidian Sainthood* (Abington, UK: Routledge, 2022); Elaine M. Fisher, “The Tangled Roots of Vīraśaivism: On the Vīramāheśvara Textual Culture of Srisailam,” *History of Religions* 59, no. 1 (2019): 1–37; and Eric Steinschneider, “Subversion, Authenticity, and Religious Creativity in Late-Medieval South India: Kaṇṇuṭaiya Vaḷḷal's Oḻiviloṭukkam,” *Journal of Hindu Studies* 10, no. 2 (August 2017): 241–71.
40. For Śivayoga see Seth Powell, “A Lamp on Śiva's Yoga: The Unification of Yoga, Ritual, and Devotion in the Fifteenth-Century Śivayogapradīpikā,” PhD prospectus, Harvard University, 2018. For ways in which it is distinct from Śivarājayoga as practiced in Tamil Nadu see Chapter 4 of this book.
41. This is in line with David White's assertion that “a history of yogis opens the way for an analysis of the extremely rich body of *narrative* accounts.” White, *Sinister Yogis*, xii. I have generally kept “yogi” in lowercase without diacritics according to English usage but have used diacritics when citing vernacular or Sanskrit references.

1

Hagiographies and Old Diary Leaves

> Know O! Sabhapathi that I, the Infinite Spirit am in all creations, and the creations are in me. You are separate from me, neither is any soul distinct from me. I reveal this directly unto you, because I see you to be Holy and Sincere. I accept you as my disciple and bid you rise and go to the residence of Agustia Rishi or Holy Saint (அகஸ்திய ஆச்ரமம்) where you will find me in [the] shape of Rishís and Yogís.
>
> —CPSPS, First Book, 2

> Whatever good opinion we may have formed of him before was spoilt by a yarn he told of his exploits as a Yogi. He had, he said, been taken up at Lake Mânsarovara, Tibet, high into the air and been transported two hundred miles along the high level to Mount Kailâs, where he saw Mahadeva!
>
> —Henry S. Olcott, *Old Diary Leaves, Second Series 1878–83*, 258–59

In this chapter I provide foundational biographical information on Sri Sabhapati Swami (Śrī Sabhāpati Svāmī or Capāpati Cuvāmikaḷ, 1828–1923/4)[1] and those associates for whom there is evidence of his physically meeting them, with special attention to (1) his gurus Vedashreni Chidambara Swamigal (Vētacirēṇi Citambara [Periya][2] Cuvāmikaḷ) and Satgurunath Shivajnana Bodha Yogishwarar (Caṟkurunāta Civañāṉa Pōta Yōkīsvarar); and (2) his students, especially Om Prakasa Swamigal (Om Pirakāccuvāmi Yokīsvarar) and Konnur Ramalinga Swamigal (Koṉṉūr Irāmaliṅka Cuvāmikaḷ).[3] I also here treat the early life and works of Sabhapati's most "translocalizing" interlocutor, the Bengali polymath Shrish Chandra Basu (Śrīś Candra Basu, aka Sris Chandra (S.C.) Vasu or Srishchandra Basu), given his considerable importance as promoting a colonial-era vision of Hindu modernity within the works of Sabhapati that he edited from 1880 to 1895, after which his involvement appears to gradually end.

Like a Tree Universally Spread. Keith Edward Cantú, Oxford University Press. © Oxford University Press 2023.
DOI: 10.1093/oso/9780197665473.003.0002

Extant Sources for Sabhapati's Life

Data on Sabhapati's life is scarce compared to many of his contemporaries, and no one has attempted until now to construct even a basic biography of his life grounded in the historical sources available. There are at least two separate semihagiographical accounts of his life from which this biographical chapter begins; they are expanded using secondary sources by or about his associates as well as material obtained through my field research in South Asia. The first account, what I prefer to call the "Ur-account," was drafted in Lahore on January 3, 1880. It was signed anonymously by "An Admirer," but at least two sources—both Shrish Chandra's biographer and the Indological scholar Friedrich Max Müller (1823–1890), of all people—attest to Shrish Chandra himself being the author.[4] The Ur-account was first published in *The Theosophist*,[5] and in identical form in Sabhapati's first English work, in print by April 1880 (VRY1).[6] It was subsequently translated by two other authors with ties to the Theosophical Society,[7] the details of which are as follows: an anonymous partial French translation published in 1897 with additional comments by Paul Gillard (d. 1901),[8] and a German translation first published in 1908 with annotations by Franz Hartmann (1838–1912).[9] This Ur-account was slightly expanded in 1884 in the first volume of Sabhapati Swami's revised and expanded two-volume English, Tamil, and Sanskrit work CPSPS,[10] the most notable difference of which is the inclusion of certain terms and places in Devanagari script that help confirm the archaic or irregular Roman transliterations in the original 1880 version.[11] Additional details were also supplied in the Ur-account's subsequent translations and modifications when rendered in Bengali (BRY),[12] Hindi (RYB),[13] and even Urdu in a small pamphlet.[14] The Ur-account, its edited reprints, and its translations seem to be written for both pan-Indian (mesolocal) and international (translocal) audiences.[15] The Ur-account and its derivations further appear intended to provide a basis for Sabhapati's religious credentials, and in addition to historical facts also includes more or less explicit hagiographical narratives that elude historical analysis, such as visions of Shiva and encounters with age-defying sages, including one of Sabhapati's gurus who is described as being "about two hundred years old."[16] At the same time, such narratives are remarkably detailed and provide much useful historical information, including names, dates, and geographical locations that are verifiable with reference to external sources and that provide many clues about the local religious contexts that Sabhapati operated in. Furthermore, there is an extant claim that the details of his life that form the basis of the Ur-account—if not the whole account—were "narrated" by Sabhapati himself,[17] and thus despite alterations by the editor, we can safely assume that the Ur-account reflects his own idiosyncratic style of self-representation. At the same time, I would argue that Sabhapati's "Admirer" prefers to situate him more squarely within the pale of more conventional currents of Advaita Vedānta and to this end mentions the reformer Shankaracharya (Śaṅkarācārya) alongside Christ and the Buddha at the end of the Ur-account. As we shall see in Chapter 3, however, Sabhapati's teachings on Vedānta were more directly mediated by his Tamil Vīraśaiva guru in Velachery, and Sabhapati also uses Śaiva Siddhānta, Vaiṣṇava, and to some extent even Śākta terminology and imagery to describe the practice and goals of his yogic system.

Practically every author writing on Sabhapati Swami to date has relied only on this English-language Ur-account or its translations to make claims about his life. However, I have discovered two other hagiographical accounts that were published in Tamil (henceforth "T1" and "T2") in 1898 and 1913 respectively, and thus were produced later in his life.[18] T1 is prefaced to CTCSPV, of which at least eight copies survive at Om Prakash Swamigal's former ashram in the Kandal area of Ooty (see the section Om Prakash Swamigal). The only known extant copy of T2 is bound as a prefatory insert—perhaps originally disseminated separately—to his main Tamil work on mantras and yoga (MCVTS). At least three copies of MCVTS survive, although the two copies respectively held by the British Library and the Library of the Tamil Nadu Archives (formerly the Library of the Madras Record Office) are incomplete, being around fifty pages long, and in any case omit the pages that include T2. The third extant copy, on the other hand, held by the Adyar Library and Research Centre in Chennai, is about 130 pages long and includes T2 as a preface, an additional woodblock print of Sabhapati as a bearded yogi (Mpvl. *yōki*, Skt. *yogī*, < *yogin*, "one who does yoga"),[19] and several other diagrams and instructions. To my knowledge, no scholar, historian or otherwise, has considered either T1 or T2 to date (or, for that matter, Sabhapati's literature published in Indic vernacular languages more broadly).

T2 was authored by Shivajnanaprakash Yogishwara (Civañāṉappirakāca Yōkīsvara), a student of Sabhapati, and, given its textual similarities with T1, it is probable that T1, although anonymous, was written by the same individual. Both were written in an early modern form of Maṇipravāla (abbreviated Mpvl.) that prefers a Sanskritic register for technical vocabulary overlaid on top of a Tamil grammatical base woven together with a stunning array of Tamil verbal participles, adverbial forms, and adjectives.[20] The substance of the account clearly outlines Sabhapati's two principal gurus' "lines" (Skt. *paramparās*), that of Vedashreni Chidambara (Periya) Swamigal and Satgurunath Shivajnana Bodha Yogishwarar, both of whom are also respectively mentioned in the title page of CPSPS (1884) in archaic Roman transliteration as "Sidhumbara Swamy" and "Brumhamaya Suthgurunadha Sivagnyanabodha Rishi Yogiswer." Based in part on this data as well as references in his other vernacular works, I have been able to conclusively confirm the continued existence of Vedashreni Chidambara (Periya) Swamigal's line in the Velachery area of Chennai as well as the site of Sabhapati's ashram in the Villivakkam area of Chennai, which was later handed down to his student Konnur Ramalinga Swamigal (see Konnur Ramalinga Swamigal). T1 and T2 also provide more clues as to the semilegendary identity of his other guru, Satgurunath Shivajnana Bodha Yogishwarar, as a four-hundred-year-old sage in the line of Agastya (Akastiyar or Agattiyar) in the Pothigai Hills (Pothigai Malai). Unlike the Ur-account, T1 and T2 seem to predominantly reflect the needs and concerns of Sabhapati's Tamilian and Malayali students, and accordingly do not appear to mention either Sabhapati's lectures in Lahore or his encounter with the founders of the Theosophical Society, which I treat in a separate section entitled A Splash on the Lahore Scene.

In addition to Ur-account, T1, and T2, there is also a remarkably helpful list in MCVTS of some of Sabhapati's principal students and financial supporters toward the end of his life, for whom the book was explicitly compiled (see Figure 1.10).[21] This has led to my acquisition of several important secondary sources that help to corroborate the accounts I have already mentioned, including a biography of Sabhapati's student Om Prakash Swamigal of the Kandal area near Ooty (the summer capital of the Madras Presidency during the British Raj, colloquially known as "snooty Ooty," and today the tourist town of Udhagamandalam),[22] who is mentioned in the list, as well as one of his independent works, *Śrīsatsampāṣiṇi*,[23] both of which refer to Sabhapati's life and career as a yogi and even show evidence that at least one of his students occasionally traveled to Mysore and back to spread Sabhapati's teachings outside of Tamil Nadu.[24] I have thus far not been able to trace any of Sabhapati's surviving letters, although it can be gathered from Om Prakash's biography that he occasionally wrote them to interested inquirers.

In addition to securing these primary textual sources about his life and secondary accounts of interviews and meetings with Sabhapati, I have also conducted interviews and consulted extant wills and government land records, such as those pertaining to his student Konnur Ramalinga Swamigal and Ramalinga's student Aanandha Aanandha Swamigal, both of which I have obtained through the assistance of his followers still living in the environs of Sabhapati's hermitage in present-day Villivakkam, Chennai (see Konnur Ramalinga Swamigal). These documents contain land survey numbers that I have been able to compare with period village maps obtained from the Central Survey Office in Chepauk. I have also consulted numerous colonial-era maps of the Madras Presidency, including Madras, Chingleput, and the forests of the Tinnevelly (modern Tirunelveli) District held in the Tamil Nadu Archives, all of which have helped confirm various placenames, roads and railway lines, and forests as they existed in Sabhapati's time throughout the development of the Presidency up to the eve of Indian independence. When all this data is taken together, a relatively comprehensive historical as well as geographical portrait of this remarkable religious innovator emerges.

Sabhapati's Childhood

Sabhapati was likely born in 1828 to a wealthy family either of Brahmin Deccani[25] or Naidu of Telugu-speaking origin[26] who lived in Vedashreni (Vētacirēṇi or Vētasrēṇi, from Skt. *vedaśrenī*, lit. "row of Vedas," an alternate name for Velachery), then a temple village about fourteen kilometers south of Madras, which at that time was expanding under the direction of the British East India Company based in Fort St. George (see Figure 1.1 for this and other relevant sites in this chapter). T2 provides the most detailed information about his birth, including astrological data as follows:

> The year was 1828, the month of Markazhi [December–January], the lunar mansion of Thiruvathirai, at the time of a celestial great moment [Mpvl. *tivya mahāmukūrttam*, < Skt. *divya mahāmuhūrta*], on an auspicious day of Mars. At the time there were six planetary bodies in the Elevated Position [Mpvl. *uccastāṉam*, < Skt. *uccasthāna*], two planetary bodies in the Position of Speech [Mpvl. *vākkustāṉam*, < Skt. *vāksthāna*],[27] and one planetary body in the Position of Happy Heat [Mpvl. *sukatapastāṉam*, < Skt. **sukhatapasthāna*].[28]

The Ur-account, by contrast, gives 1840 as the year of Sabhapati's birth, which is also reflected in T1's date of 4941 of the Kali Yuga (Tam. *kaliyukam*). I consider this to be an error of estimation either on the part of the "Admirer"

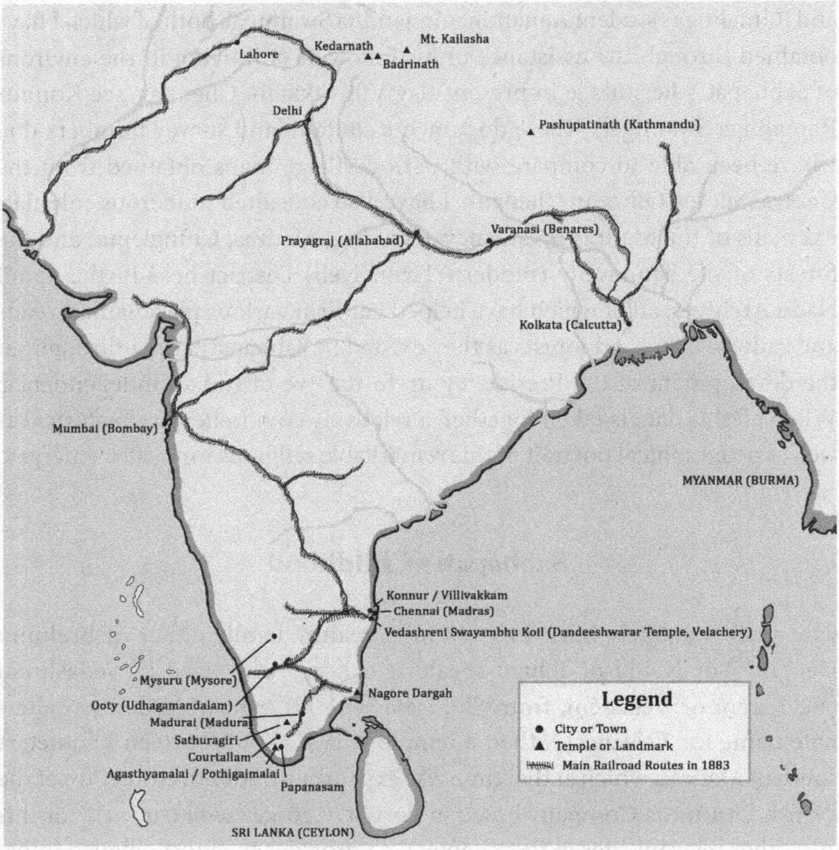

Figure 1.1 A map of several sites in South Asia associated with Sri Sabhapati Swami's life and works. Map created by the author.

who authored the account or an uncritical guess by Sabhapati himself since it does not corroborate other known details of his life, particularly his relationship with his first guru, Vedashreni Chidambara Swamigal (Vētacirēṇi Citambara Cuvāmikaḷ), who died in 1858. As we shall see, if we take T2 at its word that Chidambara met with Sabhapati when he was as old as twenty-nine or thirty, then out of the two options Sabhapati must have been born in 1828 and not 1840, as that would place this meeting in 1869 or 1870, at least a decade after Chidambara's death, widely confirmed in both textual and inscriptional evidence at his tumulus (Mpvl. *jīvacamāti*, < Skt. **jīvasamādhi*, lit. place of "individual composition")[29] in Velachery. T2's attention to minute astrological details and the specifics of his parentage also implies that the author, Shivajnanaprakash Yogishwara, had probed Sabhapati more deeply about the circumstances of his birth and had paid much more attention in general to chronological details, at least as pertains to his early life. Additionally, T1 does not provide a Gregorian equivalent to the Kali Yuga year, meaning that the calculation could possibly have reflected a different correlation closer to 1828.

Sabhapati's parentage presents further complexities, and we unfortunately know only a few details. While the Ur-account only mentions his parents in passing, T1 and T2 provide the names of his father, Gurunatha Baktar (Gurunāta Paktar), and of his mother, Punyavathi (Puṇṇiyavati), and also note his father's work as a temple restorer and his service to Vedashreni Chidambara Swamigal in the following passage:

> The creator of this work, *Compiled Instructions*, the Jnana Guru Yogi, Guru Father Rishi, Sabhapati Swami, was incarnated at the place of Natesamurthy Shivakami Amman Metalworks in Vedashreni within the southern part of India, in Tondayan Chakravartin's city of Tondama, in the city of Chennai, to a father named Gurunatha Baktar, from an illustrious family of gurus who mark their foreheads, who worked and was trained as one of the best restorers [*jīrṇōttāraṇam*] of divine temples, and to his wife named Punyavati. The directions of Gurunatha Baktar's guru Vedashreni Chidambara Swamigal, author of *The Truth of Instruction* [*Upatēca Uṇmai*), were carried out by Gurunatha Baktar along with Kumbalinga Acharya of Mylapore at the location of the auspicious Vedashreni.[30]

We know from the Ur-account that his parents were Śaiva and of Brahmin caste, so if he were a Tamil Brahmin or "TamBram," then he would have likely belonged to either the Iyer or Gurukkaḷ community. However, the Ur-account's reference to the Deccan ("Dakkan") could imply that his parents were instead of Telugu Niyogi or Maratha Deshastha descent,[31] and I have conducted an interview with a devotee who claimed he was from a Naidu family.[32] This assertion is somewhat strengthened by the fact that Sabhapati in his youth was known to have had a command at least four other languages in addition to Tamil and English, which could mean that his parents likely spoke different languages at home. He also was later was keen to produce Telugu and Marathi translations of his work, although this could have been a response to the demands of his students. While his parents were Brahmins, it is notable that Sabhapati's compositions reflect a general disdain for caste distinctions and are explicitly intended for "his male and female students of [any of] the four castes,"[33] and his works only ever mention his Brahmin heritage in passing, if at all. This attitude likely is at least partially informed by his parents' support for Vedashreni Chidambara Swamigal, who preached a more egalitarian message in line with the tradition of his Tamil Vīraśaiva guru-line (see A Search for Spiritual Truth and Chapter 3).

As for Sabhapati's childhood, both accounts agree, as is typical of biographies of religiously charismatic personalities, that he was a saintly child. While T2 focuses on his virtue and service, the author of the Ur-account notes his "precocious intellect" and "well-regulated imagination," and relates that he had the reputation of a poet and musician, earning the title "Arootpa moorti" (Tam. *aruṭpā* [*aruḷ* + *pā*] *mūrtti*, "embodiment of sacred verse") among his peers.[34]

The Ur-account gives the important historical detail, that he was educated at Free Church Mission School, a Scottish Protestant missionary school headed by John Anderson (1805–1855) and Robert Johnston (1807–1853).[35] This is confirmed by T2, which notes that by age twenty he "had read the whole Bible and had examined the truth of the Christian religion,"[36] undoubtedly a reference to his time at Free Church Mission School. The school was first opened in April 1837 as the Madras General Assembly's School after two Scottish chaplains, who two years prior had founded a school named St Andrew's School, handed control of it to John Anderson with the intent to turn it into a reputable educational institution along the lines of what Alexander Duff (1806–1878) had formed in Calcutta.[37] Anderson's involvement is historically important since, as one of his peers who witnessed the first ten years of the school's development wrote, he "was the first missionary in south India who had made the *English* language the chief medium of his instruction, and who had from the first mainly directed his efforts to the evangelization of the *higher* classes of the Hindu community."[38] As a result, I would argue that Sabhapati's interest in publishing his lectures in English a few decades later, thus transforming his system of rāja yoga from a local Tamil into a translocal English phenomenon, was at least partially informed by Anderson's pioneering emphasis on the English language as a viable medium of instruction in India.

Madras General Assembly's School was opened just six years before the Disruption of 1843, which saw a Scottish "Free Church" separate from the official Church of Scotland, hence the different name of the school given in the Ur-account, which reflects the ecclesiastical situation after 1843. The main building of the school originally was located on Armenian Street in the so-called "Black Town" area of Madras. Later it shifted to the Esplanade (now NSC Bose Road, near the Madras High Court), and the original church associated with the school still remains (see Figure 1.2).[39] It is not known when Sabhapati joined the school since no records survive of his enrollment, but if we accept the dating of T2, then he must have joined sometime in the eleven years prior to 1848 and would have figured among one of its first cohorts of students.

The school's explicit object, as stated in its prospectus first published on the eve of the school's opening in 1837, was to "convey through the channel of a good education as great an amount of truth as possible to the Native mind, especially of Bible truth."[40] It appears that Sabhapati was a direct beneficiary of the school's emphasis on biblical literacy, which greatly contributed to his command, if limited, of the English language. At the

Figure 1.2 C.S.I. Anderson Church on the Esplanade (today NSC Bose Road). Photo by the author.

same time, missionary records of the time, such as Anderson's contemporary John Braidwood's account of the school's origin, depict tensions on the one hand with the local Brahmin community in Madras, many of whom desired the educational opportunities afforded by the school but often clashed with the school's ultimate mission to convert Hindu and Muslim children by baptizing them to Protestant Christianity,[41] and on the other hand Roman Catholic missionaries who were considered rivals and whose beliefs Braidwood sourly dismissed as "Popery."[42] As a result, Sabhapati's youth was inextricably intertwined with a somewhat polarizing educational experiment during the colonial period, a chief object of which was to save him from Hindu "idolatry," a dominant concern in the missionary literature of the period. Indeed, in Braidwood's account alone the term "idolatry" appears no fewer than forty-six times, not as an abstract concept but as a scathing critique of the very same rites that Sabhapati would, perhaps somewhat ironically, wholeheartedly embrace in subsequent years and even publish instructions on.

A Search for Spiritual Truth

From 1848 to 1853, or age twenty to twenty-five, Sabhapati was working at a "big job" (Tam. *periya uttiyōkam*), which may be the same "government employment" that the Ur-account mentions he "easily obtained" a few years later. He also was married around this period to the daughter of a textile merchant, and the Ur-account indicates that he already had two sons by age twenty-nine,[43] meaning they were born before the year 1858. No names or other further biographical details are given about his wife or two sons in the Ur-account, and T2 omits mention of his wife and children altogether; T1 does mention his father-in-law, however.

The Ur-account and T2 diverge on the timing of what follows, namely Sabhapati's trip to Burma (modern Myanmar) with his father-in-law. The Ur-account frames the trip as occurring much earlier, closer to age nineteen or twenty, while the chronology of T2 clearly indicates the trip taken was at age twenty-five, upon quitting his job. The relevant passage in the Ur-account is as follows:

> His great desire to learn what the religions of other people had to teach, caused him to travel to Burmah. He lived there with his father-in-law who

> carried on a great merchandise. Here he learned from the Poongees (the Buddhist priests) the doctrines of their renowned Teacher. He stayed there for about a year.[44]

This should be compared with T2, which reads as follows:

> He investigated the truth of the Buddhist religion while carrying on a large business, through spiritual companionship [Mpvl. *catcaṅkam*, < Skt. *satsaṅga*] with exquisite Burmese monks and by using the Pali language. Realizing that the Buddhist religion, Hindu religion, and Vedānta are one and the same, he was disenchanted with this business and renounced it as illusory.[45]

From the Ur-account and T1 we learn that the "large business" was conducted with his father-in-law and that he stayed there about a year, both details of which are omitted in T2. Likewise, we learn from T2 that Sabhapati was aware of the existence of Pali and also that, curiously enough, Hinduism and Vedānta could be considered as separable religions at that time. Both accounts mention his interactions with Buddhist monks ("Poongees," or Tam. *poṅkikaḷ*, plural of *poṅki* in T2, probably a rendering of *phun: kri*, a Burmese word for monk). When faced with these divergences, I take T1 and T2 to be more trustworthy—especially for chronology—on account of their increased attention to the details surrounding Sabhapati's birth and parentage as well as his first guru in the environs of Madras. At the same time, the above example illustrates that the Ur-account also contains useful details, such as the role of his father-in-law in the business, and in many instances appears more grounded in Sabhapati's daily experiences.

If we accept that Sabhapati stayed in Burma for one year, from 1853 to 1854, then T2 contains the following critical piece of information for understanding Sabhapati's subsequent relationship with his first guru and the wider context for his philosophy:

> Leaving that business and returning to Chennai, he sustained himself by his ancestral property and special goods and, becoming the student of Vedashreni Chidambara Swamigal, the author of the guru sayings called *Instructive Truth* [*Upatēca uṇmai*], he obtained through him the knowledge of the principles of all scriptures.[46]

I have concluded with certainty that Vedashreni Chidambara Swamigal is none other than Chidambara Periya Swamigal (Citampara Periya Cuvāmikaḷ; see Figure 1.3), whose tumulus is still present in Velachery alongside a thriving temple that contains sculpted images or idols (Mpvl. *silaikaḷ*, < Skt. *śilā*) of the Tamil Siddhas (Cittarkaḷ). The main proof for this conclusion is the mention of Chidambara as the author of *Upatēca uṇmai*, or *Instructive Truth*, a collection of Tamil sayings on Vedānta and yoga published at least as early as 1881 and still in print today.[47] Vedashreni Chidambara Swamigal is sometimes confused in library records with another person, Thiruporur Chidambara Swamigal (Tiruppōrūr Citambara Cuvāmikaḷ), but they are different individuals who nevertheless are part of the same line; beyond the later date of the former, a key distinction is that Vedashreni Chidambara Swamigal, and not Thiruporur Chidambara Swamigal, authored *Upatēca uṇmai* despite

Figure 1.3 An image of Vedashreni Chidambara Swamigal at his tumulus. Photo by the author.

the fact that the work is sometimes erroneously attributed to the latter in library catalogs. Using inscriptional evidence at the shrines of both Vedashreni Chidambara Swamigal and his guru Kuzhandaivel Swamigal (Kuḻantaivēl Cuvāmikaḷ) in Velachery and Mylapore, respectively, as well as lists given in relevant published works, I have also been able to trace Vedashreni Chidambara Swamigal's line well beyond Thiruporur Chidambara Swamigal, back to the circa seventeenth-century CE Vīraśaiva authors Kumara Devar (Kumāratēvar) and his guru Perur Santhalinga Swamigal (Pērūr Cāntaliṅka Cuvāmikaḷ),[48] the implications of which I will fully treat in Chapter 3. Sabhapati would have known of Vedashreni Chidambara since childhood from his father's service as per T1 and T2, but by the time of their meeting, Vedashreni Chidambara would have been nearing the end of his life, since his apotheosis or death is clearly dated to December 24, 1858.[49]

Either just before or after Chidambara's death, Sabhapati next left Madras for the predominantly Islamic *maraikkāyar* (Tam. "kings of the boat") port city of Nagore near Nagapattinam (Nākappaṭṭiṉam; see Figure 1.4), where

Figure 1.4 A busy street around the Nagore Dargah. Photo by the author.

he interacted with fakirs at the circa sixteenth-century dargah of the late fifteenth- to sixteenth-century Sufi elder Shah al-Hamid Naguri (Shāh al-Ḥamīd Nagurī), who may have been a thirteenth-generation descendant of Abdul Qadir Gilani (ʿAbd al-Qādir Gīlānī), to whom the founding of the Qadiriyya Sufi order (Arabic *ṭarīqa*) is attributed.[50] As Narayanan points out in her ethnographic chapter on votive offerings at this shrine, not only Muslims but also "Hindus of all castes in Tamil Nadu frequent the *dargah* in Nagore as they do many other Muslim shrines," attesting to its role in a kind of unique syncretic Tamil religious milieu.[51] The Ur-account's mention of his visit is sparse, only noting that "he went to the temple of Nagoor Masthan in Nagapatam and gained the truths of Moslem faith from the well-known and learned fakirs of the place." T1 also mentions this event, noting the place's connection to fakirs (Tam. *pakkīr*). T2's mention of this is also brief but adds a few other details:

> He desired after this unity to understand the truth of Muhammad, and for this visited the shrine [*samādhi*] of Nagur Mira Sayappu Andavar [Shah al-Hamid Naguri]. There, having spiritual company with the people of the Islamic religion, he learned the truths of Muhammad and the Quran.[52]

Shah al-Hamid Naguri's hagiographical literature records that he became a close student of the Shaṭṭārī adept Muhammad Ghaus Gwaliyari (Muḥammad Ghawth Gwāliyārī, d. 1563), which is relevant for the connection of this shrine to yoga, a topic on which Sabhapati would of course later become known for discussing. This is the same Muhammad Ghaus who translated and expanded the Persian *Baḥr al-Ḥayāt* ("Ocean of Life") from an Arabic translation of a supposedly preexistent Sanskrit text entitled *Amṛtakuṇḍa*.[53] Given the special emphasis on yogic practice among Shaṭṭārī fakirs, it is therefore possible that Sabhapati may have discussed some methods of yoga during his stay at the Nagore Dargah, although this is difficult to conclusively determine from his works. In any event, an account of the Carnatic nawab Azam Jah Walajah IV (A'zam Jāh Bahādur Nawwāb Wālājāh IV, 1797–1825), who visited Nagore in 1823, three decades prior to Sabhapati, does record the presence of a fakir "of the *malang* order"[54] and also provides evidence for a Shaṭṭārī presence in Tamil Nadu.[55]

T2 does not state when exactly Sabhapati returned to Madras from Nagapattinam, but if we accept the length of time given in the Ur-account, then the trip would have lasted about two years. In any event, T2 notes that upon his return he solidified his ties to Hinduism, and we learn that he subsequently "performed the worship of the Lord of the Dance [Naṭēcar] as the Lord of All [Carvēsvarar] in mental meditation, together with severe austerities [Mpvl. *akōra tapam*, < Skt. *aghora tapas*]."[56] The Ur-account omits this reference to "tapas" and austere Śaiva religious practice, only noting that, despite these experiences of other religions, his "mind was not at ease" and that he was still "far from obtaining the true Spirituality [Skt. *brahmajñāna*]."[57] As noted earlier, the chronologies of the three accounts diverge in the order of his journeys up to his thirtieth year, but both the Ur-account and T2 agree that all of these experiences led to a turning point for Sabhapati and that he earnestly took up the study of Hindu scriptures. T2 frames this as follows:

> After obtaining the knowledge of the Four Vedas, the Seven Scriptures, the Sixty-Four Arts, and the knowledge of all the Upanishads and the Gita, he considered the world's Christian religion, Buddhist religion, and Islamic religion and, moreover, these religions' entire mysteries, truths, discourses, rites, and experiences, to be pieces of the Hindu religion. He therefore felt that evidently the Hindu religion is the father religion of the world, and the Sanskrit language of the Hindu Vedas is the mother tongue of the world.[58]

I would argue that this passage is critical since it reveals that Sabhapati's religious belief as to the truth of the "Hindu religion" was explicitly tied to his perception of the linguistic origins of Sanskrit, however erroneous such a view may be in the light of contemporary linguistics. It is not that other religions are false per se, it is that they were pieces of Hinduism that have splintered off over time, and Sanskrit therefore represents a level of linguistic purity before such a splintering occurred: the language prior to the figurative Tower of Babel, to borrow a similar metaphor from the Bible. This position of course denies independent origination and seems eerily reminiscent of perennialism, or even "Theosophical Orientalism"[59] if the latter were to have instead been delineated on exclusively Hindu lines rather than a selective mixture of Hindu and Buddhist doctrines. In any event, as we will see in A Splash on the Lahore Scene and in Chapter 4, Sabhapati did not join the Theosophical Society and continued to emphasize methods to cultivate an experience of what is only written about in the Hindu scriptures mentioned in the quotation above.

A Visionary Experience in Velachery

By the age of twenty-eight (the years 1856–57), we learn that Sabhapati was longing for more than just a theoretical knowledge of the scriptures he was consulting. He craved experience (Skt. *anubhava*), and this preoccupation with obtaining experience and exercising one's faculties would continue to pervade his entire literary corpus. I would argue that it is precisely this emphasis on cultivating religious experience that attracted occultists to his work both during and after his lifetime (see Chapter 7). T2 frames this as a distinction he made between mediated gnosis (Skt. *parokṣajñāna*, lit. "invisible knowledge") and gnosis that is not mediated, that is, unmediated or direct gnosis (Skt. *aparokṣajñāna*). Sabhapati's mental suffering is framed in the first person as follows:

> Even if I have obtained through the guru the knowledge and examination of the knowledge of teaching, the knowledge of simplicity, the knowledge of time, the knowledge of dispassion, I have not obtained this gnosis through exercise and ritual, which are permanent gnoses since they are the experience of what is manifest. What will I do? I therefore desire to become liberated while alive [Skt. *jīvanmukta*], which is the highest gnosis of Brahman.[60]

The Ur-account similarly frames this in English as his longing for "face to face communion with God," and states that "books could not teach him this knowledge."[61]

"Communion" is the most common translation for *samādhi* (lit. "composition") in Sabhapati's English works, a technical term that was translated by Mircea Eliade in his classic work as "stasis" or "enstatic experience" (as rendered into English from the original French) in the context of his own overarching theory of "reintegration" and interpretations of Pātañjalayoga.[62] Samādhi is of course a technical experience that is believed to be achieved through yogic meditation, being one of the eight "auxiliaries" (Skt. *aṅga*s) of Pātañjalayoga. While Sabhapati appears to be familiar with Patañjali's work, his idea of Śivarājayoga, which is defined as *niṣṭhā samādhi* (lit. "a fixed state of composition"), reflects a Tamil Vīraśaiva synthesis of not just Vedānta but also Saiddhāntika sources (see Chapter 3). Sabhapati's works in English, edited by Shrish Chandra Basu, almost unilaterally paint him as a Vedāntin, hence the English translation "communion," but at the same time his vernacular works also frame this experience in Saiddhāntika terminology that provides evidence that Sabhapati himself had an idea of samādhi that was more polyvalent than the Vedānta-inflected translation "communion" allows for (see Chapter 4). T2 in any case also presents other related goals, such as the experience of unmediated gnosis as mentioned above, a desire for liberation (Mpvl. *mūmkṣutva*, < Skt. *mumukṣutva*), as well as attaining a stage (Mpvl. *pātam*, < Skt. *pāda*, lit. "the feet" taken plurally) of "the Śakti who burns away the three impurities or *malas*" (Tam. *mūmmala paripākacattiṉi pātam*). This latter stage appears to be a relatively obscure reference to a supposed "fifth" stage presented in the medieval text *Tirumantiram*, attributed to Tirumular, which exceeds the traditional four stages (Mpvl. *cariyai*, *kiriyai*, *yōkam*, and *ñāṉam*; < Skt. *caryā*, *kriyā*, *yoga*, and *jñāna*).[63] Regardless of the precise terminology used for Sabhapati's motivation and experience, T2 notes that Sabhapati at this stage began praying to and mentally meditating upon the Lord of All (Mpvl. Carvēsvarar, < Skt. Sarveśvara), also mentioned in T1, whom the Ur-account glosses as "Infinite Spirit" but whom T2 more directly indicates is a form of Shiva.

Either in his twenty-ninth (Ur-account) or thirtieth year (T2), that is, in either 1857 or 1858, the accounts agree, Sabhapati had a vision-like dream. While this dream marks the beginning of Sabhapati's experiences that must ultimately be considered "hagiographical," that is, unverifiable to an empirical historian of religions, its impact was such that it greatly altered Sabhapati's life.[64] I therefore suspend judgment and consider this experience as well as those that follow as if they did really happen in Sabhapati's world, even if ultimately they may have been only "real" in his subjective experience, were simply the expressions of hagiographical myth that conceals a greater truth, and/or—on the extreme end of cynicism—were merely a literary device designed to generate social capital or religious devotion by means of literary narrative. Added to these considerations, however, is also a question of social verifiability, in that many readers in colonial-era Madras would have been at least marginally familiar with the temple in which his subsequent vision occurred, as it is a physical location, and could have visited to inquire about these kinds of experiences. Furthermore, at least some of his students would have resonated with the experiences in question and would have believed them to be within the realm of possibility, at least for a yogi if not the general public at large. In any event, suspending truth claims for the time being, I now proceed to delineate its description in each of the two accounts in order to describe the social conditions of this experience in a relatively systematic way.

Both accounts divide this experience into two parts, of which the first is a dream that Sabhapati had while sleeping, that is, neither while meditating nor in a waking state. In the Ur-account this dream is characterized by the "Infinite Spirit"—in Sabhapati's English works always a translation of Brahman—expressing a kind of pantheistic monism: "I the Infinite Spirit am in all creations, and all creations are in me. You are not separate from me, neither is any soul distinct from me."[65] The account then continues with the Infinite Spirit bidding him to go to the "Agastiya Ashrum" (Agastyāśrama), where he would be found in the "shape of Rishees and Yogis."[66] The reference to this visionary experience in T1 and T2 corroborates the Ur-account, but we encounter Shiva as the "Lord of All" (Carvesvara, < Skt. *sarveśvara*) and the Embodiment of the Lord of the Dance (Naṭēcamūrtti) instead of the Infinite Spirit, as follows:

> At the age of thirty, one day at midnight the Lord of All appeared in his dream and said: "O crest-jewel among devotees, since I have called you out as my messenger, I will give you the name Azhaitthat Kondamurtthy [Tam. *aḻaittāṭk oṇṭamūrtti*]. I honor your adherence to devotion [Skt. *bhakti*]. You, becoming free, will receive liberation [Skt. *mukti*] on the southern Kailāsa mountain called Agastyachala ["Mount Agastya"], through the discipline of an experienced guru. Go." Having said this he, whose sacred mouth blossomed with grace, disappeared. [Sabhapati's] sleep being broken, he woke up.[67]

T1 and T2 furthermore emphasize the role of Sabhapati's first guru, the aforementioned Vedashreni Chidambara (Periya) Swamigal. T2 even introduces a lengthy paragraph writing about his mother Punyavathi's acceptance of her son's renunciation (Skt. *saṃnyāsa*) that is worth quoting in full:

> His vision of engaging the Lord in a dream was made known to his mother Punyavathi as he was paying obeisance to her. That mother, being submerged in ecstasy and the bliss of Brahman by means of the gnosis of Brahman, said: "O my son, from the day you were incarnated in my womb, you were highly fortunate to not want illusion [Skt. *māyā*] to ensnare you. Today you have received renunciation [Skt. *saṃnyāsatva*], as one who is liberated by the gnosis of Brahman and as one who is the path to receiving liberation, and your soul [Skt. *ātman*][68] is the same as my soul by virtue of becoming the gnosis of Brahman. We will see each other there. Take your leave from me and go to your guru."[69]

The role of Sabhapati's mother's acceptance of his renunciation in T2 contrasts sharply with the mention of his suddenly leaving his wife and two sons in the Ur-account, although both accounts otherwise read somewhat similarly.

All three accounts go on to tell us that Sabhapati, filled with "Divine ecstasy," went directly to the Sacred Place (Skt. *sthala*) of Vedashreni Swayambhu (Vedaśreṇi Svayambhū, "The Self-Manifest [Linga] in the Abode of the Vedas"). Evidence in T2 confirms that this is none other than Dandeeswarar Vedashreni Temple (Taṇṭīsvarar Vētacirēṇi Kōvil) (see Figure 1.5), a once-rural temple now located just outside the sprawling campus of the Indian Institute of Technology and around the corner from Phoenix Mall, one of the largest shopping malls in Chennai. The temple, also called Sri Dhandapani Eswaraswamy Temple, is considered a "Swayambhu," or self-manifesting phallic stone of Shiva. The presiding deity is Shiva as the Lord of the Dance (Śrī Naṭarājar), and there is a documented legend of Thirugnana Sambandar (Tiruñāṉa Cambantar) of the sixty-three Nayanars (Nāyaṉmārkaḷ) having visited the site.[70]

Figure 1.5 Dandeeswarar Vedashreni Temple as seen from the tank (Tam. *kuḷam*). Photo by the author.

In this temple Sabhapati obtained the second part of the experience following the dream, which this time is not framed as a dream but as a vision that Sabhapati obtained after three days and nights in continual meditation (Skt. *dhyāna*). According to the Ur-account, after he "sat before the Mahadeva for three days and three nights immersed in deep contemplation," on the third night he had a vision ("darshonum," < Mpvl. *taricaṉam*, < Skt. *darśana*) of Mahadeva (Mahādeva), who expressed to him certain mysteries of Shiva's "phallic stone" (Mpvl. *liṅkam*, < Skt. *liṅga*) as follows: "Consider the Lingam to be nothing more than my Universal Infinite Spiritual Circle or Brahmasaroopa [Skt. *brahmasvarūpa*, "the inherent form of Brahman"] itself. He who thinks so receives Brahmagiyana [Skt. *brahmajñāna*, "gnosis of Brahman"]."[71] Following this, the Ur-account records that Mahadeva again bade him to go to Agastya's ashram. Compare the above with the experience in T2, which is framed as follows:

> Having reached Chidambara Swamigal at the midnight watch, he solemnly put on red ocher clothes and a tied forelap [Tam. *laṅkōṭu*] from the worship rites [Mpvl. *pūjai*, < Skt. *pūjā*]. After that he came to the sacred locale of Vedashreni, which was his family clan's [Mvpl. *kulam*, < Skt. *kula*] and his own divine, sacred place [Mvpl. *teyvastalam*, < Skt. *divyasthala*]. He remained in meditation [Mvpl. *tiyāṉam*, < Skt. *dhyāna*] both day and night in that sacred place's locale of Dhandapani Eswarar [Taṇṭapāṇīsvarar, < Skt. *Daṇḍapāṇīśvara*, "The Lord in whose Hand is a Staff"] over the course of three days. On the third day at night, a splendor of radiance [Mvpl. *cōtippirakācam*, < Skt. *jyotiḥprakāśa*] appeared at the place of the phallic stone [Mvpl. *liṅkam*, < Skt. *liṅga*]: "We are called out for truth. What is this? Recite your composition of a Garland as a Hymn of Mercy at all sacred places, and afterward go to the place of the guru." Upon hearing that, he uttered the "Garland of Mercy" ["Kirupāstippāmālai"] while full of bliss and ecstasy.[72]

This accords well with the Ur-account's emphasis on the centrality of the self-manifesting "phallic stone" (Sabhapati's own translation for Skt. *liṅga*), but we also are given some significant details. First, we learn that this is the moment where Sabhapati explicitly dons the attire of renunciation, formally breaking his ties with familial life. Second, we get confirmation that he not only considered Vedashreni to be his birthplace but also to be both his own and his clan's spiritual home. Finally, we learn that he met with his guru Vedashreni Chidambara Swamigal, and, if T1 and T2 are accurate on this point, as we have no compelling reason to doubt, this meeting would have been just prior to the guru's death in 1858, as confirmed by both inscriptional and published evidence.[73]

As noted above, in the vision above the Lord of All had communicated to Sabhapati his desire for him to travel to the hermitage (Skt. *āśrāma*) of Agastya. But, as T2 notes, his first instruction was to "Recite your composition of a Garland as a Hymn of Mercy at all sacred places." Accordingly, we next learn from T2 (omitted in the Ur-account) that "he went to all the sacred places in the lands of the Thondaman [Toṇṭa], Chola [Cōḻa], Kongu [Koṅku], Pandya [Pāṇṭiyan], and Chera [Cēra]"[74] to recite this "Garland Hymn of Mercy."[75] After Sabhapati performed this pan-Tamilian circuit through the various regions attributed to the above ancient and medieval south Indian empires, which may have been a flourish added by Shivajnanaprakash Yogishwara to demonstrate Sabhapati's authority in Tamil-speaking contexts, he then headed south to seek out Agastya's hermitage.

A Southbound Quest

Robert Caldwell (1814–1891) wrote in his colonial-era history of Tinnevelly District (modern Tirunelveli), published a few decades after Sabhapati's visionary experience, that there is a river in the district called the Thamirabirani (Tāmiraparaṇi), which "rises on a noble conical mountain called Potigai, more commonly called Potiyam, or Potiya-mā-malai, the meaning of which is probably 'a place of concealment.'"[76] He separately noted that the mountain may have been known to the Greeks,[77] was revered by the Pandya rulers, and, at least by Caldwell's time if not before, had come to be known as "Agastyar's Hill, or by the English simply 'Agastier.'"[78] The association has lasted at least a millennium, as this mountain was even mentioned in the Vaiṣṇava classic *Bhāgavata Purāṇa* (IV, 28, 29), where, as the scholar Friedhelm Hardy notes, it was called Kulācala. The Thamirabirani (as Tāmraparṇī) is mentioned along with two other unknown rivers, the Candravasā and Vaṭodaka,[79] and another passage (X, 79, 16f.) records Agastya's association with the mountain.[80] Shu Hikosaka has argued, based in part on an etymology of the mountain's earlier name Potiyil (*bodhi* + *il*, "place of awakening"), that there is a clear connection between Agastya and the Buddhist figure of Avalokiteśvara as well,[81] but this assertion has not been conclusively proven, and the history of a Buddhist presence at the mountain, while certainly very likely, remains to be fully explored.[82]

Caldwell's period descriptions of Mount Agastya and the Thamirabirani River are highly interesting for their historical references to the river in Indian and possibly even Greek sources as well, if the Solen was indeed an ancient name for this same river. His treatment is certainly dated from a scholarly perspective, and his enthusiasm to describe the nearby Thamirabirani River's civilizational appeal to a "higher class than the rude, black aboriginees" who inhabited Tinnevelly in his day is, of course, problematically racist.[83] However, Caldwell's work is important for our purposes since it is a period source, contemporary with Sabhapati's own life, which reveals that Sabhapati would not have been wandering aimlessly in his search for Agastya's hermitage but instead would most likely have had a specific destination (or destinations) in mind that by his time had already been firmly associated with the mythos of Agastya for at least a few centuries, if not earlier. The Thamirabirani River, which as Caldwell noted has its source in Mount Agastya, played the most significant role in this mythos as it was perpetuated by the Tamil Siddhas (Mpvl. *cittarkaḷ*, < Skt. *siddha*), among whom the Vedic rishi Agastya was believed to be the foremost exponent and had acquired legendary status on account of his mastery over medical and yogic arts. This Tamil Siddha form of Agastya was part of an amalgamation that also encompassed his role in receiving Śaiva religious teachings as well as revealing Tamil language and grammar.[84]

Today the mountain range is known as the Pothigai Malai, situated on the border of the modern states of Tamil Nadu and Kerala, geographically located to the south of the Nilgiri (Nīlakiri, "Blue Mountain") range in the Western Ghats of south India. Just as in Caldwell's time, the highest mountain in this range is today called Agasthya Mala (Akattiyamalai) or Agasthyarkoodam (Akastiyarkkūṭam). It is also now a popular trekking site from the Kerala side that was recently opened to women as well via a court ruling; Dhanya Sanal became the first recorded female to officially make the trek up to Agasthya Malai in 2019.[85]

The Ur-account more or less traces Sabhapati's own route of about 150 years earlier, much of which is also confirmed elsewhere in T1 and T2, providing conclusive evidence as to the fact that the location of Agastya's hermitage is indeed none other than the environs of Mount Agastya:

> Entering a thick forest he crossed it and passed through Soorooli [Suruli], Alagur [Azhagar] and Sathragiri [Sathuragiri] hill, thence through Kootala [Courtallam/Kutralam] Papanashan [Papanasam] to Agustya Ashrum [Agastya Ashram].[86]

These places along his way are themselves notable as sites historically associated with the Tamil Siddhas. Sathuragiri especially is still considered an active site for devotees interested in learning about Siddha religion, alchemy, and yoga, as attested by numerous pilgrims who flock to the site and travel guides that show where to visit.[87] Courtallam is the site of a Chola- and Pandya-era scenic site called Sri Kutralanathaswamy Temple (Aruḷmiku Tirukkuṟṟālanātacuvāmi Tirukkōyil) that is associated with a legend of Agastya changing the presiding deity by miraculous means from Vishnu (Viṣṇu) into a Shiva Lingam (Śivaliṅga).[88] Papanasam is a naturally beautiful town along the banks of the river Thamirabirani, and its circa thirteenth-century Sri Papavinasar Temple (Pāpavinācar Civaṉ Kōvil; commonly spelled Pāpanācanātar Koyil) is renowned for removing one's sins, as the name would suggest. The temple contains a sacred tree (Mpvl. *stalaviruksam*, < Skt. *sthalavṛkṣa*) behind the temple, and the presiding deity is a self-manifesting phallus (Skt. *svayambhū-liṅga*), which, as we saw in the previous section, played an important part in Sabhapati's initial visionary experiences in Velachery.[89]

All of these locations additionally contain sacred waters or waterfalls that are believed to bestow religio-magical properties upon those who bathe in them. This is especially true of the Thamirabirani River and its waterfalls near Courtallam (e.g., Five Falls) and Papanasam (Agastya's Falls), and it was the same, if not more so, in Sabhapati's day. T1 also highlights the significance of these waters by mentioning Thamirabirani directly (Tam. *tāmpara paraṇi nati*).[90] Caldwell also noted this phenomenon and emphasized that the purest water of the Thamirabiraṇi is considered to be that which is closest to the river's source: "Every portion of the stream is sacred; but bathing at the waterfalls in the upper part of its course is supposed in these times to be specially meritorious."[91] He goes on to cite Banatheertham (Bāṇatīrtham) and Kalayana Theertham (Kalyāṇītīrtham or Kalyāṇatīrtham) as two principal examples, both of which are in the vicinity of Papanasam and Mount Agastya as mentioned in the Ur-account.

Since I have established that Sabhapati's destination was somewhere in the environs of Mount Agastya and at the source of the sacred Thamirabirani River, I now turn to what the accounts themselves say about his search for the hermitage. The Ur-account does not tell us that he was searching for a monastic structure or temple building of some kind, but rather that he "searched these forests for the caves of the Rishees."[92] This was, of course, no urban hermitage or "ashram," such as was made possible by the institutionalization of various yoga ashrams in the twentieth century; Sabhapati was literally searching for caves. Both accounts mention dense jungle and roaming animals and that he survived by foraging for fruits and edible roots. While this is stock hagiographical material, it was probably not far from the truth given that Mount Agastya even today is considered one of India's (if not the world's) hotspots for biodiversity and remains heavily forested with limited human presence.

Both accounts agree that he was exhausted and sitting under one of the trees in the forest. T2 tells the following of how he finally found his guru-to-be, Shivajnana Bodha Yogishwarar (Civañāṉabōta Yogīśvar, also Civakñāṉapō:ta Ruṣi,[93] "Rishi who is the Awakening of the Gnosis of Shiva"):

> At that time Shivajnana Bodha Rishi, Agastya Rishi's righteous student on Mount Agastya and the twenty-fourth Gurupita, was in a state of samādhi. He perceived the Lord of All as communicating the following in the vision of his gnosis: "Oh servant of mine, your devotee Azhaitthat Konda Murthy has come. Make him to be your own student." After knowing everything, he called and sent out for his principal student Paramaguruyogi Siddhan (Paramakuruyōki Cittaṉ). After he arrived and his fatigue was treated, he took him along to the place of the guru.[94]

The Ur-account tells the story a bit differently, with Sabhapati instead having a vision that "three miles from the place where he was sitting was a Yogee raja to whom he must go and become disciple."[95] Upon going there, Shivajnana Bodha's "first disciple" asks Sabhapati if he is the "same person who had the vision of Mahadeva while in the temple of Vedshreni" (the same vision that was analyzed earlier in this chapter), and notes that his guru had been talking of such a person's arrival. When taken together, both accounts, while slightly divergent, do include the role of Shivajnana Bodha's principal student Paramaguruyogi Siddhan, although he is unnamed in the Ur-account, as well as the idea that Shivajnana Bodha had prior knowledge of Sabhapati's arrival, either via yogic powers or from an informant. Finally, both accounts also agree on the essential point that Sabhapati here encountered his second guru, Shivajnana Bodha and became his student in the line of Agastya.

Tracking down a physical location of the hermitage beyond the general range of Mount Agastya has proven to be fascinating, perplexing, and ultimately frustrating. The Ur-account locates Shivajnana Bodha's hermitage in a milelong cave near Mount Agastya. This cave, if it indeed existed, is

Figure 1.6 An illustration from MCVTS depicting the southern Kailāsa mountain of Agastya's succession of gurus and students (Mpvl. *takṣaṇakailāca akastiyācala parvata kurucişya pāramparaiya* [*sic*] *paṭam*). Photo by the author.

exceedingly difficult to locate, despite a maplike image provided in MCVTS that depicts the general area of Shivajnana Bodha's hermitage, possibly in the environs of the aforementioned Kalayana Theertham but certainly near a confluence of rivers (see Figure 1.6). This "map," which appears to be a simplified version of another more complex map presented in CTCSPV (see Figure 1.7), is actually a woodblock print depicting Shivajnana Bodha together with Agastya and Sabhapati, with his later title "Guru Father Rishi" (Gurupitā Ruṣi), meditating in caves (Mpvl. *kukaikaḷ*, < Skt. *guhā*) at the confluence of the Thamirabirani River and two other (possibly legendary or "yogic") rivers, the Amrita River (Mpvl. *amirutanati*) and the Siddhi River (Mpvl. *cittinati*). These form a "triple-braided" (Skt. *triveṇi*) confluence that mirrors the famous the confluence of the Ganges, Yamuna, and (subterranean) Saraswati in present-day Prayagraj. As a result, it is not impossible that this map is also similarly intended to depict yogic physiology mapped onto a landscape, or vice versa, such as has also been done with the mythic/yogic geography of Varanasi.[96]

Exploring the area today is complicated since the entire Tamil Nadu side of the Pothigai Hills is protected by the Government of Tamil Nadu Forest Department, which patrols the area via the use of police volunteers and Forest Department officials. When I visited the environs of Papanasam and

Figure 1.7 An illustration from CTCSPV depicting the "hermitage of the great rishi Agastya of the sacred Southern Kailāsa, the great Meru which is the Pothigai mountain" (Mpvl. *śrītakṣaṇakaiyilāsa mahāmēru potikācala akastiyamahāriṣi āsramam*). I am grateful to David Gordon White and Gudrun Bühnemann for respectively pointing out that a similar style of depicting yogis in pod-like caves was employed in at least one miniature by Purkhu of Kangra (ca. 1800–1815) and in a painting by Dakṣiṇāmūrti on Kailāsa (late eighteenth century, Tanjore style). Scan by the author.

Kalayana Theertham in the summer of 2018, several sadhus I spoke with along the quays of the Thamirabirani River confirmed that in Sabhapati's day westward travel in the hill areas toward the Kerala side of Mount Agastya was unrestricted, but that today such travel is impossible given that many areas, including access to the mountain itself, are simply off-limits from the Tamil Nadu side for either ecological or safety reasons. Several dam projects were also completed in the twentieth century that have further altered the landscape, and there is even a slight chance that the cave hermitage, if it was indeed a physical spot, has since been flooded.

At the same time, I have visited a publicly accessible hermitage in Kalayana Theertham that somewhat fits the description of a cave carved out of a rock (albeit not a mile long) and could have been a potential site for Sabhapati's hermitage. This site was permanently closed with the death in 2011 of one Sadhu Srila Srikrishnaveni Amma, a devotee of Agastya and the Siddhas for several decades, and the transfer of the land she occupied over to the Forest Police via a settled court case.[97] Whether that was the precise site or not, I would argue that the presence of additional cave-hermitages lurking somewhere in the mountains is not impossible. One police official I spoke with confirmed that, scattered about the area of Kalayana Theertham, a gorgeous waterfall area rich in fresh water, there are caves that yogis used to meditate inside. There are also Tamil inscriptions in the Grantha script at Kalayana Theertham that to my knowledge have not yet been deciphered and translated. Perhaps if more geographical and archaeological attention is given to this historically important site of religious activity, a more likely candidate for Agastya's cave hermitage could be discovered.[98]

All this is further complicated by the fact that there is no corroborating proof that Sabhapati's second guru, Shivajnana Bodha, ever existed, and he may have himself been a semi- or wholly legendary figure like Agastya. Unlike Vedashreni Chidambara Swamigal, about whom some basic information is known and can be confirmed due to secondary witness accounts as well as the continued existence of his shrine, Shivajnana Bodha's life remains almost entirely obscured in legend. His name is identical to a well-known medieval work related to the Śaivāgamas, the circa thirteenth-century CE *Civañāṉapōtam* (< Skt. *Śivajñānabodha*) of Meikandadevar (Meykaṇṭatēvar) of Thiruvennainallur,[99] and there was one Shivajnana Yogi (Civañāṉayōki, < Skt. *śivajñāna yogī*) of Thiruvavadutharai who wrote a commentary on this work in the eighteenth century,[100] but the precise relationship of Shivajnana Bodha with this Śaiva Saiddhāntika text, if any, remains unclear.[101] T2 gives slightly more information about him than T1 and the Ur-account, noting that he is the "twenty-fourth Guru Father" in the line of Agastya and that he considered himself to be a Mahatma who spreads "compassion (Mpvl. *kāruṇya* = Skt.) to the sentient beings of the world," a remarkably bodhisattva-like sentiment. The other factor contributing to his legendary status is his physical longevity; T2 quotes him as saying that, by the time of Sabhapati's departure from his hermitage, he had been "sitting majestically" for "four hundred and thirty-eight years,"[102] while the Ur-account mentions that the yogi was "about two hundred years old."[103]

Regardless of whether Shivajnana Bodha was a historical person or legendary mouthpiece for yogis claiming descent from Agastya's hermitage along the Thamirabirani River, both accounts claim that Sabhapati spent either nine years (Ur-account) or twelve years (T2) with this guru engaged in yogic practice.[104] This time period is critical for the purposes of this book since it is precisely when Sabhapati is mentioned as first learning the techniques that culminated in his experience of "royal yoga for Shiva" (Mpvl. *civarājayōkam*, < Skt. *śivarājayoga*, see Chapter 4; T1 calls it *ñāṉarājayōkam*, "rāja yoga of gnosis"), as the following excerpt of T2 makes clear:

> While in a cave, and while eating bulbs, roots, and so on, he received all the instructions [Mpvl. *upatēcaṅkaḷ*, < Skt. *upadeśa*], experienced all the rites [Mpvl. *cātaṉaikaḷ*, < Skt. *sādhana*], and obtained all experience [Mpvl. *aṉupavam*, < Skt. *anubhava*]. He obtained the fullness of experience in mantra, concentration [Mpvl. *tāraṇā*, < Skt. *dhāraṇā*] of vigor [Mpvl. *vayam*, < Skt. *vayas*], and the yogas of devotion [Mpvl. *paktiyōkaṅkaḷ*, < Skt. *bhaktiyoga*]. He obtained the power [Mpvl. *citti*, < Skt. *siddhi*] and experience of all yogas by means of the binding [Mpvl. *pantaṉam*, < Skt. *bandhana*] of the exhalation [Mpvl. *rēcakam*, < Skt. *recaka*], inhalation [Mpvl. *pūrakam*, as Skt.], and retention [Mpvl. *kumpakam*, < Skt. *kumbhaka*], and by the arresting [Mpvl. *stampanam*, < Skt. *stambhana*], fixing [Mpvl. *stāpaṉam*, < Skt. *sthāpana*], and the six acts [Mpvl. *ṣaṭkiriyaikaḷ*, < Skt. *ṣaṭkriyā*] of the foremost yogas of the breath [Mpvl. *cuvācam*, < Skt. *śvāsa*] and vital channel [Mpvl. *vāci*, < Skt. *vāṃśi*], the life-breath [Mpvl. *pirāṇam*, < Skt. *prāṇa*], the drop [Mpvl. *vintu*, < Skt. *vindu*], the sound [Mpvl. *nātam*, < Skt. *nāda*], the syllable *Om* [Mpvl. *piraṇavam*, < Skt. *praṇava*], and the digit [Mpvl. *kalā*, as in Skt.]. He experienced a vision of all the principles [Mpvl. *tattuva taricaṉam*, < Skt. *tattva darśana*], the divine natures of visible appearance, splendor, the womb, and power and energy. Having refuted all of these through his guidance, [his] isolated nondual self was united to Brahman by the experience of the steadfast communion with Brahman [Mpvl. *pirammaniṣaṭai camātiyaṉupavam*, < Skt. *brahmaniṣṭhā samādhyānubhava*], which is the yoga of kings for Shiva as Brahman [Mpvl. *civapiramma rājayōka*, < Skt. *śivabrahma rājayoga*]. While being in the most excellent and fully developed, unwavering, and superior samādhi, he said, "I am neither the gnosis of thinking nor the gnosis of happiness. I possess every nature and am Brahman itself."[105]

From this we learn, therefore, that Sabhapati found what he was searching for earlier while his "mind was not at ease," as we saw above, namely those techniques that lead to an experience of what is only hinted about in the Vedas, Upanishads, and other sacred texts. The balance of both accounts will subsequently go on to stress both the continued development of his abilities as well as the sharing of these abilities with his students in the role of a teacher.

Lectures and a Himalayan Flight

Sabhapati stayed with Shivajnana Bodha at Agastya's hermitage for either nine years (Ur-account) or twelve years (T2) engaged in yogic practice, when the accounts agree that he left to embark on a lecture and pilgrimage circuit that lasted at least until his arrival in Lahore toward the end of 1879. That would place his departure somewhere between 1867 and 1870. T2 provides the following additional details as to the instructions that Shivajnana Bodha gave him and, perhaps more interesting, what he was and was not permitted to share with the public:

> You know six languages. I command you therefore to complete this work of helping others. However, you must not reveal our utmost secrets, the foremost among them being alchemy [Mpvl. *vātam*, < Skt. *vāda*], sky flight [Mpvl. *kavuṉam*, possibly < Skt. *gagana*],[106] medical arts [Mpvl. *kalpam*, < Skt. *kalpa*], the entrance into other bodies [Mpvl. *parakāyappiravēcam*, < Skt. *parakāyapraveśa*], the magical ointment [Mpvl. *añcaṉam*, < Skt. *añjana*], powers [Mpvl. *sitti*, < Skt. *siddhi*], energy [Mpvl. *cakti*, < Skt. *śakti*], theurgy [Mpvl. *mūrttikaram*, < Skt. **mūrtikara*], increasing the life force [Mpvl. *āyurvirutti*, < Skt. *āyurvṛddhi*], the power of the eight acts [Mpvl. *aṣṭakkiriyācitti*], and the eight powers [Mpvl. *aṣṭacitti*, < Skt. *aṣṭasiddhi*], to the people of the world. Instead, [you should reveal] the forms of teaching on exercises [Mpvl. *aṉupavaṅkaḷ*, < Skt. *anubhava*] of devotion [Mpvl. *pakti*, < Skt. *bhakti*], meditation [Mpvl. *tiyāṉam*, < Skt. *dhyāna*], gnosis [Mpvl. *ñāṉam*, < Skt. *jñāna*], and practice [Mpvl. *cātaṉam*, < Skt. *sādhana*], which are for the benefit of the soul, for reaching the desires of now and the hereafter, and for [the sake of] desirelessness. After making a new sacred text with a sequence of instructions [Mpvl. *upatēcakkiramam*, < Skt. *upadeśakrama*] and a path of initiation [Mpvl. *tīkṣāmārkkam*, < Skt. *dīkṣāmārga*], and displaying in pictures every inquiry, ritual, and every exercise, you should send it to be printed. Worship rites [Mpvl. *pūjai*, < Skt. *pūjā*] are to be performed in the same way by people of every caste [Mpvl. *carvavarṇastarkaḷ*, < Skt. **sarvavarṇastha*]. It is your duty to go and assist the people in this way and then return to me.[107]

Again suspending truth claims as to the validity of these powers, I find that this passage presents a remarkable perspective that must have been more widespread during this period prior to the more or less rationalistic refashioning of modern yoga by both the Theosophical Society and Swami Vivekananda (Svāmī Vivekānanda), namely that many yogis also practiced alchemy, medicine, entrance into other people's bodies, and even the cultivation of powers (*siddhis*), but that these were believed to be kept secret for a select few who were the most dedicated of a given hermitage.[108] It also provides an example showing that the practices of mantra-based ritual, meditation, and devotion were to be freely taught to the public at large, while other practices such as the above powers were considered to be valid at some stages of the yogic path yet were withheld from the public gaze. This is very different from the prevailing contemporary opinion that mantra-based ritual, meditation, and devotion is separate from the cultivation of such "yoga powers," often regarded as superstition.

In any event, the Ur-account mentions that soon after his departure he published a sacred text or "science" (his translation for Skt. *śruti*) in Tamil. This original Tamil text, now apparently lost if it indeed existed, was entitled *Vētānta sittānta samarasa pirummakiyāṉa civarājayōka kaivalya aṉupūti* (< Skt. *vedānta siddhānta samarasa brahmajñāna śivarājayoga kaivalya anubhūti*, "Perception of Vedānta, Siddhānta, Samarasa, the Gnosis of Brahman, Śivarājayoga, and Isolation").[109] The title, especially the phrase *vedānta brahmajñāna śivarājayoga anubhūti* with *siddhānta samarasa* and *kaivalya* removed, is remarkably similar to the Sanskritic titles of CPSPS (*Vedhantha Siva Raja Yoga Brumha Gnyana Anubuthi*, i.e., Skt. *vedānta brahmajñāna śivarājayoga anubhūti*) and to some extent also his Hindi work RYB (*Rājayoga brahmajñānānubhūti saṃgraha veda*). As we shall see in Chapter 2, portions of this text may have formed the basis for some of Sabhapati's instructions in these later texts that were absent from his other published lectures. It is further interesting that "Siddhānta," in this case almost certainly a reference to Śaiva Siddhānta, was removed from subsequent titles that only wished to stress the text's leanings toward Vedānta. As I shall point out in Chapter 3, however, a clear innovation of Sabhapati's thinking is that the experience of Śivarājayoga could be framed in the terminologies of both Advaita Vedānta *and* Siddhānta—in simple terms, to him monism and dualism were not necessarily mutually exclusive positions in the attainment of the royal yoga for Shiva.

T2 records that Sabhapati at this time then traveled to "Malayali, Tamil, Telugu, Kannada, Marathi, Gujarati, Hindustani, Bengali, Nepali, Punjabi,

Rajputhani, Kashmiri, Sindhi, Multani, and Himachali lands,"[110] which geographically covers much of the Indian subcontinent except for parts of modern-day Assam and further northeast, Bhutan, and the Sinhalese-speaking areas of Sri Lanka. In these places he visited sacred sites to view their presiding deities (Mpvl. *stalataricaṉaṅkaḷ*, < Skt. *sthaladarśana*), bathed in rivers (Mpvl. *natisṉāṉam*, < Skt. *nadīsnāna*), and went on pilgrimage to sacred sites (Mpvl. *stalatīrttayāttirai*, < Skt. *sthalatīrthayātra*).[111] He also wrote instructions such as the above Tamil text, and others according to T2 "in the languages of Sanskrit, Urdu, Hindustani, Bengali, Telugu, Marathi, Dravidian Tamil, and English, as well as in images that depict the exercise of these rites,"[112] the content of which was perhaps incorporated into later works in those languages.[113] He likewise composed numerous poetic stanzas of praise, some of which are interspersed in both T1 and T2.

T2 even mentions a meeting in Vadalur (Vaṭalūr) with the prominent figure Chidambaram Ramalinga Swamigal (Tam.: Citampara Irāmaliṅka Svāmikaḷ, 1823–1874, not to be confused with Sabhapati's student Konnur Ramalinga Swamigal, for which see the section Konnur Ramalinga Swamigal).[114] Chidambaram Ramalinga Swamigal had established the "Satya Jnana Sabha" (or Sathya Gnana Sabha, Tam.: Catya Ñāṉa Capai) in Vadalur in 1872, and a Brahmin named "Sabhapathy Sivachariar" (Tam.: Capāpati Civācāriyār) is mentioned in some popular hagiographical accounts of this period as serving as the first priest of this shrine.[115] Although possible, it does not seem likely that they were the same Sabhapati since at least one court document states that Sabhapathy Sivachariar was from Adoor (in present-day Kerala) and died in 1903,[116] whereas Sabhapati Swami was from Velachery and likely died around 1923.

The Ur-account for its part stresses that on these journeys he corresponded and communicated with many religious practitioners at these and other temple sites across the subcontinent, noting that he had "visited nearly all the holy shrines and Ashrams of India, and in some of these places he met with genuine Yogis and Rishees," and that he "had many adventures with these depositories of ancient lore."[117] These experiences would have greatly contributed to the pan-Indian character of his instructional literature on yoga, which would have undoubtedly been an interest of the account's author. Finally, T2 also records that he "established 464 meditation societies [Mpvl. *tiyāṉa capaikaḷ*, < Skt. *dhyāna sabhā*] in various places of the land of the Hindus [Persian + Mpvl. *hintutēcam* = Skt. *hindudeśa*] for his students to carry out the practice of the rites."[118]

At this point both accounts relate a cosmic vision that he had "on the coast of Manasarovar Lake" after "crossing the Himalayas."[119] This visionary experience, as we shall see, would become somewhat of a controversial matter for Sabhapati and his followers, so I here recount it in full. In the Ur-account, he encounters "three Rishees in antique Aryan dress," two of whom are later revealed to be Shuka (Śuka) and Bhringi (Bhr̥ṅgi) from the Sanskrit epic Mahabharata, while the third does not reveal his name. They question him about his guru and Agastya's hermitage and, upon hearing his answer, they offer to grant him the "Ashtama Siddhis" (Skt. *aṣṭamāsiddhi*), which are framed as "eight kinds of psychic powers the acquisition of which enables one to perform (what is vulgarly called) miracles."[120] Sabhapati of course turns down the offer, saying that he only wishes to pass his remaining days on earth in "Nishkamya Brahmagiyana, Yoga tapam" (Skt. *niṣkāmya brahmajñāna yoga tapa*, "the austere heat of yoga that leads to the gnosis of Brahman, free from desire"). They confer upon him the title "Brahmagiyana Guroo Yogi" (Skt. *brahmajñāna guru yogī*, CPSPS: "Holy Spiritual Godheaded Ascetic") after hearing this answer, and ask if they can do anything else for him. He responds in the affirmative, saying that he has desired to see "Kailas [Kailāsa] or the celestial mountain which it is said is invisible to ordinary mortals." They accept his request, and both they and Sabhapati "began to fly in the air for a time towards the direction of the mountain . . . where he had the goodfortune [*sic*] of seeing Mahadeva sitting in Semadhi [Skt. *samādhi*] in a cave."[121] Sabhapati then spontaneously composes verses from his "overcharged emotions" that the rishis named "Shiva varnana stuti mala" (Skt. *śiva varṇanā stuti mālā*, "Garland Hymn in Praise of Shiva"). They then descend back to where they were, and Shuka and Bhringi reveal their identities.

T1 and T2 gives similar readings of this event, except there are a few minor differences. First of all, Sabhapati is not offered the eight powers since, as we read, he had already ostensibly learned these from his guru Shivajnana Bodha but was instructed to keep them secret. Second of all, Sabhapati's response in T2 after the offer is that he only wants the "liberation of unity" (Mpvl. *aikya mukti* = Skt.), and it is instead the rishis that praise him as "desireless" (Mpvl. *niṣkāmmiyam*, < Skt. *niṣkāmya*). Third, a truncated version of the poem that Sabhapati spontaneously composed is provided. A much longer version of this poem is given in both Tamil and Devanagari script with some variations in the third part of CPSPS, which mostly follows the Ur-account but with some slight modifications,[122] and it was also supplied in full in T1.[123] Fourth, in T2 there is a difference in the title conferred on Sabhapati; the rishis mention that he was "elevated as a Guru Father Rishi [Kurupitā Ruṣī] by those of your hermitage [Mpvl. *ācīrmam*, < Skt. *āśrama*] who are beloved by the guru." The title "Jñānaguru Yogī" ("Yogi who is the Guru of Gnosis"), on the other hand, had already been bestowed upon him (minus the Ur-account's prefix *brahma-* to make *brahmajñāna*) in both T1 and T2 by his guru Shivajnana Bodha following his years of yogic practice on Mount Agastya. A final embellishing detail in T2 is that the rishis, after speaking, "vanished as they entered the sky [Mpvl. *kaka:ṉam*, < Skt. *gagana*],"[124] while the Ur-account has them vanishing "on the very spot."[125]

Following this event, all three accounts agree that he went to temple complexes in "the southern region of the Himalayas"[126] associated with the pilgrimage sites of Kedarnath (Kedārnāth; Ur-account: "Pancha Kedar" ["Five Kedars"]; T2: "Kētāranāt"), Badrinath (Badrīnāth; Ur-account: "Pancha Bhadrie" ["Five Badris"]; T2: "Pattirināt"),[127] and Pashupatinath (Paśupatināth Ur-account: "Pasupati Nath in Nepal," T2: "Pacupatināt"). T2 adds that following these he also visited "Jwalamukhi [Jvālāmukhī], Triloknath [Triloknāth], Bhutanath [Bhūtanāth], the source of the Ganges [likely Gaṅgotrī], the source of the Yamuna [likely Yamunotrī], Amarnath [Amarnāth], and Manikaran [Maṇikarṇa],"[128] and then left for Kashmir, a list also mostly the same as T1. We know from both his primary accounts and secondary literary accounts that, amid travel to these sacred locations—possibly before or after visiting Jwalamukhi, which is not too far from Lahore and is the first site not mentioned in the Ur-account—he traveled to this former capital of British Punjab.

A Splash on the Lahore Scene

Sabhapati enters another stream of colonial-era history with his stay at Lahore, which was then the principal city of British Punjab (since Partition in West Pakistan, and today the Islamic Republic of Pakistan).[129] This was undoubtedly one of the most fertile stops on his pilgrimage and teaching circuit, and here he secured at least three meetings of great importance for his future publishing efforts and both pan-Indian and international fame. It is notable that T1 and T2 entirely omit mention of Sabhapati's stay at Lahore, but beyond the Ur-account there are multiple secondary sources that confirm his visit to the city. Variants of the Ur-account differ on whether he stayed either a "few days"[130] or about "six months,"[131] but it seems he broke his trip into at least two visits, one in December 1879 and another in November 1880. One source records his arriving in December 1879 to deliver "lectures on *Yoga*,"[132] and we know that he must have already met with Shrish Chandra Basu, who penned the Ur-account, in Lahore before January 1880 (the date of the account). After these initial lectures on yoga, he himself records in a published letter in *The Amrita Bazar Patrika* (see Shrish Chandra Basu and the Theosophical "Founders") that he spent "six or seven months in the solitary caves and jungles of Kangra Hills" near present-day Kangra, Himachal Pradesh, where he enjoyed a "solemn state of Samadhi."[133] As we shall see in the following section, Sabhapati had returned to Lahore by November 1880, as evident in a personal diary entry of Henry Steel Olcott, in Olcott's published work, as well as in the published letter itself.

Shrish Chandra Basu and the Theosophical "Founders"

The most instrumental meeting that Sabhapati had in Lahore was with his Bengali editor-to-be and principal "Admirer" Shrish Chandra Basu (Śrīś Candra Basu, aka S. C. Vasu, 1861–1918),[134] the most likely candidate for authorship of the Ur-account itself; the account was, after all, penned in Lahore. According to his biographer Phanindranath Bose,[135] who also interviewed his mother, at the time of their meeting Shrish Chandra was only around nineteen years old and had not yet joined any reformist societies, but would later go on to become an educated legal advocate (Hnd.: *vakīl*) and translator of Sanskrit texts, including the dissemination of the work by Panini (Pāṇini) on traditional Sanskrit grammar, the *Aṣṭādhyāyī*, first published in 1897.[136] After meeting Sabhapati he went on to join the Theosophical Society, publish widely on yoga, and, as Singleton has noted, later would emerge as an unlikely emblem of early twentieth-century Hindu reform with the release of his series "Sacred Books of the Hindus," today ubiquitous at university libraries and with print-on-demand book dealers.[137] Given Shrish Chandra's importance in the middle period of Sabhapati's life, I here briefly treat Shrish Chandra Basu's own parallel history and interactions with Sabhapati, beginning with the history of his father's relocation from Bengal to Lahore and ending with Shrish Chandra's activities as a college student at Government College Lahore,[138] during which Shrish Chandra met Dayananda Saraswati (Dayānanda Sarasvatī, 1824–1883), Sabhapati Swami, as well as the founders of the Theosophical Society,

Helena P. Blavatsky (1831–1891) and Henry Steel Olcott (1832–1907), both of whom also met with Sabhapati.[139]

Shrish Chandra's father, Shyama Charan Basu (Śyāmācaraṇ Basu or "Babu Shama Churn Bose," 1827–1867), was born to a family of Kayastha (Kāẏastha) caste in his home village (Bng. *deśer bāṛi*) of Tengra-Bhavanipur (Ṭeṃgrā-Bhabānīpur), which prior to the partition of Bengal in 1905 was in Khulna (Khulnā) and today is in Satkhira District (Ṣaṭkṣīrā Jelā), Bangladesh.[140] Shyama Charan eventually left his home to study for a few years in Calcutta (today Kolkata, West Bengal) at the General Assembly's Institution, an English-medium school founded by the Free Church of Scotland missionary Alexander Duff (1806–1878), and on Duff's recommendation found employment with an American Presbyterian missionary, Charles William Forman (1821–1894) of Kentucky, a graduate of Princeton Theological Seminary who was seeking to open the first English-medium missionary school in the Punjab. A series of events led Shyama Charan to government service, and he worked closely with Dr. Gottlieb Wilhelm Leitner (1840–1899), a Hungarian Jew who was the first nonofficiating principal of Lahore Government College, from November 1864 to April 1886,[141] during which time Shyama Charan's son Shrish Chandra would go on to attend the institution. Shyama Charan died suddenly in August 1867 of natural causes, leaving behind his wife, Bhubaneshwari Devi (Bhubaneśvarī Debī, ca. 1837–1923), and their four children, two sons and two daughters. Shrish Chandra, born on March 21, 1861, was the oldest son. His younger brother, Baman Das Basu (Bāmandās Basu, 1867–1932), was the youngest child and also went on to travel to England and become a prominent author on a variety of subjects from medicine to missionary movements (see Figure 1.8 for some of their activities together). One sister whose name is unknown was the eldest of all and was still living in 1932, while another younger sister was named Shrimati Jagatmohini Das (Śrīmatī Jagatmohinī Dās).

Shrish Chandra's behavior changed after his father's death, and we learn that he enrolled at Forman's Mission School in 1868. He soon was transferred to the Government District High School after his mother was alarmed at the missionary influence on his life, and thanks to tutoring from friends of the family who taught him English via the Shakespearean classics *Julius Caesar*, *Macbeth*, *Hamlet*, and other works, he went on to achieve top marks on the Calcutta University entrance exam in 1876 and received a scholarship to attend Lahore Government College, where he was attending when he met Sabhapati in 1879. He initially chose Arabic and Persian as his secondary

Figure 1.8 The Basu brothers and some of their activities. Published in the Bengali journal *Prabāsī*, vol. 30, and photographed with permission at the Visva-Bharati University library (out of copyright).

languages instead of Sanskrit, perhaps in honor of his father, who had been a scholar of those languages, but he would eventually pick up a serious study of Sanskrit after his departure from Lahore.

Parallel to Shrish Chandra's academic achievements was a growing interest in yoga. Phanindranath Bose informs us that Shrish Chandra met a Kanphata Nath Yogi (Kāṇphaṭa Nāth Yogī, that is, an "ear-pierced" yogi of the Nāth sect) named "Shivanath" (Śivanāth), who was in charge of a temple on the same lane as the house the Basu family moved to in 1874.[142] Not much is known about Shivanath except the description that he provides:

> There was a temple not far from the house in Lahore where Sris [Shrish Chandra] lived, in charge of a yogi, who had both his ears bored and with circular rings in them. He belonged to the sect of Guru Gorakhnath. He was learned in Sanskrit, Hindi and Panjabi and used to deliver discourses on religious subjects to the people who used to assemble almost daily in the temple. Sris was also a very frequent visitor there. He owed much of his knowledge of Hinduism and the rites and ceremonies of Guru Gorakhnath's sect to this ascetic, whom he always held in great reverence.[143]

The reference to the semimythical Nāth hero Gorakhnath (Skt.: Gorakṣanātha, Hnd.: Gorakhnāth) is notable as it connects Shivanath—and Shrish Chandra's initial fascination with yoga as a teenager—to the Punjabi milieus of Nāth activity that Mohan Singh and George Briggs explored for their respective studies over half a century later,[144] as well as to the wider historical context of the Nāth Yogī movement prior to Partition.[145]

Shrish Chandra took this interest in yoga with him as he attended Government College Lahore, where he also became interested in a few popular Hindu reform movements that were just beginning to form at that time. He attended meetings personally hosted by Shiv Narayan Agnihotri (Śiv Nārāyaṇ Agnihotrī, 1850–1929), who had taken a vow of renunciation (Skt. *saṃnyāsa*) and took the name "Swami Satyananda," although his subsequent marriages and his children caused him to receive popular criticism from those who felt his renunciation was insincere.[146] Agnihotri founded the Dev Samaj (Hnd.: Dev Samāj) in 1887 and took the name "Dev Guru Bhagavan," but by that time it seems that Shrish Chandra had lost all interest in that movement. On the other hand, Agnihotri's rival Dayananda Saraswati, the aforementioned founder of the Arya Samaj (Ārya Samāj),[147] was at that time a popular personality at the Government College. As Shrish Chandra's classmate and friend Lala Shiv Dayal (Lālā Śiv Dayāl Seṭh, 1861–1935) recounted, Dayananda paid his first visit to Lahore in 1877 and "gave a series of lectures which created commotion in the student community";[148] the Lahore Arya Samaj was founded in November of that year. These lectures inspired Shrish Chandra to study "books on religious and scientific subjects" and to take "an active part in the debates which became common in those days and especially the weekly meetings which were then held in the Brahmo Samaj."[149] Although Dayananda's hard-line reformist attitude provided an early source of inspiration for Shrish Chandra and likely informed some of the tensions he expressed toward haṭha yoga (Skt. *haṭhayoga*) and Tantra,[150] Shrish Chandra never joined the Arya Samaj due to his "scruples regarding the infallibility of the Vedas" and later would go on to publish a translation of an explicitly Tantric text, the *Śiva Saṃhitā*, with the subtitle *Esoteric Philosophy of the Tantras*. He would also go on to join the Theosophical Society in 1880, as we shall see later in this section, and the Brahmo Samaj (Brahma Samāj) in 1881, although he would sever his ties with the Brahmo Samaj two years later.[151] Nevertheless, he joined these two societies only after meeting Sabhapati, who entered Shrish Chandra's life in this world of competing visions of colonial modernity.

As Karl Baier has also noted, Sabhapati began his lectures on Vedānta and rāja yoga in December 1879, and the Ur-account—again, penned by Shrish Chandra himself—was soon after published in the occult periodical *The Theosophist* in March 1880.[152] As Baier explains, the article was a "hagiography filled with so many miraculous events that even the editors of *The Theosophist* felt obliged to distance themselves from its content in an editorial note."[153] Yet his story, however blended it seemed with the realm of fiction, was undoubtedly inspiring to Shrish Chandra, and may have resonated with the interactions or conversations he had with Shivanath in his youth. Perhaps his biographer puts it best, as follows: "If Dayananda Saraswati was instrumental in arousing his interest in the study of the sacred scriptures of the Hindus, Sabhapaty Swami and the Theosophical Society stimulated him to investigate the mysteries of life after death."[154] As we have seen in this chapter, however, there is also a surprising amount of historical material beyond these mysteries that can be gleaned between the hagiographical lines.

The next month, in April, a pamphlet was subsequently advertised in *The Theosophist* as follows:

> The "Trieste [*sic*] on Vedantic Raj Yoga," by the Madras Mahatma Giana Yogi, Sabhapaty Swami, a chapter of whose life was given in our magazine last month, has appeared, and may be had at the *Mitra Vilas* Press, Lahore, Panjab, at annas 8 per copy. It is one of the most curious pamphlets ever printed, and will doubtless have a very large sale. A review of it will appear next month.[155]

The "Mitra Vilas" Press was established in 1861 by one Pandit Mukund Ram (Paṇḍit Mukund Rām, 1831–1897), the "son of a Kashmiri Brahmin priest of Srinagar,"[156] and in this instance may have worked together with the "Civil and Military Gazette" Press, where the pamphlet was printed, to distribute the work to a wider audience. The pamphlet itself was entitled *Om: A Treatise on Vedanta and Raja Yoga* (1880, henceforth VRY1), with the Ur-account added as a preface, and became widely successful, as can be gleaned by its numerous reprints. Henry Olcott possessed a personal copy of the first edition of VRY (VRY1) that has survived in the Adyar Library and Research Centre, and also includes the only known colored diagram in Sabhapati's works that in future works was printed instead in black and white, perhaps demonstrating that an original intent was for the diagrams to be in color.

Shrish Chandra's involvement as editor helped give Sabhapati's work a pan-Indian and even international appeal, which helped transform the yogi into a widely known personality across several different vernacular linguistic worlds of India as well as abroad. As we will see in Chapter 2, the reprinted editions of VRY, in print in English until 1977 and in German translation by Franz Hartmann until 2005, went on to contain new material, including supplementary instructions, additional poems, and a question-and-answer section. Shrish Chandra also sponsored a Bengali translation of the pamphlet (BRY), translated by one Ambikacharan Bandyopadhyay (Ambikācaraṇ Bandyopādhyāẏ),[157] which still survives at the National Library in Kolkata and has since been digitized. Furthermore, Shrish Chandra continued to be mentioned in all subsequent reprints of the English editions, as well as on the address page of a trilingual English, Tamil, and Sanskrit/Devanagari edition of his work (CPSPS), and he is given honorable mention in Sabhapati's work in Hindi (RYB). Friedrich Max Müller, who would also praise Shrish Chandra's *Aṣṭādhyāyī*, even cited an edition of VRY in his classic, if considered problematic on a scholarly level today, work *The Six Systems of Indian Philosophy*, and discussed the Ur-account in the context of popular belief in what he called "miracles."[158] Shrish Chandra's involvement would last until the late 1890s, when Sabhapati's later Tamil literature (including CTCSPV and MCVTS) ceased to mention him as a contributor and instead was sponsored and edited by a new cohort of mostly Tamilian students and supporters. There is also a Telugu work mentioned in front matter of MCVTS that could potentially mention Shrish Chandra's involvement, but I consider it to be unlikely given its apparently late date of release.

Another contribution of Shrish Chandra was to edit and in some cases even compose the poetry that accompanied VRY1 AND 2, much of what was in English but attributed to Sabhapati. For example, his biographer tells us that Shrish Chandra was the author of a nationalistic poem variously titled "The Yogi's Address to His Countrymen," which was included in VRY1 and most subsequent English works, including a small pamphlet entitled *The Secret of Longevity and Verses by Yogi Sabhapathy Swami.*[159] This poem is sometimes attributed to Sabhapati in his works, but this attribution is evidently erroneous; Shrish Chandra's biographer tells us that the poem was reproduced by Babu Narendra Nath Sen (Bābu Narendranāth Sen), who had also met Swami Vivekananda in 1897,[160] in the periodical *Indian Mirror* during the partition of Bengal in September 1905, and who praised Shrish Chandra and said that "these verses deserved to be written in letters of gold."[161] While the stanzas of this poem are an important record of prevailing attitudes at the time and contain many interesting Indic references from the Yoga Sūtras of Patañjali to the Mahabharata, the poem does perpetuate Orientalist tropes about the degeneracy of Indian thought that seem much more in line with Shrish Chandra's preoccupation of the reformist societies mentioned above rather than entirely a reflection of Sabhapati's own ideas. It is possible and even likely, however, that Sabhapati would have been sympathetic to Shrish Chandra's political activism and would have supported his critique of atheism and materialism in favor of the spirituality of yoga, which as we shall see in a moment is reflected in a published letter signed by Sabhapati.

At the translocal level, Shrish Chandra's involvement was also instrumental in elevating Sabhapati into a known figure in the nascent Theosophical Society, which had only just been founded in a New York City apartment five years back, in 1875.[162] As already mentioned, both the Ur-account and an advertisement for the pamphlet (VRY1) were respectively published in *The Theosophist* in March and April 1880. The two principal "Founders," Helena P. Blavatsky and Henry Olcott, first visited Lahore in 1880 following their arrival in Bombay from New York on February 16, 1879.[163] They subsequently took a trip to explore Buddhism in Ceylon (modern Sri Lanka) and by the autumn of 1880 were staying with Alfred Percy Sinnett (1840–1921) before channeling the first of the infamous "Mahatma Letters."[164]

Olcott, who had already been lecturing regularly at that point, was invited to give a lecture on the occasion of the third anniversary of the founding of the Lahore Arya Samaj, to be held on Sunday, November 7, 1880, and Sabhapati addressed the crowd afterward. Blavatsky managed to preserve a program for the event in her scrapbook, in which the site of the lecture is given as the "Arya Samaj premises in *Bhadarkaliyali, Vachovali Bazar*."[165] The joint secretaries of the Samaj are listed on the program as one Sain Dass (Lālā Sāin Dāss, d. 1890)[166] and Ruttun Chund Bary (also transliterated Lala Rattan Chand Barry; Ratan Candra Bairī, ca. 1849–1890), a Punjabi clerk in the Lahore Accountant-General's Office[167] who would go on to join the Theosophical Society and play an important role in the publication of VRY2 and VRY3 (see Chapter 2); his independent stances would periodically clash with Arya Samaj views,[168] but he did publish a well-circulated periodical out of Lahore entitled *The Arya* on a wide range of views that clarified the Lahore Arya Samaj's religious views, often in contradistinction to Theosophy.[169] The anniversary event lasted from seven-thirty in the morning to eight at night, with Olcott scheduled to lecture last, from 7:00 to 8:00 p.m., on "The relation of Theosophical Society with the Arya Samaj." Given the date and other evidence about Olcott's lecture, some of its content likely mirrored "The Fourth Anniversary Address" of the Theosophical Society, also delivered in November 1879 but in Bombay; the text of this lecture was published in 1883.[170]

There is no mention of Sabhapati's name on the program for Lahore, but we know from Olcott's published record in *Old Diary Leaves* as well as his unpublished diary for 1880 that he addressed the crowd, and that the address took place after Olcott's lecture. Olcott's published account of the lecture in *Old Diary Leaves* is as follows:

> The Anglo-Indian papers were just then full of malevolent writings against us, which made us appreciate all the more the friendliness of the Indians. I lectured to the usual overflowing audience on Sunday, the 7th November, and among the Europeans present was Dr. Leitner, the famed Orientalist, then President of the Punjab University College. At the close, the alleged Yoga [*sic*] Sabhâpaty Swami read a rambling complimentary address in which his praises of us were mingled with much self-glorification.[171]

Contrast this with Olcott's unpublished diary entry for November 7:

> Delivered my lecture to an overflowing audience. Lalla Mulraj presided, & sundry Europeans were present, among them the Justice Lindsay, Dr. Leitner (Pres't Punjab University College) Mr.—Ass't Accountant General, and half a dozen clergymen.

> At the close Sabhapaty Swami read a complimentary address & lots of people crowded around to get a sight of the Man from Patâl.[172]

From this we can gather that Olcott's lecture and Sabhapati's address were well attended, even overflowing, and it is notable that the audience was a mix of Indians and Europeans, and even clergymen. Lalla Mulraj (Hi. Lālā Mūlrāj, pop. lit.: Lala Mul Raj), who presided, was a prominent member of the Arya Samaj who was also considered a "friend and Brother" by Olcott.[173] Lalla along with Sain Dass and one other "rewrote the original principles [of the Arya Samaj] drafted in Bombay," and would later become the president of the Lahore Arya Samaj.[174] "Justice Lindsay" most likely refers to Charles Richard Lindsay, who served on the Chief Court of Lahore from 1877 to 1880.[175] The reference to "the Man from Patâl" is obscure (*pātāla* refers in Sanskrit to the underworld or nether regions) but refers to Olcott himself and not to Sabhapati.[176]

Leitner's presence is noteworthy but expected, since almost a year earlier, on November 23, 1879, the scholar and principal had written to Olcott and "promised cooperation."[177] As we saw above, Leitner had been a personal friend of Shrish Chandra's father and would have also likely known of Shrish Chandra and his interest in Sabhapati as well. Despite his favorable disposition toward Shrish Chandra, in June 1880—only a few months prior to Sabhapati's address—Leitner apparently lost his temper and "kicked one of his students," prompting a revolt from the rest of the students called the "Students' Rebellion," led by none other than Shrish Chandra, who had to forfeit his scholarship for three months.[178]

The next day, on November 8, Sabhapati visited Blavatsky and Olcott at their residence in Lahore along with one Birj Lal and one other unnamed associate. Sabhapati stayed there from 9:30 a.m. to 4:00 p.m. Olcott wrote the following about Sabhapati's visit in his *Old Diary Leaves*, which I will quote in full for reference:

> He [Sabhapati] came to our place the next day and favored us with his company fom 9.30 A.M. until 4 P.M., by which time he had pretty thoroughly exhausted our patience. Whatever good opinion we may have formed of him before was spoilt by a yarn he told of his exploits as a Yogi. He had, he said, been taken up at Lake Mânsarovara, Tibet, high into the air and been transported two hundred miles along the high level to Mount Kailâs, where he saw Mahadeva! Ingenuous foreigners as H.P.B. and I may have been,

> we could not digest such a ridiculous falsehood as that. I told him so very plainly. If, I said, he had told us that he had gone anywhere he liked in astral body or clairvoyant vision, we might have believed it possible, but in physical body, from Lake Mânsarovara, in company with two Rishis mentioned in the Mahabharata, and to the non-physical Mount Kailâs—thanks, no: he should tell it to somebody else.[179]

Compare this with Olcott's unpublished diary entry for November 8, which reads as follows:

> Sabhapaty Swami came [to] us with Birj Lal & another & stopped from 9 ½ am to 4 pm. His talks are right, but seems to me a possible humbug as his is not a spiritual face, and he tells a ridiculous story about being able to fly bodily 200 miles through the air.[180]

Olcott is, of course, referring in both the published and unpublished entries to Sabhapati's vision of Mount Kailāsa as recounted in both the Ur-account, T1, and T2, as I have already previously summarized.

Olcott's readiness to view Sabhapati as a pretender or charlatan appears to be somewhat misplaced, especially given some of the other occult phenomena that he readily believed in, such as that related to mesmerism and spiritualism. Furthermore, it is unclear if Sabhapati would have been able to effectively communicate such a clear delineation between "spiritual" and "physical" or "mind" and "body" when faced with trying to describe what clearly must have been, if it indeed happened, a profound religious experience. Furthermore, this would have been an experience that his practices of mental isolation would have only made him more susceptible to (see Chapter 6). In any event, at least some of Sabhapati's supporters felt compelled to respond to Olcott's challenges. By both the second (1893) and third (1895) editions of VRY, published by R.C. Bary & Sons (i.e., Ruttun Chund Bary), we find the following footnote—presumably written by Shrish Chandra, who is still listed as editor—in the section of the revised Ur-account that describes Sabhapati's vision of Kailāsa:

> This need not have been in the *physical* body of the Rishis; they might have flown towards the holy mountain in their *Mayavi Rupa Kama Rupa* (astral body), which to our author (who certainly is not an Adept in the sense the Theosophists use the word) must have been as real as if he had travelled through air in his physical body.—ED.[181]

A second footnote note also disputes the identities of the "Rishies" (Skt. *ṛṣi*) as being from the Mahabharata: "We beg to differ from our venerable author in this surmise. For our own part, we have *now* come to know that these Rishis were none else but the members of the glorious fraternity of adepts, the "Brothers of the Theosophical Society.—Ed."[182] This prompted a brief response from one Damodar Mavalankar (Dāmodar Ke Māvalākar, b. 1857), an early Theosophist from Ahmedabad, Gujarat, who had been accompanying Olcott during much of this early trip in India and who was also a friend of Shrish Chandra.[183] While Damodar considered "the motives of the author and the editor no doubt perfectly benevolent," he viewed much of the work as a parable that could be potentially misleading to one not properly versed in "esoteric philosophy." In response to Sabhapati's vision he notes that "the Editor has, to some extent, in a special footnote hastened to extricate his hero and himself out of a really perilous situation."[184]

There is another factor to consider here, however, which is Sabhapati's much more positive perspective on his meeting with Olcott and Blavatsky. A little over a week after their November 8 meeting, on November 16, 1880, a letter was published in the *Amrita Bazar Patrika* by the "Madras Yogi Sabhapaty Swamy" that paints a much more positive view of the meeting. In the open letter, Sabhapati recounts the following:

> I remained with them from 8 A.M. to 4 P.M. of the 8th November 1880. [H]ad a long conversation with them on the theory and practice of ancient occult science (*Sarva Sidhoo Shastras*) and on the *Vedantic Giyana Yog Shastras i.e.*, the science and holding communion with one's Self Impersonal God—The Infinite Spirit. Their explanations of these two branches of secret knowledge of our ancestors were on the whole perfectly correct, and in harmony with my own practical knowledge of them. They agreed with all my main points, and I am fully convinced that they have gained some practical acquaintance of both these sciences.[185]

Sabhapati goes on to recollect Blavatsky's perspective on the knowledge of these two "ancient sciences," including a statement by her saying that she owes this knowledge "entirely to the *Yogis* of India" from whom she acquired it on her "first and second journeys through India." He then follows this by praising her spiritual power, noting the following:

> Now, my dear Hindoo Brothers, I have found her through my divine sight of spirit that she is on the right track and has attained considerable progress

> in *yoge* [Skt. *yog(a)*], and acquired some of the *siddhees* [*siddhis*]—psychic powers, which however ought to be ignored and discarded if a person is in earnest after *moksh* [*mokṣa*]—final absorption. . . . I as a *Yogi* advise you all to listen to these Theosophists and help them in reviving the ancient spiritual sciences.[186]

Despite Sabhapati's wholehearted endorsement of Blavatsky, likely at least partially mediated by Shrish Chandra, the prospect of any further relationships between Olcott, Blavatsky, and Sabhapati appears to have been soon abandoned after these events and especially Olcott's lack of reciprocity. Yet Sabhapati's favorable disposition toward Theosophy was not forgotten, and he continued to be considered—at least publicly—by both Blavatsky and Olcott as a "friend." For example, Blavatsky most likely had both his address and his letter in the *Amrita Bazar Patrika* in mind when she wrote the following a year later in *The Theosophist* (April 1881): "Some time ago our friend Sabhapathy Swami, the 'Madras Yogi,' publicly endorsed the truth of all that the Theosophists had said about Yoga and Yogis."[187]

In any case, while there is no evidence that Sabhapati himself ever joined the Theosophical Society, Shrish Chandra was personally initiated by Henry Olcott himself on November 8, 1880,[188] and was officially listed as a member by November 20 of the same year.[189] Shrish Chandra was not the only one initiated that day, but we see in Olcott's diary the following names:

1. Ruttun Chand Bary [Ratan Candra Bairī]
2. Birnassi Das [possibly Banārasī Dās][190]
3. Kasul Nair[191]
4. Chandra Lal [Candra (or Chandu) Lāl][192]
5. Bhavani Das Batra [Bhavānī Dās Batrā][193]
6. Ramprasad [Rāma Prasād][194]
7. Siris Chundra Basu [Shrish Chandra Basu]

It is likely no accident of timing that Shrish Chandra and these others' initiations were the day after Sabhapati's address and the very same day that Sabhapati had visited Olcott and Blavatsky. Despite Olcott's personal reservations about Sabhapati, it seems that the swami's welcome in conjunction with a favorable turnout for the Lahore Arya Samaj's anniversary had an unintended—or perhaps intended all along—consequence of persuading these Indian intellectuals away from some of the more hard-line antiritual positions of the Arya Samaj as delineated by Dayananda Saraswati (both the

Samaj and Dayananda would later break ties with the Theosophical Society) and toward more embracing, if limiting in some other ways, visions of Theosophy and yoga instead. As we will see in Chapter 7, the publications of a few of these figures would go on to significantly affect the world of yoga and occultism at both the mesolocal and translocal levels.

It appears that Sabhapati and Shrish Chandra likely parted company sometime around 1881, as there is no subsequent mention of their interactions after this date, and, as mentioned previously, there is no further mention of him in Sabhapati's Tamil-language works from the late 1890s onward. By 1882 we find Shrish Chandra working toward the "Vakilship" of the Allahabad High Court. In 1883 his efforts to launch a Lahore branch of the Theosophical Society were halted when Olcott heard of a controversial meeting presided over by one Bishan Lal (Biśān Lāl), a well-educated and influential Theosophist of Bareilly, who apparently in his struggle with mental illness decided to "convince the people as to the reality of occult forces."[195]

Shrish Chandra by 1886 had passed the Allahabad legal bar, left his post as the principal of a Bengali school in Lahore, and was working in Meerut, then part of the North-Western Provinces, where he became more interested in the study of Sanskrit. It appears there were at least some limited interactions between him and Sabhapati concerning the publication of the First Book of CPSPS in 1884, in which his Meerut court details are listed, but unfortunately no record of their correspondence has been traced at present, and it seems that they gradually fell out of touch; his name is not even mentioned in the Second Book of CPSPS, published in 1890.

John Campbell Oman and "Sadhuism"

Aside from Shrish Chandra, another important meeting Sabhapati had in the Lahore "scene" was with John Campbell Oman (1841–1911), who would later obtain considerable fame as a popular author of various aspects of Indian life, especially the "fakir-yogi" and what he called "sadhuism."[196] Oman, the son of one John Oman, a planter, and Maria Eweler, was described as of "Eurasian or Domiciled European" origin.[197] He was educated in the "La Martiniere Institution" of Calcutta, the city where he appears to have been born. He was employed in the Accounts Department and apparently left from there to England, where he studied science, earning his MA. From

1866 to 1877 he worked in the Public Works Department of the British Raj, and joined the staff of Government College Lahore in 1877.

At the time of his meeting with Sabhapati, Oman was working as a "Professor of Natural Science" at the college, a post he would hold until his retirement in 1897.[198] During this time he was accordingly also an academic mentor to Shrish Chandra Basu, and he would also invite students to his home on some occasions to meet with his wife, who was named Ellen Agnes Hodges. Oman apparently had an interest in spiritualism and even held séances with the planchette with his students. His occult leanings likely informed his earnest interest in what he called the "sadhuism" of India, an eclectic interest for the time, about which he would later publish a tome including many interesting photographs, illustrations drawn by his son, and personal insights of an ethnographic nature.[199] Somehow or another he heard of Sabhapati during the latter's visit to Lahore, and they even met sometime between 1879 and 1880. Oman devotes almost three pages to Sabhapati and his rāja yoga—contrasting it with haṭha yoga, which is somewhat reductive, as we shall see in Chapter 4—in his work *Indian Life: Religious and Social* (1899).[200] This analysis was also included in his expanded and revised edition entitled *Cults, Customs and Superstitions of India* (1908).[201] The following is an extract from his original treatment:

> The *Raj yog* philosophy, as expounded in English by the Madras yogi Sabhapaty Swami, with whom I had the pleasure of conversing on one occasion, teaches that man's existence, as distinct and separate from the Infinite Universal Spirit, is a mere delusion, which arises from the genesis of the so-called twelve faculties, due to the circulation of the Universal Spirit through the human body, in a triple set of hollow vessels, answering in some way to animal functions, mind, and soul—reminded one of [E. Bulwer-]Lytton's impressive description of the red, the azure, and the silvery light circulating through Margrave's prostrate frame in the museum under the power of Sir Philip Derval's spells.[202]

The "twelve faculties" that Oman mentions, as we shall see, are none other than the cakras (< Skt. *cakra*), of which for Sabhapati there are twelve and four superseding principles, making sixteen in all (see Chapter 4). The reference at the end of the extract is to Bulwer-Lytton's occult novel *A Strange Story*, first published in 1862, and underscores the remarkable way in which Europeans, often independently of each other, would continue to read

Sabhapati's teachings through the lens of occult literature and practice (see Chapter 7).

A Vision of Agastya Once in Fifty Years

While the Ur-account only treats Sabhapati's life up to January 1880, when the account was written, other sources show that Sabhapati permanently departed Lahore in or after December 1880 to return back to the Madras Presidency and his guru's ashram on Mount Agastya. CPSPS tells us the following about his subsequent activities:

> Our Yogísver after the expiration of a few days at Lahore, he went to Jelander [Jalandhar], with the Rajah of that place, and spent a few days there, wherefrom he started directly, to his holy cave Agustia mountain of Neilgiri mountain *ācīrmam* [< Skt. *āśrama*], touching Benares, Madras &c., reached his Guru's place very soon, lest he will be loser of the visitation of Agustia Rishí which is once in 50 years.[203]

This is corroborated by T2, which gives the following sequence of events, interspersing the text of several poems of praise:

> While he was in Kashmir his guru Civaññāṉapōtaruṣi was at Agastya's Hermitage, and Akastiya Mahāruṣīsvarar was going to come to his hermitage, as he does once in every fifty years, to grant the Beloved Students of the Guru a little time to have a vision of him. The Guru Yogi of Gnosis [Sabhapati Svāmī] realized this by means of his sequence of initiation [Mpvl. *tīkṣākirama*, < Skt. *dīkṣākrama*] into the sight of the gnosis of Brahman [Mpvl. *pirammaññāṉa tiruṣṭi*, < Skt. *brahmajñānadṛṣṭi*], in his formulated sight of gnosis, and through the sight of gnosis. Both merged with each other, and he perceived the connection. Akastiyaruṣi came within his vision and said, "You must come and join us at our hermitage." Bewildered by this command [Mpvl. *ākñā*, < Skt. *ājñā*], he came from his place to the three banks [along the Ganges] of Rishikesh, Haridwar, and then Vindhyachal. After coming to Vedashreni via Kishkindha and Srisailam, he worshiped with a poem of praise. . . . Afterward he came to Chidambaram and expressed a song of praise. . . . After that, he visited Thirukkadaiyur, Tirupperunturai, Rameswaram, Madurai, Courtallam and then came to

> the mount called "Agastya's Mountain," which is his guru's hermitage and the Kailāsa of the South. Having worshiped his teacher's feet, he composed the "Poem of Keeping the Teacher's Command."[204]

The notion that Agastya only appears once every fifty years had already been expressed in the Ur-account's publication in *The Theosophist* (March 1880, see Shrish Chandra Basu and the Theosophical "Founders") as well as a section of VRY1 appended to the Ur-account, which I will reproduce in full here to facilitate a proper understanding of T2's mythological subtext that informed Sabhapati's compulsion to return to Mount Agastya:

> The founder of our Ashram viz. His Holiness the Agastiya Moonee [< Skt. *muni*] who died according to the common chronology many thousand years [ago], *is still living*, with many of the other Rishees of his time. He lives in a cave on top of the hills. The entrance of the cave is three feet long and one foot broad. The present Yogies who live around this cave go to have the darshanam [< Skt. *darśana*] once in fifty years. At all other times the cave is inaccessible, and if any Yogi wants to pay special reverence, for some special reason he assumes the shape of a bird and then enters the cave. But at the appointed time (after fifty years) all the Yogies of the Ashram go in a procession, the door is spontaneously opened, and they prostrate themselves at the feet of the Holy Rishee who blesses them, and enjoins them to keep secret what passes in his presence and in the Ashram. All Shastras [Skt. *śāstras*] and Vedas and many other books which are now supposed to be lost, are also preserved in that cave: but our Holy Agustya Moonee has not allowed us to open them and reveal their contents to mankind, as the time has not come.[205]

The claim that Agastya is still alive prompted a question from at least one member of the Theosophical Society, and the editors' response compared Sabhapati's conviction of the reality of immortal rishis to a belief that the "moon is made of green cheese"—in other words, a belief that must be suspended.[206] Yet there is something more being expressed in Sabhapati's accounts that appears to transcend the level of argumentation over whether something is merely "true" or "false," and it is here that we must again read between the hagiographical lines.

Sabhapati here appears to be perpetuating a mythology of yoga, similar to the "mythology of Tantric alchemy," a phrase coined by David Gordon

White to describe the diversity of Indian alchemical literature, some of which extends beyond mere laboratory instructions into the realm of myth.[207] The poems of praise that accompany the hagiography, especially at this stage of T1 and T2, serve to deepen this literary force even further. To see the course of events as merely false or unbelievable—while admittedly it is so, at least on a physical level—is to dismiss its function as a literary meaning-making apparatus that breathes life and purpose into the raw instructions of Sabhapati's manual of Śivarājayoga.

The mythology of T2 goes on to recount the arrival of the Gnostics (Ñāṉikaḷ), the Rishis (Ruṣikaḷ), the Siddhas (Cittarkaḷ), and the Yogis (Yōkikaḷ) on Mount Agastya from the eleven mountain ranges, namely the Himalayas (Himāñcalam), Kush Mountain (Kuṣācalam) Mount Abu (Apā:calam), Vindhya Mountain (Vintācalam), Kishkindha Mountain (Kiṣkintācalam), the Holy Kailasa Mountain (Śrī Kailācam), Bala Mountain (Pā:lācalam), Udhaga Mountain (Utakācalam) and Velliangiri (Veḷḷiyaṅ:ri) in the Nilgiris (Nīlakiri), Mahendragiri, and "Kandy Mountain" of the mountains on Lanka. It also recounts the profound experience of Sabhapati's vision (*darśana*) of Agastya in very detailed terms, which I treat in Chapter 3, since it pertains more to the mythology of the Tamil Siddhas and certain intersections with Śaiva cosmology, although the experience also reads like a visualization to be performed in meditation (Skt. *dhyāna*). RYB, by contrast, provides a much more succinct account of the events that were believed to have transpired (translated from Hindi):

> When he came this second time to the hermitage, he obtained the sight of Agastya Muni and of many rishis of his time. The people believed that this Agastya Muni was not alive, but such a thought was untrue.[208]

T2 records that the title "Rishi who is the Father of Gurus" (Kurupitāruṣi, henceforth translated "Guru Father Rishi") was bestowed upon him soon after receiving this vision of Agastya, both supplementing and superseding his earlier title of "Guru Yogi of Gnosis" (*jñānaguruyogī*).

T2 dates Sabhapati's vision of Agastya to "the full moon in the asterism of Chaitra" (April/May, i.e., Chitra Pournami) in 1880, but this appears to be based on a calculation from a parallel date from the Kali Yuga given in T1. As I have already demonstrated, we conclusively know that Sabhapati would have been in Lahore or the Kangra Hills during 1880. As a result, one possible conjecture is that Sabhapati instead returned to the hermitage on

Mount Agastya in the Pothigai Hills a few years later, sometime between 1881 and 1884, and from there returned to Madras (see Agastya and the Konnur Meditation Hall). CPSPS mentions that he made a promise to his guru before leaving Mount Agastya to fulfill two of his desires: (1) bringing the mode of worshiping the "imitated divine spiritual universal circle of the holy stone as Personal God," that is, the "phallic stone" (Skt. *liṅga*) both in its "Kasi Lingum" and "Bana Lingum" forms, to both north and south India; and (2) teaching the people the "Spiritual Divine Vision."[209] After making this promise to his guru, our "Yogísver all in a sudden came to Madras," which is where the biographical additions of CPSPS to the Ur-account, entitled "The second visit of our Yogísver to his Guru and the second order of Guru to our Yogiswamy," end.[210]

Another argument for Sabhapati's presence in Madras by 1884 is that his followers would have been interested in his whereabouts and would have been able to verify his presence in the city, especially once the First Book of CPSPS was published in 1884. Indeed, by 1884 we learn of a network of "Admirers" starting to emerge across India, especially in Madras, who seem to have been partially responsible for disseminating Sabhapati's works and assisted with publication efforts in various places (see Figure 1.9). The two places listed from which CPSPS could be obtained were Meerut, where we know Shrish Chandra was living at this time, and Mylapore (Tam. Mayilāppūr) in Madras, where by this time a new "disciple" named M. S. Mooroogasa Moodelliar (Murukēca Mudaliyār) was living near the eastern road (*māṭavīti*) surrounding the historic Kapaleeshwarar Temple (Kapālīcuvarar Kōyil).[211] On the other hand, Shrish Chandra's details are given, but he is only listed as an "Admirer," not a "student" or "disciple."

Beginning with the First Book of CPSPS, which marks Sabhapati's historical reemergence in Madras, we also see a "seal of REALITY" occur over

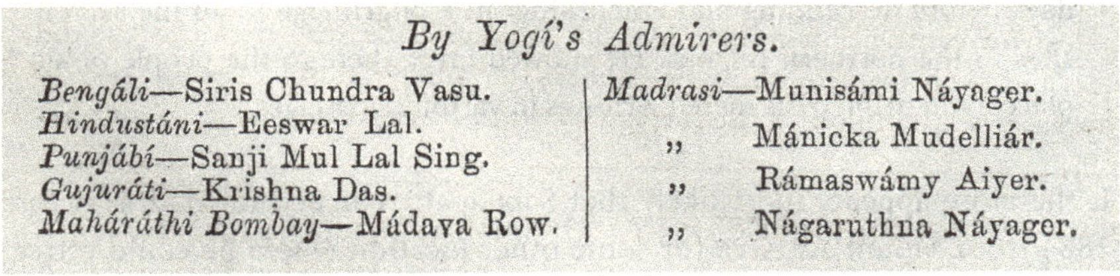

By Yogí's Admirers.

Bengáli—Siris Chundra Vasu.
Hindustáni—Eeswar Lal.
Punjábi—Sanji Mul Lal Sing.
Gujuráti—Krishna Das.
Mahárâthi Bombay—Mádava Row.
Madrasi—Munisámi Náyager.
" Mánicka Mudelliár.
" Rámaswámy Aiyer.
" Nágaruthna Náyager.

Figure 1.9 The "Yogí's Admirers" (CPSPS, First Book, 24). Scan from copy of 1884 edition, courtesy of Bill Breeze.

a span of almost three decades, from 1884 to 1913, in the title pages of CPSPS, RYB, CTCSPV, and even MCVTS. This seal includes the names and/or titles of three "succeeding disciples" along with their relevant "callings" (Skt. *āvāhana*) or titles: (1) Nagaratna Yoginath (Nākarattiṉa Yōkināt), whose "calling was the gnosis of the constituents of reality" (Mpvl. *tattuvakkiñāṉ-āvāhaṉa*, < Skt. *tattvajñānāvāhana*); (2) Murugesa Yoginath (Murukēca Yōkināt), whose "calling was the vision of the gnosis of Brahman" (Mpvl. *pirmakkiñāṉatiruṣṭiyāvāhaṉa*, < Skt. *brahmajñānadṛṣṭyāvāhana*); and (3) Shishyanath (Ciṣṣiyanāt), whose calling was "initiation into the vision of the gnosis of every instruction" (Mpvl. *carvōpaṭēcakkiñāṉatiruṣṭi tīkṣkṣāvāhaṉa*, < Skt. *sarvopadeśajñānadṛṣṭidīkṣāvāhana*). Two of the names, "Nagaratna" and "Murugesa," are recognizable (although there is unfortunately no additional information about "Shishyanath"), which confirms that Sabhapati Swami by 1884 had attracted two additional disciples in Tamil Nadu to help carry out his work. The first was undoubtedly "M. Nagaruthanum Moodliar [Tam.: Ma Nākarattiṉam Mutaliyār], Gnyan Guru Yogi Sabhapati Swami's Son and disciple," whose address was in the Mylapore area of Madras, opposite a large tank called Chitrakulam, still extant but undergoing renovation as of 2018.[212] The other disciple was one M. Mooragasa Moodliar (Ma Murukēca Mudaliyār, possibly the same as M.S. Mooroogasa Moodelliar). These two disciples were instrumental in publishing Sabhapati Swami's first extant full-length work in Tamil, CTCSPV, published in Madras in 1889, accompanied by numerous vivid diagrams (see Chapter 2).

T2 for its part omits mention of Madras but records that after Sabhapati obtained his vision of Agastya he stayed for two years on Agastya's eponymous mountain before descending from his mountaintop experience:

> In this manner he dwelt for a period of two years in the hermitage's cave, and afterward at his guru's command again set out for the Nilgiris for a few days before descending and embarking on a pilgrimage to all the sacred sites in the northern regions. He showed favor there to the people of all places, and printed his sacred writings in various languages.

It therefore appears most likely that Sabhapati returned to Madras before 1884 from Mount Agastya (or some other location where he could retreat from his supporters, if the hermitage is in fact entirely mythical). From Madras he took yet another trip north after overseeing the publication of

CTCSPV, likely after 1889. This time part of the journey included a trip, probably via rail, to Bombay, the City of Dreams.

Sabhapati in Bombay

The historical thread of Sabhapati's life resurfaces in March and April 1890, when we discover him lecturing in Bombay, as attested by one Muncherjee M. Shroff, librarian of the Bombay Branch of the Theosophical Society:

> Swami Sabhapatee, who is known to have come out of the Agastya Rishi's Ashramum in the Nilgherries, has been in Bombay for the past two months and delivered a series of six lectures in the Framjee Cowasjee Institute on Creation and Evolution and Purification of mind and soul. The lectures were illustrated by diagrams. He has been initiating some hundreds of men into the practical system of Raj-yoga, as he calls it. The Swamy says that he will persuade all his disciples to join the Theosophical Society. It is a question whether the Theosophical Society should or should not identify itself with such Guru-Yogis, and Swamis, and it is hoped our beloved Colonel will throw some light on this subject.[213]

The foundation stone for the Framjee Cowasjee Institute, mentioned in the excerpt and named after the Parsi trader and humanitarian Framji Cowasji Banaji (Phrāmjī Kavasjī Bānājī, 1767–1851), was posthumously laid in 1862, and lectures on a wide variety of various topics were regularly held at the institute (now a Hall and Reading Room). Colonel Olcott responded to Shroff's query in a snarky note:

> The "beloved Colonel" repeats what he has often said already, that all this running after Yogis, Gurus and Hermetic Brotherhoods of sorts, that promise to put students into a short cut to adeptship, is criminal folly and sheer childishness. The particular Yogi in question I have known for years, and while it is kind of him to advise people to join the Theosophical Society, I should like to see his credentials before undertaking to believe that he ever went into or came out of Agasthya's Ashrum.

Olcott's response is notable for its criticism of "Hermetic Brotherhoods" alongside yogis and gurus, which indicates that by this time he may have been aware of the growth of rival occult societies following the Theosophical Society's start in 1875, such as the Hermetic Brotherhood of Luxor (founded in 1885), some members of which were interested in acquiring some of Sabhapati's publications,[214] or the Hermetic Order of the Golden Dawn (founded in 1887; see Chapter 7).

Credentials or no, Olcott's skepticism about Agastya did little to dampen Sabhapati's popularity in Bombay; on the contrary, the Second Book of CPSPS was published out of Bombay in 1890 with an additional section in Marathi specifically for readers of that language, and his Hindi and Sanskrit work (RYB, almost entirely in the Devanagari script) would be published only two years later, in 1892, by Bombay's Tattvavivecak Press (see Chapter 2 for its relationship with VRY and Sabhapati's other works). This book does not name an editor or translator but does provide a song praising Sabhapati by the pandit Jwalaprasad Mishra (Jvālaprasād Miśra, 1862–1916) of Moradabad (Murādābād), an important figure in the formation of Hindi literature who likely assisted with its publication in that language.[215]

An order slip in the copy of CPSPS held by the British Library serves to further confirm these dates, noting Sabhapati's temporary address "up to 1st of June 1891" as in the care of "Jamsetjee Pestonjee Patel Esqr: 47 Frere Road, Mody Baug, Bombay." His permanent address "after the Ist of June 1891," however, is "M. Mooragasa Moodliar, Gnyan Guru Yogi Sabapathy Swami's Son and Disciple," residing at "Door No. 2 Brahmin Street, South to Chitracolum, Mylapore, MADRAS." This is the same Mooragasa Moodliar who had, together with Nagaruthanum Moodliar, assisted with the publication of CTCSPV, as we saw in the previous section.

Agastya and the Konnur Meditation Hall

Following this trip to Bombay and the "northern regions," T2 records that he returned to Madras (Ceṉṉai). However, the place that caught his eye was not Mylapore or Velachery, as one might expect, as the following excerpt makes clear:

> He then approached the city of Chennai and was in Holy Konnur in Villivakkam. In ancient times [here was] established a pilgrimage bathing site for Agastya and a temple for Agastya at a forest of bael trees [Mpvl.

> *vilvava$\underline{n}$am*, < Skt. *bilvavana*] where Agastya slew the asuras Vātāpi and Ilvala. [Sabhapati] established a large pool, called the Offering Pool [Yākakuṇṭam, < Skt. *yajñakuṇḍa*], and made an offering [Mpvl. *yākam*, < Skt. *yajña*] upon coming to Holy Konnur. He approached the large pool and was in his gnostic vision of the past, present, and future [Mpvl. *tirikāla ñā$\underline{n}$atiruṣṭi*, < Skt. *trikālajñānadṛṣṭi*] while on the ground in steadfast devotion. By means of his steadfast devotion, he also established a hermitage and abode of instruction [Mpvl. *maṭālayam*, < Skt. **maṭhālaya*] after a short time. He dwelled there in that place and made offerings at the great lake called the Offering Pool. On the ground at the north side of this Pool of Offering was where the Lord of All [Carvēsvara, < Skt. Sarveśvara] had given a vision of his dance [Mpvl. *naṭa$\underline{n}$am*, < Skt. *naṭana*] of five activities [Mpvl. *pañcakiruttiyam*, < Skt. *pañcakṛtya*] to Agastya, and where his disciples had gone to perform worship rites to 1,008 lingas and 108 shaligrams.[216]

Holy Konnur (Thirukoṇṇūr, pop. lit.: Konnur, Connoor) was a village in the Saidapet Taluk of Chingleput District that today has been almost entirely subsumed within the northwest Chennai suburb of Villivakkam (Villivākkam), a name also mentioned in the previous quote; Villivakkam began as a neighboring village immediately to the south of Konnur but must have already been expanding to encompass Konnur even by that time. In any event, Konnur by the time of Sabhapati's arrival in the late 1890s was still a tiny village at a good distance away from Fort St. George, Black Town, or the Esplanade, then some of the main urban centers of Madras. The Chennai to Arrakonam railway line—still running today—connected the village to Madras, however, making it accessible to the city, the rest of the Presidency, and India more broadly (cf. Figure 1.15). The village had a post office and a still-active large temple to Perumal (Tam.: Perumāḷ, a Tamil name for Vishnu [Viṣṇu], but the village otherwise would have been quite sleepy and rural.

A temple to Agastya named the Arulmigu Agatheeswarar Temple (Tam.: Aruḷmiku Akastīsvarar Tirukkōyil) along with a large tank is also still extant at the location alluded to in the quote from T2 above. The 1961 census of India surveyed this temple and dated it to the sixteenth century, and the architecture and the sculptures of the temple reveal some artistic similarities with Vijayanagara-era temples in Hampi and Srisailam;[217] in any case the temple must have predated Sabhapati's arrival by at least several centuries. A published pamphlet about this site in Tamil, entitled *Vilvāraṇyat tala purāṇac curukkam* ("Summary of the Legend of the Sacred Site of the Bael

Forest"), refers not only to T2's bael forest in its very title but also to the same destruction of Vātāpi and Ilvala by Agastya in Villivakkam.[218] The earliest known mention of this story appears to be in the third book (Skt. *parvan*) of the Mahābhārata epic, entitled the "Āraṇyakaparvan," chapter 99 according to Sørensen's order[219] and chapter 97 according to Sukthankar's numbering of the *parvan*.[220] Agastya's digestion of the two "daemon" (Skt. *daitya* or *āsura*) brothers Ilvala and Vātāpi—the latter of whom even has an ancient temple site named after him in Badami, Karnataka—accords precisely with their mention in T2, and deepens our understanding of the textual mythos of Agastya that is constantly referred to in Sabhapati's works (see Chapter 3).

Yet we know that Sabhapati was not simply a devotee (Skt. *bhakta*) but a "guru of gnosis," after all. According to T2, it was not long before he founded "the Guru Father Rishi Meditation Hall [Mpvl. *maṭālayam*, < Skt. *maṭha* + *ālaya*] of the order of Agastya" in Konnur.[221] There he also "facilitated the establishment of 1,008 lingas and the establishment of 108 shaligrams."[222] The word *maṭālayam* is of course difficult to translate, and it could be argued that the Indic loan-words "matha" (< Hi. *maṭh*, < Skt. *maṭha*) or "ashram" (< Hi. *āśram*, < Skt. *āśrama*) are closer approximations to *maṭālayam* than what the phrase "meditation hall" communicates today. However, we know that Sabhapati had an interest in teaching through the use of "meditation halls" (using that exact phrase in English), and RYB calls them *maṭh sthāns* that included a "Hall for the maintenance of a library and residence of chief guiders and mesmerisers."[223] It is highly possible that the *maṭālayam* in Konnur was at least partially built on this model. By "mesmerisers" he mostly meant initiatory gurus, as evident by a diagram that directly translates the Sanskrit word *dīkṣā* with the English word "mesmerism," which is as interesting as it is potentially misleading.[224]

We can be certain that the Guru Father Rishi "meditation hall" was at least partially established by 1889, as CTCSPV mentions the presence of this hall directly in the main text. It also refers to it in an insert as "Konnur Guru's Meditation Hall" (Tam. *koṉṉūr kirāma kurumaṭālayam*). In the main text the Chief of the Meditation Hall (Mpvl. *maṭātipati*) is referred to as none other than this same Mooragasa Moodliar (Murukēcacuvāmi), whom we have seen earlier, and in both cases the village number is given as 73, which matches a survey map from this period (see section Konnur Ramalinga Swamigal).

Furthermore, a few relatively short texts from 1894 survive, authored by Sabhapati, that also mention his name in conjunction with the *maṭālayam*. One is a multi-part series entitled "Synopsis of all the Āgamas" (Tam.

Cakālākama tiraṭṭu) (CĀT), which was published in Madras, distributed by one Mayilai Munisami Nayager (Mayilai Muṉicāmi Nāyakar), and authored (lit. "examined," Tam. *pārvaiyiṭuppaṭṭu*) by none other than Jnanaguru Sabhapati Yogishwara (Jñānaguru Sabhāpati Yogīśvara) of the Konnur Meditation Hall (Koṇṇūr Maṭālaya Ñāṉakuru Capāpati Yōkīsvarar).[225] The series of booklets contain various instructions for different rituals to be conducted on various holy days of the Hindu and astrological calendar, such as Vinayaga / Ganesh Chaturthi (Mpvl. *viṉāyakacaturtti*, < Skt. *vināyakacaturthī*), Diwali (Mpvl. *tīpāvali*, < Skt. *dīpāvali*), Navaratri (Mpvl. *navarāttiri viratam*, < Skt. *navarātri vrata*), the day of the winter solstice (Mpvl. *caṅkirāntti*, < Skt. *saṃkrānti*), and for rituals of "pradosham" (Mpvl. *piratōṣam*, < Skt. *pradoṣa*). Another pamphlet that Sabhapati released this same year (1894) was *Aṭukkunilai pōtam*, "The Order of the State of Awakening" (ANB) a work attributed to Agastya. The original edition appears to be no longer extant, although the work was reprinted without Sabhapati's name listed. The original book was registered with the Madras Record Office and a short description of it exists in the catalog page of the aforementioned *Cakālākama tiraṭṭu* (Part 1-A), indicating it was published for the same audience as "Synopsis of all the Āgamas."

The next we read of the Konnur Meditation Hall is in 1898, in a booklet entitled "Instructions on the Exercises and Practice of the Rites that are Engaged by Jñāna Guru Yogīśvara Sabhāpati Svāmī of the Hermitage of Asceticism that is Konnur Meditation Hall" (Tam. *Koṇṇūr kñāṉa kurumaṭālaya tapācīrmattiṉuṭaiya ñāṉakuru yōkīsvara capāpati svāmikaḷ aṉukkirakitta cātaṉāppiyāsāṉupava upatēcam*) (CU). This booklet, only eleven pages long, contains some basic practices, mantras, and meditations to be done at various times of the day. Yet notice the expansion of the name of Konnur Meditation Hall to now include "Hermitage of Asceticism" (Mpvl. *tapācīrmam*, < Skt. *tapāśrama*). The indication is clear that this is now not just a "meditation hall" but a hermitage for *tapas*, that frustratingly untranslatable word that has a range of semantic meanings from various physical ascetic practices that were later incorporated into haṭha yoga to cultivating an inner heat.

The next decade and a half seems to have been fortunate for Sabhapati, who attracted a wide range of new students and devotees, both male and female, to the Konnur Meditation Hall and Hermitage of Asceticism. Little is known about his precise activities in the fifteen years between 1889 and 1913, but we know that he was definitely still living in 1913, at around age eighty-five, since instructions are given on how to travel to Konnur and meet him or write him via post. It is evident that Sabhapati channeled his efforts more specifically into Tamil students and the Tamil language, culminating in a new work (MCVTS) published that year. T2 records the following:

> He created and graciously bestowed a revealed scripture, recollected teaching, and sacred writing, which facilitates instruction in the Dravidian language of Tamil, and in it he showed the performance of action, the gnosis of yoga, and all kinds of austerities, practices of the rites, exercises, and gnoses of all the principles of being, as well as in forty diagrams of the principles of being and in diagrams of meditation [*tiyāṉapaṭaṅkaḷ*].[226]

This new work appears to be Sabhapati Swami's last independent work (i.e., that is not a reprint). As mentioned earlier, two versions exist; a short version of around forty-four pages (plus front matter) and a long version of 108 pages, the original front matter plus some additions, such as T2. The additional pages are not listed in the table of contents (Tam. *aṭṭavaṇai*), which is a remarkable amount of text (sixty-four pages in all) to not be accounted for. It is possible that the larger version may have been designed for teachers, or was added later, or was only released to the public on a limited basis, especially since it was the shorter version that was registered with the Madras Record Office, a copy of which found its way into the collection of the British Library in London. In any event both versions of the work included a veritable wealth of instructions on mantras and meditations not only pertaining to Śaiva, Vaiṣṇava, and Śākta ritual devotion but also include mantras for many other gods, forms of the Goddess, and astrological bodies. Most importantly of all for the purposes of this book, both versions also include a coherent explanation of Śivarājayoga and where it stands in relation to haṭha yoga and rāja yoga (or Haṭha Rājayoga, as he calls rāja yoga; see Chapter 4). In short, the establishment of the Konnur Meditation Hall and the Hermitage of Asceticism as early as 1889 had all but inspired a new wave of growth for Sabhapati and his students, the latter of whom were eager to put his teachings into practice.

South Indians to the Fore

By 1913, Sabhapati's followers were spread out around the Nilgiri Hills in Ooty (present-day Udhagamandalam), Coonoor, as well as elsewhere in what is today Tamil Nadu, including Madras and Trichy (present-day Tiruchirappalli), as attested by a list of names given in his Tamil work (see Figure 1.10).

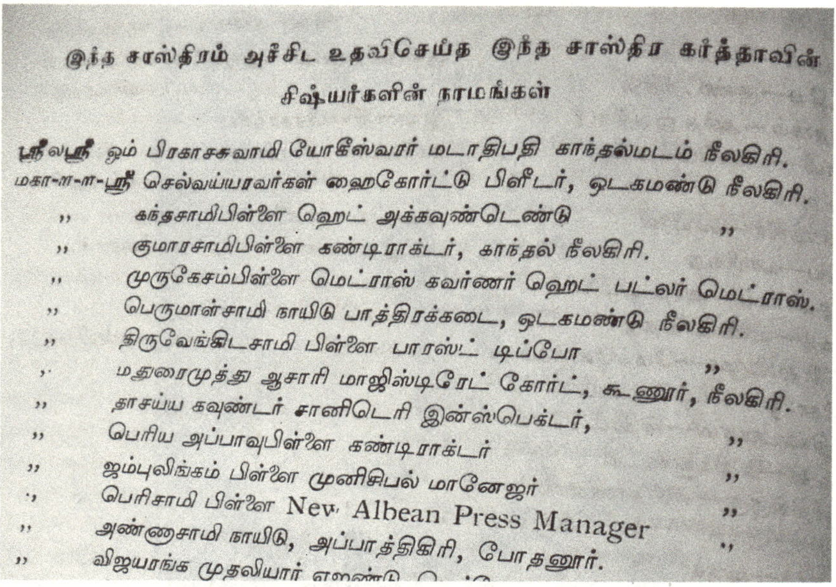

இந்த சாஸ்திரம் அச்சிட உதவிசெய்த இந்த சாஸ்திர கர்த்தாவின்
சிஷ்யர்களின் நாமங்கள்

ஸ்ரீலஸ்ரீ ஓம் பிரகாசசுவாமி யோகீஸ்வரர் மடாதிபதி காந்தல்மடம் நீலகிரி.
மகா-ா-ா-ஸ்ரீ செல்வய்யரவர்கள் ஹைகோர்ட்டு பிளீடர், ஒடகமண்டு நீலகிரி.
" கந்தசாமிபிள்ளை ஹெட் அக்கவுண்டெண்டு "
" குமாரசாமிபிள்ளை கண்டிராக்டர், காந்தல் நீலகிரி.
" முருகேசம்பிள்ளை மெட்ராஸ் கவர்ணர் ஹெட் பட்லர் மெட்ராஸ்.
" பெருமாள்சாமி நாயிடு பாத்திரக்கடை, ஒடகமண்டு நீலகிரி.
" திருவேங்கிடசாமி பிள்ளை பாரஸ்ட் டிப்போ "
" மதுரைமுத்து ஆசாரி மாஜிஸ்டிரேட் கோர்ட், கூனூர், நீலகிரி.
" தாசய்ய கவுண்டர் சானிடெரி இன்ஸ்பெக்டர்,
" பெரிய அப்பாவுபிள்ளை கண்டிராக்டர் "
" ஜம்புலிங்கம் பிள்ளை முனிசிபல் மானேஜர் "
" பெரிசாமி பிள்ளை Nev Albean Press Manager "
" அண்ணுசாமி நாயிடு, அப்பாத்திகிரி, போதனூர். "
" விஜயரங்க முதலியார்

Figure 1.10 A list of Sabhapati's new wave of Tamilian students who helped make MCVTS possible, published in MCVTS, 6. Photo by the author.

Many of these followers had various occupations, which are also listed as English words rendered into Tamil, such as "head accountant" (Tam. Eng. *heṭ akkavuṇṭeṇṭu*), "contractor" (*kaṇṭirākṭar*), and even "Madras governor's head butler" (*meṭrās kavarṇar heṭ paṭlar meṭrās*). While the central point was still the Konnur Meditation Hall and Hermitage of Asceticism, as mentioned in MCVTS, the network by this time and grown to encompass new areas of Tamil Nadu that don't appear to have been previously reached.

Om Prakash Swamigal

The most notable name on the Tamil list of Sabhapati's supporters in Figure 1.10, also evident by his name at the top of the list, is Om Prakash Swamigal (Om Pirakāca Cuvāmikaḷ; Om Pirakāccuvāmi Yokīsvaraṛ, August 11, 1872—December 14, 1947, See Figure 1.11). The full name and title on the list could be translated as "The highly auspicious Om Prakash Swami Yogishwarar, chief of the Kandal meditation hall in the Nilgiris" (Tam. *śrīlaśrī om pirakāccuvāmi yōkīsvarar maṭātipati kāntalmaṭam nīlakiri*). Om Prakash was born in a suburb

Figure 1.11 An undated (early twentieth-century) photograph of Om Prakash Swamigal on display at his hermitage and adorned with a garland. Photo by the author.

of Chennai called "Varata Rājappēṭṭai" (possibly Varadharajapuram) to one Rayavelur Ve. Mu. Gopalaswamy Pillai (Rāyavēlūr Ve. Mu. Kōpālacuvāmi Piḷḷai) and Sironmani Amaravathi (Cirōṉmaṇi Amarāvati). In his childhood he received the holy name "Tulsilinga" (Mpvl. *tuḷaciliṅkam*, < Skt. *tulasīliṅga*) at a temple to Perumal. As is the case with many hagiographical accounts of saintly people, his only known biographical account stresses his positive qualities and virtues during childhood and adolescence, but it is otherwise a very useful starting point to construct a history of this elusive figure.[227] He attended school, but even while there he had a constant attraction to temple rituals, and appears to have been religiously-minded from an early age. A few brief narrative sketches are given in the account that illustrate this, which I summarize here to give some context for his interest in yoga and religious rituals leading up to his meeting with Sabhapati.

One day a well-known person from the "land of Malayalam" (Mpvl. *malaiyāḷa tēcam*; at that time Travancore State, much of which is now modern Kerala) came by chance to his house from an adjacent street.

Impressed with his devotion, he wrote a song for use in his ceremonies that both of them would sing regularly in the morning and night. Apparently Om Prakash could not get enough of what the man could teach him, and after a few months would sneak out the window regularly with his friends while his parents were sleeping so that he could learn more from him about the "wealth of worship rites" (Mpvl. *pūjā tiraviyaṅkaḷ*, < Skt. *pūjā dravya*).[228]

He seems to have been especially fond of Ganesh (Gaṇapati, Vināyakar) as a child, so much so that one day the idol of Ganesh that had been worshiped during the festival of the "Fourth Lunar Day of Vinayagar" (Mpvl.: *vināyaka caturtti*) had been submerged and left behind in some water according to tradition, and Om Prakash without anyone knowing pulled it out of the water and hid it in a room of his house behind a stack of earthen pots. When his mother found it and asked why he put it there, he started crying and gave it to his mother and told her to put it in their room for worship rites (Mpvl./Tam. *pūjai aṟai*).[229]

His account also recounts an interesting childhood story where he and his friends acted in a play depicting the story of Markandeya (Mārkkaṇṭēyar) and Yama (Yamaṉ). One of his friends, dressed as Yama, cast the noose over Markandeya, who was hiding in a basket. Om Prakash, who was dressed as Shiva, emerged furiously and started kicking Yama to preserve Markandeya's life.[230] This particular anecdote in the account seems to at once highlight his ability to immerse himself in a role, useful in ritual worship, as well as the difficulty he could have in separating his own identity from such a dramatic simulation.

The account also devotes some attention to Om Prakash's interest in books, noting that along the way to Chennai some booksellers had set up shop. Approaching one, he asked for a recommendation since he had no idea what book to get. The seller gave him a book entitled *Civāṉantapōtam*, "The Awakening of the Bliss of Shiva," the price of which was one anna (at that time a currency denoting one-sixteenth of a rupee).[231] After taking that home and reading it thoroughly, he was then given a book of the songs of one Kunangudi Masthan Sahib (Kuṇaṅkuṭi Mastāṉ Cāyapu, also Cākipu), a scholar from a Muslim family who appears to have been active in the Royapuram (Irāyapuram) area of Chennai in the early nineteenth century and composed songs relating to the Tamil Siddhas, among other topics.[232]

Om Prakash apparently also enjoyed composing poems and hymns on the gods (Mpvl. *teyvaṅkaḷ*), and would visit Thiruttani (Tiruttaṇi) and Thiruporur (Tiruppōrūr) out of devotion to Murugan (Murukaṉ, identified with Kartikeya and Skanda).[233] The account also reveals that by this time he had two idols for contemplative worship (Mpvl. *upācaṉā mūrttikaḷ*, < Skt. *upāsanā mūrti*) in his personal temple room (Mpvl./Tam. *pūjai aṟai*), Gaṇapati (Tam.: Kaṇapati, i.e.,

Ganesh) and Daṇḍapāṇi (Tam. Taṇṭapāṇi), in this case most likely a form of Murugan although it could also be a form of Vishnu.

After his initial "schooling on the veranda" (Tam. *tiṇṇaippaḷḷikkūṭa*)[234] was complete, Om Prakash was sent to "Wesley High School" (Tam. Eng.: Vesli Haiskūl) in Royapettah (Irāyapeṭṭai) to learn English. The school, today Wesley Higher Secondary School, was founded in 1818 and boasts a considerable amount of famous alumni, such as the politicians C. P. Ramaswami Aiyar (1879–1966) and M. C. Rajah (1883–1945),[235] who would have attended slightly later if not around the same time as him.

In 1890, the same year Sabhapati was lecturing in Bombay, Om Prakash left for Ooty in the Nilgiris (Nīlakiri) to visit the home of his paternal uncle (lit. "father's younger brother," Tam. *ciṟiya takappaṉ*). While he was there, his father and uncle wished to take him to the Dakshinamurthy Madalayam (Takṣiṇāmūrtti Maṭālayam) to obtain the sight of Balathandayuthapani (Pālataṇṭāyutapāṇi), a deity usually associated with the worship of Murugan.[236] Popular evidence suggests that this hermitage had been established eight years prior, in 1882, by one Shri Ekambara Desikar (Śrī Ēkāmparatēcikar) who was roaming in the Nilgiris looking for a place to meditate and had settled in Kandal (Kantal), then a village outside of Ooty.[237] Our account mentions that Om Prakash met both Shri Ekambara Desikar and a female ascetic named Shrimati Ratnam Ammani (Śrīmati Irattiṉam Ammaṇi), and they are both pictured in Om Prakash's book *Śrī Satsampāṣiṇi*, first published in 1915.[238] The account also claims that Shri Ekambara Desikar was someone who was "acquainted with the rituals of haṭha yoga," or the "yoga of force."[239] This is the first mention we have of Om Prakash's encounter with yoga, so we can assume that his serious interest in its study and practice started at this time, as an eighteen-year-old. He only stayed with his uncle for about a year, leaving for Chennai in 1891 to take his academic examination for university placement. Yet a year later, in 1892, both his mother father decided to permanently move to the Nilgiris, and Om Prakash accompanied them both. During this period he also studied literature and grammar with a student of the nineteenth-century scholar Sri Sabhapati Mudaliar (Śrī Capāpati Mutaliyār, not to be confused with Sabhapati Swami) who was knowledgeable in "picture poems" (Mpvl. *cittirakkavi*, < Skt. *citrakavi*), in which the visual arrangement of letters makes for different combinations of poetry.[240]

Shortly after this he joined a "Draftsman" (Tam. *piḷāṉ eḻutum*, lit. "plan-writing") section of the Office of the Army Chief Engineer, but he left when the office transferred to Bangalore (today Bengaluru in the state of Karnataka) and his parents didn't give him permission to move. Yet they allowed him travel to Mysore (today Mysuru, also in Karnataka), where he joined the Maharaja's Palace (Mpvl./Tam. *mahārājā araṇmaṉai*) as a draftsman instead. This would have been just at the time of a transition of power between Chamarajendra Wadiyar X (r. 1881–94) and his son Krishna Raja Wadiyar IV (r. 1894–1940). Despite these prestigious appointments he appears to have had anxiety about worldly pursuits, and his mind was always elsewhere.

While traveling to Chennai for some work, his account records that Om Prakash met one Saangu Siddha Sivalinga Nayanar (Cāṅku Citta Civaliṅka Nāyaṉār, d. 1900), a swami whose tumulus (Skt. *jīvasamādhi*, for which see Sabhapati's Childhood) is still extant and active in the Guindy (Tam. Kiṇḍi) area of the city, northwest of Velachery. The story goes that Saangu Siddha embraced him upon seeing him, initiated him, and gave Om Prakash the name Sadhu Swamigal (Cātu Cuvāmikaḷ). A few days later he returned to the Nilgiris, reciting the mantras he received day and night.

It is here where the parallel stories of Om Prakash and Sabhapati finally converge. The account of their interaction, at first via a dream and later via letters in the post, is subtitled the obtaining of his "initiation into the gnosis of Brahman" (Mpvl. *pirammaññāṉa tīkṣai*, < Skt. *brahmajñānadīkṣā*), a section that I will produce here in full:

> While at the palace of the Mysore raja he read the sacred writing *Pirammaññāṉa Anuṣṭāṉa*, which he had obtained from a friend, and which was composed by the yogi who is the Guru of Gnosis Sri Adi Sabhapati Swamigal [Ñāṉakuru Yōki Śrī Āti Capāpati Cuvāmikaḷ], who is of the guru lineage of the great sage Holy Agastya, that great Siddha of the Pothigai Mountain. He wanted intensely to come forth in a state of steadfastness in the gnosis of Brahman, and he sent a poem in a letter to Chennai with reverence toward this great man. That great man, consenting to his wish, bestowed the favor of initiation [Mpvl. *tīkṣānukraham*, < Skt. **dīkṣānugraha*] in the direction of Ooty on a full-moon night. A wise man [Mpvl. *ñāṉi*, < Skt. *jñānin*] of mature age appeared in Sadhu Swamigal's dream. He paid him respect with an abundance of devotion [Mpvl. *pakti*, < Skt. *bhakti*] and overflowing tears. His soul, being satisfied, was taken away to his caves. The great man, abundant with compassion, there gave him instruction in gnosis [Mpvl. *ñāṉōpatēcam*, < Skt. *jñānopadeśa*] and then, after blessing him, vanished. When he woke up and looked around, he saw that his bed had been soaked with tears, and his bliss was fulfilled. He did not sleep and was reflecting again and again on the holy guru's

instruction until the break of dawn. The night had passed in a dream, and that day he told everything to his dear mother. His mother, her heart [Mpvl. *akam*] being so very delighted, recorded the language of that instruction. She said that it was mysterious that such a method of practicing the rites had not been explained by anyone. Three days later he received via mail the book *Pirammañāṉa Anuṣṭāṉa*, along with a sacred portrait [Tam. *tiruvuruvappaṭam*) of the Yogi who is the Guru of Gnosis, some offering of ashes, and a letter. He became filled with great joy as he read the letter written by the Gurunātha, and he realized that he had received initiation in a dream into the instruction of gnosis as well as some practices on the yoga of gnosis [Mpvl. *ñāṉa yōkāpyācaṅkaḷ*, < Skt. *jñānayogābhyāsa*) and words of blessing. He was astonished and filled with an ecstasy of bliss. He performed the practice according to his holy guru's command. After some time passed, he went to Elk Hill, then Pajē Swami Cave,[241] and then he reached the mountains to the south of the maharajah's palace in Mysore, all the while singing praises to the groups of Siddhas [Mpvl. *cittar kaṇaṅkaḷ*, < Skt. **siddhagaṇa*] with his eyes tearful from devotion and his thoughts full of tenderness. He returned to his little room in the palace and would perform a practice [Mpvl. *apyācam*, < Skt. *abhyāsa*] until it became a habit [Tam. *vaḻakkamāyiruntatu*].[242]

From the previous excerpt we can glean at least a few interesting points. First, Om Prakash's experience of a dream immediately recalls Sabhapati's own vision-like dream, analyzed earlier in this chapter. As referenced earlier, this motif also uncannily resembles the Tirumalai Krishnamacharya's own trance-like vision of his guru. Yet here we have a further practice being alluded to, that of "initiation" (Mpvl. *tīkṣai*, < Skt. *dīkṣā*), which, as earlier mentioned, was directly translated as "mesmerism" in one of his English works, despite the fact that in his vernacular Indic-language works it equally recalls Tantric systems of initiation. Translation aside, initiation, as we will see in Chapter 4, is an important technique in his works of yoga, to which are devoted several pages and diagrams. This excerpt in particular shows that Sabhapati (and Om Prakash for that matter) believed that initiation could be conferred not just through physical contact but also at a distance through the medium of dreams, in this case while the student is dreaming but the guru is awake and consciously bestowing this initiation on a full-moon night. Second, the excerpt shows that Sabhapati was involved in active correspondence through the mail, including the shipment of his English- and vernacular-language books via post (see Chapter 2). Third, Om Prakash's devotion to the Siddhas directly after this visionary of Sabhapati demonstrates that the latter by this time had been firmly considered to partake in the tradition of Agastya and the Tamil Siddhas in addition to the Vīraśaiva leanings of his first guru, Vedashreni Chidambara (Periya) Swamigal. This alone is a strong example of how Vīraśaiva-inflected Vedānta philosophy and the teachings of the Siddhas could be perceived as harmonious and overlapping categories and not as mutually exclusive (see Chapter 3).

Om Prakash's story continues with more relevant details about Sabhapati and his students. It wasn't long of course, before he had another dream:

> He had steadfast devotion and love even while working, and therefore would meditate on these men who were Siddhas [Mpvl. *citta puruṣarkaḷ*, < Skt. *siddhapuruṣa*] and would praise them. One time at night, and moreover in a dream, a great man who was a Siddha appeared. The swami worshiped him with reverence and devotion and rejoiced at the divine speech: "The instruction of gnosis was previously given to you. Henceforth a name of initiation will be consecrated for you by a great man named Sri Suparna Swamigal [Śrī Cuparṇa Cuvāmikaḷ], and you will receive from him the mystery of "*om acalapīṭhakīlaka*" [lit. "Om, the fastener of the altar of the mountain"]. After saying this, he blessed him and vanished.[243]

Four days later, he learned "some news that one of Adi Sabhapati Swamigal's students had come to Ooty on the way to the Palace of the Maharaja of Mysore." After delivering his lectures there and returning to the mountains, Om Prakash went out to meet him. It was, of course, the same person in his dream, and he embraced him with tears of joy. A few weeks later, they went together to "Tiger Hill Cave" (Tam.: Pulikkukai), a still-extant cave temple site outside of Ooty. Here Sri Suparna Swamigal gave Om Prakash his initiatory name of "Lord of Yoga" (Tam.: Yōkīntirar, < Skt. Yogīndra). He also instructed him to read the books *Vairākya Catakam* and *Vairākya Tīpam*, two works attributed to the seventeenth-century Śaiva author Perur Santhalinga Swamigal (Pērūr Cāntaliṅka Cuvāmikaḷ), a figure known for his connections to Vīraśaiva philosophy through his student Kumara Devar (Kumāratēvar), who in turn was a part of Sabhapati's own guru lineage, as we saw in the section Sabhapati's Childhood and will analyze further in Chapter 3. Finally, we learn that this is the first time that Om Prakash began to experience this steadfast devotion as a renunciate (Mpvl. *canyāci*, < Skt. *saṃnyāsin*). This experience would prove to have a profound impact on his subsequent life and interest in yoga, including his membership in the organization Latent Light

Culture, which had explicit connections to modern occultism through its founder, T. R. Sanjivi of Tinnevelly (today Tirunelveli).

Om Prakash straddled the modern and contemporary yoga worlds, having even lived to see the independence of India in 1947, although he died only four months later. He was born only nine years after Swami Vivekananda yet outlived him by forty-five years. Om Prakash's time of death (Mpvl. *camāti*, < Skt. *samādhi*, lit. "composition") is still annually celebrated at the hermitage bearing his name in Kandal at the former site of Dakshinamurthy Madalayam. While Om Prakash is still commemorated in this way, I have noted during my visits that Sabhapati has been essentially forgotten in Kandal apart from the mentions in Om Prakash's biographical account, and the presence of some of Sabhapati's works in the hermitage library (see Chapter 2) was surprising to the current temple leadership and trustees. I would argue that this "source amnesia" is due to the fact that Om Prakash's own body of work was reinterpreted by more mainline Vedānta thinkers associated with Swami Vivekananda and the Ramakrishna Mission, and their popularity by this time is accounted for by their prefatory remarks to his biographical account with praise for his devotion.[244] In the process of this reinterpretation, Sabhapati's own contribution to his works and separate guru-lineage appear to have been largely forgotten or possibly even obscured by the all-encompassing mythos of Agastya and the Siddhas. Yet the details of Sabhapati and Om Prakash's collaboration are critically important since, as I will indicate in Chapter 3, Om Prakash would have supported Sabhapati's elevation of Śivarājayoga ("the subjugation of gnosis") as a higher form of Rājayoga ("the subjugation of the breath and mind"), while at the same time we know he continued to practice and teach the postures and breathing exercises of Haṭhayoga ("the subjugation of the breath"). We know that Swami Vivekananda, on the other hand, eschewed haṭha yoga in general, partially contributing to the split between meditative, Patañjali-inflected Vedānta and postural haṭha yoga that still exists to this day.[245] As a result, Om Prakash's example and literature offer an alternative vision of yoga that is worth comparing with more dominant translocal flows of modern yoga in the twentieth century and beyond.[246]

Konnur Ramalinga Swamigal

Sabhapati must have died between 1913 and 1936, and as I demonstrate below the evidence suggests he died in either 1923 or 1924. In MCVTS he is mentioned as still being alive and accepting visitors in 1913, and by that time he would have already been around eighty-five years old. The last new information about his activities is provided in T2, which notes the following:

> He also spent a little time in each place, such as this Holy Konnur Meditation Hall and Hermitage of Asceticism, the Nilgiri Hermitage of Austerities, and the Hermitage of Austerities of the mountain and cave of Mount Agastya, realizing the steadfast devotion of experiencing the nonconceptual communion of the gnosis of Brahman.[247]

This indicates that at the end of his life he split his time principally between three places, (1) his Meditation Hall in Konnur; (2) a Hermitage of Austerities in the Nilgiris, which is likely none other than Om Prakash's ashram in the Kandal area of Ooty/Udhagamandalam; and (3) Agastya's Hermitage of Austerities, which as I have demonstrated was located somewhere between Papanasam and Mount Agastya in the Pothigai Malai of the present-day Tirunelveli District. Sabhapati therefore likely died in one of these three places, although, as we shall see, there is evidence suggesting that his final resting place was in Konnur.

The missing link in this story is Konnur Ramalinga Swamigal (Koṉṉūr Irāmaliṅka Cuvāmikaḷ, 1856–1936), Sabhapati's student who himself was given the title "Guru Yogi of Gnosis" (Mpvl. *ñāṉakuruyōki*, < Skt. *jñānaguruyogī*) and who was the "appointed chief" of "Guru Father Rishi's meditation hall" (Tam. *kurupitāruṣiyiṉ maṭattiṟku maṭātipatiyāy niyamikkappaṭṭa*), which was in Konnur, as I demonstrated in the section Agastya and the Konnur Meditation Hall and will further show below. As already noted, CTCSPV, published in 1889, clearly states that one Murugesa Swami—most likely the same as Mooroogasa Moodelliar (Murukēca Mudaliyār)—at the time was the chief of Konnur Meditation Hall. Ramalinga Swamigal's name (along with his title of Ñāṉakuruyoki) is mentioned separately from Murgesa Swami's in a section of this text dedicated to "praises for the guru" (*kurustuti*), which demonstrates that they were two different individuals.[248]

However, by the time of MCVTS, published in 1913, Konnur Ramalinga Swamigal is clearly mentioned as the chief of the Konnur Meditation Hall, and it is noted that the publication of the book "was overseen" (Tam. *pārvaiyiṭappaṭṭu*) by him.[249] As a result, Murugesa Swami by 1913 must have either died or resigned his position. Ramalinga Swamigal in this work also supplied a poem for publication in this work in praise of Sabhapati:

> He who has complete gnosis, who has perceived finality;
> he who is learned, who is eminent, who practices truth;
> he who is the ultimate teacher, whose worship is free from attachment;
> he whose austerities are abundant, he who is Guru Father Rishi![250]

Essentially nothing has been published about Konnur Ramalinga Swamigal to date, and it has been difficult to conduct archival research on him. Part of this is due to his sharing a name with the much more popular Chidambaram Ramalinga Swamigal (Citambara Irāmaliṅka Cuvāmikaḷ), who died in 1874. Even were this not an issue, it is unlikely that archival or library research would get very far; it does not appear that Konnur Ramalinga Swamigal was prolific, like Sabhapati, or even wrote religious books at all, like Om Prakash, although there could be some shorter works still extant that have yet to surface since he did practice yoga in Sabhapati's lineage of practice.

As a result, the quest to discover more details about this student of Sabhapati required a shift to a combined methodology based principally on ethnography and geography, and I took my first trip in person in the summer of 2018 to the general area of Konnur and Villivakkam to track down remnants of Guru Father Rishi's meditation hall, which I had read mention of in the copy of MCVTS held in the British Library. There is only one extant candidate for the hall, a relatively small site near the present-day Baliamman Temple that at that time was called in Tamil "Aruḷmiku Śrī Capāpati Liṅkēsvar Jīvacamāti Ālayam" ("The Place of the Tumulus of the Blessed and Holy Sabhapati Lingeshwar").[251] The name "Sabhapati" immediately stuck out, of course, but there were still doubts, especially since Sabhapati is a common name in Chennai and throughout Tamil Nadu and can also be an epithet of Shiva. Yet, when I entered, I was struck by the ambience of the shrine and in particular the emphasis on the Siddhas—for example, a huge portrait of Agastya stood before me, and there were other images depicting Siddhas as well. When I interviewed the head of the "Managing Trust" (Tam. Eng.: *mēṉējiṅ ṭirasṭ*), named P. P. R. Hariharan Swamigal (Tam.: Pi. Pi. Ār. Hariharaṉ Cuvāmikaḷ, ca. 1935—September 30, 2019),[252] he happily took me to the back of the building, where I saw a photograph of none other than one Ramalinga Swamigal, a bearded yogi, along with his dates of birth and death. Ramalinga Swamigal's portrait was flanked by the portrait of his student Aanandha Aanandha Swamigal (Ananta Āanantā Cuvāmikaḷ, alias Raman Nair, d. October 29, 1983),[253] a former military officer from Kerala, and both were in turn located above the shrine containing the remains of Aanandha Aanandha Swamigal's body.

In interviews with Hariharan and other friends from Villivakkam, a confusing claim arose: on the one hand, Hariharan was clear that Sabhapati lived to be ninety-five years old and was from a Naidu family;[254] on the other hand, there was also a lingering assumption—given without proof—that Sabhapati must have lived several centuries ago, an assumption most likely generated by missing historical data on his life. I later learned that thieves had broken in upon his student Aanandha Aanandha Swamigal's death and were believed to have stolen goods as well as books and documents, which may have contributed to the lack of historical materials. This created some confusion since Ramalinga Swamigal in published literature as well as interviews with Hariharan and others was unequivocally referred to as Sabhapati's direct student and not an idealized figurehead of some kind. Ergo this same Sabhapati must have been alive in the late nineteenth to early twentieth century to meet and initiate Ramalinga Swamigal, who died in 1936.

Gathering this information during the August 2018 visit, I had established that there was still extant, in Konnur, a shrine devoted to a "Siddha" or "Mahan" named Sabhapati, and this Sabhapati had a student named Ramalinga Swamigal. As for the epithet Lingeshwar, I later learned that this had been added by P. P. R. Hariharan Swamigal after the shrine's principal phallic stone was excavated and that phrase was discovered to be inscribed upon it.[255] The burden of the evidence suggested that it was part of the same site, but there were still doubts remaining. To determine if this Ramalinga Swamigal conclusively matched the Ramalinga Swamigal in Sabhapati's literature, upon my return in 2019, I went with P. P. R. Hariharan Swamigal's son Vinayagam Swamigal to Ramalinga Swamigal's own tumulus, which is not located in Chennai but in Murugambakkam Village, Madurantagam Taluk, in Kanchipuram District, where he had started organizing his own meditation hall (Mpvl. *maṭam*, < Skt. *maṭha*) in 1905. There I met and interviewed one V. Subramaniya Chettiar (Vi. Cuppiramaṉiya Ceṭṭiyār, born ca. 1933), whose father was a personal friend and devotee of Ramalinga Swamigal.[256]

During this interview I learned that Ramalinga Swamigal was indeed one of Sabhapati's students, and also received confirmation that his guru Sabhapati's own tumulus is in Konnur, which is of course strong evidence that Sabhapati died in Konnur and not elsewhere. V. Subramaniya also asserted that Ramalinga Swamigal around the age of forty was living near Madurai and had an experience of "communion" (Mpvl. *camāti*, < Skt. *samādhi*) that led to his association with Sabhapati. Since we know from extant portraits that Ramalinga Swamigal was born in 1856, that would place the date of his experience of samādhi in or around 1896, which, as we saw above, is precisely the same period in which Sabhapati's meditation hall in Konnur was established. This offers additional confirmation that they are indeed one and the same Ramalinga Swamigal.

V. Subramaniya also provided me with copies of his legal will that establish the upkeep and regular worship rites at the shrine of Ramalinga Swamigal. After interviewing him, both Vinayagam and I went to visit this shrine along with his associate who conducts the worship rites. The shrine is currently kept locked except for visitors and the occasional ritual *pūjā*. An old painting of Ramalinga Swamigal was hanging in the shrine and, upon enquiring about it, it was kindly gifted to me by V. Subramaniya. The resemblance between this painting and Sabhapati's own woodcut portrait as provided in MCVTS, such as the posture (Skt. *āsana*) and threefold mark (Mpvl. *tiripuṇṭaram*, < Skt. *tripuṇḍra*), lends a further argument that they were of the same guru lineage (see Figures 1.12 and 1.13). In fact, one would almost think they are the

Figure 1.12 A woodblock portrait of Sabhapati as Guru Father Rishi from MCVTS. Photo by the author.

Figure 1.13 A painting of Konnur Ramalinga Swami now in the personal collection of the author.

same person were it not for Sabhapati's wearing what appears to be the sacred thread (Tam. *pūṇūl*) of a Brahmin in the form of a sash. Sabhapati was either from a Brahmin or a Naidu family, or a combination of both (which may have been more common while he was alive). By contrast, P. P. R. Hariharan Swamigal noted in an interview that Ramalinga Swamigal was from a Mudaliyar family,[257] while V. Subramaniya noted that he was Malayali, so this information when taken together could mean Ramalinga was from a Kerala Mudali family.

An inscription at the shrine conclusively shows the identity of the yogi buried inside: the name given is "Koṉṉūr Śrī Irāmaliṅka Cuvāmikaḷ," which is the first time I had seen the name of the village Konnur (contemporary spelling: Koṉṉūr) explicitly attached to his name (see Figure 1.14). As I quoted from MCTVS above, we know that the Ramalinga Swamigal known to Sabhapati is also inextricably attached to Konnur, being the "appointed chief" of "Guru Father Rishi's meditation hall" in Konnur. As there is no

Figure 1.14 An inscription showing the establishment of a *maṭam* in Murugambakkam by "Koṉṉūr Śrī Irāmaliṅkasvāmi" and the date of his *samādhi* or "composition" (i.e. death). Photo by the author.

other person who would remotely fit the description, dates, and identity of Konnur Ramalinga Swamigal, Konnur being a small village even at that time, I have concluded that they are indeed the same person.

In this context, however, ethnography is most convincing when supplemented by published primary sources, and by 2019 I had also discovered the longer version of MCVTS at the Adyar Library that provided further geographical details that help to confirm the location of the site and the identity of Konnur Ramalinga Swamigal. Sabhapati's address is given in English as follows:

> Those who like to see G. P. Rushi Sabapathy Swamy and learn from him anything may come through train from Madras Central Station to Villivakam [*sic*] Station, which is in the Arakonam Railway Line and from here to Guru Pitha Rushi Madam of Connur Village, which is within Villivakam Village, where the Guru Swamy can be seen.[258]

The village "Connur" is an archaic anglicized spelling of Konnur, as confirmed by maps of the Madras Presidency that I have consulted at the Tamil

Nadu Archives. The Tamil version of this statement is similar but with a notable addition (emphasis added):

> After boarding a train at Madras Central Station and getting off at Villivakkam Station on the Arakkonam Railway Line, upon reaching there the Guru Father Rishi's meditation hall *will be to the west of Konnur Perumal Temple.* Upon arriving there you can see Sabhapati Swamigal. You can receive instruction for yourself and also buy his sacred writings.[259]

Apart from the fact that books were for sale, the main notable difference in the directions given in Tamil, namely that the meditation hall is to the west of the Perumal temple, is significant. This Perumal temple is none other than Sri Sowmya Damodara Perumal Temple (Tam.: Cavumiya Tāmōtarapperumāḷ Kōyil), the only temple surveyed in Konnur in the 1961 census of India. The Vaiṣṇava temple is believed to have been constructed in the fifteenth century CE and was renovated in 1901.[260] The present-day tumulus at Sri Sabhapathy Lingeshwarar Koil is located in walking distance to the west of this temple, about 150 meters away according to Google Maps. These directions further accord with earlier directions by rail given in the prefatory matter of CTCSPV.

For additional proof, I went to the Central Survey Office (Tam. *mattiya nila aḷavai aluvalakam*) in Chepauk (Tam. Cēppākkam) and obtained village maps of Konnur (No. 71, see Figure 1.15) and Villivakkam (No. 73). These maps were drafted to scale, with sixteen inches equal to one mile (with conversion to the metric system, one inch is equal to just over 100 meters), enabling me to locate Sabhapati Swami's temple sites with relative precision. Furthermore, the map provides a legend for the various symbols, including the location of "Tanks" or bodies of water and "Pagodas" or temples. The map is also populated by old survey numbers that are linked to what is called a Re-settlement Register, ostensibly made for each village.[261] These numbers on the village map have since been transformed into town survey numbers and incorporated into an urbanized system of blocks and wards as the Greater Chennai Corporation has gradually assumed jurisdiction over the area. However, the old survey numbers are still listed in the legal documents pertaining to Konnur Ramalinga Swamigal's bequest of his lands to his student Aanandha Aanandha Swamigal upon the former's death in 1936. These numbers include, among other numbers that have since been mortgaged or sold, 341, 342, and 343, which are located on Figure 1.15. Documents that were in the possession of Hariharan Swamigal and now his son Vinayagam show that

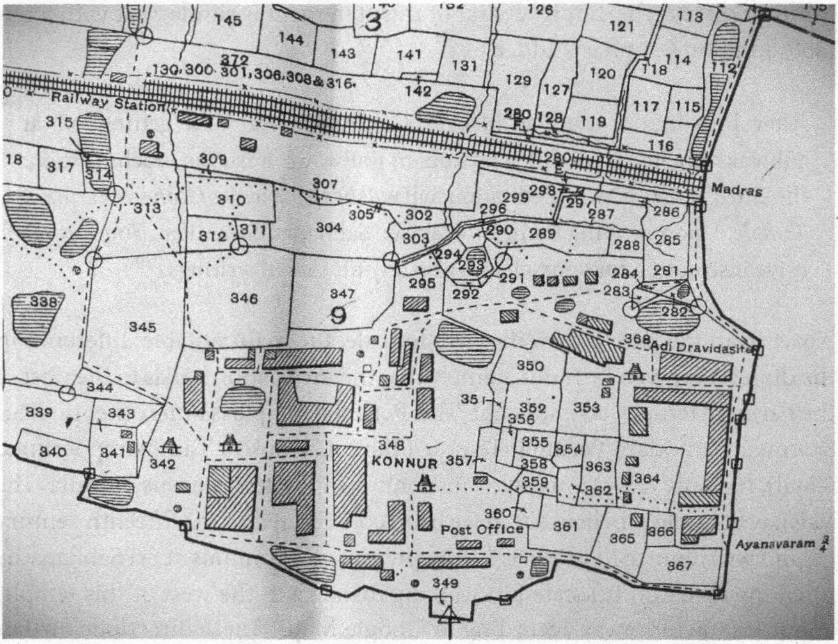

Figure 1.15 A portion of the village survey map of "Konnur," "No. 71," traced "from the Original map of 1906" and obtained upon request at the Central Survey Office in Chepauk, Chennai. Sri Sabhapathy Lingeshwarar Koil is located in or near No. 343 with Sowmya Damodara Perumal Temple to the east with a still-extant temple tank (*kuḷam*), matching directions given in MCVTS. Photo by the author.

number 341 is the location of the present-day Sri Sabhapathy Lingeshwarar Koil and tumulus. I have been able to conclusively determine the location of the Sowmya Damodara Perumal Temple on the old village map based on the placement of the temple "Tank" and upon comparing the measurement of the distance from the village map with that of present-day Google Maps.

More information on these old survey numbers could potentially reveal Sabhapati's place of death and a potential transfer of ownership between Murugesa Swami and Konnur Ramalinga Swamigal. However, it is a highly complex bureaucratic process to find further information about these numbers, though the scrutiny upon citizens or noncitizen researchers who take an interest in land titles has fortunately somewhat lessened due to the Right to Information Act passed in 2005. I have applied both in person and via post to the relevant government offices with assistance from both the Tamil Nadu head archivist and other graduate students in the Tamil Nadu Archives.[262] The two applications I have sent were to the public information officer (Tam. *potu takaval aluvalar*) at the Central Survey Office as well as to the direct assistant to the collector (Tam. *āṭciyariṉ nērmuka utaviyāḷar*) at the District Collector Office (*māvaṭṭa ācciyar aluvalakam*). The response I received was that no information exists on the Re-settlement Register for these numbers between 1913 and 1936, which was the date range I requested, so it may be fruitful to request an earlier date range. An opportunity to appeal was given and I sent a letter to the officer of appeals (Tam. *mēlmuṟaiyīṭṭu aluvalar*) to conduct an additional search, but heard no further news before my research trip ended.

Furthermore, the name of the adjacent village to the south, Villivakkam, number 73, accords with "No. 73" given in multiple places in CTCSPV (Tam. *73-vatu nempar koṉṉūr kirāma kurumaṭālayam*, "the Guru's Meditation Hall of Konnur Village, No. 73"). Although number 73 by 1938 had been assigned to neighboring Villivakkam and not Konnur, as evident from the village map of each, it is clear that the Meditation Hall was on the border between Villivakkam (number 73) and Konnur (number 71) and that the precise border between them would have been tenuous and possibly altered over subsequent decades. If the numbering was not been amended, is also possible that the Meditation Hall moved to its present location after starting just to the south, in Villivakkam, in 1889, or that Villivakkam's number was more readily known by the general public of Madras and its environs.

On account of (1) the details gleaned in personal interviews and material evidence such as books and photographs demonstrating that Konnur Ramalinga Swamigal was the student of an celebrated yogi named Sabhapati, and (2) the geographical location of the present-day Sri Sabhapathy Lingeshwarar Koil generally matching the location of the Konnur Meditation Hall given in CTCSPV and MCVTS, including the specific directions given in MCVTS showing it is west of the Perumal temple, I am compelled to claim with relative certainty that Konnur Ramalinga Swamigal is indeed the same Ramalinga Swamigal mentioned in CTCSPV and MCVTS, and that he remained a guru after Sabhapati died both in Konnur and in Murugambakkam, where he first arrived in 1905 and which he appears to have visited on multiple occasions. Registration details of the land or another document mentioning Sabhapati's name and date of death alongside mention of Konnur Ramalinga

Swamigal would make this claim absolutely conclusive and provide much-needed detail corroborating the accumulated evidence, but in lieu of more concrete evidence, it is as close as we can come to a definite conclusion about Ramalinga Swamigal's identity.

Sabhapati Swami's Death and Disappearance

As I have demonstrated in the previous section, Konnur Ramalinga Swamigal is the most likely—and so far only—candidate for Sabhapati's own student and successor at the Konnur Meditation Hall. This enables us to make two further claims that neither the Ur-account, nor T1, nor T2 addresses, since they were all written while the swami was alive. First, Hariharaṉ Swami recalled with relative certainty in an interview that Sabhapati lived to be ninety-five years old. As we have already treated, T2 appears to give the most concrete data on his birth, placing it in Mazhkali in (December or January) 1828, which, unlike the 1840 date of the Ur-account or the Kali Yuga date of T1 (which, converted according to contemporary reckoning, gives 1840 or 1841), accords with the relatively well-documented dates of Vedashreni Chidambara Periya Swamigal. This enables us to tentatively situate Sabhapati's year of death as either 1923 or 1924, depending on whether he was born at the beginning of the year, in January 1828, or at the end of the year, in December 1828. An alternative, if Sabhapati was indeed born in or closer to 1840, is that Sabhapati died in 1935.

Second, V. Subramaniya Chettiar was clear in his interview that Sabhapati's "meditation hall" (he used the word *maṭam* instead of the archaic *maṭālayam*) was in what is today Villivakkam, and was clear that this place is none other than the still-extant Sri Sabhapathy Lingeshwarar Koil in present-day Konnur/Villivakkam. This shrine has been maintained by each of its caretakers, from Aanandha Aanandha Swamigal onward, who have held that it contains the remains of Sabhapati's body in his tumulus (see Figure 1.16). V. Subramaniya's interview also confirms that Villivakkam was Sabhapati's place of death, although precisely where in the village still appears inconclusive. The current phallic stone installed at the site of the Sri Sabhapathy Lingeshwarar Koil extends around seventeen feet deep into the earth, and Sabhapati's body would have been buried underneath the stone in "sitting position only," although there is also a traditional belief that "Mahans" like Sabhapati would "bring themselves to the earth and perform miracles and

Figure 1.16 The *liṅga* traditionally associated with Sabhapati Swami's *jīva-samādhi* or tumulus at Sri Sabhapathy Lingeshwarar Koil. Photo by the author.

disappear into the lingam."[263] While there is no indication his head was encased in the above-ground portion of the tumulus or tumulus, the current phallus is ceremonially adorned with a face, as is the case with other Tamil Vīraśaiva temples. If Sabhapati's physical body were indeed buried there, it would, according to tradition, have been covered in flowers, sacred ash (Tam. *vipūti*, < *vibhūti*), and rose water prior to being placed in seated position.[264] While in Chennai I explored the possibility of hiring an archaeologist to excavate the stone in collaboration with temple authorities, but this idea was abandoned because it might have upset local religious sensibilities and created controversy in a charged political climate. A solution was raised of instead utilizing radar to see beneath the surface of the phallic stone without physical excavation, but this takes the research outside the realm of what I as a scholar of religious studies am currently capable. Perhaps in the future a collaborative team can be organized to conclusively solve the mystery of the swami's resting place once and for all.

Notes

1. Issues surrounding the precise dating of Sabhapati's birth and death will be addressed throughout this chapter.
2. Vedashreni Chidambara Swamigal is today more commonly referred to as Chidambara Periya Swamigal to distinguish him from Thiruporur Chidambara Swamigal (Tiruppōrūr Citambara Cuvāmikaḷ). See the section A Search for Spiritual Truth and Chapter 3.
3. For the sake of readability, I have rendered most proper names and places first according to contemporary transliteration styles according to each language followed by a precise transliteration with diacritical marks in parentheses. Unless otherwise indicated the transliteration in parentheses derives from a version of transliteration adapted from ISO15919 without adjustment for ē and ō in Sanskrit and Bengali. Some proper nouns with common English forms as well as texts or published works are given without (e.g., Shiva for Śiva, Upanishad for Upaniṣad), but with clarifying diacritics when deemed appropriate.
4. Phanindranath Bose, *Life of Sris Chandra Basu* (Calcutta: R. Chatterjee, 1932), 86; F. Max Müller, *The Six Systems of Indian Philosophy* (New York: Longmans, Green, 1899), 462. We know from Bose's account that Shrish Chandra is the "author" in correspondence with Müller. See also the chapter by Donald Lopez in Erik Sand and Tim Rudbøg, eds., *Imagining the East: The Early Theosophical Society* (Oxford: Oxford University Press, 2019), for Müller's critical perspective on Theosophy in general.
5. An Admirer, "The Madras Yogi Sabhapaty Swami," *The Theosophist: A Monthly Journal Devoted to Oriental Philosophy, Art, Literature and Occultism: Embracing Mesmerism, Spiritualism, and Other Secret Sciences* 1, no. 6 (March 1880): 145–47.
6. The Mahatma Giana Guroo Yogi Sabhapaty Swami, *Om: A Treatise on Vedantic Raj Yoga Philosophy* (Lahore: "Civil and Military Gazette" Press, 1880), i–vii. I have elected to cite the page numbers from this text for the Ur-account.
7. For the historical interactions between Sabhapati and the "Founders" of the Theosophical Society, see the section A Splash on the Lahore Scene.
8. Theosophist [Anonymous], "Un Yogui," *Le Lotus Bleu: Revue Theosophique Mensuelle* 8, no. 1 (1897): 18–20; and Paul Gillard, "Le pas décisif," *Le Lotus Bleu: Revue Theosophique Mensuelle* 8, no. 1 (1897): 20–24.
9. Franz Hartmann, trans., "Aus dem Leben des indischen Mahātmā Jñāna Guru Yogī Sabhapatti Svāmī," *Neue Lotusblüten*, vol. 1 (Leipzig: Jaeger'sche Verlagsbuchhandlung, 1908), 259–70.
10. Mahathma Brumha Gnyana Mavuna Guru Sabhapathy Swamy Rishi Yogiswer, *Om: The Cosmic Psychological Spiritual Philosophy and Science of Communion with and Absorption in the Infinite Spirit, or Vedhantha Siva Raja Yoga Samadhi Brumha Gnyana Anubuthi* (Mylapore: Hindu Press, 1884 [First Book] and Bombay: Karnatak Press, 1890 [Second Book]).
11. For the phenomena of translations, publications, and the various scripts see Chapter 2.

12. Śrīmat Sabhāpati Svāmī, *Bedāntadarśan o rājayoga*, trans. Śrī Ambikācaraṇ Bandyopādhyāẏ (Kolkata: Śrīśacandra Basu, 1885).
13. Mahātmā Jñānaguruyogī Sabhāpati Svāmī, *Rājayoga Brahmajñānānubhūti saṅgraha veda* (Mumbai: Tattvavivecaka Chāpakhānemem Chāpe, 1892).
14. Sabhāpati Svāmī, *Yogī Sabhāpati Svāmīke hālāt* (Bareilly [Barelī]: The Rohilkhand Theosophical Society, 1883). I am grateful to Gwendolyn Kirk, instructor of Urdu at Lahore University of Management Sciences, and Piotr Borek of Jagiellonian University, for helping me examine this account, which is written in a Persian *nastaliq* script and appears to follow the Ur-account closely.
15. For an analysis of this interplay between mesolocal and translocal, see the introduction.
16. Ur-account, iii.
17. For evidence that Sabhapati narrated this account see Bose, *Life of Sris Chandra Basu*, 86–87. In any event, it is highly unlikely (if not impossible) that Sabhapati's principal "Admirer" (most likely Shrish Chandra Basu) would have known the specificity of certain placenames and dates without receiving this information directly from him. As we shall see, many of these locations are highly localized sites in Tamil Nadu that would have been unfamiliar to north Indian authors—this is exemplified by recourse to these placenames' perceived phonetic pronunciation when rendering them into Roman script.
18. See Appendix 1 for a translation of most of T2.
19. Common terms relating to yoga are often given without italicization to partially conform to OUP's preferred style of rendering such terms as English words (e.g., yogi, haṭha yoga, rāja yoga, samādhi, cakra, tattva) and to make the book more readable. Diacritics are adapted from ISO 15919 when used, except for some strengthening of vowels.
20. See Chapter 2 for a more detailed treatment of the language used in Sabhapati's literature and issues with its translation.
21. Capāpati Cuvāmikaḷ, *Carva māṉaca nittiya karmānuṣṭāṉa, carva tēvatātēvi māṉaca pūjāttiyāṉa, pirammakñāṉa rājayōka niṣṭai camāti, carva tīkṣākkramattiyāṉa, cātaṉā appiyāca kiramāṉucantāṉa, caṅkiraha vēta tiyāṉōpatēca smiruti* (Tiruccirāppaḷḷi: Ṣaṇmukavilās Piras, 1913), 6.
22. Śrī Ti. Ku Piḷḷai, *Nīlakiri, utakamaṇṭalam, tirukkāntal Śrī Takṣiṇāmūrtti Maṭam Lōkōpakāra Vityātāṉa Capai stāpakar acalapīṭam Śrīmat Ompirakāsa Cuvāmikaḷ carittirac curukkam* (Tirupparāytturai: Śrīmat Citpavānanta Cuvāmikaḷatu muṉṉuraiyuṭaṉ kūṭiyatu, 1957), 13–20.
23. Ōm Pirakāca Cuvāmikaḷ, *Śrīsatsampāṣiṇi* (Nīlakiri: Śrī Carasvati Ācramam, 1915). This work was reprinted a couple of decades later as Śrīmat Om Pirakāca Cuvāmikaḷ, *Śrī Satsampāṣiṇi* (Madras: Eveready Press, 1939).
24. Piḷḷai, *Nīlakiri*, 13–20.
25. Ur-account, i.
26. Hariharaṉ Cuvāmikaḷ, interview at Aruḷmiku Śrī Capāpati Liṅkēsvar Jīvacamāti Ālayam, audio recording, August 12, 2018.
27. An asterisk next to a Sanskrit compound indicates that it is rare or unused in Sanskrit, despite the compound having separate Maṇipravāla components that are each

individually derived from Sanskrit. Such a distinction not only highlights the lack of adequate lexicons that include Maṇipravāla forms but also demonstrates the creative way in which Maṇipravāla authors could gradually create new compounds that didn't need to be previously attested yet still retained their communicative value when parsed.

28. T2, 3. Tam. "*naṭēcamūrtti civakāmiyammaṉ vārppaṭam vētasrēṇiyil ceytaruḷiya āṟukkirakam uccastāṉattil, iraṇṭu kirakam vākkustāṉattil oru kirakam cukatapastāṉattiluḷḷa kālamākiya 1828 varuṣam mārkaḻi mātam tirūvātirai naṭcattira tivya mahāmukūrttakāla maṅkaḷ cupatiṉattil.*" For a description of these astrological terms, see Caterina Guenzi, *Le discours su sestin: La pratique de l'astrologie à Bénarès* (Paris: CNRS Editions / Bibliothèque de l'Anthropologie, 2013). I am grateful to Peder Pedersen and Martin Gansten (Lund University) for their attempts to decipher the horoscope, which yielded December 29, 1830, as another possibility for Sabhapati's birth given the available data.
29. For a summary of the function of these tumuli among Tamil Siddha milieus, see Chapter 3. The compound *jīvasamādhi* appears to have entered Tamil somewhat irregularly, perhaps an adaptation from *jīvanmukti* or via an early form of Hindi/Urdū, as it does not appear to be an attested Sanskrit compound.
30. T2, 3. Tam.: "*intutēca taṭcaṇa kāṇṭattil, toṇṭayāṉ cakkiravarttiyiṉ toṇṭamā nakarattil, ceṉṉaipuriyil, taṉattil, tēvālaya jīrṇōttāraṇa paṇiyil, kalviyil, cirēṣaṭarāy viḷaṅkiya kurukula tilakarākiya kurunāta pakttarrām pati:kkum, puṇṇiyavati eṉṉum cati:kkum kurunāta pakttarāl tiruvēta cirēṇi kṣēttirattiṟkāka, tirumayilai kumpaliṅka ācāriyaik koṇṭu, kurunāta pakttariṉ kuruvākiya (upatēcavuṇmai) cāsttirakarttā vētacirēṇi citampara svāmikaḷiṉ ākñāpirakāram.*"
31. For these categories and their relation to Brahman identity in Tamil Nadu, see C. J. Fuller and Haripriya Narasimhan, *Tamil Brahmans: The Making of a Middle-Class Caste* (Chicago: University of Chicago Press, 2014), esp. 62–65.
32. Hariharaṉ Cuvāmikaḷ, interview, August 12, 2018.
33. MCVTS, [19]. Tam. "*taṉatu caturvarṇa stirīpuruṣa ciṣyarkaḷukku.*"
34. VRY1, i. This could also imply he was skilled in the tradition of songs known as the "Arutpas" of Chidambaram Ramalinga Swamigal.
35. Rev. John Braidwood, *True Yoke-Fellows in the Mission Field: The Life and Labours of the Rev. John Anderson and the Rev. Robert Johnston, Traced in the Rise and Development of the Madras Free Church Mission* (London: James Nisbet, 1862).
36. T2, 3–4. Tam.: "(20) *vayatukkuḷ iṅkiliṣil purōpacarāy, paipil muḻutum vācittu kirustumatavuṇmai ārāyntum.*"
37. Braidwood, *True Yoke-Fellows*, 59.
38. Colonel M. J. Rowlandson, quoted in ibid., 558.
39. Today the school has been reconstituted as Madurai Christian College and is one of the more prestigious colleges in the city, being especially known for its historical commitment to female education.
40. Braidwood, *True Yoke-Fellows*, 61.
41. Ibid., 206–8.
42. Ibid., 33–34, 207, 542.

43. Ur-account, ii.
44. Ur-account, i.
45. T2, 4. Tam.: "*piṉpu atai viṭṭu viṭṭu raṅkōṉukkum pōy pāriyavarttakañceytukkoṇṭum pavattamata uṇmaiyai yariya parmātēca poṅkikaḷ catcaṅkattāl pālipāṣaiyiṉāl ārāyntu pavuttamatamum intumata vētāntamum oṉṟeṉatterintukkoṇṭum, inta vartakam māyaiyil viratticeykiṉṟateṉṟu veruttu.*"
46. T2, 4. Tam.: "*avvarttakattai nīkki ceṉṉaipurikku vantu taṉ piturārjita vicēṣa cottāl jīvittuk koṇṭum taṉ kuruvākiya upatēcavuṇmai cāstira karttāvētas cirēṇi citampara svāmikaḷukku ciṣyarāy avariṭam carva cāstira tatatuvakiñāṉamataintu.*"
47. Citampara Cuvāmikaḷ, *Upatēcavuṇmaiyum*, ed. Ciṅkāravēlu Piḷḷai (Koṇṇūr: Maṉōṉmaṇivilācavaccukkūṭam of Māṇikka Mutaḷiyār, 1881). The current version in print and still circulating at his tumulus in Velachery is Citampara Periya Cuvāmikaḷ, *Upatēca uṇmai, viḷakka uraiyuṭaṉ* (Vēḷaccēri, Chennai: Vēḷaccēri Makāṉ Patippakam, 2014). An English translation is forthcoming.
48. For the relevance of these figures in Tamil Vīraśaiva literature see Eric Steinschneider, "Beyond the Warring Sects: Universalism, Dissent, and Canon in Tamil Śaivism, ca. 1675–1994" (PhD dissertation, University of Toronto, 2016), 20–21. I am very grateful to Eric for taking the time to personally share with me over the phone his insight and perspective on these figures.
49. Inscription at Vedashreni Chidambara Swamigal's tumulus, photographed by Keith E. Cantú.
50. Vasudha Narayanan, "Religious Vows at the Shrine of Shahul Hamid," in *Dealing with Deities: The Ritual Vow in South Asia* (Albany: State University of New York Press, 2006), 67; cf. Susan Bayly, *Saints, Goddesses and Kings: Muslims and Christians in South Indian Society, 1700–1900* (Cambridge: Cambridge University Press, 1989), 91–92.
51. Narayanan, "Religious Vows," 67, 80–84.
52. T2, 4. Tam.: "*avar aikkiyamāṉa piṟaku makamat uṇmaiyai aṟiyavēṇṭumeṉṟu nākūr mīrā cāyappu āṇṭavar camātikkucceṉṟu aṅku makumat matastāṉkaḷōṭu catcaṅkam ceytu makamat kurāṉ uṇmaikaḷai aṟintu.*"
53. For more on this text see Carl Ernst, "The Islamization of Yoga in the Amṛtakuṇḍa Translations," *Journal of the Royal Asiatic Society of Great Britain & Ireland* 13, no. 2 (2003): 199–226; and "Situating Sufism and Yoga," *Journal of the Royal Asiatic Society*, 3rd series 15, no. 1 (April 2005): 15–33.
54. Ghulām 'Abdu'l-Qādir Nāzir, *Bahār-i-a'zam Jāhī*, trans. S. Muhammad Husayn (Madras: University of Madras, 1950). 29. The term *malang*, "robust," may reveal an association with the Madari *tariqa*, but in South Asian Islamic sources it can also refer to any nonaligned cannabis-imbibing ascetic who acts on the margins of normative society; cf. Ja'far Sharīf, *Islam in India or the Qānūn-i-Islām*, trans. G. A. Herklots (London: Oxford University Press, 1921), 290. I visited this dargah in the summer of 2015, spent the night with a cannabis-imbibing fakir at the site, and collected some literature there for further analysis.
55. For example, the Nāzir account states that Shah Rahmatullah, a descendent of Muhammad Ghawth's brother and one of his four khalifas, Hazrat Shah Phul Shattari

(Shaikh Phul or Shaikh Buhlul), received an endowment village (*in'ām*) of Samiwaram (modern Samayapuram, not far from Thiruchirappalli).

56. T2, 4: "*carvēsvararākiya naṭēcar upācaṉai māṉacēka tiyāṉattil akōra tapam ceytukoṇṭum.*" The adjective *aghora* literally could be translated as "nonterrific" (privy *a*-suffix + *ghora*, "frightful," "sublime," "terrible"); however, at least by the time of Sabhapati's nineteenth-century Tamil *akōram*, it came to mean "vehemence," "severity," often with a connotation of heat. See Johann Philipp Fabricius, *J. P. Fabricius's Tamil and English Dictionary*, 4th ed. (Tranquebar, Tamil Nadu: Evangelical Lutheran Mission Pub. House, 1972), s.v. *akōram*.
57. CPSPS, First Book, 2.
58. T2, 4: "*piṉṉum ceṉṉai purikku vantu carvēsvararākiya naṭēcar upācaṉai māṉacēka tiyāṉattil akōra tapam ceytukoṇṭum, caturvēta, ṣaṭ cāstira 64 kalaikkiñāṉa carva upaniṣatam kītaikaḷiṉ kiñāṉamaṭaintu, inta ulakattiṉ kirusttumatam pavutta matam, makamat mataṅkaḷākiya inta mataṅkaḷukku mēlāka cakala rahasyaṅkaḷaiyum, uṇmaikaḷaiyum vicāraṇaikaḷaiyum cātaṉaikaḷaiyum aṉupavaṅkaḷaiyum uṭaiyatu inta intumatam ākaiyāl intumatam jekat pitā matamāyum intuvēta camuskiruta pāṣai jekat mātā pāṣaiyāyum viḷaṅkukiṉṟateṉṟu uṇarntaṉar.*"
59. For the nuances of this phrase and its coinage see Karl Baier, "Theosophical Orientalism and the Structures of Intercultural Transfer: Annotations on the Appropriations of the Cakras in Early Theosophy," in *Theosophical Appropriations: Esotericism, Kabbalah and the Transformation of Traditions*, ed. Julie Chajes and Boaz Huss (Be'er Sheva, Israel: Ben-Gurion University of the Negev Press, 2016), 309–54. For a much more critical analysis of Theosophical Orientalism see Christopher Partridge, "Lost Horizon: H.P. Blavatsky and Theosophical Orientalism," in *Handbook of the Theosophical Current*, ed. Olav Hammer and Mikael Rothstein (Boston: Brill, 2013), 309–33.
60. T2, 4: "*nāṉ aṭainta vicāraṇakkiñāṉamākiya cāṅkiya parōkṣakkiñāṉattāl kuruviniṭam vicāraṇaikkiyāṉam kirahitakyāṉam, teḷivukkiyāṉam, yukakkiyāṉam niṣcamisciyakkiyāṉam yaṭaintēṉēyaṉṟi aṉupava aparōkṣa stirakkiyāṉamākiya cātaṉā aṉupava kiñāṉam yaṭaintilēṉē eṉ ceyvēṉ evvaṇṇamucup pirammakkiyāṉiyāy jīvaṉ muktaṉ ākavēṇṭum.*"
61. Ur-account, ii.
62. Mircea Eliade, *Yoga: Immortality and Freedom*, trans. Willard Trask (New York: Routledge & Kegan Paul, 1958), 69–70, 76.
63. For a summary of, and the problems with, dating this text see Richard S. Weiss, *Recipes for Immortality: Medicine, Religion, and Community in South India* (New York: Oxford University Press, 2009), 57–62; for a reference to these four stages see ibid., 212, n. 81. See also Chapter 4.
64. Similar visionary experiences of initiation surround the legends of Tirumalai Krishnamacharya (1888–1989); see David Gordon White, *The Yoga Sutra of Patanjali: A Biography* (Princeton, NJ: Princeton University Press, 2014), 197–201; cf. Mark Singleton, *Yoga Body: The Origins of Modern Posture Practice* (New York: Oxford University Press, 2010), 175–90. Sabhapati's student Om Prakash Swamigal also was visited in a dream, which may point to this being a south Indian yogic episteme.

65. Ur-account, ii.
66. Ur-account, ii.
67. T2, 4–5: "*taṉ (30-vatu[)] vayatākiya or tiṉ irāttiri uccikālattil taṉ coṟpaṉattil carvēcuvarar tōṉṟi o pakta cirōṉmaṇiyē uṉṉai yaḻaittāṭkoḷḷa vantapaṭiyāl uṉakku (yaḻaittāṭkoṇṭamūrtti) eṉṉum nāmamiṭṭēṉ, uṉ paktik [5] kirakkamuḷḷēṉ, nī muktaṉāki muktipeṟa akastiyācala takṣaṇakailāsa parvatattil uṉakkaṉupava kuruvai niyamittēṉ-avariṭañ celleṉat tiruvāy malarntaruḷi maṟaintaṉar appoḻuta coṟapaṉāvastaipōy jākkirāvastaiyaṭaintu caravapraka.*"
68. I have translated *ātman* as "soul" rather than "self" as per Sabhapati's own usage in his English works. See the introduction and Chapter 2 for notes on translation.
69. T2, 5: "*taṉ mātāvākiya puṉṉiyavatiyai namaskarittu taṉ coṟpaṉattilīcuvaraṉaṉ ukkirahitta kākṣiyait terivikka anta mātā pirmma kñāṉiyākaiyāl prahamāṉanta paravacattil mūḻki o puttirā nī avataritta eṉke:rppamiṉṟē kirutārttamāyiṟṟu nī māyaiyiṟ cikkavēṇṭām, iṉṟē caṉṉiyācittuvampeṟṟu prahammakñāṉi muktaṉāy muktipeṟakkaṭavāy, uṉṉātmamumeṉṉātmamum orē pirammakñāṉamākaiyāl, aṅkiruvarun taricittukkoḷvōm nī eṉṉiṭattu viṭaipeṟṟu ku:ruviṭañ celleṉa.*"
70. P. K. Nambiar and N. Krishnamurthy, *Census of India 1961*, vol. 9, *Madras*, Part XI-D: *Temples of Madras State, 1. Chingleput District and Madras City* (Delhi: Manager of Publications, 1965), 74.
71. Ibid.
72. T2, 5. Tam.: "*arttajāmattil citampara svāmikaḷiṭam peṟṟu pūjaipilirunta kāvivastiram, laṅkōṭu kapī:rṇamaṉintu, attuṭaṉē taṉ kulattiṟkku ātmārttateyvastalamākiya tiruvētacirēṇi kṣēttirattiṟku vantu yantastala taṇṭapāṇīsvararukketiril mūṉṟutiṉam irāttiri pakal orē tiyāṉattiliruntuviṭṭār mūṉṟām nāḷirāttiri anta liṅkattiṉiṭam cōtippirakācam tōṉṟi acarīravākkāy, (nām ummaiyaḻaittāṭkoṇṭōm) ēṉ stalaṅkaḷtōrum kirupāstuti karuttu naṭaippā mālaiccāṟṟi piṉṉar kuruviṭam pōkuka) eṉṟataittāṉ kēṭṭu yāṉanta paravacaṉāy (kirupāstippāmālai) cāṟṟiṉar.*"
73. Inscription at Vedashreni Chidambara Swamigal's tumulus, photographed by the author.
74. T2, 6. Tam.: "*atiṉ piṟaku toṇṭanāṭṭiṉ cōḻanāṭṭiṉ koṅkunāṭṭiṉ pāṇṭiyanāṭṭiṉ cēranāṭṭiṉ stalaṅkaḷtōruñceṉṟu.*"
75. See Chapter 5 for the role of music and poetry in Sabhapati's works.
76. Robert Caldwell, *A Political and General History of the District of Tinnevelly, in the Presidency of Madras, from the Earliest Period to Its Cession to the English Government in A.D. 1801* (Madras: E. Keys, at the Government Press, 1881), 6.
77. Robert Caldwell, *A Comparative Grammar of the Dravidian or South-Indian Family of Languages*, 2nd ed. (London: Trübner, 1875), 100–101.
78. Caldwell, *Political and General History*, 6.
79. Friedhelm Hardy, *Viraha-Bhakti: The Early History of Kṛṣṇa Devotion in South India* (Delhi: Oxford University Press, 1983), 637.
80. Ibid. I am grateful to Aleksandar Uskokov for pointing these references out to me.
81. Shu Hikosaka, "The Potiyil Mountain in Tamil Nadu and the Origin of the Avalokiteśvara Cult," in *Buddhism in Tamil Nadu: Collected Papers* (Chennai: Institute of Asian Studies, 1998), 119–41.

82. For example, see the pessimism about Hikosaka's argument in Marcus Bingenheimer, *Island of Guanyin: Mount Putuo and Its Gazetteers* (New York: Oxford University Press, 2016).
83. Caldwell, *Political and General History*, 5.
84. For the history of the amalgamation of various "Agastyas" in Tamil literature, see Appendix 3 of Kamil Zvelebil, *Companion Studies to the History of Tamil Literature* (New York: Brill, 1992). For a detailed history and overview of the Siddhas, see Ramaswamy Venkatraman, *A History of the Tamil Siddha Cult* (Madurai: Ennes Publications, 1990). For a treatment of primarily their medical expertise, see Weiss, *Recipes for Immortality*. For their connections with the wider phenomenon of "Siddhas" in Indian medieval literature, see David Gordon White, *The Alchemical Body: Siddha Traditions in Medieval India* (Chicago: University of Chicago Press, 1996). For Agastya as a recipient of the Śivadharma in the ca. sixteenth-century Tamil *Civatarumōttaram* attributed to Maṟaiñāṉa Capantar, see Margherita Trento, "Translating the Dharma of Śiva in Sixteenth-Century Chidambaram: Maṟaiñāṉa Campantar's Civatarumōttaram," in *Śivadharmāmṛta: Essays on the Śivadharma and Its Network*, ed. Florinda De Simini and Csaba Kiss (Naples: UniorPress, 2022), 101–45. For Agastya as grammarian see Jean-Luc Chevillard, "The Pantheon of Tamil Grammarians: A Short History of the Myth of Agastya's Twelve Disciples," in *Écrire et transmettre en Inde classique*, ed. Colas Gérard and Gerdi Gerschheimer (Paris: École française d'Extrême-Orient, 2009), 243–68. I am grateful to Whitney Cox for sharing this latter reference with me.
85. Samuel Osborne, "Woman Becomes First in India to Climb Sacred Mountain Agasthyakoodam after Ban on Females Lifted," *The Independent*, January 16, 2019, https://www.independent.co.uk/news/world/asia/agasthyakoodam-climb-mountain-woman-first-india-sacred-dhanya-senal-kerala-a8731146.html.
86. Ur-account, ii.
87. See, for example, Pi Cuvāminātaṉ, *Caturakiri yāttirai / Sadhuragiri yaththirai* (Chennai: Vikaṭaṉ Piracuram, 2014).
88. Nambiar and Kurup, *Census of India 1961*, 298–99.
89. Ibid., 350.
90. T1, 5.
91. Caldwell, *Political and General History*, 7–8.
92. Ur-account, ii.
93. MCVTS often adds colons (:) between syllables. Their placement is irregular but could have been intended to indicate syllabic stress or some kind of pause. A different symbol is used to indicate the *visarga*.
94. T2, 7: "*appoḻutu akastiya ruṣiyiṉ nēr ciṣyarākiya akastiyācala parvatattil (24 vatu kurupīṭamākiya (civakñāṉapō:taruṣiyiṉ[)] camāti lakṣiyattil nāṉaṭumaikoṇṭa (aḻaittāṭkoṇṭamūrtti) varukiṟāṉ avaṉai ciṣyarākkikkoḷ yeṉṟu carvēsvaraṉ terivikka taṉ kñāṉatiruṣṭiyil yāvum terintukoṇṭu taṉ piratama ciṣiyaṉākiya (paramakuruyōkicit:ta:ṉai) yivarai yaḻaittuvarayaṉuppa, yavar vantu yivar yāyācattai tirttu yiṭṭukkoṇṭupōy kuruviṭam viṭṭaṉar*."
95. Ur-account, ii.

96. White, *The Alchemical Body*, 225–28.
97. "Sadhu Srila Srikrishnaveni Amma vs The State Rep. By Its Secretary," a legal document, March 18, 2015.
98. It remains a point of humor that, when I was first starting to research Sabhapati, one of the only sources online for him ("Minotaur Labyrinth") was about Agastya really being an extraterrestrial alien and his ashram being a point of visitation for said aliens.
99. See Alexis Sanderson, "The Śaiva Literature," *Journal of Indological Studies*, nos. 24–25 (2012–13, 2014): 86.
100. J. M. Nallaswami Pillai, *Sivagnana Botham of Meikanda Deva* (Tinnevelly: South Indian Saiva Siddhanta Works Publishing Society, 1984).
101. See Chapter 3 for a more detailed analysis of this question.
102. T2, 8. Tam.: "*inta (438) varuṣakālamāy vīṟṟirukkiṉṟatu.*"
103. Ur-account, iii.
104. A period of yogic practice or *sādhanā* lasting nine or twelve years is also common in hagiographies of other legendary yogis, such as the Nāth yogis and Siddhas of Sanskrit alchemical literature; see White, *The Alchemical Body*, 295.
105. T2, 7. Tam.: "*avar kuhaiyilēyē, kantamūlāti pakṣkṣaṇai ceytukoṇṭu carva upatēcaṅkaḷaippeṟṟu carva cātaṉaikaḷaiyuṟṟu, carvāṉupavamaṭaintu, mantira, vaya, tāraṇā, paktiyōkaṅkaḷil pūrṇāṉupavappeṟṟu cuvācam vāci, pirāṇam, vintu, nātam, piraṇavam, kalā mutaliya yōkaṅkaḷiṉ rēcaka, pūraka kumpaka pantaṉa, stampaṉa stāpaṉa ṣaṭkiriyaikaḷāl carva yōkāṉupava cittiyaṭaintu carva tattuva taricaṉam kākṣi; mākṣi, yākṣi, kukṣi, citti cakti mūrttīkaraṅkaḷaiyaṉupavittu nayatiyāl nivāraṇañ ceytu kēvavāttuvaita ātma piramma aikya civapiramma rājayōka pirammaniṣaṭai camātiyaṉupavattāl cittukñāṉiyallātacukñāṉiyāya nāhañ carvam etpirakāramayam ahañcuvappirammam) eṉṉum cuvāṉupava variṣṭta [8] pakkuva nirvikalpa kāṣṭṭa camātiyilirukkum camayattil.*"
106. I have translated *kavuṉam* (an alternate form of *kevuṉam*) as flight, which seems to be the connotation here; see the entry in the University of Madras Tamil Lexicon, which suggests its derivation from *gagana*. Based on the term's usage in Siddha alchemical texts, it could also refer to competency in the use or purification of mica, mercury, or another similar substance.
107. MCVTS, 8. Tam.: "*nī āṟu pāṣai terntavaṉ ākaiyāl nāṉ āññāpikkum inta parōpakāra kiriyai muṭikkuka, āṉulum nammuṭaiya yatirahasyaṅkaḷākiya, vātam, ka:vuṉam, kalpam, parakāyappiravēcam, añcaṉam, citti, cakti, mūrttikaram, āyurvirutti aṣṭaṭakkiriyācitti aṣṭacitti mutaliyatukaḷai ulakattavarkaḷukkut terivikkāmal, ātma lāpattiṟkum, ihaparakāmya niṣkāmyattiṟkumuṟiya pakti tiyāṉa ñāṉa cātaṉāṉupavaṅkaḷai pōtaṉārūpamāyum, upatēcakkiramamāyum, tīkṣāmārkkamāyum inta carva vicāraṇai, cātaṉai, yaṉupavaṅkaḷai, paṭaṅkaḷil kāṭṭi nūtaṉa cāstirañceytu accipaṭukkoṭuppatāyum, carvavarṇastarkaḷūñ camamāy pūjai ceyvatumākiya inta parōpakārattaiceytukoṇṭum eṉṉiṭam vantu koṇṭum pōykkoṇṭumirukkakkaṭavāyeṉṟu ākñā pittapirakāram.*"
108. See Chapter 4. For examples of these aspects of what it meant to be a "yogi," see Somadeva Vasudeva, "Powers and Identities: Yoga Powers and the Tantric Śaiva Traditions," in *Yoga Powers: Extraordinary Capacities Attained Through Meditation*

and Concentration, ed. Knut A. Jacobsen (Leiden: Brill, 2012), 264–302, and David Gordon White, *Sinister Yogis* (Chicago: University of Chicago Press, 2009).

109. See Chapter 3 for some indications as to how these terms are intertwined in Sabhapati's literature.
110. T2, 9. Tam.: "*malaiyāḷam, tamil̲, teluṅku, kan̲n̲aṭi, mahārāṣṭṭi, kujarāṭṭi hintustāṇi, peṅkāli, nēpāḷam, pañcāp, rajaputṭāṇā, kāṣmiyar, cintu, mulṭān̲ himāñcalam, mutaliyatēcaṅkaḷukkuccen̲r̲u.*"
111. T2, 9.
112. T2, 9: Tam.: "*cātan̲ai an̲upavarūpamāy paṭaṅkaḷōṭu camaskirutam, urutu, hintustān̲i, peṅkāli, teluṅku, maharāṣṭi, tirāviṭa tamil̲, iṅkilīṣ mutaliya pāṣaikaḷil ceytu acciṭṭu veḷippaṭuttiyum.*"
113. It is also possible that Shivajnanaprakash Yogishwara was unaware of the precise dates that many of Sabhapati's works were published in various languages, from 1880 onward. See Chapter 2 for the textual history of his many works.
114. T2, 9. For more on the significance of this figure see Srilata Raman, *The Transformation of Tamil Religion: Ramalinga Swamigal (1823–1874) and Modern Dravidian Sainthood* (New York: Routledge, 2022); and Richard Weiss, *The Emergence of Modern Hinduism: Religion on the Margins of Colonialism* (Oakland: University of California Press, 2017).
115. For example, see Ma. Po. Civañān̲am, *The Universal Vision of Saint Ramalinga: Vallalar Kanda Orumaippadu*, trans. R. Ganapathy (Annamalainagar: Annamalai University, 1987).
116. Justice K. Chandru, "Thiru Sabanatha Oli Sivachariyar v/s The Commissioner, H.R. & C.E. Department & Others," March 24, 2010.
117. Ur-account, iii.
118. T2, 9. Tam.: "*hintutēcattir̲kuḷ tan̲ ciṣyarkaḷ appiyāca cātan̲aiceyya (464) tiyān̲a capaikaḷai āṅkāṅku stāpittan̲ar.*"
119. Ur-account, iii.
120. Ur-account, iv.
121. Ur-account, iv.
122. CPSPS, First Book, 6–15.
123. T1, 7–9.
124. T2, 10. Tam.: "*kaka:n̲appiravēcamāy maraintan̲ar.*"
125. Ur-account, iv.
126. T2, 10. Tam.: "*himāñcal takṣaṇapāricattiluḷḷa.*"
127. For traditional pilgrimage routes associated with Kedarnāth and Badrināth, see Shivaprasad Dabral, *Shri Uttarakhand Yatra Darshan* (Narayankoti: publisher unknown, 1960), 242–82. The grouping of "Five Kedars" is also treated in an undergraduate paper by William "Bo" Sax that refers to their presence in the *Kedārkhaṇḍ*, a text on the mythology of Kedārnāth allegedly deriving from the *Skandapurāṇa* of which there are many local recensions; the list that Sax cites refers to Madhyamaheśvara, Tuṅganāth, Kalpeṣvara, and Mahālaya (apparently synonymous with Rudranāth) in addition to Kedārnāth proper. I am grateful to William for sharing with me his paper and sources on these two temple complexes in Uttarakhand.

128. T2, 10. Tam.: "*jūvālāmuki tirilōkanāt, pūtanāt keṅkōtpatti, yamuṉōtpatti, amarnāt, maṉikarṇikā mutaliya kṣēttira tiricaṉam, natisnāṉam ceytu.*"
129. For more on the history of Lahore's role and development in the Punjab during the colonial period see Ian Talbot, *Punjab and the Raj, 1849–1947* (New Delhi: Manohar Publications, 1988); and William J. Glover, *Making Lahore Modern: Constructing and Imagining a Colonial City* (Minneapolis: University of Minnesota Press, 2008).
130. CPSPS, First Book, 19: "Our Yogísver after the expiration of few days at Lahore . . ."
131. BRY, 12. BRY is the only text that mentions Sabhapati's length of stay at Lahore, so this dating is tentative.
132. Bose, *Life of Sris Chandra Basu*, 86.
133. Sabhapaty Swamy, "The Madras Yogi Sabhapaty Swamy, Madame Blavatsky and Colonel Olcott at Lahore," *Amrita Bazar Patrika*, letter dated November 16, 1880, in Blavatsky's unpublished scrapbook held at the Theosophical Society Archives in Adyar, Chennai.
134. Vasu's family name is transliterated as "Basu" according to Bengali orthography, which is the version I have used throughout for the sake of consistency.
135. Bose, *Life of Sris Chandra Basu*. For other sources in Bengali that inform this treatment of his life see Śrījñānendramohan Dās, *Baṅger Bāhire Bāṅgālī (Uttar Bhārat)* (Kalikātā: Śrī Anāthanāth Mukhopādhyāẏ, 1322 [1915]); Śrīrāmānanda Caṭṭopādhaẏ, "Bāmandās Basu," *Prabāsī* 30, no. 2nd khaṇḍa, 3 (January 1339): 400–408.
136. Pāṇini, *The Ashtadhyayi*, trans. Srisa Chandra Vasu (Benares: Published by Sindhu Charan Bose at the Panini Office, 1897).
137. Singleton, *Yoga Body*, 44–53.
138. Government College Lahore was established in 1864 in accordance with Wood's Educational Despatch of 1854, which mandated that an education department be established in every East India Company–controlled province and that at least one government school should be opened in every district. For a history of the institution see H. L. O. Garrett, ed., *A History of Government College, Lahore, 1864–1914* (Lahore: "Civil and Military Gazette" Press, 1914); and Syed Sultan Mahmood Hussain, *50 Years of Government College Lahore (1864–1913)* (Lahore: Izhar Research Institute of Pakistan, 2005).
139. For Shrish Chandra's subsequent publications of yoga, such as the first known English translation of *Gheraṇḍa Saṃhitā* as well as the *Shiva Samhita* (Sanskrit: *Śivasaṃhitā*), a ca. fifteenth-century work of haṭha yoga that was widely utilized by occultists, from the Austrian industrialist Carl Kellner (1851–1905) to the British poet and mountain-climber Aleister Crowley (1875–1947, See Chapter 7), see Keith Cantú, "Shrish Chandra Basu and Modern Occult Yoga," in *Occult South Asia*, ed. Karl Baier and Mriganka Mukhopadhyay (forthcoming).
140. I am grateful to Idris Ali for visiting this village, confirming its location, and taking photographs.
141. For more on Leitner's role at Lahore Government College see Hussain, *50 Years*.
142. Bose, *Life of Sris Chandra Basu*, 77.
143. Ibid.

144. Mohan Singh, *Gorakhnath and Mediaeval Hindu Mysticism* (Lahore: Dr. Mohan Singh, Oriental College, Lahore, 1936); George Weston Briggs, *The Religious Life of India: Gorakhnāth and the Kānphaṭa Yogīs* (Calcutta: Y.M.C.A. Publishing House, 1938).
145. For more on the Nāth Yogīs see White, *Sinister Yogis*, as well as his earlier works; James Mallinson, "The Nāth Saṃpradāya," *Brill Encyclopedia of Hinduism* 3 (2011): 407–28; David Lorenzen and Adrián Muñoz, *Yogi Heroes and Poets: Histories and Legends of the Nāths* (Albany: State University of New York Press, 2011); and Gordan Djurdjevic and Shukdev Singh, trans., *Sayings of Gorakhnāth: Annotated Translation of the Gorakh Bānī* (New York: Oxford University Press, 2019).
146. Bose, *Life of Sris Chandra Basu*, 68.
147. For the rivalry between Agnihotri and Dayananda see Kenneth W. Jones, *Arya Dharm: Hindu Consciousness in 19th-Century Punjab* (Berkeley: University of California Press, 1976). For a more recent take on Dayananda's reformism and its role in shaping Hindu modernity, see J. Barton Scott, *Spiritual Despots: Modern Hinduism and the Genealogies of Self-Rule* (Chicago: University of Chicago Press, 2016).
148. Lala Shiv Dayal Seth, quoted in Bose, *Life of Sris Chandra Basu*, 68.
149. Ibid.
150. For Dayananda's views on Tantra and a response to them by some Indian Theosophists, see Baier, "Theosophical Orientalism," 326–27. For Shrish Chandra's complicated views on haṭha yoga see Singleton, *Yoga Body*; and Cantú, "Shrish Chandra Vasu."
151. Bose, *Life of Sris Chandra Basu*, 96, 117. The Brahmo Samaj was founded in Calcutta in 1828, but it wasn't established in Lahore until the 1860s by one Nabin Chandra Ray (Nabīn Candra Rāẏ), a contemporary of Shrish Chandra's father Śyāmācaraṇ.
152. Baier, "Theosophical Orientalism," 328–30; the first scholarly treatment of this meeting was in Karl Baier, *Meditation und Moderne: Zur Genese Eines Kernbereichs Moderner Spiritualität in der Wechselwirkung Zwischen Westeuropa, Nordamerika und Asien* (Würzburg: Königshausen & Neumann, 2009).
153. Ibid., 328.
154. Bose, *Life of Sris Chandra Basu*, 249.
155. Helena Blavatsky and Henry Olcott, eds., "The 'Trieste [*sic*] on Vedantic Raj Yoga,'" *The Theosophist: A Magazine of Oriental Philosophy, Art, Literature and Occultism* 1, no. 7 (April 1880): 190.
156. Francesca Orsini, *The History of the Book in South Asia* (New York: Routledge, 2016).
157. Unfortunately the dates of this translator could not be traced at the time of writing.
158. Müller, *Six Systems*, 456, 462–65.
159. Anonymous, *The Secret of Longevity and Verses by Yogi Sabhapathy Swami* (Coimbatore: K.N. Easwariah at the Literary Sun Press, 1895). It appears that only the "Verses" (i.e. "The Yogi's Address to his Countrymen") are attributed to Sabhapati, and not the story about one Prince Dharmapalu that precedes it.
160. Advaita Ashrama, *Reminiscences of Swami Vivekananda*, new ed. (Kolkata: The Ahyaksha, Advaita Ashrama, 2018).

161. Bose, *Life of Sris Chandra Basu*, 87.
162. Joscelyn Godwin, "Blavatsky and the First Generation of Theosophy," in *Handbook of the Theosophical Current*, ed. Olav Hammer and Mikael Rothstein (Leiden: Brill, 2013), 15–31.
163. Ibid., 22.
164. Ibid., 23. For more on these letters and the early Theosophical Society in India in general, see the chapters by various authors in Sand and Rudbøg, *Imagining the East*; and Hans Martin Krämer and Julian Strube, eds., *Theosophy across Boundaries: Transcultural and Interdisciplinary Perspectives on a Modern Esoteric Movement* (Albany: SUNY Press, 2020).
165. H.P.B. Scrapbook, vol. 10, part 2, *1879–80*, 493. This unpublished scrapbook is held in the Archives of the Theosophical Society at Adyar, Chennai. *Vachovali* in Blavatsky's scrapbook and Bose's biography is also variously transliterated "Vachchowali," "Vachhowali," and "Vachoovāli." *Bhadarkaliyali* is also transliterated "Bhadarkálli Galee." This area may refer to the south of the Walled City or somewhat outside its gates, near Queens Road.
166. Jones, *Arya Dharm*, 37, 89.
167. See Bose, *Life of Sris Chanda Basu*, 117–19.
168. Jones, *Arya Dharm*, 46.
169. The first annual volume of this periodical, from 1882 to 1883, exists in the library collection of the University of Toronto, and a full run is present in the catalog of the National Library of India in Kolkata.
170. H. S. Olcott, "The Fourth Anniversary Address," in *A Collection of Lectures on Theosophy and Archaic Religions, Delivered in India and Ceylon by Colonel H.S. Olcott, President of the Theosophical Society* (Madras: A. Theyaga Rajier, 1883), 18–25.
171. Henry S. Olcott, *Old Diary Leaves. Second Series, 1878–83* (London: Theosophical Publishing Society and the Theosophist Office, 1900), 258.
172. Henry Olcott's personal diary for 1880, entry "November 7," held at the Theosophical Society Archives in Adyar, Chennai.
173. Olcott, "The Fourth Anniversary Address," 23.
174. Jones, *Arya Dharm*, 37, 38 n. 20.
175. Supreme Court of India, *Courts of India: Past to Present* (Delhi: Supreme Court of India, 2017).
176. The phrase appears in Olcott's address in Bombay earlier that year, where he writes the following ("The Fourth Anniversary Address," 19): "How often since we came to India have I heard it said by Natives, that it was a strange anomaly that white men had to journey from the antipodes—from *Patál*—to tell them about their forefather's religion!"
177. Henry Olcott's unpublished personal diary for 1879, entry "Sunday, November 23, 1879," held at the Theosophical Society Archives in Adyar, Chennai.
178. Bose, *Life of Sris Chandra Basu*, 80–85.
179. Olcott, *Old Diary Leaves*, 258–59.
180. Henry Olcott's unpublished personal diary for 1880, entry "Monday, November 8, 1879," held at the Theosophical Society Archives in Adyar, Chennai.

181. VRY3, iv.
182. VRY3, iv.
183. For more on the life of this figure from the Theosophical perspectives of his associates see Sven Eek, *Damodar and the Pioneers of the Theosophical Movement* (Adyar, Madras: Vasanta Press, 1978).
184. D. K. Mavalankar, "The Philosophy and Science of Vedantic Raja Yoga," *The Theosophist: A Magazine of Oriental Philosophy, Art, Literature and Occultism* 5, no. 6 (March 1884): 146.
185. Sabhapaty Swamy, "Madras Yogi Sabhapaty Swamy."
186. Ibid.
187. H. P. Blavatsky, "A Hindu Professor's Views on Indian Yoga," *The Theosophist: A Magazine of Oriental Philosophy, Art, Literature and Occultism* 2, no. 7 (April 1881): 158–59. This piece is also included in volume 3 of Blavatsky's *Collected Writings*.
188. Henry Olcott's personal diary entry for 1880, held by the Theosophical Society in Adyar, Chennai, which I consulted in February 2020.
189. I am grateful to Kurt Leland for sharing with me the dates of Shrish Chandra's formal membership in the Theosophical Society.
190. It is not clear who this refers to.
191. It is not clear who this refers to.
192. This could refer to a few different figures active in Lahore during that time. Olcott's handwriting also makes it difficult to distinguish if the first name is "Chandu" or "Chandra." If it is the latter, then he was a respected and wealthy leader in the local community; see Jones, *Arya Dharm*, 158–59.
193. This could be the same person as Lala Bhawani Das; see Jones, *Arya Dharm*, 53.
194. This is likely Rama Prasad Keshyap (Rāma Prasād Keśyap), who did his MA at Punjab University in Lahore and later went on to be president of the Meerut Theosophical Society and publish a translation of the Sanskrit text *Śivasvarodaya*, entitled *Nature's Finer Forces* (1890), probably read by Yogi Ramacharaka (William Walker Atkinson).
195. Bose, *Life of Sris Chanda Basu*, 126–27.
196. Cf. Singleton, *Yoga Body*, 44, 69–70 for some consideration of Oman's subject matter and inspiration on other authors and artists.
197. Ibid, 87. His parentage is given in *Who Was Who*, vol. 1, *1897–1915: A Companion to Who's Who Containing the Biographies of Those Who Died during the Period 1897–1915*, 7th ed. (London: A. & C. Black, 2014).
198. Garrett, *History of Government College*, Appendix B, iii; Hussain, *50 Years*, 374.
199. John Campbell Oman, *The Mystics, Ascetics, and Saints of India: A Study of Sadhuism, with an Account of the Yogis, Sanyasis, Bairagis, and Other Strange Hindu Sectarians* (London: T. Fisher Unwin, 1905). Oman's work is also cited by Daniela Bevilacqua, "Let the Sādhus Talk: Ascetic Understanding of Haṭha Yoga and Yogāsanas" (2017).
200. John Campbell Oman, *Indian Life, Religious and Social*, 1st ed. (London: T. Fisher Unwin, 1889), 30–33.
201. John Campbell Oman, *Cults, Customs and Superstitions of India, Being a Revised and Enlarged Edition of "Indian Life, Religious and Social," Comprising Studies and*

Sketches of Interesting Peculiarities in the Beliefs, Festivals and Domestic Life of the Indian People; Also of Witchcraft and Demoniacal Possession, as Known amongst Them (London: T. Fisher Unwin, 1908), 17–19.

202. Oman, *Indian Life, Religious and Social*, 30–31.

203. CPSPS, First Book, 19.

204. T2, 11. Tam.: "*kāṣmīrattilirukkum poḻutu akastiyarāsramattilirukkun taṉ kuruvākiya civañāṉapōtaruṣiyāṉavar (50) varuṣattiṟku oruvicai, akastiya mahāruṣīsvarar, taṉ āsrama ciṣyakurupīṭastarkaḷukku vantu taricaṉaṅkoṭukkuñcamayam vantuviṭṭamaiyāl, taṉ pirammañāṉa tiruṣṭi tīkṣākiramattāl avar ñāṉa tiruṣṭiyai inta ñāṉakuruyōki ñāṉatiruṣṭiyil kalappittatai yivararintu iruvaruṅkalantavuṭaṉ akastiyaruṣi taricaṉantaravaruñcaṅkatiyai terivittu nī vuṭaṉē nammāsramam vantucērakkaṭavāyeṉṟu ākñāpittavuṭaṉē taṉṉiṭattilirunta mūṉṟu karaikkuṭu-kaiyakkoṇṭu ruṣikēcam harattuvāram vintācalam vantu piṉpu kiṣkintā, śrī kailam vētacirēṇi vantu oru stauttiyappāvālarccittaṉar. . . . piṉpu citamparattukku vantu ekārccaṉaippā cāṟṟiṉār. . . . piraku, tirukkaṭaiyu, tirupperunturai, rāmēsvaram, maturai, kuṟṟālam, pāpanācam taricittu taṉṉuṭaiya kuruvīṉāsramamākiya takṣaṇakailācamākiya akastiyācalaparvatattiṟku vantu taṉ kurupātam vaṇaṅki kurākñaparipālaṉappā ceytaṉar.*"

205. Ur-account, *vi*.

206. Another Hindu Theosophist, "Do the Rishis Exist?," *The Theosophist: A Magazine of Oriental Philosophy, Art, Literature and Occultism* 4 (May 1883).

207. White, *The Alchemical Body*, 74.

208. RYB, page *kai* [the work uses the order of the Devanagari characters, beginning with "ka," to paginate prefatory materials]. Hi.: "*yaha dūsare daphe jab āśrammẽ gaye tab agastya muni aur unõke kālke anek ṛṣiyõke darśan pāye. yaha agastya muni haiyāt nahī hai ēsā log samajate hai; lekīn ēsā vicār asatya hai.*"

209. CPSPS, First Book, 19–21.

210. CPSPS, First Book, 19–21.

211. CPSPS, First Book, vi. The address given is "Kapali Eeswarer East Madaveedi, Car Street Door No. 28, Mylapoor, Madras."

212. The address listed is "No. 2, Brahmin Street, south of Chitracotum [*sic*], Mylapore, Madras." I visited this address in the summer of 2018 and discovered the streets have since been renumbered. When I found the old number, I discovered the home had since been replaced with a modern apartment building.

213. M. Muncherjee Shroff, "The Work in Bombay," supplement to *The Theosophist: A Magazine of Oriental Philosophy, Art, Literature and Occultism* 11 (April 1890): cxxiv. I am grateful to Kurt Leland for bringing this reference to my attention.

214. Patrick D. Bowen, "'The Real Pure Yog': Yoga in the Early Theosophical Society and the Hermetic Brotherhood of Luxor," in Sand and Rudbøg, *Imagining the East*, 143–65.

215. Haramohana Lāl Sūda, *Bhāratendu maṇḍal ke samānāntara aur āpūrak Murādābād maṇḍal* (New Delhi: Vāṇī Prakāśan, 1986), 78–84. I am grateful to Jason Schwartz for pointing out Jwalaprasad Mishra's broader significance in the development of Hindi literature.

216. T2, 13. Tam.: "*vilvavaṉattil ātiyil akasttiyar vātāpi, vilvāpiyacurāḷaikkoṉṟu akasttiyāralayamum, akasttiya tīrttamum stāpittu ipperēri ye:ṉpatil yākakuṇṭam eṟpaṭutti yākañceytupōṉa tirukkoṇṇūriṟkuvantu pērērikku yaṭutta nilattil niṣṭaiyilirukkumpoḻuthu taṉ tirikāla ñāṉatiruṣṭiyil, tāṉ niṣṭaiyilirukkumiṭam akasttiyaruṣi koñcakālam maṭālayayācīrmam eṟpaṭutti, vacittupōṉayiṭamāyum, pērēri avar yākañceytayākakuṇṭamāyum inta yākakuṇṭavaṭapuṟanilattil akastiyarukku carvēsvarar taṉ pañcakiruttiya naṭaṉa taricaṉam koṭuttatāyum, 1008 liṅkaṅkaḷai 108 cālikkirāmaṅkaḷai taṉ ciṣyarkaḷ pūjittu pōṉatāyum.*"
217. I am grateful to Seth Powell for introducing me to the significance of using figures "etched in stone" to help date temples and explore previously unknown connections between disparate sites.
218. Aruṭkavī Śrī Tēvī Karumārī Tāsar, *Vilvāraṇyat tala purāṇac curukkam* (Villivākkam, Ceṉṉai: Iḷaiñar Aruṭpaṇi Maṉṟam, 2000). Cf. Sanderson, "The Śaiva Literature," 88, for the importance of *sthalapurāṇa* literature in Tamil.
219. Søren Sørensen, *An Index to the Names in the Mahābhārata* (London: Williams and Norgate, 1904), 237 (Ilvala); 720 (Vātāpi).
220. Vishnu S. Sukthankar, *The Āraṇyakaparvan (Part 1), Being the Third Book of the Mahābhārata the Great Epic of India* (Poona: Bhandarkar Oriental Research Institute, 1942), 339–41. See also Zvelebil, *Companion Studies*, 238 and Appendix 3.
221. MCVTS, 14. Tam.: "*koṇṇūril akastiyavarkka kurupitāruṣi maṭālayam stāpittu.*"
222. T2, 13. Tam.: "*yatil (1008) liṅkappiratiṣṭaiceyya (108) cālikkirāmapiratiṣṭaiceyya.*"
223. CPSPS, Second Book, 419–26.
224. Compare CPSPS, Second Book, 390–91; RYB, 118–19; and MCVTS, inserted diagrams between pages 44 and 45 of the main text. For the way that this would have compared and contrasted with the "mesmerism" of Henry Olcott and other Theosophists see Karl Baier, "Mesmeric Yoga and the Development of Meditation within the Theosophical Society," *Theosophical History* 16, nos. 3–4 (October 2012): 151–61.
225. Ñāṉakuru Capāpati Yōkīsvarar, *Amcumati cūriyamūrttikkup pōtitta cakalākama tiraṭṭu. itil civālayamātapūjai, viṉāyakacaturtti, caṅkaṭacaturtti . . . tira aṭaṅkiyirukkiṉraṉa*, part 1 (Madras: Printed by N. Kupusawmy Chettiar at the Duke of Edinburgh Press, 1894); Ñāṉakuru Capāpati Yōkīsvarar, *Amcumati cūriyamūrttikkup pōtitta cakalākama tiraṭṭu. itil caṅkirāntti, tiruvūcaluṟcavam, tīpāvali (naraka caturttaci) aṭaṅkiyirukkiṉraṉa*, Part I-A (Madras: Printed by N. Kupusawmy Chettiar at the Duke of Edinburgh Press, 1894); Ñāṉakuru Capāpati Yōkīsvarar, *Amcumati cūriyamūrttikkup pōtitta cakalākama tiraṭṭu. itil tēppōṟcavam, navarāttiri viratam, parācatti ānanta taricaṉap pūjai āṭaṅkiyirukkiṉraṉa*, Part I-C (Madras: Printed by C. Murugesa Mudalyar at the Hindu Theological Press, 1894); Ñāṉakuru Capāpati Yōkīsvarar, *Amcumati cūriyamūrttikkup pōtitta cakalākama tiraṭṭu. itil vināyakar, cuppiramaṇiyar, cukkiravāram, caṣṭi, aṅkārakacaturtti, tiruvātirai viratam mutaliyavai āṭaṅkiyirukkiṉraṉa*, Part I-D (Madras: Printed by C. Murugesa Mudalyar at the Hindu Theological Press, 1894). A bibliographical reference exists for Part I-B, which seems nonexistent, but not Part I (without a letter), so it is possible that Part I is in fact Part I-B or that the order is switched in another way.

226. T2, 13. Tam.: "*karmakkiriyā yōkakñāṉa carvavita tapaṅkaḷaiyum, cātaṉāppiyā-caṅkaḷaiyum, aṉupavaṅkaḷaiyum, tattuvakñāṉaṅkaḷaiyum (40) tattuvapaṭaṅkaḷil, tiyāṉapaṭaṅkaḷil kāṭṭi upatēcāṉukkirahamāy tamiḻ tirāviṭa pāṣaiyil curuti smiruti cāstirañceytaruḷi (carva vicāraṇā cātaṉāṉupava caṅkiraha vētōpatēcam) eṉṉum cāstira nāmantaṉṉācīrma kurupīṭastarkaḷāl tarappaṭṭa nāmattōṭu acciṭappaṭṭirukk-iṉṟatu.*"
227. Piḷḷai, *Nīlakiri*, 13–20.
228. Ibid., 5.
229. Ibid., 5–6.
230. Ibid., 6.
231. This could have been an earlier edition of *Civāṉantapōtam* (Ceṉṉai: Manoṉmaṇivilācam Accukkūṭam, 1897).
232. Piḷḷai, *Nīlakiri*, 7. For a short summary of Kuṇaṅkuṭi Mastāṉ Cāyapu's literary contributions, see Ci. Pālacuppiramaṇiyaṉ, *Tamiḻ ilakkiya varalāṟu* (Ceṉṉai: Maṇamalarp patippakam, 1998), 231–32.
233. Piḷḷai, *Nīlakiri*, 8.
234. This refers to a common form of primary schooling during the colonial period in which a teacher would conduct classes on the raised veranda (*tiṇṇai*) of a house.
235. "Photo Gallery: Prominent Alumni," Wesley Higher Secondary School website, http://www.wesleyschool.in/photogallery5.html. Accessed February 16, 2020.
236. Temples to Balathandayuthapani also exist in Malaysia, such as the Arulmigu Balathandayuthapani Temple in Penang.
237. "Ooty Kasiviswanathar Temple," in *Wanderings of a Pilgrim*, a blog on south Indian temples with focus on unique features and sthalapuranams. http://wanderingtamil.blogspot.com/2017/11/ooty-kasiviswanathar-temple.html. Accessed February 16, 2020.
238. Cuvāmikaḷ, *Śrīsatsampāṣiṇi*.
239. Piḷḷai, *Nīlakiri*, 10. Tam.: "*śrī ēkāmpara tēcika cuvāmikaḷ haṭayōka anuṣṭāṉamum uḷḷavarkaḷ.*"
240. Ibid., 11.
241. It is unclear to which cave this refers, so I have left it untranslated with diacritics.
242. Piḷḷai, *Nīlakiri*, 13–14. Tam.: "*maicūr aracar araṇmaṉaiyil iruntapōtu mahācittarām potikācalam śrī akastiya māmuṉivar paramparaiyil vanta ñāṉakuru yōki śrī āti capāpati cuvāmikaḷ iyaṟṟiya pirammañāṉa anuṣṭāṉa cāstiram oru naṇpar vāyilākak kiṭaikkap peṟṟu paṭittuvaravē, anta pirammañāṉa niṣṭaiyiṉiṭattu mikunta avar piṟantu ammahāṉukku mikka vinayattuṭaṉ pācuram mūlamāka viṇṇappam oṉṟu tapālil ceṉṉaikku aṉuppiṉār. ivaratu kōrikkaikku iṇaṅki ammahāṉum oru pauṟṇimai iravilē utakai ticaiyai nōkkit tīkṣānukraham puriyavē ivviṭam cātu cuvāmikaḷuṭaiya cuvapṉattil vayatu mutirnta or ñāṉi puruṣar tōṉṟiṉār. avarai pakti mikutiyāl kaṇṇīr perukki upacarittu ātaṉattirutti taṉ kuhaikaḷai eṭuttuccollavum, mahāṉ karuṇaikūrntu ñāṉōpatēcam ceytu ācīrvatittu maṟaintaṉar. viḻippaṭaintu pārkkumpōtu uṇmaiyākavē tam paṭukkai kaṇṇīriṉāl naṉaintirukkakkaṇṭu āṉantamuṟṟu tūṅkāmalē śrī kuruviṉ upatēcattai mīṇṭum mīṇṭum cintittukoṇṭiruntu, poḻutu pularntatum iravu coppaṉattil nikaḻntavaṟṟai*

ellām tamatu arumait tāyāriṭam colla, avvammaiyār akam mika makiḻntu avvupatēca moḻikaḷaik kuṟittuvaittukkoṇṭu ataṉai irakaciyamāka cātaṉai ceytuvarumpaṭiyākavum, ataṉai yāriṭamum terivikkāmal irukkumpaṭiyākavum coṉṉārkaḷ. itu nikaḻnta mūṉṟāmnāḷ tapāl mūlamāka pirahma ñāṉānuṣṭāṉa pustakam anta ñāṉakuru yōkikaḷuṭaiya tiruvuruvappaṭam, vipūtippiracātam maṟṟum or kaṭitamum varappeṟṟup pērāṉantamuṇṭāki kurunātar eḻutiya nirupattaip paṭittapōtu tām cuvapṉattil peṟṟa ñāṉōpatēca tīkṣaiyum, maṟṟum cila ñāṉa yōkāpyācaṅkaḷum ācīr vacaṉaṅkaḷum irukkakkaṇṭu āccaryamum, āṉanta paravacamum aṭaintārkaḷ. śrī kuruviṉ ākñaiyiṉpaṭi apyācamum ceytuvantārkaḷ. camayam nērum pōtellām (Elk Hill) elk hil malaikkuppōy pajē cuvāmi kuhaikkum, maicūr makārājā araṇmaṉaikkut teṟkiluḷḷa malaikkum ceṉṟu aḻuta kaṇṇum paktiyāl urukiya cintaiyumāka cittar kaṇaṅkaḷaip pāṭittutittu tirumpuvatum, araṇmaṉaiyil or ciṟiya aṟaiyil apyācam ceytuvaruvatum vaḻakkamāyiruntatu."

243. Ibid., 15. Tam.: "*ivvāṟu utyōkattil iruntukoṇṭē niṣṭai purivatum citta puruṣarkaḷait tiyāṉittut tutippatumākavē irukkuṅkāl oru iravil piṉṉum oru kaṉavil oru mahā citta puruṣar tōṉṟavum avarai cuvāmikaḷ pakti vinayattuṭaṉ pūjikka avar tiruvuḷam makiḻntu "uṉakku muṉṉarē ñāṉōpatēcam ceytāyiṟṟu. iṉi uṉakku śrī cuparṇa cuvāmikaḷ eṉap peyariya periyār oruvarāl tīkṣā nāmamum nām anuṣṭittu varum om acalapīṭakīlaka irakaciyamum kiṭaikkum" eṉa ācikūṟi maṟaintaṉar.*"
244. Ibid., i–ii.
245. See Singleton, *Yoga Body*, 70–75.
246. For example, of other such translocal flows, see Foxen, *Biography of a Yogi* and *Inhaling Spirit*.
247. Tam.: "*ivarum inta tirukkoṇṇūr maṭālaya tapācīrmattilum nīlakiri tapācīrmattilum taṉ kuruviṉ akasttiyācala parvata kuhai tapācīrmattilum koñcam koñcaṅkālamāṅkāṅku pirammakñāṉa nirvikalpa camāti niṣṭai purintu varukiṉṟaṉar.*"
248. CTCSPV, 12.
249. MCVTS, 32/1.
250. MCVTS, 12/3. Tam.: "*muṟṟumuṇarntamūḻuñāṉiyākuvāṉ / kaṟṟavarēttuṅkaruṇaiyāḷaṉākuvāṉ / paṟṟaṟṟavarparavumparamakuruvākuvāṉ / naṟṟavamuṭaiyāṉnaṟkurupitāruṣiyē.*"
251. Cuvāmi Pi. Pi. Ār. Hariharaṉ, *Aruḷmiku Śrī Capāpati Liṅkēsvar Jīvacamāti Ālayamstala varalāṟu* (Maṇavūr: Kaviñar Murukāṉantam Accakam, 2017).
252. Ibid. I attended his funeral the following year after he died of health-related causes.
253. Aanandha Aanandha Swamigal's alias is given in Koshi Muthalali, "Proceedings of the Tahsildar of Saidapet Taluk, Ref: Transfer of Registry-Saidapet Taluk 71, Konnur Village Patta Nos. 54 and 68," 1936. I am grateful to Hariharan Swamigal's son Vinayagam for sharing this document with me.
254. Hariharaṉ Cuvāmikaḷ, interview at Aruḷmiku Śrī Capāpati Liṅkēsvar Jīvacamāti Ālayam, interview by Keith Cantú, with assistance from Sivasakthi, Mathan, and Beulah. Audio recording, July 2018.
255. I am grateful to Vinayagam for sharing this information with me.
256. V. Cuppiramaṇiya Ceṭṭiyār, interview with V. Cuppiramaṇiya Ceṭṭiyār, interview by Keith Cantú and Vinayagam, audio recording, August 17, 2019.

257. Hariharaṉ Cuvāmikaḷ, interview at Aruḷmiku Śrī Capāpati Liṅkēsvar Jīvacamāti Ālayam, 2018.
258. MCVTS, [4] (in unnumbered prefatory material to the work proper).
259. MCVTS, [4]. Tam.: "*matirācu ceṉṭiral sṭeṣaṉil rayilēṟi arakkōṇam rayilvē layṉilirukkum villivākkam sṭēṣaṉiliṟaṅki, itaic cērnta koṇṇūr perumāḷ kōyilukku mēṟkilirukkum kuru pitāruṣi maṭālayattiṟku vantu, kurupitāruṣi capāpati cuvāmikaḷait taricikkalām. upatēcam peṟṟukkoḷḷalām, cāstiramum vāṅkikkoḷḷalām.*"
260. Nambiar and Krishnamurthy, *Census of India 1961*.
261. See Appendix 23 in *A Manual of Instructions for Conducting Resettlements in the Madras Presidency (Under the Simplified System)* (Madras: The Superintendent, Government Press, 1937), 49.
262. I am especially thankful to Umamaheshwari, Balachand, and Yuvaraj Sir at the Tamil Nadu Archives for their assistance with drafting these letters and in some cases providing court stamps to accompany the requests.
263. Personal communication via WhatsApp with Vinayagam Swamigal, the current trustee and presiding swami of the Sabhapati Lingeshwarar Koil, February 11, 2021.
264. Personal communication with Vinayagam Swamigal.

2
A Vast Forest of Printed Words

> All rights of the Publication of this Philosophy only in English Language reserved by the Author and His Disciples themselves as Registered Copy Right for only Thirtyfive [*sic*] Years after which the Author gives liberty to each and every *Press* throughout the world to have self publication of this Philosophy.
>
> —CPSPS, First Book, iv

> No book of this kind concerning the Gnosis of Brahman and Rāja Yoga is yet circulating in vernacular languages to date. Studying this book will allow one to practice and understand what yoga is even without instruction from a guru.
>
> ব্রহ্ম-জ্ঞান ও রাজযোগ সম্বন্ধে এরূপ গ্রন্থ এপর্যন্ত প্রচলিত ভাষায় প্রচারিত হয় নাই। ইহা পাঠ করিলে গুরূপদেশ ব্যতিরেকেও যোগ যে কি তাহা বুঝিতে ও করিতে পারা যায়।
>
> —BRY, 2

In this chapter I assess the scope and textual history of Sabhapati's published literature and their subsequent translations in English and vernacular languages. I also provide a summary and list of contents for each of his works, some lists of which are entirely new and some of which are adapted, annotated, and in some cases translated from extant lists of contents in a given work. The dissemination of Sabhapati's published texts runs parallel to his own life, as already demonstrated (Chapter 1), and separately analyzing these works provides much additional data of relevance to the translocalization of his Śaiva philosophy (Chapter 3) and, more directly, to his system of Śivarājayoga (Chapter 4).

I would argue that the most immediately helpful method to make sense of the geographical and linguistic spread of Sabhapati's literature is to loosely apply the philological technique of categorizing texts and variants into language-based "stemmas" of transmission. This is only a loose application of a much more intricate and technical practice of

Like a Tree Universally Spread. Keith Edward Cantú, Oxford University Press. © Oxford University Press 2023.
DOI: 10.1093/oso/9780197665473.003.0003

textual criticism since we here do not need to reconstruct a genealogy of a single archetype with multiple manuscript variants. Instead, the goal is to better apprehend Sabhapati's wide dissemination of published sources and variants of printed text in several different languages in Roman and Indic scripts. At the same time, Sabhapati's publications were often reprinted and translated in at least partial isolation from other stemmata, and the contents of each individual textual stemma does sometimes point to archetypal content in a given language that is then translated, rendering useful a stemmatic method of analysis. The process of separating information about the development of each textual stemma additionally enables one to more properly appreciate the local, pan-Indian, and international flows of Sabhapati's works and system of Śivarājayoga when taken as a whole. The reader should however keep in mind that such a separation is not intrinsic to the texts themselves and is only presented here for the sake of convenience in order to help scholars and the public at large more properly contextualize his texts' various audiences and reception histories.

Before proceeding with a description of Sabhapati's three textual stemmata, I wish to here also briefly clarify my use of a linguistic concept in this chapter (and in the book more broadly). As will be seen throughout this chapter, there is certain stratum of technical Sanskrit language found in Sabhapati's textual stemmata (with the possible exception of his works in Hindi and Bengali, which are inextricably intertwined with Sanskrit) that I prefer to frame for convenience as a nineteenth-century variant of Maṇipravāla (Mpvl. *maṇippiravāḷam* "Ruby and Coral"), a hybrid language that in this case operates between Sanskrit and Tamil linguistic worlds but that is also used to describe a certain interplay between Malayalam and Sanskrit, and other similar blends between (principally) south Indian languages.[1] Sabhapati's literature, despite its overwhelming preference for Sanskrit nouns and Tamil verbs deriving from Sanskrit roots, does not typically go as far as to employ Sanskrit nominal case endings, so as a result his literature does not entirely qualify as "real" Maṇipravāla; in many cases his language could alternatively be described as a local form of "Tamilized Sanskrit" that emerged in some communities across Tamil Nadu, such as among Brahmins and some musical communities.[2] However, even this is complicated since Sabhapati and his followers do in some of their more Sanskrit-centric compositions use Sanskrit grammatical particles and verbal forms that are sometimes given separate translations into Tamil for Sabhapati's Tamil-speaking audience (such lists or word banks are common in CTCSPV and MCVTS, especially following poetic compositions). In any event, while recognizing that the Maṇipravāla label is not wholly satisfactory, I nevertheless find it to be a useful marker in lieu of a better term for distinguishing Sabhapati's own use of Sanskrit terms (with their erratic Tamil spellings) from their more readily recognizable dictionary spellings based on their rendering in north Indian scripts. My main reason for this distinction is practical: Sabhapati's spelling and usage of Sanskrit could appear highly erratic, even erroneous, to a scholar trained only in Sanskrit or the languages of north India more generally, while a scholar trained in Maṇipravāla—or simply familiar with the general way Sanskrit is rendered in Tamil script and pronounced accordingly—would find such renderings commonplace, highly readable, and even intuitive.

Textual Stemmata of Sabhapati's Works

Sabhapati's works have been published in Chennai, Lahore, Kolkata, Mumbai, and New Delhi, to name a few cities in South Asia, as well as abroad in Leipzig, Germany, and Excelsior Springs, Missouri. The texts of these various publications can be divided chronologically according to their earliest known witnesses as follows (see Figure 2.1):

Stemma α, an English textual stemma with Sanskrit technical terms that resemble Maṇipravāla spellings transliterated into the Roman script, and later rendered into Tamil and Devanagari scripts; portions of this stemma were translated from English into Bengali and German (pan-Indian mesolocal and international translocal levels);

Stemma β, a north Indian Hindi and Sanskrit textual stemma, containing diagrams either derived from or translated into Tamil and Telugu equivalents (north Indian mesolocal level); and

Stemma γ, a south Indian stemma composed almost entirely of Tamil and Maṇipravāla in Tamil script; there is also a no-longer-extant Telugu work that was registered in Madras (south Indian local level).

We are fortunate to still have at least one extant original exemplar of Sabhapati's books from each of these interconnected stemmata, although

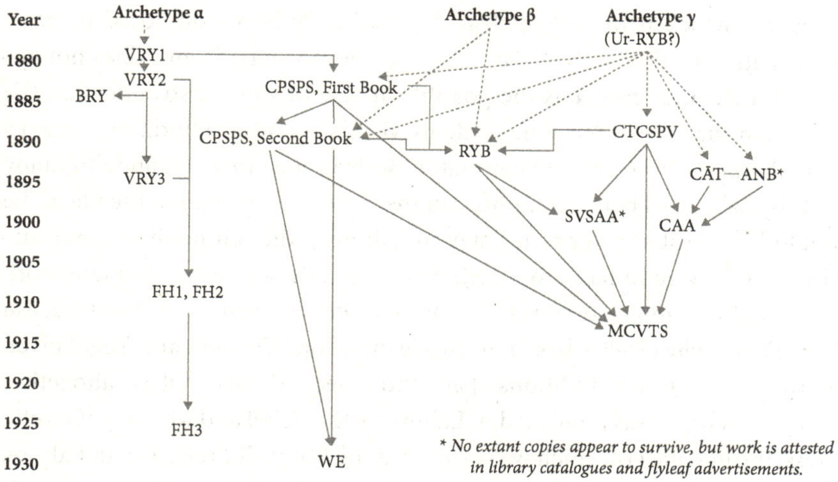

Figure 2.1 A chart depicting three principal textual stemmata of Sabhapati's works from 1880 to 1930 and their date of publication. Lines without arrows indicate parallel sources or intertextual references, while lines with arrows indicate a source relationship.

original editions are today very rare and are mostly held by research libraries or private collections. However, texts from each of these stemmata—especially those in the Alpha Stemma (α)—were circulated widely at the time of their publication, as indicated by the presence of reprinted editions and their mention in publisher's catalogs in Britain, Germany, and elsewhere. They would have also been readily available for purchase from Sabhapati's Meditation Hall in Konnur either in person or via post.

The Alpha Stemma

Three Original Editions of VRY

The introduction of Shrish Chandra Basu as Sabhapati's editor (see Chapter 1) marks the beginning of the latter's extant publications and most if not all of their subsequent translation history to date, although the Ur-account does mention one earlier work in Tamil, "Vedanta Sidhanta Samarasa Brahmagiyana Shiva raja Yogue Kaiulia anubhooti" (Mpvl. conjecture *Vētānta cittānta camaraca pirammakñāṉa civarājayōka kaivalya aṉupūti*), which if indeed published would have been composed prior to Sabhapati's meeting with Shrish Chandra. However, this work does not appear to be extant except as the possible ur-text of some instructions in the Beta Stemma, which has a near-identical title extant in Hindi, or in CPSPS (see The Beta and Gamma Stemmata). Both T1 and T2 also allude to many texts by Sabhapati being composed in the various languages of the places he would have visited prior to his stay in Lahore, although none of these survive, if they were in fact produced. As a result, the earliest still-extant work attributed to Sabhapati (VRY1) is entitled *Om: A Treatise on Vedantic Raj Yoga Philosophy* (1880), based on two lectures on "Vedanta and Yoga" given in 1879 with "much additions" [*sic*] and a second part that is "altogether new."[3] This work was published in Lahore by the "Civil and Military" Gazette Press, the first part of which was printed at the Mitchell Press, also in Lahore, and sold for eight annas (half a rupee). Shrish Chandra's involvement as editor is clearly cited in the title page. The only copy extant today of this first edition was originally owned by Henry Olcott (see Chapter 1), as evident by his signed initials on the cover, and was found in the collection of the Adyar Library and Research Centre. This first edition was out of print for ninety-seven years until a facsimile of VRY1 was reprinted in New Delhi in 1977 by Pankaj Publications with the revised title *Vedantic Raj Yoga: Ancient Tantra Yoga of Rishies* [*sic*].[4] The reprint appended an additional section entitled "A Historical View of the Theories of the Soul" by the Scottish philosopher Alexander Bain (1818–1903), although this was not present in the first edition of VRY1.

A second edition of this work (VRY2) was published in 1883 by R. C. Bary at the "Arya Press." Only a single copy of VRY2 appears to have survived, at the British Library, and a reference is found in *Probsthain's Oriental Catalogue*.[5] VRY2 was also advertised and mentioned in the preface to the second edition of Rama Prasad Kasyapa's *Occult Science of Breath* (1892), part of a notable series that would see later forms and editions circulating among occultists interested in yoga and breath cultivation, both in India and abroad (see Chapter 7);[6] the price listed was twelve annas (three-fourths a rupee). VRY2 marks the beginning of the publishing involvement of Ruttun Chand Bary, an active member of the Lahore Arya Samaj who had interacted with the founders of the Theosophical Society in Lahore (see Chapter 1). Ruttun Chand that same year also published *Sandhyāpaddhati*, a prayer book for "Sandhia" (*saṃdhyā*) or the twilight time of dusk as well as the "Gayutree" (Gayatrī) mantra.[7]

A reprint of VRY2 was published in 1950 by Chaitanya Prabha Mandali, a community founded by one Swami Krishna Chaitanya that was based in Bombay; Swami Sivananda (1887–1963) visited the community for one of his lectures and was greeted by this same Krishna Chaitanya.[8] Another author and retired accountant general, one T. K. Rajagopalam (also Rajagopalan) of Madras, had discovered an original copy of VRY2 and offered the text to Chaitanya Prabha Mandali for its reprinting, assisted by one Sriyuth Manilal K. Desai.[9] T. K. Rajagopalam had devoted two chapters to interpreting Sabhapati's yogic teachings in a separate work (see also Chapter 7). While the text of VRY1 is undoubtedly the foundation of VRY2, certain spelling changes were made to the Sanskrit terms and some other minor adjustments to the English syntax that readily distinguish the two.[10] Other more major changes are also discernible, including the following:

1. VRY2 adds notes to the Ur-account that seek to clarify Sabhapati's vision of Mount Kailāsa as taking place in the "astral" rather than physical body, and to change the rishis he encountered to the " 'Brothers' of the Theosophical Society" (see Chapter 1).
2. VRY2 omits a prefaced poem entitled "Poems on the Purification" that was included in VRY1.[11]
3. VRY2 omits the Sanskrit verses entitled "Shlokas composed by the Madras Yogi Sabhapaty Swami on the state of Smadhi [*sic*]"[12] and replaces this with Sanskrit verses attributed to "Lord Shankaracharya" entitled "Nirvan" as well as a poem entitled "Verses on Atma" that was translated by the editor.[13]
4. The title of the poem "The Yogi's advice to his Country" is changed to "Sabhapaty's advice to his Country," which as we saw in Chapter 1 appears to have actually been written by Shrish Chandra Basu.
5. The Sanskrit portions of the text in the "Supplementary Instructions" of Part II are considerably abbreviated.
6. VRY2 appends two additional sections to the end of the work that are not present in VRY1: a section entitled "Search after Knowledge of Spirit" from the *Mahānirvāṇa Tantra*[14] and a question-and-answer section entitled "A Brief Sketch of Vedantism and Yoga."

While the above alterations between VRY1 and VRY2 are for the most part quite minor, I would argue that especially points 3 and 4 serve to further reinforce Sabhapati's connection to Advaita Vedānta at the expense of his debt to other philosophical perspectives (see Chapter 3). Point 1, as mentioned in Chapter 1, is of course a clear response to Olcott's criticism of Sabhapati's visionary experience that he framed in physical terms.

A third edition of this work was subsequently published in 1895 (VRY3), also by Ruttun Chand Bary but this time under his new Lahori publishing house R.C. Bary & Sons, which was established in 1890 and oversaw the publication of works as varied as (1) a commentary by Pandit Rama Prasad on the *Śivasvarodaya* (as evident from Rama Prasad's later publications that produced a translation of this text);[15] (2) a reprint of the aforementioned *Sandhyāpaddhati* by R. C. Bary; (3) an edition of *The Science and Art of Organic Magnetism* by Chandos Leigh Hunt Wallace,[16] (4) an Urdu story of a journey of one Lala Jhinda Ram, (5) a response to an article in *The Theosophist*, (6) a booklet of Indian national songs, and (7) "Middle School Examination Papers" from 1869 to 1882. The price of VRY3 was again set at twelve annas, making it the most expensive work in an R.C. Bary & Sons' for-sale list, which included many of the above books as well as additional titles for sale like *The New Science of Healing* and *Am I Well or Sick*. A typescript of this third edition, omitting the Ur-account and other prefatory material, is extant in the possession of Munish Kumar of Latent Light Culture, a still-extant Indian occult society currently based in New Delhi.[17] Published editions are also extant at the British Library, the Connemara Public Library, and possibly the library of the late Kenneth and Steffi Grant.[18] The text of VRY3 is only slightly changed from VRY2, with a few alterations being made to the spelling of certain Sanskrit technical terms and capitalization, but otherwise it is much closer to VRY2 than VRY2 is to VRY1.

CPSPS as Alpha Stemma

In addition to the above three editions of VRY proper, there is another English work that Sabhapati Swami released that could be said to also partake directly in the Alpha Stemma since it includes a modified and expanded version of the base text of VRY. This work is *The Cosmic Psychological Spiritual Philosophy and Science of Communion with and Absorption in the Holy and Divine Infinite Spirit* (CPSPS), of which the First Book was published on May 1, 1884, at the Hindu Press in Mylapore, Madras, with the subtitle *Vedhantha Siva Raja Yoga Brumha Gnyana Anubuthi* (Skt. *vedānta śiva rāja yoga brahmajñānānubhūti*, "Perception of the Gnosis of Brahman that is the Vedāntic Rāja Yoga for Shiva"). The Second Book was published with the revised subtitle *Survopadhasa Survanoobhava Raja*

Yoga Bruhma Gnyana Anubhuthi (Skt. *sarvopadeśa sarvānubhava rāja yoga brahmajñānānubhūti*, "Every Instruction and Every Practice for the Rāja Yoga That Is the Perception of the Gnosis of Brahman") in 1890 by the Karnatak Press in Bombay. The price of each was initially advertised in the work itself for one rupee and two annas, and by 1913 the price had increased to two rupees for both volumes together. Both the First Book of CPSPS and a short portion of the Second Book contain the full text of VRY1 with many alterations and valuable additions, such as the inclusion of technical terms in both Tamil and Devanagari script as well as in Roman script and translation.[19] This effort facilitates a much greater understanding of the original context of such terms and their definitions, and also allows for a reflexive understanding of Sabhapati's translations of certain Sanskrit terms into English. Certain distinguishing features of the text reveal that the republished portions of VRY in CPSPS were taken from VRY1 (1880) and not from VRY2 (1883).[20]

In addition to two volumes, CPSPS divides itself into four parts, which are self-described as follows:

1st. Part is Divine and Holy Infinite Spiritual Theory or instructions of Creations and of Non-creations of the Spiritual Faculties and Functions from the Infinite Spirit and of Rishi Yogiswara Author's life and Poems.

2nd. Part is of the different Practicable and Practical Divine and Holy Infinite Spiritual Processes, Modes and Practices or full of the instructions of Practices of attaining Infinite Spriritual Godhead and of holding Communion with the Infinite Spirit and of Becoming and Being the Infinite Spirit and of Chess Play of the Punishment and Transmigration by the Tree of Vice and Sins, and of Godhead and Salvation by the Tree of Virtue and Righteousness and of practising Infinite Spiritual Trance and the Ecstasy in different ways.

3rd. Part is of Instructions of the full of the Infinite Spiritual Secrecies and Mysteries, of the Hatta Yoga Practice, of the defects of Religions, and of clearing the doubts of Atheist by pointing out the untruth of Atheism, and of the Creational Table of the Spiritual Creations, Occultism, Psychic Powers, &c.

4th. Part is full of different instructions of secret, moral, and Spiritual Truths as Public Lectures and Speeches by the Author Yogi and of the Articles and the Catechisms of this Yogi's Disciples on the instructions, practice and success in the Spiritual search and attainment from Guru Yógi, and of the alphabets in English, Sanskrit and Tamil.[21]

The Second Book saw the inclusion of a fifth part, some of which overlaps with what the fourth part appears intended to describe. In any event, some of the material in these latter parts mirrors instructions provided in Sabhapati's vernacular literature in Hindi/Sanskrit (RYB) and Tamil (MCVTS and CTCSPV), which will be clear from an examination of their contents in the relevant sections below.

While the above language may appear erratic to a scholar of Indian religions, Sabhapati is consistent with the English terms he uses. For example, "Vice" and "Virtue" always directly refer to the equivalent concept of (Skt.) *pāpa* and *puṇya*, the "Infinite Spirit" and the adjective "Infinite Spiritual" are always direct translations of "Brahman" (or "of Brahman" in the adjectival usage; for Sabhapati, Brahman is also sometimes synonymously referred to as Shiva in his form of Sarveśvara, "The Lord of All"), and "Communion" or "Ecstasy" are placeholders for samādhi. As a result, while such English translations may on the surface appear to be misleading, they also serve two functions for scholars today: (1) they provide an example as to how Sanskrit yogic terminology could be variously interpreted in an English philosophical frame during the colonial period, before dictionary usage was standardized; and (2) they enable a phenomenon of reverse-translation. By the second point I mean that, regardless of how one feels about "Infinite Spirit" as a translation for Brahman, one can go back with the knowledge of this translation and read in "Brahman" for "Infinite Spirit" if one likes, and still make sense of a wide variety of passages in his English works. The same goes for his other terms, which points to the need for a comprehensive linguistic lexicon that pieces together these translations and their vernacular equivalents over time.[22]

Finally, CPSPS integrates in its reprinting of material from VRY additional sections not extant in any edition of VRY, such as a section on sixteen "Rays" and four forms of "Brightness," additional poems composed by Sabhapati Swami in Sanskrit and Tamil,[23] a page that treats of Pātañjalayoga, additional social and political commentary, and extended practical instructions. As I shall consider when treating the Beta Stemma and Gamma Stemma, CPSPS also contains material that was later integrated or written parallel to vernacular north and south Indian stemmata, so in that respect could be said to "bridge" or link both the Alpha Stemma and the Beta and Gamma Stemmata. The remaining text of the Second Book (about three hundred additional pages in all) is not found in any edition of VRY and represents material that had previously been unpublished.

Detailed Contents of the Alpha Stemma

None of the three main editions of VRY included a table of contents, although the Second Book of CPSPS did include an index for both books, and therefore provided the first real condensation of VRY's material, albeit in very short phrases, and it did not reproduce the headings in VRY in full. To satisfactorily present the contents of this entire textual stemma I will first synthesize the contents of the various editions of VRY. I will then separately reproduce the index of those portions of VRY that were integrated into CPSPS to allow for an easier side-by-side comparison between both representations.

The main subjects of VRY are reproduced as follows from the main headings, with the original formatting (italics and capitalization) mostly preserved and with distinctions being made when a certain section is only found in a given edition or editions. I have preserved the archaic transliterations of VRY1 but have added updated transliterations in notes according to contemporary academic standards whenever the terms referred to are not clear and have supplied translations, sometimes with assistance from CPSPS. I have also noted variations in the titles of the headings between editions of VRY wherever possible.

Contents of VRY (VRY1, VRY2, and VRY3; with CPSPS variants in notes)

1. [Dedication]
2. *THE LIFE OF THE AUTHOR.*[24]
3. . . . *how the Yogies and Rishees pass their lives in the Ashrum.*[25]
4. [The Yogi and the Nawab of Arcot][26]
5. [VRY1 only] *Poems on the Purification*[27]
6. *Verses on Purification.*[28]
7. *Prayer to the Infinite Spirit.*
8. *Introduction.*[29]
9. *Purification of the Jivatma*[30] *or soul by itself.*[31]
10. *Jivatma becomes the disciple to Parmatma*[32].[33]
11. *Instructions of Parmatma or Guru to Jivatma or disciple on the truths of Tatwa Gyana*[34].[35]
12. *Holy commandments of voidness and purification by Parmatma.*[36]
13. *Instructions on Sankalpa Kalpana Bhranti*[37].[38]
14. *Knowledge of soul with Maya or delusion.*[39]

15. *Instructions on Tatwa Vritti through Kalpana and Bhranti.*[40]
16. *Parmatma instructs Jivatma the practice and truth of Tatwa Laya Kaivalya Anubhuti*[41].[42]
17. *Paramatma instructs Jivatma the Vedantic Raja Yogue, and Siva Yogue Layabodh Jivanmookti, Anubhuti.*[43]
18. *Parmatma shows to Jivatma the secret state of Samadhi*[44] *or Vedantic Raja Yogue or Shiva Yogue success.*[45]
19. [VRY2 and VRY3 only] NIRVAN[46]
20. [VRY2 and VRY3 only] VERSES ON ATMA. (Translated by the Editor).
21. [VRY1 only] *Shlokas composed by the Madras Yogi Sabhapaty Swami on the state of Smadhi* [*sic*].[47]

PART II

22. *The Yogi's advice to his Country.*[48]
23. INSTRUCTION. *The fear of Transmigration or on Navabarana Dukhabhaya Atidheevera Bhukti verukti avasha utpuna Moomuktchu Adhikara Pukvum.*[49,50]
24. *Tatwagiyana Paroksha Giyananoobhavam.*[51]
25. *The Apaváda or the absorption of Tatwagiana.*[52]
26. POEM OF BLESSING.
27. [VRY2 and VRY3 only] SEARCH AFTER KNOWLEDGE OF SPIRIT. (*Translated by the Editor.*)[53]
28. [VRY2 and VRY3 only] A BRIEF SKETCH OF VEDANTISM AND YOGA.

The contents of VRY1 (and possibly VRY2) are usefully compared with the index printed at the end of the Second Book of CPSPS, which demonstrates that the entire First Book and a good amount of the Second Book are sourced from the contents of VRY1.[54] Since the First Book of CPSPS was printed four years later, we can assume that VRY1 was reworked into CPSPS and the technical terms produced in Tamil and Devanagari were added, most likely with the assistance of Sabhapati himself, although it is still unclear how the writing process unfolded (i.e., whether Sabhapati himself wrote the manuscript or dictated it to a scribe).[55] The three editions of VRY are no longer advertised in Sabhapati's vernacular-language material from 1892 onward, and CPSPS appears to entirely eclipsed its importance; CPSPS is advertised as Sabhapati's principal work in English by 1913 (see Figure 2.2).

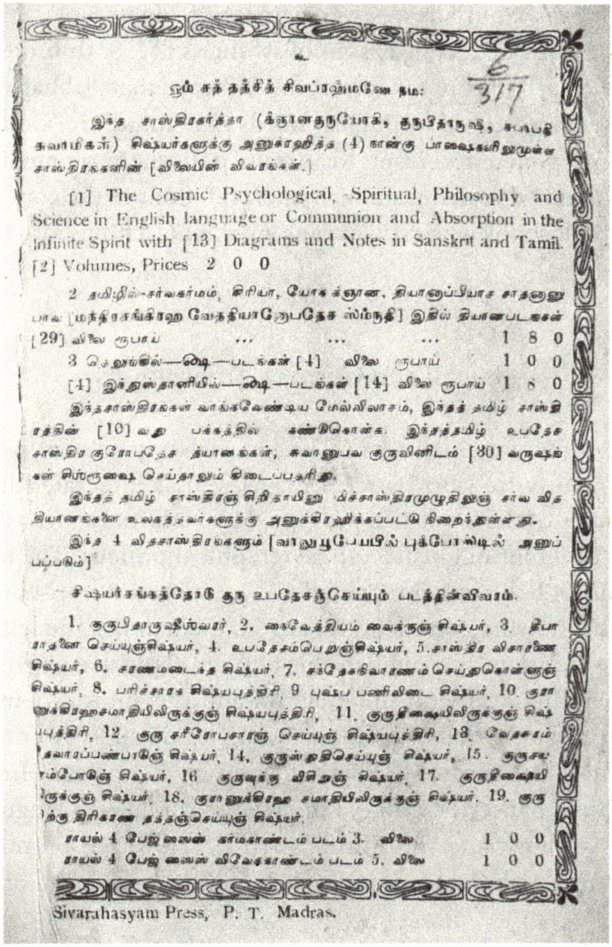
[1] The Cosmic Psychological, Spiritual, Philosophy and Science in English language or Communion and Absorption in the Infinite Spirit with [13] Diagrams and Notes in Sanskrit and Tamil. [2] Volumes, Prices 2 0 0

Sivarahasyam Press, P. T. Madras.

Figure 2.2 An advertisement found in the long edition of MCVTS that provides an example as to how CPSPS, not editions of VRY, was advertised among Sabhapati's works in three vernacular languages (Tamil, Hindi, and Telugu). Photo by the author.

Finally, at the end of the so-called "Index" (what today's readers would consider a table of contents) of CPSPS, a text that is remarkable in its attempt to render Sabhapati's technical instructions on yoga in intelligible (if now somewhat archaic) English, there is the following note clarifying some of his translations on key religious concepts: "Mind or Mun [< Skt. *manas*] means Consciousness as Thoughts of Darkness; Soul or Atma [*ātmā*,

< *ātman*] means Consciousness as witness of Light; God or Brahmam [Brahman] means Consciousness as blissfulness of I. S. [Infinite Spiritual] Sight only." Clarifying notes like these indicate that Sabhapati and his followers were aware of how English words like "mind" or "God" could be variously interpreted according to various philosophies or religions and that they attempted to delineate such interpretations in the context of their own yogic philosophy while still expanding their teachings into the English language.

Bengali and German Translations

The demand for VRY1 upon its release is certainly evident by it having been reprinted twice (VRY2 and VRY3) as well as integrated into CPSPS. Yet the success of the book also prompted two additional translations intended for different linguistic and geographical milieus. The text of VRY from the outset had even anticipated and invited such translations by including the following comment: "If any gentleman has the leisure or inclination to translate and publish this book in Bengalee or Hindustanee or any other language with the diagram and the author's name, he has the full permission of our venerable Swamy to do so."[56] A note in CPSPS clarified these languages further, including "Bengálee, Hindoostáni, Punjábi, Tamil, Sanscrit, Telugu, Kanarese, and Malayali languages only, with the Diagrams, and the Author's name." However, permission was not given to publish the work in English "till the expiration of the registered time."[57]

The first of these translations was accordingly into Bengali by Ambikācaraṇ Bandyopādhyāẏ in 1885 (BRY), offering tantalizing proof that Tamil teachings on a different kind of "rāja yoga" had already spread to Bengal around a decade prior to Swami Vivekananda's own reformulation of Râja Yoga,[58] a reformulation at least indirectly assisted by the Theosophical Society. BRY, published privately by Shrish Chandra Basu himself, still survives at the National Library of India in Kolkata and possibly a few other libraries in West Bengal, such as the Bagbazar Reading Library in Kolkata (as a stamp on one surviving digital copy attests), and textual evidence demonstrates it was a translation from VRY2 and not from VRY1.[59] A diagram of the "mark(ed) body" (*liṅgaśarīra*, see Chapter 4), based on the one included with the original VRY, was also included with the translation according to Sabhapati's above instruction, and the original English caption below the diagram was translated into Bengali as the following:

> *ye rūpe upabiṣṭa haiẏā yog praṇālī dvārā samādhi yog abhyās pūrbbak sthul śarīr sūkṣma śarīre pariṇata haẏ tāhāi māndrājī yogī pūjyapād śrīmat sabhāpati svāmi karttr̥k pradarśita hailo*
>
> "The form of composure [*samādhi*] in which the gross body [*sthula śarīr* (*sic*)] being seated, by means of the yogic system becomes changed into the subtle body [*sūkṣma śarīr*] after yogic practice; this is what has been shown by the venerable Madrasi Yogī Śrīmat Sabhāpati Svāmi.

The most notable part of this translation of the caption is the change from *liṅga-śarīr* "body of the phallus [*liṅga*]" in VRY to *sūkṣma śarīr*, "subtle body," in BRY, which may appear to be a minor change but carries with it important implications for yogic physiology (see Chapter 4). Although little or nothing can presently be found on the life of Ambikācaraṇ, this highly literate Bengali translator provided a compelling new Bengali-language introduction to VRY with references to continental philosophers like Immanuel Kant (1724–1804) and the British biological philosopher Herbert Spencer (1820–1903). He also notes that he took the liberty of creatively rendering Sabhapati's Sanskritic English songs into Bengali, rendering them into a lyrical meter that can be easily set to music. Indeed, the songs and their range of vocabulary forms a striking fusion between Sabhapati's terminology on Vedānta that loosely mirrors language used by nineteenth-century Bāuls and other kinds of religious musical composers in Bengal (see Chapter 5).

The second translation of the VRY series was a partial translation into German by the occultist and novelist Franz Hartmann (1838–1912), first published between 1908 and 1909 in the journal *Neue Lotusbluthen* (FH1) and again as a stand-alone work in 1909 (FH2), which was in turn reprinted in 1926 (FH3) and 2015; this German-language edition of VRY is thus the only one of Sabhapati's works still readily available for purchase at the present time of writing. This edition, translated from either VRY2 or VRY3,[60] also contains numerous extra notes by Hartmann that interpret Sabhapati's philosophy through the lenses of the Bhagavadgita, the Bible, the *Tattvabodha* attributed to Śaṅkarācārya (Shankaracharya), the Theosophical literature of H. P. Blavatsky and C. W. Leadbeater, Swami Vivekananda, and even the thirteenth- to fourteenth-century late medieval mystic Meister Eckhart. The translation, while highly important for the translocalization of Sabhapati's teachings, ends with Part One and does not include the "Supplementary Instructions" of Part Two of VRY2 or 3.

William Estep's *Esoteric Cosmic Yogi Science*

Text from the Alpha Stemma directly reached American shores due to the pioneering efforts of William Estep, a New Thought guru who took the alias "Mahatma Gotam Rishi" and was active in the 1920s.[61] Estep published a version of CPSPS entitled *Esoteric Cosmic Yogi Science, or Works of the World Teacher* (WE), out of Excelsior Springs, Missouri, in 1929. The publisher was called "Super Mind Science Publications," which had previously released a variety of works such as *The Path of Light*, *Mysteries of God and Man*, *Threads of Wisdom*, and *The White Prophecy*, and three years later (in 1932) would publish *Eternal Wisdom & Health*, a work of over seven hundred pages on mental healing that also included an exegesis of certain books of the Bible and claimed to present "Super Mind Science" as the "restored message of Jesus Christ."[62] As I will show in Chapter 7, Estep claimed to be a direct disciple of Sabhapati Swami, although there is no validation of this claim in Sabhapati's own published writings, and Estep used the Super Mind Science imprint to market an occult correspondence course of instruction that likely partook at least partially in some of Sabhapati's teachings.

WE was published in two volumes that include most of the contents of the original two books of CPSPS, although notably all of CPSPS's text and notes in the Devanagari and Tamil scripts were removed. The diagrams, however, were preserved, although significantly shrunk (especially in the cases of foldout diagrams). WE claims in the foreword that the original work consisted of "manuscripts" published in 1888—rather than 1884 (CPSPS, First Book) and 1890 (CPSPS, Second Book)—that were later used in Sabhapati's "Schools of Yoga" by his disciples, and that the "Swami consented to let them be published in English after the expiration of 35 years,"[63] which could be a reference to the registered time mentioned in the previous section. The foreword also mentions that one "Professor Vithal Hari Khoth of Bombay" had possessed the "manuscript" (probably the original source volumes of CPSPS) and "helped in their translation and correcting of terms from Sanscrit [*sic*] and Tamil."[64]

The Beta and Gamma Stemmata

Contextualizing Sabhapati's Vernacular Works

Sabhapati Swami's English works of the Alpha Stemma were cataloged by libraries on a given spelling of the name Sabhapati, of which there are many variations (including, but not limitied to, Sabhapaty Swami, Sabhapathy Swamy, Sabapatty Swami, Sabhapatti Svami, and Swami Sabhapatee). Yet, as previously alluded to, the Ur-account did mention that Sabhapati had composed at least one earlier work in Tamil prior to 1880, entitled "Vedanta Sidhanta Samarasa Brahmagiyana Shiva raja Yogue Kaiulia anubhooti." In attempting to locate this work mentioned in the Ur-account, I added proper diacritics to portions of the title of this work, especially combinations of the key words *brahmajñāna*, *rājayoga*, and *anubhūti*, and made several searches in a few catalogs. What resulted was a catalog hit of *Rājayoga Brahmajñānānubhūti saṅgraha veda* (RYB), "A Compiled Scripture on Rāja Yoga as the Perception of the Gnosis of Brahman," specifically what I thought at the time was probably the only surviving copy in the world, held by the library of the University of Chicago. It is unclear why the term *samarasa* disappeared along with "Vedanta" (Vedānta) and "Sidhanta" (Siddhānta), although it would reemerge by 1889 in Sabhapati's Tamil work CTCSPV.[65] It is possible that Sabhapati's attempt to promote a soteriological "equal flavor" between Vedānta and Śaiva Siddhānta was not as large concern for Sabhapati outside of south India during this time period.[66]

In any event this work, published in 1892, was composed by one "Sabhāpati Svāmī" in a Sanskritic register of Hindustani, also called *Urdū*, which the OED defines as an "Indo-Aryan language of northern South Asia widely used as a lingua franca, from which modern Hindi and Urdu derive."[67] After I acquired and began to analyze the work, I noted that there was much information in it that was not present in the texts of the Alpha Stemma, particularly VRY1 and VRY2, and that the structure of the book's contents was relatively different from those of these English works.

While I consider RYB to be separate from the unknown Tamil work mentioned in the Ur-account (Ur-RYB), I do think the partial connection between the two titles provides an illustrative example of the presence of vernacular-language content both preceding and running parallel to the Alpha Stemma. I have already indicated that publications grouped under

Alpha Stemma were principally based on Sabhapati's English-language lectures in Lahore (along with additional supplementary instructions and a great deal of transliterated Sanskrit terminology) that took place after he had already been on quite a few journeys abroad from the environs of Madras. Sabhapati's vernacular-language works, in which English is almost nonexistent, by contrast, can be further divided into two distinct stemmata, what I call a "north Indian" Beta Stemma that was centered on this Hindi work (RYB) and that was also intended to be accessible to Gujarati- and Marathi-speakers; and a "south Indian" Gamma Stemma centered on CTCSPV, the Tamil pamphlets of Konnur Meditation Hall, and later MCVTS that was directly intended for readers of Tamil. Some vernacular-language content had already been integrated with the Alpha Stemma as early as 1884 in CPSPS, a uniquely hybrid trilingual work, but in most cases the vernacular-language content was intended to be accessible on its own and does not resort to English except in discrete sections or in isolated circumstances. See Figure 2.3 for a joint advertisement in RYB (1892) for CPSPS and CTCSPV indicating the cross-pollination of the English and "Dravid Language" content during this period between 1884 and the mid-1890s.

CPSPS as Beta and Gamma Stemmata

CPSPS was a two-book hybrid work composed in English, Tamil, and Devanagari, with portions in Marathi, published in 1884 and 1890, as we have already seen (see CPSPS as Alpha Stemma). The Sanskritic title of the First Book, "Vedhantha Siva Raja Yoga Brumha Gnyana Anubuthi," reveals some of the same key terms, such as *rājayoga*, *brahmajñāna*, and *anubhūti*, that connect it to Sabhapati's vernacular literature in Tamil and Hindi. Although I have already demonstrated that the First Book and a short portion of the Second Book are clearly part of the Alpha Stemma, CPSPS's addition of Tamil and Devanagari scripts alongside English shows that Sabhapati's literature was already beginning to participate in a process of vernacularization so as to be readable to individuals more comfortable with languages apart from English and scripts other than Roman. The Second Book's inclusion of a lengthy portion in "Maharashtrian" (Marathi) on "Shiva Rāja or Jñāna Yoga" (*śivarāja athavā jñānayoga*) is also evidence of this,[68] and marks the first clear expression of north Indian vernacularization (i.e., the Beta Stemma), as

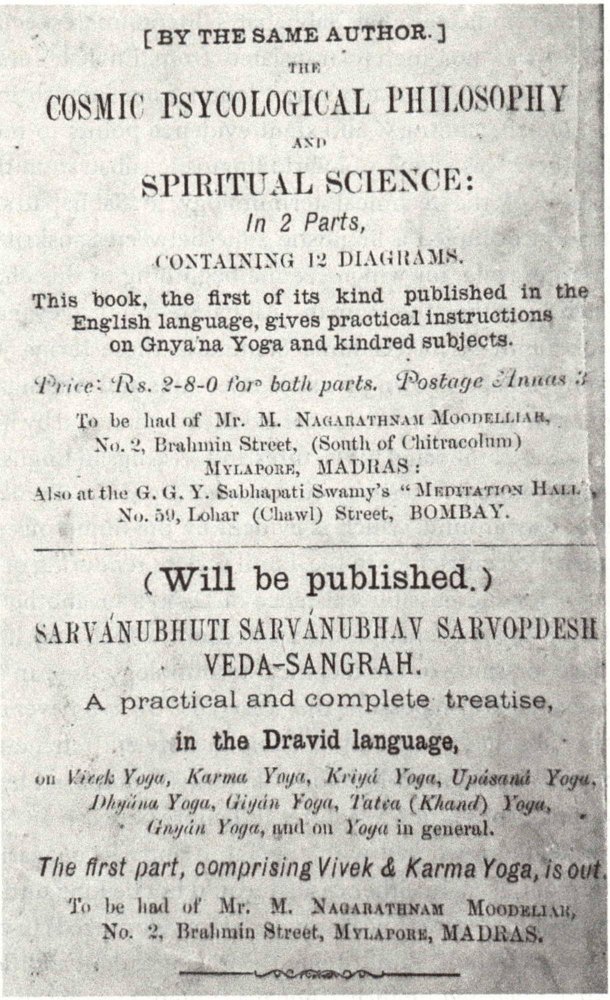
[BY THE SAME AUTHOR.]
THE
COSMIC PSYCOLOGICAL PHILOSOPHY
AND
SPIRITUAL SCIENCE:
In 2 Parts,
CONTAINING 12 DIAGRAMS.
This book, the first of its kind published in the English language, gives practical instructions on Gnya'na Yoga and kindred subjects.
Price: Rs. 2-8-0 for both parts. Postage Annas 3
To be had of Mr. M. Nagarathnam Moodelliar, No. 2, Brahmin Street, (South of Chitracolum) Mylapore, MADRAS:
Also at the G. G. Y. Sabhapati Swamy's "Meditation Hall", No. 59, Lohar (Chawl) Street, BOMBAY.
(Will be published.)
SARVÁNUBHUTI SARVÁNUBHAV SARVOPDESH
VEDA-SANGRAH.
A practical and complete treatise,
in the Dravid language,
on Vivek Yoga, Karma Yoga, Kriyá Yoga, Upásaná Yoga, Dhyána Yoga, Giyán Yoga, Tatva (Khand) Yoga, Gnyán Yoga, and on Yoga in general.
The first part, comprising Vivek & Karma Yoga, is out.
To be had of Mr. M. Nagarathnam Moodeliar, No. 2, Brahmin Street, Mylapore, MADRAS.

Figure 2.3 An advertisement for CPSPS and CTCSPV found in the copy of RYB held at Om Prakash's *āśrama* in Kandal, near Ooty. Photo by the author.

does the inclusion of several of Sabhapati's poetic and spiritual compositions throughout CPSPS, some of which were not translated into English but simply left in Tamil and/or Devanagari script. These Tamil works in particular are intimately connected to Sabhapati's literature as spread in south India (i.e., the Gamma Stemma), and some of these compositions were even intended to be set to Carnatic musical modes.

CPSPS further indicates that Sabhapati's literature (especially in the Second Book) was not merely translated from English into Tamil or Devanagari, as we saw from BRY's translation from English into Bengali (see above). On the contrary, all extant evidence points to the other direction, that there was a kind of hybrid linguistic substratum that formed the foundation of the technical terminology in Sabhapati's literature. This substratum occupied a linguistic zone between Sanskrit and Tamil (possibly Maṇipravāla, for which see the beginning of this chapter), and was mediated by either the Roman (Alpha Stemma), Devanagari (Beta Stemma), or Tamil script (Gamma Stemma). These terms were either sourced from Sabhapati's own preexistent lectures and writings—possibly manuscripts or texts that are no longer extant—or dictated by him directly at the time he was composing his lectures and writings in English or Tamil. The Devanagari notes of CPSPS were rendered from the Tamil script and not the other way around, which is evident by the numerous spelling issues that mirror eccentricities in the Tamil script's rendering of Sanskrit.[69] This all allows for the possible existence of Ur-RYB or another text composed in Tamil, as mentioned in the Ur-account, which may have formed a general base for some of the technical terminology used in Sabhapati's works. However, it is also possible that a text like Ur-RYB never existed and the contents published in the Alpha Stemma were entirely new teachings in English (with Romanized Maṇipravāla terms) composed by Sabhapati himself for the purposes of his lectures in Lahore between 1879 and 1880, and then gradually reworked with the Tamil and Devanagari scripts in the formation of CPSPS. In either case, it would not be long until these and many other teachings were to be re-rendered (or relocalized) in vernacular-language editions (Hindi, Tamil, Telugu) with a wealth of additional material, and which relegated English-language content to a few comparatively short pages or instances alongside vernacular content (see Figure 2.2, for example).

CTCSPV and the Gamma Stemma

Sabhapati's first full-length vernacular-language published work that is still extant was *Carvōpatēsa tatvañāṉa civarājayōka svayap pirammañāṉāṉupūti vētapōtam* (CTCSPV), published in Madras in 1889 by the "Empress of India Piras" (Empress of India Press). A notice about this book had been included as early as 1884 as a detached insert in some copies of CPSPS, which explained the following:

> Donations for Swami's Tamil Philosophy, coming out with about 50 practically explained Diagrams and whose publication is principally delayed in consequence of want of funds, will be thankfully accepted on the addresses given above from those who like to assist for public Spiritual good and prosperity.[70]

Over four years of rigorous searching for Sabhapati's texts failed to bring this book to light in any library catalog, either inside or outside of India, and I had given it up as either lost or delayed for several decades prior to the publication of MCVTS (see the section Sabhapati's Tamil Work MCVTS). However, I discovered in March 2020 that at least eight copies (out of a total of twelve that were cataloged) of CTCSPV happened to survive at the former Meditation Hall of Om Prakash Swamigal in the Kandal area of Ooty, including Om Prakash's own personal copy. As a result, the funds must have been eventually secured for its publication, at least partially. The resulting work, over 130 pages plus prefatory and appended material, was divided into two principal parts (following T1 as a preface), a "A Ritual Section for the Realization of Daily Rites through the Exercise of Theory" (Mpvl. *vivēkāppiyāsa nittiyakarmāṉupūti karmakāṇṭam*)[71] and a "A Ritual Section for the Realization of Daily Rites through the Exercise of Action" (Mpvl. *karmāppiyāca nittiyakarmmāṉupūti karmma kāṇṭam*).[72] It appears that this work was originally intended to have additional parts (Mpvl. *kāṇṭaṅkaḷ*), but these don't appear to ever have been published, and the relevant information may have been folded over into MCVTS, published twenty-four years later.

CTCSPV was Sabhapati's first (still-extant) work composed almost entirely in Tamil, including even the page numbering in the Tamil script, the only one of Sabhapati's works to mark the pages in this traditional way. It therefore represents a critical piece of the Gamma Stemma, or the traceable genealogy of his works designed specifically for south Indian and not Anglophone or north Indian audiences. An easy but useful distinction from other textual stemmata is that the first name of the author in the Gamma Stemma is rendered neither as one of the myriad renderings of Sabhapati's name in English nor as a Sanskritized or Hindi "Sabhāpati," but rather is given in Tamil, the transliteration of which would be "Capāpati" in the prevailing system, often with the epithets Cuvāmikaḷ, Svāmi (using characters derived from Grantha), or Yōkisvarar appended; in other words, the phoneme "ca" replaces "sa" according to Tamil convention. While Tamil is accordingly dominant, there are also some isolated instances of English terminology. Such phrases as "The Infinite Spiritual Phenomena," "The Void Ether of Blissfulness," "Fixing the mind in the centre seat of the skull," and so on, are directly parallel to the kinds of English phrases used in CPSPS. This indicates a kind of harmonization between these two works and further confirms CPSPS's role as an important "bridging" node in the vernacularization of Sabhapati's works, even if CPSPS itself was primarily an English work and not fully vernacular. Many, though not all, of the instructions and diagrams also appear similar to those given in CPSPS, although it must be added that CTCSPV contains a vast array of stunning new visual material and yoga-related depictions, including what may be the first published illustration of Agastya's ashram in the Pothigai Hills (see Chapter 1).

RYB and the Beta Stemma

The reception of the two lavishly illustrated works CPSPS and CTCSPV must have prompted interest in a full-length Hindi work that followers in north India could more readily consult. As mentioned in Chapter 1, the Ur-account had been rendered into Urdu and, as mentioned above, Marathi instructions were provided in the Second Book of CPSPS, but no full-length works had been extant that would have been intelligible to native speakers of the "language of the North" (*vaṭamoḻi*), a generic categorization by south Indians to describe the general intelligibility among speakers of Persian- and Sanskrit-derived languages of north India, especially variants of so-called Hindustani. This changed with the publication of RYB in 1892, marking the most important node of the Beta Stemma, or what could even be described more generally as the dissemination of a systematic work on Sabhapati's philosophy and methods of Rāja Yoga for Shiva in north India. As mentioned above, the full title, *Rājayoga brahmajñānānubhūti saṅgraha veda*, "A Compiled Scripture on Rāja Yoga as the Perception of the Gnosis of Brahman," bears some similarity to Ur-RYB as well as the Sanskritic title of CPSPS. The book itself was printed at the "Tattvavivecak Chāpkhānā" in Bombay and also contains a poem praising Sabhapati by Shri Jwala Prasad Mishra (Jvālāprasād Miśra, 1862–1916) of Moradabad, who, I noted in Chapter 1, was an important colonial figure in the development of Hindi literature.[73]

The text of RYB is divided into prefatory material and eight chapters (Hnd. *adhyāys*) on subjects as varied as purifications (*śuddhis*), meditative absorptions (*dhyāns*), meditative cultivations (*bhāvanās*), and mantras, and also includes eight diagrams and a portrait of Sabhapati Swami that exactly matches one given in CTCSPV, demonstrating some continuity (see Figures 2.4 and 2.5). Many of the same diagrams were also released with text in Tamil and Telugu (see Chapter 5), pointing to a certain model being followed across Sabhapati's vernacular works at this time. An order form prefaced to RYB advertises the sale of CPSPS, in two books, and an invitation to remit payment to the address of M. Nagaruthanum Moodliar, "Gnyan Guru Yogi Sabhapati Swami's Son and Disciple" in Mylapore (see Chapter 1). It also mentions Sabhapati's publication of a large nine-part book in the "Dravid language" (Hnd. *draviḍ bhāṣā*, here referring to Tamil), which must undoubtedly be CTCSPV;[74] the division into nine parts either takes into account the text's

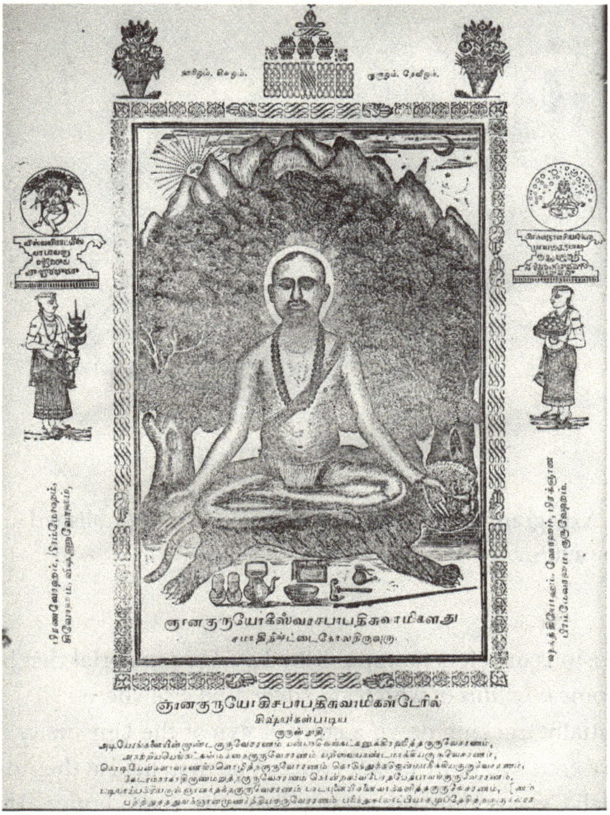

Figure 2.4 A diagram of Sabhapati Swami given in CTCSPV, published in 1889. Photo by the author.

द्राविडदेशमें पोधियाचलपर्वतके अगस्त्यऋषि-आश्रममें रहै गुहावासि ऋषि
ज्ञानगुरु योगी सभापति स्वामी.

Figure 2.5 A diagram of Sabhapati Swami given in RYB, published in 1892. Photo by the author.

smaller divisions or refers to unpublished parts or material that have not yet surfaced, some *khaṇḍa*s of which are advertised elsewhere.

Since initially tracking down a copy of RYB at the University of Chicago, I have discovered two more extant copies. The first, held at the Adyar Library and Research Centre, contains a stamp from the Youth Lodge, Theosophical Society, located on Sandhurst Road in Bombay. Another later stamp mentions that the book was gifted to the Adyar Library by the Theosophical World University in 1946. The stamps are interesting since they demonstrate that not only Sabhapati's English works but also his works in vernacular languages were circulating around at least some Theosophical lodges regardless of Henry Olcott's critical skepticism (see Chapter 1). The other extant copy I have traced was preserved in the library of Om Prakash's former Meditation Hall in Ooty. An inscription in the book records that it was presented by Om Prakash Swamigal in the Nilgiris to his disciple, one Jashabhai Bhailal Bhai Patel of "Bhadraw," Baroda State, in present-day Gujarat (see Figure 2.6). This indicates, in juxtaposition to the spread among Theosophical lodges,

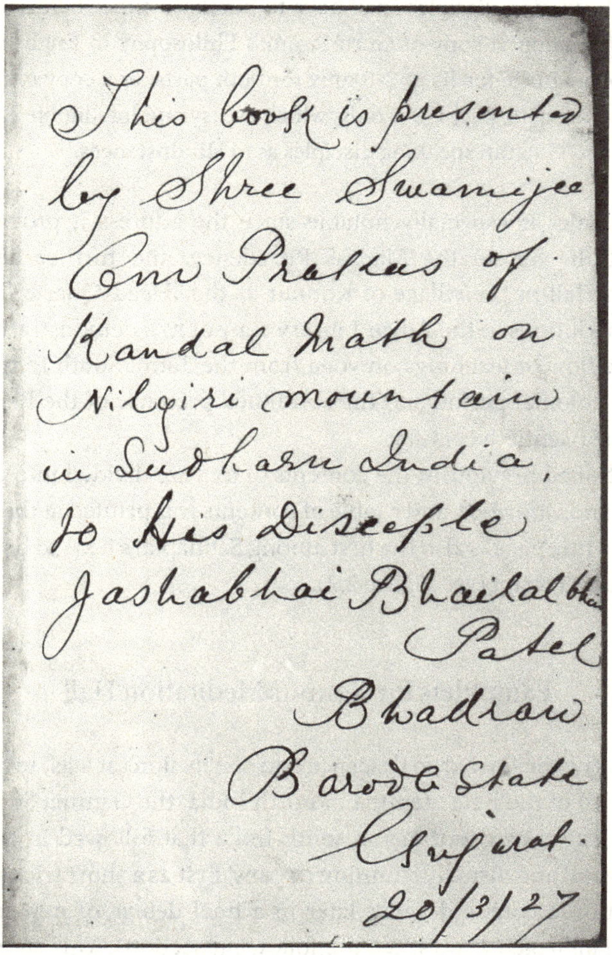
This book is presented
by Shree Swamijee
Om Prakas of
Kandal Math on
Nilgiri mountain
in Sudharn India,
To His Disceple
Jashabhai Bhailalbhai
Patel
Bhadraw
Baroda State
Gujarat.
20/3/27

Figure 2.6 A handwritten dedication in a copy of RYB by Sabhapati's student Om Prakash Swamigal to one of his own disciples, Jashabhai Bhailal Bhai Patel of Gujarat. Photo by the author.

that there was an additional dissemination of Sabhapati's works in north India among Sabhapati's "grand-disciples," or disciples of his immediate disciples, as late as the 1920s.

Further evidence for the dissemination of RYB among not only readers of Hindi but also his north Indian disciples more broadly is provided by an insert to at least one edition of RYB that is entitled "Rules to be Observed by Disciples Seeking Initiation from Gnyan Guru Yogi Sabhapati Swami," specifically Rule II, which states the following:

> Persons becoming disciples shall have to purchase either before or at the time of Initiation, a copy of Guru Swami's Philosophy in English, if they know the language for Rs. 2-8-0 only for both parts; or a copy of his Hind Philosophy, for Re. [*sic*] 1-0-0 only, which is easy and intelligible equally to Marathi and Gujarati speaking disciples as to Hindustanees.[75]

The set of rules is especially notable since the address it provides is not in north India but in the Madras Presidency, and further denotes the Meditation Hall in the village of Konnur as the "Head-Quarter." Both this and the inscriptions in the Adyar Library copy of RYB demonstrate a rare but remarkable flow of teachings on yoga from the Tamil South to north India during the colonial period and the continued presence of the Beta Stemma well into the twentieth century.

As mentioned previously, the contents of RYB are divided into eight main chapters (Hnd. *adhyāy*s), and a table of contents was printed at the end of the work.[76] The title page is also the first among Sabhapati's texts to be printed in the Devanagari script (see Figure 2.7).

Pamphlets for Konnur Meditation Hall

While RYB saw the formal coalescence and conclusion (at least in Sabhapati's own lifetime) of the Beta Stemma in north India, the Gamma Stemma continued to inspire new writings in south India that followed in the wake of the magisterial and visually stunning CTCSPV, first as a short trickle and then a culmination a couple decades later in a final deluge of new material in the Tamil language (MCVTS; see the following section). This short "trickle" consists of three short Tamil works, one of which was divided into at least four parts, all of which were published in Madras in the latter half of the

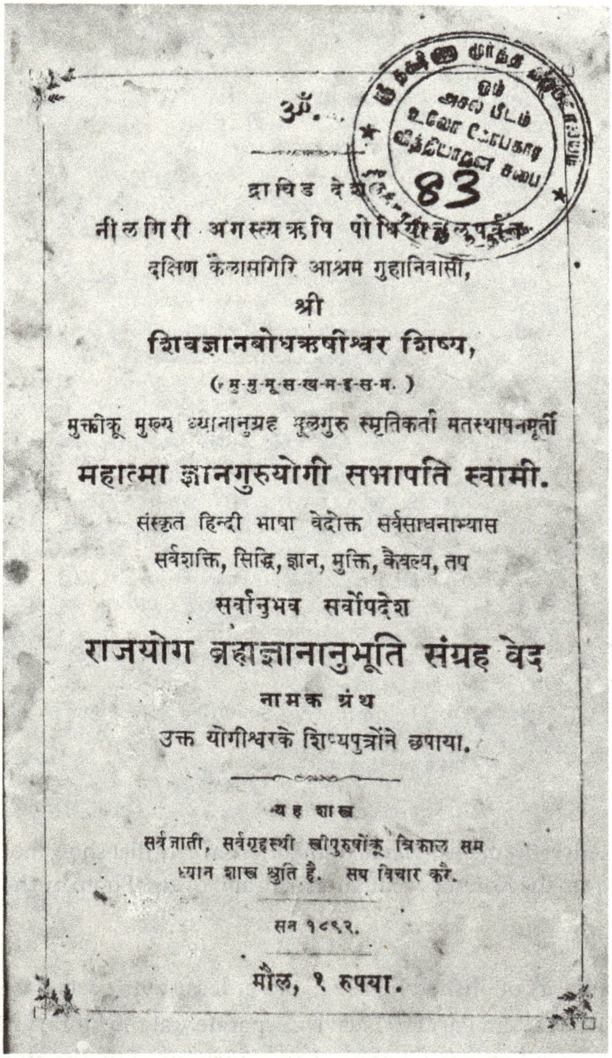

Figure 2.7 The title page of the copy of RYB dedicated to Jashabhai Bhailal Bhai Patel. Photo by the author.

1890s and which refer to the Konnur Meditation Hall (Koṇṇūr Maṭālayam) (see Figure 2.8).

The first of these bears the title *Amcumati cūriyamūrttikkup pōtitta cakalākama tiraṭṭu* ("A Compilation of All Agamas, as Taught by the Divine Embodiment of the Beautiful and Benevolent Sun," here abbreviated CĀT).

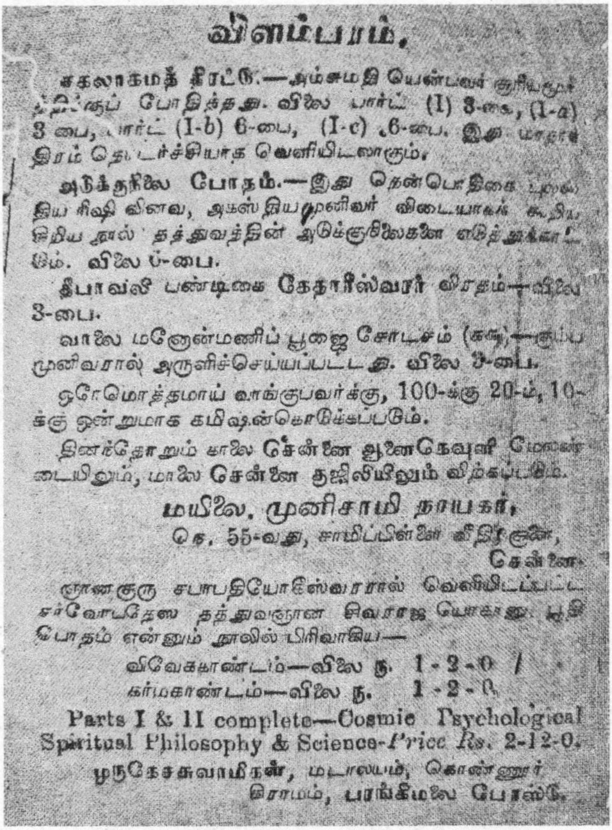

விளம்பரம்.

சகலாகமத் திரட்டு.—அம்சமதி யென்பவர் [illegible]க்குப் போதித்தது. விலை பார்ட் (I) 3-பை, (I-a) 3 பை, பார்ட் (I-b) 6-பை, (I-c) 6-பை. இது மாதாந்திரம் தொடர்ச்சியாக வெளியிடலாகும்.

[illegible] போதம்.—இது தென்பொதிகை [illegible]திய ரிஷி வினவ, அகஸ்தியமுனிவர் விடையாகக் கூறிய நூல் தத்துவத்தின் அடுக்குநிலைகளை எடுத்துக்காட்டும். விலை [illegible]-பை.

தீபாவலி பண்டிகை கேதாரீஸ்வரர் விரதம்—விலை 3-பை.

வாலை மனோன்மணிப் பூஜை சோடசம் (கரு)—[illegible] முனிவரால் அருளிச்செய்யப்பட்டது. விலை [illegible]-பை.

ஒரேமொத்தமாய் வாங்குபவர்க்கு, 100-க்கு 20-ம், 10-க்கு ஒன்றுமாக கமிஷன்கொடுக்கப்படும்.

தினந்தோறும் காலை சென்னை ஆனைகேவுனி [illegible]டையிலும், மாலை சென்னை தஜிலியிலும் விற்கப்படும்.

மயிலை. முனிசாமி நாயகர்,
நெ. 55-வது, சாமிப்பிள்ளை வீதி[illegible],
சென்னை.

ஞானகுரு சபாபதியோகீஸ்வரரால் வெளியிடப்பட்ட சர்வோபதேச தத்துவஞான சிவராஜ யோகானுபூதி போதம் என்னும் நூலில் பிரிவாகிய—

விவேககாண்டம்—விலை ரூ. 1-2-0

கர்மகாண்டம்—விலை ரூ. 1-2-0

Parts I & II complete—Cosmic Psychological Spiritual Philosophy & Science-Price Rs. 2-12-0.

[illegible], மடாலயம், கொன்னூர்
கிராமம், பரங்கிமலை போஸ்டு.

Figure 2.8 Advertisements (*viḷamparaṅkaḷ*) from CĀT that show the pamphlets from the Konnur Meditation Hall and CPSPS. Photo by the author.

The first part was published in 1894, and at least four parts, labeled Part I, Part I: A, Part I: C, and Part I: D, survive separately at the Library of the Tamil Nadu Archives in Egmore, Chennai. Large portions of these pamphlets were unfortunately eaten by bugs and, as a result, portions of the text are missing, although many portions are also still readable. Another copy of this text also survives in the British Library that is in much better condition and includes additional pages and sections.[77] It is labeled "Part I: A to E" on the title page but it appears to actually be a compilation of sections I: A through I: K, as a capital letter was printed on the lower right corner of each page that denoted a beginning of each new part. Even the British Library compilation is not complete, however, as a "final" sentence runs onto the next page, so it appears that there were additional pages or sections published or intended to be published that have since been lost.

It becomes clear when comparing the text of both the separate and compiled versions of CĀT that the separate pamphlet labeled "Part I" was actually "Part I: A," and the work labeled "Part I: A" is actually "Part I: B." The separate work labeled "Part I: C" is in fact Part I: C, but it is missing the first sixteen pages, and it also includes twelve additional pages of Part I: D. The separate work physically labeled "Part I: D" as a result begins on the thirteenth page of Part I: D and actually extends all the way to the eighth page of Part I: E. The extant separate works end here, while the compiled version extends for eighty more pages, excluding material printed on the back cover; and, as mentioned above, this version appears to terminate at what separately would be Part I: K. Despite these irregularities with the labeling of the sections, the four surviving separate parts of CĀT were submitted individually to the Office of the Registrar of Books, Madras, and formally registered, along with their date, quarter, and number of registration, under the category "Tamil—Religion."[78]

The substance of these Tamil pamphlets differs from Sabhapati's other works in its emphasis not on yoga per se but on Hindu ritual observances of holidays, arranged according to Tamil month, annual celebrations, and astrological events, some of which would have undoubtedly been celebrations intended for the general public. It is accordingly a valuable record of what kinds of rituals took place on a regular basis at the Konnur Meditation Hall. As alluded to in Chapter 1, these included more prominent observances like Shivaratri (Mpvl. *civarāttiri viratam*, < Skt. *śivarātri*) and Vinayaga / Ganesh Chaturthi (Mpvl. *viṉāyakacaturtti*, < Skt. *vināyakacaturthī*), but also less-common festivals and observances that may reflect Sabhapati's travels outside of south India (e.g., "Dol," or "the Observance of Lord Kedar").[79]

Another notable aspect of CĀT are the advertisements (Tam. *viḷamparaṅkaḷ*) on the back-cover pages that promote the sale of other of Sabhapati's works (see Figure 2.8), linking these manuals of observances to his wider corpus of literature, including on yoga. In addition to CĀT itself, other advertised works include ANB (for six paisa), the two parts of CTCSPV (Mpvl. *kāṇṭam*, < Skt. *khāṇḍa* or *khaṇḍa*), advertised separately for one rupee, two annas each), and CPSPS ("Parts I & II complete," for two rupees and twelve annas). There are also references to what appears to be material overlapping with some sections of CĀT, advertised separately, such as *Tīpāvali* and *Kētārīsvarar viratam*, for three paisa each. The point of contact given for ordering CĀT and

ANB was one Munisami Naicker of Mylapore (Mayilai. Muṉicāmi Nāyakar), and for CTCSPV and CPSPS we find Murugesa Swami (Murukēca Cuvāmikaḷ) of Konnur Meditation Hall (Maṭālayam, Koṇṇūr Kirāmam; see Chapter 1).

As mentioned in Chapter 1, Sabhapati released another pamphlet the same year as the first sections of CĀT (1894). This work was *Aṭukkunilai pōtam*, "The Order of the State of Awakening" (ANB), a series of verses attributed to Agastya that appear to derive from extant manuscripts known by the same title. Sabhapati's original edition of *Aṭukkunilai pōtam* appears to be no longer extant, although editions have since been published by other authors and publishers that allow for at least a general understanding of the text that Sabhapati had consulted, deepening our understanding of the mythos of Agastya he had presented in his works. A description in the advertisements to CĀT (see the previous paragraph), where it is listed at a price of six paisa, also helps further our understanding of what this small work consisted of:

> Agastya Muni composed his replies to questions asked by Pulastya Rishi, also of the honeyed Pothigai Hills, in the form of a poem [*pattiyam*] that is in this book called "Awakening to the Ordered State." Pulastya wishes to attain to the perception of his inherent nature [Mpvl. *corūpānupūti*, < Skt. *svarūpānubhūti*] and to delve into the ordered states of reality [Mpvl. *tattuvam*, < Skt. *tattva*].... There are the three voids [Tam. *muppāḻ*], the first void [Tam. *mutaṟpāḻ*], the contraction of the five elements [Tam. + Mpvl. *aimpūtavoṭukkam*], the hexagon [Tam. + Mpvl. *aṟukōṇam*], the beginning and the end [Mpvl. *ātiyantam*, < Skt. *ādyanta*] the two heads [Tam. *irutalai*], the ruby [Mpvl. *māṇikkam*, poss. < Skt. *māṇikyā*], the mute syllable [Om] [Tam. *ūmaiyeḻuttu*], the imperishable support [Tam. *cākātakāl*], the imperishable head [Tam. *cākāttalai*], he who extends the five faces [Mpvl. + Tam. *pañcamukavīcaṉ*], the thousand-eyed Indra [Tam. + Mpvl. *āyiraṅkaṇṇintiraṉ*], and so on. After understanding these many subjects he will have the mind of the lofty king of sages. This book takes up and shows the spoken answers as the bliss of his inherent nature [Mpvl. *corūpāṉantam*, < Skt. *svarūpānanda*].[80]

An examination of another extant published edition of this poem shows that Pulastya is rhetorically asking "where" (Tam. *eṅkē*) these cosmic principles are, most of which are reproduced verbatim in the advertisement and reflect various cosmological concepts entertained by the Tamil Siddhas, especially those reflected in the text *Tirumantiram*. It does not appear that there are direct answers given to Pulastya's questions in the poem itself, which is only ten stanzas of eight lines each, so it is possible that Sabhapati's edition may have included some general answers or commentaries to his questions, albeit in a condensed fashion since the library record at the Tamil Nadu Archives notes that the work was no more than ten or twenty pages at most. The book was registered as no. 125 in the category "Tamil—Religion" in the catalog of books, which states it was published in the first quarter of 1894.[81]

The last of the extant pamphlets of Konnur Meditation Hall published during the 1890s was released four years later, in 1898, and was entitled *Cātaṉāppiyās-āṉupava upatēcam* (< Skt. *Sādhanābhyāsānubhava upadeśa*, "Instruction on the Exercises and Practices of the Rites," here abbreviated CU). It was published in Vellore, a city west of Chennai, by "Natasun & Co." and "V.N. Press." The library of the Tamil Nadu Archives appears to hold what is the sole surviving copy of this small work, of which there are eleven numbered pages. Some portions of the text have been eaten by bugs, but most of the text is still legible. The contents of the text were divided into several headings, including among others an "Instruction on the Order of Ceremonies That Must Be Carried Out in the Morning" (Mpvl. + Tam. *kālaiyil ceyyavēṇṭiya aṉuṣṭāṉaviti upatēcam*), "Śaiva and Vaiṣṇava Assignments of the Limbs and Assignments of the Arms" (Mpvl. *caiva vaiṣṇava aṅkarnniyācam, karnniyācam*), "Meditation on the Recitation of the Gāyatrī [Mantra]" (Mpvl. *kāyattiri jepattiyāṉam*), "Instruction on the Sacrifice and Meditation of the Nine Celestial Bodies" (Mpvl. *navakkirakattiyāṉam yākam upatēcam*), and several other topics.

A survey of CU indicates that its topics would later be treated in a remarkably expanded form in MCVTS (see Sabhapati's Tamil Work MCVTS). In particular, here we find a wide array of mantras and the "assignment" (*nyāsa*) of deities to parts of the body as presented alongside instructions for the meditative visualizations (*dhyāna*) that accompany Śivarājayoga (in heading 5 termed *pirammakñāṉayōka niṣṭai camāti*, < Skt. *brahmajñānayoga niṣṭhā samādhi*, which is used synonymously for Śivarājayoga in MCVTS). There was also a sequence of triadic correspondences included in a section called the "Instruction on the Details of the Experience of the Mystery of the Characteristics of This Yoga of Knowledge" (Mpvl. *inta pirakñāṉayōka lakṣiyarahasyāṉupava vipara upatēcam*).

Sabhapati's Literature in Telugu

Sabhapati Swami's hagiographical accounts in Tamil as well as MCVTS (see Sabhapati's Tamil Work MCVTS) both record that he composed for Telugu-speaking audiences, meaning that his published material in Telugu was available for purchase prior to 1913, but other evidence demonstrates it was released at least thirteen years earlier, in 1900. An advertisement to MCVTS explicitly notes that Sabhapati Swami had composed his writings in four languages for his students, English (with notes in Sanskrit and Tamil, a reference to CPSPS), Tamil (most likely MCVTS itself), Telugu, and Hindi (RYB). The Telugu work advertised was almost undoubtedly a work listed in the Madras catalog of books under the title "Sarvavidha Vicharana Sadhana Abhyasa Anubhava, Sarva Tapa Dhyana Upadesa Sangraha Vidha" (Tel. conj. *Sarva vēda vicāraṇa sādhana abhyāsa anubhava, sarva tapa dhyāna upadēśa saṅgraha vēda*, abbreviated SVSAA), and its price was listed as one rupee. This work, authored by one "Brahma Gnana Guru Yogisvara Sabhapati Swami," was registered as number 146 in the section of the catalog called "Telugu—Religion," and its entry notes that it was published in the third quarter of 1900.[82] If this work is indeed the same as that advertised in MCVTS, then we can assume that it included four diagrams and that its price upon release was one rupee. Unfortunately further details about this work, such as its publisher or provenance, are still unknown, and it is unclear if there are any surviving copies anywhere in the world. Based on the advertisement in MCVTS, however, we can assume that its contents were generally parallel to those of CPSPS, RYB, or MCVTS.

While none of Sabhapati's complete works in Telugu appear to survive, multiple copies of a packet of ten diagrams containing parallel text in both Telugu and Tamil do survive at Om Prakash's ashram in Ooty.[83] Eight of these diagrams match those produced in RYB, as alluded to above, which contains either copies or the original versions of these illustrations but with the text not in Telugu and Tamil but in Hindi. There is no date listed on these diagrams, but since they are stylistically closer to RYB than to CPSPS, CTCSPV, or MCVTS, it is possible that they were produced in the 1890s or early 1900s. It is unclear if they were stand-alone diagrams for teaching or if they were intended to be published as the diagrams for Sabhapati's work in Telugu (e.g., SVSAA). If they were intended to be published in SVSAA, however, then the advertisement in MCVTS, which clearly notes that the work only had four diagrams, would be in error, so this seems unlikely. I would argue that it is therefore more likely that this set of diagrams, bound together by a string, were used as stand-alone teaching aids; eight different sets of such diagrams are advertised separately from Sabhapati's published books in the prefatory material to the copy of MCVTS held by the Adyar Library and Research Centre, so we know that such published material circulated separately.

Other isolated instances of Telugu are also scattered throughout some of Sabhapati's published works, especially CTCSPV, indicating that there were at least some readers for whom the Telugu script would be intelligible. For example, a short verse in Telugu was printed alongside the same verse rendered in the Devanagari script in CPSPS.[84] CTCSPV contains many more scattered instances of Telugu, especially on the margins of printed diagrams. These latter instances of Telugu are names that are almost definitely the signature of two different artists that illustrated most if not all of the diagrams, although the spelling of the names vary; they are Gu. Je. Subramaṇyaṃrājuhuśiṃdi (also transliterated Gu. Je. Subramaṇyaṃrājuhuśiṃdhi, Gu. Je. Subram aṇyaṃrājuhuśinadi, and Gu. Je. Subramaṇyaṃrājuhuśinadi) and Gu. Je. Ceṃggalvarāyaṃrājuhuśinaddi.[85]

Sabhapati's Tamil Work MCVTS

The last of Sabhapati Swami's known vernacular works published while he was alive was given the following extended title: *Carva māṉaca nittiya karmāṉuṣṭāṉa, carva tēvatātēvi māṉaca pūjāttiyāṉa, pirammakñāṉa rājayōka niṣṭai camāti, carva tīkṣākkramattiyāṉa, cātaṉā appiyāca kiramāṉucantāṉa, caṅkiraha vēta tiyāṉōpatēca smiruti* (< Skt. *sarva mānasa nitya karmānuṣṭhāna, sarva devatādevī mānasa pūjādhyāna, brahmajñāna rājayoga niṣṭhā samādhi, sarva dīkṣākramadhyāna, sādhanā abhyāsa kramānusaṃdhāna, saṃgraha veda dhyānopadeśa smṛti*), "Inspired Treatise on the Instructions of Meditation, as Compiled from the Scriptures, on Every Mental Ceremony to Be Performed Daily, on a Mental Ritual Meditation for Every God and Goddess, on the Steadfast Composition in the Yoga of Kings That Is the Gnosis of Brahman, on Every Meditation on the Sequences of Initiation, and on an Inquiry into the Sequence of the Practice of the Rites." No date is given on the cover (see Figure 2.9), but a label affixed to the copy held by the British Library notes that it was published on October 7, 1913. This accords with its entry in a catalog published by the Madras Record Office, which notes its registration number as 178 in the category of "Tamil—Religion" and dates its publication to the fourth quarter of 1913.[86] The title in the Madras Record Office catalog entry is shortened to "Mantira Sangraha Veda Dyanopadesa Smriti," an Anglicization of *Mantira caṅkiraha vēta tiyāṉōpatēca smiruti*, which is a shortened or alternate title also given in the work itself (hence

Figure 2.9 A photograph of the title page and/or cover page for MCVTS, from a laminated copy held by the Adyar Library. Photo by the author.

the abbreviation MCVTS). The main work was published by the Office of Shanmuga Vilasa Press (Ṣaṇmuka Vilāsa Piras Āpīc) in the Puttur (Puttūr) area of Tiruchirappalli (formerly Trichy), today an important metropolis in Tamil Nadu. Additionally, some of the prefatory material in the copy held by the Adyar Library and Research Centre was published by "Sivarahasyam Press, P. T." in Madras. The initial price of the whole work was listed as one rupee.

As mentioned in the first chapter, at least three copies of MCVTS survive, although there are two variants, a short version and a long version. The two copies respectively held by the British Library and the library of the Tamil Nadu Archives (formerly the Madras Record Office)[87] are identical short versions, both only around fifty pages long. The third extant copy, on the other hand, held by the Adyar Library and Research Centre in Chennai, is a longer version of about 130 pages and includes an important hagiographical account (T2, partially based on T1) and some additional advertisements for Sabhapati's books as a preface. The table of contents (Tam. *aṭṭavaṇai*) affixed to both versions only reflects the contents of the short version and does not index the additional pages. As a result, it is possible that the long version was released separately or did not circulate as widely; additional evidence for this is that it was the short version, and not the long version, that was registered with the colonial authorities at the Madras Record Office. In any event, the long version would have been known to the core of Sabhapati's students and also constitutes an important record of his literature and instructions on ritual and yoga.[88] Its contents span everything from mantras to a wide variety of deities (as the title suggests), poetry, instructions on ritual based on attributive correspondences, a wide array of visual diagrams, and lengthy instructions on Śivarājayoga (see Chapter 4).[89] It is arguably Sabhapati Swami's most comprehensive and cohesive work and an invaluable record of the development of modern Tamil yoga as well as of modern blending of Tamil and Sanskrit language worlds.

Notes

1. I am grateful to Manasicha Akepiyapornchai for presenting her research and sharing with me her informed insights on Maṇipravāla as a kind of "hybrid language" (neither Sanskritized Tamil nor Tamilized Sanskrit).
2. For a survey of the role of Maṇipravāla in Tamil literature and a delineation as to what constitutes "pure Maṇipravāla," see David Dean Shulman, *Tamil: A Biography* (Cambridge, MA: Belknap Press of Harvard University Press, 2016), 215–33.
3. VRY1, v.
4. Maahtma [*sic*] Giana Guroo Yogi Sabhapaty Swami, *Vedantic Raj Yoga: Ancient Tantra Yoga of Rishies* (New Delhi: Pankaj Publications, 1977).
5. *Probsthain's Oriental Catalogue, No. XXVIII. Indian Literature: Art and Religion* (London: Probsthain 1913), 27.
6. Pandit Rama Prasad Kasyapa, *Occult Science: The Science of Breath*, 2nd ed. (Lahore: R.C. Bary & Sons, Printed at the "New Lyall Press," 1892).

7. The first edition of this work was published as R.C. Bary, *The Prayer Book of the Aryans, Being a Translation in English of Sandhia and Gayutree, with Original Mantras in Sanscrit, as Well as Rules for Their Observance, with Scientific Explanation* (Lahore: R.C. Bary, printed at the "Arya Press," 1883).
8. Swami Sivananda and Swami Venkatesananda, *Sivananda's Lectures: All-India Tour* (Rishikesh: Sivananda Publication League, 1951), 495–96.
9. The Mahatma Jnana Guru Yogi Sabhapathy Swami, *The Philosophy and Science of Vedanta and Raja Yoga*, ed. Siris Chandra Vasu (Mahim, Bombay: Chaitanya Prabha Mandali, 1950), 6, 9–10.
10. For the full list of the table of contents of this and other of Sabhapati Swami's works, see Chapter 2 of Keith Cantú, "Sri Sabhapati Swami and the 'Translocalization' of Śivarājayoga" (PhD dissertation, University of California, Santa Barbara, 2021).
11. VRY1, vii.
12. VRY1, 28–30.
13. VRY2, 53–55.
14. This portion is from *Mahānirvāṇa Tantra* and was added later by Shrish Chandra Basu or another editor; see Chapter 6.
15. Pandit Rama Prasad Kasyapa, *Occult Science*.
16. It is not clear if the R.C. Bary & Sons edition survives separately or if it was simply imported from another publisher. The most readily available edition is Miss Chandos Leigh Hunt, *Private Instructions on the Science and Art of Organic Magnetism*, 3rd ed. (London: Printed for the authoress by G. Wilson, 1885).
17. I am very grateful to Munish Kumar for tracking this typescript down and allowing me to photograph it at his apartment in New Delhi.
18. At the time of writing it is still unclear which edition of VRY was possessed by the Grant library. The name and publisher (R.C. Bary & Sons) mostly matches VRY3, but the date initially provided to me from his library was 1890, which does not accord with the publication year of VRY3 (1895). In any event I am grateful to both Michael Kolson and Henrik Bogdan for separately querying the caretakers of their library.
19. The text is almost entirely integrated into CPSPS, First Book, 1–122, and CPSPS, Second Book, 123–42.
20. For example, CPSPS omits mention of Sabhapati's stay in Lahore for six months and reprints a time-specific detail printed in VRY1 that he is currently residing in Lahore, which was true in 1880 but not in 1884; CPSPS itself notes that he had left Lahore by then (see Chapter 1). CPSPS also does not include "Nirvan" or "Verses on Atma" and instead prints Sabhapati's verses composed after his recounted experience of flying to Kailāsa.
21. CPSPS, First Book, iii–iv.
22. See Appendix 2 for a start at such a lexicon, which includes most of the technical terminology in the Alpha stream and English, Sanskrit, and Tamil equivalents for each term.
23. CPSPS, First Book, 90–96.
24. CPSPS: "The life of the Author."

25. The full heading in VRY1 reads, "These pages were already in print when the writer received the following communication from the venerable Swamy describing how the Yogies and Rishees pass their lives in the Ashrum." VRY2 and VRY3 shortened and emended this to "*How the Yogis and Rishis pass their lives in the Ashram.*" CPSPS: "*How the Yogís and Rishís pass their lives in the holy residence of Caves* *ஆசிர்ம்ம்."
26. This short section does not have a distinct heading but is marked off by a section line and recounts a distinct story from the rest of the work.
27. CPSPS: "*(Poems of the Caution).*"
28. CPSPS: "Verses on Purification from Transmigration."
29. CPSPS: "*INTRODUCTION.*"
30. "Jivatma" < Skt. nominal form *jīvātmā*, from *jīvātman*, individual "soul" or "self," often translated into English by Sabhapati in VRY1 as "Finite Spirit."
31. VRY2 and VRY3: "*The longing of Jivatma for purification.*" CPSPS: "*Purification of Finite Spirit or Jiváthmá or soul by itself.*"
32. "Parmatma" and "Paramatma" < Skt. *paramātmā*, from *paramātmā*, supreme "soul" or "self," often translated into English by Sabhapati in VRY1 as "Spirit of Spirits."
33. VRY2 and VRY3 emend "*Parmatma*" to "*Paramatma.*" CPSPS: "*Finite Spirit or Soul* [in Tam.:] *jīvātmā becomes the disciple to the Infinite Spirit or Priest* [in Tam.:] *pirmmam.*"
34. "Tatwa Gyana" and "Tatwa Jnana" < Skt. *tattva jñāna*, "gnosis of the principles." CPSPS (First Book, 39) interprets this as "truths of the faculties of the Phenomena of creations." See Chapter 3 for the way in which Sabhapati interprets the term *tattva* alone and in certain phrases.
35. VRY2: "*Instructions of the Paramatma or Guru to the Jivatma or Disciple on the truths of Tatwa Jnana.*" VRY3: "*Instructions of the Paramatma or Guru to the Jivatma or disciple on the truths of Tatwa Jnana.*" CPSPS: "*Instructions of the I. Spirit or Guru to F. Spirit or disciple on the truths of the faculties of the Phenomena of creations* [in Tam.:] *tattuvakñāṉam.*"
36. VRY2 and VRY3: "*Holy commandments of voidness and purification by the Paramatma.*" CPSPS: "*Holy Commandments of Voidness and Purification to F. Spirit by the I. Spirit.*"
37. "*Sankalpa Kalpana Bhranti*" < Skt. *saṃkalpa kalpana bhrānti*, "delusion [that arises] from [mental] fabrication and wishful thinking." CPSPS (First Book, 45) translates this similarly as a kind of "False" illusion (see note 38).
38. VRY2: "*Classification.*"; VRY3: "*Calssification* [*sic*]." CPSPS: "*Instructions on False contrivances, False Introduction, False show and False appearenaces* [*sic*]."
39. VRY2 and VRY3: "*Maya or delusion.*" "*Maya*" = Skt. *māyā*, "illusion," "delusion." CPSPS: "*Knowledge of soul with delusion* [in Tam.:] *māyai* [note in Skt.: *māyā*]." CPSPS groups the final paragraph in this section starting with "I shall now enter upon the discussion . . ." and ending with "active principle" into a separate section.
40. "*Tatwa Vritti*" < Mpvl. *tatvavirtti*, either < Skt. *tattvavṛtti*, "devotion or addition to the principles" or *tattvavṛddhi*, "growth of the principles" (both are possible when the Sanskrit is rendered into Tamil (and here Romanized) due to loss of voicing and aspiration. CPSPS: "*Instruction on the reflection of faculties* [in Tam.:] *tatvavirtti* [note in Skt.: *tatvavṛddhi* (*sic*)] *through false belief* [in Tam.:] *kalpaṉai* [note in Skt.: *kalpanai*

(*sic*)] and false appearance or show [in Tam.:] *pirānti* [note in Skt.: *bhrānti*] or explanation of the seeming state of Active Personal Soul or Finite Spirit [in Tam.:] *ātmasvarūpalakṣaṇam* [note in Skt.: *ātmasvarūpalakṣaṇaṃ* (*sic*)]."

41. "*Tatwa Laya Kaivalya Anubhuti*" and "*Tattwa Laya Kaivalya Anubhuti*" < Skt. *tattva laya kaivalya anubhūti*, "perception of isolation through the dissolution of the principles."
42. VRY2 and VRY3: "*Paramatma instructs Jivatma the practice, and the truth of Tattwa Laya Kaivalya Anubhuti.*" CPSPS: "*Infinite Spirit* [Tam.:] *pirmmam* [note in Skt.: *brahmaṃ* (*sic*)] *instructs Finite Spirit* [in Tam.:] *ātmā* [note in Skt.: *ātmā*] *the Practice and the Truth of the absorption of the above faculties* [in Tam.:] *tattuvalayakaivalliyāṉupūti* [foonote in Skt.: *tatvalayakaivalyānubhūti* (*sic*)]."
43. VRY2 and VRY3: "*Paramatma instructs Jivatma in the Vedantic Raja Yoga.*" CPSPS: *The Infinite Spirit* [in Tam.:] *paramātmā* [note in Skt.: *paramātmā*] *instructs the Finite Spirit* [in Tam.:] *jīvātmā* [note in Skt.: *jīvātmā*] *the Absorptional Communion with the Infinite Spirit* [in Tam.:] *vētānta rājayōka civayōka layapōta vitēka muktiyāṉupūti aikkiyakaivalyam* [note in Skt.: *vedāṃta rājayoga layabodha jīvanmuktiyānubhūti aikyakaivalyaṃ* (*sic*)]."
44. "*Samadhi*" < Skt. *samādhi*, "composition," most often translated "communion" or "ecstasy of communion" in Sabhapati's English works.
45. VRY2 and VRY3: "*Paramatma shows to Jivatma the secret state of Samadhi or Vedantic Raja Yoga or Shiva Yoga success.*" CPSPS: "*Infinite Spirit* [in Tam.:] *paramātmā* [note in Skt.: *paramātmā*] *shows to Soul* [in Tam.:] *jīvātmā* [note in Skt.: *jīvātma*] *the secret Infinite Spiritual state of Ecstasy* [in Tam.:] *camāti* [note in Skt.: *samādi* (*sic*)] *by Védantic Raja Yoga or Shiva Yoga Success* [in Tam.:] *civañāṉa rājayōka nirvikalpa pirmmañāṉa camātikaivalliyastiti* [note in Skt.: *śivañāna rājayoga nirvikalpa brahmañāna samādi kaivalya stiti* (*sic*)].
46. "Nirvan" < Skt. *nirvāṇa*, "extinction," "cessation."
47. "Shlokas" < Skt. *śloka*, "verse." "*Smadhi*" < Skt. *samādhi*, see note above. CPSPS (First Book, 90ff.) includes these verses in separate Tamil and Devanagari sections entitled "*mahāvākkiyāyaikkiya nirvikalpa vitēkamukta pirmañāṉa camātiyāṉupūtistiti*" and "*atvaita mahāvākkiyārtta ēkamēva pirummalayapōta mavuṉattiyāṉa stuti*" (Tamil); and "*mahāvākāyaikya nirvikalpa videhamukta brahmañāna samādhyānubhūtistiti* [*sic*]" and "*advaita mahāvākyārtha ekameva brahmalayabodha maunadhyānastuti*" (Devanagari).
48. VRY2: "SABHAPATY'S ADVICE TO HIS COUNTRY"; VRY3: "SABHAPATY'S ADVICE TO HIS COUNTRY." CPSPS: "Yogi's advice to his Country." In CPSPS this poem is placed earlier in the text with Sabhapati's other English poems (sections 5–7 in the list above).
49. "*Navabarana Dukhabhaya Atidheevera Bhukti verukti avasha utpuna Moomuktchu Adhikara Pukvum*" < Skt. *navāvaraṇa duḥkhabhaya atitīvra bhakti virakti avasthā utpanna mumukṣu adhikāra pakva* (see next note for Maṇipravāla variants), "The nine states of blindness, sorrow, and fear, [and the nine] states of indifference and intense devotion that arise in he who has the competency and sovereignty to desire liberation."

50. VRY2: "*SUPPLEMENTARY INSTRUCTIONS. The fear of Transmigration.*" VRY3: "SUPPLEMENTARY INSTRUCTIONS. *The fear of Transmigration.*" CPSPS renders this heading as "The fear of Transmigration and of 9 sorts of imperfections, unholiness, impurities and sinfulness, and of 9 sorts of purifications, holiness, purity and goodness when of being as Infinite Spirit's holy state of indifference of Faculties [in Tam.:] *navāvaraṇa tukkapayayacuttavācaṉā* and [in Tam.:] *navappirakācavirtiyāṉantacuttavācaṉā* of [in Tam.] *atitīvaravirākaviraktipaktiyāvēcayuṭpaṉṉamummūkkṣūyatikārapakkuvam* [note in Skt.: *navārvarṇa duḥkha bhaya aśuddhavāsanā* and *navaprakāśa vṛddhiyānanda śuddha vāśanā* of *atitīvara virāgavirakti bhaktiyāveṣa yutpanna mumukṣu adhikāraḥ* (*sic*)]."
51. VRY2: "TATWAJNANA PAROKHSHA JNANANUBHAVAM"; VRY3: "*Tatwajnana Parokhsha Jnanubhavam.*" CPSPS: "The Knowledge and The Wisdom of Creations" [in Tam.:] *parōkṣatattuvakñāṉāṉupūti* [note in Skt.: *parokṣatatva jñānānubhūti*].
52. VRY2 and VRY3: "*The Apavada or the absorption of Tatwajnana.*" CPSPS: "*The Knowledge and Wisdom of the Absorption of Creations.*" [in Tam.:] *parōkṣattuva kñāṉayapavātalaya kñāṉāṉupūti* [note in Skt.: *parokṣatatva jñānāpavāda laya jñānānubhūti*].
53. VRY3 omits the period after "*Translated by the Editor.*"
54. For this index see the forthcoming second volume of Sabhapati Swami's collected works or Cantú, "Sri Sabhapati Swami."
55. A diagram in CTCSPV depicts a scribe who is writing in the presence of Sabhapati seated as a guru, so it is possible that one was employed in the initial stages of creating his works, especially for those in Tamil.
56. VRY1, v.
57. CPSPS, First Book, 16.
58. See Chapter 4; Elizabeth De Michelis, *A History of Modern Yoga: Patañjali and Western Esotericism* (reprint, London: Continuum, 2008); and Jason Birch, "Rājayoga: The Reincarnations of the King of All Yogas," *International Journal of Hindu Studies* 17, no. 3 (2013): 399–442.
59. For example, its translation of the Ur-account notes that Sabhapati stayed in Lahore for six months, a detail only present in VRY2 and VRY3 (which was published after BRY so could not have been the source text).
60. The differences between VRY2 and VRY3 are so minor as to prevent easily discerning which edition Hartmann translated from.
61. For more on Estep see Chapter 7 and the forthcoming research of Philip Deslippe. I am grateful to Philip for showing me newspaper clippings of Estep and continuing to highlight his importance in American religious contexts.
62. Professor W. M. Estep, *Eternal Wisdom and Health with Light on the Scriptures* (Excelsior Springs, MO: Super Mind Science Publications, 1932), 10.
63. WE, 8.
64. WE, 9.
65. For an alchemical usage of this term among the Nāth yogīs, see David Gordon White, *The Alchemical Body: Siddha Traditions in Medieval India* (Chicago: University of Chicago Press, 1996), 185.

66. For the bitter debates between Vedānta and Siddhānta that prompted religious entrepreneurs to navigate a mediating path that tried to include or even transcend both perspectives, see Eric Steinschneider, "Beyond the Warring Sects: Universalism, Dissent, and Canon in Tamil Śaivism, ca. 1675–1994" (PhD dissertation, University of Toronto, 2016). While sectarianism was an issue in north India too during the colonial period, debates between Vedāntins and Saiddhāntikas do not seem to have reached the same fever pitch.
67. OED (3rd ed., June 2020), s.v. Hindustani, B.1.
68. CPSPS, Second Book, 427–34.
69. The notion that such eccentricities in Devanagari are merely due to their rendering from the Prakrits or Pali is untenable in this case given the clear transcription of many words first in Tamil and then second in Devanagari.
70. CPSPS, detached insert printed prior to 1889 found in the copy held by the British Library.
71. CTCSPV, 7. The Sanskrit compound *Karmakāṇḍa* has a specific meaning in Vedic literature, which refers to sections (of the Veda) that pertain to ritual, as opposed to *Jñānakāṇḍa*.
72. CTCSPV, 67.
73. Haramohana Lāl Sūda, *Bhāratendu maṇḍal ke samānāntara aur āpūrak murādābād maṇḍal* (New Delhi: Vāṇī Prakāśan, 1986), 78–84.
74. RYB, *kai* (RYB uses the phonemes of the Devanagari script, beginning with *ka*, to paginate prefatory material instead of i, ii, iii, etc.).
75. This is the first page in the copy of RYB held by the Adyar Library & Research Centre.
76. For a translation of this table of contents see the forthcoming edition of RYB that will be published as part of the collected works of Sabhapati Swami or Cantú, "Sri Sabhapati Swami."
77. I am grateful to Philip Deslippe for photographing this copy for me that I had not been able to access on an earlier trip to the British Library.
78. Madras Record Office, *Classified Catalogue of Books Registered from 1890–1900 at the Office of the Registrar of Books* (Madras: Controller of Stationery and Printing, Madras, on Behalf of the Government of Madras, 1962), 157. Registration no. 208 was assigned to Part I: A, no. 15 to Part I: B, no. 16 to Part I: C, and no. 17 to Part I: D.
79. For a translation of the contents of CĀT see the forthcoming edition that will be included as part of the collected works of Sabhapati Swami or Cantú, "Sri Sabhapati Swami."
80. Tam.: "*teṉpotikai palastiyariṣi viṉava, akastiya muṉivar viṭaiyākak kūṟiya (aṭukku nilai pōtam) eṉṉum pattiya rūpamāyiyaṟṟi yuḷḷa ciṟiya nūl tattuvattiṉ aṭukku nilaikaḷai āyntaṟintu taṉ corūpānupūtiyai aṭaiyavēṇṭiyavar kiṉṟiyamaiyā tuṇarttu māṟu pulastiyar-muppāḻ, mutaṟpāḻ, aimpūtavoṭukkam, aṟukōṇam, ātiyantam, irutalai, māṇikkam, ūmaiyeḻuttu, cākātakāl, cākāttalai, pañcamukavīcaṉ, āyiraṅkaṇṇintiraṉ ittiyātipala viṣayaṅkaḷai yucarava, munīntirar maṉam pūrittu corūpāṉantamāyc colliya viṭaikaḷai apputtakam eṭuttukkāṭṭum, vilai 6-pai.*"
81. Madras Record Office, *Classified Catalogue of Books.*
82. Madras Record Office, *Classified Catalogue of Books*, 210.

83. I am grateful to Isa Thompson for confirming that the text of these diagrams is indeed Telugu and not Kannada, given certain resemblances between the scripts. There was another locked cabinet of books at Om Prakash's ashram that I was unable to obtain access to at the time of writing due to having to terminate my fieldwork early, so there is a slight possibility that Sabhapati's text in Telugu may survive either there or elsewhere, perhaps at the library of the Tamil Nadu Archives but filed under a different author.
84. CPSPS, First Book, 25.
85. I am grateful again to Isa Thompson for transliterating these names of the artists from Telugu script.
86. Madras Record Office, *Classified Catalogue of Books Registered from 1911–1915 at the Office of the Registrar of Books* (Madras: Controller of Stationery and Printing, Madras, on Behalf of the Government of Madras, 1965), 257.
87. This copy has since been digitized and is available at the Tamil Digital Library website (https://www.tamildigitallibrary.in).
88. A xerox copy of the longer version was made by the Adyar Library prior to laminating the original, and the position of several of the diagrams varies between the copy and the original, both of which I have consulted. The use of diagrams in CTCSPV and RYB clearly shows that Sabhapati usually intended the diagrams to be positioned near portions of the text that treat on a given diagram.
89. The author is currently preparing an English translation and edition of the full contents of both the short and long versions of MCVTS as part of the collected works of Sabhapati Swami.

3
Seeds of a Cosmological Religion

Oh! hear! my dear disciples all, Oh! head [sic],
The Universal truth and church and creed,
Oh! thine, thine is that unlimited bliss,
Of Infinite Spirit; Oh! never miss
Oh! think, indeed of me and my process,
I do in might of Mighty God possess
The blessing power pure to bless thee all,
And in the Infinite Spirit install.
But, Oh! fail not to read the book minute,
Waste not a single second or minute,
Oh! understand the contents all therein
With head quite calm and quiet, pure and serene,
Oh! practise my process Spiritual
With all the fifteen pious principles
Oh! hear! Oh! hear! all Souls of all the world,
Oh! this philosophy divine and pure.

—"Swami's personal blessing to his disciples,"
in CPSPS, Second Book, 418

Search after the Infinite Spirit, and its powers which seem to descend and ascend in circle . . .

—VRY1, 35

In this chapter I describe how Sabhapati's cosmological system reflects a syncretic Tamil Śaiva (< Skt. *śaiva*, followers of Shiva = Skt. *śiva*) worldview that is deeply embedded in the Vīraśaiva milieus in which his gurus operated their own "meditation halls" (Sabhapati's own translation for Tam. *maṭālayam*, < Skt. *maṭha* + *ālaya*; see Chapter 1). By "syncretic" in this case I do not intend the adjective's frequent connotation as a haphazard hybridization of collected theories and doctrines, but rather a historical process specific to Tamil Nadu in which the soteriologies of monistic Vedānta (< Skt. *vedānta*, lit.

Like a Tree Universally Spread. Keith Edward Cantú, Oxford University Press. © Oxford University Press 2023.
DOI: 10.1093/oso/9780197665473.003.0004

"end of the Veda") and dualistic Saiddhāntika philosophy were idiosyncratically and eclectically harmonized with the poetry and praxis of the Siddhas (Tam. *cittarkaḷ*) in the context of yogic experience. As was demonstrated in Chapter 2, the diversity of Sabhapati's literary corpus on this yogic experience of "communion" or literally "composition" (< Skt. *samādhi*), or Śivarājayoga, spans local Tamil Śaiva vernacular milieus to works intended for pan-Indian and international audiences in English. As a result, I would argue that to adequately understand the full scope of his system of yoga it is critical to also analyze the "seeds"—to continue our tree metaphor—of his cosmological and philosophical perspectives in the context of the genealogies of his teachers and the cultural setting of colonial-era India more broadly.

Sabhapati's literature outlines theories of a truly infinite proportion that describe a descent of "cosmic principles" or tattvas (Skt. *tattva*, which he translates as "faculties") that make up the universe as well as the individual's sense faculties. In this perhaps he is not so original as far as Indian philosophy goes, as this has been a feature since at least the development of Saṃkhyā (or Sāṅkhya) philosophy and the Upanishads, despite a wide variety of different philosophical positions on the nature of monism and dualism, spiritualism and materialism. However, attempts to limit Sabhapati's work to more prevalent cosmological frames, such as that of Advaita Vedānta or Śaiva Siddhānta, eventually fail to satisfactorily account for the range of doctrines he espouses. The 108 so-called Yoga Upanishads, the corpus of which Bouy has argued were compiled in south India around the eighteenth century, also would appear on the surface to be the best starting point for making sense of Sabhapati's cosmology given its recourse to the terminology of Vedānta to describe his system of yoga (see Chapter 4).[1] However, these texts do not account for other material that Sabhapati includes, such as the following: (1) his teachings on the cancellation of twelve Tantric cakras (< Skt. *cakra*, "wheel") that equally facilitate a cancellation of the aforementioned cosmic principles and the attainment of Śivarājayoga, (2) his reverence for the mythos of Agastya and by extension the Tamil Siddhas (Cittars), (3) his detailed prescriptions on and mantras for the ritual worship of Vishnu and the Shakti in addition to Shiva and a whole host of other gods and forms of the Goddess, and (4) and the eccentricity of some of his limited engagement with other religions as well as Theosophy, Hindu reformist societies, and atheism, which for Sabhapati is generally synonymous with what he perceived as a narrow view of scientific materialism.

One reason for the difficulty of categorizing his philosophy is that many of the nineteenth- to early twentieth-century Śaiva milieus that

Sabhapati engaged have remained relatively uncharted by scholars, which is perhaps one reason he himself has not been considered by virtually any author writing on the development of Śaivism (or Indian philosophy more broadly, modern or classical for that matter). Alexis Sanderson in his masterful overview of the "Śaiva Age" does hint in a note at a notable synthesis that occurred many centuries earlier, in the circa twelfth-century work *Tirumantiram*, attributed to Tirumūlar.[2] This is a work that in many instances bears striking resemblance to Sabhapati's cosmology and teachings on yoga, even if it is to my knowledge never explicitly cited by him (see the section Shivajnana Bodha and the Tamil Siddhas, and Chapter 4). This is perhaps not surprising considering his *paramparā*'s own indebtedness to the soteriology of the *Tirumantiram* (via Shivajnana Bodha) and the Tamil Vīraśaiva position that Tirumūlar was actually a Vīraśaiva.[3] Yet the syncretic contents of the *Tirumantiram* and related forms of Tamil Śaivism, such as later successive waves of Tamil Vīraśaiva and Siddha authors who inspired Sabhapati's own work, are seldom treated in scholarship on Śaiva philosophy. Sanderson's comprehensive research on earlier developments of Śaiva philosophy and literature has, however, provided an important academic impetus to define and delineate this relative lack of material on what occurred "after the Śaiva Age,"[4] and I anticipate that Sabhapati's own interpretation of, and innovation upon, Śaiva philosophy and cosmology will accordingly emerge into much clearer focus as this broader trajectory of related currents begins to gradually attract more scholarly attention.

In this chapter I take a more limited approach to these broader questions of Śaiva genealogy in my focus on certain key sources for Sabhapati's philosophy and cosmology that were eventually translocalized across India as well as internationally. I accordingly take Sabhapati's published literature and corroborative ethnographic data that I have obtained in Chennai as my main starting point, both of which help clarify the main philosophical currents that informed Sabhapati's main period of literary activity between 1880 and 1913. I have accordingly divided this chapter into four parts. In the first section I delineate the milieus of his two guru *paramparās*, one explicitly linked to a celebrated Tamil Vīraśaiva *parampāra* that extends back to at least the seventeenth century, and another more or less mythological one that I interpret as primarily linked to the Tamil Siddhas and by extension the aforementioned Tamil text *Tirumantiram*. In the second section I describe some of the salient cosmological features of Sabhapati's system and his system of transmigrations. In the third section I describe the connection of Sabhapati's cosmology with Tamil Śaiva religious milieus. In the fourth section I note Sabhapati's doxographical engagement with other points of view such as other religions (including Buddhism, Islam, Christianity, and Zoroastrianism), atheism, reform societies, and early Theosophy, as such engagement serves to bring his own colonial-era views into sharper focus.

Sabhapati's Two Gurus

As previously noted, Sabhapati Swami's own inheritance of Śaiva (and to some extent also Vaiṣṇava and Śākta) doctrines and practices as expressed throughout his own published literature is informed by wide-scale developments subsequent to the "Śaiva Age," specifically developments in Tamil Śaivism from the sixteenth to eighteenth centuries. Steinschneider in particular has skillfully analyzed early modern literary attempts to overcome rigid divisions between "warring sects," that is, between teachers of a monistic Vedānta and a dualistic Saiddhāntika persuasion, or for that matter even between those of Vaiṣṇava or Śaiva persuasion.[5] As Steinschneider narrates, a critical mediating factor between these "warring sects" was the spread of Vīraśaiva philosophical doctrines to Tamil Nadu. Vīraśaivas, or Vīramāheśvaras as they had previously been called in emic discourses, appear to originally have had an antipathy toward Vedānta but gradually came to accept it as a valid mode of framing religious soteriology.[6] The context of this acceptance of Vedānta also allowed for the development of a system of yoga known as Śivayoga or "Yoga for Shiva," which was exported from Kannada- and Telugu-speaking milieus to (what is today) Tamil Nadu by at least the seventeenth century, if not earlier.[7] Steinschneider in particular aims to show that "the polyvocality of Tamil Śaiva theology, literary culture, and sectarian identity compels us to reconsider the supposed unity of this tradition,"[8] and this is certainly relevant to keep in mind when considering Sabhapati's relationship to more dominant currents of Śaiva philosophy, whether Vedānta or Siddhānta. Indeed, by Sabhapati's time this "polyvocality" had created enough space for a tenuous but remarkable synthesis between the monism of Vedānta and the dualism of Śaiva Siddhānta, often considered contrasting philosophical expressions, and with it space for new soteriological rationales for yogic practice. This synthesis did not start with Sabhapati but began several centuries earlier, as Raman has astutely noted in the following correspondence:

> The bringing together of the Vedānta and the Siddhānta as one continuum already begins with Aruḷnanti Civācāriyār, and is cemented in the commentaries on the *Civañāṉacittiyār* between the fifteenth and sixteenth centuries. Integrated into its soteriology is the idea of a path of knowledge (*ñāṉa*) called the *caṉmārkkam*, which by the late fourteenth century integrates a yogic path ostensibly called the *aṣṭāṅgayoga* ["yoga of eight auxiliaries"], but in reality also incorporating other yogic modes within it.[9]

I would argue that Sabhapati is likewise partaking in a wider centuries-old trend that was shared by some of his contemporaries like Chidambaram Ramalinga Swamigal, and, as a result, his philosophical integration of these currents into his yoga is not as idiosyncratic as it may initially appear.

Steinschneider's historical and literary analysis is not only relevant to Sabhapati's work on a general philosophical level but is also directly intertwined with the yogi's personal life and web of human relationships. The discursive currents that he analyzes includes one of Sabhapati's two principal guru-lines (*paramparā*s) from which he claims descent, that of Kumara Devar (Kumāratēvar) and his guru Perur Santhalinga Swamigal (Pērūr Cāntaliṅka Cuvāmikaḷ). As a result, while a comprehensive treatment of the wider picture of these many centuries of historical developments would require an additional research project in and of itself, we are fortunate that Sabhapati did provide some concrete details about his specific religious "credentials" that enable us to more properly contextualize him within the wider shifts taking place in modern Tamil Śaiva and Vaiṣṇava discourse, especially at the periphery where these discourses often intersected with Vīraśaiva and the remnants of Tamil Siddha milieus.

Chidambara Swamigal and "Instructive Truth"

As stated in Chapter 1, CPSPS, T1, and T2 all clearly state that Sabhapati Swami's first guru—and, as T1 and T2 add, his father's guru—was Vedashreni Chidambara Periya Swamigal (Vētacirēṇi Citampara Periya Cuvāmikaḷ, d. 1858), a fact that his followers in Madras would have been readily able to verify (see Chapter 1 for a treatment of their interaction). While today the site of a major campus of the Indian Institute of Technology and a thriving suburb near Chennai's international airport, Vedashreni (an old name for Velachery)[10] in Sabhapati's time was a separate temple village that already been an important Śaiva religious site for at least almost a millennium.[11] As cited in Sabhapati's own literature, Velachery Chidambara Swami was the author of *Upatēca uṇmai*, or "*Instructive Truth*," an as-yet-untranslated collection of 192 verses on Vedānta and yoga published at least as early as 1881 and still in print today along with useful paraphrases and commentaries for each verse, which was originally composed in an archaic style of Tamil religious verse.[12] His earlier name was Veeraswamy Swamigal (Vīrācuvāmi Cuvāmikaḷ), but he is said to have received the name Vedashreni Chidambara Swamigal upon his initiation (Skt. *dīkṣā*) from his guru, Kuzhandaivel Swamigal (Kuḻantaivēl Cuvāmikaḷ).[13] Vedashreni Chidambara Swamigal is sometimes confused in library records with another person, Thiruporur Chidambara Swamigal (Tiruppōrūr Citambara Cuvāmikaḷ), but they are different individuals who nevertheless are part of the same line; beyond the later date of the former, a key distinction is that Vedashreni Chidambara Swamigal, and not Thiruporur Chidambara Swamigal, authored *Upatēca uṇmai* despite the fact that the work is sometimes erroneously attributed to the latter in library catalogs.[14]

The most recent edition of *Upatēca uṇmai* emphasizes Vedashreni Chidambara Swamigal's connection with the circa seventeenth-century CE Vīraśaiva author Kumara Devar. The edition offers a short life-sketch of Kumara Devar and Vedashreni Chidambara Swamigal and also interprets one of the latter's verses (189) as a praise of his guru Kumara Devar.[15] This is the same Kumara Devar analyzed by Steinschneider, who notes that no fewer than sixteen individual works were attributed to him, "including the *Cuttacātakam*, the *Attuvitavuṇmai*, and the purportedly autobiographical *Makārājāturavu* (*The Renunciation of the Great King*)."[16] These along with some other Tamil works have been included in a publication entitled *Cāstirakkōvai* (*Series of Scriptures*), which was published at least as early as 1908,[17] and possibly as early as 1871.[18] Kumara Devar's guru Perur Santhalinga Swamigal also authored four major works, including *Vairākya Catakam* (< Skt. *Vairāgya Śataka*, "One Hundred Verses on Dispassion") and *Vairākya Tīpam* (< Skt. *Vairāgya Dīpa*, "Lamp of Dispassion"),[19] which as I noted in Chapter 1 were recommended by one of Sabhapati's students to Om Prakash Swamigal; there is thus evidence that Sabhapati and his students were directly familiar with the literature of both Kumara Devar and Santhalinga Swamigal. Many of these works have not been yet translated into English, and some remain fairly obscure outside of Tamil Nadu. Since this book is primarily focused on the "translocalization" of Sabhapati's yoga, I will not here attempt to conduct a comparison of these works' contents with Sabhapati's own cosmological views on Vedānta and Siddhānta, although pursuing this kind of systematic comparison in the future would undoubtedly help further situate Sabhapati's position in the context of Tamil Śaiva literature.

While a full list of the swamis' names between Kumara Devar and Vedashreni Chidambara Swamigal is absent in the edition mentioned above, based on available data I have been able to populate the names of Vedashreni Chidambara Swamigal's line through his guru Kuzhandaivel to Thiruporur Chidambara Swamigal and even further to Kumara Devar and his guru Perur Santhalinga Swamigal (Pērūr Cāntaliṅka Cuvāmikaḷ), as well as Santhalinga Swamigal's own guru Thuraiyur Sivaprakasa Swamigal (Tuṟaiyūr Civappirakācacuvāmikaḷ). The populated list of names is as follows:

1. Thuraiyur Sivaprakasa Swamigal (Tuṟaiyūr Civappirakācacuvāmikaḷ)
2. Perur Santhalinga Swamigal (Pērūr Cāntaliṅka Cuvāmikaḷ)
3. Kumara Devar (Kumāratēvar)
4. Thiruporur Chidambara Swamigal (Tiruppōrūr Citambara Cuvāmikaḷ)
5. Retty Chidambara Swamigal (Reṭṭi-Citamparacuvāmikaḷ)
6. Pazhani Swamigal (Paḻaṉicuvāmikaḷ)
7. Kuvalattu Swamigal (Kūvālattuccuvāmikaḷ)
8. Puliyur Swamigal (Puliyūrccuvāmikaḷ)
9. Mylapore Kuzhandaivel Swamigal (Mayilāppūr Kuḻandaivēl Cuvāmikaḷ)
10. Muttaiya Swamigal (Muttaiyacuvāmikaḷ) and Vedashreni Periya Chidambara Swamigal (Vētacirēṇi Citampara Periya Cuvāmikaḷ)
11. Sabhapati Swamigal (Capāpati Cuvāmikaḷ), via Vedashreni Periya Chidambara Swamigal

The relationships between Thuraiyur Sivaprakasa Swamigal, Perur Santhalinga Swamigal, and Kumara Devar are all well established in scholarship. The second part of the connection, from Kumara Devar to Kuzhandaivel, is provided in some editions of *Cāstirakkōvai*, the aforementioned collection of Kumara Devar's works (see Figure 3.1).[20] The

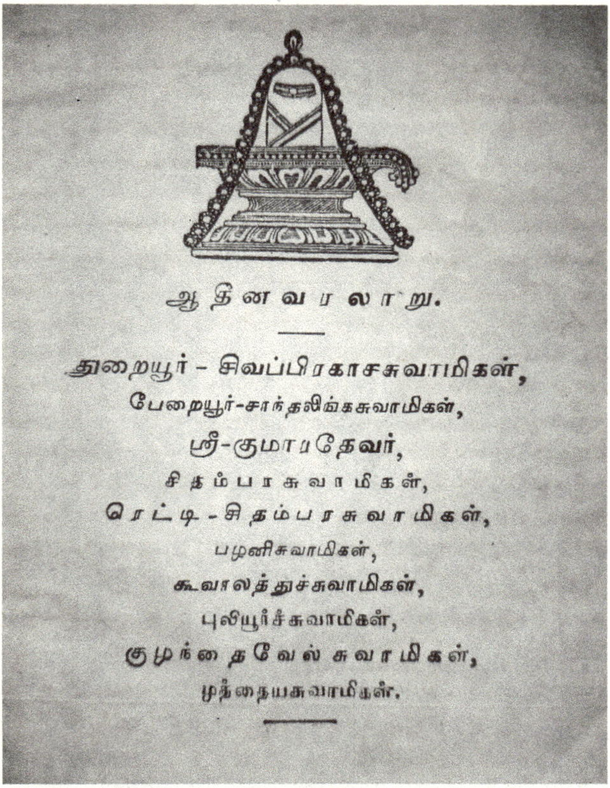
ஆதினவரலாறு.

துறையூர் - சிவப்பிரகாசசுவாமிகள்,
பேறையூர்-சாந்தலிங்கசுவாமிகள்,
ஸ்ரீ-குமாரதேவர்,
சிதம்பரசுவாமிகள்,
ரெட்டி-சிதம்பரசுவாமிகள்,
பழனிசுவாமிகள்,
கூவாலத்துச்சுவாமிகள்,
புலியூர்ச்சுவாமிகள்,
குழந்தைவேல்சுவாமிகள்,
முத்தையசுவாமிகள்.

Figure 3.1 A page from Śrī Kumāratēvar, *Tiruvāymalarntaruḷiya cāstirakkōvai* that lists the names as part of a "history of the monastery" (*ātīṉavaralāṟu*). Photo by the author.

third part of the connection is inscriptional evidence that I have obtained at the tumulus of Vedashreni Chidambara Swamigal's guru Kuzhandaivel Swamigal in Mylapore (see Figures 3.2 and 3.3). The fourth part of the connection is Vedashreni Chidambara Swamigal's own literature that mentions his initiation by one Kuzhandai Velar (Kuḻandai Vēlar, another name for Kuzhandaivel Swamigal) in the line of Kumara Devar.[21] It is clear from this literature and on account of the Kumara Devar connection that Kuzhandaivel Swamigal mentioned in the collection of Kumara Devar's works and Vedashreni Chidambara Swamigal's own guru Kuzhandaivel Swamigal were one and the same person.[22] The fifth and final link pertains to the link between our Sabhapati Swami and

Figure 3.2 The tumulus of Mylapore Kuzhandaivel Swamigal (Mayilāppūr Kuḻandaivēl Cuvāmikaḷ), guru of Vedashreni Chidambara Swamigal (Vētacirēṇi Citampara Cuvāmikaḷ). Photo by the author.

Vedashreni Chidambara Swamigal, which as I already mentioned is referred to throughout Sabhapati's extant literature (especially CPSPS, CTCSPV, and MCVTS). Sabhapati's opening pages of his Tamil work MCVTS (see Figure 3.3) confirms that his guru was none other than this same Vedashreni Chidambara Swamigal: Sabhapati claims that he is the "student of Vedashreni Chidambara Swamigal, author of *Upatēca uṇmai*, of the monastic line of Kumara Devar" (see Figure 3.3).[23]

Figure 3.3 An inscription at the tumulus of Mylapore Kuzhandaivel Swamigal that records his guru as Kumara Devar (Kumāratēvar) and another of his students as Muttaiya Swamigal (Muṭṭaiyacuvāmikaḷ). Photo by the author.

Shivajnana Bodha and the Tamil Siddhas

As can be seen in Figure 3.4 and throughout Sabhapati's literature, Vedashreni Chidambara Swamigal is not the only guru whom Sabhapati Swami cites, as he always adds a second figure: Shivajnana Bodha Yogishwarar (Civañāṉabōta Yogīśvar), also referred to as Shivajnana Bodha Rishi (Civañāṉabōta Ruṣi). This latter figure is mentioned in the context of the guru succession (*paramparā*) of Agastya (Akattiyar, Akasttiyar; see Chapter 1 for more details on Sabhapati's claim to be a part of Agastya's line). While next to nothing can currently be traced about Shivajnana Bodha beyond what details Sabhapati himself gives, it is clear from the woodblock prints and descriptions that he is supposed to be a representative from what would today be described as a Tamil Siddha (Cittar, also commonly transliterated Siddhar) milieu.[24] The Pothigai Mountains are held

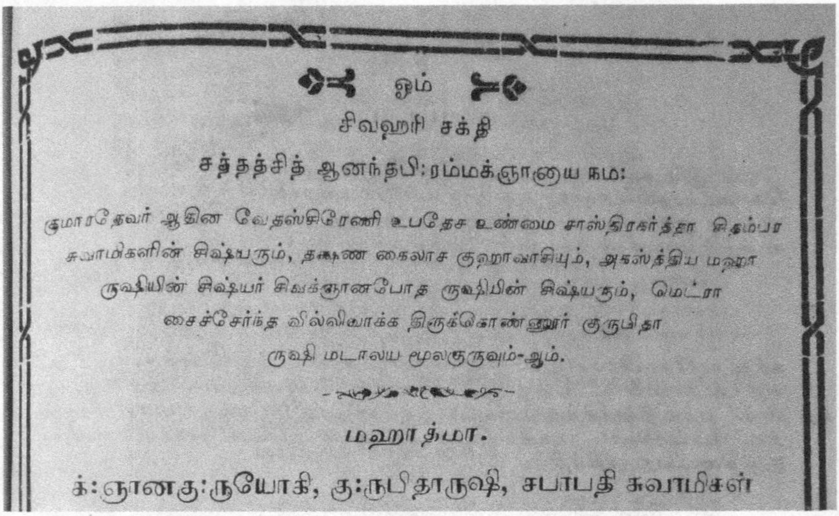
ஓம்

சிவஹரி சக்தி

சத்தத்சித் ஆனந்தபி:ரம்மக்ஞாஞய நம:

குமாரதேவர் ஆதின வேதஸ்சிரேணி உபதேச உண்மை சாஸ்திரகர்த்தா சிதம்பர
சுவாமிகளின் சிஷ்யரும், தக்ஷிண கைலாச குஹாவாசியும், அகஸ்திய மஹா
ருஷியின் சிஷ்யர் சிவக்ஞானபோத ருஷியின் சிஷ்யரும், மெட்ரா
சைச்சேர்ந்த வில்லிவாக்க திருக்கொண்ணூர் குருபிதா
ருஷி மடாலய மூலகுருவும்-ஆம்.

மஹாத்மா.

க்:ஞானகு:ருயோகி, கு:ருபிதாருஷி, சபாபதி சுவாமிகள்

Figure 3.4 The opening praise of MCVTS that mentions Sabhapati as a student of both Vedashreni Chidambara Swamigal (Vētacirēṇi Citampara Cuvāmikaḷ) in the *ātiṉam* of Kumara Devar (Kumāratēvar) as well as Shivajnana Bodha Rishi (Civañāṉabōta Ruṣi), the student of Agastya (Akasttiyar). Photo by the author.

even to this day to be sacred to the devotees of Agastya, who as I have already described in Chapter 1 have revered its highest peak, Mount Agastya or Agastyamalai, as his embodiment for several centuries if not longer.[25] The mythology is rooted in the Puranic notion that Agastya needed to come to south India to "correct" the imbalance of so much ascetic *tapas* in the north, an idea that appears to have been reflected in the *Tirumantiram*.[26] The Tamil Siddhas are often intertwined with Tamil Vīraśaiva movements, and in some temple contexts they are even worshiped alongside Vīraśaiva gurus (see Figure 3.5).

The Tamil Siddhas have been the subject of a few book-length studies, of which one of the earliest appears to be by A. V. Subramania Aiyar, which includes sketches of some of the principal Siddha poets, starting with Tirumūlar.[27] However, at present R. Venkatraman's work *A History of the Tamil Siddha Cult* is the most extensive study as far as their broader history and texts are concerned.[28] Venkatraman builds on a wide variety of primary and secondary sources, including Kamil Zvelebil's more or less groundbreaking exploration into this subject from the perspective

Photo 3.5 Idols of some Tamil Siddha figures, including Tirumūlar and Irāmatēvar, in the tumulus of Vedashreni Chidambara Swamigal. Photo by the author.

of Siddha poetry.[29] A few years after Venkatraman published his study, Zvelebil published a fascinating (if somewhat eccentric) work on the "Siddha preoccupation with medicine, healing and therapies, with sexual attitudes and yoga, as preserved and expressed in ancient texts composed in Tamil as well as the living practices of contemporary Siddha physicians."[30] Weiss's more recent study is a more refined academic treatment of the range of topics covered by Zvelebil but, while extremely valuable in its own right and useful for its perspective on Agastya, is focused more or less exclusively on the political uses of Siddha traditions and their medical practices by Tamil nationalists and accordingly does not go into much detail about the Siddhas' cosmological beliefs or yogic practices as informed by Śaiva literature.[31] More recently, R. Ezhilraman has produced a relevant thesis on the Siddhas that supplies very useful details about their connection to local temple cultures and also includes numerous images related to individual Siddhas and their rites of worship.[32] Numerous books published in Tamil also treat on various aspects of the Siddhas such as their yoga, medicine, and songs.[33] While outside of Tamil Nadu, scholars have also noted evidence of Siddha presence at Srisailam in Andhra Pradesh, on the Telangana border.[34] Finally, David Gordon White has also examined aspects of the Siddhas in his book on Tantric alchemy.[35]

Venkatraman divides the Tamil Siddhas into four overarching categories: (1) the Sanmārgasiddhas or "Siddhas on the right path" who followed the *Tirumantiram* and similar works that were adopted into the Śaiva canon;[36] (2) the Ñānasiddhas or "Siddhas of Gnosis" who considered "the physical body as perishable and the world as unreal"; (3) the Kāyasiddhas or "Siddhas of the Body" who aimed at "physical immortality, perpetuation of youth and acquisition of occult powers"; and (4) individuals whom Zvelebil has termed later "Siddha-like" poets who "have been 'appended' to the Siddha school by posterior generations, or who called themselves *cittar* (*siddhas*) without properly belonging to the esoteric group itself."[37] Any significant distinction between Venkatraman's first three categories is subject to debate among scholars, but Sabhapati Swami and his guru Shivajnana Bodha Yogishwarar do appear to generally fit the fourth category given their relatively late date. In other words, they are inheritors of the legacy of the medieval Siddhas while not necessarily being Siddhas themselves, although one of Shivajnana Bodha's students did have the title Siddha (*cittaṉ*) and the Siddhas (*cittarkaḷ*) are one of the four groups in Sabhapati's hagiographical accounts who visit Agastya's hermitage to catch a vision of Agastya (see Chapter 1). In any case, Sabhapati Swami's literature in various places expresses discernible tendencies toward each of the other three groups that Venkatraman outlines and is not easily mapped onto such a scheme.

As noted in Chapter 1, T2 records that Sabhapati not only learned yoga but also alchemy and related arts from his guru Shivajnana Bodha, but was instructed to keep these latter practices secret from the public. These arts stem from the teachings of Agastya, and indeed Sabhapati's claim of being part of the guru-*paramparā* of Agastya himself, who assumes many forms and functions in Tamil literature (see Chapter 1 for more on the Agastya amalgamation and his mountain). This connection inextricably links him to what are widely considered to be Siddha milieus, even if his literature is ultimately more reflective of a Vedānta-inflected form of Śaiva "rāja yoga" and even if there is little evidence that he practiced any of their techniques and arts apart from yogic meditation. Some aspects of his yogic practice, however, such as his descriptions of embodied initiations (*dīkṣā*) and sexual rites, do seem to point to some familiarity with Siddha practices, albeit framed and expressed in a more sanitized terminology (see Chapter 4).

An Embodied Cosmos

The introduction to CPSPS states the overarching aim of Sabhapati's philosophical literature, which he saw as a kind of spiritual "science": "The object of this Philosophy and Science is to show the method by which the human soul is sure to *gain* success in Holding Communion with the Universal Infinite Spirit, and thereby to become the very I[nfinite]. Spirit itself."[38] Indeed, in all his works—both in English and in vernacular languages—Sabhapati's main intention is to show the "method" of "Holding Communion," which as I have already stated is his translation for *samādhi* (Mpvl. *camāti*), more literally a state of mental "composition" or "composure." The method referred to is none other than Sabhapati's system of the "royal yoga for Shiva" (Skt. *śivarājayoga*; Mpvl. *civarājayōkam*), which resonates with but is nevertheless distinct from the compound *śivayoga* as well as the name of its practitioners or *śivayogīs*, a common epithet of identity among early Vīraśaivas in Kannada milieus.[39] While I analyze the distinguishing features of Sabhapati's method of Śivarājayoga in Chapter 4, it is important to emphasize at the outset that there is evidence for Śivarājayoga being distinct from Śivayoga (and Pātañjalayoga for that matter) in Tamil-speaking milieus at least as early as the circa eighteenth-century poem *Cittarkaṇam*, or "The Troops of Siddhas," composed by the Tamil poet Tāyumāṉavar.[40]

There is a broader philosophical postulate undergirding all of this, however, namely the existence of a "Universal Infinite Spirit"—with all of its so-called faculties, or tattvas—from which all things arose and to which one can return and eventually become. The assertion of an Infinite Spirit from which faculties "emanate" or "descend" (to use Sabhapati's own words) pervades Sabhapati's literature and also informs his antagonism toward a narrow form of atheism, which to him is a "nonreligion" that only recognizes the final faculty, that of elemental matter, as true (see the section Sabhapati and Atheism). In this section I will describe the philosophical and cosmological presuppositions as expressed in Sabhapati's literature and connect it—insofar as possible—so similar assertions in other related currents of Indian and particularly Śaiva philosophy.

Shiva as "Infinite Spirit"

The phrase "Infinite Spirit" (sometimes abbreviated "I. Spirit"), while it may appear eerily Hegelian,[41] is Sabhapati's English translation of choice for the Brahman of the Upanishads. This is made clear in CPSPS, in which notes are given for many English technical terms; for "Infinite Spirit" we most often find *pirmmam* noted in the Tamil script and *brahma* in Devanagari. However, the first invocation of "Infinite Spirit" in CPSPS is noted as *civamayappirmō* in Tamil and *śivamayabrahmo* in Devanagari, which could be literally rendered as the "Brahman which consists of Shiva."[42] I do not think this is an accidental or mere passing gesture, as a consideration of Sabhapati Swami's Tamil works reveals that Mahādeva ("The Great God") or Shiva as Sarveśvara ("The Lord of All") is used synonymously in those instances where "Infinite Spirit" or "Brahman" is mentioned in his English works. For example, in the English accounts of Sabhapati's dream at the age of twenty-nine or thirty that led to his quest to find Agastya's hermitage (see Chapter 1), it is the "Infinite Spirit" that appears to him. In T1 of MCVTS, however, we find Sarveśvara (variously rendered *carvasvarar*, *carvēsvarar*, or *carvēcuvarar* in the Tamil script). While if left unclarified this compound could be a generic epithet for Brahman, a few sentences earlier we find the terminology clarified: Sabhapati's severe devotion (Mpvl. *akōra tapam*) is to the "Lord of the Dance (Naṭēcar) as the Lord of All" (*carvēsvararākiya naṭēcar*), who is the presiding deity of Dandeeswarar Vedashreni Temple (Taṇṭīsvarar Vētacirēṇi Kōvil), where Sabhapati was said to remain for three days and nights in continual meditation when he was twenty-nine or thirty years old. In other words, here Sarveśvara does not indicate an abstract "Infinite Spirit" but Shiva in his assumed form as the Lord of All. Despite this precedent for Brahman to be equated with Shiva, MCVTS makes it clear that Sabhapati's philosophy does allow for Vaiṣṇava and Śākta paradigms that can equally lead to the experience of Śivarājayoga, and it accordingly allows space for alternate cosmologies and provides devotional instructions, mantras, and visualizations for a wide range of deities outside the confines of what is typically considered to be Śaiva. In other words, Sabhapati's synthesis is not exclusively limited to a Śaiva frame nor does it require devotion to Shiva to accomplish; in this his approach is perhaps most similar to the *Tirumantiram*'s allowance for Vaiṣṇava and Śākta cosmological views.[43] Finally, some degree of inspiration from a local Tamil form of Shiva cannot be entirely discounted, although evidence is lacking. Sarveśvara in Tamil (Carvēcuvarar) is sometimes conflated with Sarpeśvara (Carppēcuvarar, "The Snake Lord") on account of the similarities in spelling between *pa* and *va* phonemes. The latter is a serpentine deity, a shrine I have personally visited at Vedashreni Chidambara Swamigal's tumulus. He is also depicted in some Śaiva temples in the environs of Chennai that Sabhapati would have undoubtedly known of, such as Marundeeswarar Temple in Thiruvanmiyur, a village adjacent to Velachery.

A Cosmogonic Separation of "Faculties"

Sabhapati's literature in English (the three editions of VRY) as well as his trilingual work in English, Tamil, and Sanskrit (CPSPS) present a dialogue between the Infinite Spirit (who, as we have seen above, is connected with Shiva's identification with Brahman) and what he calls in at least one place the "*Soul* anxious of salvation" (Mpvl. *mummukṣujīvātmā*, < Skt. *mumukṣujīvātman*) and in other instances the "Finite Spirit" (*jīvātmā*). The connection in Sabhapati's literature between "finite" (here *jīva*, more literally "individual life-form") and "infinite" (an interpretation of Brahman's quality as *parama*, or "supreme") is not accidental, as the Infinite Spirit is not a principle abstracted or separate from the human "body" (Mpvl. *tēkam*, < Skt. *deha*), but is in fact intertwined with the body itself along with its mental processes, emotions, and capacity for feeling. This is all explained in the context of "two main branches" of the "Raja Yogá [*sic*] system": (1) the "knowledge of soul," predicated upon removing the "doubts of faculties"; and (2) the "method by which the soul is enabled to hold Communion with, and thence become the Infinite Spirit."[44] In this section I only describe the salient features of the first "branch," as the second branch will occupy Chapter 4 given that it consists of the practical aspects of Sabhapati's yoga. It should be kept in mind while considering either branch that both engage the same cosmogonic principles and are intended to describe two motions of the same process, one "descending" toward finite matter and the other "progressing" toward infinite spirit.

Sabhapati's cosmogonic system, like many other systems of Indian philosophy, is predicated on the existence of tattvas, which he consistently translates as "faculties."[45] The Sanskrit term *tattva* can have a variety of meanings that can be grouped under two semantic "clouds of meaning," so to speak. The first semantic cloud describes a "true or real state," "truth," or "reality" as a more or less abstract conception.[46] The second cloud is undoubtedly connected to the first cloud but more specifically refers to a discrete "ground principle" of being (*Grundprinzip* in German),[47] of which two common enumerations in

Indian philosophy are twenty-five, as derived from Sāṃkhya, and thirty-six, as derived from the Śaivāgamas. Dominic Goodall has noted the following phenomenon of their expansion as it pertains to early Śaiva Tantras, which also informs Sabhapati's own integration of these principles in a different way than what is understood in Sāṃkhya:

> The tantras of the Śaiva Siddhānta modified [the structure of the twenty-five *tattva*s of Sāṃkhya] in two ways: they added principles to the top, demonstrating that the Sāṅkhyas had correctly grasped the nature of only the inferior levels of the universe, and they attempted to place worlds inherited from older Śaiva scriptures on the levels of these various principles (*tattva*). The latter change meant that *tattva* in some contexts approximates to a "reality level" of the universe in which various worlds are placed rather than a constitutive "principle" of the universe.[48]

I would argue that it is in this same sense of "reality level" that Sabhapati uses the term. For Sabhapati, however, to merely intellectually map these levels of reality as a "cosmography" (*prakriyā*, to use Goodall's translation) is not enough—one must conquer them as one would conquer a "kingdom," to use Sabhapati's own terminology. As Goodall makes clear, this attitude toward conquering the tattvas is not unique to Sabhapati but has a long history in Śaiva Tantra, being at least as old as the Mūla Sūtra layer of the circa fifth- to sixth-century *Niśvāsatattvasaṃhitā* and its notion of "*tattvajaya*, in other words a yogic conquest of the *tattvas* that extends the notion of *bhūtajaya*, 'conquest of the elements,' that we find in Yoga Sūtra 3.43 to reach well beyond the ontological ladder of the Sāṅkhyas."[49] A similar form of conquest is also found in the *Mālinīvijayottaratantra*, which was commented upon by the ninth- to tenth-century Kashmiri philosopher Abhinavagupta.[50] Indeed, Sabhapati claims that it is necessary to remove "nearly 1,008 doubts" about the tattvas "before we obtain the knowledge of Soul and Spirit."[51] To remove these doubts, he offers three ways to explain them: (1) an "illustration by examples," (2) a "detailed account of the introduction of the Infinite Spirit into the Finite Spirit," and (3) the "emancipation of the Finite Spirit from this earthly bondage."[52] Since these three ways reveal the bulk of Sabhapati's cosmogonic and philosophical presuppositions as expressed in his English literature (the Alpha stream), I will here explain them before considering in the subsequent section how they are represented in his vernacular literature (Beta and Gamma streams; see Chapter 2 for a consideration of these different streams).

"Illustration by Examples"

The first way, the "illustration by examples" (his translation for Mpvl. *tiruṣṭāntam*, < Skt. *dṛṣṭānta*), is relatively short. These examples are more like analogies, some of which are taken from other Indic texts. The first example is seeing the soul as a reflection of the Infinite Spirit, but that by the "curtain of delusion" one considers oneself to be separate until the curtain is removed. The second example is that of seeing the Finite Spirit as a merely the Infinite Spirit's reflection in a mirror, without independent existence. The third and fourth analogies are mistaking the Finite Spirit for the Infinite Spirit the way someone would mistake a rope for a snake, or a block of wood for a thief, on a dark night. The fifth analogy is the imagination of one's "conscious soul" to be separate from the Infinite Spirit as akin to a thirsty traveler thinking a "glittering mirage" in a "vast and sandy desert" to be a "pond of sweet water" on account of "delusion" (Mpvl. *māyai*, < Skt. *māyā*). To this analogy the result of removing this delusion is also given: "When he holds deep communion with the [Infinite Spirit], he neither sees his soul nor is conscious of the attributes of the soul, such as intellect, memory, imagination, and ideas of sensation and perception, and finds himself absorbed in the I. Spirit."[53] The sixth analogy is seeing the Infinite Spirit as akin to a sun that "illuminates every object of this universe as long as it is in the heavens" but with "infinitely more luminous rays."[54]

Sabhapati then adds three additional analogical examples, many of which resemble parallel analogies in Advaita Vedānta, to explain how "the pure essence of I. Spirit [Mpvl. *pirammam*, < Skt. *brahman*] becomes so many different objects." The first additional analogy is seeing the Infinite Spirit as akin to a "brilliantly polished mirror stone [*spaṭikam*, < Skt. *sphaṭika*, lit. "crystal," "quartz"] in which many forms, figures, shapes and colours will be seen." The second additional analogy is seeing the Infinite Spirit as akin to a metal such as gold from which many different ornaments and jewels are made, yet all from the same original metallic substance. The third and final additional analogy is perhaps the most striking, namely that the Infinite Spirit is like someone who constructs a building from an initial idea of it in his mind. Just as the idea of the building is what is transformed into the building, so Sabhapati argues that it is the "idea of separate existence has brought the separate existence into existence."[55] This latter category echoes the idealism of the *Yogavāsiṣṭha*, which was absorbed into Tamil Vīraśaivism as well as Tamil Advaita Vedānta by the seventeenth-century via its Tamil translation.[56]

The Tree Universally Spread

The second way of removing doubts about the tattvas is by understanding the "introduction of the Infinite Spirit into the Finite Spirit," although Sabhapati in the actual section that describes this way makes an important switch from "Infinite Spirit" to the phrase "Universal Spirit," which is marked as a translation of *civamayam* (Mpvl.) and *śivamaya* (Skt.), literally "that which consists of (or is fully) Shiva." Sabhapati states that this Universal Spirit "resides in your brain," which is perhaps a surprisingly modern notion although it must be kept in mind that in subsequent pages it is clear that "brain" is sometimes Sabhapati's translation of *kapāla*, lit. "skull" or "head" and also is used in the phrase "top of the brain" to describe the *brahmarandhra*, or "crevice of Brahman." However, there is evidence from his descriptions of the bodily attributions of the higher cakras as well as from his critique of atheism, which I will treat below, that his use of "brain" can also mean the physical brain, but not the brain as an organ from which thought originates. Sabhapati further defines this Universal Spirit as the "same Spirit which is everywhere invisible, omnipotent, all-knowing, all-seeing, perfectly pure and the only witness with 4 sorts of Brightness and 16 sorts of Rays," the terms of which he describes in the pages that follow.

Perhaps most important for the subject of cosmogony, however, is Sabhapati's division of this original Universal Spirit into two parts, what he terms (1) a Universal Infinite Spirit and (2) a Universal Finite Spirit. The first part, or the Universal Infinite Spirit, is Brahman, which is an "Impersonal God" and "Passive Principle" and does not create or act alone, but only witnesses such activity. The second part, or the Universal Finite Spirit, by contrast, is the "Personal God" and "Active Principle," and is described as the "Creations and all the Souls of the creation, always acting and creating, preserving and destroying."[57] This hierarchical distinction between the passive "Universal Infinite Spirit" and the active "Universal Finite Spirit" resonates with the Śaiva Saiddhāntika distinction between Shiva's highest form Paramaśiva as "limitless, formless, undifferentiated" and Sadāśiva as the "body of mantras with which Śiva acts in the world."[58] While Sabhapati explicitly takes issue with what he perceives as the dualism of Saiddhāntika doctrine (see Connections with Tamil Śaiva Discourse), his cosmology is clearly informed by many of its principles.

The Universal Infinite Spirit has what Sabhapati calls the "4 sorts of Brightness" or "4 Spiritual Brightnesses" (Mpvl. *caturpirmatārakamayam*,

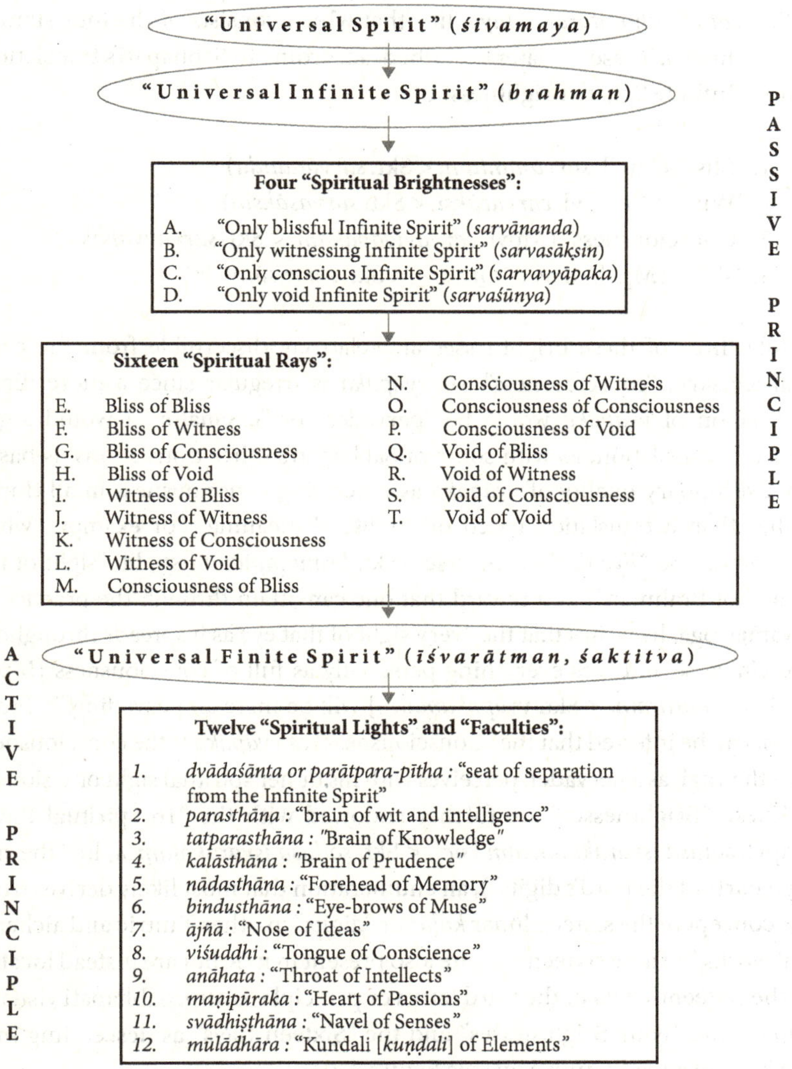

Figure 3.6 A diagram of the "descent" or "emanations" of the Universal Spirit in the "thirty-two faculties," as outlined in editions of VRY and CPSPS. The idiosyncratic translations of "Prudence" for *kalā*, "Memory" for *nāda*, and so on are not direct translations but rather an attempt to communicate the embodied characteristics and qualities of each tattva or cakra in question.

< Skt. *caturbrahmatārakamaya*, lit. "that which consists of the four stars of the Brahma"). These are later described, according to Sabhapati's translation, as the "Infinite Spirit's Brightness" of

1. "Bliss" (Mpvl. *sarvāṉantam*, < Skt. *sarvānanda*)
2. "Witness" (Mpvl. *carvacākṣi*, < Skt. *sarvasākṣin*)
3. "Consciousness" (Mpvl. *carvaviyāpakam*, < Skt. *sarvavyāpaka*)
4. "Void" (Mpvl. *carvacūṉṉiyam*, < Skt. *sarvaśūnya*)[59]

While three of these brightnesses are relatively discernible from the original Sanskrit, "consciousness" for *vyāpaka* is irregular since a more direct translation of *vyāpaka* would be "pervader" or "emanator." I would argue that this translation, as with some of Sabhapati's other translations, is based on a secondary quality of *vyāpaka* as perceiving consciousness in all things rather than a translation based on its literal meaning. For example, when describing the "*Eye* to the Universe" (Skt. *brahmajñānadṛṣṭi*, lit. "sight of the gnosis of Brahman") as a reward that one can attain through the practice of Śivarājayoga, he writes that the "very sight of that eye as it spreads throughout the Universe and sees everything personally as full of consciousness [Mpvl. *viyāpakamāttiram*, < Skt. *vyāpakamātra*] will be mere all pervading."[60] From this it can be inferred that the "Consciousness" of *vyāpaka* is the consciousness that the yogi, as a pervader, perceives with his or her spiritual sight or vision.[61]

These "Brightnesses" are further endowed with the "16 Spiritual Rays" (Mpvl. *sōṭasa īsvarakalāñcam* [*sic*], < Skt. *ṣoḍaśa īśvarakalāṃśa*, lit. "the sixteen parts of the Lord's digits"), an enumeration that most likely derives from the concept of the sixteen lunar *kalā*s or "digits" in other Tantric and alchemical works.[62] These sixteen rays are also present in RYB, but are instead located in the sixteenth *kalā* of the third tattva or principle, *īśvara*. Sabhapati visually depicts the "Four Brightnesses" and the "Sixteen Rays" as descending into the head of a meditating yogi (see Figure 3.7).

The Universal Finite Spirit or Active Principle, by contrast, is endowed with "12 Spiritual Lights" (Mpvl. *tuvātasayāttama corūpam*, < Skt. *dvādaśātmasvarūpa*, lit. "the inherent form of twelve selves"), a solar number on account of its correspondence to the twelve months in a year. Each of these twelve "Lights" is a Tantric lotus (Mpvl. *kamalam*, < Skt. *kamala*, lit. "lotus," synonymous with the cakra), which in Sabhapati's English works are also called "Kingdoms." These lotuses are not just isolated cakras but are twelve cosmic "faculties" that form the very core of Sabhapati's system of

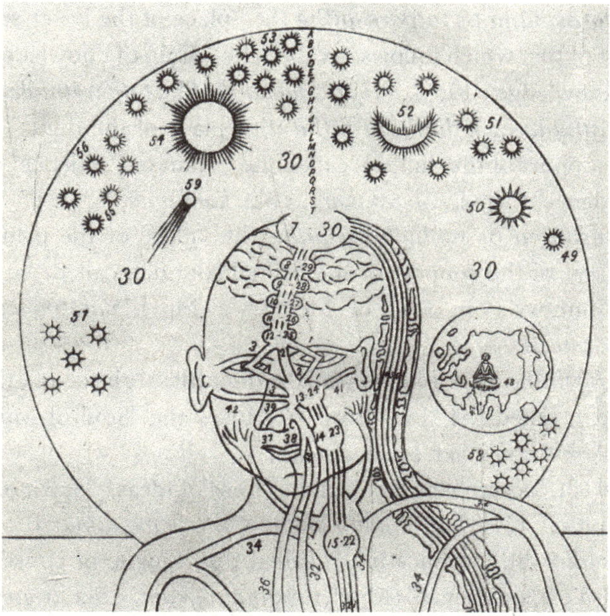

Figure 3.7 A portion of the first main diagram in the First Book of CPSPS, between pages 24 and 25, entitled "The Posture of Brumha Gnyana Siva Raja Yoga Samadhi or Infinite Spiritual Communion." The letters (A through T) refer to the "Four Brightnesses" and the "Sixteen Rays," and the numbers 7 to 12 are the higher six of the twelve "Spiritual Lights" or cakras (see Figure 3.6 above). Scan from copy of 1884 edition, courtesy of Bill Breeze.

emanations, which are creative principles that structure the invisible and visible cosmos. Their role in cosmology is also clear in his reliance on them in a philosophical context in his apologetic critique of atheism (see the section Sabhapati and Atheism).

From the top of the head to the "bottom of the spinal chord [*sic*]," Sabhapati's location for Skt. *kuṇḍali*, lit. "ring," they are as follows:

1. ***parātpara-pīṭha*** (lit. "seat of that which is superior to the best" or "the supreme of the supreme") or ***dvādaśānta*** (lit. "the end of the twelve"), called "self Consciousness and Wisdom" (< Mpvl. *parātparātmakam*, < Skt. *parātparātmaka*)
2. ***parasthāna*** (lit. "place of the supreme"), called the "Brain of wit and intelligence" or the "soul of Wit" (Mpvl. *parātmakam*, < Skt. *parātmaka*)

3. ***tatparasthāna*** or ***tatpara-pīṭha*** (lit. "place of the lesser supreme" or "seat of that which follows"), called the "Brain of knowledge" or "Soul of Knowledge" (Mpvl. *tatparātmakam*, < Skt. *tatparātmaka*)
4. ***kalāsthāna*** or ***kalādhāra pīṭha*** (lit. "place of the digits" or "seat of the support of the digits"), called the "Brain of Prudence" or "Soul of Prudence" (Mpvl. *kalātmakam*, < Skt. *kalātmaka*)
5. ***nādasthāna*** or ***nādadhāra pīṭha*** (lit. "place of the primal sound" or "seat of the support of the primal sound"), called the "Forehead of Memory" or "Soul of Memory" (Mpvl. *nātātmakam*, < Skt. *nādātmaka*).
6. ***bindusthāna*** or ***bindodhāra pīṭha*** (lit. "place of the primal drop"), called the "Eye-brows of Muse," the "Soul of Muse" (Mpvl. *vintātmakam*, < Skt. *bindvātmaka*)
7. ***ājñā*** (lit. "command,"), called the "nose of ideas," "Spirit of Ideas and Ambition" (Mpvl. *tirimalātmakam*, < Skt. *trimalātmaka*)
8. ***viśuddhi*** (lit. "purification"), called the "tongue of conscience" and "Spirit of Conscience" (Mpvl. *tirikuṇātmakam*, < Skt. *triguṇātmaka*)
9. ***anāhata***, called the "throat of intellects" and "Spirit of Intellect" (Mpvl. *antakkaraṇātmakam*, < Skt. *antaḥkaraṇātmaka*)
10. ***maṇipūraka*** (lit. "city of jewels"), called the "heart of passions," "Spirit of Passions," and "Soul of Notion" (Mpvl. *irākakōsayavastātmakam*, < Skt. *rāgakośāvasthātmaka*)
11. ***svādhiṣṭhāna***, called the "navel of senses" and "Spirit of Senses" (Mpvl. *intiriyātmakam*, < Skt. *indriyātmaka*)
12. ***mūlādhāra*** (lit. "root support"), called the "*kuṇḍali* of elements,"[63] "Spirit of Natures" (Mpvl. *pūtātmakam*, < Skt. *bhūtātmakam*)

As is likely immediately evident to any Sanskritist, the names that Sabhapati gives for these cakras in English, such as "Spirit of Natures" for *mūlādhāra*, "Spirit of Senses" for *svādhiṣṭhāna*, and so on, are not intended to be direct translations of a cakra, but are instead functional descriptions in that they either describe a part of the body at which a cakra resides or denote its sphere of activity that is to be refuted, negated, and/or "canceled" in yogic meditation (see Chapter 4). This is clear by comparing their names in English to the cosmic function that they correspond to in RYB, Sabhapati's Hindi text, as well as Sabhapati's Tamil works CTCSPV and MCVTS. This also clarified when considering their role as part of Sabhapati's scheme of seven or eight *svarūpas* (see Figure 3.8 and Chapters 5 and 6). Additionally, in Sabhapati's descriptions of these cakras he often goes into extended detail about their

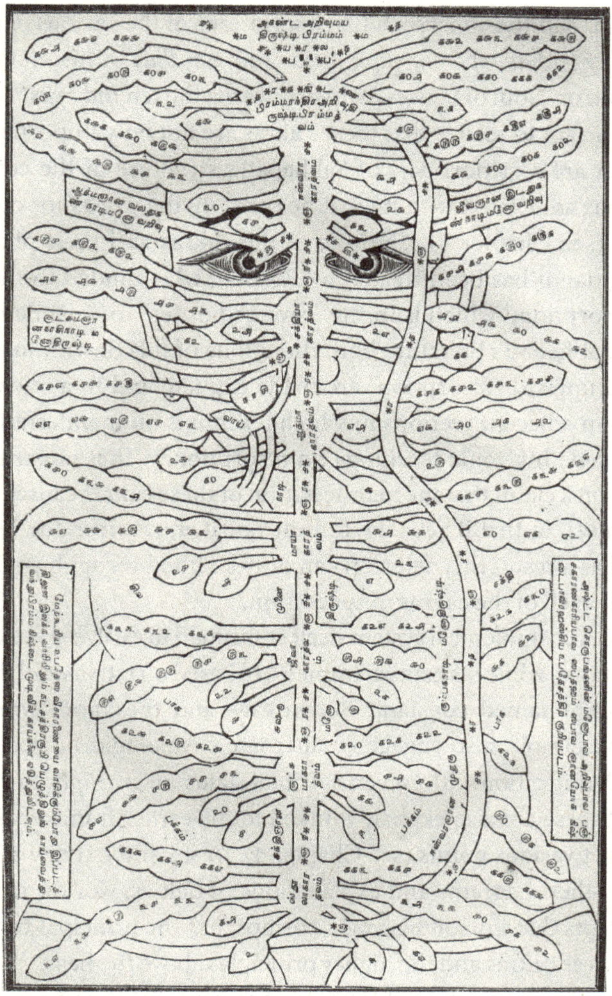

Figure 3.8 A diagram in CTCSPV containing "instruction on the mystery of the steadfast state of the yoga of gnosis, [namely] the states of mind, the states of knowledge, the states of the actions of the five causes, and the seven self-states of the eight inherent natures *(svarūpa)*" (*aṣṭta corupaṅkaḷiṉ maṉōpāva aṟivupāva pancakāraṇakāriyapāva saptaham sapāva nāṉayōka niṣṭaipāvarahasciya upatēcattiṟ kuṟiyapaṭam*), the cosmic svarūpas being located along the central channel where one would expect to find cakras. Scan by the author.

divisions and subdivisions, such his descriptions of the various parts of each sense faculty (*śabda*, *sparśa*, *rūpa*, *rasa*, and *gandha*) in his section on the *svādhiṣṭhāna* or "Soul of Senses," which governs the ten *indriyas*.[64]

It is important to realize that these cakras are not only important to yogic practice but are a critical part of Sabhapati's structure of the cosmos, and each also has associated with it what he calls "divine words" or cosmogonic phonemes (see Chapter 4). The role of the cakras and their phonemes in raising kuṇḍalinī has been treated by Padoux, who alluded to their role in "cosmic resorption," which is in the "reversed order" to "cosmic manifestation."[65] In Sabhapati's literature both directions of this downward "manifestation" and upward "resorption" are made explicit, and in a few cases even referred to in adjacent sections in which teachings on manifestation immediately precede his yogic teachings on resorption.[66] These instructions are predicated on a claim that the manifestation of these cakras causes "delusion" (< Skt. *bhrānti*) in that it veils the Infinite Spirit above from the Finite Spirit below, and as a result this delusion can only be lifted through yogic practice that cancels each of the cakras in succession.

Sabhapati's cosmological system itself continued to evolve and expand over his publications, while his general framework based on tattvas and their bodily correlations remained constant. Both CPSPS and the Tamil work CTCSPV (1889), for example, also engage an alternate cosmological discourse of the practical identification with "seven Spiritual states" or *svarūpas* through meditation, but these are also explicitly linked to the earlier framework of tattvas and cakras at various points (see Chapter 4). CPSPS and CTCSPV also provide numerous other diagrams and explanations of deities, worlds, temples, and other concepts that inhabit his yogic cosmos, but the principal framework is of the tattvas as cakras and the higher principles above the head.

By 1913, which saw the publication of MCVTS, Sabhapati would refer to as many as fourteen sites instead of the original twelve cited in his earlier works. While he retains a description of six lower and six higher cakras, he adds two additional parts of the "thousand-petaled lotus" that he calls *piraṇavastāṉam* (< Skt. *praṇavasthāna*, "place of the syllable Om") and *pirammakñāṉātmakastāṉam* (< Skt. *brahmajñānātmakasthāna*, "place of the soul of the gnosis of Brahman"), both of which are located between *kalāsthāna* and *nādasthāna*.[67] In MCVTS Sabhapati also revised his earlier bodily assignment of *maṇipūraka* to the heart and *anāhata* to the throat, which was somewhat irregular when compared to many other Tantras, including the *Śivasaṃhitā*. Sabhapati instead reassigned *anāhata* to the heart and made some other changes (see Table 3.1 for a comparison of these attributions).

Table 3.1 A comparison of the cakras and assignment to places in the body from VRY1 (1880), CPSPS (1884/1890), RYB (1892), and MCVTS (1913)

Cakra (or related site)	Bodily location (VRY1/CPSPS)	(RYB)	(MCVTS)
parātpara	"Centre of the Skull"	*dvādaśānta* ("end of the twelve") (bodily location not stated)	*pirammarantira ātistāṉam* ("beginning of the fontanelle")
parasthāna	"Top of the Brain"	*mastakādi* ("beginning of the brain")	*pirammarantira mattiyastāṉam* ("middle of the fontanelle")
tatparasthāna	"Middle of the Brain"	*mastakamadhya* ("middle of the brain")	*pirammarantira yantastāṉam* ("end of the fontanelle")
kalāsthāna	"Bottom of the Brain"	*mastakānta* ("end of the brain")	*sahasttirakamala ātistāṉam* ("beginning of the thousand-petaled lotus")
[*praṇavasthāna*]	(not present)	(not present)[a]	*sahasttirakamala mattiyastāṉam* ("middle of the thousand-petaled lotus")
[*brahmajñānātmaka-sthāna*]	(not present)	(not present)	*sahasttirakamala yantasttāṉam* ("end of the thousand-petaled lotus")
nādasthāna	"Centre of the Forehead"	*lalāṭamadhya* ("middle of the forehead")	*lalāṭa mattiyastāṉam* ("middle of the forehead")
bindusthāna	"Centre between the two Eyebrows"	*bhrumadhya* ("middle of the brow")	*puruvamattiyam* ("middle of the brow")
ājñā	"Tip of the Nose"	(bodily location not stated; shown at the nose on Diagram 3)	*nācikārantiram* ("the nostrils of the nose")
viśuddhi	"Centre of the Tongue"	(bodily location not stated; shown at the throat on Diagram 3)	*kaṇṭam* ("throat")
anāhata	"Centre of the Throat"	(bodily location not stated; shown at the heart on Diagram 3)	*hirutayam* ("heart")

(*continued*)

Table 3.1 Continued

	Bodily location		
Cakra (or related site)	(VRY1/CPSPS)	(RYB)	(MCVTS)
maṇipūraka	"Centre of the Heart"	(bodily location not stated; shown at the solar plexus on Diagram 3)	*unti* ("belly" or "navel")[b]
svādhiṣṭhāna	the "Navel"	(bodily location not stated; shown at the navel on Diagram 3)	*nāpi* ("navel")
mūlādhāra	*kuṇḍali* (five inches below navel)	*kuṇḍalisthān* ("place of the *kuṇḍali*)	*kuṇḍali*

[a]RYB refer to what Sabhapati calls *praṇavagāyatrī*, but this is part of *parātpara* and not an independent extension of the cakras.

[b]The Tamil word *unti*, like *nāpi* (< Skt. *nābhi*), can also be translated as "navel."

Note: CTCSPV has been omitted since it depicts these cakras in diagram form but does not present as clear an arrangement as in Sabhapati's other works.

Sabhapati's cosmological system includes thirty-two tattvas in all in the editions of VRY, BRY, and CPSPS (four "Brightnesses," sixteen "Spiritual Rays," and twelve "Spiritual Lights" or "Faculties"; see Figure 3.6) and sixteen tattvas in RYB (Parabrahman/Svayabrahman, Māyā/Śuddhabrahman, Īśvara, Śakti, followed by the twelve "Spiritual Lights" using slightly different terminology).[68] According to Sabhapati, the tattvas gradually "descend" or "emanate" from the Infinite Spirit in the context of an embodied yogic physiology that is connected by what Sabhapati idiosyncratically translates as "pipes" or "organs" (Mpvl. *vāci*, < Skt. *vāśi*, used synonymously with *nāḍī*, "stream" or "channel"), such as what he calls the "Becoming Spiritual Organ" (Mpvl. *suṣumuṉaivāci*, < Skt. *suṣumnāvāśi*, lit. "channel of Suṣumnā"). The agent that moves through these "pipes" is noted as *jñānākāśa* or *prāṇākāśa*, which plays a role in the cancellation of each cakra (see Chapter 4). This alternative cosmological system of thirty-two tattvas incorporates and adapts elements from other systems of tattvas as well as Tantric notions of subtle physiology. To facilitate an apprehension of its unique qualities, I will first enumerate the more standard systems before describing how they contrast with Sabhapati's own system.

The best-known "enumeration" of tattvas is the system of classical Sāṃkhya as exemplified by the *Sāṃkhyakārikā* of Īśvarakṛṣṇa, a work of seventy-three verses (called *kārikās* or "concise statements"), which we know was composed no later than the sixth century CE on account of a translation into Chinese.[69] In this work twenty-five tattvas are enumerated as follows:

1. *puruṣa* "consciousness"
2. *prakṛti* "primal nature or materiality"
3. *buddhi* "intellect or will"
4. *ahaṃkāra* "ego"
5. *manas* "mind"

   buddhīndriyas **"sense capacities"**

6. *śrotra* "hearing"
7. *tvac* "feeling"
8. *cakṣus* "seeing"
9. *rasana* "tasting"
10. *ghrāṇa* "smelling"

    karmendriyas **"action capacities"**

11. *vāc* "speaking"
12. *pāṇī* "grasping" / "apprehending"
13. *pāda* "walking" / "motion"
14. *pāyu* "excreting"
15. *upastha* "generating"

    tanmātras **"subtle elements"**

16. *śabda* "sound"
17. *sparśa* "touch"
18. *rūpa* "form"
19. *rasa* "taste"
20. *gandha* "smell"

    mahābhūtas **"gross elements"**

21. *ākāśa* "space" or "ether"
22. *vāyu* "wind"
23. *agni* "fire"
24. *ap* "water"
25. *pṛthivī* "earth"[70]

In the classical system the goal of *puruṣa* is isolation (*kaivalya*) from *prakṛti* and the generation of the subsequent tattvas that comprise mental and sensible (un)reality.[71] The sets of *indriyas*, subtle elements, and gross elements that make up this "dance" of reality are further correlated as systems of five (i.e., *vāc* is linked to *śabda* and *ākāśa*, and so on). Sabhapati was aware of these lower tattvas and their correlations and describes them in his literature, although they are not independent tattvas but are subordinated into his larger system of thirty-two tattvas as mapped onto the physiology of the subtle or yogic body.[72]

Sabhapati's systems also contrast with the more typical Śaiva enumeration of thirty-six, which became canonical in Śaiva Tantras and was also reflected in the *Tirumantiram*,[73] although this latter text does refer to multiple sets of possible enumerations of the tattvas. Authors of early Śaiva Tantras gradually, and with some variation, added eleven additional principles to the twenty-five tattvas known to Sāṃkhya; these were as follows: (1) Shiva (Śiva), (2) Shiva's power, or Shakti (Śakti), (3) Sadāśiva, (4) Īśvara, (5) (higher) *vidyā*, (6) *māyā*, (7) *kalā*, (8) (lower) *vidyā*, (9) *rāga*, (10) *kāla*, and (11) *niyati*.[74] Numbers seven through eleven (*kalā*, *vidyā*, *rāga*, *kāla*, and *niyati*) came to be known as the five "jackets," "cuirasses," or "sheaths" (Skt. *kañcukas*), which separate pure/transcendent and impure/manifest levels of being.[75]

Another important feature of Sabhapati's system(s) is that they map many but not all of the Sāṃkhyan and/or Śaiva tattvas onto the lower six faculties or cakras of what he terms the "Universal Finite Spirit."[76] Sabhapati's descriptions of Śivarājayoga accordingly have much in common with descriptions of other kinds of "Tantric yoga" as framed according to contemporary scholarly usage.[77] A characteristic feature of Tantric yoga in this context is the cultivation of—and in Sabhapati's case, subsequent cancellation of—a "subtle body" or "yogic body." These latter phrases are both common contemporary translations of *liṅgaśarīra* (lit. "mark[ed] body") or *sūkṣmaśarīra* ("subtle body"), both terms of which were employed by Sabhapati in his literature and diagrams (see Chapter 4). The concept of the subtle body in Hinduism has roots in Upanishads like the *Bṛhaddāraṇyaka Upaniṣad* and the *Kaṭha Upaniṣad*, the *Bhāgavata Purāṇa*, early Tantras like the *Niśvāsatattvasaṃhitā* and *Sārdhatriśatikālottara*, medieval Tantric and yogic works like the *Siddhasiddhāntapaddhati*, *Netratrantra*, *Kubjikāmatatantra*, *Yogabīja*, *Śivasaṃhitā*, *Gorakṣaśataka*, the Tamil *Tirumantiram*, and countless other Sanskrit and vernacular texts throughout South Asia.[78]

By the nineteenth century, however, descriptions of Tantric yoga usually were standardized or simplified to include "wheels" or cakras, three principal "channels" or *nāḍīs* (*suṣumṇā*, *iḍā*, and *piṅgalā*), and the "power of she who is coiled" or *kuṇḍalinīśakti*.[79] The Arthur Avalon collaboration between the Calcutta-based judge John Woodroffe and Indian scholars is perhaps the best-known mediator of this popular standardization, which saw the model of "6+1" cakras presented in the *Kubjikāmatatantra* and Woodroffe's much later classic *The Serpent Power* (itself a translation of *Ṣaṭcakranirūpaṇa*, also of relatively late date) become the most readily recognizable by the public at large.[80] This enumeration of cakras, which correlates with descriptions given in the *Śivasaṃhitā* as well as Swami Vivekananda's lectures on "Râja Yoga", is typically given as follows:

1. *mūlādhāra* "root support" at the perineum
2. *svādhiṣṭhāna* "self-sovereignty" at the genitals
3. *maṇipūra* (or *maṇipūraka*) "city of jewels" at the navel
4. *anāhata* "unstruck" at the heart
5. *viśuddhi* "complete purification" in the throat's region
6. *ājñā* "command" between the eyes
7. *sahasrāra* "thousand-fold" atop the head[81]

As I demonstrate in Chapter 4, Sabhapati's own system of "12 + 4" or sixteen cakras, which he usually calls lotuses (Mpvl. *kamalam*, < Skt. *kamala*), differs from this list in some respects while maintaining some of the names and characteristics of the lower six cakras. Some of the higher eleven Śaiva tattvas additionally appear to be mapped onto Sabhapati's higher six faculties or cakras, such as *rāga* and *kalā*, but somewhat irregularly.

I would argue that the omission or subsummation of certain tattvas in Sabhapati's case (e.g., *sadāśiva*, *vidyā*, and *niyati*) reflects additional shifts and transformations of the Śaiva tattvas as they gradually departed the world of formal Sanskrit texts and entered vernacular yogic milieus, not only in Sabhapati's time but also in preceding centuries. Varying arrangements of tattvas were known to have circulated in premodern Tamil Vīraśaiva milieus, and these lists sometimes differed from formulations of the tattvas in other traditions of Advaita Vedānta and Śaiva Siddhānta.[82] For example, Steinschneider has noted the presence of several additional stages in the circa fifteenth-century text *Oḻiviloṭukkam* "Subsiding upon Annihilation" of Kaṇṇuṭaiya Vaḷḷal through which the "soul comes to shed its ego-consciousness and 'become the godhead' (*civam āy*)."[83] Several of these stages bear direct resonance to Sabhapati's own formulation of tattvas, such as "seeing *parai*" (*parai taricaṉam*), "the state beyond bliss" (*āṉantātītam*), and "annihilation of the ego-consciousness" (*taṟpōta oḻivu*).[84] Steinschneider further notes that these stages resemble another "better-known list of soteriological stages known in Tamil as the 'ten acts' (*taca kāriyam*, Skt. *daśakārya*)," which were elaborated in the circa fourteenth-century *Uṇmaineṟiviḷakkam* "Light on the Path to Truth" attributed to Umāpati Civācāriyar or Cīkāḻi Tattuvanātar and described elsewhere in Tamil Śaiva literature.[85] Related stages were described in Cīkāḻi Ciṟṟampalanāṭikaḷ's *Tukaḷaṟupōtam* "Knowledge that Severs Falsity", which included a verse on *parai yōkam* "yoga for the supreme." The cosmological importance placed on *parai* (< Skt. *parā*) in these texts resonates with Sabhapati's own tripartite division of *parā* "supreme" in his elaboration of Śivarājayoga (see Table 3.1 and Chapter 4), which itself appears genealogically linked to the triad of goddesses (Parāparā, Parā, and Aparā) in the Trika Śaivism of Kashmir.[86]

Such innovations on these tattvas, understood by yogis as spiritual stages, were still happening in Sabhapati's own lifetime; there is evidence that his Vīraśaiva guru Vedashreni Chidambara Swamigal engaged the *tanmātras*, or so-called subtle elements, and these Sāṃkhyan principles are then further reinterpreted and elaborated upon in Sabhapati Swami's own work.[87] At the present time of writing, such innovations in Śaiva yogic cosmology between the *Tirumantiram* of the circa twelfth century, these premodern Tamil Śaiva texts in subsequent centuries, and Sabhapati's late nineteenth-century literature still remain largely uncharted by scholars. There could be other texts, including the writings of Vīraśaivas or the extant songs of the Tamil Siddhas, that would show idiosyncrasies similar to Sabhapati's own integration of the Sāṃkhyan and Śaiva tattvas into the Tantric cakras with their own subtle physiology and could more precisely show their development.[88]

Sabhapati does not interpret these cakras as physical sites in the body—with the possible exception of *mūlādhāra*, which presides over the material elements—but rather these are part of the *liṅgaśarīra* (lit. "mark[ed] body") or the *sūkṣmaśarīra* (translated by him as "sensual and mental body," lit. "subtle body"), both of which are used synonymously. He also alludes to the attainment of a "Conscious and Finite Spiritual body" (*kāraṇaśarīra*) and an "Infinite Spiritual body" (*mahākāraṇaśarīra*), both of which appear to be superior to the *liṅgaśarīra* or *sūkṣmaśarīra*.[89] In his main diagram accompanying each of the three editions of VRY, the sensual and mental body is contrasted with the *sthūlaśarīra* (translated by Sabhapati as the "physical body," lit. "gross body"), from which the *liṅgaśarīra* or *sūkṣmaśarīra* arises through the practice of Śivarājayoga. The "mark" in the Sanskrit compound *liṅgaśarīra* refers to the marker of a person's individuality in transmigration, a meaning that is certainly salient to Sabhapati's literature given his attention to transmigration (see Emancipation and Transmigration).

Given that some of Sabhapati's diagrams explicitly map the body onto Shiva's *liṅga*, it is tempting to assume that Sabhapati also interpreted the compound *liṅgaśarīra* somewhat idiosyncratically as the body of Shiva's *liṅga*, but there is no direct evidence for this and this reading would be irregular. However, there is evidence that Sabhapati did allow for the yogi's body to potentially assume the shape of *liṅgasvarūpa*, or the "inherent form of the *liṅga*," during his prescribed meditations on what he idiosyncratically translates as the "shapes of God."[90] The latter idea is especially prominent in Tamil Siddha cosmology, as reflected both in visual art and in the *Tirumantiram*, where this notion is explicitly expressed in the following verse (v. 1726): *māṉuṭar ākkai vaṭivu civaliṅgam*, "The human body is in the shape of Shiva's phallus."[91] It is therefore most likely that his diagrams depicting the body of the yogi in a similar shape as Shiva's *liṅga* are intended to depict a meditational assumption of the *liṅgasvarūpa* and not the *liṅgaśarīra* as the body that transmigrates.

Finally, it must be mentioned that the Universal Spirit's division into a cosmogonic pair (Universal Infinite Spirit and Universal Finite Spirit) may seem semantic, but it masks a critical point. We have already seen that the Universal Infinite Spirit is essentially another name for Shiva operating in his passive capacity as Brahman. However, Sabhapati's division of this Universal Spirit into "active" and "passive" roles indicates one of two probable options: (1) that the Universal Finite Spirit could also be related to the Shakti (< Skt. *śakti*, "power"), or active feminine principle of creation, as made more explicit in other texts of Tantric philosophy that describe a kind of interplay (*līlā*) between Shiva and the Shakti as the source of the cosmos; or (2) that these two roles are part of Shiva's own dual nature. As Padoux has pointed out, it is the first idea that is salient in Kashmir nondual Śaivism, where "Śiva assumes two aspects," the first being an "utterly transcendent principle" and the second, or the Shakti, being the "source of the entire manifestation" and the "Word aspect of the primary principle."[92] This is corroborated by Sabhapati's citation of the Indic terms from which he arrives at the interpretive translation "Active Principle," which is described as not only *īsvarattuvam* (< Skt. *īśvaratva*, lit. "lordship") but also *saktittuvam* (< Skt. *śaktitva*, "a state of power" or more colloquially "Shakti-ness"). Furthermore, the idea of a division of the ultimate Brahman into a Paraśiva and his *śakti* or *parai* (< Skt. *parā*, see above) is common to the Pratyabhijñā school as well as to Tamil Vīraśaivism, which is possibly the source of Sabhapati's own cosmological division here.[93]

Other parts of his literature also variously reflect a division into Shiva and Shakti. A similar pairing is also reflected in his heavily Sanskritized Hindi work (RYB), which mentions that each of the Tantric lotuses or cakras has a "division of Shiva" (Hi. *śivabhāg*) and a "division of Shakti" (Hi. *śaktibhāg*), albeit this division refers to the twelve faculties themselves and not the primal cosmogony.[94] Sabhapati also instructs his followers to meditate upon the physical stone of Shiva's phallus (Skt. *śivaliṅga*) as being joined to the "seat" (*pīṭha*, which refers to the sculpted *yoni* portion of a *liṅgam-yoni*) of Gaurī, or Parvatī, the consort of Shiva, which also reflects his attentiveness to the Shakti despite the fact that depictions of such a "joining" are considered to be rather late Tantric aniconographic developments in the material history of *śivaliṅgas*.[95] Finally, the role of the Shakti in cosmogony is more explicitly reflected in a chart of familial relationships provided in his Tamil work CTCSPV that openly describes a "father" and "mother" that together create the individual (non-Universal) Finite Spirit or *jīvātman*, for which see the section Household of the Body's Truth (*dehatattva*).

Emancipation and Transmigration

Another principal expression of Sabhapati's cosmogonic system is found in the third way of removing doubts about the tattvas, namely the "emancipation of the Finite Spirit from this earthly bondage." This is part of Sabhapati's broader instructions on his idea of reincarnation, which he calls "transmigration" or "evolution," instructions designed to encourage the student to "distinguish between the everlasting and transitory things and the momentary pleasures of this and of the heavenly world."[96] In a section entitled "Instructions on the mystery and theory of the successive emanation and evolution," Sabhapati notes two kinds of evolution, "Progressive evolutions for the Meditations" and "Decreasing evolutions for the Vice and sin."[97] The first kind is what Eliade and other academics as well as philosophers before him would have likely perceived as a form of "eternal return," and is described by Sabhapati as follows:

> From grass to herbs to trees; from trees to insects; from insects to fishes; from fishes to birds; from birds to beasts; from beasts to mankind; from mankind to Deotas [= Skt. *devatā*, a kind of "local deity"]; from Deotas to astral bodily deities; from deities to spiritual powers; from spiritual powers

> to the Infinite spirit, whence the emanation called the final salvation takes place.[98]

While the first evolution is accomplished by following out Sabhapati's prescribed techniques of yogic meditation, the second evolution is caused by actions of vice, and is described as follows:

> From deotas to men; from men to any of the abovementioned [*sic*] lower stages according to the degree of their sins, whence they have again to recover their stages as said above; the lowest stages of creatures if they become ferocious and more sinful are even transmigrated to the degraded stages of herbs and grass &c: with full capacity to revive the progressive state according to the scale of their vice and virtue.[99]

Sabhapati adds to this a clarification that once the stage of deota/*devatā* is reached, there is no longer any decreasing evolution but only a "progressive state to attain its self universal Infinite Spiritual state."[100] He closes his treatment on "evolution," which bears some resemblance to the Great Chain of Being, by noting that transmigrations can be grouped in three categories, which he calls "firmamental worldly divisions" that correspond to the three *guṇa*s or "qualities":

> The souls of meditation are transmigrated into the worlds of silence and peacefulness [Mpvl. *cattuvalōkam*, < Skt. *sattvaloka*], The souls of virtue are transmigrated into the worlds of suffering and enjoyments [Mpvl. *rajalōkam*, < Skt. *rajaloka*]. The souls of vice are transmigrated into the worlds of punishments and reformations [Mpvl. *tamōlōkam*, < Skt. *tamoloka*].[101]

The addition in this final paragraph of a transmigration for "souls of virtue" is notable since it underscores Sabhapati's belief that being "virtuous" or "good" is not good enough; meditation is required to enter the highest *sāttvika* world of "silence and peacefulness."

The above system warrants further comparison with H. P. Blavatsky's own later system of reincarnation that she adopted during a period between the publication of *Isis Unveiled* (1877) and *The Secret Doctrine* (1888), a period during which she met Sabhapati Swami, in November 1879 (see Chapter 1).[102] While there is no evidence that Blavatsky obtained any of her teachings on reincarnation directly from Sabhapati, the topic could very well have arisen during their meeting and been thought-provoking for both parties.[103] We know that her associate Henry Olcott possessed a copy of the first edition of VRY (VRY1, published in 1880), which mentions Sabhapati's teachings on transmigration, but this work does not go into much detail about his views on the matter. On the contrary, the Second Book of CPSPS, published in 1890, contains the bulk of Sabhapati's doctrines on transmigration in English, and it is plausible that the success of Blavatsky's *The Secret Doctrine* prompted Sabhapati to articulate his own views on transmigration further since we know he was in contact with Theosophical circles in Bombay around this time; he also mentions Blavatsky and Olcott by name as well as "Theosophical Societies" in CPSPS (see Chapter 1 and Sabhapati and the "Theosophical Societies").

Additionally, Sabhapati in at least three of his main works (CPSPS, RYB, and CTCSPV) included elaborate diagrams, each slightly different (see Figure 3.9 for one example), which visually depict an individual's transmigration based on the karmic deeds of virtue or vice (*Skt. pāpa-puṇya*). These diagrams are anthropomorphic and are part of a larger type of game sometimes called the "Board of Knowledge" (Hi. *gyān chaupar*). This game was also developed in Jaina, Vaiṣṇava, and even Muslim religious milieus and, as Jacob Schmidt-Madsen has also demonstrated, provided inspiration for the modern "Snakes and Ladders" board game.[104]

Household of the Body's Truth (*dehatattva*)

Sabhapati's English-language works (the editions of VRY and CPSPS), the Bengali translation (BRY), and his Hindi work (RYB) all participate in the philosophical system I have outlined in the previous sections. However, his Tamil works (especially CTCSPV) provide a connected but nevertheless distinct cosmological scheme that is worth considering separately. A chart published in CTCSPV is entitled "Instruction on the mystery that is the sprout of truth in the body, [described in terms of] familial and domestic life" (Tam. *tēkatattuvavampu samcāra vāḻkkai rakaciyōpatēcam*). The phrase "truth of the body" (or "reality of the body," "doctrine of the body," Mpvl. *tēkatattuvam*, < Skt. *dehatattva*) accords with what we saw in the previous section about the Universal Spirit residing in one's body, specifically, the head (Skt. *kapāla*), which means that the rest of the universe is also embodied in the various networks of yogic physiology. This chart provides another way of seeing

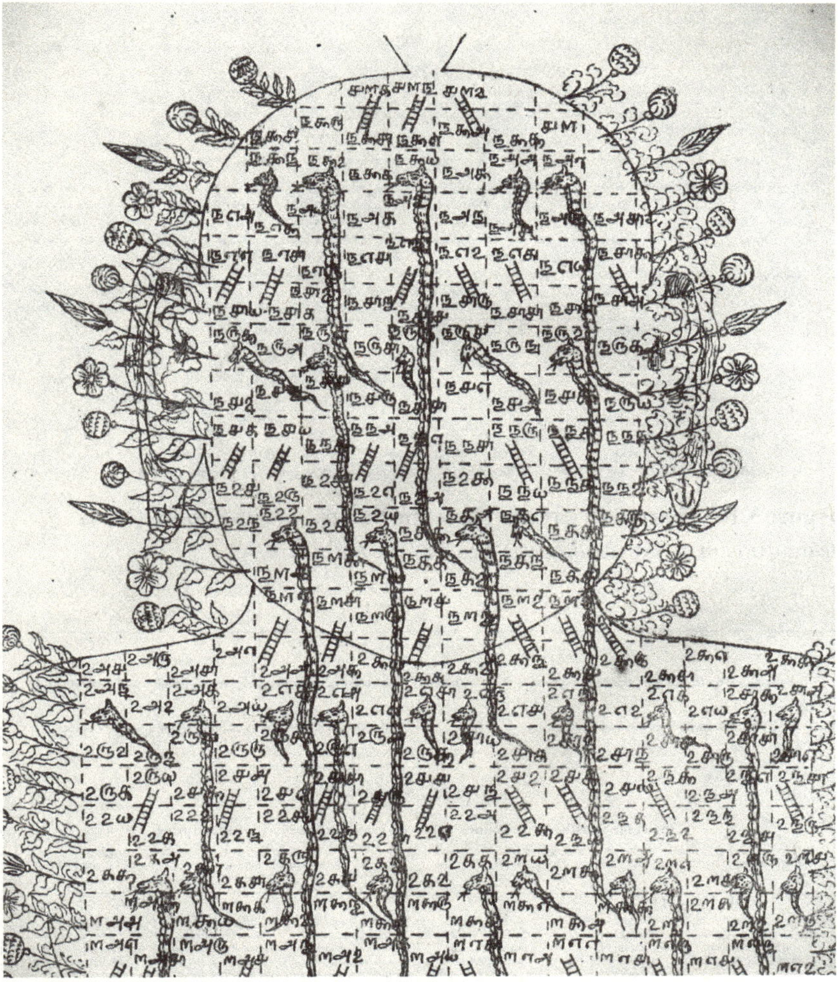

Figure 3.9 Diagram Eight of CTCSPV that shows transmigrations in a "Snakes and Ladders" form. Scan by the author.

these correspondences as formulated in terms of domestic relationships rather than the list of "kingdoms" or cakras.

As can be seen from Figures 3.10 and 3.11, there are two cosmic principles that lead to the generation of the "Finite Spirit," which as we saw above is Sabhapati's translation of Sanskrit *jīvātman*, today more often translated "animate self" or "individual soul," in contrast to *paramātman*, "supreme self" or "supreme soul." Here we find "Universal Spirit" for *paramātman*, as expected,

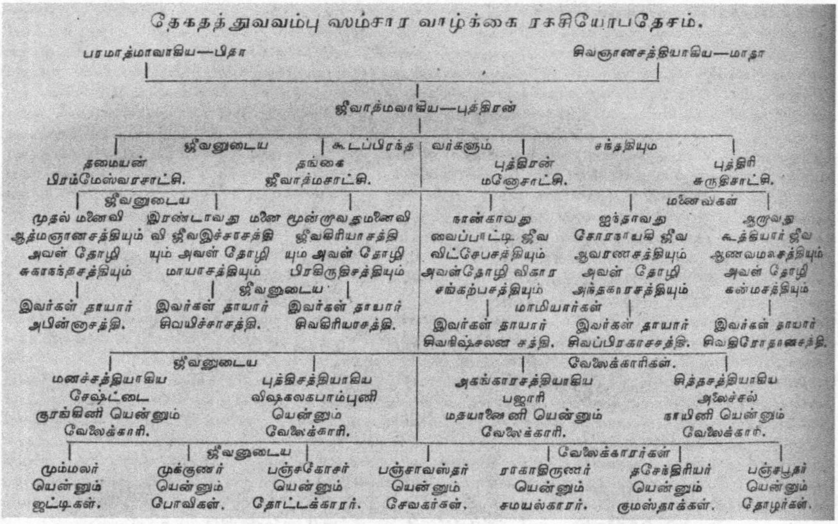

Figure 3.10 Chart from CTCSPV depicting the "truth of the body" (Mpvl. *tēkatattuvam*, = Skt. *dehatattva*). Scan by the author.

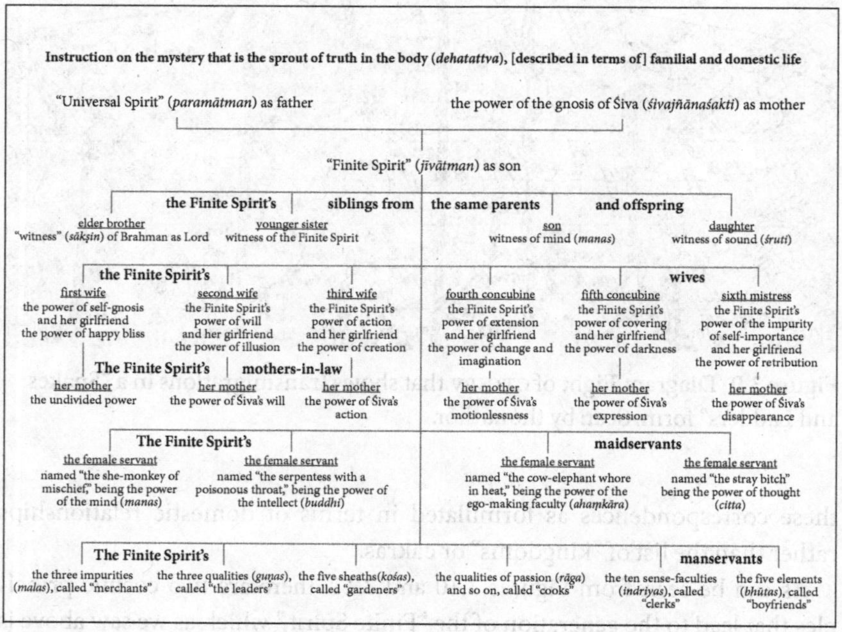

Figure 3.11 English translation of Figure 3.10 (original is in Tamil only), maintaining some of Sabhapati's own translations in his English works (such as "Finite Spirit" for *jīvātman*) for ease of comparison and contrast with the principles of VRY1 and CPSPS.

but we also have a principle occupying the spot of "mother": "Shiva's power of the gnosis" (Mpvl. *civañāṉacatti*, < Skt. *śivajñānaśakti*). The Finite Spirit is not alone, either, but has two siblings, an elder brother (Tam. *tamaiyaṉ*) and a younger sister (*taṅkai*), both of whom are "witnesses" (Mpvl. *cāṭci*, < Skt. *sākṣin*, lit. "eyewitness"), a recurrent term we saw in Sabhapati's works in English (see Figure 3.6 above). Also noted are two other "witnesses" described as the Finite Spirit's offspring, a son named the "witness of mind" (Mpvl. *maṉōcāṭci*, < Skt. *manaḥsākṣin*) and a daughter named the "witness of sound" (Mpvl. *curuticāṭci*, < Skt. *śrutisākṣin*), the latter of which perhaps has a scriptural connotation as a revelation obtained through hearing (*śruti* interpreted as sacred text).

This primal Shakti (Śakti) is further differentiated as six "wives" (Tam. *maṉaivikaḷ*) of the Finite Spirit, each of whom represent a different "power" (Mpvl. *catti*, < Skt. *śakti*):

1. "power of self-gnosis" (Mpvl. *ātmañāṉacatti*, < Skt. *ātmajñānaśakti*)
2. "power of will" (Mpvl. *iccācatti*, < Skt. *icchāśakti*)
3. "power of action" (Mpvl. *kiriyācatti*, < Skt. *kriyāśakti*)
4. "power of extension" (Mpvl. *viṭcēpacatti*, < Skt. *vikṣepaśakti*)
5. "power of covering" (Mpvl. *āvaraṇacatti*, < Skt. *āvaraṇaśakti*)
6. "power of the impurity of self-importance" (Mpvl. *āṇavamalacatti*, < Skt. *āṇavamalaśakti*)

Three of these wives, numbers 4 through 6, are "concubines" or "mistresses" (Tam. *vaippāṭṭi*, *cōranāyaki*, *kūttiyār*) rather than wives proper, adding an interesting social dimension to these powers. These six are in turn accompanied by a "female companion" or "girlfriend" (Tam. *tōḻi*) who further clarifies the nature of the above powers, and are respectively as follows:

1. "power of happy bliss" (Mpvl. *cukānantacatti*, < Skt. *sukhānandaśakti*)
2. "power of illusion" (Mpvl. *māyācatti*, < Skt. *māyāśakti*)
3. "power of creation" (Mpvl. *pirakiruticatti*, < Skt. *prakṛtiśakti*)
4. "power of change and imagination" (Mpvl. *vikāra caṅkaṟpacatti*, < Skt. *vikāra saṃkalpaśakti*)
5. "power of darkness" (Mpvl. *antakāracatti*, < Skt. *andhakāraśakti*)
6. "power of retribution" (Mpvl. *kaṉmacatti*, < Skt. *karmaśakti*)

Finally, these "wives" also themselves have mothers, who are in turn the Finite Spirit's "mothers-in-law" (Tam. *māmiyārkaḷ*) and are also linked to the Shakti on account of their nature. They are ascribed to various powers of Shiva specifically, and are as follows:

1. "undivided power" (Mpvl. *apiṉṉācatti*, < Skt. *abhinnaśakti*)
2. "power of Shiva's will" (Mpvl. *civayiccācatti*, < Skt. *śivecchāśakti*)
3. "power of Shiva's action" (Mpvl. *civakiriyācatti*, < Skt. *śivakriyāśakti*)
4. "power of Shiva's motionlessness" (Mpvl. *civaniṣcalaṉa catti*, < Skt. *śivaniścalana śakti*)
5. "power of Shiva's expression" (Mpvl. *civappirakācacatti*, < Skt. *śivaprakāśaśakti*)
6. "power of Shiva's disappearance" (Mpvl. *civatirōtāṉacatti*, < Skt. *śivatirodhānaśakti*)

Toward the bottom of the chart we find two more sets of relationships to the Finite Spirit, "female workers" or "maidservants" (Tam. *vēlaikkārikaḷ*) and "male workers" or "manservants" (Tam. *vēlaikkārarkaḷ*). These are none other than the principal and recognizable tattvas of Sāṃkhya philosophy that emerge following "pure consciousness" (*puruṣa*) and "primordial materiality" (*mūlaprakṛti*), with the difference that Sabhapati's list adds "thought" (*citta*) as a tattva in addition to "mind" (*manas*), omits the five subtle elements (*tanmātras*), and adds gendered qualities and creative names that were not present in the original enumeration of Sāṃkhya.[105] The four "female workers" are as follows, described in Tamil in not-so-flattering animalistic terms in addition to their more technical Sanskritic referents:

1. "the she-monkey of mischief" (Tam. *cēṣṭai kuraṅkiṉi*), as the "power of the mind" (Mpvl. *maṉaccatti*, < Skt. *manaḥśakti*)
2. "the serpentess with a poisonous throat" (Tam. *viṣakalakapāmpuṉi*), as the "power of the intellect" (Mpvl. *putticatti*, < Skt. *buddhiśakti*)
3. "the cow-elephant whore in heat" (Tam. *pajāri matayāṉaiṉi*) as the "power of the ego-making faculty" (Mpvl. *ahaṃkāracatti*, < Skt. *ahaṃkāraśakti*)
4. "the stray bitch" or "wandering female dog" (*alaiccal nāyiṉi*) as the "power of thought" (Mpvl. *cittacatti*, < Skt. *cittaśakti*)

Such an equation of tattvas with animals is not unique to Sabhapati but is also found in the *Tirumantiram*, where the *indriyas* are also compared to animals, including an elephant in rut.[106] The manservants are six in number, and round out the lower tattvas, which are given personal suffixes in Tamil that turn them into the equivalent of a *bahuvrīhi* in Sanskrit:

1. The "man of the three impurities" (Tam. *mummalar* = Skt. *trimala*), called "the merchants" or "wrestlers" (Tam. *jaṭṭikaḷ*)
2. The "man of the three qualities" (Tam. *mukkuṇar* = Skt. *triguṇa*), called "the leaders" or "they who make things go" (Tam. *pōvikaḷ*)
3. The "man of the five sheaths" (Mpvl. *pañcakōcar*, < Skt. *pañcakośa*), called "the gardeners" (*tōṭṭakkārar*)
4. The "man who feels passion and so on" (Tam. *rākātiruṇar*, partially < Skt. *rāgādi*), called "the cooks" (Tam. *camayalkārar*)
5. The "man of the ten sense-faculties" (Mpvl. *tacēntiriyar*, < Skt. *daśendriya*), called "the clerks" (Tam. *kumastākkaḷ*)
6. The "man of the five elements" (Mpvl. *pañcapūtar*), called "boyfriends" or "male companions" (Tam. *tōḻarkaḷ*)

These six "manservants" serve as an important connecting point between this Tamil *dehatattva* cosmology and Sabhapati's descriptions of the twelve faculties or cakras in his English, Bengali, and Hindi works. If one looks carefully, the order of these six "manservants" somewhat matches the order of the lower six cakras, with the exception of *anāhata* (see Table 3.2).

The higher cakras that correspond to *bindu*, *nāda*, *kalā*, *tatpara*, *para*, and *parātpara* are not directly reflected on the above *dehatattva* chart, but appear to be an alternate model of framing the same doctrine of the "descent" or

Table 3.2 A partial correlation of the "manservants" of CTCSPV with the lower six cakras and their locations in CPSPS and the three editions of VRY

Manservant (CTCSPV)	Cakra (CPSPS/VRY)	Corresponding principles (both texts)
"merchants" or "wrestlers"	*ājñā*	the three impurities
"leaders"	*viśuddhi*	the three qualities
"gardeners"	*anāhata*	the five sheaths (CTCSPV) or the internal instrument (CPSPS/VRY)
"cooks"	*maṇipūraka*	the passions and so on
"clerks"	*svādhiṣṭhāna*	the ten sense faculties
"boyfriends"	*mūlādhāra*	the five elements

"emanation" of Shiva's powers into the internal body and external cosmos. The inclusion of multiple ways of framing this cosmology in his works could also reflect Sabhapati's exposure to yogic teachings in north India during his travels (see Chapter 1) and his attempts to reconcile disparate details.

While Sabhapati's system of faculties is unique in its synthesis of Tamil familial roles and the Śaiva and Sāṃkhya systems of tattvas, the Sanskritic phrase *dehatattva* understood in more general terms is not limited to his Tamil literature or even Śaiva philosophy more broadly. Instead, *dehatattva* is a pan-Indian concept, being also prevalent in Bengali Tantric milieus where it is a *tatsama* from Sanskrit (Bng. *deha+tattva*). For example, Carol Salomon has correctly noted that the doctrine is prevalent among the Bāuls of Bengal, who have harmonized Vaiṣṇava, Islamic Sufi, Buddhist Tantric, and other currents:

> The Bāul saying, "Whatever is in the universe is in the receptacle [that is, the body]," sums up the doctrine of *dehatattva*, "the truth in the body." The Bāuls, like other tantrics, take this saying literally and locate cities, mountains, rivers, pilgrimage places—virtually everything on the map—in the human body.[107]

Hans Harder has additionally noted that this concept is present among the Maijbhandaris of Bangladesh, where it is interpreted even more directly in Sufi Islamic contexts.[108] The link between these Bengali sources and Sabhapati's similar use of *dehatattva* to describe his own embodied system of cosmogony appears to be linked to some kind of common denominator on the body's formation that historically informed both. While there is evidence of cross-pollination in Sanskrit between these contexts (e.g., via texts like the *Kularṇava Tantra*, and the *Bhāgavata Purāṇa*), the separation of language between vernacular Tamil and Bengali is such that by the modern period a translation of Sabhapati's own work into Bengali (BRY) was deemed necessary.

I would postulate based on the available evidence that the most likely historical link for these striking kinds of connections on *dehatattva* is Buddhist Tantra. Some of the earliest teachings on *dehatattva* in Bengali are documented in the Caryāpadas, medieval Buddhist songs about the universe in one's body, among many other topics, which were later interpreted by Sufi mediators. While the connections between Buddhist so-called *sahajiyā* or "innate" Tantra and Bengali conceptions of *dehatattva* have been relatively well documented, especially by Bengali scholars,[109] unfortunately little research has yet been done to trace Buddhist Tantric antecedents in Tamil vernacular yogic milieus that would enable such historical divergences and reformulations to be better understood via recourse to surviving texts and inscriptions. On the one hand, one possible link could be the yogic and/or Nāth traditions based in Srisailam (and more broadly across the Deccan) in the early centuries of the second millennium, which were heavily cross-pollinated with Buddhist Siddha traditions. We now have convincing manuscript and material evidence that the early roots of haṭha yoga (< Skt. *haṭhayoga*) that later informed the Nāth Yogīs in both south and north India were at least partially cultivated in Buddhist Tantric milieus.[110] The Nāth Yogīs were also known to have a presence in the city of Nagapattinam, a port city on the Bay of Bengal adjacent to the Nagore Dargah where Sabhapati resided for at least several months (see Chapter 1). While the precise connections are elusive, the tumulus or *jīvasamādhi* of the Tamil Siddha Kōrakkar, traditionally held to be identical to the semilegendary figure Gorakṣanātha, is located in North Poigainallur (Vaṭakku Poykainallūr), a mere four miles south of Nagore, and traditionally believed to be part of a wider network of Nāths in the region.[111] Additionally, a so-called Cave of Kōrakkar is located in Sathuragiri, one of Sabhapati's stops according to his hagiographies. On the other hand, while the presence of Nāth yogic communities in Bengal remains a point of scholarly contention,[112] there is no doubt that *dehatattva* nevertheless remains an important part of Bāul fakiri *sādhana* that was to some extent derived from Buddhist Tantra; even the term itself greatly informed Vaiṣṇava, Sufi, and Śaiva and Śākta Tantric cosmology as expressed in music and literature.[113]

Connections with Tamil Śaiva Discourse

As mentioned at the beginning of this chapter, Sabhapati's guru-*paramparā* explicitly connects his literature to Tamil Vīraśaiva circles, such as that related to the circa seventeenth-century author Kumara Devar (Kumāratēvar) and his guru Perur Santhalinga Swamigal (Perūr Cāntaliṅka Cuvāmikaḷ). This connection is clear from Sabhapati's references to his gurus in his literature, especially CPSPS and his extant literature in the Tamil language. However, Sabhapati's own teachings on Śivarājayoga also independently reflect a connection with a kind of Śaiva philosophy, including a Śivayoga or "Yoga for Shiva," which is specific to south India. In other words, his literature did not appear in a vacuum and reflects developments in Tamil Saivism in the centuries that follow what Alexis Sanderson has described as the "Śaiva Age."[114] While there are many specific developments that could be minutely traced by means of a comprehensive analysis of Sabhapati's literature, in this section I will highlight three among the most evident: (1) the Tamil-specific development of Śivayoga (Tamil *civayōkam*) as reflected in texts like the *Oḻiviloṭukkam*, (2) the notion of a "doctrine of unity" (Tam. *aikkiyavātam*) that came to occupy a kind of in-between zone between Vedānta (*māyāvātam*) and Śaiva Siddhānta (*caiva cittāntam*), and (3) a south India-specific framing of a "fourfold internal instrument" (*caturantaḥkaraṇa*).

The first aspect is the broader development of Śivayoga (Mpvl. *civayōkam*), which Sabhapati more often calls Śivarājayoga (*civarājayōkam*) but, in at least one instance in VRY1, simply "Shiva yoga" (Śivayoga), implying that the two for him were interchangeable. As I have already pointed out and will return to in detail in the following chapter, Śivayoga was also linked to a Kannada milieu via the Sanskrit text *Śivayogapradīpikā* and its reception history, but it is important to keep in mind that there were Tamil-specific developments that more clearly informed its philosophical development and context in Sabhapati's literature.

One of the most important texts to anchor Sabhapati's contextual understanding of Śivayoga and its accompanying cosmology was the aforementioned circa fifteenth-century work *Oḻiviloṭukkam*, translated by Steinschneider as "The Subsiding [into the godhead] upon the annihilation [of the ego-consciousness],"[115] or, translated another way, "concealment [*oṭukkam*] in dissolution [*oḻivu*]." This text, attributed to one Kaṇṇuṭaiya Vaḷḷal, is principally known through its earliest commentary, attributed to the circa seventeenth- to eighteenth-century Vīraśaiva thinker Thiruporur Chidambara Swamigal (Tiruppōrūr Citampara Cuvāmikaḷ). It was also later published by Chidambaram Ramalinga Adigal (Citampara Irāmaliṅka Aṭikaḷ), whom as I mentioned in Chapter 1 is referred to in one of Sabhapati's accounts as his childhood friend.[116] The connection between Thiruporur Chidambara Swamigal and Sabhapati Swami is more explicit, however, as the former is in Sabhapati Swami's own guru-*paramparā* (see the beginning of this chapter). While an analysis of this text is outside the scope of this book, it is clear that several of its concepts, such as the dissolution of the tattvas; the knowledge of the *paṟai*, or supreme principle, as "the fulfillment of Grace"; an emphasis on the dissolution of "I-ness" (Mpvl. *taṟpōtam*) that leads to a mingling with the supreme Shiva (*civam*, akin to Sabhapati's *śivamaya*; see Figure 3.6); and the emphasis on various states of "beyond" (Mpvl. *atīta*) are all also foundational themes that also inform the practice of Śivarājayoga in Sabhapati's literature. As mentioned in the previous section, Sabhapati's division of this supreme principle into his three highest cakras also resembles the Trika division of the Goddess into three forms (Parāparā, Parā, and Aparā), and he may have also been inspired by this formulation during his travels in northwestern India and Kashmir (see Chapter 1). At the same time, it is clear from his vernacular literature in Tamil that another source of his inspiration was an already extant corpus of Tamil Śaiva literature that included texts like *Oḻiviloṭukkam*.

The second and related Tamil Śaiva-specific factor is that Sabhapati's work is also a late reflection of the increasing "Vedanticization" of the Śaiva Siddhānta and Vīraśaivism that had already been taking place for at least three centuries prior to his publications.[117] In other words, Sabhapati was not the first to equate the gnosis or knowledge (Skt. *jñāna*) of Vedānta with the gnosis of Siddhānta, perhaps most succinctly expressed by what later came to be framed as an "equal flavor" or *samarasa* (Mpvl. *camaracam*), which we know Sabhapati was aware of given the title of his (now nonextant) first work in Tamil as well as its use in his other publications (see Chapter 2). Sabhapati was instead participating in a long tradition of discursive reconciliation that had led to aspects of Vedānta gradually informing Śaiva Siddhānta to the extent that, by the time Sabhapati was writing, there was little real distinction perceived between the two in at least some religious milieus.[118] This was a notable development since "neo-Saiddhāntika" works like the *Civakñāṉacittiyār*, one of the most important texts of Tamil Śaiva philosophy, refuted the view of Vedānta that "Brahma jnana is knowledge that the Ego is Brahman. And when the self becomes self, and enjoys the self in the self, and when such things as body, senses, prāṇa, lose their form and name, when the great elements are destroyed, and the self remains unchangeable, this knowledge is possible."[119]

By Sabhapati's time, however, an acceptable point of view emerged for Tamil Vedantins and exponents of Siddhānta alike. This middle ground was likely inspired by the Vīraśaiva concept of *liṅgaikyabhāva*, or "the state of being united with [Shiva's] phallus" as well as the later *liṅgāṅgasamarasa*, or "equanimity as an auxiliary of [Shiva's] phallus"; both appear to have been states of interiorization that end in a unity or culmination with Shiva. The former concept, for example, is found in the *Śivayogapradīpikā* as *liṅgaikyādvaitabhāva*, "or the state of non-dual unity with [Shiva's] phallus."[120] Among Tamil Vīraśaiva authors such as those in Sabhapati's own *paramparā*, however, this unity was more abstractly framed as *aikkiyavātam* (< Skt. *aikyavāda*), or the doctrine that one could achieve a kind of unity with Shiva. Sabhapati engages such discourses in his own literature, citing (1) "Atheism" (Mpvl. *nāstīkamatam*, < Skt. *nāstikamata*), (2) "Dualism or Manicheism" (Mpvl. *tuvaitamāyāstāpaṉamatam*, < Skt. *dvaitamāyāsthāpana-mata*), (3) "Theism" (Mpvl. *caivacittāntamatam*, < Skt. *śaivasiddhāntamata*), (4) "Vadantism" [*sic*] (Mpvl. *vētāntamatam*, < Skt. *vedāntamata*), and finally (5) "Believing the Soul is ever and ever the very Universal Infinite Spirit or the Self" (Mpvl. *aikkiyapirmmakñāṉa attuvaitamatam*, < Skt. *aikyabrahmajñāna advaitamata*).[121] For Sabhapati these are gradual stages, and he considered only the last (number 5) to be "perfectly true" and to "prove with Head and Heart that truth."[122] The main philosophical hurdle to overcome in this ideal of self-identification would have been the presence of the *āṇavamala*, or the "filth of particles," which in more hard-line expressions of Saiddhāntika doctrine always separated the *jīva* or individual from Shiva.[123] By Sabhapati's time, however, it was possible to relax this doctrine, and the idea of *āṇavamala* no longer had the explanatory force it may have once had. Instead, the assumed existence of the three *mala*s (including *āṇavamala*) were a development embodied in the *ājñācakra*, and the *mala*s were to be abolished relatively early in the schema of refutations and cancellations of the cakras as part of the practice of Śivarājayoga.

The third and final point is more technical than doctrinal, however, and can therefore serve as a check on the above broader philosophical commonalities, which, as clear and historically traceable as they may be in Sabhapati's case, must nevertheless to some extent remain imprecise and contextual. This is Sabhapati's consistent and technical use of *caturantaḥkaraṇa*, or "four-fold internal instrument," in his English, Tamil, and Hindi works alike. As mentioned previously, the *antaḥkaraṇa*, or "internal instrument," is an important concept in classical Sāṃkhya that has pervaded many systems of Indian thought since. In Sabhapati's literature, however, one finds "thought" (*citta*) in addition to "mind" (*manas*) (see Figures 3.10 and 3.11), whereas only "mind" was present in the original categorization of the *antaḥkaraṇa* known to classical Sāṃkhya; *citta* was not considered as a separate part of the *antaḥkaraṇa*.[124] While this may strike a scholar of yoga philosophy as idiosyncratic, this idea of a "fourfold" *antaḥkaraṇa* is not Sabhapati's own invention. Instead, the *caturantaḥkaraṇa* is a technical idea that is traceable to relevant texts in Tamil Vedānta and Śaiva philosophy, adding even more evidence of Sabhapati's inextricable connection to these milieus.

For example, the circa fourteenth-century text *Tukaḷaṟupōtam*, or "Knowledge That Severs Falsity," attributed to one Ciṟṟampala Nāṭikaḷ, offers instructions for "the obtaining of Shiva" (Tam. *civappēṟu*) and includes many topics that are clearly resonant with Sabhapati's cosmological system, including "states" (Mpvl. *avattai*, < Skt. *avasthā*) and stages of "blaming the elements" (Tam. *pūtap paḻippu*) and "feeling beyond the sense-capacities" (Tam. *poṟiyaṟa uṇartal*). However, whereas these three previous topics could be found in other Śaiva religious texts even outside of Tamil milieus, the *Tukaḷaṟupōtam* also includes a section (verses 14–15) on the "purification of the internal organ" (Mpvl. *antakkaraṇacutti*, < Skt. *antaḥkaraṇaśuddhi*). This internal organ, as in Sabhapati's literature, is not tripartite as in Sāṃkhya but rather is explicitly fourfold, and likewise consists of the "mind" (*manas*), "intellect" (*buddhi*), "thought" (*citta*), and the "ego-faculty" (*ahaṃkāra*), each of which is attributed to the *a*, *u*, *m*, and *bindu* of the *praṇava* or syllable Om.[125]

In Sabhapati's Tamil literature, as mentioned above, each part of the fourfold internal instrument is grouped with the others as the four "female workers": (1) "the she-monkey of mischief" (Tam. *cēṣṭai kuraṅkiṉi*), as the "power of the mind" (Mpvl. *maṉaccatti*, < Skt. *manaśakti*); (2) "the serpentess with a poisonous throat" (Tam. *viṣakalakapāmpuṉi*), as the "power of the intellect" (Mpvl. *putticatti*, < Skt. *buddhiśakti*); (3) "the cow-elephant whore in heat" (Tam. *pajāri matayāṉaiṉi*) as the "power of the ego-making faculty" (Mpvl. *ahaṃkāracatti*, < Skt. *ahaṃkāraśakti*); and (4) "the stray bitch" (or "wandering female dog," *alaiccaḷ nāyiṉi*) as the "power of thought" (Mpvl. *cittacatti*, < Skt. *cittaśakti*). This concept of a fourfold internal instrument is not limited to Sabhapati's vernacular Tamil literature but is also embedded in his earliest English works that reached translocal audiences. For example, in the editions of VRY the "Sadurantakarana" (i.e., *caturantaḥkaraṇa*) is attributed to the "Ninth Kingdom" or *anāhata cakra*, and is also at one point related to the emanation of the *maṇipūraka cakra* below the *anāhata*, as in the following passage:

> Consider that in the centre of the heart the above Jivatma [Skt. *jīvātmā*, < *jīvātman*] becomes the finite Spirit of Notions and Passions. These notions are either of Mana-antakarana,[126] Booddhi anta-karana (or intellectual ideas),[127] and Ahankar anta-karana (egotistic ideas),[128] chitta antukkarna (doubtful ideas).[129]

The concept of the fourfold internal instrument is also found in Sabhapati's Hindi work RYB, proving that it was considered a key point of Sabhapati's cosmology that could be exported and "relocalized" for his readers in north India.[130] Just as in Sabhapati's Tamil and English works, where the four components of *manas*, *buddhi*, *ahaṃkāra*, and *citta* are clearly outlined, in RYB the *caturantaḥkaraṇ* is, in addition to being linked to the Sanskrit phonemes *sa* and *śa*, distinguished by the same four components: (1) "the emergence of the thought that is full of fabrication" (Hi. *saṃkalpamaya cittodaya*); (2) "the emergence of the mind full of doubts" (*saṃśayamaya, manodaya*); (3) the "emergence of the intellect full of stubbornness" (*niścayabuddhyodaya* [*sic*]); and (4) the "emergence of the ego-faculty full of self-illusions" (*abhimānamaya, ahaṅkārodaya*).[131]

The above indicates that Sabhapati's teachings reflect concepts intertwined with south Indian sources that are found embedded in his literature or "went along for the ride," so to speak, as his teachings on Śivarājayoga were translocalized for pan-Indian audiences in English as well as relocalized for not only Hindi-speaking audiences but also Bengali and Telugu audiences (see Chapter 2). This speaks to the importance, I would argue, of more deeply analyzing the contexts of Sabhapati's terminology, which often appears idiosyncratic on the surface but, upon a more critical inspection, connects to a wider Tamil Śaiva milieu that goes far beyond simply Sabhapati himself. I would posit, therefore, that it is reductive to assume that Sabhapati's terminology is automatically indicative of a kind of post hoc pan-Indian and colonial-era neo-Vedānta,[132] despite the fact that this is how many of his followers—his editor Shrish Chandra Basu foremost among them—sought to portray and package his teachings on the cakras, Tantric and yogic subtle physiology, and so on to an educated colonial audience. Instead, I would suggest that it is more productive to engage in a bit of textual excavation and first determine whether the sources for a given idea may also be located in extant Tamil Śaiva literature in the centuries preceding Sabhapati's publications. Only in those cases where no correlate is found does it seem logical to proceed to the possibility that Sabhapati integrated a given idea from some kind of pan-Indian textual milieu or other published source, or that it is his own syncretic innovation.

Views on Other Religions and Movements

Sabhapati's cosmological system, as outlined in preceding sections, is largely a reflection of a Hindu (and particularly Tamil Śaiva) worldview that integrates doctrines from the Vīraśaiva milieus of his gurus that harmonized the soteriologies of Vedānta (Advaita Vedānta) and Saiddhāntika philosophy (see also Chapter 4 for "yoga" as a goal described in the terminologies of both). The work of doxographers to represent and deconstruct other points of view is obviously nothing new in Indian philosophy, and the research of Bouthillette and Halbfass has analyzed the nuances of such engagement.[133] Yet Sabhapati's work also engages with other points of view that were dominant in the colonial period, making it of great interest to the philosophical discourses of early modernity, as also engaged to some degree by Steinschneider. This engagement, while relatively brief relative to the bulk of his literary contents, is most explicitly found in his trilingual work CPSPS, which includes engagement with Buddhism, Christianity, Islam, the Parsi religion or Zoroastrianism (as "Parsism"), and various societies ("Brahma Samaj, Arya Samaj, Prarthana Samaj" and even a paragraph on "Theosophical Societies"). The fact that he takes special interest in Buddhism, Christianity, and Islam here was likely part of the nascent "world religions" discourse that included not only the emergence of the Theosophical Society but also the Parliament of the World's Religions meeting in Chicago in 1893 within a few years of the publication of the Second Book of CPSPS.[134] A separate section of CPSPS also offers a critique of atheism, a recurrent theme in that work. These discourses were likely included at the behest of Sabhapati's Hindu pan-Indian "Admirers" who helped to sponsor Sabhapati's publication of CPSPS and appear to have been concerned with adapting his spiritual teachings more directly to prevailing social and political contexts. Additionally, a section of CTCSPV briefly engages other religions in the context of describing "the shape of the Lord in the truth of the six religions" (Tam. *īcuvaraṉ āṟumata uṇmaikkōlamāy*). None of his works appear to explicitly address either Jainism or Judaism, whether out of lack of interest or Sabhapati's own unfamiliarity with their doctrines. In this section I will summarize this interfaith engagement since it provides evidence that his cosmological views, although deep-rooted in the currents of Śaivism that I mentioned above, did not exist in a vacuum. His writing on the subject emerged at a time in which teachings from other religions and societies were also prevalent, and it is notable that Sabhapati or his editor felt the need or pressure to engage with these other worldviews to justify Sabhapati's system of Śivarājayoga and the cosmology upon which it was based.

Before treating Sabhapati's engagement with each religion or group individually, it is necessary to first point out that Sabhapati's comparative engagement in CPSPS with each of the above religions is mapped onto a progressive sequence of self-realizations that he calls the "six sorts of truths of Adhikari" (Mpvl. *atikāri*, < Skt. *adhikāritva*, lit. "authority").[135] These six truths are described as follows:

1. **"Hero"**: The Finite Spirit (*jīvātman*) is dwelling in the "delusion" of "separate real Self existence" from the Infinite Spirit.
2. **"Weapons"**: The Finite Spirit, engaging in the "fifteen sorts of the purifications of the Mind and Soul," is able to burn down the "delusive curtain" of the Hero stage.
3. **"Enemies"**: The Finite Spirit, having destroyed the previous delusion, is disturbed by the "five vitals" and sensual phenomena, and if these are overcome, then the Finite Spirit notices the "mental phenomena standing as Commander-in-Chief over a gigantic troop of hosts such as wrath, rage, revenge, anger, egotism, pride, arrogance, passions, &c."
4. **"Ministers"**: The Finite Spirit becomes two kinds of "Ministers" or "Mediators," of which the first kind is one's own "Self-state" that is "situated in the centre seat of the brain," and the second kind is the Infinite Spirit coming down in human form to perservere in the yoga of gnosis (*jñānayoga*) as the "Suthguru" (Sadguru) or "Rishees [*ṛṣis*], Yogees [*yogīs*], Gnyanees [*jñānins*], Christ, Mahomed [Muhammad], Budha [Buddha] and Zaraster [Zoroaster] as secondary indirect Spiritual Priests Ministers or Mediators."
5. **"Ruling Power"**: The Finite Spirit is constantly practicing seeing itself as "void, witnessing, conscious, and blissful" (*śūnya*, *sākṣin*, *vyāpaka*, and *ānanda*; these are the "Four Spiritual Brightnesses" of Brahman or "Passive Principle" in Figure 3.6 above).
6. **"Spiritual Emperor"** or **"Success of Ever Being Your Own Self"**: The Finite Spirit overcomes both trinity (Mpvl. *tiripuṭapētattuvam*, < Skt. *tripuṭabhedatva*) and duality (Mpvl. *tuvitapētattuvam*, < Skt. *dvaitabhedatva*) and is finally "lost in the real existence of the Infinite Spirit" through attainment in "Gnyana Yogue Nirvikulpa Samadhi" (< Skt. *jñāna yoga nirvikalpa samādhi*).[136]

As one can see from the fourth truth above, Christianity, Islam, Buddhism, and the religion of the Parsis/Zoroastrianism all reach to this fourth truth but essentially stop there, which is one of Sabhạpati's major arguments for his doctrinal disagreement with these religions. However, his specific analysis of each religion (as well as societies that don't map as neatly onto this scheme) are worth separately analyzing since they draw out certain nuances of his own philosophical and cosmological system.

Sabhapati may appear narrow-minded, argumentative, and rhetorical in these debates to a contemporary reader, although it is important not to neglect his overarching message of universalism. He seems to never have been concerned with proselytizing or converting non-Hindu peoples, and a concept of what he calls a "Universal truth, Church and Creed" for all castes and genders permeates his literature. As is seen in the subsequent section on atheism, his strongest criticism was reserved for what he perceived to be a narrow preoccupation with "material ideas," and he appreciated religious impulses even when his view the teachings were imperfect. In other words, he believed that teachings from religions other than Hinduism may therefore contain "parables" or "sacred sentences," but perceived the interpretation of these teachings to be mostly lost by their followers. For example, he states with regard to Christianity that "even the present most ardent followers, without understanding the true meaning of the secret sentences spoken in parables, have attached unreal meaning to such sacred sentences in accordance with the material ideas."[137] I would argue that this kind of perspective brings Sabhapati's interpretive frame more in line with contemporary discourses on esotericism, and he was likely inspired by his interactions with both the "Founders" and South Asian members of the Theosophical Society (see Chapter 1 and Chapter 7) as well as Tamil notions of *uḷ* ("inner") of *maṟai* ("something hidden") as frameworks for interpreting Vedic knowledge.[138] In any event, Sabhapati's analysis of each religion is situated in the context of determining whether or not they have the potential to show a practical method of what he termed "communion" with the Infinite Spirit, that is, the samādhi of Śivarājayoga, described as the experience of the tree universally spread.

Sabhapati and Buddhism

Sabhapati's engagement with Buddhism is relatively brief and positive, and he appears to have interacted with Buddhist monks in Rangoon, Burma (modern Yangon, Myanmar), as I already noted in Chapter 1. Sabhapati explains that "Budha Rishee is still living in the sacred caves of Himalaya in deep Yogue Samadhi [*yoga samādhi*]," a claim similar to Agastya's continued life in the Pothigai Hills in Chapter 1.[139] The reason for the Buddha's travels to what Sabhapati calls the "other side of the Himalaya i.e., east not blest with the truths of the secret doctrines of Hinduism" is linked to his idea that "Viasa Rishee [Vyāsa Ṛṣi] in India began to introduce the other minor doctrines in the Vedas."[140] According to Sabhapati, Vyāsa was warned by the Buddha that the "introduction of such doctrines will cause much confusion, difference of castes, creed, sect, religious, and divine truths in India," but that Vyāsa didn't listen. As a result, the Buddha set out to "reveal the truths of Vedantism in their true shape throughout those countries," and Sabhapati notes that his teachings "admit the veracity of my two principles and other four truths,"[141] which refers to the Universal Spirit and Finite Spirit and Sabhapati's aforementioned four principles that he calls "hero, weapon, enemy and the minister." Sabhapati unfortunately does not appear to consider the Buddhist doctrine of *anātman*, or "not-self," which contrasts with his own views on *paramātman* and *jīvātman* and would have made for a much more interesting dialogical engagement. Instead, Sabhapati simply blames the "Budhist [*sic*] priests of middle ages" for leading the people away from his original "secret truths."[142] This is somewhat ironic given that some of haṭha yoga's principal roots are in medieval Buddhist Tantra and that the exponents of Buddhist Tantra believed they were faithfully interpreting Mahayana doctrines in a new frame.[143] Sabhapati's work CTCSPV, however, mentions Buddhism (Tam. *pauttamatam*) in the context of one of six religions that contain the truth of the Lord (Īśvara). This work considers the Buddha as a great rishi who descended to the "northeast part of the world" (Tam. *ulakattiṉ vaṭakiḻa pākam*) as an avatar to "establish meditation on the state of formless gnosis" (Tam. *nirākāra ñāṉapāva tiyāṉattai nilaināṭṭu*).[144]

Sabhapati and Christianity

As mentioned in Chapter 1, Sabhapati's hagiographical accounts record that he attended the Scottish-origin Free Church Mission School when he was a youth, meaning that he would have obtained a firsthand knowledge of Christian teachings from this denomination of Protestant Christianity even though he was raised by Śaiva parents in the service of his own guru-to-be,

Vedashreni Chidambara Swamigal. In addition to these accounts of his own personal experience of missionary school, Sabhapati devotes over three full pages in CPSPS to reconciling his own philosophy with that of Christianity, which he describes as "the most extended religion" that consists of "all truths essential for the purification of the Mind and Soul, but irregularly."[145] He argues that Christianity professes the "first passive principle" and the "second active principle," that is, the Universal Infinite Spirit (Brahman) and the Universal Finite Spirit (Īśvara and, by extension, the Shakti), and that it accepts his first four "truths" of the "hero, weapon, enemy, and the minister" (see Views on Other Religions and Movements). Sabhapati admires Christianity's doctrine of the soul being bound by "sin and vice," although this binding in his view is not on account of disobeying God's commandments as much as the result of one's delusionary separation from the Infinite Spirit. Similarly, he admires what he sees as its doctrine of the world being a "delusion," which is based not so much on an understanding of Christian doctrine as much as his personal interpretation of a verse including the statement "Ye are Gods." Despite this conciliatory tone, he argues that the religion "does not teach the way to hold communion with me [the Infinite Spirit], which Christ, the incarnation of my Spiritual power, and his disciples, who established his true doctrines, did and got salvation."[146] He further offers a dissenting view on the "Judgment Day" or "Last Judgment," a reference to the biblical book of Revelation attributed to St. John. This Judgment Day is typically interpreted in Protestantism as a future day when Jesus Christ will return to judge each and every soul. In contrast to most Protestant eschatologies, however, Sabhapati argues through the lens of his own doctrine of evolution and transmigrations (see Emancipation and Transmigration) that "Judgment day" is not some date "millions of years" from now, but actually "the very moment when Souls depart from their bodies."[147] This on the surface appears less in line with Protestantism than with the Catholic idea of Purgatory, which Protestants rejected. However, Sabhapati makes it clear that for him the real "judgment day" is karmic retribution, or an individual soul's repositioning, immediately after death, in a new form either higher or lower on *saṃsāra*'s board game of Snakes and Ladders (or in exceptional cases a liberation from the board altogether).

In addition to the above, Sabhapati's apologetic engagement with Christianity is on three other fronts, namely (1) quotations from quite a few biblical passages (such as the Psalms, the Gospels, and the Epistles of Paul, though he does not supply these references himself) that are intended to show that one's so-called "self state" is the Infinite Spirit; (2) an interpretation of the "inward real meaning" of the Trinity (Father, Son, and Holy Ghost); and (3) a critique on the Christian view of creation ex nihilo.

The first opens with the assertion that "Ye are Gods" (a reference to Psalms 82:6, but also a verse cited by H. P. Blavatsky in *Isis Unveiled* to express a similar message of human divinity, which could have in turn inspired Sabhapati).[148] This is then qualified by the idea that the "Soul" only seems limited in the body on account of its delusion, and that in reality the Infinite Spirit pervades it. The rest of the verses contain similar quotations and interpretations. Sabhapati then proceeds to interpret the Trinity as follows:

> The Father means the whole of the unlimited Infinite Spiritual state throughout the Universe called God.
>
> The Son means the whole of the unlimited Infinite Spiritual state that seems as limited in the body of every creature called the Soul.
>
> The Holy Ghost means the power of absorptive state that reveals the secret and real truth that the Soul which seems as limited is not in reality so, but is the real unlimited self Infinite Spirit throughout the Universe by making the faculties of the Soul to be entirely lost in the Self Infinite Spiritual State.[149]

It is clear that Sabhapati is trying to bring the Christian doctrine of the Trinity in line with his own philosophical postulates by identifying the Father with the "Universal Spirit" (*śivamaya*), the Son with the "Universal Infinite Spirit" (Brahman), and the Holy Ghost (or Holy Spirit) with the individual soul or Finite Spirit's experience of the "absorptive state," which is Sabhapati's translation for *samādhi*.

Sabhapati's section on Christianity in CPSPS closes with an argument that the "creation is not created merely by the will of God as said in the Bible," but that instead there is a "primary evolution" (the initial creation at the beginning of time) and "secondary evolution" (creations resulting from transmigration that have happened since the primary evolution).[150] Sabhapati is likely here referring to Puranic doctrines of primary creation at the beginning of a *kalpa*, or a "day of Brahmā," and secondary creation at the beginning of a *yuga*, or "age."[151] In several Puranas the primary cause of creation is the god Brahma (Brahmā), who in turn is divided into a primary and secondary cause: a supreme unmanifest form and a manifested form as the Trimūrti (often Brahma [Brahmā] as creation, Vishnu as preservation, and Shiva as dissolution, along with their Shaktis,

< Śakti, (feminine) "Power").[152] Implicit in this creation is also a cosmic dissolution, called the "Maha Pralayakala" (< Skt. *mahāpralayakāla*, lit. "time of the great dissolution"), or what he calls the "active Godship taking rest and silence at the termination of every four Yoogums" (< Mpvl. *yukam*, < Skt. *yuga*).[153] The "active Godship" for Sabhapati is what he elsewhere calls the "Universal Finite Spirit" (*īśvarātman* or *śaktitva*; see Figure 3.3). This principle, embodied in the subtle physiology of the individual's cakras and tattvas, accordingly not only sets creation at rest but also stirs creation to activity. However, this activity is not devoid of origin (*anādi*) but has an origin (*ādi*) to which there is a periodical reabsorption.[154] At the same time, Sabhapati is clear that someday there will be a "final and real" time of dissolution in which the "active Godship" and its creation will permanently cease to exist.[155] Sabhapati's main concern here is mostly a criticism of the Christian doctrine of creation ex nihilo, "out of nothing," but his criticism also clarifies his relationship to Śaiva Siddhānta (see Connections with Tamil Śaiva Discourse), which he called "Theism." In other words, he allows that the "passive Godship" (or "Universal Infinite Spirit," i.e., Brahman or its higher form, *śivamaya*; see Figure 3.6), being *anādi*, or "without beginning," survives beyond the *mahāpralayakāla* of the "active Godship" with its point of origin (*ādi*).

Sabhapati's Tamil work MCVTS also contains a brief reference to Christianity, just as with Buddhism above, as of one of six religions that contain the truth of the Lord (Īśvara). Sabhapati sepcifically notes that the people from "countries in the western part of the world" (Tam. *ulakattiṉ mēṟpākatēcaṅkaḷ*) established a devotion (Skt. *bhakti*) of meditating on Jesus Christ in the shape of a "formless" or "invisible" (Skt. *arūpa*) being (Tam. *arūpākāramākap pāvittut tiyāṉikkum pakti*).[156] Given the prevalence of physical forms of devotions in Catholicism, especially in India, such a description of Christianity as *arūpa bhakti* is likely based on Sabhapati's own familiarity from childhood of Protestant forms of devotion that tend to favor aniconic representations of Jesus and the Trinity.

Sabhapati and Islam

As mentioned in Chapter 1, Sabhapati's sources record that he spent several months to a couple of years in the port city of Nagore near Nagapattinam (Nākappaṭṭiṉam), where he interacted with fakirs at the Dargah or shrine of Shah al-Hamid Naguri (Shāh al-Ḥamīd Nagurī). While Sabhapati later turned more directly to Hinduism, his encounters and conversations at the shrine would have facilitated a general contextual understanding of Islam as mediated through Tamil regional forms of Sufism. In contrast to his treatment of Christianity, however, which as I noted spanned over three pages in CPSPS, explicit consideration of Islam (which he calls "Mahomedanism") only gets half a page. Curiously, Sabhapati claims that Muhammad after his birth "came with some Caravan merchants to Punjab and there was initiated into Veda[n] tic Yogue [*sic*] of Hinduism," which could reflect his confusion of Muhammad with a Punjabi Sufi *pīr* such as Goga, for example.[157] From there he "went to Palestine and gathered some truths there as regards Christianity and began to establish the truths learned from Christianity and Hinduism."[158] As far as the teachings of the "great Mahomed" are concerned, Sabhapati notes he "inculcated the doctrine of Hero, Weapon, Enemy and Minister" (four of six "truths" listed above) but that his followers have misrepresented his teachings on the "fifteen weapons of purifications of Mind and Soul" (see Chapter 4) and instead interpreted as literally referring to the use of "real weapons of polished iron" that are to be used in beheading physical enemies of Islam.[159]

His Tamil work MCVTS, just as with Christianity and Buddhism, describes Islam in a more positive light as one of six religions that contain the Lord's truth (Tam. *uṇmai*). In this context Muhammad (Mōhamatu) is considered to have come in the shape of an avatar (Tam. *avatārakōlamāy*) from the "place of the middle portion of the virtuous world" (Tam. *pūlōkakaṇṭattiṉ mattiyakaṇṭa stāṉam*) to expound the mystery of "inebriation" (Tam. *mayakkam*) as the "inebriation of gnosis" (Tam. *ñāṉamayakkam*) out of a "desire for liberation" (Mpvl. *mōkṣakāmiyam*, < Skt. *mokṣakāmya*). Like Christianity, it also describes the Quran (Tam. *korāṉ*) as teaching devotion for meditating on the Lord in a "formless" or "invisible shape" (Mpvl. *arūpākāram*, < Skt. *arūpākāra*).

Sabhapati and Zoroastrianism, or "Parsism"

Another traditional religion that Sabhapati engages in his CPSPS is Zoroastrianism, specifically the religion of the Parsi community, which he calls "Parsism."[160] Sabhapati's engagement with Zoroastrianism only spans between one and two pages, and likely emerges out of the context of his desire to attract followers in Mumbai and northwest India, although this interest could have also arisen in conversations in Lahore with members of the newly founded Theosophical Society (see Chapter 1).

Sabhapati's apology is notable in its description of a mythological connection of both Parsis and Hindus to the "Aryans of Yore" when they were both settled together at a town he calls "Vedekia Puree" (< Videha Purī, most likely a spurious reference to the Videha Kingdom) on the Indus River and headed by one "Veda Deva Rishee" (Vedadevarṣi).[161] Veda Deva Rishee in turn had two children, an elder son named "Vedha Dhatha" or "Vedha Dhata" (Vedadatta) and a younger son named "Vedha Dhesa" (Vedadeśa). The elder son settled west of the Indus and introduced a "new Sanskrit tongue" called "Zind" (Zend), which refers to commentaries to the Avesta, a collection of Zoroastrian sacred texts.[162] The younger son in turn came south and became the ancestor of the present-day Hindus.

The story doesn't end there, however, as the elder son Vedha Dhatha had a fifth descendant named "Parashara Maha Rishee" who "married the daughter of one of the Rishees of India and settled his Ashrumum [< Skt. *āśrama*] in the caves of Kushachalum [Kuśācala, "the Kush Mountains"], now called the Hindu Kusha." Parashara was said to have "mastered the truths of the four Vedas" and to have initiated his followers into those truths as well as "Agni Hotra worship." This Parashara is almost certainly a reference to Parāśara, a well-known rishi in Hinduism who in the Mahabharata epic is the son of Śaktri and Adṛśyantī, and the father of Vyāsa.[163] There is a connection of him with yoga as well; the *Parāśarasmṛti*, or "Recollection of Parāśara," includes an aphorism about yogis who pierce the orb of the sun, and he also offers a teaching on yoga to the king Janaka in the twelfth book (*parvan*) of the Mahabharata.[164]

The twelfth descendant of this Parashara Maha Rishee was in turn none other than "Zhoraster" or Zoroaster, who "translated all the four Vedas of the Hindus into the Zend language." These Vedas were taken away by the "Rishies" and "Yogees" of both Hinduism and Zoroastrianism following an unspecified "change over the nations of the western world," and were hidden in the ashram hermitage of the Kush Mountains for preservation.

Sabhapati claims that the term "Parsee" (Parsi) comes from the name "Parashara" of Parashara Maha Rishee. The ethnic marker "Parsi" does not actually derive from a specific person, however, but refers to inhabitants of Pars, a region in Iran (from which the Hindustani adjective *phārsī* and English adjective "Persian" are ultimately derived).[165] This aforementioned mythology therefore has no grounding in the historical development of the Parsi community, who fled to India between the eighth and tenth centuries following the Islamic conquest. However, the reference to the Kush Mountains does provide additional data for constructing the yogic mythology of Agastya's hermitage; as I noted in Chapter 1, the Kush Mountains (Tam. Kuṣācala) are one of the eleven mountain ranges from which the Gnostics (Ñāṉikaḷ), the Rishis (Ruṣikaḷ), the Siddhas (Cittarkaḷ), and the Yogis (Yōkikaḷ) were said to travel to Mount Agastya to catch the vision of Agastya that was said to occur only once every fifty years. As a result, this mythology tells us that the other ten mountain ranges very likely had similar mythologies associated, some of which have likely been long forgotten or obscured.

In addition to his mythological account, Sabhapati appends a short paragraph entitled "Instructions on the fire worship of Hindus and Parsees." These instructions, which are more descriptive than practical, do not appear to come from a Parsi ritual context but are likely Sabhapati's own invention, possibly to promote harmony between Parsis and Hindus and to encourage Parsis to embrace the "Universal truth, Church and Creed" predicated on Sabhapati's Hindu yogic system. Earlier he had noted a commonality between the "Devata woaship" [*sic*] of the two religions, which is at least terminologically inaccurate since Parsis "clearly differentiate between Ahuras/Yazatas (positive divine entities) and Daevas (demons)."[166] Yet these practices, five in number, perhaps intentionally do not include any worship to gods and goddesses but are meditations on the fire itself. They are as follows, with Sabhapati's own idiosyncratic English followed by a transliteration of the accompanying Maṇipravāla phrases provided):

1. "The worship [lit. "meditation"] of the fire of satisfying Godly powers" (Mpvl. *tēvatārpaṇayākṉitiyāṉ*, < Skt. *devatārpaṇāgnidhyāna*)
2. "The worship of the fire of good thoughts, good words and good deeds" (Mpvl. *cuttakuṇavācā kiriyākṉitiyāṉ*, < Skt. *śuddhaguṇavācākriyāgnidhyāna*)
3. "The worship of the fire of the purification of the Mind and Soul" (Mpvl. *ātmamaṉocuttiyākṉitiyāṉ*, < Skt. *ātmamanaḥśuddhyagnidhyāna*)
4. "The worship of the fire of absorption of the functions and faculties" (Mpvl. *carvatattuvalayākṉitiyāṉ*, < Skt. *sarvatattvalayāgnidhyāna*)
5. "The worship of the fire of the identification of the Soul and Spirit in deep meditation by holding communion with God" (*pirmmēsvarakñāṉākṉitiyāṉ*, < Skt. *brahmeśvarajñānāgnidhyāna*)

These descriptions are additionally accompanied by rewards for their practice, perhaps intended to provide additional incentive.

Sabhapati and "Samajees"

In additional to the aforementioned religions, Sabhapati also offered a scathing critique in CPSPS of Indian "Samajees" (< Hi. *samājī*, "a member of a society"), specifically of Brahmo Samaj (Brahma Samāj, the "Society of Brahman"), Arya Samaj (Ārya Samāj, the "Noble Society"), Prarthana Samaj (Prārthana Samāj, the "Society of Prayer"), and "others."[167] It is very likely that Sabhapati had his own former editor Shrish Chandra Basu in mind as he wrote, dictated, or at least reviewed this section of his Second Book of CPSPS, which was published in 1890. As already mentioned in the first chapter, Sabhapati had delivered an address on the anniversary of the Lahore Arya Samaj in November 1879. He had already met Shrish Chandra by that time, who edited VRY1 (published in 1880) and who would go on to join the Brahmo Samaj in 1881, only to sever his ties with that society two years later, in 1883. Shrish Chandra had also flirted with joining the Arya Samaj while still a student after attending lectures in Lahore by Dayananda Saraswati, but never joined and refused to sign a pledge form, although he continued to further his sympathetic interest in the politics of Hindu reformation. Shrish Chandra also joined the Theosophical Society after meeting Sabhapati Swami, a society that the swami considered separately (see the subsequent section). Given Shrish Chandra's activities, it is interesting that Sabhapati by 1890 had distanced himself from all these societies, many of which his own followers, such as Shrish Chandra himself, had various degrees of relationship to or invested membership in. As I will argue, Sabhapati's perspective seems on the one hand designed to reflect his gradual disillusionment with the leadership of these societies and on the other hand intended to promote his own yogic system of initiation and "meditation halls" as a viable alternative to membership in these societies.[168]

Sabhapati opens his critique with the declaration that the societies "were once nothing more than the Vedantic societies in the true shape" and that their leaders had established them to "extend this oriental and ancient Vedantic Yogue [*sic*] truth of Aryans of yore."[169] In contrast to the aforementioned religions, he notes that these societies accept the truth of the "first passive" and "second active" principles as well as all six of the truths of "Adhikari" (see Views on Other Religions and Movements). However, he laments what he perceives as "evil alternations and changes" introduced by the present members of these societies, specifically their denial of the doctrine of "punishment by transmigrations" and, even more "absurd" and "foolish," their denial that the "self nature of the Soul" is the "Infinite Spirit of everywhere (which it really was, is, and will be)." The source of the problem, Sabhapati argues, is "their belief in the seeming scientific and Atheistic studies of the western nations without practising or caring to comprehend what is the Vedantic Yogue Philosophy." As I shall show in a separate section below, this is just one example of a whole host of responses to a certain discursive current of atheism that must have been beginning to spread in India around that time, and is a preoccupation that does not figure prominently (or at least as explicitly) in his other works.

Sabhapati continues his critique of "societies and samajees" on other fronts as well, and perhaps in no other section is he quite as explicit as to the social importance of his spiritual teachings. He pointedly asks members of these societies the following line of questioning as a kind of challenge:

> Why for you pray? and to whom you pray? The Meditation of praying without understanding God's nature (to whom the prayer is devoted) and the nature of the Soul (by whom the prayer is devoted) is as ignorant and senseless as that praise, which a man without knowing what for he praises and to whom he praises and who is it that praises, gives to a man whom he does not see, and knows not whether he exists or hears and what is his state.[170]

Sabhapati's overarching critique in all of this is his perception that the leaders of these reform societies in his day had failed to delve deep into understanding "God's nature," that is, the interplay between the Infinite Spirit and the Finite Spirit, or between Brahman and the *jīvātman*, as predicated on the descent of the tattvas and their canceling and reabsorption through the practice of yoga (see Chapter 4). He goes on to emphasize that the "real Universal truth, church and creed is the Infinite Spirit or God or whole," reiterating that there is actually "no such thing as Finite or Soul or part"—there is only a delusion of separateness prior to engaging in the rituals of purifications and yoga. This is made explicit in a later point, in which Sabhapati reiterates that all one has to do is to "understand that there is no created thing and truly to cancel all seeming creations together with the seeming existing functions and faculties by the Vedantic Gnyana Yogue [= Skt. *jñāna yoga*] practice of this philosophy."[171]

Beyond Sabhapati's metaphysical instructions, however, there are also discernible forces and social implications. For example, it is clear that Sabhapati is advocating that members of these societies return to a more traditional mode of spiritual instruction in the guru-disciple model, a model that would have already been significantly declining in importance by the peak of the colonial period when British-inspired forms of standardized education and the prospects of urban mobility were rapidly replacing any perceived benefits of traditional apprenticeship under a renunciate guru. In other words, it is clear that the social worlds of colonial cities like Madras, Calcutta, Bombay, and Lahore would have encouraged or even necessitated the rise of religious communities and organizations that talked more in terms of "membership" and "pledge-forms" than "initiation," for example, of which the Arya Samaj is perhaps the textbook example.[172] At the same time, the old structures and politics of initiation and renunciation never really disappeared, and Sabhapati could also be read as criticizing these new societies for "outgrowing" their traditional religious source of authority.[173] This phenomenon is reflected in Sabhapati's own words as follows:

> The members of different sorts of Societies and Samajees under different designations lead their meditation themselves in accordance with their untrue, unreal, misused, misled, misguided opinions without having Saniasee Sadhoos [= Skt. *saṃnyāsī sādhus*] as their Spiritual precepters to guide them in the proper channel.[174]

As we saw in Chapter 1, Sabhapati had taken his sannyasi vows from his guru Vedashreni Chidambara Swamigal around the age of thirty. As a result, he would have thought of himself as an exemplary model of a "Sannyasi Sadhu" who would have been capable of guiding members of the "Societies and Samajees" in the proper way that he suggests.

At the end of this section in CPSPS he even summarizes his prescriptive guidance for members of these societies into four pithy steps as follows, which I have edited slightly for clarity:

1. Realize the nature of God, the Universal Infinite Spirit [Mpvl. *pirmmēsvarasvarūpam*, < Skt. *brahmeśvarasvarūpa*], upon which the meditation is carried out.
2. Realize the nature of the Soul [*ātmasvarūpam*, < Skt. *ātmasvarūpa*], by which the meditation is carried out.
3. Make the Soul to lose its nature in God by means of purity, communion, concentration and absorption, through the Gnyan Yogue [*jñāna yoga*]

practice with identification [Mpvl. *ātma piramma aikkiyasvarūpam*, < Skt. *ātmabrahma aikyasvarūpam*].

4. Pray, meditate and make Manasa Puja [= Skt. *mānasa pūjā*, "mental worship rites"] through the piety of duality [=Mpvl. *ātmapirammesvara pakttisvarūpam*, < Skt. *ātmabrahmeśvara bhaktisvarūpa*] to get the grace of God and to obtain relief from sorrows, sins, and transmigrations.

While these prescriptions are intended to be more or less applicable to any reader, he closes his apology with the following blunt statement: "This is the initiation of mine come and learn."[175] This closing statement underscores the fact that, while Sabhapati's books were intended to faithfully communicate his teachings and methods, there was still an additional component of personal instruction and initiation offered to serious students who took the time to "come and learn" from Sabhapati or his followers at their Meditation Hall.

Sabhapati and the "Theosophical Societies"

As treated in Chapter 1, Henry Olcott and H. P. Blavatsky, the so-called founders of the Theosophical Society, which had been established in New York City in 1875,[176] first arrived in Bombay in February 1879 and met with Sabhapati Swami nine months later, in November 1879, after he and Olcott had addressed the same crowd. Both Olcott and Blavatsky had previously been corresponding with Dayanada Saraswati, the founder of the Arya Samaj, with whom they would break ties in 1882.[177] There is evidence that Olcott and Blavatsky in this earlier period of Theosophy's history were searching for instruction in yoga to further their knowledge of "astral" travel (see Chapter 7), although they shifted their focus after their falling out with Dayananda. They remained interested from the beginning, however, in assuming roles in reviving what they perceived to be the wisdom of the Aryas, or "Nobles."[178] While there is no evidence that Sabhapati Swami himself joined the newly founded society, he remained mostly sympathetic to this cause, and his editor Shrish Chandra Basu did join and remained a lifelong member.

In the First Book of CPSPS, published in 1884, Sabhapati mentions Blavatsky and Olcott by name in the context of a note of "Caution" that admonishes the reader to get over "*Shame* and *Pride*" that may prevent one from "going to *Gnyanís* and *Yógís*":

> You must hear also Foreign Brother's and Sister's, (such as Col. Olcott's and Madame Blavatsky's) advices of Reviving our Beliefs on Aryan Forefather's Religious Spiritual Instructions and Gaining Success over the practices of those Ancestral Instructions, by being a member and biding [*sic*] thanks to such foreign successful advisers.[179]

The note celebrates these "ancestral Aryans" as "*Teachers and Gurus of any of the four Castes* from whom to learn Spirituality" (italics as original here and in all quotations in this section), meaning that for Sabhapati the adjective "Aryan" referred to a pan-Indian ancestral heritage that was not only limited to the Brahmin caste. The note further provides an important justification for Sabhapati's translocalization of his yogic knowledge to "*Foreigners* or *Non-Aryans*," noting that the "ancestral Aryans" were "*Teachers* to the Foreign nations of the World" and not vice versa, with "Hindu learned mean of the present age becoming students and disciples to the *Teachers* or *Missionaries* from other shores."[180] A deep sense of loss pervades the tone of this note mingled with encouragement at the prospect of reviving ancestral teachings and spreading them throughout the world, as the following statement makes clear:

> We have *lost* already the ruling *powers* to the foreigners but we may have them as Brothers and Sisters from foreign Land, and try our best to give them every means of possible and practicable instructions of Spiritual truths what we hold of, enabling them to spread it in their own lands and also everywhere of the World if possible.[181]

This openness to spreading yogic instructions to foreigners, expressed in 1884, over a decade before Swami Vivekananda's lecture at the Parliament of World Religions in 1896, is exemplary of a larger zeitgeist of the late nineteenth century. Yogis and authors on yoga, like Sabhapati's editor Shrish Chandra Basu, who would go on to publish separately, were trying to revive teachings that were perceived to be in danger of dying out in the colonial period due to several factors, including conversion efforts undertaken by missionaries on the one hand, and on the other hand the advent of Western-style standardized forms of education for elites that for the most part dismissed local forms of knowledge like yoga and its accompanying cosmological system as mere superstition.

Sabhapati more directly engages what he calls "Theosophical Societies" in a separate section appended to his aforementioned treatment of "Samajees."

His consistent use of the plural form (rather than a singular, specific Theosophical Society) is itself interesting since it indicates that by 1890 he could imagine the presence of "Theosophical Societies" as a category that could encompass other groups of occultists who followed a similar line of thinking, both Indian and foreign, rather just the Theosophical Society founded in 1875 or its regional branches. It is also notable that Sabhapati treats such societies in a separate section from his critique of the Arya Samaj, Brahmo Samaj, and so on, but at the same time it is understandable; their doctrines on yoga and rebirth to a certain extent could more closely be framed as in alignment with his own, despite some clear differences on specific points.[182] Sabhapati's criticism of "Theosophical Societies" accordingly takes a warmer tone than with those other societies:

> Ye brotherly members of the Theosophical Societies you all deal much in theoratical [*sic*] knowledge of Vedantism, Yogism, purification, benevolence, indistinction of caste and religion, brotherhood, search after the knowledge of God and search and love of the Psychic powers, good thoughts, good words and good deeds but not practical knowledge.[183]

His final point is reiterated in an injunction for these "brotherly members" to "follow the practical experience more earnestly than the theoratical [*sic*] knowledge."[184] This criticism of overtheorizing likely reflects a shifting interest among the early members of the Theosophical Society away from the occult practice of astral travel, which at least some members thought yoga could help facilitate, and toward an emphasis on theoretical speculation on the metaphysics of Vedānta and Buddhism, as Deveney and others have indicated.[185]

Another aspect of Theosophy that must have inspired Sabhapati was in his adoption of the rhetoric of a "Universal Church" and "Creed," which he mentions throughout his works alongside his apologetic engagement with the different religions. Theosophy's motto, "There is no religion higher than truth," is certainly resonant with Sabhapati's description of the ideal guru or spiritual preceptor: "*He has no castes, no sects, no sexes, no religion therefore men of castes, sects, sexes, religions must take him to be preceptor of all castes, all sects, all sexes, all religions* and as a child of the world in General."[186] Sabhapati, therefore, preached a universalist ideal of the guru despite the methods to achieving this ideal being predominantly framed in a Hindu soteriological context.

Sabhapati and Atheism

In addition to the religions and societies previously treated, Sabhapati intersperses a pointed critique of "Atheism" throughout the two volumes of CPSPS, a critique that is minimized or even absent in his other works and appears to be a reaction to colonial-era secular attitudes inspired by his encounters with educated and urban elites, especially in developing areas of cities like Madras, Bombay, and Calcutta. His critique is accordingly not so much aimed at modern revivals of an indigenous form of Cārvāka materialism, but at a worldview that had been imported from outside. At the same time, his discourse follows a long history of critiques against materialism (as it arose in India as well as outside) by religious authors, a discourse that would later be engaged by Swami Vivekananda in the context of his teachings on *ākāśa* ("space" or "ether").[187] Sabhapati specifically mentions the words "atheism" or "atheist" at least forty-five times in CPSPS, and even devotes over ten full pages to it in a section subtitled "Atheism condemned by the Practical proofs of reason and logic."[188] In that section he offers a string of synonymous concepts, namely "non-religion or atheism or naturalism or scientific untruism or materialism of the present day,"[189] all of which are subsumed under his criticism of atheism. Perhaps the most generalized and socially descriptive of his arguments are as follows:

> Therefore, ye! atheists! ye? atheists? do not be puffed up with vain egotism, pride, arrogance, self-conceit, ignorance, because you or your parents have amassed for you sufficient wealth to suitably preserve your material body, because you can dress well with beautiful vest in seasons cold and hot, because you can live in comfortable place, because you can command your brother-man, whom you in your ignorance and cruelty, have made your slave, because he cannot maintain himself, because he cannot dress well, cannot lodge in comfortable place in consequence of his not having arts of wit to amass money (to live virtuously) as you or your parents did, because you can temporarily enjoy joyfully in impure, unnatural, undivine, unholy, unsacred things.[190]

Sabhapati could be responding to a certain body of literature that he encountered on atheism as well as to interactions he would have had with followers who likely expressed their own doubts about Sabhapati's framework of emanations and evolutions when confronted with their own colonial-era education or books on philosophical and scientific topics acquired from overseas.

The term "atheism" itself derives from the French *athéisme*, which in turn derived from Greek *átheos*, the privy prefix *a-* being added to *theos*, or "God," and gained currency as a concept in the context of seventeenth-century literary attempts to grapple with the Greek philosophies of Stoics and Epicureans who had distinctive views on the existence of God or gods.[191] In the eighteenth century, French thinkers such as Paul-Henri Thiry (Baron) d'Holbach (1723–1789) expanded these literary conceptions of atheism to promote a "mechanistic" kind of materialism, as outlined in the two volumes of his *Système de la nature* (1770).[192] By the late nineteenth century British figures like Charles Bradlaugh (1833–1891), a contemporary of Sabhapati, were also self-appropriating and inverting the term "atheism" as an affirmation rather than a negation, such as in the following comment taken from Bradlaugh's "Plea for Atheism": "Atheism, properly understood, is nowise a cold, barren negative; it is on the contrary, a hearty, fruitful affirmation of all truth, and involves the positive assertion and action of highest humanity."[193] For Bradlaugh, an affirmation of atheism went hand in hand with an affirmation of the identity of "matter," "substance," and "existence," expressed in logical principles and proofs that are presented in a format similar to Sabhapati's own critique.[194] While we do not know for sure if Sabhapati read or was otherwise familiar with Bradlaugh, he would have certainly taken issue with his philosophical account since for Sabhapati matter is not an essential substance, and separate existence itself is simply an illusion brought about through the emanation of faculties from the Infinite Spirit.

Sabhapati's main treatment on atheism is accordingly synonymous with his critique of "naturalism" or "materialism" in that he describes atheists as people who "blindly say and believe that the last creations i.e. five vitals of the last Spiritual creation of the second active principle have the elements themselves to act what God, the Infinite Spirit, in his second active principle can do."[195] Sabhapati's terminology would be incomprehensible here unless one considers what the "five vitals" of the "second active principle" are in the context of his system of "emanation" and "evolution" of the tattvas (see the section The Tree Universally Spread). The five vitals are the five elements (*bhūtas*), in the body located in the *mūlādhāra*, which Sabhapati calls the "kundali [*kuṇḍali*] of elements." In other words, these elements are where Sabhapati locates material or physical reality. The idea that the atheists of his day could take these physical elements, reframe them as the elements known to modern chemistry, and then argue that nothing else exists apart from them (no faculty of *manas* or mind, no faculty of *buddhi* or intelligence, or much less no Universal Finite or Infinite Spirit) is perhaps the biggest existential threat to Sabhapati's cosmology that he spends hundreds of pages outlining in various ways in his literature. It appears simply inconceivable to Sabhapati that atheists could "vainly maintain that the sensual and mental phenomena are the results of the unconscious movements of the brain" instead of realizing that such phenomena result from the emanations of the higher "eleven faculties" or cakras from the Universal Spirit through the active Universal Finite Spirit.[196] Although Sabhapati places some of the highest of these other eleven faculties in the brain or head of the yogic body, such as the "crevice of Brahman" (*brahmarandhra*) or seat of the Universal Finite Spirit, their origin is not limited to the functions of the physical brain but are ultimately believed to be caused by the emanations of these faculties as part of his wider cosmological system. The section immediately previous to his main critique of atheism describes this system of thirty-two emanations in a relatively succinct form, which to some extent can be read as his counterpoint to his construction of an antagonistic atheist worldview, whether real or imaginary, that only accounts for the lowest of the emanations, that of physical matter or the elements.[197]

There is another related critique that Sabhapati offers, namely that the physical methods and instruments by which atheists attempt to observe and analyze spiritual or subtle principles are inadequate. He writes that the atheists judge "Spiritual things, that are imperceptible, invissible [*sic*], unseen, by the assistance of all the instruments of microscope, telescope &c: but which will surely be perceived vissibly [*sic*] by the mental vision."[198] Sabhapati's contention is accordingly that physical things are observed with physical instruments, but that spiritual things are observed by the "mental vision" that is cultivated through the consistent application of his prescribed practices; as a result scientists are misled in their endeavor to deny God by noting his absence in the world of matter. This notion of the "mental vision" of the yogi is linked to his promise that the yogi will obtain an "*Eye* to the Universe" (*brahmajñānadṛṣṭi*; see The Tree Universally Spread).[199] Sabhapati's views were, of course, expressed prior to the spread of modern psychoanalysis as propounded by Sigmund Freud (1856–1939) and more especially the analytical psychology of Carl Jung (1875–1961), both of whom would become famous around the world for their explorations into the powers of the mind and its relationship to the physical matter of the brain; it would have been interesting to know how Sabhapati would have responded to Freud's theories on dream interpretation or Jung's theories on archetypes, for example.

While Sabhapati himself (or his editor) was mostly content to critique the modern philosophical literature of his day as narrowly focused on the world of matter, he did attempt to engage with scientific materialist theories, albeit in a limited way. In a section of his Tamil work CTCSPV entitled "Instruction on the Divine Way, Having Left Behind the False Way" (Tam. *poymmārkkan tavirttameymmārkka upatēcam*), which spans a few pages, Sabhapati attempts to link his doctrine of the seven *svarūpa*s (lit. "inherent forms," "essential natures"), which he translates as "Spiritual states" in CPSPS and links with his frameworks of tattvas outlined above,[200] with "seven types of elemental expansion" (Tam. *pirapañcam ēḻuvakaittākum*). These include (1) "Spirit or Space," (2) "Presence and Atoms," (3) "Power," (4) "Essence," (5) "Force and Motion," (6) "Action and Creation," and (7) "Visible Show," and he also mentions oxygen and nitrogen as invisible elements of life.[201]

It was left to one of Sabhapati's followers, however, to take up the task even further to reconcile certain theories of "Western pandits" (*pāścātya paṇḍitgaṇ*) that were prevailing in Sabhapati's day with his own yogic cosmology. Ambikacharan Bandyopadhyay (Bengali: Ambikācaraṇ Bandyopādhāẏ) supplied (1885) an additional introduction to Sabhapati's work translated into Bengali (BRY), published by Shrish Chandra Basu. In this piece he takes recourse to the opinions of Immanuel Kant (1724–1804), Herbert Spencer (1820–1903), William Hamilton (9th Baronet, 1788–1856), and Henry Longueville Mansel (1820–1871) in the context of such topics as "contraction and expansion," the "relative realities" of time and space, the "negation of conceivability," the "unconditioned consciousness," the "inconceivable and imperceptible," and "mechanical motion." These are figures and ideas related to the worldview of what Asprem has called Victorian scientific naturalism,[202] and must have offered possibilities to Ambikacharan for a kind of reconciliation between Western science and Sabhapati's yogic system of emanation and evolution, however problematic from a contemporary scientific perspective. Chajes has shown that a similar sympathetic trend toward the scientists of her day, specifically those who espoused alternative approaches to Darwinian evolution, can be detected in the writings of Helena Blavatsky, and this also applies to the writings of Swami Vivekananda and the Christian Science of Mary Baker Eddy (1821–1910).[203] This approach may have inspired Ambikacharan, who like Shrish Chandra appears to have had connections to the Theosophical

Society. Furthermore, some of the authors that Ambikacharan cited would also be engaged a couple decades later by the occultist Aleister Crowley (1875–1947) to justify his own teachings of yoga and ceremonial magic in a loosely scientific frame; Crowley, unlike Blavatsky, would, however, often praise the evolutionary approach of "Darwin's bulldog," Thomas Henry Huxley (1825–1895) (see Chapter 7).[204]

In addition to the lines of argument above, Sabhapati offers fifteen so-called "proofs" that the "untruths" of the "non-religions" of atheism are "full of absurdities."[205] They are as follows, summarized from Sabhapati's original, more lengthy arguments:

1. The elements, being of pure matter, cannot combine themselves into the eleven higher faculties, nor can they be the "first principle" that is devoid of the twelve faculties.
2. The cause of death is not a material "suffocation" of elements, but a kind of bidding "farewell" on the part of the "spiritual chemist or the Alchemist" who had initially brought the eleven higher faculties into existence to act upon the "machine of the body."
3. The elements do not create the "Spirits" of the higher eleven faculties, but rather the "Spirits" create the elements; the force of the elements is like the "light of the gun powder" that vanishes upon combustion.
4. Force, or the "result of the combinations of such elements," is not stopped on account of a portion of matter being taken away; instead, "Spirits create the faculties by resting in different places of matter" and thus need a material basis "to rest upon." The faculties are no longer physically perceived when the material basis is "taken away or stopped or absorbed."
5. If one supposes the eleven conscious faculties to be the "result of the force of combinations of unconscious elements," how are they "Universally diffused" in the "body of every man," which varies vastly from one to another?
6. The "combination of elements" is temporary and transient and so cannot have the Infinite Spirit as its cause; no "internal or external combination of elements" takes place in the Infinite Spirit or the higher eleven faculties.
7. When someone knows his true self to be the "first faculty," he is "not affected" by the other faculties, yet atheists still believe the "unconscious elements" to be "the cause of the conscious eleven faculties," which is "totally absurd."

8. When elements are combined by "material proofs and examples," it creates a "different and separate thing from the original element without Spiritual power" but not a "new creation of elements or more creation of the same nature."
9. Combining these elements does give "motion" and "action" but not in a self-impelled way, and not the power of the "consciousness of eleven faculties."
10. There cannot be a "combination of elements without anyone to combine them," that is, without the "Supernatural one Supreme being." The elements cannot be "self masters for actions and motions," since when a person dies, the body is always dead with "self-existence, self-action, self-emotion, self-notion, self-creation," and the elements do not continue "with their combinations or forces as they once did."
11. The idea that "sensual and mental phenomena are nothing more than unconscious movement of the brain is quite absurd in theory and practice," since the "self-consciousness which reveals as a wisdom that there is such thing as brain and faculties is unquestionably the above thing that commands over the unconscious movement of sensual and mental phenomena" by means of the brain.
12. If the eleven faculties are "the result of the self combination of the unconscious matter" of the brain, how is it possible for one combination of the brain to "create contrary faculties one at the same time"?
13. When a man begins to die, the "combinations of the matter of the organs of every part" decrease rapidly, while the "mental phenomena of the brain are augmenting." This is because the "Spiritual conscious man, who had created that body by extending the eleven faculties at their destined seats to work the physical phenomena, in obedience with the appointed time by God, begins to draw with all the acquired treasure of sin and vice, those eleven faculties to enter another body."
14. If the elements were the "true Gods," as atheists suppose, then whatever "is consciously thought, spoken or done in accordance with . . . the unconscious material movement of the brain" would "never become the cause for pain, sorrow, repentance," but this is not the case.
15. "If the eleven faculties are as actions, the body . . . must move to act first before the faculty," and it is "quite absurd and ignorant . . . to think that action is cause and emotion is effect of cause."[206]

It is evident that the arguments that Sabhapati proposes are predicated upon his system of the twelve faculties, of which the material elements are the lowest or twelfth faculty, associated with *kuṇḍali* and the *mūlādhāra* cakra. However, his interpretation of the atheist argument more broadly is that it maintains that everything resides in matter, which according to Sabhapati is false since matter is not a cause but an effect—indeed, the final effect prior to death, dissolution, or withdrawal back to the Infinite Spirit.

Sabhapati then offers four more proofs by which atheists can have the truth revealed to them: (1) "the proof of the internal self conscious phenomena," (2) "the proof of the internal mental phenomena," (3) "the proof of the internal physical phenomena," and (4) "the proof of the external phenomena by Yogue [= "yog" < Skt. *yoga*] (in doing miracles) and Gnyana [= Skt. *jñāna*] (by sitting in trance, putting entire stop without remembrance of all the mental and physical phenomena several days and months together when yet living but not when dead)." He then offers an abbreviated set of instructions on a sequence of meditations to be engaged "in some lovely place where your mind may not have any disturbance either by any sound or shake of thought."[207]

This sequence, which is related to his more specific practices of Śivarājayoga (see Chapter 4), begins with an examination of the flow of one's thought and an attempt to trace the source of one's "self consciousness," which he elsewhere defined as the

> seeing presence, knowing presence, understanding presence, and conceiving presence, both in the body and everywhere in the Universe as the only one aether-like, space-like, clear void sight and eye, which is the Universal Infinite Spirit or the God of Omni-presence as all witnessing, all knowing, all seeing, all understanding, and all conceiving in the body at the centre seat of the skull or Brahma, Rundhra [*sic*, < Skt. *brahmarandhra*, "crevice of Brahman"].[208]

Here the Maṇipravāla term that Sabhapati translates into "consciousness" is most likely *viyāpakam*, literally "diffusion, universality, ubiquity," which is a kind of abstract noun formed from the Sanskrit *vyāpaka*, "pervading, diffusive, comprehensive," and in this context an attribute of Brahman or "passive principle" as *sarvavyāpaka* or "omnipresence" (see "C" on Figure 3.6).[209]

Perhaps most importantly, Sabhapati in this section allows that the "faculties come out from the brain," a rare context in which he appears to use brain both in the sense that his atheists use it (according to his previous critique) as well as the bodily region of the brain more generally (Skt. *kapāla*).[210] However, he adds that the meditator will perceive that the "self consciousness is not in the brain," but that it is "aloof" and "in the vacant void space between the skull and brain." For Sabhapati, then, the physical brain does not create mental phenomena on its own (the position of his atheists), but rather the brain "creates mental phenomena" when self-consciousness, as ultimately an emanation from the Infinite Spirit via the "self consciousness of eternal bliss" (Mpvl. *carvakñāṉāṉantam*, < Skt. *sarvajñānānanda*, lit. "the bliss of all gnosis") and the "self consciousness of witness" (Mpvl. *carvaviyāpakakñāṉatiruṣṭi*, < Skt. *sarvavyāpakajñānadṛṣṭi*, lit. "gnostic vision of omnipresence"), rests upon the brain. In other words, for Sabhapati the creation of thought itself is predicated on an interplay between emanations from the Infinite Spirit, framed in his system of twelve faculties or cakras, and the physical location of the brain.

Notes

1. Christian Bouy, *Les Nātha-Yogin et les Upaniṣads* (Paris: Diffusion de Boccard, 1994).
2. See Alexis Sanderson, "The Śaiva Age—the Rise and Dominance of Śaivism during the Early Medieval Period," in *Genesis and Development of Tantrism*, ed. Shingo Einoo (Tokyo: Institute of Oriental Culture, University of Tokyo, 2009), 286 n. 686. Elaine Fisher has argued that its contents reflect influence from Śrīvidyā, a "goddess-centered (Śākta) esoteric ritual tradition, whose origins have been definitively traced back so far as early second millennium Kashmir." See Elaine Fisher, "A New Public Theology: Sanskrit and Society in Seventeenth-Century South India" (PhD dissertation, Columbia University, 2013), 53, 229–30. For more information on this text, which has been translated but never critically edited, see Tirumūlar, *Tirumūlar Tirumantiram: mūlamum—viḷakka uraiyum*, ed. Ñā. Māṇikkavācakaṉ and Pattām Patippu (Ceṉṉai: Umā Patippakam, 2016); the introduction in Tirumular, *Tirumantiram: A Tamil Scriptural Classic*, trans. B. Natarajan and N. Mahalingam (Madras: Sri Ramakrishna Math, 1991); Maithili Thayanithy, "The Concept of Living Liberation in the Tirumantiram" (PhD dissertation, University of Toronto, 2010). A helpful translation of this text with multiple descriptions in English was released in multiple volumes by Babaji's Kriya Yoga and Publications; see Tirumūlar, *The Tirumandiram*, trans. T. N Ganapathy et al., 10 vols. (Eastman, Quebec, Canada: Babaji's Kriya Yoga and Publications, 2013).
3. Srilata Raman, personal correspondence, July 17, 2020.
4. For example, see the schedule for "After the Śaiva Age: Transformation and Continuity in the Regional Śaivisms of South India," Symposium, Forty-Seventh

Annual Conference on South Asia in Madison, Wisconsin, October 11, 2018 (available at https://www.academia.edu/37558595/After_the_Saiva_Age_Schedule).

5. Eric Steinschneider, "Beyond the Warring Sects: Universalism, Dissent, and Canon in Tamil Śaivism, ca. 1675–1994" (PhD dissertation, University of Toronto, 2016).
6. See ibid., 19–20. For more background on the Vīraśaivas and their relationship to Vedānta (especially outside of Tamil Nadu) see also Elaine M. Fisher, "Remaking South Indian Śaivism: Greater Śaiva Advaita and the Legacy of the Śaktiviśiṣṭādvaita Vīraśaiva Tradition," *International Journal of Hindu Studies* 21, no. 3 (December 2017): 319–44; Jonathan Duquette, "Is Śivādvaita Vedānta a Saiddhāntika School? Pariṇāmavāda in the Brahmamīmāṃsābhāṣya," *Journal of Hindu Studies* 8 (2015): 16–43; Rohini Bakshi, "The Vedānta of the Vīraśaivas," talk by Jonathan Duquette, *Sanskrit Reading Room* (blog), May 23, 2018.
7. For the Sanskrit (and Kannada) Vīraśaiva perspective on Śivayoga see Seth Powell, "A Lamp on Śiva's Yoga: The Unification of Yoga, Ritual, and Devotion in the Fifteenth-Century Śivayogapradīpikā" (PhD prospectus, Harvard University, 2018), 7, 31 n. 28.
8. Steinschneider, "Beyond the Warring Sects," 21.
9. Srilata Raman, personal correspondence with the author, July 17, 2020. For more on this theme see Srilata Raman, *The Transformation of Tamil Religion: Ramalinga Swamigal (1823–1874) and Modern Dravidian Sainthood* (New York: Routledge, 2022).
10. Citampara Periya Cuvāmikaḷ, *Upatēca uṇmai, viḷakka uraiyuṭaṉ* (Vēḷaccēri, Chennai: Vēḷaccēri Makāṉ Patippakam, 2014), 15.
11. Em. Irājakōpālaṉ, *Vēḷaccēri tiruttalam* ["The Sacred Sites of Velachery"] (Chennai: A4 Āṉant, 2003).
12. Citampara Cuvāmikaḷ, *Upatēcavuṇmaiyum*, ed. Ciṅkāravēlu Piḷḷai (Koṇṇūr: Maṉōṉmaṇivilācavaccukkūṭam of Māṇikka Mutaḷiyār, 1881); for a current edition that contains an explanation (*urai*) and commentary (*viḷakkam*) for each verse see Citampara Periya Cuvāmikaḷ, *Upatēca uṇmai, viḷakka uraiyuṭaṉ*. The latter at the time of writing is available for purchase at Vedashreni Chidambara Swamigal's tumulus (*jīvasamādhi*).
13. Pā. Cu Ramaṇaṉ, *Cittarkaḷ vāḻvil*, vol. 2, Kindle ed. (2018).
14. For example, the Roja Muthiah Research Library erroneously listed at least one copy of *Upatēca uṇmai* as the work of Thiruporur Chidambara Swamigal and not Vedashreni Chidambara Swamigal, which has also been reflected in the library microfilm catalogs of the University of Chicago.
15. Citampara Periya Cuvāmikaḷ, *Upatēca uṇmai, viḷakka uraiyuṭaṉ*, 12–14, 220–21.
16. Steinschneider, "Beyond the Warring Sects," 20–21.
17. Śrī Kumāratēvar, *Tiruvāymalarntaruḷiya cāstirakkōvai*, ed. Caccitānantacuvāmikaḷ and Āṟumukamutaliyār (Ceṉṉai: Manōṉmaṇivilāca Acciyantiracālai, 1908). This edition was at least partially reprinted in 1909. I am enormously grateful to Brinda at the library of Senthamil College for tracking down this publication for me and allowing me to photograph it.
18. Kumāratēvar, *Virutācalattil śrīperiyanāyakiyār varapiracātiyāy eḻuntaruḷiyirunta cāttirakkōvai*, ed. Āṟumuka Mutaliyār and Koṇṇūr Māṇikka Mutaliyār

(Ceṉṉai: Parappiramamuttirākṣaracālai, 1871). I have been unable to consult this edition to confirm its identity.

19. Ibid. *Vairāgya Śataka* is also the title of a different work by the ca. fifth-century philosopher Bhartṛhari.
20. Śrī Kumāratēvar, *Tiruvāymalarntaruḷiya cāstirakkōvai.*
21. Citampara Periya Cuvāmikaḷ, *Upatēca uṇmai, viḷakka uraiyuṭaṉ*. This is also discernible when physically visiting the still-extant *jīva samādhi*s or "tumuli" of each—upon my visits to both (in 2018 and 2019) I noted a resonance on every level, from the rituals to the art to the attitude toward and integration of Siddha iconography.
22. At least one independent account of Vedashreni Chidambara Swamigal's account also corroborates this: see Pā. Cu Ramaṇaṉ, *Cittarkaḷ vāḻvil*. The account clearly mentions that his guru Kuzhandaivel Swamigal was of Kumara Devar's *paramparā* at Virudhachalam (Viruttācalam).
23. Tam. "*kumāratēvar ātiṉa vētascirēṇi upatēca uṇmai cāstirakarttā citampara cuvāmikaḷiṉ ciṣyarum.*"
24. The Sanskrit word *siddha* is rendered *cittar* (*citta* + *-r* suffix, denoting a person) in Tamil on account of the lack of separate letters for voiced and aspirated consonants in Tamil. I have retained "Siddha" for the sake of consistency with Sabhapati's non-Tamil literature.
25. This is also asserted independently in the introduction to Tirumular, *Tirumantiram: A Tamil Scriptural Classic*.
26. Tirumūlar, *Tirumantiram: mūlamum—viḷakka uraiyum*, 148–49; Tirumular, *Tirumantiram: A Tamil Scriptural Classic*, 52 (Tantra 1, verses 337–38).
27. A. V. Subramania Aiyar, *The Poetry and the Philosophy of the Tamil Siddhars: An Essay in Criticism* (1957; Chidambaram: Manivasakar Noolakam, 1969).
28. R. Venkatraman, *A History of the Tamil Siddha Cult* (Madurai: Ennes Publications, 1990).
29. Kamil Veith Zvelebil, *The Poets of the Powers* (London: Rider, 1973).
30. Kamil Veith Zvelebil, *The Siddha Quest for Immortality* (Oxford: Mandrake, 1996).
31. Richard S. Weiss, *Recipes for Immortality: Medicine, Religion, and Community in South India* (New York: Oxford University Press, 2009).
32. R. Ezhilraman, "Siddha Cult in Tamiḻnādu: Its History and Historical Continuity" (PhD dissertation, Pondicherry University, 2015).
33. For example, see Yōki Kailaṣnāt, *Cittar kaḷañciyam* (Ceṉṉai: Kaṟpakam Puttakālayam, 2017).
34. For the presence of Siddha iconography at Srisailam see Prabhavati C. Reddy, *Hindu Pilgrimage: Shifting Patterns of Worldview of Srisailam in South India* (New York: Routledge, 2014); and Robert N. Linrothe, ed., *Holy Madness: Portraits of Tantric Siddhas* (New York: Rubin Museum of Art, 2006); see also P. V. Parabrahma Sastry, *Srisailam, Its History and Cult* (Guntur: Lakshmi Mallikarjunna Press, 1985).
35. David Gordon White, *The Alchemical Body: Siddha Traditions in Medieval India* (Chicago: University of Chicago Press, 1996), 57–77.
36. For an example of this direction see also Thayanithy, "Concept of Living Liberation."

37. Venkatraman, *Tamil Siddha Cult*, 8–9.
38. CPSPS, First Book, 29.
39. See Powell, "Lamp on Śiva's Yoga." For another bhakti perspective see also Gil Ben-Herut, *Śiva's Saints: The Origins of Devotion in Kannada according to Harihara's Ragaḷegaḷu* (New York: Oxford University Press, 2018).
40. See Nā. Katiraivēr̲ Piḷḷai, *Tāyumāṉa cuvāmi pāṭalkaḷ: mūlamum uraiyum* (Chennai: Cantiyā Patippakam, 2010), 149–63; cf. Steinschneider, "Warring Sects," 92–122. I am grateful to Srilata Raman for sharing with me this early source for Śivarājayoga that predates Sabhapati's literature by around a century or more.
41. Although there is no concrete evidence, its use with "Finite Spirit" appears to have been a conscious (or unconscious) translation choice by Sabhapati's editor Shrish Chandra Basu, who would have almost certainly been exposed to nineteenth-century translations of Hegel during his time at Government College Lahore and in the student circles he frequented. Swami Vivekananda would have also likely been exposed to Hegel during his education at St. John's in Delhi, pointing to a wider philosophical interface among elite colonial-era authors of yoga; cf. David Gordon White, *The Yoga Sutra of Patanjali: A Biography* (Princeton, NJ: Princeton University Press, 2014), 116–43.
42. CPSPS, First Book, i.
43. Sanderson, "The Śaiva Age," 286 n. 686.
44. CPSPS, First Book, 45.
45. CPSPS, First Book, 45.
46. M. Monier-Williams, *A Sanskrit-English Dictionary: Etymologically and Philologically Arranged with Special Reference to Cognate Indo-European Languages* (Oxford: Clarendon Press, 1899), 432
47. Otto Böhtlingk, *Sanskrit-Wörterbuch in kürzerer Fassung*, part 3 (St. Petersburg: Buchdruckerei der Kaiserlichen Akademie der Wissenschaften, 1882), 3.
48. Dominic Goodall and Harunaga Isaacson, "How the Tattvas of Tantric Śaivism Came to Be 36: The Evidence of the Niśvāsatattvasaṃhitā," in *Tantric Studies: Fruits of a Franco-German Collaboration on Early Tantra*, ed. Dominic Goodall and Harunaga Isaacson (Pondicherry: Institut Français de Pondichéry and École française d'Extrême-Orient, 2016), 77–78.
49. Dominic Goodall, ed., *The Niśvāsatattvasaṃhitā: The Earliest Surviving Śaiva Tantra* (Pondicherry: Institut Français de Pondichéry and École française d'Extrême-Orient, 2015), 74.
50. Somadeva Vasudeva, ed., *The Yoga of Mālinīvijayottaratantra: Chapters 1–4, 7–11, 11–17* (Pondicherry: Institut Français de Pondichéry and École française d'Èxtrême-Orient, 2004).
51. CPSPS, First Book, 45.
52. CPSPS, First Book, 45.
53. CPSPS, First Book, 46.
54. Ibid. Michael Allen's new book (2022) on Niścaldās shows similar analogies.
55. CPSPS, First Book, 46.

56. I am grateful to Srilata Raman for this insight (personal communication, July 17, 2020).
57. CPSPS, First Book, 47.
58. Richard H. Davis, *Ritual in an Oscillating Universe: Worshiping Śiva in Medieval India* (Princeton, NJ: Princeton University Press, 1991), 185–86; see also 42–52.
59. Ibid., 67.
60. CPSPS, First Book, 87–88.
61. For more on this yogic power of the eye and its perception, see David Gordon White, *Sinister Yogis* (Chicago: University of Chicago Press, 2009), 154–61.
62. White, *The Alchemical Body*, 36–45. See also Manon Hedenborg White, *The Eloquent Blood: The Goddess Babalon and the Construction of Femininities in Western Esotericism* (New York: Oxford University Press, 2020), 157–95, for the way *kalās* were interpreted in the occultist Kenneth Grant's literature.
63. Sabhapati explains (CPSPS, First Book, 126) that "Kundali" (< Skt. *kuṇḍalī*, "ring") is so called since it is the place where the subtle *nāḍīs* "join with the lingam and bend downwards to ascend upwards" (see Chapter 4). CPSPS in at least one other place (First Book, 75) curiously refers to this location as the "bottom and centre of the Spiritual Organ of throwing Urine."
64. VRY1, 15–16; CPSPS, First Book, 57–61.
65. André Padoux, *Vāc: The Concept of the Word in Selected Hindu Tantras* (Albany: State University of New York Press, 1990), 135 n. 38.
66. For example, see CPSPS, First Book, 51–66, for "manifestation" and First Book, 75–80, for "resorption" along the same system of cakras. The second and third chapters of RYB also deal with manifestation (Hi. *parabrahm, māyā, tatva, ādi kram vicār*) and resorption (Hi. *tatvalay*), respectively, along this same model.
67. MCVTS, 73.
68. RYB, 21–33. The sixteen "rays" are part of the sixteenth digit of the third or Īśvara tattva.
69. Gerald James Larson, *Classical Sāṃkhya: An Interpretation of Its History and Meaning* (Delhi: Motilal Banarsidass, 1979), 4.
70. The translations follow those given in ibid., 236; and Gerald James Larson and Ram Shankar Bhattacharya, "Philosophy of Sāṃkhya," in *Encyclopedia of Indian Philosophies*, vol. 4, *Sāṃkhya: A Dualist Tradition in Indian Philosophy*, ed. Gerald James Larson and Ram Shankar Bhattacharya (Delhi: Motilal Banarsidass, 1987), 49. See those sources for more detailed charts and analysis of these tattvas and their relationships.
71. *Sāṃkhyakārikā*, 78; see Larson, *Classical Sāṃkhya*, 275. For more on this text the reader may also consult Philipp Maas's online course with Yogic Studies entitled *The Sāṅkhyakārikā*: Stanzas on All-Embracing Insight.
72. See VRY1, 10–19.
73. See Tirumular, *Tirumantiram: A Tamil Scriptural Classic*, 411 (v. 2656); Tirumūlar, *Tirumūlar Tirumantiram: mūlamum—viḷakka uraiyum*, 1184 (v. 2656).
74. Goodall and Isaacson, "Tattvas of Tantric Śaivism," 78. For their embodiment in some Śaiva traditions see also Davis, *Ritual in an Oscillating Universe*, 44–45, 52–53.

75. Goodall and Isaacson, "Tattvas of Tantric Śaivism," 78. The chapter that Goodall and Isaacson cite is Raffaele Torella, "The Kañcukas in the Śaiva and Vaiṣṇava Tantric Tradition: A Few Considerations between Theology and Grammar," in *Studies in Hinduism II: Miscellanea to the Phenomenon of Tantras*, ed. Gerhard Oberhammer (Vienna: Der Österreichischen Akademie der Wissenschaften, 1998), 55–86.
76. See, however, Figures 3.8 and 3.9 for an alternative way these tattvas are expressed in his Tamil work CTCSPV.
77. See, for example, the use of "Tantric yoga" as a category of yoga in Mark Singleton, *Yoga Body: The Origins of Modern Posture Practice* (New York: Oxford University Press, 2010), xvii–xx. While not entirely satisfactory, a similar phrase has been used to describe Sabhapati's yoga since at least the 1970s, when a reprint of his work described his yoga as "Tantra Yoga" in the title: Maahtma Giana Guroo Yogi Sabhapaty Swami, *Vedantic Raj Yoga: Ancient Tantra Yoga of Rishies* (New Delhi: Pankaj Publications, 1977). This descriptor "Tantra Yoga" to my knowledge is not used in any of Sabhapati's works published during his lifetime.
78. Singleton, *Yoga Body*, 171–227; David Gordon White, *Kiss of the Yoginī: "Tantric Sex" in its South Asian Contexts* (Chicago: University of Chicago Press, 2006), 177–87.
79. For *kuṇḍalinī* in a Trika Śaiva perspective, see Lilian Silburn, *La Kuṇḍalinī, ou, L'énergie des profondeurs: Étude d'ensemble d'après les textes du Śivaïsme non dualiste du Kaśmir* (Paris: Deux océans, 1983) or its English translation.
80. James Mallinson and Mark Singleton, eds., *Roots of Yoga* (London: Penguin Books, 2017), 175–80; John Woodroffe, *The Serpent Power: Being the Shat-Chakra-Nirupana and Paduka-Panchaka: Two Works on Tantrik Yoga* (London: Luzac, 1919). For the spread of the Avalon literature see Julian Strube, *Global Tantra: Religion, Science, and Nationalism in Colonial Modernity* (New York: Oxford University Press, 2022).
81. Mallinson and Singleton, *Roots of Yoga*, 176–77.
82. Srilata Raman, personal correspondence, July 17, 2020.
83. Eric Steinschneider, "Subversion, Authenticity, and Religious Creativity in Late-Medieval South India: Kaṇṇuṭaiya Vaḷḷal's Oḻiviloṭukkam," *Journal of Hindu Studies* 10, no. 2 (August 2017): 253.
84. Ibid., 268–69 n. 23.
85. Ibid. These ten acts are *tattuva rūpam* (< Skt. *tattvarūpa* "form of the principles"), *tattuva taricaṉam* (< Skt. *tattvadarśana*, "vision of the principles"), *tattuva cutti* (< Skt. *tattvaśuddhi*, "purification of the principles"), *āṉma rūpam* (< Skt. *ātmarūpa*, "form of the self"), *āṉma taricaṉam* (< Skt. *ātmadarśana*, "vision of the self"), *āṉma cutti* (< Skt. *ātmaśuddhi*, "purification of the self"), *civa rūpam* (< Skt. *śivarūpa*, "form of the godhead"), *civa taricaṉam* (< Skt. *śivadarśana*, "vision of the godhead"), *civa yōkam* (< Skt. *śivayoga*, "union with the godhead"), and *civa pōkam* (< Skt. *śivabhoga*, "enjoyment of the godhead").
86. For these see Alexis Sanderson, "Mandala and Āgamic Identity in the Trika of Kashmir," in *Mantras et diagrammes rituelles dans l'Hindouisme*, ed. Andre Padoux (Paris: Éditions du Centre National de la Recherche Scientifique, 1986), 169–214. As indicated above, the Tamil *parai* is a phonetic transformation of Parā, a principal goddess of the Trika, for which consult early Trika scriptures from the

Siddhayogeśvarīmata onward through Trika/Pratyabhijñā literature in Kashmir. For an analysis of the historical contexts in which Kashmiri forms of Śaivism had a major influence on south India in the medieval period, see Whitney Cox, "Making a Tantra in Medieval South India: The Mahārthamañjarī and the Textual Culture of Cōḻa Cidambaram: Volume I" (PhD dissertation, University of Chicago, 2006), 14–17 and throughout.

87. See Vētacirēṇi Citampara Cuvāmikaḷ, *Upatēcavuṇmaiyum upatēcavuṇmaikkaṭṭaḷaiyum tōttiramālaiyum aṭaṅkiyirukkiṉṟatu*, ed. Tirumayilai Vaitiliṅkatēcikar (Chennai: Cakalakalānilaiyaccukkūṭam, 1881), 52–53. For Sabhapati's engagement with subtle elements see CPSPS, First Book, 61–66.

88. According to Srilata Raman (personal correspondence, July 17, 2020), Sabhapati Swami's childhood friend and contemporary Chidambaram Ramalinga Swamigal also experimented with the levels of the tattvas so as to "create a Śaivite cosmogony which would supersede both that of the Tamil Śaivasiddhānta as well as that of the Vīraśaiva, placing his above both of the others."

89. CPSPS, Second Book, 232.

90. CPSPS, Second Book, 326. Sabhapati calls this the "Meditation of the Universal Self-Infinite Spiritual state or Shiva Linga Swaroop [*śivaliṅgasvarūpa*]" (Mpvl. *pahirpāva antarapāva civaliṅka pahirpūjā antarapūjā*, < Skt. *bahirabhāva antarabhāva śivaliṅga bahirapūjā antarapūjā*, lit. [meditation on] the internal and external state and internal and external worship of the *liṅga*). The word "shapes" appears to be Sabhapati's (or his editor's) eclectic translation here of *svarūpa*.

91. Tirumūlar, *The Tirumandiram*, 1895–97. Tirumūlar, *Tirumūlar Tirumantiram: mūlamum—viḷakka uraiyum*, 746; Tirumular, *Tirumantiram: A Tamil Scriptural Classic*, 270–71.

92. Padoux, *Vāc*, 88–89.

93. I am grateful to Srilata Raman for this insight (personal correspondence, July 17, 2020), which alludes to a genre of texts known to Tamil Vīraśaivism in which "the reabsorption soteriologically happens when one crosses *parai* and then reaches Paraśiva who is beyond all the *tattvas*"; one such text to indicate this reabsorption is Cīkāḻi Ciṟṟampalanāṭikaḷ's *Tukaḷarupōtam*. As noted previously, this "crossing" is strikingly similar to Sabhapati's descriptions of Śivarājayoga (see Chapter 4).

94. RYB, Fifth Chapter, 60–78. See also CPSPS, Second Book, 246–50.

95. CPSPS, First Book, 118. For a criticism of this view of the *liṅga* see Gritli V. Mitterwallner, "Evolution of the Liṅga," in *Discourses on Śiva: Proceedings of a Symposium on the Nature of Religious Imagery* (Philadelphia: University of Philadelphia Press, 1984), 26–27. For a counterpoint to Mitterwallner, see Hélène Brunner, "The Sexual Aspect of the Liṅga Cult According to the Saiddhāntika Scriptures," in Oberhammer *Studies in Hinduism*, 87–103.

96. CPSPS, First Book, 72.

97. CPSPS, Second Book, 405.

98. CPSPS, Second Book, 405.

99. CPSPS, Second Book, 405.

100. CPSPS, Second Book, 405.

101. CPSPS, Second Book, 405.
102. See Julie Chajes, *Recycled Lives: A History of Reincarnation in Blavatsky's Theosophy* (New York: Oxford University Press, 2019),for an overview of Blavatsky's views on transmigration. While she does not mention Sabhapati Swami, there is a substantial section of the views of other South Asian authors she engaged.
103. For more on the broader context of these kinds of exchanges, of which Sabhapati was a part for a brief period, see Hans Martin Krämer and Julian Strube, eds., *Theosophy across Boundaries: Transcultural and Interdisciplinary Perspectives on a Modern Esoteric Movement* (Albany: State University of New York Press, 2020); and Erik Sand and Tim Rudbøg, eds., *Imagining the East: The Early Theosophical Society* (Oxford: Oxford University Press, 2019).
104. Andrew Topsfield, "The Indian Game of Snakes and Ladders," *Artibus Asiae* 46, no. 3 (1985): 203–26. The versions in Sabhapati's texts most closely resemble the Jaina examples in this article (see especially Topsfield's Figure 4) in that the squares are situated in an anthropomorphic form that includes a head and body.
105. For an organized enumeration of the tattvas in Sāṃkhya see Larson and Bhattacharya, "Philosophy of Sāṃkhya," 49.
106. Tirumular, *Tirumantiram: A Tamil Scriptural Classic*, 318–19 (verses 2023–26); Tirumūlar, *Tirumūlar Tirumantiram: mūlamum—viḷakka uraiyum*, 879–82 (verse 2656).
107. Carol Salomon, "Bāul Songs," in *Religions in India in Practice*, ed. Donald Lopez (Princeton, NJ: Princeton University Press, 1995), 193.
108. Hans Harder, *Sufism and Saint Veneration in Contemporary Bangladesh: The Maijbhandaris of Chittagong* (Hoboken, NJ: Taylor & Francis, 2011).
109. See especially Ahmad Śarīph, *Bāul tattva* (Dhaka: Bangla Academy, 1973). A dated but still relevant discussion of this topic is found in Shashi Bhusan Das Gupta, *Obscure Religious Cults*, 3rd ed. (Calcutta: Firma K.L. Mukhopadhyay, 1969).
110. James Mallinson, "Kālavañcana in the Konkan: How a Vajrayāna Haṭhayoga Tradition Cheated Buddhism's Death in India," *Religions* 10, no. 4 (2019): 1–33.
111. For one attempt to describe these connections between the Nāths of the north and of the south see Ezhilraman, "Siddha Cult in Tamiḻnādu," 14–34.
112. For an example of this contestation, see the lecture by Lubomír Ondračka, "Is the Bengali Nāth Literature Really Nāth?," January 13, 2021, https://www.youtube.com/watch?v=5-u6yjETgus, sponsored by the Centre of Yoga Studies at the School of Oriental and African Studies (SOAS).
113. Salomon, "Bāul Songs." For some of these connections see also Keith Cantú, "Islamic Esotericism in the Bengali Bāul Songs of Lālan Fakir," *Correspondences* 7, no. 1 (2019): 109–65; Carola Lorea, "Playing the Football of Love on the Field of the Body: The Contemporary Repertoire of Baul Songs," *Religion and the Arts* 17, no. 4 (2013): 416–51; Jeanne Openshaw, *Seeking Bāuls of Bengal* (Cambridge: Cambridge University Press, 2002); Glen Hayes, "The Necklace of Immortality: A Seventeenth-Century Vaiṣṇava-Sahajiyā Text," in *Tantra in Practice*, ed. David Gordon White (Princeton, NJ: Princeton University Press, 2000), 308–26; and Rahul Peter Das, "Problematic Aspects of the Sexual Rituals of the Bāuls of Bengal," *Journal of the American Oriental Society* 112, no. 3 (1992): 388–432, among many others.

114. Sanderson, "The Śaiva Age," 41–351. I am grateful to Srilata Raman for allowing me to participate in a course she offered entitled After the Śaiva Age that helped make better sense of these developments between medieval Śaiva Siddhānta and the early modern Śaiva religious movements that informed Sabhapati's literature.
115. For a treatment of this text see Steinschneider, "Subversion."
116. Ibid.
117. For the wider south Indian context of this development, see Fisher, "Remaking South Indian Śaivism"; also Alexis Sanderson, "The Śaiva Literature," *Journal of Indological Studies* 24–25 (2012–13, 2014): 83–91.
118. For the social and historical contexts of this see Sanderson, "The Śaiva Literature," 87, 87 nn. 356–57.
119. J. M. Nallaswāmi Pillai, trans., *Śivajñāna Siddhiyār of Aruṇandi Śivāchārya* (Madras: Meykandan Press, 1913), 96, II.14; cf. Sanderson, "The Śaiva Literature," 86.
120. ŚYP 3.63; see Sadāśivayogīśvara, *Śivayogadīpikā*, ed. Hari Nārāyaṇa Āpṭe (Ānandāśrama: Pune, 1907), 13; Sadasiva Yogindra, "Sivayogadipika," *The Brahmavâdin* 8, no. 12 (December 1903): 691. I am grateful to Seth Powell for pointing out the salience of this concept to the ŚYP. His forthcoming critical edition of this text may result in a change in the numbering or substance of this verse.
121. I have retained Sabhapati's idiosyncratic translations in English on account of their interpretive value for understanding how he viewed these doctrines. CPSPS, First Book, 148–52.
122. CPSPS, First Book, 152.
123. While *āṇavamala* can be translated the "filth of materiality," it didn't have the same meaning, at least for Sabhapati, as physical materiality; see Chapter 6.
124. Larson and Bhattacharya, "Philosophy of Sāṃkhya," 49; Larson, *Classical Sāṃkhya*, 187–89.
125. Cikāḻic Ciṟṟampalanāṭikaḷ, *Tukaḷaṟu pōtam* (Paruttitturai [Point Pedro], Sri Lanka: Kalānitiyantiracālai, 1950), 10–11.
126. Mpvl. *maṉōyantakaraṇam*, < Skt. *mano antaḥkaraṇa*.
127. Mpvl. *puttiyantakkaraṇam*, < Skt. *buddhyantaḥkaraṇa*.
128. Mpvl. *ahaṅkārayantakkaraṇam*, < Skt. *ahaṃkārāntaḥkaraṇa*.
129. Mpvl. *cittayantakkaraṇam*, < Skt. *cittāntaḥkaraṇa*. This passage is found in VRY1, 42. CPSPS in its version adds "with 5 Cosa [Skt. *kośa*], Avusta [*avasthā*], and 13 Guna [*guṇa*]."
130. RYB, 29 (end of the second chapter).
131. RYB, 29.
132. This is also relevant to some extent to the consideration of Vivekananda's own "neo-Vedānta"; see James Madaio, "Rethinking Neo-Vedānta: Swami Vivekananda and the Selective Historiography of Advaita Vedānta," *Religions* 8, no. 101 (2017).
133. Karl-Stéphan Bouthillette, *Dialogue and Doxography in Indian Philosophy: Points of View in Buddhist, Jaina, and Advaita Vedānta Traditions* (Abingdon, Oxon: Routledge, 2020); Wilhelm Halbfass, *India and Europe: An Essay in Philosophical Understanding* (Delhi: Motilal Banarsidass, 1990), 349–69.

134. See Tomoko Masuzawa, *The Invention of World Religions, or, How European Universalism Was Preserved in the Language of Pluralism* (Chicago: University of Chicago Press, 2005).
135. CPSPS, Second Book, 362–65.
136. This use of allegorical language here, as with Sabhapati's above discussion of the tattvas, serves to connect his ideas with other works relating to allegories of Vedānta, such as the eleventh-century *Prabodhacandrodaya* of Kr̥ṣṇamiśra; see Sita Krishna Nambiar, ed., *Prabodhacandrodaya of Kr̥ṣṇa Miśra* (Delhi: Motilal Banarsidass, 1971); Kr̥ṣṇamiśra and Matthew Kapstein, *The Rise of Wisdom Moon* (New York: New York University Press, 2009).
137. CPSPS, Second Book, 377.
138. For more on this see the article by Keith Cantú, "Translating Esotericism: Tamil," in the special issue "Translating Esotericism," ed. Wouter Hanegraaff and Mriganka Mukhopadhyay, *Correspondences: Journal for the Study of Esotericism*, forthcoming.
139. CPSPS, Second Book, 373–74.
140. CPSPS, Second Book, 373–74.
141. CPSPS, Second Book, 373–74.
142. Sabhapati on this front may have been influenced, at least indirectly, by Rhys Davids and others in the Pali Text Society who were critical of native Buddhist customs in the colonial period; see Philip C. Almond, *The British Discovery of Buddhism* (Cambridge: Cambridge University Press, 1988).
143. Ibid. For the Buddhist roots of haṭha yoga see James Mallinson, "The Amr̥tasiddhi: Haṭhayoga's Tantric Buddhist Source Text," in *Śaivism and the Tantric Traditions: Essays in Honour of Alexis G.J.S. Sanderson*, ed. Dominic Goodall et al. (Leiden: Brill, 2020), 409–25; and Jason Birch, "The Amaraughaprabodha: New Evidence on the Manuscript Transmission of an Early Work on Haṭha- and Rājayoga," *Journal of Indian Philosophy* 47 (2019): 947–77.

    For an example of the kind of Indian Buddhism that was prevalent in the medieval period and how it had its roots in earlier Mahayana doctrine, see Vesna A. Wallace, *The Inner Kālacakratantra: A Buddhist Tantric View of the Individual* (New York: Oxford University Press, 2001).
144. CTCSPV, 38.
145. CPSPS, Second Book, 374.
146. CPSPS, Second Book, 375.
147. CPSPS, Second Book, 375.
148. See Chajes, *Recycled Lives*, 55–56. The verse in question reads, "I have said, Ye *are* gods; and all of you *are* children of the most High" (King James Version).
149. CPSPS, Second Book, 366–67.
150. CPSPS, Second Book, 377.
151. For these definitions and their time frames, especially in the context of *avatārs*, see Madeleine Biardeau and Charles Malamoud, *Le sacrifice dans l'Inde ancienne* (Paris: Presses Universitaires de France, 1976), 119–20.
152. Ibid.
153. CPSPS, Second Book, 377.

154. This may be a response to the Śaiva Saiddhāntika position that Shiva is without origin (*anādi*).
155. CPSPS, Second Book, 377.
156. CTCSPV, 38.
157. CPSPS, Second Book, 378.
158. CPSPS, Second Book, 378.
159. CPSPS, Second Book, 378.
160. For more on this community and its religious history see Michael Stausberg and Yuhan Sohrab-Dinshaw Vevaina, eds., *The Wiley Blackwell Companion to Zoroastrianism* (Chicester, West Sussex: John Wiley & Sons, 2015), 157–73; Helmut Humbach, "Mithra in India and the Hinduized Magi," in *Études Mithriaques: Actes du 2e Congrès International Téhéran, du 1er au 8 Septembre 1975* (Leiden: Brill, 1978), 230–52.
161. CPSPS, Second Book, 378–79. The rest of the quotations in this section, unless otherwise noted, are from these pages.
162. I am grateful to Mariano Errichiello for reading this section of Sabhapati's work and offering his comments, some of which inform this section. He explains the following about Zend (email correspondence, July 1, 2020): "It is a Middle Persian term proceeding from the Avestan *zanti* 'interpretation' which refers to commentaries to the Avesta (collection of Zoroastrian sacred texts). However, in the 18th and 19th [centuries], Orientalists were referring to the term Zend as the holy Zoroastrian scripture, probably due to the assonance with Pazand (a writing system based on the Avestan script and used for Middle Persian language)."
163. Søren Sørensen, *An Index to the Names in the Mahābhārata* (London: Williams and Norgate, 1904), 538.
164. See White, *Sinister Yogis*, 144–45.
165. Errichiello, email correspondence, July 1, 2020.
166. Ibid.
167. CPSPS, Second Book, 381. It is possible that Sabhapati could have also had the Dev Samaj (Dev Samāj) in mind (see Chapter 1).
168. See Karl Baier, "Mesmeric Yoga and the Development of Meditation within the Theosophical Society," *Theosophical History* 16, nos. 3–4 (October 2012): 156–57.
169. CPSPS, Second Book, 380.
170. CPSPS, Second Book, 381.
171. CPSPS, Second Book, 383.
172. For the latter, see Kenneth W. Jones, *Arya Dharm: Hindu Consciousness in 19th-Century Punjab* (Berkeley: University of California Press, 1976).
173. In this Sabhapati somewhat resembles Traditionalist reactions against modernity but coming from an Indian rather than European voice; for more on this phenomenon see Mark Sedgwick, *Against the Modern World: Traditionalism and the Secret Intellectual History of the Twentieth Century* (New York: Oxford University Press, 2009).
174. Ibid., 384.
175. Ibid., 385.

176. Joscelyn Godwin, "Blavatsky and the First Generation of Theosophy," in *Handbook of the Theosophical Current*, ed. Olav Hammer and Mikael Rothstein (Leiden: Brill, 2013), 15–31.
177. Chajes, *Recycled Lives*, 29; Karl Baier, *Meditation und Moderne: Zur Genese eines Kernbereichs moderner Spiritualität in der Wechselwirkung zwischen Westeuropa, Nordamerika und Asien* (Würzburg: Königshausen & Neumann, 2009), 329–35.
178. See Chapter 2 of Julian Strube, *Global Tantra: Religion, Science, and Nationalism in Colonial Modernity* (New York: Oxford University Press, 2022). At this early date (1880s–1900s) the adjective "Aryan" (< Skt. *ārya*) referred to a shared conception of Indian philosophical heritage and did not yet have the overtly racist connotations that it would acquire a half-century later under the Third Reich. Nevertheless, at that time it was salient to a budding colonial-era nationalism; *aryāvarta*, or "cyclic home of the Aryas," had been cited at least as early as the "Laws of Manu" (*Manusmṛti* 2.22–23), and Sabhapati and his editor Shrish Chandra Basu do tend to conceptualize "India" more broadly as a cultural and geographical entity.
179. CPSPS, First Book, 106–7.
180. CPSPS, First Book, 106.
181. CPSPS, First Book, 106.
182. For some of the specifics of these exchanges, see Chajes, *Recycled Lives*, 160–83; and Karl Baier, "Theosophical Orientalism and the Structures of Intercultural Transfer: Annotations on the Appropriations of the Cakras in Early Theosophy," in *Theosophical Appropriations: Esotericism, Kabbalah and the Transformation of Traditions*, ed. Julie Chajes and Boaz Huss (Be'er Sheva, Israel: Ben-Gurion University of the Negev Press, 2016), 309–54.
183. CPSPS, Second Book, 385.
184. CPSPS, Second Book, 385.
185. John Patrick Deveney, *Theosophical History Occasional Papers*, vol. 6, *Astral Projection or Liberation of the Double and the Work of the Early Theosophical Society* (Fullerton, CA: Theosophical History, 1997); see also Chajes, *Recycled Lives*, 29.
186. CPSPS, Second Book, 220.
187. Magdalena Kraler, "Tracing Vivekananda's Prāṇa and Ākāśa: The Yogavāsiṣṭha and Rama Prasad's Occult Science of Breath," in *The Occult Nineteenth Century: Roots, Developments, and Impact on the Modern World*, ed. Lukas Pokorny and Franz Winter (London: Palgrave Macmillan, 2021), 373–99. I am grateful to Magdalena for sharing with me an early draft of her chapter, much of which should be read in conversation with Sabhapati's own discourse in this chapter.
188. CPSPS, Second Book, 405–16.
189. CPSPS, Second Book, 416.
190. CPSPS, Second Book, 413.
191. Christopher Brooke, "How the Stoics Became Atheists," *Historical Journal* 49, no. 2 (2006): 387–402. I am grateful to Joseph Blankholm for sharing with me the historical understanding of the origins of atheistic philosophy that are reflected in this paragraph.

192. Michael LeBuffe, "Paul-Henri Thiry (Baron) d'Holbach," in *The Stanford Encyclopedia of Philosophy*, ed. Edward N. Zalta, 2020, https://plato.stanford.edu/archives/spr2020/entries/holbach/.
193. Charles Bradlaugh, "A Plea for Atheism," in *A Few Words about the Devil, and Other Biographical Sketches and Essays* (New York: A.K. Butts & Co., 1874), 2.
194. Ibid., 11.
195. CPSPS, Second Book, 406.
196. CPSPS, Second Book, 406.
197. CPSPS, Second Book, 403.
198. CPSPS, Second Book, 403.
199. For more on the wider theory of yogic perception that Sabhapati is probably contrasting with the science of physical optics, see White, *Sinister Yogis*, 154–61.
200. CPSPS, Second Book, 212–16.
201. CTCSPV, 24–25. See also Chapter 6.
202. Egil Asprem, *The Problem of Disenchantment: Scientific Naturalism and Esoteric Discourse, 1900–1939* (Albany: State University of New York Press, 2018), 67–72.
203. Chajes, *Recycled Lives*, 132–59.
204. For Crowley's response to Victorian scientific naturalism see Egil Asprem, "Magic Naturalized? Negotiating Science and Occult Experience in Aleister Crowley's Scientific Illuminism," *Aries* 8 (2008): 139–65.
205. CPSPS, Second Book, 408.
206. CPSPS, Second Book, 408–13.
207. CPSPS, Second Book, 414.
208. CPSPS, Second Book, 217–18.
209. See also CPSPS, First Book, 120, for a description of consciousness as "Universally pervading."
210. CPSPS, Second Book, 414–15.

4

Breathing into Śivarājayoga

> Among the main yogas there are three kinds, the *first* of which is the "yoga of force," being the binding of the breath. . . . The *second*, being the binding of the breath and the mind, is the "royal yoga of force." . . . The *third*, being the subjugation of gnosis, is the "royal yoga for Śiva."
>
> —MCVTS (long version), 39

> This Raja Yoga practice is Gnyana Pranayamam of conceiving or பாவம் [*pāvam*, < Skt. *bhāva*] . . . Finding . . . Absorbing . . . Becoming . . . and Being.
>
> —MCVTS (long version), 47

As outlined in the previous chapter, Sabhapati's descriptions of the "descent" or "emanations" of the tattvas are predicated upon a subtle physiology of cakras (< Skt. *cakra*, "wheel"). These are enlivened by the presence of a subtle principle that he variously refers to as *prāṇākāśa* ("vital ether"), *jñānākāśa* ("gnostic ether"), or simply *jñāna* ("gnosis" or "knowledge") (see Chapter 6 for his place in the contemporary discourse around "ether"). These descriptions, however, are not just theoretical "maps" of the body but are intertwined with a wide variety of interconnected practices, including mental visualizations, the recitation of correspondent mantras and hymns that are to be chanted at certain times, as well as a whole host of other rituals, meditations, and mantras for specific occasions.[1] Since an analysis of all his practices could fill volumes, in this chapter I limit my analysis to the main topic of relevance to this book: Sabhapati's instructions on how to experience the universally spread treelike state of Śivarājayoga ("royal yoga for Shiva"). The central part of these instructions is a process by which these cakras are to be canceled out by means of meditative refutations so as to attain a state of "composure," or "communion" (Skt. *samādhi*), which Sabhapati usually translates as "communion" or "ecstasy."

Like a Tree Universally Spread. Keith Edward Cantú, Oxford University Press. © Oxford University Press 2023.
DOI: 10.1093/oso/9780197665473.003.0005

Three Branches of Yoga

The term "rāja yoga" (< Skt. *rājayoga*) in its early history denoted a form of yogic samādhi that is characterized by the "absence of mental activity" (*cittavṛttirahitaḥ*), but it later came to denote a wide variety of practices that drew from textual sources as varied as the Brahma Sūtra, the Yoga Upanishads, and the Tantras.[2] Sabhapati maintains this earlier meaning of rāja yoga as samādhi, which he qualifies throughout his works as *brahmajñāna śivarājayoga niṣṭhā samādhi*, "The unwavering composure that is the royal yoga for Śiva, which is the gnosis of Brahman." However, as his texts were composed very late in the history of rāja yoga, he is also clearly drawing (consciously or not) upon a variety of innovative practices to help facilitate this samādhi, perhaps foremost among which are his techniques of "canceling" the Tantric cakras or "Twelve Spiritual Lights" of the Finite Spirit that are part of his cosmology (see Chapter 3 and the section Śivarājayoga or "Royal Yoga for Shiva" in this chapter).

While Sabhapati's understanding of rāja yoga as a qualified kind of samādhi does resonate with its definition in other medieval and early modern texts on this subject, he departs from most if not all known systems in his distinction between three main kinds of yoga: (1) "Haṭha Yoga" (Tam. *aṭayōkam*, < Skt. *haṭhayoga*), (2) "Haṭha Rājayoga," and (3) "Śivarājayoga."[3] This triadic sequence contrasts, on the one hand, with the sequence of Mantrayoga, Layayoga, Haṭhayoga, and Rājayoga as found in some seminal medieval texts of yoga such as the *Amaraughaprabodha* and the *Śivayogapradīpikā* (ŚYP),[4] and on the other hand with the more contemporary dichotomy in modern yoga and Theosophy between haṭha yoga and rāja yoga as "physical" versus "mental" methods of yoga, a dichotomy that did not address any "supplementary" form of rāja yoga (whether Śivayoga, as salient in the ŚYP, or Śivarājayoga as in the writings of Sabhapati Swami). Sabhapati's triadic sequence is consistent and recurs throughout his published literature; he explicitly mentions the full sequence in at least two instances in both his English and Tamil works and also offers an entirely separate chapter on Śivarājayoga in his Hindi work (see Śivarājayoga: From Purification to Nonbeing).

While the phrase occurs in VRY1, Sabhapati's first use of the full classification is found in a section entitled "A Brief Sketch of Vedantism and Yoga" appended to the second and third editions of VRY (VRY2 and VRY3), respectively published in 1883 and 1895, and likely added by Shrish Chandra Basu (see Chapter 1 for his editorial involvement). After noting that many kinds of yoga have been enumerated by "ancient authors," such as "Karma Yoga or Hatha Yoga, Mantra Yoga, Raj Yoga," the author says that only "Hatha Yoga and the Raj Yoga need to be mentioned here."[5] When asked to distinguish between the two, he notes the following: "Hatha Yoga is a process of physical training, in order to strengthen the will. The Raja Yoga is a process of pure mental training for the same purpose. The Hatha Yoga is the lowest, the Raja Yoga the middle, and the Shiva Raja Yoga (i.e., spiritual method) the highest." He then goes on to describe "Raja Yoga" (not "Shiva Raja Yoga") in terms of Patañjali's "auxiliaries" or "limbs" (*aṅgas*, see Haṭha Yoga or "Yoga of Force") and divides it into three parts.[6] Interestingly, he does not continue this section with a description of Śivarājayoga but appears to be content to describe the "middle" process, or rāja yoga, after which the dialogue and the book concludes.

Three decades later, Sabhapati would elaborate in much more detail on this sequence of his three yogas in his Tamil work MCVTS, a translation of which is as follows (my personal translation from Tamil, using some of Sabhapati's own terminology such as "Infinite Spirit" for Brahman, "Finite Spirit" for *jīvan*, and "communion" for samādhi, more literally "composition" or "composure" for the sake of consistency with his English cosmology outlined in Chapter 3):

> [Haṭha Yoga]
> Listen, O students: Among the main yogas there are three kinds, the *first* of which is the "yoga of force" [Mpvl. *aṭayōkam*, < Skt. *haṭhayoga*), being the binding of the breath [Mpvl. *cuvācapantaṉam*, < Skt. *śvāsabandhana*]. If the downward-flowing breath is stopped by means of inhalation, retention, and exhalation in the *suṣumnā*, *iḍā*, and *piṅgaḷā* pipes, and if there is a binding, arresting, or fixing of the upward-flowing [breath] in the *suṣumnā* pipe up to the fontanelle, there is a restraint of the vital breath [Mpvl. *pirāṇāyāmam*, < Skt. *prāṇāyāma*]. With this the gnosis of the Infinite Spirit and release is impossible. [Instead,] the result of this is long life and the dissolution of the principles. This breath is the agent of the Finite Spiritual mind. Such a one is dissolved [Tam. *oṭuṅku*] in the gnosis of the absolute void [Mpvl. *carva cuṉyakñāṉam*, < Skt. *sarva śūnyajñāna*].[7]
>
> [Haṭha Rājayoga]
> The *second* [kind of yoga], being the binding of the breath and the mind, is the "royal yoga of force" [Mpvl. *haṭa rājayōkam*, < Skt. *haṭha rājayoga*].

Here the breath and the mind, going up to the nostrils from the coiled organ [Mpvl. *kuṇṭali*, < Skt. *kuṇḍali*] via the *suṣumnā*, *iḍā*, and *piṅgaḷā* streams, are joined together in the *suṣumnā* pipe that runs from the anus and is connected to the end of the fontanelle via the nostrils. In such a way these [the breath and mind] are arrested like a pillar [that is] devoid of stirring, moving, unsteadiness, wishing, doubting, thinking, or denying, and is without self-delusion. This is the dissolution of breath and mind [Mpvl. *cuvācamaṉōlayam*, < Skt. *śvāsamanolaya*], and their stopping is as the fullness of abiding in the joy of awakening and in ecstasy, being the vitality-restraint of breath and mind [Mpvl. *cuvācamaṉō pirāṇāyāmam*, < Skt. *śvāsamano prāṇāyāma*]. By this the gnosis of the dissolution of mind [Mpvl. *maṉōlayakñāṉam*, < Skt. *manolayajñāna*] is attained.[8]

[Śivarājayoga]

The *third* [kind of yoga], being the subjugation of gnosis [Mpvl. *kñāṉavaciyam*, < Skt. *jñānavaśya*], is the "royal yoga for Śiva" [Mpvl. *civarājayōkam*, < Skt. *śivarājayoga*]. In Vedānta modes of knowledge and discourse it is defined as a kind of gnosis, being the nature of unified oneness between the self and Brahman, the nature of nonduality, the nature of unity. In Saiddhāntika modes of knowledge and discussion it is defined as the dissolution of Brahman and the self, the nature of "I am a servant" [Skt. *dāso 'ham bhāva*], the nature of duality, the nature of dissolution. With steadfastness in the communion of meditation there is steadfastness in the communion of gnosis.[9]

From this it is clear that Sabhapati intended Śivarājayoga to be a distinct category of practice apart from Haṭha Yoga and Haṭha Rājayoga, and in this sense it is perhaps more akin to the Śivayoga of the ŚYP. However, there are also certain key differences with Śivayoga, such as the lists of cakras and other defining features; see the third part of Chapter 3 for the ways in which Śivayoga could be distinguished from Śivarājayoga in Tamil literary discourse.[10] As a result, Sabhapati's interpretations of Haṭha Yoga and Haṭha Rājayoga must first be analyzed to distinguish how Śivarājayoga differed in his view.

Haṭha Yoga or "Yoga of Force"

Sabhapati's first category, Haṭha Yoga or the "yoga of force," is an area of research that keeps evolving as scholars continue to reexamine sources in Sanskrit literature and to compare these sources with ethnographic investigation.[11] Current consensus is that it emerged in a Buddhist Tantric milieu with the circa eleventh-century text *Amṛtasiddhi*, but was formally codified by the circa thirteenth-century *Dattatreyayogaśāstra*.[12] As evident from his definitions, Sabhapati's own engagement with haṭha yoga is predicated on the binding of the breath and the physical techniques of *prāṇāyāma*. Scholars today agree, however, that haṭha yoga can refer to a much broader assortment of practices, some of which likely derive from ancient Indian practices of *tapas*, which in classical Sanskrit literature referred to a kind of ascetic heat produced through austerities carried out by various heroes, sages, or divine beings. In subsequent centuries haṭha yoga was represented as an alternative to Pātañjalayoga, and by the nineteenth century it was viewed as largely synonymous with the "eight auxiliaries" or "limbs" (*aṣṭāṅga*) of Patañjali.[13] At the time Sabhapati was writing, which was prior to its resurgence in the mid-twentieth century, haṭha yoga was also stigmatized as "black magic" in at least some colonial-era milieus on accounts of its claim to produce powers or *siddhi*s, as traceable in Theosophical literature, and numerous warnings were issued against its misuse without guidance from a guru.[14]

Despite facing a colonial-era stigma against haṭha yoga, Sabhapati's multilingual work CPSPS does include a general section on this kind of yoga entitled "Instructions on the Hata Yogue,"[15] a section that is relatively evenhanded in its approach for the time. In this subject he warns against injury in case haṭha yoga is wrongly practiced but also states that it is "perfectly harmless" when blended with "Shiva Raja Yogue."[16] This form of practice is centered on a theory that breath arises as the syllable "om" in the center of the heart and the *kuṇḍali* (i.e., the *mūlādhāra*; see Chapter 3), and that this breath can be manipulated to become like a "magnet" in the "centre seat of the skull" to "draw the Self Universal Infinite Spiritual aether" and thereby "spread the Infinite Spirit everywhere and in the three nerves as well."[17] As we saw in Chapter 3, the "Universal Infinite Spirit" is Brahman or Shiva or Sarveśvara, construed as a "passive" principle. The three nerves, part of the "active" principle, are the *suṣumnā*, *iḍā*, and *piṅgalā nāḍī*s.[18]

The process by which this breath is manipulated includes two parts. The first part is an instruction to perceive exhalations (Skt. *recaka*) and inhalations (*pūraka*) in both (1) the feminine *sthūla vāyu* and *sthūla svarūpa* associated with the Shakti and the "Onkara Pranava Nadhum (< Skt. *oṃkāra praṇava nāda*) as Skt. *śiva*, and (2) the masculine *sūkṣmā vāyu* and *sūkṣmā svarūpa* associated with Shiva and the same "Onkara Pranava Nadhum" but of *ham*. The combination of exhaling and inhaling air, the sounds of which together make *śivo ham*, "I am Shiva," makes what Sabhapati calls the "embracing connection" or a

> third air, which is as mild, absorptive, intoxicative, blissful, conscious air called Karana Vayu [Skt. *kāraṇa vāyu*, lit. "the wind of causation"], which forcibly penetrates up in the Spiritual organ [*suṣumnā*] and hits the centre of the skull in the perceptible invisible unheard Onkara Pranava Nadhum of (Om) which is therefore called the blissful intoxicative absorptive establishing sound or common air in Karana Swaroop [*kāraṇa svarūpa*].[19]

This mention of a *kāraṇa vāyu* is somewhat irregular and it is not part of the more widespread list of ten yogic *vāyus* (*apāna*, *devadatta*, *dhanaṃjaya*, *kṛkara*, *kūrma*, *nāga*, *prāṇa*, *samāna*, *udāna*, and *vyāna*).[20] Some indication is given by a reference to number 39 of the main diagram that accompanies the First Book of CPSPS, but this simply describes it as the "Absorbing breath in the I[nfinite]. Spirit" in the legend.

The second part traces this "embracing connection," or union between the airs of Shakti and of Shiva, in detail. The union of these two, the *kāraṇa vāyu*, ascends the *suṣumnā* that is connected to the "wind pipe at the centre seat of the nostril," and this *vāyu* is then divided into three equal parts that travel through the *iḍā*, *piṅgalā*, and *suṣumnā nāḍīs*. These are in turn each associated with what Sabhapati calls a "Mudra" (< Skt. *mudrā*, "seal"), a "Stambhana" (< Skt. *stambhana*, "fixing"), and a "state" (his translation of Skt. *svarūpa*, lit. "inherent form," "essential nature") (see Table 4.1).[21] The

Table 4.1 Sabhapati's attributions of the "wind of causation" (*kāraṇa vāyu*) in the three channels

Nāḍī	Type of *stambhana* ("fixing")	*Mudrā*	*Svarūpa*
iḍā (left channel)	*kumbhaka stambhana*	*khecarī mudrā*	*laya svarūpa* "absorptive state"
suṣumnā (center channel)	*sthāpana stambhana*	*bhūcarī* or *śiva mudrā*	*ānanda svarūpa* "blissful state"
piṅgalā (right channel)	*bandhana stambhana*	*śambhavī mudrā*	*bodha svarūpa* "intoxicative state"

three parts of the *kāraṇa vāyu* enter the head and travel to the left, right, and center of the eyebrows, where they meet at the center and shift direction from facing downward (*adhomukha*) to upward (*ūrdhvamukha*). Once they meet, the *kāraṇa vāyu* "ascends up to the centre seat of the skull as absorptive, blissful and intoxicative states in three electric lines," and then is completely absorbed in the "Self Universal Infinite Spirit" while "in the midst of three Infinite Spiritual aetherial holes."[22]

Sabhapati's consideration of haṭha yoga in his English works is not limited to the above section, and he mentions it in another short section of CPSPS on the yogic auxiliaries of Patañjali's circa fifth-century CE Yoga Sūtras and their commentary, together which form the *Pātañjalayogaśāstra*.[23] Sabhapati also engaged Patañjali's teachings on yoga in an appendix to the second edition of VRY, edited by Shrish Chandra Basu.[24] However, his allusions in CPSPS to Patañjali's *aṣṭāṅga* (Mpvl. *aṭṭāṅkam*) or "eight auxiliaries" or "eight limbs" in addition to *saṃyama*—without reference to Patañjali's name—appear to be mediated at least partially by the second chapter (*paṭala*) of the circa fifteenth-century text *Śivayogapradīpikā* and/or the third "tantra" (*tantiram*) of the circa twelfth-century *Tirumantiram*.[25] He also would have come across these auxiliaries in the main work of his guru Vedashreni Chidambara Swamigal, *Upatēca uṇmai* (see Chapter 1 for more on this guru and his text), which Sabhapati cites in the front matter of MCVTS.[26] I have outlined Sabhapati's list and descriptions of the auxiliaries as follows, along with their subdivisions (English translations are Sabhapati's own):

1. "Eyamum" (Mpvl. *iyamam*, < Skt. *yama*), which includes "five states of *Purity* and *Holiness of Soul*," namely:
   a. "Unmurdering" (Mpvl. *najīvanācam*, < Skt. *najīvanāśa*)
   b. "Not giving pains to other creations" (Mpvl. *najīvahimsā*, < Skt. *najīvāhiṃsā*)
   c. "Not speaking lies" (Mpvl. *aṉyasattiyavākkōtayam*, < Skt. *anyasatyavākudaya*)
   d. "Not stealing" (Tam. *tiruṭaramai*)
   e. "Not coveting others property" (Mpvl. *parastirī puruṣastiti ākiruṣṇa nayiccā*, < Skt. *parastrī puruṣasthiti ākarṣaṇa nayicchā*) or "preventing senses from *vice*" (Mpvl. *intiriyaviṣayanācam*, < Skt. *indriyaviṣayanāśa*).
2. "Niyamum" (Mpvl. *niyamam*, < Skt. *niyama*), which also includes five additional "states of Purity and Holiness of Soul," namely

a. "Devotion and Piety" (Mpvl. *tapam*, < Skt. *tapas*)

b. "Purity of heart and body" (Mpvl. *ācāracuttātma hirutayattuvam*, < Skt. **ācāraśuddhātmahṛdayatva*)

c. "Attaining knowledge of delusions and creations" (Mpvl. *māyāvaṉityacekacīva paravicāraṇā* and *aṉāti nitya pirmaññāṉavicāraṇā cintaṉā*, < Skt. **māyāvanityajagaccīva paravicāraṇā* and **anādi nitya brahmajñānavicāraṇā cintana*).

d. "Satisfaction, Patience and Bliss" (Mpvl. *tirupti sāntāṉantam*, < Skt. *tṛpti śāntānanda*).

e. "Always Praying and Devoting" (Mpvl. *īsvara pakti stuticintā*, < Skt. *īśvara bhakti stuticintā*).

3. "Asanum" (Mpvl. *ācaṉam*, < Skt. *āsana*), which includes "10 sorts of posture . . . to hold Spiritual Communion steadily."

a. *svastikāsana* (Mpvl. *cuvattikāsaṉam*): "Sitting as legs and feet folded one upon another."

b. *gomukhāsana* (Mpvl. *kōmukācaṉam*): "Sitting in a cross folded legs or feet, catching the toes by two hands separately."

c. *padmāsana* (Mpvl. *patmāsaṉam*): "Sitting by crossly placing left foot on right thigh and right foot on left thigh."

d. *vīrāsana* (Mpvl. *vīrāsaṉam*): "Sitting on the right leg or foot and folding the left leg or foot on right thigh."

e. *kesaryāsana* (Mpvl. *kēsariyāsaṉam*): "Sitting squeezing legs so as to place . . . hands on their respective knees, seeing the tip of nose by two eyes steadily."

f. *bhadrāsana* (Mpvl. *pattiramāsaṉam*): "Sitting squeezed two legs being tied stead fastly [*sic*] by two hands."

g. *muktāsana* (Mpvl. *muttāsaṉam*): "Sitting in a posture, so that the left leg folded and right leg lifted squeezedly, having paws on their respective knees."

h. *mayūrāsana* (Mpvl. *mayūrāsaṉam*): "Sitting in a posture, so that two knees squeezed across, having two respective paws one on each."

i. *sarvasukhāsana* (Mpvl. *carvacuhāsaṉam*): "Doing Samádhi or Ecstasy of Communion in whatever comfortable, easy and suitable posture untroubled."

j. *sahajapādāsana* and *sahajaśayanāsana* (Mpvl. *sahajapātāsaṉam* and *sahajakṣaiyāsaṉam*): "Being in Ecstasy in Standing and in Lying posture."

4. "Pránáyámum" (Mpvl. *pirāṇāyāmam*, < Skt. *prāṇāyāma*), which includes "different sorts of pressing breath through Réchaka, Púraka, Koombaka [Skt. *recaka, pūraka, kumbhaka*] to help keep mind steadily fixed on certain attention which are the process of Hatta Yogue ["haṭha yog," Skt. *haṭhayoga*]."
5. "Pretthiyáhárum" (Mpvl. *pirattiyāhāram*, < Skt. *pratyāhāra*), a "state of enduring and removing all the internal and external sufferings and difficulties that rise from the practice of Yoga by forgetting himself."
6. "Sannyámum" (Mpvl. *caṉyāmam*, < Skt. *saṃyama*), the "state of all cancelled consciousness of all internal and external faculties."[27]
7. "Dharanum" (Mpvl. *tāraṇam*, < Skt. *dhāraṇā*) and
8. "Thiyanum" (Mpvl. *tiyāṉam*, < Skt. *dhyāna*), which are listed together as the "state of making deep Spiritual communion or Ecstasy with fixing mind in Throat, Heart, centre of Eye-brows Forehead, Navel, and in the centre of Skull or Brain."
9. "Samádhi" (Mpvl. *camāti*, < Skt. *samādhi*), the "state of Holding Communion steadfastly and perfectly day and night together void of all Delusions and Emotions of faculties in deep Ecstasy as I. Spiritual Consciousness of Bliss in everywhere" (Mpvl. *catāpirmmañāṉasamāti*, < Skt. *sadābrahmajñānasamādhi*).[28]

Sabhapati's list of *yamas* and *niyamas* or "restraints" in this list may have either been composed from his memory or derived from an extant list in Tamil Maṇipravāla that was subsequently translated into English and also rendered in Devanagari for publication in CPSPS (see Chapter 2 for these linguistic considerations). They differ slightly from those originally given in the thirtieth and thirty-second sutras of Patañjali's *sādhanapāda*, namely *ahiṃsā*, "non-violence"; *satya*, "truthfulness"; *asteya*, "not stealing"; *brahmacarya*, "celibacy"; and *aparigraha*, "not possessing" (the five *yamas*); and *śauca*, "cleanliness"; *santoṣa*, "contentment"; *tapas*, "asceticism"; *svādhyāya*, "one's own study"; and *īśvarapraṇidhāna*, "the worship of Īśvara" (the five *niyamas*), although most are synonymous.[29] They also differ slightly from the lists given in the *Tirumantiram* (Tantra 3, verses 553–57) and *Upatēca uṇmai* (verses 168–69), so may be derived from any combination of sources that variously interpreted the restraints of Pātañjalayoga.[30]

To make matters more confusing, an appended question-and-answer section was appended to the second edition of VRY (VRY2), entitled "A

Brief Sketch of Vedantism and Yoga," most likely added or edited by Shrish Chandra Basu, which lists the *yamas* and *niyamas* according to Patañjali's terminology.[31] Philological evidence suggests, however, that Sabhapati had more recourse to Tamil and Sanskrit hybrid vernacular sources for his teachings in CPSPS, the two volumes of which were not edited by Shrish Chandra (see Chapter 2). I would argue that the presence or relative absence of Shrish Chandra, who by 1883 (the publication date of VRY2) would have been certainly aware of translations of Patañjali from his involvement in educated circles and the Theosophical Society, likely accounts for the difference in lists between CPSPS and VRY2. The instruction on *āsana* given in "A Brief Sketch" also differs significantly from the list provided in CPSPS (see Sabhapati's list and descriptions); it merely states that one should adopt "any posture which is steady and convenient" and "not change it at all," and offers no specific postures.[32]

More specific information on Sabhapati's sources can be gleaned from the list of his *āsanas* in CPSPS, however, which lists postures that were not codified in the time of Patañjali but are relatively well-documented in extant sources of medieval haṭha yoga.[33] As seen above, Sabhapati lists ten or eleven *āsanas* depending on how one counts (the last has two parts) along with short postural descriptions. These descriptions are somewhat vague, but this could be due to the fact that serious students would not have had to rely only on the book's instructions but would be able to obtain in-person instruction from Sabhapati or one of his students at a meditation hall. One of the earliest sources for most of these *āsanas* that Sabhapati lists appears to be the *Tirumantiram*, which gives a list of at least nine (Mpvl. *pattiram*, *kōmukam*, *paṅkayam*, *kēcari*, *cottiram*, *vīram*, *cukātaṉam*, and *svattikam*, in addition to *kukkuṭācaṉam*), many of which match or are synonyms (e.g., *paṅkayam* for *padmāsana*).[34] Another source appears to be the ŚYP on account of many of the *āsanas* matching exactly, while others (e.g., *mayūrāsana*, *padmāsana*) are clear synonyms (see Table 4.2).[35] Several of these *āsanas* were also mentioned in the *Haṭhapradīpikā*.[36] Only one of the postures is not a discernible match from either of these sources, namely Sabhapati's inclusion of both *sahajapādāsana* and *sahajaśayanāsana* as together comprising his tenth *āsana*.

As for *prāṇāyāma*, Sabhapati (or his editor Shrish Chandra Basu) frames this auxiliary more explicitly as a practice of "Hatta Yogue" (haṭha "yog"), and he further notes that he will drop consideration of it "lest the Public will be misled."[37] As a result, we unfortunately cannot know whether Sabhapati also

Table 4.2 A list of Sabhapati's eleven *āsanas* in CPSPS and their likely correlates in ŚYP, the *Tirumantiram*, and the *Haṭhapradīpikā*

Sri Sabhapati Swami, CPSPS, 104–5	*Śivayogapradīpikā* 2.14	*Tirumantiram* 3, verses 558–63	Haṭhapradīpikā 1.18–56	English translation
svastikāsana (Mpvl. *cuvattikāsaṉam*)	*svastikāsana*	*svattikam*	*svastikāsana*	"Auspicious Posture"
gomukhāsana (Mpvl. *kōmukācaṉam*)	*gomukhāsana*	*kōmukam*	*gomukhāsana*	"Cow-faced Posture"
padmāsana (Mpvl. *patmāsaṉam*)	*ambujāsana*	*paṅkayam*	*padmāsana*	"Lotus Posture"
vīrāsana (Mpvl. *vīrāsaṉam*)	*vīrāsana*	*vīram*	*vīrāsana*	"Hero Posture"
kesaryāsana (Mpvl. *kēsariyāsaṉam*)	*kesaryāsana*	*kēcari*	*siṃhāsana*	"Lion Posture"
bhadrāsana (Mpvl. *pattiramāsaṉam*)	*bhadrāsana*	*pattiram*	*bhadrāsana*	"Blessed Posture"
muktāsana (Mpvl. *muttāsaṉam*)	*muktāsana*	[not present]	*siddhāsana* (?)	"Liberated Posture"
mayūrāsana (Mpvl. *mayūrāsaṉam*)	*ahibhujāsana*[a]	[not present]	*mayūrāsana*	"Peacock Posture"
sarvasukhāsana (Mpvl. *carvacuhāsaṉam*)	*sukhāsana*	*cukātaṉam*	[not present]	"Most Comfortable Posture" / "Comfortable Posture"
sahajapādāsana and *sahajaśayanāsana* (Mpvl. *sahajapātāsaṉam* and *sahajakṣaiyāsaṉam*)	[not present]	[not present]	[not present – *śavāsana* (?)]	"Easy Standing Posture" and "Easy Lying Down Posture"

[a]*Ahibhuj* literally means "snake-eater," and only by extension "peacock."

Note: English translations of *āsanas* found in ŚYP taken from Powell, "Advice on Āsana in the Śivayogapradīpikā," *The Luminescent* (blog), June 30, 2017, https://www.theluminescent.org/2017/06/advice-on-asana-in-sivayogapradipika.html.

derived his techniques on *prāṇāyāma* from the ŚYP, although I would argue that such a derivation is likely on account of his association of *prāṇāyāma* with haṭha yoga, which completely makes sense if he derived some of his teachings from the *Pātañjaliyogaśāstra* as mediated by either the ŚYP, the *Tirumantiram*, or another text on haṭha yoga, a fact evident from the *āsanas* he cites, as shown above. In any event, Sabhapati does not deny the efficacy of haṭha yoga but adds that it is not necessary to practice *prāṇāyāma* separately since the process of the "Siva Rája Yóga" (i.e., Śivarājayoga) already includes it, since it will "suppress itself the Breath and its Emotion and devour it entirely after all without its existence ever, as the Magnet draws the Pins."[38] The allusion to a "Magnet" serves to link this statement with his instructions on haṭha yoga that pertain to observing the ascent of the *kāraṇa vāyu*, mentioned above, so perhaps the earlier section is what Sabhapati was more interested in authorizing—or, perhaps more accurately, internalizing—as a prescribed practice of *prāṇāyāma*. The mention of a kind of magnetic energy is also probably connected to discourses around mesmerism happening in the Theosophical Society and, a decade later, in the works of Swami Vivekananda.[39]

Despite the lack of any direct emphasis on *prāṇāyāma* in his English works, it does figure prominently in his vernacular works, and their positive recommendation to practice haṭha yoga shows a marked contrast with his literature in English. For example, the Hindi work RYB contains an entire chapter entitled the "instruction on the sequence for experiencing the practice of nine types of haṭha yoga and three types of *prāṇāyāma* [*navavidh haṭayog trividh prāṇāyāmābhyāsānubhav kramopedeś*], and also includes a diagram for reference (see Figure 4.1).[40]

The larger version of MCVTS also describes certain techniques of haṭha yoga at length, complete with descriptions and a numbered diagram (labeled number 13 in MCVTS; see Chapter 5, Figure 5.5) that depicts the subtle physiology of yoga, complete with its *nāḍīs*, cakras, and so on.[41] In an adjacent section Sabhapati describes seven kinds of *prāṇāyāma*:

1. "the yoga of binding [*bandhanayoga*] that is the *prāṇāyāma* of the channel of the *prāṇa*" (Mpvl. *cuvācavācip pirāṇāyāma pantaṉayōkam*).
2. "the yoga of binding that is the *prāṇāyāma* of the channel of channels" (*vācivācip pirāṇāyāma pantaṉayōkam*).
3. "the yoga of binding that is the *prāṇāyāma* of the channel of the vital breath [*prāṇa*]" (*pirāṇavācip pirāṇāyāma pantaṉayōkam*).
4. "the yoga of binding that is the *prāṇāyāma* of the channel of the drop [*bindu*]" (*pi:ntu:vācip pirāṇāyāma pantaṉayōkam*).
5. "the yoga of binding that is the *prāṇāyāma* of the channel of the sound [*nāda*]" (*nāta:vācip pirāṇāyāma pantaṉayōkam*).
6. "the yoga of binding that is the *prāṇāyāma* of the channel of the syllable Om [*praṇava*]" (*piraṇavavācip pirāṇāyāma pantaṉayōkam*).
7. "the yoga of binding that is the *prāṇāyāma* of the channel of the digit [*kalā*]" (*kalāvācip pirāṇāyāma pantaṉayōkam*).[42]

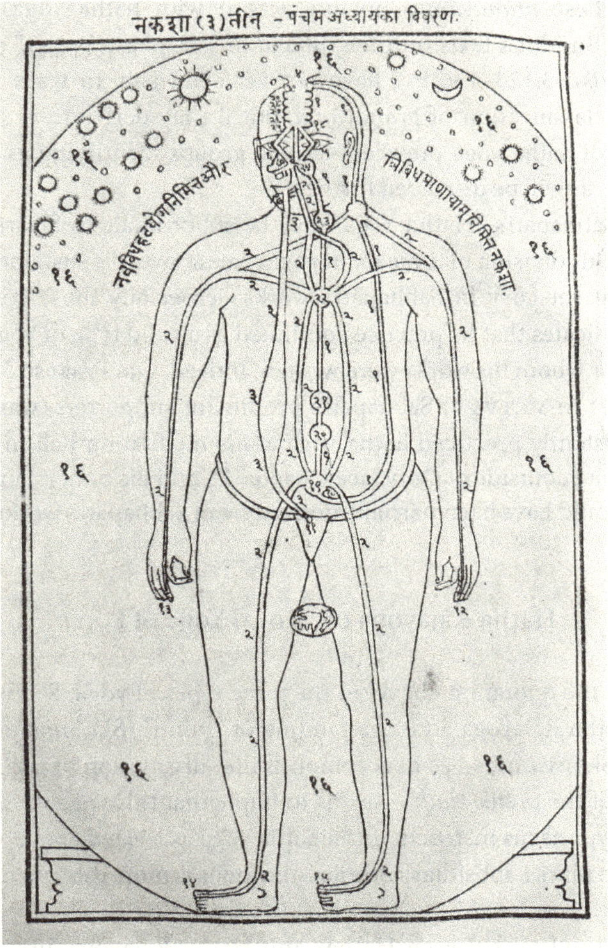

Figure 4.1 "Diagram Number Three, for the Description of Chapter Five / A diagram for the nine types of haṭha yoga and three types of *prāṇāyāma*" (Hi. *nakśā* (3) *tīn pañcam adhyāykā vivaraṇ / navavidh haṭayoga nimita aur trividh prāṇāyām nimitta nakśā*). This diagram is between pages 60 and 61 of RYB. Photo by the author of a copy held by the Adyar Library and Research Centre.

Some of these *prāṇāyāma*s notably accord with haṭha yoga as defined in Tantric Buddhist texts on the *sādhana* of "six-phased yoga," such as the *Sekoddeśaṭīkā* 3.123–136.[43] I have not yet been able to trace Sabhapati's sevenfold classification of *prāṇāyāma*, but it may derive from local Tamil traditions of haṭha yoga prevalent among groups identifying as Siddhas or Swamigals, as will be discussed further.

While Sabhapati's "Haṭha Yoga" may be subordinate to Śivarājayoga according to his division of three main yogas (see above), its sustained presence as a salient category in Sabhapati's works—especially those composed in Tamil—indicates that its practice continued as a valid type of yoga for those students for whom his works were written. Indeed, Om Prakash Swami, who tops the list in MCTVS of Sabhapati's prominent supporters, was known to have consistently practiced haṭha yoga at his meditation hall in the village of Kandal, just outside of Ooty (see Chapter 1), and his understanding of the practice would have been partially derived from Sabhapati's works.

Haṭha Rājayoga or "Royal Yoga of Force"

As seen in the quotation above on the three types of yoga, Sabhapati's concept of Haṭha Rājayoga adds the binding of "mind" (Skt. *manas*) to that of "breath" (Skt. *śvāsa*), so as to accomplish the "dissolution of the mind." The inclusion of the prefix *Haṭha-* seems to imply that this yoga is essentially of the same type as his instructions on haṭha yoga as treated above, except that here breath plays a subsidiary role and the focus is more directly on the mind (Skt. *manas*).

This distinction between Haṭha- and Haṭha Rājayoga also appears to have been Shrish Chandra Basu's way of separately delineating instructions on the four latter auxiliaries of Pātañjalayoga, namely *pratyāhāra*, *dhāraṇa*, *dhyāna*, and *samādhi*. In the appended text "A Brief Sketch of Vedantism and Yoga," mentioned above, the author divides "Raja Yoga" into three parts: (1) *indriya-saṃyama*, which he calls "subjugation of the senses," (2) *manosaṃyama*, "subjugation of the mind," and (3) *laya*, which he calls "absorption." *Saṃyama* in Patañjali's third section, or "Vibhūtipāda," only refers to the three auxiliaries *dhāraṇa*, *dhyāna*, and *samādhi*, not *pratyāhāra* (see reference above). However, the author attributes *indriya-saṃyama* to *pratyāhāra*, so we can assume that *mano-saṃyama* would refer to *dhāraṇa* and *dhyāna* and *laya* would refer to *samādhi*. For *pratyāhāra*, he instructs the would-be yogi (Skt. *yogī*, < stem *yogin*) to "strongly *imagine* that you are out of the body and moving in *akas* [= Skt. *ākāśa*]." He then goes on to offer a short description of the results of this bewildering practice, as follows:

> Practise this for months till you attain the power of throwing your body into catalepsy whenever you like. It will be easier if you begin step by step, e.g., will strongly that you will not *hear* any external sound, so much so that you should be able to make yourself deaf whenever you like. This is hard of course, but not impossible, and requires patience. Having subdued the ear, try to subdue in a similar way the senses of sight, taste, smell and touch.[44]

Unfortunately Shrish Chandra or the actual author ends "A Brief Sketch" with this instruction and does not treat the other two *saṃyama*s.

In Sabhapati's main teachings, however, his description of Haṭha Rājayoga is not limited to Pātañjalayoga. In his work he introduces a kind of *prāṇāyāma* for both the breath (*śvāsa*) and the mind (*manas*) together, which underscores the salient distinction for him between *śvāsa*, ordinary "breath," and *prāṇa*, a vital and more animate "breath" that in Sabhapati's literature is sometimes compounded with *ākāśa*, "ether," and used synonymously with *jñānākāśa*, "gnostic ether," as principles that course through the body (see Chapter 5 and the next section in this chapter Śivarājayoga or "Royal Yoga for Shiva"). Both breath and mind are to be "arrested" like "a pillar [that is] devoid of stirring, moving, unsteadiness, wishing, doubting, thinking, or denying, and is without self-delusion."[45] In this context it is notable that the binding, not only of breath and mind but also of the body's fluidic correlate, semen (*bindu*), has been a defining feature of Tantric alchemy and haṭha yoga for centuries. Such associations appear to have been first formulated in Sanskrit literature of relevance to haṭha yoga in the *Amṛtasiddhi*, composed in a Buddhist Tantric milieu, as previously mentioned.[46]

Sabhapati appears to have been aware of these connections between breath, mind, and semen, as he explicitly refers to them in a section designed to "show how to enjoy the I[nfinite]. Spiritual blissfulness in coition with females . . . or the Spiritual trance of blissfulness in the momentary blissful female enjoyments of Mental love and attraction on the beauties and attributes of Female and Male appearances."[47] In this section Sabhapati describes a "Generative Fluid . . . in both of the Males and Females" (Mpvl. *vintu*, < Skt. *bindu*) as the "Essence of Physical Creation or body as blissful bright fluid" of various qualities. The idea that both males and females can possess semen (usually Skt. *bindu*, *bīja*, or *vastu*) is not unique to Sabhapati but also occurs in other Tantric contexts, such as among the Bāul fakirs of Bengal, although in this case Sabhapati is likely referring to menstrual blood since male/female sexual fluids were sometimes called the white and red *bindu*s, respectively.[48] In any event the Finite Spirit's "Delusive Faculties" all stand upon this "Generative Fluid," implying that it is the sourse of the tattvas of the Finite Spirit, or *jīvātman* (see Chapter 3), all of which are unreal compared to the Infinite Spirit. Sabhapati then lists six kinds of "Coitional momentary blissfulnesses," or in modern language, temporary forms of happiness during "ordinary" sex, which follow a certain fixed order:

1. the "momentary bliss of fixed attention on the ruinous false beauties of attracting appearance of the face," which is thrown from the "brightness of Spiritual **Fixing** Bliss in the centre of the brain"
2. the "momentary bliss of sight on the ruinous false attributes of the bodily appearances," which is thrown from the "rays of Spiritual **seeing** Bliss in the centre of the two eyes on eyebrows"
3. the "momentary bliss of emotional and actional embracing on the runious, vain false and lovely show of the joining appearances," which is thrown from the "emotions and actions of Spiritual **embracing** bliss"
4. the "momentary Bliss of attraction and lovely absorption on the ruinous vain false idea of the pleasure by the pressure of breast to breast, touch to touch of the whole body of the mixing appearances," which is thrown from the "attraction and love of Spiritual **absorbing** bliss in the centre of the Heart"
5. the "momentary imitating bliss on the ruinousness vain false state of imitating appearances," which is thrown from the "force of throwing out its fluid state through the generative organ and becoming as **void** bliss in the centre seat of the Kundali [*kuṇḍali*]"
6. the "momentary bliss of Spiritual perfection and self state on the ruinous vain false truth of ascertaing [*sic*] appearance," which is thrown from the "perfection and self state of **being** Spiritual bliss in the place from the bottom of the Kundali and up-to the top of Brahmmarundhram [*brahmarandhra*] through back-bone."[49]

He states that these temporary experiences of bliss should be changed into six kinds of "Spiritual everlasting blissfulness," which are less descriptive than prescriptive:

1. "You must meditate as the Spiritual **fixing** bliss in the brain when you throw your attention on the beauties of the females or males attractive appearance."
2. "You must meditate as the Spiritual **seeing** bliss in the eyes when you throw your attention on the attributes of female's or male's bodily appearance."
3. "You must meditate as the Spiritual **embracing** bliss in the nose when you throw your attention on the false lovely show of female's or male's joining appearance."
4. "You must meditate as the Spiritual **absorbing** bliss in the heart when you throw your attention on the false form of female's or male's mixing appearance."
5. "You must meditate as the Spiritual **becoming** bliss in the Kundali when you throw your attention on the false state of imitating appearance."
6. "You must meditate as the Spiritual **being** bliss in the middle of the Kundali and Brahmmarandhram through back-bone when you throw your attention on the false truth of females' or male's ascertaining appearance."[50]

Sabhapati's overarching point is that one should "see those six sorts of blissfulnesses' coitional sensual pleasures, not like those momentary blisses on their features and shapes, but like eternal and everlasting blisses." In other words, one should mentally transmute the momentary experiences of bliss into an experience of the eternal sources from whence they derive. He is perhaps intentionally vague about whether he means that this transmutation should occur while one is actually engaging in physical attraction and sex or merely imagining it, although in any case he does state that this practice is to be engaged during a state of "enjoyment" of attractive "features and shapes."[51]

Part of this practice is further designed to induce a kind of spiritual state of what he reductively translates as "Conscious sleeping" (Mpvl. *jarkkiraturiya pirmmakñāṉamaya cuṣuptti avastā*, < Skt. *jāgratturīya brahmajñānamaya suṣupti avasthā*, lit. "the waking fourth state [*jāgrat* + *turīya*] in sleeping that consists of the gnosis of Brahman"). These terms refer to three out of four or (sometimes) five technical "states" (*avasthā*s) often found not only in the literature of Vedānta and yoga but also later Śaiva Siddhānta, including waking (*jāgrata*), dreaming (*svapna*), deep dreamless sleep (*suṣupti*), the fourth state (*turīya*), and that which is beyond the fourth state (*turīyātīta*).[52] Sabhapati also refers to them repeatedly in VRY1, 2, and 3 and CPSPS. The general idea is that only yogis in their samādhi know how to access levels of consciousness beyond deep sleep, although here there is a kind of highest consciousness that arises in sleeping that results from the aforementioned practices.

While the above may seem tangential to yoga, for Sabhapati it is directly relevant; he wraps up this instruction by saying that the "above secret practices" will help one to "gain the Rajayoga practice in getting absorption and ecstasy of Communion."[53] While he could be implying Śivarājayoga here, the mental association makes it also relevant to his description of Haṭha Rājayoga as the binding of not just the breath but the mind as well (and in this case, also the "Generative Fluid," or *bindu*).

Another factor that is likely salient to Sabhapati's distinction between Haṭhayoga and Haṭha Rājayoga is that rāja yoga in the colonial period was sometimes considered to be a "mental" yoga to still the mind, in contrast to the physical techniques of haṭha yoga. As De Michelis has noted, the Theosophical Society was likely "the first group to propogate this idea."[54] This demarcation between the physical techniques of breath-retention and mental practice was salient to Swami Vivekananda's own reformulation in his published lectures *Yoga Philosophy* (1896) on "Râja Yoga" as the "cessation of the turnings of the mind" (Skt. *yogaścittavṛttinirodhaḥ*).[55]

Vivekananda was not the only reformer during this period, however, but was preceded by earlier reinterpretations of rāja yoga by Indian authors such as Manilal Nabhubhai Dvivedi, who first published his *Rája Yoga, or the Practical Metaphysics of the Vedanta*, in 1885 (eleven years prior to Vivekananda's *Rāja Yoga*).[56] Manilal Dvivedi's friend in Bombay, the influential Theosophical author Tookaram Tatya, would reprint Dvivedi's translation specifically for a Theosophical audience three years later, in 1888.[57] In their introduction and commentaries "Rája Yoga" is framed as the culmination of the Vedānta of Śaṅkara (Shankaracharya) rather than the philosophy of Patañjali, as Vivekananda and subsequent authors would later frame it, although both frames are somewhat intertwined since the auxiliaries of Pātañjalayoga (as interpreted through the lenses of Vedānta) do figure into the text's instructions.[58]

Manilal Dvivedi and Tookaram Tatya primarily derived their Vedānta-influenced understanding of "Rája Yoga" from the text *Aparokṣānubhūti*, a circa twelfth- to fourteenth-century text that, as Birch notes, "is unique in using the term 'rājayoga' to denote a system of Yoga without the connotation of *samādhi*."[59] In Dvivedi's translation of *Aparokṣānubhūti*, "Rája Yoga" is explicitly defined as "mental *yoga*" and haṭha yoga as "physical *Yoga*."[60] To make matters more confusing, however, Dvivedi adds a note present in both editions interpreting rāja yoga as the "attainment of the condition of eternal *Samádhi* or concentration or identification with the principle of the universe," and this despite the fact (as Birch noted) the text itself does not support the connotation of rāja yoga as samādhi.[61] In any event, Dvivedi's interpretation of haṭha yoga is that it "holds that the mind will be naturally and easily controlled by shutting up all the avenues of its communication with the external world—viz. the breath &c."[62] By contrast, rāja yoga oxymoronically

> holds and perhaps correctly holds—that the shortness of length of the breath, is but an indication of the State of the mind and that therefore instead of fruitlessly and unnaturally stifling this breath we had much better curb the cause of all this breath and everything *viz.* the giant *manas* or the mind.[63]

As a result, Dvivedi's main argument for the higher position accorded rāja yoga is that it addresses the mind directly, whereas haṭha yoga only addresses its symptom: breath as an effect of and physical indication of the mind.

Sabhapati Swami himself would, at least by 1883 or 1884 (the first mention he makes of haṭha yoga), contrast the meditative aspects of his third type of yoga, Śivarājayoga, with the physical breath techniques of his second type Haṭha Yoga, a distinction that would also indirectly apply to his mental methods of Haṭha Rājayoga.[64] However, as we see throughout his literature, he consistently described Śivarājayoga in all languages as *niṣṭhā samādhi*, a "composure that is steadfast." This samādhi is genealogically linked to Patañjali but, as I have demonstrated, has its own distinct definition as the "subjugation of gnosis" (Mpvl. *kñāṉavaciyam*, < Skt. *jñānavaśya*) and accompanying ritual apparatus (the canceling of the Tantric cakras and so on; see Śivarājayoga or "Royal Yoga for Shiva") that was not present in Pātañjalayoga or the *Aparokṣānubhūti*. Sabhapati's idea of "subjugation" does not imply that jñāna is a lower state to be subdued than, say, *vijñāna* or "[power of] discerning," but rather implies that the yogi who subjugates jñāna has also subjugated the supreme principle of the cosmos by uniting with (in the Vedānta view) and/or melting into (in the Saiddhāntika view) that which possesses *brahmajñāna*, "gnosis of Brahman," or *śivajñāna*, "gnosis of Shiva," used synonymously in Sabhapati's works. This gnosis is an experience that is perceived to be far beyond the stilling of mental processes, that is, beyond *manas*, "mind," or *citta*, "thought," which are part of the fourfold internal instrument (Skt. *caturantaḥkaraṇa*) consisting of (in his interpretive translation) (1) "emotional faculties" (Skt. *citta*, lit. "thought"), (2) "mental faculties" (Skt. *manas*, lit. "mind"), (3) "faculties of volition" (Skt. *buddhi*, lit. "intelligence"), and (4) "faculties of pride and negligence" (*ahaṃkāra*, lit. the "ego-making" faculty).[65] In Sabhapati's earliest formulation this fourfold internal instrument was located in the "ninth kingdom" or lotus that is situated in the center of the throat. As a result, the turnings of mind and thought would have—at least theoretically—been subdued prior to one's experience and subjugation of *jñāna*. By contrast, the *Aparokṣānubhūti* makes it relatively clear that its samādhi, mentioned in the context of the auxiliaries of Patañjali and the union with Brahman, is predicated on "forgetting the turnings [of the mind]" (Skt. *vṛttivismaraṇa*). As a result, Sabhapati's system of Śivarājayoga departs from the way rāja yoga was more typically understood by the global audiences who would, thanks to the spread of the Theosophical Society and later Swami Vivekananda's lectures, interpret rāja yoga either through the lenses of Dvivedi and Tookaram Tatya's editions and interpretations of *Aparokṣānubhūti* or Vivekananda's *Rāja Yoga*. Indeed, Sabhapati's delineation of a "middle" category between Haṭha Yoga and Śivarājayoga, namely Haṭha Rājayoga, has much more in common with rāja yoga as presented by either Dvivedi or Vivekananda and could be viewed as an attempt by Sabhapati to address these emerging colonial-era interpretations of rāja yoga.

Śivarājayoga or "Royal Yoga for Shiva"

Sabhapati's third principal kind of yoga, Śivarājayoga, is also called the subjugation of gnosis (Mpvl. *kñāṉavaciyam*, < Skt. *jñānavaśya*). The word "subjugation" (Tam. *vaciyam*, < Skt. *vaśya*) can imply a magical charm or influence that exerts control over an object, in this case over gnosis. As noted above and in Chapter 3, this yoga refers to the practice described in his English works as the Finite Spirit, or *jīvātman*'s conquering of itself, that is, each of the twelve "kingdoms" or cakras in succession, which leads eventually to an identity with the Universal Infinite Spirit, or Shiva. The emphasis on the subjugation of *jñāna* ("gnosis," "knowledge") is also important, as in some instances he refers to this yoga in abbreviated form simply as *jñānayoga*, which in that context does not simply refer to yoga as an act of intellectual understanding but as an act of subjugating or controlling gnosis. Sabhapati also gives an additional list of other synonyms for Śivarājayoga:

> Infinite Spiritual Pranava Yoga [Skt. *praṇavayoga*], Nirákára Yoga [*nirākārayoga*], Onkára Yoga [*oṃkārayoga*], Brimha Gnyana Kala Yoga [*brahmajñāna kalāyoga*], Vási Yoga [Tam. *vāciyōkam*], Brimha Bávana Yoga [*brahmabhāvanāyoga*], and Gnyana Lutchiadhiana Yoga [*jñānalakṣya-dhyānayoga*], Brimha Gnyana Dhrishti Ubasana Raja Yoga [*brahmajñāna-dṛṣṭyupāsanarājayoga*], Parotchagnyana Siva Yoga [*parokṣajñānaśivayoga*], Surva siddhi Sorooba Yoga [*sarvasiddhi svarūpayoga*], Surva Surva sukthi Angsa Yoga [*sarva sarvaśakti aṃśayoga*], Surva Surva Sátcháthkara Maya Yoga [*sarva sarva sākṣātkāramayayoga*].[66]

Many of these names are either uncommon as types of yoga or appear to be more descriptive of various aspects of the practice. While largely forgotten today, however, they may have been more salient in the milieus that Sabhapati frequented; for example, a form of yoga called "Vási Yoga" continued to be salient as a synonym for Śivarājayoga over a century after Sabhapati's last publication.

According to Srilata Raman, "The compound Śivarājayoga appears to have emerged in Vīraśaiva circles, after the ca. seventeenth-century author Kumāratēvar definitely but perhaps even earlier, as a word to describe the process of Vīraśaiva worship and to distinguish it, clearly, from the Tamil Śaivasiddhānta's *śivayoga*" (see Chapter 3).[67] As mentioned in the introduction, one of the first mentions of it is in the poetry of the circa eighteenth-century Tamil poet Thayumanavar (Tāyumāṉavar), where it is used in connection with the Tamil Siddhas. I agree with Raman's position and would additionally argue that Sabhapati's form of yoga appears to also be partially connected to the Śivayoga of the ŚYP, albeit with many technical changes introduced on account of its teachings being translated away from the world of Sanskrit (or Kannada, for that matter) and entering milieus that today we would consider more or less connected to the Tamil Siddhas.[68] One notable change is Sabhapati's departure from the Vīraśaiva idea of "six stages" (Skt. *ṣaṭsthala*) of devotion (Skt. *bhakti*) as articulated by the circa twelfth-century reformer Basava, toward a ritualized cancellation of the twelve Tantric cakras to obtain identity with Shiva and to understand the body's functions through "divine pilgrimage."[69]

As I have already pointed out at the beginning of this chapter, his hierarchy of yogas also departs from the ŚYP's fourfold system of Mantra, Laya, Haṭha, and Rāja, in which Śivayoga is equated with Rājayoga. In any event, Tamil Vīraśaiva attitudes on the reconciliation of Saiddhāntika or Advaita Vedānta soteriology, as analyzed and recorded by Raman and Steinschneider, are also clearly reflected in Sabhapati's description of Śivarājayoga, despite the fact that in Sabhapati's English parlance the yoga was in its early formulation called "Vedantic Rajayoga" or "Vedhanta Siva Raja Yoga."[70] Yet the importance given to Shiva and the *liṅga* is ever-present in his work, and this importance is also reflected in many of Sabhapati's diagrams that map yogic physiology onto the *liṅga* and internalize Śaiva temple architecture (see, for example, Figure 4.2).

The full extent to which Kumara Devar and his line of students, including Sabhapati's guru Vedashreni Chidambara Swamigal and Sabhapati Swamigal himself, innovated upon Vīraśaiva forms of Śivayoga remains an open question that would benefit from a much more comprehensive analysis of their entire *paramparā*'s surviving literature that treats on topics relevant to yoga. However, there is a parallel titular phenomenon to this historical integration that can serve as a useful guide: prior to the nineteenth century, many figures who would today be considered as "Siddha" or "Siddhar" if they had lived in the medieval period, instead began to affix the title "Swamigal" (Tam. *cuvāmikaḷ*, < Skt. *svāmī* "Lord" + honorific Tamil *-kaḷ* suffix) to their names. The most notable example of this is Chidambaram Ramalinga Swamigal (1823–1874), whose work also reflects some degree of inspiration from Vīraśaiva movements.[71] To my knowledge the historical dynamics of this shift from "Siddha" to "Swamigal" have not yet been analyzed in scholarship, although they could be more broadly located in Venkatraman's "fourth category" of Siddhas who were only later added to the group or category, as mentioned in Chapter 3.

On the topic of definitions, it is finally worth pointing out Śivarājayoga is known in Tamil as Civarāja yōkam (= Skt. *śivarājayoga*), which today remains a localized genre of Tamil yogic practices that is associated not with Sabhapati Swami but with the *Tirumantiram*, Agastya, and the Tamil Siddhas. I have located at least two paperback books that deal with this subject, both of which I was able to relatively easily order online through Indian book dealers.

The first book, *Vāciyōkam eṉṉum civarāja yōkam*, equates Civarāja yōkam with *vāciyōkam*, "the yoga of breath-channels" in the very title, which Sabhapati himself also accepted as another name for Śivarājayoga

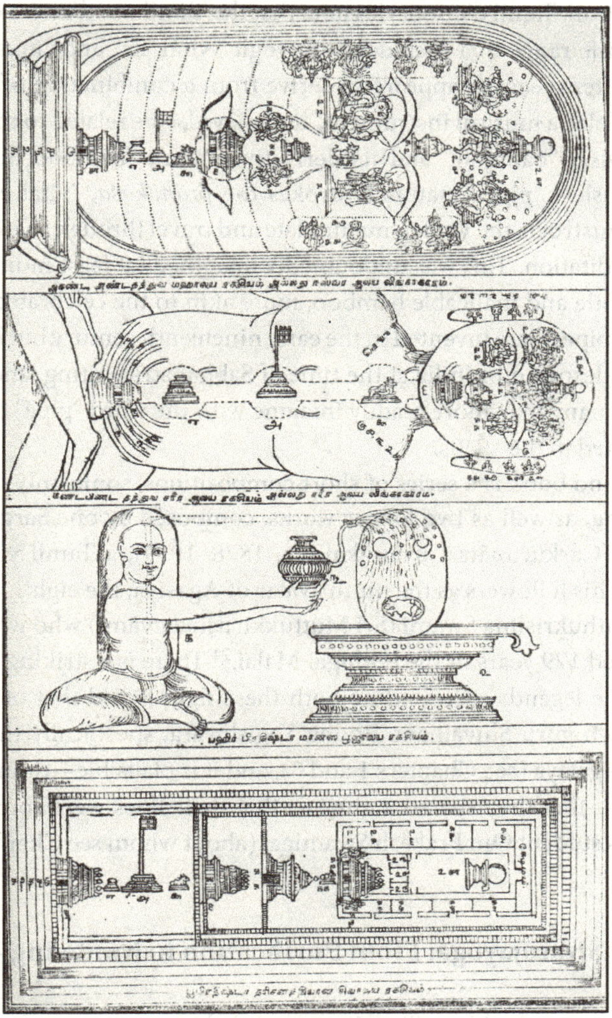

Figure 4.2 "Mysterious instruction on the four kinds of [temple] abodes" (*caturvita ālayaṅkaḷiṉ rakaciya upatēcam*), found in CTCSPV. Scan by the author.

(see above).[72] The Tamil word *vāci* in yogic contexts, especially Sabhapati's own literature, is used synonymously with *nāḍī*, a part of the body's subtle physiology that in contemporary scholarship is often translated as "channel," "nerve," or "conduit." However, in Sabhapati's works *vāci* (transliterated in VRY1 as "vasee," "vasees") is translated as "pipe," which is not an accident or mistranslation. Tamil dictionaries note that the Tamil word *vāci* is connected to a semantic range that includes both yogic "vital-air" and "musical pipe," and this latter meaning appears to derive from a combination of the Tamil verb *vāci*, "play a musical instrument," and may also be related to the Sanskrit nouns *vāṃśa*, "bamboo," and its derivative *vāṃśī*, "bamboo flute."[73] The idea of musical "pipes" naturally evokes the *prāṇākāśa*, "vital ether," that Sabhapati instructs the yogi to manipulate and travel through these channels during meditation. This was undoubtedly imagined (at least indirectly) as a kind of subtle and malleable bamboo, more akin to the celebrated "pipes of Pan." Steel pipes were invented in the early nineteenth century but likely were still not widespread in India at the time of Sabhapati's writing, and the PVC pipes that many may more readily imagine with the word "pipe" today were only invented in the 1930s.

The second book is a series of short compositions, some only one or two stanzas long, as well as two longer works, composed by one Sargurunathar Swamigal (Caṟkurunāta Cuvāmikaḷ (ca. 1878–1919), a Tamil yogi who is revered by his followers as the ninth avatar of Agastya; the eighth avatar was one Sri Muthukrishna Swami (Śrī Muttukkiruṣṇacuvāmi) who was believed to have lived 179 years in the Pothigai Malai.[74] There is a striking resonance between the legends surrounding both these figures and that of Sabhapati Swami's own guru Shivajnana Bodha Yogishwara, specifically the connection with Agastya (see Chapters 1 and 3), and it is plausible—though not yet conclusive—that they shared a guru or that their lines were connected via Sabhapati's student Om Prakash Swamigal (about whom see Chapter 1).[75]

Śivarājayoga: From Purification to Nonbeing

The techniques to achieve Śivarājayoga and the experience of samādhi as being like a "tree universally spread" are found in various places throughout Sabhapati's vividly illustrated body of work. These techniques, or *sādhana*s as they are called in several of his works, most often include meditatively inscribing and then refuting or "canceling" the twelve cakras of his cosmology, called "Kingdoms" in his English works, as illusionary parts of oneself that create a delusion of separation from Brahman and, by extension, from the absolute as a cosmic, nongendered Shiva (Tam. *civam*). Sabhapati's supplementary instructions on Śivarājayoga also include fixing the mind upon the spine as a "pole" and imagining, in his language, the "head to be removed and its place occupied by the universally and in-all-creations pervading I[nfinite]. spiritual void witnessing and blissful consciousness." These pervading principles are the "Four Spiritual Brightnesses" of the Universal Infinite Spirit, which are *sarvānanda*, *sarvasākṣin*, *sarvavyāpaka*, and *sarvaśūnya* (see Chapter 3 and Figure 4.4).[76] In other words, therefore, the whole process is framed in terms of Vedānta as a removal of the delusion of separation between the Finite Spirit (Skt. *jīvātman*) and the Universal Infinite Spirit (*brahman*) so as to facilitate a reintegration with the Universal Spirit (the cosmic Shiva; see Chapter 3 for more on these terms and their Sanskrit correlates in Sabhapati's literature), and also in Saiddhāntika terms as a dissolution (*laya*) of the Finite Spirit into Shiva, as salient to the definition of Śivarājayoga given in the epigraph to this chapter.

The process to achieve success in Śivarājayoga is multitiered and includes several steps over the course of which the yogi attains to various titles. After this consciousness is pervading and "universally spread," one attains the first and second of several titles, which is "Bachelor of Practicing I. spiritual ecstasy" (Mpvl. *pāvaṉā pirmmakñāṉapirmmaccāri*, < Skt. *bhāvanā brahmajñānabrahmacārī*) as well as a "Bachelor in the spiritual Pilgrimage."[77] This latter title, which he doesn't provide a direct Sanskrit phrase for, refers to mastery of an experience of "divine pilgrimage" (Skt. *yātrā*) into a universe that is simultaneously external and internal to the body, which by this point in the practice of yoga is permeated by the gnosis of the Universal Infinite Spirit (*brahmajñāna*). Sabhapati's own words on this pilgrimage is as follows:

> Now you should make a divine Pilgrimage in the universe of your body in order to find out how the I. Spirit [Mpvl. *cutta caitaṉṉiya pirmmakñāṉākāsamayam*, < Skt. *śuddha caitanya brahmajñānākāśamaya*], descends to the Kundalee [= Skt. *kuṇḍali*] through Sushoomna Nadi [= *suṣumnā-nāḍī*] or I. spiritual nerve and ascends up to Brahmarunthram [= *brahmarandhra*] or skull through Kumbaka-Nadi [= *kumbhaka-nāḍī*] or spinal cord; it is by this descent and ascent of the spirit the whole creation of your body is maintained till the time of death.[78]

As noted in Chapter 3, the embodied principles or, in his words, "faculties" (Skt. *tattvas*) of Sabhapati's cosmology have emanated down from the Infinite Spirit to the elemental world, that is, physical (un)reality. Now its perceived connection with bodily vitality becomes clear, which also serves to link the subtle body with the vital breath (Skt. *prāṇa*). After further practice in understanding the ascent and descent of subtle principles and their infinite correlates, one becomes what he translates as the "practical Professor in Spiritual ecstasy" (Mpvl. *pāvaṉāpirmakñāṉapirmacārirājayōka appiyāci*, < Skt. *bhāvanābrahmajñānabrahmacārirājayoga abhyāsī*) or the "Pilgrim in the Divine Kingdom of Infinite spirit's Ecstasy" (Mpvl. *civarājayōka pirmmakñāṉayāttiri*, < Skt. *śivarājayoga brahmajñānayātrī*), the latter of which makes explicit reference to Śivarājayoga.[79] At this point a list of "divine mantras," which are more like qualities of the Absolute, are provided for recitation during one's ascent from the *kuṇḍali* or *mūlādhāra*. Following success in the aforementioned practices, one becomes a "knower of the principles" (*tattvajñānī*) and obtains a lengthy title that I will here shorten to a "family-man of the knowledge of Truth or the Soul" (*ñāṉōkirahastaṉ*, < Skt. *jñānagṛhastha*, lit. "householder of gnosis").[80] After further examining delusions and "false dreams of faculties, happiness and worldly enjoyments," one is able to renounce them and obtain the highest title: "Sanniasi Mowna Gnyani" (= Skt. *saṃnyāsī mauna jñānī*, "Sannyasi who is the Knower of Silence") or "Brumma Gnyani" (= Skt. *brahmajñānī*, "Knower of Brahman"), who is the "spiritual man whom Maya or delusions will never assail."[81] As is evident, this list of titles follows three out of the four traditional "stages" (*āśrama*s) of life as codified in the Dharmaśāstras, but ascribes to them a quality of yogic attainment rather than referring literally to their social, economic, and political functions.

The rewards of pursuing this practice to completion are nothing short of epic and occupy three full pages, including promises that the yogi will be the "Universal Infinite Spirit," the "*Eye* to the Universe" (Skt. *brahmajñānadṛṣṭi*, lit. "sight of the gnosis of Brahman"), the "Linga Sorúpam [Mpvl. *liṅkacorūpam*, < Skt. *liṅgasvarūpa*, "inherent nature of (Shiva's) phallus] embracing the Sun, the Moon, the Stars, the Earth and all their Creations," a "perfect moral God, a perfect social God, a Yógí full of God," a "witness to all the wisdom and notions of every Soul," and, among many other promises, a more obvious one, seemingly added as an afterthought, which simply promises success in the subject of Sabhapati's books, namely Śivarājayoga itself: "the Infinite Spiritual Perfection of the Cosmic Psychological I. Spiritual Philosophy's Védantic Brummagnyana Anubúthy Siva Raja Yoga Practice."[82] Sabhapati also refers to the more typical list of the eight "Psychic powers" (his translation of *siddhi* in his hagiography [Mpvl. *aṣṭamāsitti*, < Skt. *aṣṭamāsiddhi* / *aṣṭasiddhi*]), which he rejects in favor in favor of a vision of Shiva, and also refers to additional powers elsewhere in his literature.[83]

Finally, he also includes a story of a "Yogi of his Ashram" (i.e., of Agastya Ashram; see Chapter 1) who, upon passing through Mysore, displayed to the Nawab of the Deccan his power over weather and his power to create precious stones out of nothing. This seems to also—if indirectly—indicate the fruits of success in Śivarājayoga as mentioned previously.

Sabhapati's works, especially CPSPS, CTCSPV, and MCVTS, explicitly describe the practice of Śivarājayoga as being compatible with Śaiva, Vaiṣṇava, or Śākta forms of devotion, and they accordingly provide mantras and diagrams for a whole host of forms of Vishnu and the Goddess and/or many other deities that one can meditate upon and obtain "communion" with, not just Shiva. Sabhapati also states that this technique can be practiced by an individual of any caste, and is not exclusive to Brahmins or even Hindus; as we saw in Chapter 3, even atheists, members of "Theosophical Societies," and adherents to other religions were encouraged to orient themselves toward the practice of this yoga so as to dispel their doubts. Furthermore, many of his diagrams depict female devotees, and his works explicitly include both women and men as being fully capable of carrying out Śivarājayoga.

Sabhapati's descriptions of the tattvas in the Alpha Stemma, beginning with his English work VRY1 (1880),[84] do include lengthy guided meditations on each tattva, but these practices of cancellation (*śuddhi*, lit. "purification," and *apavāda*, lit. "refutation" see Table 4.3), while not discounting their practical relevance, also seem to have a didactic function in that they enable the yogi to become intimately familiar with the attributions of his or her body's subtle physiology.[85] To some extent they prepare the student for the clearest synopsis of Sabhapati's direct teachings on Śivarājayoga in English, which is separately given in a section aptly called "Instruction" that occupies around thirteen pages and refers to fixing the mind to a "straight pole" or "rocky pole" (see Appendix 3).[86] In CPSPS (1884/90) this same section on Śivarājayoga, slightly modified, occupies about eleven pages.[87] Sabhapati says that the yogi, after practicing the *sādhanā* (Mpvl. *cātaṉai*), should "sing by silent meditation" a sequence of *śloka*s entitled "The Great Utterance, or Unity of abiding in the perception of the non-conceptual state of composure, the disembodied liberation of the gnosis of Brahman" (Mpvl. *Mahāvākkiyāyaikkiya nirvikalpa vitēkamukta pirmaññāṉa camātiyāṉupūtistiti*, < Skt. *mahāvākyaikya nirvikalpa videhamukta brahmajñāna samādhyānubhūtisthiti*) that he included with the book in both Tamil and Devanagari script.[88]

The idea of "disembodied liberation" (*videhamukti*), which as Malinar and White have argued, has roots in the Pātañjalayogaśāstra and was reflected in epics like the Mahabharata, warrants interesting comparisons with *jīvanmukti*, "liberation in life," a concept that would go on to largely eclipse *videhamukti*.[89] Sabhapati notably uses both compounds, however, albeit *videhamukti* only sparsely. He describes *jīvanmukti* as "full absorption even while in body" and uses it in the context of describing those rishis and yogis who would, in contemporary Tamil discourse, be considered Siddhas. These yogis "change their body and *bless* it to become Swambhu Maha Lingam [Skt. *svayambhū mahāliṅga*, "the great phallus that is self-manifesting"] and their spirit joins the Infinite Spirit."[90] The phrase *svayambhū mahāliṅga* (Mpvl. *svayampu mahāliṅkam*) more explicitly refers to naturally occurring *śivaliṅga*s found inside or under trees, such as the kadamba or burflower tree at the Meenakshi Amman Temple in Madurai,[91] or as self-manifesting geological phenomena. In pan-Indian contexts they often form part of "canonical" lists of important or famous Śaiva temple sites and their accompanying *śivaliṅga*s. I learned during my fieldwork at the remnants of Sabhapati's meditation hall in the Konnur/Villivakkam area of Chennai (currently named Sabhapaty Lingeswarar Koil), however, that the epithet *svayambhū* is not just for celebrated or famous sites but can also be applied to *liṅga*s that are present at more minor or lesser-known *jīvasamādhi*s, or "tumuli" relating to the Siddhas in Tamil Nadu. In any event, the presence of a *svayambhū liṅga* is considered highly auspicious and even a mark of distinction; the Dhandeeswaram Temple in Velachery (where Sabhapati was said to have obtained a vision; see Chapter 1), for example, advertises the fact that its *liṅga* is accordingly *svayambhū*, or "self-manifesting."

While the *liṅga* could also be interpreted as a kind of transmigrating subtle body (*liṅgaśarīra*) or even an inherent nature (*liṅgasvarūpa*) that the yogi obtains at death, the passage by Sabhapati quoted above implies that the body quite literally becomes part of the physical stone idol itself, conceived of as a universal symbol, thus granting the yogi a kind of immortal presence. CPSPS offers further clarification in its translation of this passage as "The Self divine Spiritual Universal fully pervaded Circle of stone to worship as Personal God." Indeed, a common practice at "tumuli" of swamis in the same category as Sabhapati Swami and his *paramparā* (see Chapter 3) is to bury the yogi's body following his or her state of final samādhi and to install a sacred *liṅga* over the interred body (see Chapter 1). A notable example of this is the *liṅga* worshiped at the Sri Sabhapathy Lingeshwarar Koil, which is currently revered as the tumulus of Sabhapati Swami himself, although

Table 4.3 The mantras and purifications associated with each of Sabhapati's twelve cakras, lotuses, or kingdoms

Cakra	Sanskrit mantras	Functions (Sabhapati's "translation")
mūlādhāra	*oṃ namaḥ śivāya namaḥ*	*bhūta-śuddhi* ("purification of elements")
svādhiṣṭhāna	*oṃ brahmā, viṣṇu, rudra, maheśvara, sadāśiva namaḥ* (VRY1); *nam* (CPSPS)	*indriya-śuddhi* ("purification of senses")
maṇipuraka	*oṃ ā ī ū e o śivāya namaḥ* (VRY1); *mam—oṃ ā ī ū e o śivāya namaḥ* (CPSPS)	*rāgadveṣa-śuddhi* ("purification of passions")
anāhata	*auṃ hrīṃ śrīṃ aiṃ kliṃ sauṃ nāmaḥ* (VRY1); *auṃ śiṃ śivayavaśi-namaḥ* (CPSPS)	*antaḥkaraṇa-śuddhi* ("purification of intellect")
viśuddhi	*la-hum, va-hum, ra-hum, ya-hum, kha-hum, namaḥ* (VRY1); *vam śivayavaśi-namaḥ* (CPSPS)	*triguṇa-śuddhi* ("purification of conscience")
ājñā	*yam śivayavaśi śivāya namaḥ*	*trimala-śuddhi* ("purification of ideas and ambition")
bindusthāna	*śiva caraṇa* (VRY1) *oṃ śivāya guruve namaḥ* (CPSPS)	*vindumaya-śuddhi* ("purification of muse")
nādasthāna	*śiva śiva potṛ namaḥ* (VRY1) *haṃ śiva śiva potṛ namaḥ* (CPSPS)	*nādamaya-śuddhi* ("purification of memory")
kalāsthāna	*śiva śiva śivā namaste namastu* (VRY1) *ṣam śiva śiva śivā namaste namastu* (CPSPS)	*kalāmaya-śuddhi* ("purification of prudence")
tatparasthāna	*ahameva brahman, śiva śiva śiva śivā śiva śivaḥ aikyārpaṇa namaḥ* (VRY1) *u śiva śiva śiva śivā śiva śiva śiva aikyārpaṇakaro namaḥ* (CPSPS)	*tatparamaya-śuddhi* ("purification of knowledge")
parasthāna	*śiva śiva śiva śiva śivaḥ namaḥ śambhu śivo 'ham* (VRY1) *ā oṃ śiva śiva brahma brahma śivo 'ham ekamevādvita tat-tvam-asi-ham* (CPSPS)	*paramaya-śuddhi* ("purification of wit or intelligence")
dvādaśānta	See full mantra in text.	Identity with Brahman / "purification of wisdom"

Note: These cakras are to be gradually canceled as part of the preliminary process of Śivarājayoga (CPSPS, First Book, 80–86; VRY1, 24–26). Many of Sabhapati's translations are nonliteral and refer to technical principles in his cosmology (see Chapter 3). Mantras in VRY1 are corrected from archaic transliterations that are clarified in the version from CPSPS. See Chapter 3 for the way in which these further intersect with the broader cosmologies as outlined in his vernacular works in Tamil and Sanskritized Hindi.

there unfortunately is still no conclusive proof of his body residing there.[92] When I asked Vinayagam Swamigal, the current trustee of the temple, what he thought *svayambhū liṅga* meant, he replied that it meant a "self-generated idol," and that centuries-old Mahans like Sabhapati were known to "bring themselves to the earth and perform miracles and disappear into the lingam."[93] The *liṅga* at Sri Sabhapathy Lingeshwarar Koil is believed to extend around seventeen feet deep into the ground, and during a previous excavation the word *liṅgeśvara* (Tam. *liṅkēsvar*) was found inscribed on the *liṅga*, which is how the temple acquired its name. Whether or not this was Sabhapati's own *svayambhū liṅga*, it has nevertheless been associated with a human yogi named Sabhapati Swami by the caretakers of the shrine for at least a century now (see Chapter 1).[94]

As seen in the quotation above, however, *videhamukti* is accomplished at the final stage of Śivarājayoga while singing the "Great Utterance."[95] Furthermore, many other instructions in CPSPS were also added that are of direct relevance to various aspects of the practice of Śivarājayoga, such as on music and mantra (see Chapter 5), the aforementioned instruction on "coitional blissfulness," various kinds of purification, and even initiations between guru and student (*dīkṣā*), uncannily translated as "mesmerism."[96] In any event, his instructions of Śivarājayoga all assume both familiarity and memorization of Sabhapati's cosmological descriptions, meditations, and associated mantras upon which they are based (see Table 4.3).

Sabhapati's most notable work of the Beta Stemma in Marathi and Hindi, RYB (1892), also includes practices of "purification" (*śuddhi*, see Table 4.3) and even devotes nearly thirty pages of its seventh chapter (Hi. *saptamādhyāy*) to the subject of Śivarājayoga, called *śivarāja jñānayoga* or shortened to simply *jñānayoga*. The practice (*sādhan*) is to be observed at four o'clock in the morning by either men or women (*strī puruṣ*) of any household after waking from sleep and washing the hands and face.[97] In contrast to his English work, Sabhapati here says that "there are seven methods to this practice of *śivarāja jñānayoga*."[98] The seven methods, framed as *bhāvanā*s (lit. mental "cultivations"), each consist of a different "path" (*mārg*) that pertains to interacting with the subtle physiology of Tantric yoga, also depicted in a unique diagram referred to throughout the chapter (see Figure 4.3). As in Sabhapati's Tamil works, the act of penetrating what he calls the "mystery of the eyewitness of being and nonbeing" [*bhāvābhāv sākṣātkār rahasya*] is not only limited to a frame of Vedānta as Sabhapati affirms that "Siddhānta, Vedānta, [and] Advaita have the goal

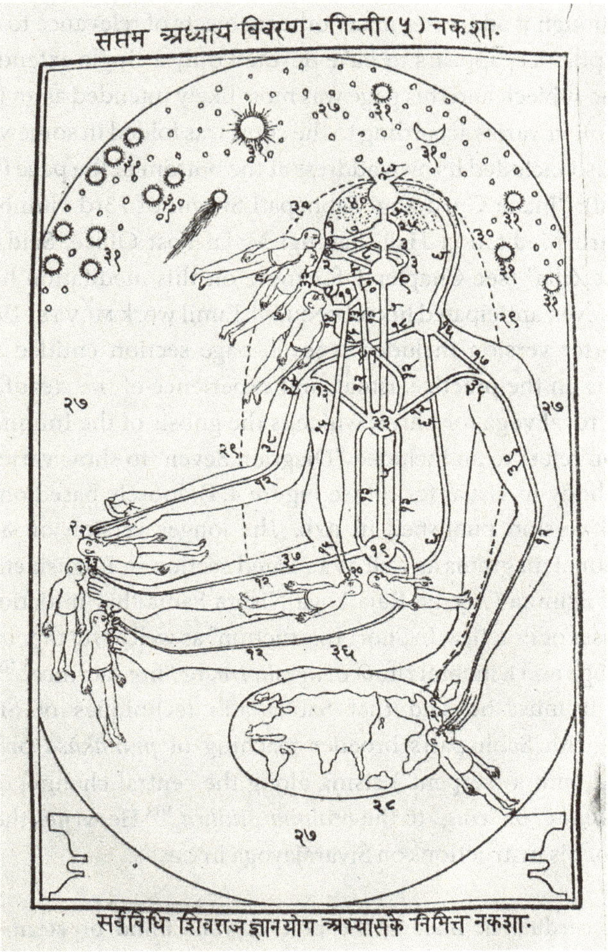

Figure 4.3 "Diagram Number Five, for the Description of Chapter Seven / A diagram for the purposes of practicing all types of Śivarāja Jñāna Yoga" (Hi. *saptam adhyāy vivaraṇ—gintī (5) nakśā / sarvavidhi śivarāja jñānayoga abhyāske nimitt nakśā*). This diagram is between pages 88 and 89 of RYB, immediately preceding the seventh chapter. Photo by the author of a copy held by the Adyar Library and Research Centre.

of knowing the gnosis of Brahman, which is the practice of the yoga of [subjugating] gnosis."[99]

Sabhapati's Tamil works in the Gamma Stemma also engaged the topic of Śivarājayoga, albeit a comprehensive treatment came relatively late. CTCSPV

(1889), although it addresses many other subjects of relevance to cosmology and ritual practice, appears to have devoted only a single extended page in Tamil to the subject, and this page was most likely intended as an insert since its page number varies according to the copy, was folded in somewhat irregularly, and also included its own address at the bottom of the page (translation from Tamil): "Jnana Guru Yogi Sabhapati Swami of 73rd Number Konnur Village Guru Meditation Hall, Parangi Malai Post Office, Saidapet Taluk, Chingleput Zilla" (see Chapter 1 for more on this meditation hall).[100] The insert, however, anticipated his subsequent Tamil work MCVTS (1913), which in the shorter version included a seven-page section entitled "Compiled instructions on the practice, ritual, and experience of the steadfast absorption of the royal yoga for Shiva, which is the gnosis of the Infinite Spirit."[101] This section refers to an included "Diagram Seven" to show various parts of the subtle body in visual form (see Figure 4.4), loosely based on the aforementioned version published in RYB. The longer version of MCVTS adds four additional diagrams as well as a related section in English entitled "The Practice of Brimha Gnyana Raja Yoga Nishta Samadhi's Initiational modes and processes of Practice, In Short Instruction" as well as further instructions on haṭha yoga and a mental ritual of *agnihotra*, or "fire sacrifice."[102]

Finally, it must be said that Sabhapati's techniques of Śivarājayoga are linked with Sabhapati's broader teaching of *jñānākāśa* or *prāṇākāśa* (analogized with a "serpent") rising along the central channel or *suṣumnā* from the *kuṇḍali* or "ring" to the *brahmarandhra*.[103] He writes the following at the end of his instructions on Śivarājayoga in CPSPS:

> After succeeding in making the pole of your mind or eternal Divine Conscious Sight, straight and steady by the foregoing process, join the Conscious Sight of the two Eyes with the top of mind in the Brummaranthra. Thus it forms a triangle whose vertex is the Mind, and the two keenness, that proceed from the eyes to join the former, are the two sides. Now drop these three Visions jointly as one Vision of conscious witnessing blissfullness to Kúndali and make itself rise like a serpent through Spinal Cord or backebone [*sic*] meeting it again in Birmharuntra.[104]

This description is somewhat similar to what John Woodroffe and the Arthur Avalon collaboration would popularize in their publications, such as *The Serpent Power*, an English translation and interpretation of the Sanskrit text *Ṣaṭcakranirūpaṇa* that was first published in 1919.[105] However, at least one

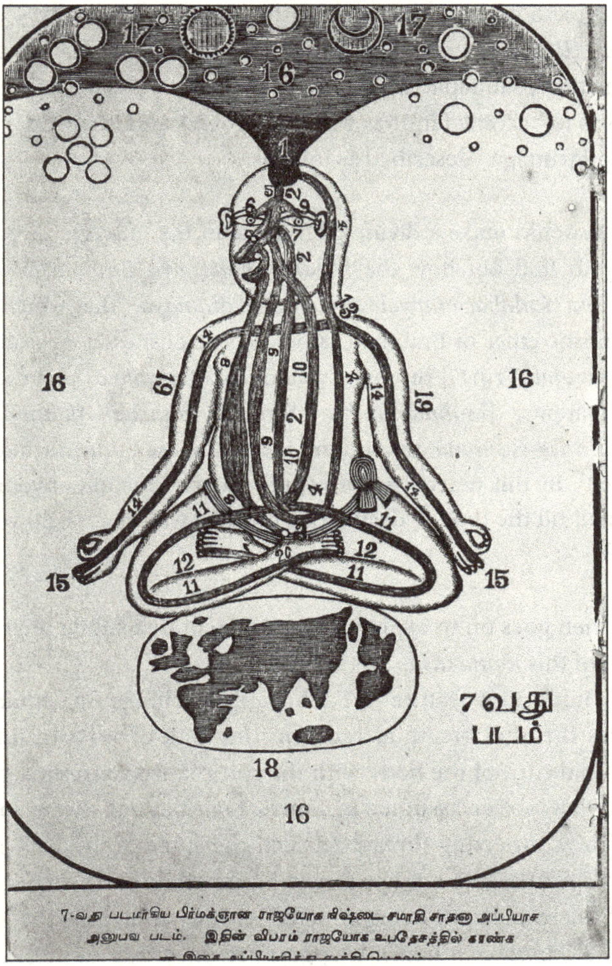

Figure 4.4 "The Seventh Diagram, being an image of the ritual, practice, and experience of the steadfast composure of the Royal Yoga for Shiva, which is the gnosis of the Infinite Spirit." From a copy of MCVTS held by Saraswathi Mahal Library in Thanjavur.

Indian author has noted several differences between their and Sabhapati's interpretation of *kuṇḍalinī*, or "she who is coiled," such as the way that kundalini descends and then reascends in the head.[106] Although Sabhapati uses the compound *jñānākāśa* rather than *kuṇḍalinī*, his description apart from this in accordance with the general Tantric understanding that *kuṇḍalinī* descends at birth and lies dormant in the lower abdomen by yoga, rises to cranial vault (*brahmarandhra*), and then redescends to rise again until death. At the same time, Sabhapati is keen on the yogi manipulating this ascent and descent so as to become familiar with the process and to become competent of "divine pilgrimage," described as follows:

> Now you should make a divine pilgrimage in the universe of your body in order to find out how the *suddha chaitannya Brahma giyanakasha mayam* [Skt. *śuddhacaitanyabrahmajñānākāśamaya*, "that which consists of the gnostic ether of Brahman as pure consciousness"] descends to the kundli [*kuṇḍali*, "ring"] through sushoomana [*suṣumnā*] and ascends up to Brahmarantar [*brahmarandhra*] through *kumbhak* [*kumbhaka*, another word for *suṣumnā* on account of it being the *nāḍī* in which breath is arrested]. By this descent and ascent the whole creation of your body is maintained till the time of death. This practice will much help you in the Yogue.[107]

Sabhapati then goes on to explain more of the body's subtle physiology and the motion of this *jñānākāśa*.

Another important feature of Sabhapati's teachings on *kuṇḍalinī* is the way he uses the vital breath as a connecting link of sorts to integrate the physical spinal cord of the body with the spiritualized *suṣumnā* channel, an integration that is often assumed in Tantric texts but not always so clearly articulated. The connecting thread between the spine's "physical" and purely "subtle" or "spiritual" aspects appears to be the vital breath, or Skt. *prāṇa*, on account of the spinal cord being equated with what he calls the "Kumbaka-Nadi" (= Skt. *kumbhaka nāḍī*). It appears to have this name since it is the site where the breath is arrested during retention (*kumbhaka*) in the context of *prāṇāyāma* (see his instructions on haṭha yoga at the beginning of this chapter). The left and right (in this case subtle) channels *iḍā* and *piṅgalā* are also equated with *recaka* "inhalation" and *pūraka* "exhalation," and together with the spine comprise the "three Nadies or Organs of Rechek, Puruk, and Kumbuk Vasi."[108] At a certain point upon the upper end of the spinal cord, however, this *kumbhaka nāḍī* is "prolonged" as the *suṣumnā*, and the three channels as *nāḍī*s or "hollow nerves" "rise up through kumbaka nadi [*sic*] or backbone spinal cord which is the upward prolongation of the Sushumna as three visions running up as one."[109] These three *nāḍī*s, rising up together, are visually depicted in Sabhapati's main diagram of the *liṅgaśarīra* or "body of the *liṅga*," which in his Bengali translation is a synonym for *sūkṣmaśarīra*, or "subtle body." Since the *suṣumnā nāḍī* is also glossed as the "I. spiritual nerve," that is, the nerve of Brahman, I would argue that Sabhapati conceived the breath by this point to be "spiritualized" and no longer physical breath in the spine. This is because it is no longer part of the *jīvātman* or Finite Spirit, and in any event it no longer resides in the *kuṇḍali* (i.e., the *mūlādhāra*), which is where Sabhapati locates the physical elements or faculties. This process of "de-physicalizing" the vital breath may be therefore assumed to have started even before the *kumbhaka nāḍī* is prolonged as the *suṣumnā*, possibly once the breath travels down from the nostrils to the *kuṇḍali* and ascends upward therefrom. In any event, it serves to connect the retention of the vital breath with the subjugation of *jñāna* and the accompanying rising of the *kuṇḍalinī* "serpent" in the context of Sabhapati Swami's system of Śivarājayoga.

Notes

1. For some of these other aspects see Keith Cantú, "Mantras for Every God and Goddess: Folk Religious Ritual in the Literature of Sabhapati Swami," in *Folk Religion (Re)Considered*, ed. Aaron Ullrey and Sravana Borkataky-Varma (Abingdon: Routledge, 2023).
2. Jason Birch, "Rājayoga: The Reincarnations of the King of All Yogas," *International Journal of Hindu Studies* 17, no. 3 (2013): 399–442; see also Jason Birch, "The Amaraughaprabodha: New Evidence on the Manuscript Transmission of an Early Work on Haṭha- and Rājayoga," *Journal of Indian Philosophy*, no. 47 (2019): 947–77; and Jason Birch, "Haṭhayoga's Floruit on the Eve of Colonialism," in *Śaivism and the Tantric Traditions: Essays in Honour of Alexis G.J.S. Sanderson*, ed. Dominic Goodall et al. (Leiden: Brill, 2020), 451–79. Birch elaborated on his research in his talk "Yoga on the Eve of Colonialism" for the Embodied Philosophy online conference "Yoga Reconsidered" (February 16–18, 2018), which I find compelling. He argued that the physical techniques of haṭha yoga ultimately derive from Buddhist and Jaina ascetic traditions, while the meditative techniques of haṭha yoga derive from earlier Tantric traditions. One example of a meditative technique of Tantric provenance is Śambhavīmudrā, the "Seal of Śambhu," for which see Paul Muller-Ortega, "On the Seal of Śambhu: A Poem by Abhinavagupta," in *Tantra in Practice*, ed. David Gordon White (Princeton, NJ: Princeton University Press, 2000), 573–86.T. K. Rajagopalan, a later author who engaged Sabhapati's works, would connect this *mudrā* to what he interpreted (correctly or not) as Tārakāyoga, or the "yoga of the pupil of the eye."
3. MCVTS, 38–42.
4. For the *Amaraughaprabodha* see Birch, "Haṭhayoga's Floruit," 452–53; Birch, "The Amaraughaprabodha," 947–77. For threatment of this sequence in the

Śivayogapradīpikā see Seth Powell, "A Lamp on Śiva's Yoga: The Unification of Yoga, Ritual, and Devotion in the Fifteenth-Century Śivayogapradīpikā" (PhD prospectus, Harvard University, 2018), 5–6, and his forthcoming dissertation.

5. VRY2, 79.
6. VRY2, 80–81.
7. MCVTS, 39. Tam.: "*(mutalāvatu) cuvācapantaṉamākiya aṭayōkamām. itil cuvācattai cuṣumṉā iṭā piṅkaḷā nāṭikaḷil atō:mukamāy pūraka kumpaka rēkṣakañ ceytu niṟuttalum, ūrt:tuvamukamāy cuṣumṉā nāṭiyil pirammarantira pariyantiram pantaṉa stampaṉa stāpaṉañ ceytu niṟuttalumākiya cuvācap pirāṇāyāmamām. itāl pirammakñāṉamum muktiyumaṭaiya oṇṇāvām. itiṉāl āyuḷ virttiyum tatva layamumuṇṭām, inta cuvācam maṉōjīvattiṉ kāriyamām. itu carva cuṉyakñāṉattil oṭuṅkum.*"
8. MCVTS, 39. Tam.: "*(iraṇṭāvatu) cuvāca maṉōpantaṉamākiya haṭa rājayōkamām. itil cuvācamum maṉamum kuṇṭaliyiliruntu cuṣumṉā iṭā piṅkaḷā nāṭikaḷ vaḻiyāy mēlceṉṟu nācikārantirattil cuṣumṉānāṭiyil cērntum ataippōṉṟu kutāviliruntu nācikāyantirattil cērntum pirammarantira pariyantiram oru stampampōṉṟu stampittu acaivaṟṟu calaṉam cañcalam, caṅkalpam vikalpam niṉaippu maṟappu kaṟpaṉaiyaṟṟu cuvācamaṉōlaya pōtāṉanta paravaca vācimayamāy niṟuttalākiya cuvācamaṉō pirāṇāyāmmākum. itiṉāl maṉōlayakñāṉa maṭaiyalākum.*"
9. MCVTS, 39. Tam.: "*(mūṉṟāvatu) kñāṉavaciyamākiya civarājayōkam itu vētānta vicāraṇai kñāṉappirakāram ātma piramma aikkiya ēkōhampāva, yattuvaita pāva, aikkiyapāva lakṣiyamāyum, cittānta vicāraṇai kñāṉampirakāram ātma pirammalaya tāsōhampāva, tuvaitapāva, layapāva lakṣiyamāyun tiyāṉa camāti niṣṭaiyilikkum kñāṉacamāti niṣṭaiyām.*"
10. Nā. Katiraivēṟ Piḷḷai, *Tāyumāṉa cuvāmi pāṭalkaḷ: mūlamum uraiyum* (Chennai: Cantiyā Patippakam, 2010), 149–63.
11. For recent findings see James Mallinson, "The Amṛtasiddhi: Haṭhayoga's Tantric Buddhist Source Text," in *Śaivism and the Tantric Traditions: Essays in Honour of Alexis G.J.S. Sanderson*, ed. Dominic Goodall et al. (Leiden: Brill, 2020), 409–25; Birch, "Haṭhayoga's Floruit"; James Mallinson and Mark Singleton, eds., *Roots of Yoga* (London: Penguin Books, 2017), xx–xxi. For current ethnographic observations see Daniela Bevilacqua, "Let the Sādhus Talk: Ascetic Understanding of Haṭha Yoga and Yogāsanas" (2017). For the connection between haṭha yoga and Indian alchemy, see David Gordon White, *The Alchemical Body: Siddha Traditions in Medieval India* (Chicago: University of Chicago Press, 1996).
12. Mallinson, "The Amṛtasiddhi"; Mallinson and Singleton, *Roots of Yoga*, xxi–xxii.
13. Mallinson and Singleton, *Roots of Yoga*. See also David Gordon White, *The Yoga Sutra of Patanjali: A Biography*, Lives of Great Religious Books (Princeton: Princeton University Press, 2014).
14. See Keith Cantú, "Haṭhayoga as 'Black Magic' in Early Theosophy and Beyond," in *Proceedings of the ESSWE6 Conference on Esotericism and Deviance*, ed. Tim Rudbøg and Manon Hedenborg White (Leiden: Brill, forthcoming).
15. CPSPS, Second Book, 356–59.
16. CPSPS, Second Book, 356.

17. CPSPS, Second Book, 358.
18. For a history of these *nāḍīs* see Mallinson and Singleton, *Roots of Yoga*, 172–74.
19. CPSPS, Second Book, 357. The *kāraṇa svarūpa* is also not one of the "Seven Spiritual States," or *svarūpas*, detailed in CPSPS, Second Book, 213–21, and its origin is obscure.
20. Mallinson and Singleton, *Roots of Yoga*, 171–74. The term *kāraṇa* in a Tantric context can refer to the five deities Brahmā, Viṣṇu, Rudra, Īśvara, and Sadāśiva, but this does not seem to fully account for this context either; see Hélène Brunner-Lachaux, Gerhard Oberhammer, and André Padoux, eds., *Tāntrikābhidhānakośa: Dictionnaire des termes techniques de la littérature hindoue tantrique = A Dictionary of Technical Terms from Hindu Tantric Literature = Wörterbuch zur Terminologie hinduistischer Tantren* (Vienna: Verlag der Österreichischen Akademie der Wissenschaften, 2000), 90–91.
21. For more on the significance of the *mudrās* in haṭha yogic and Tantric literature, see Mallinson and Singleton, *Roots of Yoga*, 228–58.
22. Ibid., 358.
23. For more on the history of this text see Philipp Maas, "A Concise Historiography of Classical Yoga Philosophy," in *Periodization and Historiography of Indian Philosophy*, ed. Eli Franco (Vienna: Sammlung de Nobili, Institut für Südasien-, Tibet- und Buddhismuskunde der Universität Wien, 2013), 57–58; White, *Yoga Sutra of Patanjali*.
24. VRY2, 80–81.
25. For an early translation of the ŚYP see Sadasiva Yogindra, "Sivayogadipika," *The Brahmavâdin* 8, no. 8 (August 1903): 439–50 and in subsequent numbers of the journal. See also Powell, "Lamp on Śiva's Yoga," and his forthcoming dissertation and critical edition of this text. For treatment of Patañjali's *aṅgas* in the third *tantiram* of the *Tirumantiram* (verses 549–640 in the editions I have consulted) see Tirumūlar, *The Tirumandiram*, trans. T. N. Ganapathy et al., 10 vols., vol. 3 (Eastman, Quebec, Canada: Babaji's Kriya Yoga and Publications, 2013), 661–764; Tirumūlar, *Tirumūlar tirumantiram: mūlamum—viḷakka uraiyum*, ed. Ñā. Māṇikkavācakaṉ and Pattām Patippu (Chennai: Umā Patippakam, 2016), 244–85; Tirumular, *Tirumantiram: A Tamil Scriptural Classic*, trans. B. Natarajan and N. Mahalingam (Madras: Sri Ramakrishna Math, 1991), 86–100, verses 549–639.
26. Citampara Periya Cuvāmikaḷ, *Upatēca uṇmai, viḷakka uraiyuṭaṉ* (Vēḷaccēri, Chennai: Vēḷaccēri Makāṉ Patippakam, 2014), 202–10. In this edition the relevant verses on the *aṣṭāṅga* are from 167 to 175.
27. In Pātañjalayogaśāstra 3.4, *saṃyama* is treated as *dhāraṇa*, *dhyāna*, and *samādhi* taken together (*trayamekatra saṃyamaḥ*). Sabhapati here lists it separately, perhaps on account of the fact that many *saṃyamas* are treated in Patañjali's third or *vibhūtipāda*. See Hari Nārāyaṇa Āpṭe, trans., *Pātañjalayogasūtrāṇi* (Pune: Ānandāśramamudraṇālayā, 1919), 4.
28. This outline is derived from the list and descriptive paragraphs provided in CPSPS, First Book, 104–5.
29. These translations of the *yamas* and *niyamas* follow those given in Jason Birch and Jacqueline Hargreaves, "The Yamas and Niyamas: Patanjali's View," *Yoga Scotland*, January 2016, 33.

30. Tirumular, *Tirumantiram: A Tamil Scriptural Classic*, 86–87; Citampara Periya Cuvāmikaḷ, *Upatēca uṇmai*, 202–4.
31. VRY2, 80.
32. VRY2, 80.
33. For visual descriptions of some of these *āsanas* and references to them see M. L. Gharote et al., eds., *Encyclopedia of Traditional Asanas* (Lonavla: The Lonavla Institute, 2006).
34. It remains unclear what *cottiram / cottirācaṉam* (also translated "sothiram" refers to, although it may be a generic kind of *sthīrāsana*, or "fixed posture." The editors of the most recent translation of the *Tirumantiram* note the following: "According to Aruṇai Vaḍivēlu Mudaliār, the āsana named sothiram may refer to *kukkuḍāsana*"; see Tirumūlar, *The Tirumandiram*, 677.
35. I am grateful to Jason Birch for his assistance in helping me to track down the origin of these *āsanas* and sharing with me sources that helped this section. For a detailed history of these *āsanas* as they are present in the ŚYP see Seth Powell, "Advice on Āsana in the Śivayogapradīpikā," *The Luminescent* (blog), June 30, 2017, https://www.theluminescent.org/2017/06/advice-on-asana-in-sivayogapradipika.html.
36. Svātmārāma, *Haṭhapradīpikā of Svātmārāma*, ed. Swami Digambarji and Raghunatha Shastri Kokaje, 3rd ed. (Lonavla: Kaivalyadhama, 2016).
37. CPSPS, First Book, 105.
38. Ibid.
39. Dominic S. Zoehrer, "From Fluidum to Prāṇa: Reading Mesmerism through Orientalist Lenses," in *The Occult Nineteenth Century: Roots, Developments, and Impact on the Modern World*, ed. Lukas Pokorny and Franz Winter (New York: Palgrave Macmillan, 2020); Magdalena Kraler, "Tracing Vivekananda's Prāṇa and Ākāśa: The Yogavāsiṣṭha and Rama Prasad's Occult Science of Breath," in *The Occult Nineteenth Century: Roots, Developments, and Impact on the Modern World*, ed. Lukas Pokorny and Franz Winter (London: Palgrave Macmillan, forthcoming); Karl Baier, "Mesmeric Yoga and the Development of Meditation within the Theosophical Society," *Theosophical History* 16, nos. 3–4 (October 2012): 151–61.
40. RYB, chap. 5, 59–78.
41. For an overview and the broader history of this yogic subtle physiology, see Mallinson and Singleton, *Roots of Yoga*, 171–227. See also the dissertation of Magdalena Kraler for the practice among other modern yoga "pioneers."
42. MCVTS, 91.
43. Vesna Wallace, "The Six-Phased Yoga of the *Abbreviated Wheel of Time Tantra* (*Laghukālacakratantra*) according to Vajrapāṇi," in *Yoga in Practice*, ed. David Gordon White (Princeton, NJ: Princeton University Press, 2012), 220–21 Some degree of historical connection is all the more plausible given current scholarship that locates at least some of the roots of haṭha yoga in Buddhist milieus; see Mallinson, "The Amṛtasiddhi."
44. VRY2, 81.
45. MCVTS, 92.

46. For Tantric alchemy see White, *The Alchemical Body*. For the *Amṛtasiddhi* see Mallinson, "The Amṛtasiddhi." For the broader context of alchemical literature in India, see Dagmar Wujastyk, "Acts of Improvement: On the Use of Tonics and Elixirs in Sanskrit Medical and Alchemical Literature," *History of Science in South Asia* 5, no. 2 (2017): 1–35.
47. CPSPS, Second Book, 143–48.
48. See Carol Salomon, *City of Mirrors: Songs of Lālan Sā̃i*, ed. Keith Cantú and Saymon Zakaria (New York: Oxford University Press, 2017), 65 n, 14 and Jeanne Openshaw, *Seeking Bāuls of Bengal* (Cambridge: Cambridge University Press, 2002), 216–24.
49. CPSPS, Second Book, 144–45. In the first point "Firing" is changed to "Fixing" in accordance with Sabhapati's rubric. I have added boldface on the key terms that are repeated in both enumerations for ease of reading and comparison.
50. CPSPS, Second Book, 145–46.
51. CPSPS, Second Book, 147.
52. See J. M. Nallaswāmi Pillai, trans., *Śivajñāna Siddhiyār of Aruṇandi Śivāchārya* (Madras: Meykandan Press, 1913), xxix.
53. CPSPS, Second Book, 148.
54. Elizabeth De Michelis, *A History of Modern Yoga: Patañjali and Western Esotericism* (reprint, London: Continuum, 2008), 178–80.
55. De Michelis, *History of Modern Yoga*, 178–80.
56. Manilal Nabhubhai Dvivedi, *Rája Yoga, or the Practical Metaphysics of the Vedánta, Being a Translation of the Vákyasudhá or Drigdrishyaviveka of Bháratitirtha, and the Aparokshánubhuti of Shri Shankarácharya, with an Introduction, Appendix Containing the Sanskrit Text and Commentary of the Vákyasudhá, and Notes Explanatory and Critical* (Bombay: "Subodha-Prakasha" Printing Press, 1885). Cf. Birch, "Rājayoga," 409.
57. Tookaram Tatya, *A Compendium of the Raja Yoga Philosophy, Comprising the Principal Treatises of Shrimat Sankaracharya and Other Renowned Authors* (Bombay: Subodha-Prakash Press, 1888).
58. See verses 118–28 for mention of the *aṅgas* of Patañjali.
59. Birch, "Rājayoga," 409.
60. Tookaram Tatya, *Compendium*, 32.
61. Dvivedi, *Rája Yoga*, 28; Tookaram Tatya, *Compendium*, 27.
62. Dvivedi, *Rája Yoga*.
63. Ibid.
64. MCVTS, 46–47.
65. VRY1, 13. This fourfold *antaḥkaraṇa* may be one distinguishing feature of Sabhapati's debt to Vedānta and Śaiva Siddhānta in south India; see Chapter 3.
66. CPSPS, First Book, 119.
67. Srilata Raman, personal email correspondence, June 15, 2020. I am grateful to Srilata for helping to confirm my suspicion that Śivarājayoga is not Sabhapati's own invention but is part of a larger Vīraśaiva genre of Śivayoga.
68. On this text see Powell, "Lamp on Śiva's Yoga," and Powell's forthcoming dissertation.

69. For Basava see R. Blake Michael, *The Origins of Vīraśaiva Sects: A Typological Analysis of Ritual and Associational Patterns in the Śūnyasaṃpādane* (Delhi: Motilal Banarsidass, 1992); and Velcheru Narayana Rao and Gene H. Roghair, *Siva's Warriors: The Basava Purana of Palkuriki Somanatha* (1990; Princeton, NJ: Princeton University Press, 2016); for their Śaiva philosophy more generally see Elaine M. Fisher, "Remaking South Indian Śaivism: Greater Śaiva Advaita and the Legacy of the Śaktiviśiṣṭādvaita Vīraśaiva Tradition," *International Journal of Hindu Studies* 21, no. 3 (December 2017): 319–44.
70. Eric Steinschneider, "Beyond the Warring Sects: Universalism, Dissent, and Canon in Tamil Śaivism, ca. 1675–1994" (PhD dissertation, University of Toronto, 2016).
71. See Richard Weiss, *The Emergence of Modern Hinduism: Religion on the Margins of Colonialism* (Oakland: University of California Press, 2017), and Srilata Raman, *The Transformation of Tamil Religion: Ramalinga Swamigal and Modern Dravidian Sainthood* (Abingdon, UK: Routledge, 2022).
72. Eṉ Taṃmaṇṇa Ceṭṭiyār, *Vāciyōkam eṉṉum civarāja yōkam* (Chennai: Śrī Indu Papḷikēṣaṉs, 2016).
73. Through the Sanskrit *vāṃśī* the word became Bengali *bāṃśi*, a common name used for the bamboo flute used in Bengali folk music and the word most commonly used for Krishna's flute.
74. Yōki Kailaṣnāt, *Caṟkurunāta yōkam: śrīcaṟkurunāta svāmikaḷ aruḷiya civarāja yōkam, taṉarāja yōkam, yōkarāja yōkam, oṭṭirāja yōkam, yavarāja yōkam (mūlamum—uraiyum)* (Chennai: Kaṟpakam Puttakālayam, 2012). Prem Manavai and Padmashree Vijayakumar have created a documentary of this yogi entitled "The Failed Samadhi," available on YouTube: https://www.youtube.com/watch?v=GNFAKlb6VZY; I am grateful to Karisal Sathish for putting us in touch.
75. According to Karisal Sathish and Vijay Kumar's research (email correspondence, January 8, 2021), Sabhapati's student Om Prakash Swamigal mentions in one of his early publications that he met Sargurunathar personally in the Nilgiris. At present time of writing I am still trying to locate this reference.
76. CPSPS, First Book, 124.
77. CPSPS, First Book, 124.
78. CPSPS, First Book, 124–25. Much of this bears relevance to the model of subtle pilgrimage as attested in Kubjikā sources; see Mark S. G. Dyczkowski, *A Journey in the World of Tantras* (Varanasi: Indica Books, 2004), 93–175 and Chapter 6.
79. CPSPS, First Book, 127.
80. CPSPS, First Book, 129.
81. CPSPS, First Book, 129.
82. CPSPS, First Book, 87–89. Cf. VRY1, 26–28.
83. CPSPS, First Book, 4–5; VRY1, iv. For the other powers see CPSPS, Second Book, 389–91. For more on the powers that yogis were believed to be able to obtain see Somadeva Vasudeva, "Powers and Identities: Yoga Powers and the Tantric Śaiva Traditions," in *Yoga Powers: Extraordinary Capacities Attained through Meditation and*

Concentration, ed. Knut A. Jacobsen (Leiden: Brill, 2012), 264–302; David Gordon White, *Sinister Yogis* (Chicago: University of Chicago Press, 2009).

84. See Chapter 2 for the division of Sabhapati's works into several "streams."
85. For more examples of this in Tantric literature see Gavin D. Flood, *The Tantric Body: The Secret Tradition of Hindu Religion* (London: I.B. Tauris, 2006).
86. VRY1, 33–46.
87. CPSPS, First Book, 105–16.
88. CPSPS, First Book, 90–96.
89. See White, *Sinister Yogis*, 112–14; Angelika Malinar, "Something Like Liberation: *prakṛtilaya* (Absorption in the Cause/s of Creation) in Yoga and Sāṃkhya," in *Release in Life: Indian Perspectives on Individual Liberation*, ed. Andreas Biggar et al. (Bern: Peter Lang, 2010), 129–56.
90. VRY1, V.
91. See Trilochan Dash, *The Story of the Deities and the Temples in Southern Indian Peninsula* (Bhubaneswar: Soudamini Dash, 2010), 113–15.
92. For more on this temple and the worship of the *liṅga* there as it was prior to the discovery outlined in this book that it is likely a former meditation hall of Sabhapati Swami (for which see Chapter 1), see Cuvāmi Pi. Pi. Ār. Hariharaṉ, *Aruḷmiku śrī capāpati liṅkēsvar jīvacamāti ālayamstala varalāṟu* (Maṇavūr: Kaviñar Murukāṉantam Accakam, 2017).
93. Personal communication via WhatsApp with Vinayagam Swamigal of the Sri Sabhapathy Lingeshwarar Koil, November 2, 2011.
94. Hariharaṉ Cuvāmikaḷ, interview at Aruḷmiku Śrī Capāpati Liṅkēsvar Jīvacamāti Ālayam, interview by Keith Cantú and Sivasakthi, audio recording, July 2018.
95. *Mahāvākyas* taken more literally are the "great sayings" of the Upanishads as interpreted by authors of Vedānta, of which the most famous is *tattvamasi*, "that thou art."
96. For more on the integration of yogic ideas with mesmerism, see Baier, "Mesmeric Yoga"; Zoehrer, "From Fluidum to Prāṇa."
97. RYB, 90. "*isa kāraṇ siddhānta vedānta advaita brahmajñān jānneke nimitta jñānyog sādhanā hai.*"
98. RYB, 91: "*isa śivarāja jñānayogameṅ sapta prakār hai.*"
99. RYB, 91: "*siddhānta vedānta advaita brahmajñān jānneke nimitta jñānyog sādhanā hai.*"
100. *ñāṉakuruyoki capāpati cuvāmi 73-vatu nempar koṉṉūr kirama kurumaṭālayam, paraṅkimalai pōsṭāpīcu, caitāpēṭṭai tālūkā, ceṅkalpaṭṭu jillā.* The number 73 refers to number of the adjacent village Villivakkam (which to this day overlaps with Konnur) in old survey records, as attested by extant village maps from that time period; see *No. 73, Villivakkam, Saidapet Taluk, Chingleput District, Traced from the Original Map of 1906*, 16 inches = 1 mile (Madras: Vandyke Survey Office, 1938).
101. MCVTS (short version), 38: "*parhmak ñāṉa civarājayōka niṣṭā camāti appiyāca cātaṉā aṉupava upatē:cāṉuk:kiraham.*" The section on Śivarājayoga spans pages 38–44.
102. MCVTS (long version), 45.

103. For scholarly treatments of this see Lilian Silburn, *La Kuṇḍalinī, ou, L'énergie des profondeurs: Étude d'ensemble d'après les textes du Śivaïsme non dualiste du Kaśmir* (Paris: Deux océans, 1983); Mallinson and Singleton, *Roots of Yoga*, 178–83.
104. CPSPS, First Book, 114.
105. Arthur Avalon, *The Serpent Power, Being the Shat-Chakra-Nirūpana and Pāduka-Panchakā* (1919; Madras: Ganesh & Co., 1950). For the global influence of this text and others on the spread of Tantra worldwide see Julian Strube, *Global Tantra: Religion, Science, and Nationalism in Colonial Modernity* (New York: Oxford University Press, 2022), 52.
106. Arjan Dass Malik, *Kundalini and Meditation* (Delhi: Motilal Banarsidass; Borehamwood: Motilal, 2002); see also T. K. Rajagopalan, *Hidden Treasures of Yoga: Revealing Certain Ancient and Secret Methods of Practical Mysticism* (Delhi: Oriental Book Centre, 2005), 21–23.
107. VRY1, 38.
108. VRY1, 38.
109. VRY1, 126.

5

Singing Mantras and Visualizing Flowers

> The disciples, who are not personally initiated by Gnyana Guru Yogi Sabapathy Swamy must have his Photo as his presence.
>
> —CPSPS, Second Book, 299

> Ye! my dear disciples! you must utilize the Slokas on Saguna and Nirguna and Bruhma Dhianum sung by me at the Darashana of Mahadeva in Kailas, which is found in my life, considering the body as Mount Kailas and the head as the cave-like temple on the bodily Kailas Mountain and the Spiritual sight or Gnyana Drishti in the Bruhmarmddhra as Bruhmeshwar Mahadev, when you are in the full ecstacy of mental pious worship.
>
> —CPSPS, Second Book, 402

> The mind must be fixed stead fastly and firmly at the centre seat of the skull, called Brimha Randhram (1) of the 7th diagram by the maditation [*sic*] of the Mantras ("Om Aham—Aham Om" "Om Siva Siva Om" "Om Hari—Hari Om.").
>
> —MCVTS (long version), 45

In this chapter I consider the aural and visual artistic aspects of Sabhapati's texts and instructions, specifically the use of poetry and music, mantric chanting, and diagrams, all of which were integrated into his system of Śivarājayoga. I base my claims on an evaluation of Sabhapati's corpus of literature (see Chapter 2) as well as my ethnographic engagement at the still-extant site of Sabhapati's former meditation hall in Konnur (today called Sabhapaty Swami Koil or Sabhapaty Lingeswarar Koil; see Chapter 1), including a recorded interview with Narayanaswamy Raju, a singer and yogi (Skt. *yogī*, < stem *yogin*).[1] I would argue that, far from being marginal,

Like a Tree Universally Spread. Keith Edward Cantú, Oxford University Press. © Oxford University Press 2023.
DOI: 10.1093/oso/9780197665473.003.0006

these aesthetic aspects played a crucial role in Sabhapati's instructions. All his works to varying extents also include poetry, several of which include a reference to the appropriate musical mode or raga, implying that these compositions were not just recited but also intended to be sung, at least on certain occasions. The recitation or chanting of mantras in his yogic instructions is also sometimes given a musical quality, the function of which appears to differ from the recitation of poetic compositions that appeared to have served either a more devotional (Skt. *bhakti*) or didactic purpose. Finally, Sabhapati's works are some of the first visual works on yoga following the advent of publishing; at least one diagram, and in most cases multiple diagrams, occupies each of Sabhapati's main (nonpamphlet) works, and most often these are numbered to directly correspond to ideas presented in the texts themselves.

Lyrical Compositions and Musical Poems

Anyone who picks up and begins to read one of Sabhapati's works, both in English and in vernacular languages, will immediately encounter the presence of poems or metered prose compositions ("prose poems") that complement his standard writing in unmetered prose. Even his hagiographical accounts noted that he had the reputation of a poet and musician from an early age (see Chapter 1). Sabhapati was said to have composed some of these poems, such as his "Garland of Praise for Shiva" (Mpvl. "Civastutimālā," < Skt. "Śivastutimālā"),[2] during or following his own personal experiences in his career and travels as a yogi (see Chapter 1). Others were composed to serve a didactic function, and still others were meant to be recited at certain phases during the experience of Śivarājayoga. Many of the poetic compositions written by Sabhapati during his experiences were assigned a musical mode and meant to be set to interpretive music.

Sabhapati's compositions have a clear affinity with an extant genre of songs that are colloquially known as "Siddha songs" (Tam. *cittar pāṭal*, pl. *pāṭalkaḷ*),[3] many of which also intersect with or innovate upon the style of older or more traditional Tamil devotional songs such as those attributed to the circa ninth-century Śaiva poet Māṇikkavācakar (Manikkavacakar), including his celebrated work *Tiruvācakam*.[4] They were likely also influenced by Tamil Śaiva poets such as Thayumanavar (Tāyumāṉavar, 1705–1742, see Chapter 3) who preceded him by a century and possibly also his contemporary and childhood friend (if his hagiography is to be believed) Chidambaram Ramalinga Swamigal (Citampara Rāmaliṅka Cuvāmikaḷ, 1823–1874). The genre and musical structure of these songs allow for interpretive performances of compositions based on attention to syllables (Tam. *acai*) and rhythm (Skt. *tāla*).[5] Even though Sabhapati's own compositions are no longer performed, they are likewise still able to be set to music and rhythm within this same interpretive frame, as with more popular Tamil compositions. I have confirmed this in my interview with Narayanaswamy Raju, who opened his interview by singing "Shiva's Ancient Deeds" (Tam. "Civapurāṇam," different from the Sanskrit text *Śivapurāṇa*), considered the first of Māṇikkavācakar's *Tiruvācakam* (although it may have been composed later), and who spoke of his personal journey in learning the songs of the Siddhas.[6] The performance of Sabhapati's own songs during his lifetime likely were mediated by similar performative contexts as the songs of the Siddhas, Thayumanavar (see Chapter 3), and those of Māṇikkavācakar before them. They would also have been improvised upon by the creative impulse and skill of the singer. Singing these songs would also have required some degree of training in Tamil musical structure and meter, even if this was based on oral instructions or immersive experience in temple sites, especially since in the case of his longer compositions there is reference to the appropriate musical scale-type or mode that a singer would need to be familiar with. Given Sabhapati's attention to poetry and song and the depiction of it as part of the guru's instructions (see Figure 5.1), it is likely that he would have also offered direct instruction in musical techniques.

There is also evidence from one of Sabhapati's diagrams (see Figure 5.1) that his meditation halls would have welcomed the presence of music within the context of ritual practice, and that it formed part of Sabhapati's "curriculum" of sorts. This diagram, entitled "Image of the students and community carrying out the instructions of the guru" (Tam. *ciṣyarkaḷ caṅkattōṭu kuru upatēcañ ceyyum paṭam*), is located in the longer version of MCVTS that prefixed an order form for his publications in other languages and for two additional diagrams the size of four pages (Tam. Eng. *4 pēj sais*). The image, a numerical diagram, depicts activities that would have surrounded Sabhapati

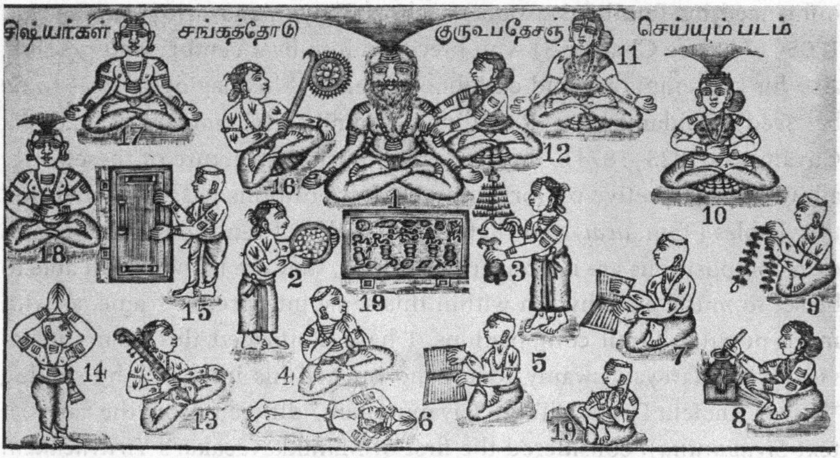

Figure 5.1 "Diagram on the students and community (Tam. *caṅkam*, < Skt. *saṅgha*) carrying out the instructions (< Skt. *upadeśa*) of the guru" (Tam. *ciṣyarkaḷ caṅkattōṭu kuru upatēcañ ceyyum paṭam*). This diagram was only preserved in two longer versions of MCVTS held at the Adyar Library and the Saraswathi Mahal Library in Thanjavur. Scan courtesy Siddhanai of the Tamil Digital Library, originally from the Saraswathi Mahal Library version (out of copyright).

Swami while he was engaged in meditation. The numbers in the diagram refer to the following activities:

1. "Guru Father, Lord among Rishis" (Sabhapati Swami) (*kurupitaruṣisvarar*)
2. "A male student setting an oblation" (*naivēttiyam vaikkuñ ciṣyar*)
3. "A male student working the lamp and musical sound" (*tīpānātaṉai ceyyuñciṣyar*)
4. "A male student receiving instruction" (*upatēcamperuñciṣyar*)
5. "A male student contemplating scripture" (*cāstira vicāraṇai ciṣyar*)
6. "A male student attaining the feet [of the guru] (*caraṇamaṭainta ciṣyar*)
7. "A male student dispelling his own doubts" (*cantēkanivāraṇam ceytukoḷḷuñ ciṣyar*)
8. "A female student as a servant" (*pariccāraka ciṣyaputtiri*)
9. "A male student working on the flowers" (*puṣpa paṇiviṭai ciṣyar*)
10. "A female student in a state of composure (Skt. *samādhi*) with assistance from the guru" (*kurāṉukkirahacamātiyilirukkañ ciṣyaputtiri*)

11. "A female student in initiation from the guru" (*kurutīkṣaiyilirukkuñ ciṣyaputtiri*)
12. "A female student attending to the body of the guru" (*kuru carīrōpacārañ ceyyuñ ciṣyaputtiri*)
13. "A male student singing the gamut of the Vedas and the musical scale-types (Tam. *paṇ*) of the *Tēvāram*" (*vētacuram tēvārappaṇpāṭuñ ciṣyar*)
14. "A male student enacting praise for the guru" (*kurustuticeyyuñ ciṣyar*)
15. "A male student laying out the guru's bed" (*kurucayaṉampōṭuñ ciṣyar*)
16. "A male student fanning the guru" (*kuruvukku viciṟuñ ciṣyar*)
17. "A female student in initiation from the guru" (*kurutīkṣaiyilirukkuñ ciṣyar*)
18. "A male student in a state of composure (Skt. *samādhi*) with assistance from the guru" (*kurāṉukkiraha camātiyilirukkuñ ciṣyar*)
19. "A male student making a gift out of his three constituents (body, speech, and mind) to the guru" (*kuruviṟku tirikaraṇa tattañceyyuñ ciṣyar*).

As is evident from the list, two of the students (numbers 3 and 13), depicted as male, are in charge of musical activities. One student (number 3) appears to have a more ritualistic role since he is holding a bell as well as a lamp. The other student (number 13), however, is seated and is holding what appears to be a tanpura, and the caption informs us that his is a more devotional role that included singing according to two different systems.

The *Tēvāram*, mentioned in Sabhapati's key under this student (number 13), is a foundational part of the Tamil Śaiva bhakti literature of the Nāyaṉārs ("leaders," "masters") and was believed to have been composed between the sixth and eighth centuries CE.[7] The foundations of its musical performance were "ancient Tamil scale-types" (Tam. *paṇ*, plural *paṇkaḷ*), which were traditionally "associated with particular times of day and particular moods" and were sung by singers who were called *ōtuvars*.[8]

From the sixteenth to the nineteenth centuries these ancient scales were gradually replaced by Carnatic raga scales,[9] so it is possible that Sabhapati refers to *paṇ* out of tradition but that in practice the singer depicted in the diagram would have been singing forms of Carnatic ragas. Some of Sabhapati's poetic compositions do specify that they were to be sung in specific *paṇ*s, but these also seem to be linked to Carnatic ragas instead. For instance, Sabhapati composed a set of Tamil and (Tamilized) Sanskrit verses, entitled "The Hymn of Following: A Gift of the Abandonment of All" (Tam.

carvattiyākatatta aṭumaistuti),[10] upon his abandonment of everything for his guru Shivajnana Bodha Rishi Yogiswarar in the Pothigai Hills (see Chapter 1). This composition is supposed to be performed in *ārapirākapaṇ*, that is, the *paṇ* of the *rākam* (Tam. *rākam* = Skt. *rāga*) of *ārapi*, which is a known Carnatic raga. Another composition, published in CPSPS, was entitled "Garland of the Body" (Mpvl. *aṅkamālai*, < Skt. *aṅgamālā*) and was to be sung in the *paṇ* of the Sahana raga (Tam. *rākam—sahāṉā—paṇ*), also a known Carnatic raga.[11] This latter composition is interesting as it also serves a Tantric function akin to the practice of "depositing" mantras (Skt. *nyāsa*) on various parts of the body, except instead of mantras one is to recite devotional statements while touching parts of the body. One of these statements, attributed to the ear (Tam. *cevi*), explicitly mentions "perceiving the gnosis of Śivarājayoga" (Tam. *civarājayōkaññāṉamuṇarntu*).[12]

Sabhapati in the above diagram also alludes to his student singing the "gamut of the Vedas" (Mpvl. *vētasuram*), which refers to the collection of seven musical notes (Mpvl. *curam*, < Skt. *svara*), similar to the theory behind the solfège of Western music (i.e., "do re mi fa so la ti do" in the modern usage): (1) *sa* for Ṣaḍja ("Sixth-born"), (2) *ri* for Ṛṣabha ("Bull"), (3) *gā* for Gāndhāra ("Prince of the Gāndhāris"), (4) *ma* for Madhyama ("Middle"), (5) *pa* for Pañcama ("Fifth"), (6) *dhā* for Dhaivata ("Clever"), (7) *ni* for Niṣāda ("Rest"); then back to *sa* to complete the octave. Some of Sabhapati's compositions, like the aforementioned "Garland of Praise of Shiva," were to be sung in the "mode of the gamut of the vedas" (*vētasvara rākam*, < Skt. **vedasvararāga*).[13] Since the Carnatic ragas are also based on the seven *svaras*, the compound *vedasvararāga* may be Sabhapati's way of distinguishing the Tamil modes (*paṇ*) and Carnatic ragas from Hindustani ragas.

It is important to keep in mind that the wider context for Sabhapati's incorporation of music in his literature and instructions is informed by the intersections between traditional temple culture and the environment of Sabhapati's "meditation hall" as depicted in his visual diagrams (see especially CTCSPV for his visual instructions on temple worship). The performance of a wide variety of arts, especially singing but also dancing and ascetic practice, appears to once have been more common in Hindu temple settings in Tamil Nadu despite the fact that today it is sometimes frowned upon, especially in more modernized temple settings that primarily focus on the laity's participation in the rites of ritual worship (*pūjā*).[14] Sanderson has also noted this, writing that the role of temple "singers of sacred hymns" (*tiruppatiyampāṭuvār*) is attested from as early as the ninth century CE.[15] A contemporary example of this is my experience while attending a Shivaratri observance at Sabhapaty Swami Koil in Konnur, during which Narayanaswamy Raju sang compositions by Māṇikkavācakar in the inner sanctum during ritual puja. As Raju indicated in an interview, part of the justification of the presence of devotional songs during ritual puja is that it was believed to constitute the real "worship" (Tam. *ārccaṉai*, < Skt. *arcana*) of the deity in contrast to the recitation of mantras by the appointed ritual specialist (*pūjārī*).[16] It is possible that this reflects an implicit tension between the magical efficacy ascribed to sacrificial mantras in a Tantric context and the bhakti of devotion toward a given deity, as well as an attempt to reconcile both through music, although it would be necessary to conduct more interviews to adequately understand this phenomenon. In any event the environment of openness to music at more established temples nearby would have undoubtedly informed the environment at Sabhapati's meditation halls, and singing songs was clearly viewed as complementary to Sabhapati's emphasis on the practice of Śivarājayoga (see Chapter 4).

Incantation of Tones and Mantras

Sabhapati, in addition to lyrical songs and poetic compositions, also included instructions on the incantation of the musical *svara*s and Mantric seed-syllables (Skt. *bījamantra*) to aid in the attainment of Śivarājayoga. While Sabhapati's instructions on these incantations are distinct from lyrical compositions, his overarching musical theory informs and includes both branches, as I subsequently indicate. Sabhapati unfortunately does not provide a source for his musical theory as it relates to yoga, and a result its origins are somewhat unclear. They may have been ultimately informed by the *Saṃgītaratnākara* (a ca. thirteenth-century Sanskrit text on music that includes similar cosmological descriptions and references to yoga),[17] mediated by another Sanskrit or Tamil text on music, derived from his own experience of Siddha or Sufi devotional singing and oral instructions obtained during his travels, gathered from another as-yet-undiscovered source on music or mantra, or any combination of the above.

CPSPS provides the most readily accessible example of Sabhapati's instructions on mantric incantation, which is as follows:

> Now when you begin to sing in different ways in a sweet and charming tone, so as your mind to be absorbed in the solemn happiness and pleasure

> and in a great delight and blissfulness in the sweetness and the charm of singing, as you go on uttering in different styles and changes with the different musical sounds of your tone, having your absorbing muse presiding over Lyric songs, especially on the praise of God, let your mind be absorbed in the Zenith and Top of the charming sweetness of singing as they are simultaneously modulated so as to please the ears, and as the sound of Ah or *ākārasvaram*, E *ikārasvaram* of Oo or *ukārasvaram* of A or *ekārasvaram* of O or *okārasvaram* of Um and Num or *amkāra namkārasvaram* of O'm and Rum or *oṅkāra*, *ramkārasvaram* and of Na, Ma, C, Vau, Ya, Sau, Ree, Gau, Ma, Pa, Dha, Nee, Sau *na, ma, ci, va, ya, ca, ri, ka, ma, pa, ta, ni, ca, svaraṅkaḷ*, get absorption in its own charm and sweetness as these sounds are of Spiritual sounds.[18]

There are several aspects of this text worth analyzing. First is the reference to the "absorbing muse presiding over Lyric songs." As I pointed out in Chapter 4, Sabhapati most often uses the English words "ecstasy" or "communion" to translate Skt. *samādhi*, not "absorption," probably the most common—if slightly misleading—translation of *samādhi* (lit. "composition," "composure") today. Instead, the English verb "absorb," the noun "absorption," and their derivatives, which together occur around 150 times in CPSPS, are almost always used to translate *laya* either on its own or as part of a compound. Based on this context as well as others, I would argue that *laya* not only has a technical soteriological meaning for Sabhapati as dissolution into Shiva, but can also imply a more general (but still cosmologically related) absorption into bliss, in this case the bliss of music, which is naturally quite common across the spectrum of human experience.

Sabhapati's use of the word "muse" (< Latin *musa*, Greek *mousa*, itself etymologically linked to the word "music") is also intentional and a technical word in his literature, being the sixth of the twelve cosmological "faculties" (*tattva*) or "Kingdoms" (*kamala*, *cakra*, to use Sabhapati's translation) that make up the Finite Spirit (*jīvātman*) (see Chapter 3 for this cosmology); its location is between the eyebrows.[19] This faculty is called the "place of the *bindu*" (Hi. *bindusthān*) or the "soul of the bindu" (Mpvl. *vintātmakam*, < Skt. **vindvātmaka*), which is also the "generative fluid" in Sabhapati's cosmology (see Chapter 4). Sabhapati states that in this faculty "spring up the powers of false imaginations, poetical conceptions and inventions of themes of all kinds," and that the faculty has "the responsibility of regulating the emotional faculties of the mind . . . by removing the Curtains of its own Emotion or

Losing the presence of its own Self [Mpvl. *āvaraṇacakti*, < Skt. *āvaraṇaśakti*] or Hiding faculty, and Emotion of Doing creation [Mpvl. *vikṣēpacakti*, < Skt. *vikṣēpaśakti*] or Creating faculty."[20] Sabhapati's reference to "poetical conceptions" arising in this location confirms that the "muse" of Sabhapati's musical theory is inextricably linked, as with everything else, to his cosmological system of the tattvas and cakras (< Skt. *cakra*, "wheel"). This is further confirmed in a line of one his English poems entitled "Prayer to the Infinite Spirit," which reads as follows: "I am not muse, nor the notes of thy voice / That make thee in poetical themes rejoice." This line, which are words set in the voice of the Infinite Spirit, imply that this faculty of "muse" and the music that results therefrom are conceived by Sabhapati as part of the twelve faculties of the Finite Spirit or individual self (*jīvātman*) and not of the Infinite Spirit or Brahman. At the same time, the Infinite Spirit can pervade or witness these faculties, and the yogi who has become this Infinite Spirit—one of the stated results of success in Śivarājayoga—would also obtain power over this faculty of muse and musical expression in general.

In the quotation above we also find reference to the phonetic sounds that comprise lyrical music, which appears to be part of Sabhapati's way of encouraging the reader or aspiring yogi to think beyond the bliss that arises from singing musical lyrics and to meditate on the sounds from which these lyrics are molded, which in turn correspond to cosmogonic inherent natures (Mpvl. *svarūpam* or *cuvarūpam*, < Skt. *svarūpa*, see the section Svarūpa and Yoga). The vowels (Skt. *svara*) are the obvious place to start, but this also includes the labial and nasal humming associated with *am*, *nam*, *oṅ*, and *ram*. This then gives way to the bliss of the Śaiva five-syllabled mantra (Skt. *pañcākṣaramantra*), in Tamil rendering *na*, *ma*, *ci*, *va*, *ya* (< Skt. *namo śivāya*), which are all integrated in the *praṇava* or syllable *om* (see Table 5.1).[21] We return finally to the "gamut of the Vedas" (*vedasvara*), which are what Sabhapati calls "Spiritual sounds" (*piraṇavasvarasaptalaya saṅkītam*, < Skt. **praṇavasvarasaptalaya saṅgīta*, lit. "music of the sevenfold absorption in the sounds of the syllable *om*"). This sevenfold absorption in sound (Mpvl. *saptalayam*) are the seven *svaras* plus their octaval resolution (Mpvl. *ca*, *ri*, *ka*, *ma*, *pa*, *ta*, *ni*, *ca*, < Skt. *sa*, *ri*, *gā*, *ma*, *pa*, *dhā*, *ni*, *sa*; see the beginning of this section).

This practice is framed as a kind of yoga, or more specifically, *nāṉā-piraṇavanātasvarākkirutipirmmesvarātmakñāṉa svarūpākāratiyāṉa yōkam* (< Skt. *jñānapraṇavanādasvarākṛtibrahmeśvarātmajñānasvarūpākāra-dhyānayoga*), the "yoga of meditation on the shapes of the inherent natures, which is the gnosis of the self as the Lord who is Brahman, [as manifest in

Table 5.1 The correspondence of musical syllables with cosmological inherent forms as found in CPSPS, Second Book, 156–57 (Mpvl. followed by Skt. in parentheses)

Phonetic syllable (*kāra*)	Inherent nature (*svarūpa*) of the sounds (*nāda*) of the gnosis of the fragmented powers (*kalā*)[a] of the syllable Om
a (a)	*pirmasvarūpam* (*brahmasvarūpa*)
i (i)	*pirmaṣakttisvarūpam* (*brahmaśaktisvarūpa*)
u (u)	*ātmasvarūpam* (*ātmasvarūpa*)
e (e)	*maṉōjīvasvarūpam* (*manojīvasvarūpa*)
o (o)	*īsvarasvarūpam* (*īśvarasvarūpa*)
am, nam (am, nam)	*maunasvarūpam* (*maunasvarūpa*)
oṅ, ram (oṃ, ram)	*ṣāntisvarūpam* (*śāntisvarūpa*)
na (na)	*curuṣṭṭipiraṇavanātakalākñāṉasvarūpam* (*sṛṣṭipraṇavanādakalājñānasvarūpa*)
ma (ma)	*titīpiraṇavanātakalākñāṉasvarūpam* (*sthitipraṇavanādakalājñānasvarūpa*)
ci (śi)	*caṅhārapiraṇavanātakalākñāṉasvarūpam* (*saṃhārapraṇavanādakalājñānasvarūpa*)
va (vā)	*turoṟpava piraṇavanātakalākñāṉasvarūpam* (*tirobhavapraṇavanādakalājñānasvarūpa*)[b]
ya (ya)	*yaṉukkirahapiraṇavanātakalākñāṉasvarūpam* (*anugrahapraṇavanādakalājñānasvarūpa*)
sa (sa)	*tatpirmmakñāṉa svarūpam* (*tadbrahmajñānasvarūpa*)
ri (ri)	*ṣaktti kñāṉa svarūpam* (*śaktijñānasvarūpa*)
ka (gā)	*ātmakñāṉasvarūpam* (*ātmajñānasvarūpa*)
ma (ma)	*māyākñāṉasvarūpam* (*māyājñānasvarūpa*)
pa (pa)	*jakajaṭapantakñāṉasvarūpam* (*jagajaḍabandhajñānasvarūpa*)
ta (dhā)	*tayākāruṇṇiyakirupākñāṉasvarūpam* (*dayākārūṇyakṛpājñānasvarūpa*)
ni (ni)	*nirākārakñāṉa svarūpam* (*nirākārajñānasvarūpa*)
sa (sa)	*cattiyapirmmakñāṉasvarūpam* (*satyabrahmajñānasvarūpa*)

[a] The term *kalā* literally means "digit," "bit," or anything tiny, often in reference to sixteen lunar *kalās* that are related to the waxing and waning moon. However, in Tantric Śaiva contexts it often refers to a "fragmented power" of Shiva, and this seems to be the sense that Sabhapati often uses the term; see Lilian Silburn, *Le Vijñāna Bhairava* (Paris: Éditions E. de Boccard, 1961), 18–19.

[b] Given the context I have interpreted *turoṟpavam* as *tirobhāva* (Tam. *tiropāvam*), the fourth of the "five activities" (Skt. *pañcakṛtya*) of Shiva, the other four of which (Tam. *ciruṣṭi*, *stiti*, *samhāram*, and *aṉukkiraham*) are listed (with variant spellings).

the] twenty-two syllables of the many notes and sounds of the syllable Om."[22] "Twenty-two syllables" translates *ākṛti*, which has the general meaning of "form," "figure," "appearance" but also can mean a poetic meter with twenty-two syllables per line as well as the number twenty-two, the same total number of syllables that Sabhapati gives in this principal section on mantra and music. Success in this yoga of soundscapes leads to two visions, the "vision of the gnosis of the principles" (Mpvl. *tatvakñāṉaterisaṉam*, < Skt. *tattvajñānadarśana*) and the "vision of the inherent natures of the gnosis of the Lord's syllable Om" (Mpvl. *īsvarapiraṇavakñāṉa svarūpatericaṉam*, < Skt. *īśvarapraṇavajñāna svarūpadarśana*). The first vision links this practice to Sabhapati's instructions on the "gnosis of the principles" (Mpvl. *tatvañāṉam*, < Skt. *tattvajñāna*) found in the three editions of VRY and two books of CPSPS, and includes the knowledge of cosmological principles that anticipates the practice of Śivarājayoga.

A final point to consider are the gender roles to be assumed during the musical incantation of these syllables. The singer should perceive him- or herself (since Sabhapati also accepted female students) as feminine, namely as the "personal Godly Spirit or Soul as wife." The attitude is clarified as being like a "sincere wife" who "when embracing her husband begs and requests in a mournful style for Grace of love and deliverence [*sic*] from her desires of jewels &c. for release from her poverty for holding continual communion and for becoming one in mind." The assumption of a feminine role in bhakti traditions is not unique to Sabhapati, and also occurs in Gauḍīya Vaiṣṇava contexts as well as among the Bāul fakirs of Bengal.[23] While in this context it may reify a gendered social norm of a colonial-era South Asian wife requesting assistance from her husband, it also underscores a broader point that I have already discussed in the context of Sabhapati's cosmology: the Finite Spirit or *jīvātman* that contains the faculty of "Muse" along with its power of music is conceived as feminine, being part of the Universal Finite Spirit or Shakti (Śakti), while the Infinite Spirit is conceived as masculine. To some degree this accords with the theory of the goddess Vāc (the "Word," cognate with "vox," or voice), who was "conceived from the very beginnings as a creative power, the 'mother of the gods.'"[24] The Universal Spirit (*śivamaya*), by contrast, includes both these masculine and feminine components and could be said to be an androgynous Godhead like the *civam* of Tamil Śaiva works; see Chapter 3).

Sabhapati's texts contain many more instructions on mantras, but not all of them are to be intoned or sung with the bliss of "Muse" as outlined above or even spoken, but silently recited in the mind. For example, a section following the one summarized above contains vivid descriptions on how each of the twelve faculties or Tantric cakras or lotuses (Mpvl. *kamalam*, < Skt. *kamala*) is "created as puffing and swelling as bubbles."[25] Each of these lotuses has what Sabhapati calls "Divine words" (Mpvl. *pījamantiram*, < Skt. *bījamantra*, lit. "seed-mantras" or "seed-spells"). There are five such words (or, perhaps more properly, "seed-syllables") in the case of the "Kundali [Skt. *kuṇḍali*] of elements or Mooladharum [*mūlādhāra*]." Each of these words has what Sabhapati translates as "Spirit" (Mpvl. *tēvatamsam*, < Skt. *devatāṃśa*, lit. "part of a deity"), which dwells in what he again calls a "bubble" (an idiosyncratic translation of *kamala*, lit. "lotus"): the Spirit of Om creates ether in the center, and the spirits of *va*, *ca*, *śa*, and *sa* respectively create air, fire, water, and mud (i.e., earth). These words create five faculties (tattvas) that accordingly contain "sins, vices, impurities and unholiness" that "must be purified by silent and dumb meditation" (Mpvl. *maunajapatiyāṉam*, < Skt. *maunajapadhyāna*, lit. "meditation of silent [mantra]-recitation). The impurities arise on account of *māyā*, what Sabhapati translates as "delusion," which is analogized with "impure water." The "pure water," by contrast, is the divine word or seed-spell of each Spirit that, when daily recited by the yogi, can wash away the impurity and cause the tattva to eventually be reabsorbed into the Infinite Spirit. These considerations show that the power of speech has two aspects for Sabhapati: on the one hand, speech (including musical expression) is linked to a cosmogonic and creative process that leads to gnosis of the tattvas, while on the other hand silence is linked to reabsorption of these tattvas into the infinite, which eventually leads to the samādhi of Śivarājayoga. In other words, in Sabhapati's system the yogi has the capacity to wield the powers of both expression and nonexpression according to the specifics of a given practice, enabling him or her, like the epic *kavirāj*, or poet-king, to dispel the "delusions" of *māyā*.

Sabhapati's Visual Diagrams

In addition to the presence of aural artistic forms, Sabhapati's literature also included a wide variety of visual diagrams. These diagrams are, for the most part, not merely aesthetic or ornamental depictions, but have a pedagogical quality that connects them to Sabhapati's instructions on Śivarājayoga and related religious subjects. Artistic depictions of yoga and meditating yogis and Siddhas have a long and rich history in South Asia, as demonstrated in the art-historical record.[26] There are many different types of these depictions, however, and most of Sabhapati's diagrams would fall into the general categories of what Debra Diamond and other art-historical contributors to the Freer and Sackler Galleries have described as the "Cosmic Body" and the "Subtle Body," which depict the universe in the form of a deity or the subtle physiology of yoga.[27] Sabhapati also includes diagrams, especially in his work CTCSPV, that would fall in line with the genres of "Portraying the Guru," "Austerities," "Meditation," and the "Landscapes of Yoga." Prior to Sabhapati's time these paintings were produced on paper, often in watercolor, and by the eighteenth and nineteenth centuries they were also released on scrolls.[28] Sabhapati may have been the first to fully explore the potential of incorporating these diagrams into printed books using what appear to be woodblock prints, which in some cases were colorized after publishing. Another of Sabhapati's innovations was to number these diagrams and connect the number to descriptive material in his printed text, which does not appear to have been a feature of yogic diagrams prior to the late nineteenth century or even afterward; most verbal descriptors for yogic diagrams prior to this time were labeled with words on the painting itself, if words were present at all. Examples of numerical diagrams may have been shown to Sabhapati during his education in colonial Madras or by Theosophical admirers and followers in Lahore amd Bombay, who could have further encouraged him to depict his ideas with numeric references for the sake of clarity.

Sabhapati's impulse to visually catalog the yogic body may have also been inspired by advancements in anatomy in Madras, which were early relative to most of India; only Calcutta appears to have an earlier tradition. Madras Medical School was opened by one Dr. William Mortimer (1782–1842) in 1835, forty-five years prior to Sabhapati's first publication, and was open to Indian students by 1842. By 1850 it was granted a charter to become Madras Medical College, and women were first admitted in 1875.[29] Dr. Mortimer, who was the surgeon of the Presidency General Hospital of Madras and superintendent of the Madras Medical School, was known to use "pasteboard models" to depict anatomy in his lectures, and an early textbook was produced entitled *Mortimer's Manual of Anatomy*, first published in 1842.[30] While *Mortimer's Manual* does not contain pictures, it does contain detailed (for the time) descriptions of the body's anatomy, including the brain and its nerves, and was explicitly designed for "Indo-British" and "Native youths" entering the medical profession.[31] While much of this anatomy would have been unknown to Sabhapati, aspects of this knowledge would have undoubtedly "trickled out" of the academy and informed his and his followers' general understanding of the body. Some of Sabhapati's diagrams (see Figure 5.3 and Figure 5.5) also depict rudimentary anatomical details that are not found in earlier visual depictions of yoga, and he uses the English terms "brain" and "spinal cord" with some basic degree of understanding as to what they are, while also being somewhat antipathetic to "mechanistic" scientific materialism (unlike some of his followers or interpreters, e.g., Ambikacharan Bandyopadhyay in his prologue to BRY; see Chapter 6).

Another interesting point of comparison is with the development of medieval and early modern Western alchemical diagrams. As Barbara Obrist has demonstrated, the visualization of alchemical procedures was a "relatively late phenomenon" that emerged in full force in the early fifteenth century, when "illustrations no longer merely punctuated alchemical texts but were organized into whole series and into synthetic pictorial representations of the principles governing the discipline."[32] She further noted that visualization can have both verbal forms (e.g., lists and tables) and nonverbal forms (e.g., shapes and depictions of people and objects), which is a distinction also salient to Sabhapati's visual material. A gradual proliferation of pictorial forms can be independently perceived throughout the span of Sabhapati's corpus of literature itself, and with it a subordination of the written text to the presence of pictorial forms. What began as a single diagram in his first work (VRY1) that is only seldom alluded to expanded into as many as seventeen diagrams by his last work (MCVTS). Additionally, in his later texts the diagrams to a large extent become the foundation of the text itself, most of which is devoted to simply clarifying the diagrams rather than vice versa (i.e., the diagrams clarifying or adding visual descriptions to the text).

In the subsections that follow I analyze the phenomenon of visual diagrams in Sabhapati's works, first by giving an overview of their presence in Sabhapati's literature and second by examining the idea of *svarūpa* in his diagrams, which offers one lens for an interpretation of his visual aesthetics.

Changing Visual Representations

A discerning eye will note subtle changes and developments in Sabhapati's diagrams throughout his publications in English, Tamil, Hindi, Bengali, and Telugu between 1880 and 1913. In many ways the differences in these diagrams reflect, in a parallel way, the various streams of his literature as analyzed in Chapter 2, and they also help clarify the date ranges and linguistic contexts of various streams.

Sabhapati's first diagram, published in 1880 and also extant in color (see Figure 5.2 for a replica), would become the principal diagram of the Alpha stream, and was included in all subsequent reprintings and translations, albeit in subsequent printings the diagram only survives in black and white. Numbers given on the diagram connect to numeric references in the text of VRY1 itself, which were carried over to CPSPS, although no separate key or legend is provided in VRY1, as with CPSPS. The original diagram was first entitled "The Posture of Samathy or Trance through Vadantic Yogue practice

Figure 5.2 A hand-painted replica by Sai Sampath, a local Chennai artist, of the original diagram in VRY (1880), with minor corrections in Photoshop by the author to make a few details match more closely. Original artwork in the author's personal collection.

by The Madras Yogi Sabapathy Svamy [& How sth]oolsarir becomes the lingasarir. Mitra Vilas Piras, Lahore."[33] While the preposition "by" is ambiguous in this diagram, its later version (see Figure 5.3) makes it clear that the posture is not depicting an abstract yogi but actually Sabhapati Swami himself in his "Posture" of samādhi. Also, according to Orsini, Mitra Vilas Press was founded in Lahore in 1861 by one Pandit Mukund Ram (1831–1897), the son of a Kashmiri Brahmin priest from Srinagar, as mentioned in Chapter 1[34] Given that some of Sabhapati's cosmology derives from Tamil Vīraśaiva sources and the *Tirumantiram*, which itself had borrowed from earlier Kashmiri Śaiva milieus (see Chapters 3 and 4), it is fascinating to entertain the possibility that these embodied ideas, albeit in greatly modified form, reconnected full circle between Tamil Nadu and Kashmir—for one of the first times in over a millennium—via the medium of printed diagrams.

The archaic transliterations of "Samathy" for *samādhi* and "Vadantic" for "Vedantic" are also notable and underscore the relative lack of standardization for Sanskrit transliterations at that early date. By the third edition (VRY3, published in 1895) the caption was slightly changed, and "Samathy" corrected: "The pasture [*sic*] of Samâdhi or Trance through Vadantic Yoga-practice by The Madras yogï Sabapathy Sivamy & How sthoolsarir becomes the lingasarir." The stated depiction of the diagram remains constant, however, namely how the "sthoolsarir" (= Skt. *sthūlaśarīra*) becomes the "lingasarir" (= *liṅgaśarīra*), which connects back to the "gross" or material body becoming the "marked" or transmigrating subtle body through the process of Śivarājayoga (see Chapter 3). This caption was translated in the Bengali translation of VRY2 (BRY; see Chapter 3), with *liṅgaśarīra* being replaced by Bng. *sūkṣma śarīr* (< Skt. *sūkṣmaśarīra*). It is also notable how in this series of diagrams from the one in VRY1 onward one finds the body of Sabhapati inextricably connected with the Śivaliṅga, implicitly connecting this body to the *liṅgasvarūpa* of which the illusionary body is the seat (*gaurīpīṭha*, "seat of Gaurī") (see Chapter 3).

The First Book of CPSPS, partaking in the Alpha stream, included a new version of this same diagram of Sabhapati Swami, albeit greatly expanded and with a numeric key or legend added to the bottom (see Figure 5.3).[35] This new version is much more intricate in terms of the detail of the subtle channels or *nāḍī*s, and also contained rudimentary anatomical depictions of the lungs and the brain, among other organs, that may have been the result of the spread of ideas from Dr. Mortimer's anatomical textbook or reflect the general increase in anatomical understanding in Madras during

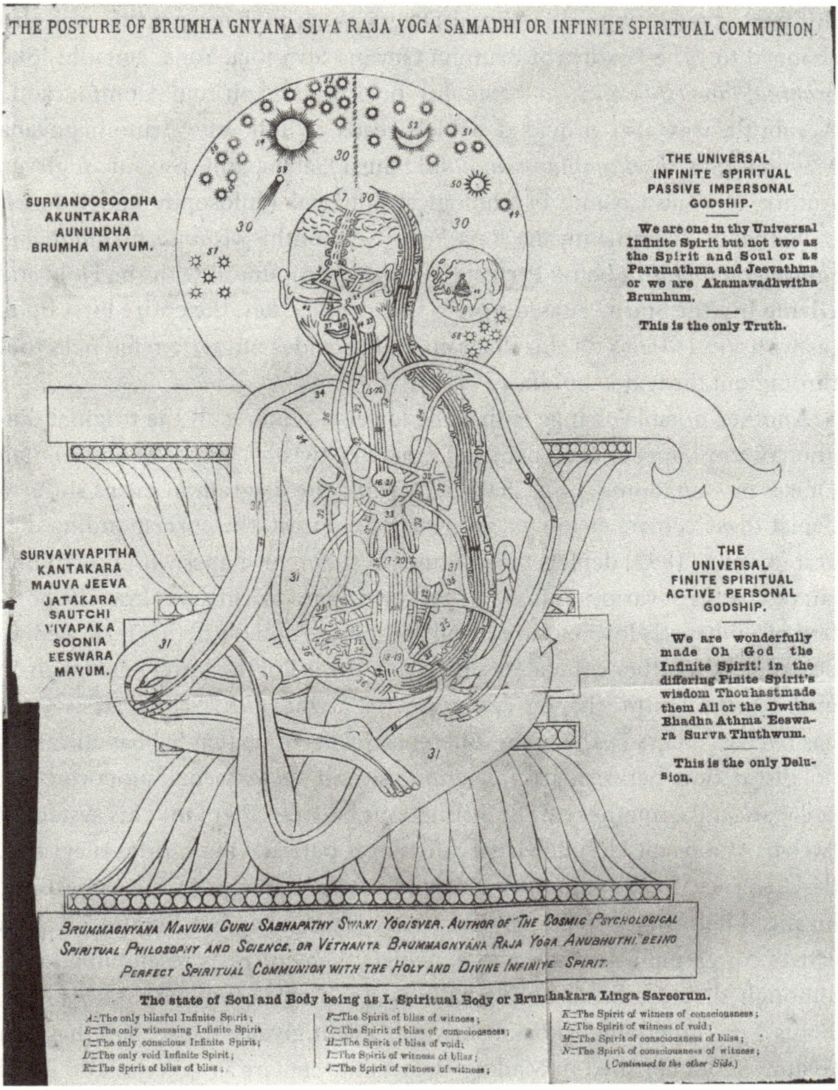

Figure 5.3 The new version of the VRY1 diagram on the posture of samādhi, published in CPSPS, First Book (1884). Notice the addition of a legend at the bottom as well as the inclusion of new anatomical details, such as the brain and lungs, which were absent in the original diagram. Scan courtesy Bill Breeze (now in public domain).

this period (see Sabhapati's Visual Diagrams). The diagram's title was also changed to "The Posture of Brumha Gnyana Siva Raja Yoga Samadhi [Skt. *brahmajñāna śivarājayoga samādhi*] or Infinite Spiritual Communion." A subtitle was also provided, which reads as follows: "Brummagnyana Mavuna [Skt. *brahmajñāna mauna*] Guru Sabhapathy Swami Yogisver. Author of "The Cosmic Psychological Spiritual Philosophy and Science, or Vethanta Brummagnyana Raja Yoga Anubhuthi [*vedānta brahmajñāna rājayoga anubhūti*], being Perfect Spiritual Communion with the Holy and Divine Infinite Spirit." In addition to the included key, the entire First Book (as with VRY1) relies on this diagram and provides numeric references to it throughout the text in boldface.

Another notable change is that the lower six lotuses in the original diagram of VRY1 appear to be depicted more like twisted "knots" (*granthi*) than lotuses or "kingdoms" (see Chapter 3), while the diagram in CPSPS shifts to depict these centers as more spherical. By contrast, the corresponding diagram in RYB (1892) depicts these lotuses as different shapes with protruding curved petals of various numbers that correspond to a given cakra. The position of Sabhapati's lower lotuses in all of these are notable in that they seem to best match, whether coincidentally or not, the list of the lower centers given in the *Netra Tantra*, chapter 7, verses 27–29, which like Sabhapati's system has twelve centers.[36] The main difference seems to be that Sabhapati makes no distinction between cakras, *granthi*s, and *adhāra*s or "supports", but collapses and combines earlier distinctions between them into his system of twelve. As a result, despite visual differences between his various diagrams, they do refer to the same principles in his cosmology. At the same time, localized tendencies could play a role: his earliest diagram (Figure 5.2 as an artist's copy), published in Lahore, depicts the centers as resembling knots although they are listed as "kamalums" (< Mpvl. *kamalam*, Skt. *kamala*, "lotus") or "kingdoms" (no Sanskrit equivalent given); the second diagram (Figure 5.3), published in Madras, depicts the centers as spheres, also listed as "kamalums" but in the context of more anatomical detail; and the third diagram (Figure 5.4), published in Bombay, depicts the lotuses (explicitly identified as cakras and not *kamala*s) with petals. His Tamil work MCVTS would combine many of the previous elements in its diagrams (see Figure 5.5), although never returning to his original diagram's style of depicting the centers as resembling knots.

The version of the diagram in CPSPS also contains instructions on how the diagram is to be colorized, which indicates that some diagrams that are not

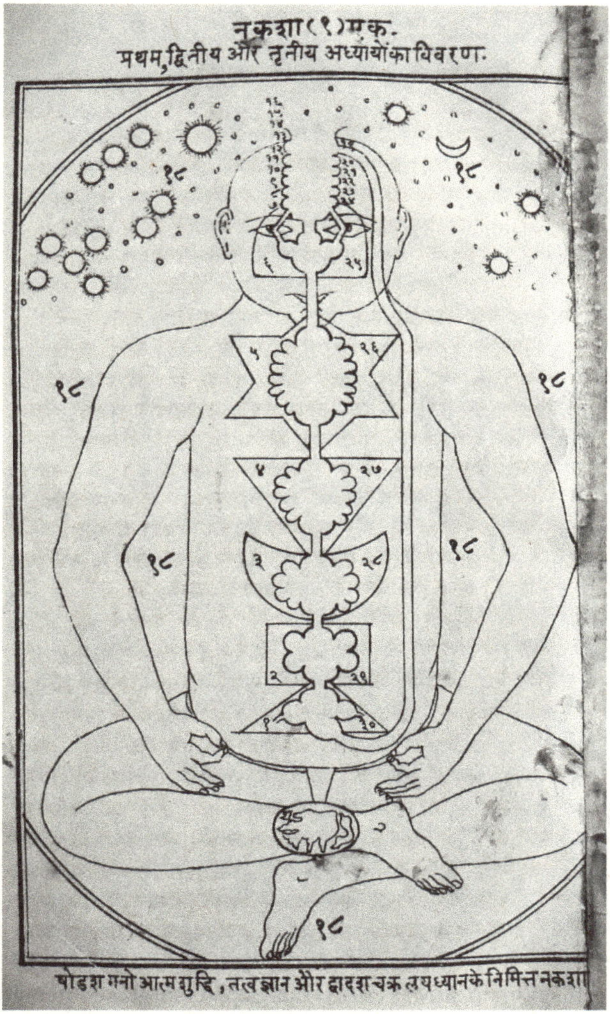

Figure 5.4 A diagram in RYB (1892) entitled "Diagram Number Five, for the Description of Chapters One, Two, and Three / A diagram for the sixteen self-purifications of the mind, the knowledge of the principles, and meditation on the dissolution of the cakras" (Hi. *nakśā* (1) *ek / pratham, dvitīya aur tṛtīya adhyāyoṅkā vivaraṇ / ṣoḍaśa mano ātmaśuddhi, tatvajñān aur dvādaś cakra layadhyānke nimitta nakśā*). Photo by the author.

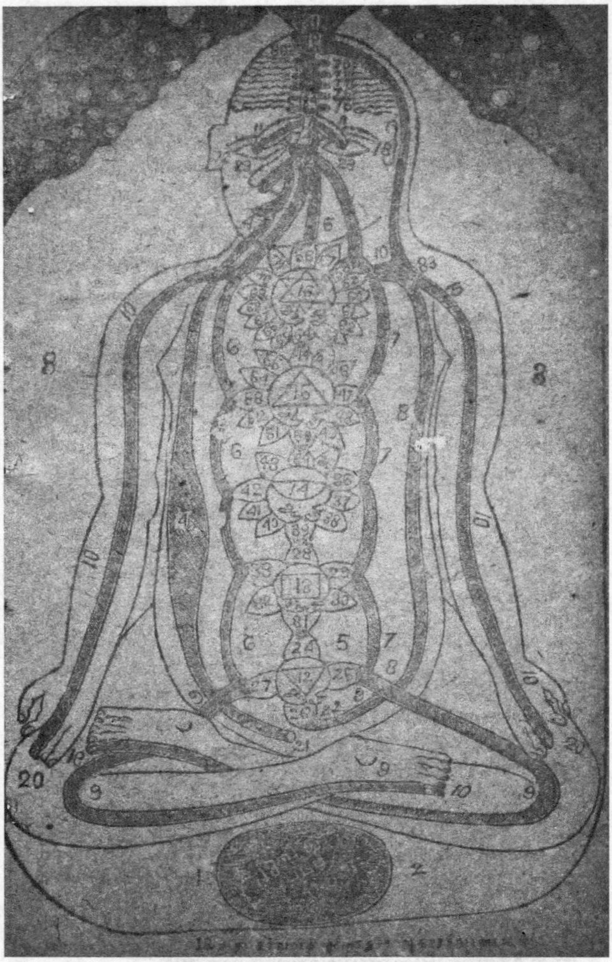

Figure 5.5 A diagram in MCVTS (1913) that depicts similar content to Figures 5.2 through 5.4. Here the lotuses are numbered in more detail and the brain is also anatomically depicted as simple wavy lines. I am grateful to Scott Wilde for restoring this image from a distorted laminated version. Photo by the author at the Adyar Library and Research Centre.

in color had the potential to colorized, if not by Sabhapati's publisher, by the owner of the book him- or herself. The legend refers in passing to the method being that of "glazing," which in the early 1920s was defined as "a method used in oil painting by which a brilliancy of finish is obtained by means of a coat of a bright but transparent colour applied over another colour having much less brilliancy but much more body."[37] While Sabhapati's other diagrams as extant in his publications are for the most part not colorized, there is some evidence for this kind of glazing subsequent to publication. One of the original copies of CTCSPV, held in the former library of Om Prakash Swamigal in Kandal, Ooty (see Chapter 1), does contain a colorized diagram of Sabhapati Swami, whereas the other copies do not. This indicates that copies obtained directly from the publisher were likely not immediately colorized, but that they were sometimes colorized either by Sabhapati Swami's students prior to distribution or by the new owner of the book.

Around the late 1880s to early 1890s, which saw the publication of CTCSPV (1889), the Second Book of CPSPS (1890), and RYB (1892), the number of diagrams in Sabhapati's literature starts to rapidly expand. CTCSPV contains at least nine diagrams (Tam. *paṭam*, pl. *paṭaṅkaḷ*, lit. "pictures") numbered as such, in addition to several unnumbered smaller drawings, and is notable for its inclusion of images that also depict the social lives of yogis, rituals to be performed at temples and temple architecture, and much more attention to what has been called the "landscapes of yoga" (see Figures 5.6, 5.7 and 5.8).[38] The diagrams of CTCSPV are elaborately illustrated, and most have a legend in Tamil that uniquely extends on all four sides describing what each part of the diagram was intended to depict.

The Second Book of CPSPS also contains ten new diagrams in addition to the portrait of Sabhapati Swami published in its First Book and the posture of samādhi that formed part of the Alpha stream, mentioned previously. RYB contains eight numbered diagrams (Hi. *nakśā*, < Persian *naghshe*) in addition to a different portrait of Sabhapati Swami, and some of its diagrams are connected in design to the diagrams found in the Second Book of CPSPS, albeit drawn differently. The diagrams from RYB, in addition to other diagrams not included in that book, were also rendered with Tamil and Telugu scripts, although with the same drawing as a base, and survive in separate packets, bound by a simple string, which are held at the library of Om Prakash Swamigal in Kandal, Ooty. This tends to offer material support to an advertisement found in some surviving copies of MCVTS that many of the diagrams were available for order as stand-alone documents from Sabhapati's published books. Since no copies of Sabhapati's Telugu work SVSAA (1890) appear to survive, there is no way of knowing whether these diagrams also formed part of this book, although that also appears likely.

Sabhapati's publications in the 1890s, mostly of pamphlets for the Konnur Meditation Hall, were much smaller works and are exceptional in that they

Figure 5.6 A depiction in CTCSPV (1889) of Sabhapati Swami, his ritual implements, three of his students (including, notably for the time, a female student in the center), and a scribe. Scan by the author.

do not contain any diagrams or additional visual material apart from text. After a relative absence of publications in the decade of the 1900s, the artistic content of Sabhapati's works only re-emerged after two decades, with the publication of MCVTS in 1913, the long version of which contains seventeen numbered diagrams (as before called Tam. *paṭam*, "picture," but mostly numbered diagrams), a couple of which appear to be missing or duplicated

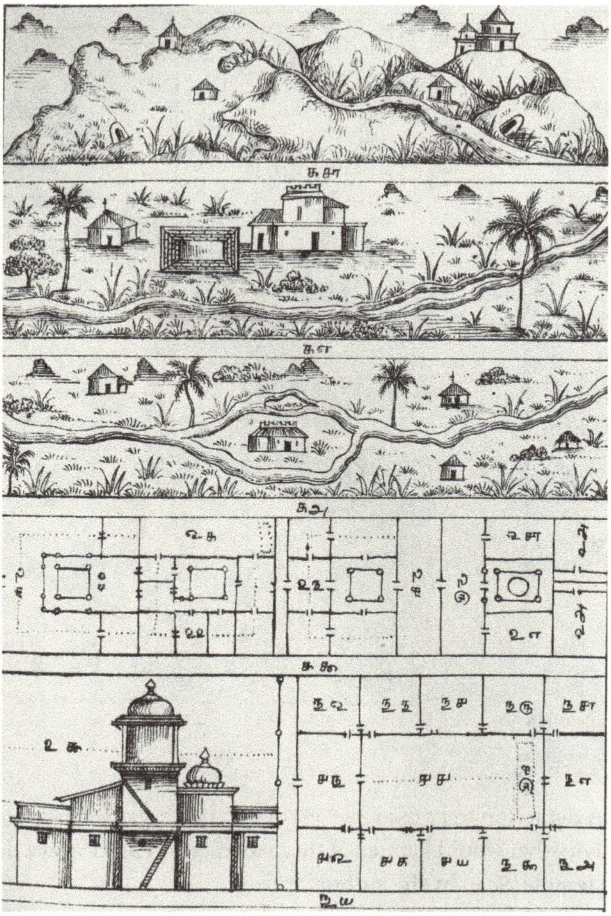

Figure 5.7 A depiction in CTCSPV (1889) of the landscapes of yoga, or different areas where *maṭālayams* or what Sabhapati called "meditation halls" were to be located, and details on their construction. Scan by the author.

in extant versions, as well as a new bearded portrait of Sabhapati and a few other small visual images. At seventeen diagrams, MCVTS is the most image-heavy of any of Sabhapati's works, and seems to reflect the culmination of what Obrist noted in the context of alchemy as a shift from the pictorial representation of text to textual representation of pictures. The diagrams are further presented in a new style that is unique to this Tamil work's own yogic instructions and contextual audience, and in some cases are much more playful and experimental in their shape and design.

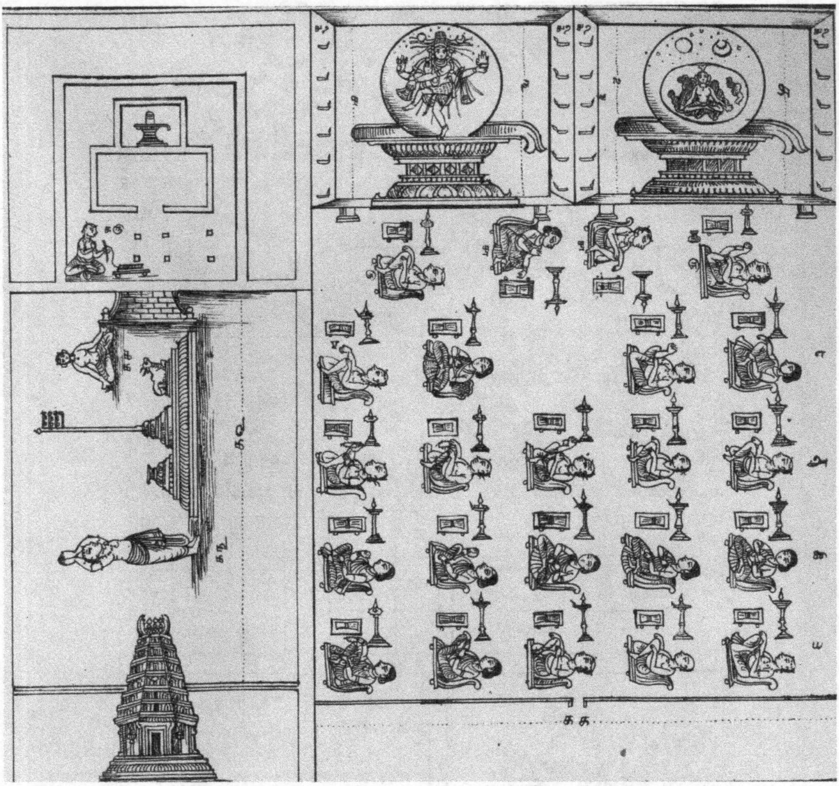

Figure 5.8 A depiction in CTCSPV (1889) of the training, meditative, and postural activity that would happen at these meditation halls, and a depiction of worship at a temple. Scan by the author.

Svarūpa and Yoga

In this final subsection I will give an example to show how Sabhapati's diagrams are employed in his literature, and will also note the salience of the term *svarūpa* for his visual aesthetics more generally. As noted in Chapter 4, Sri Sabhapati Swami's literature contains detailed yogic practices that are designed to subjugate gnosis (*jñāna*). While the central practice is the refutation of twelve lotuses or cakras, Sabhapati also introduces the notion of various "inherent natures" or "essential forms" (*svarūpas*), which he variously glossed in English as "spiritual visions," "spiritual states," or "spiritual phenomena."

The term *svarūpa* in the context of yoga philosophy can be traced back to the Pātañjalayogaśāstra (comprising the sutras and their *bhāṣyas*, "commentaries"), where it came to denote the primary condition of yoga as isolation or "aloofness" (*kaivalya*) following the cessation of the turnings of the mind (*yogaś cittavṛtti nirodhaḥ*).[39] For example, verse 1.3 reads (my translation): "Then the condition [*avasthānam*] of the beholder [*draṣṭṛ*] is in its inherent nature [*svarūpa*]" (*tadā draṣṭuḥ svarūpe 'vasthānam*).[40] The *bhāṣya* adds the term *kaivalya* in the locative, but curiously leaves *svarūpa* without a gloss,[41] and seems to indicate a condition in which the being or object is "isolated" (or, alternatively, "whole"), somewhat linked to the goal of Pātañjalayoga itself (*kaivalya*). The term *svarūpa* has accordingly been translated often as "essential nature" or "inherent form," and has been largely treated as a tangential clarifier rather than a technical term in and of itself. In Patañjali's day the term *svarūpa* probably was also informed by Sāṃkhya, although the term *rūpa* does not occur together with the reflexive prefix *sva* in Īśvarakṛṣṇa's *Sāṅkhyakārikā*.[42] The term *drāṣṭṛtvam*, "beholding-ness," is present, however, and applied abstractly in verse 19 of *Sāṃkhyakārikā* as an epithet of the Puruṣa, the aloof tattva (separate from the other twenty-four) who is also called *jñaḥ*, "the knower."[43] Since *drāṣṭṛ* is a synonym for the Puruṣa of Sāṃkhya and Pātañjalayoga philosophy, *drāṣṭṛtvam* would imply the condition of being the Beholder, or Puruṣa. By extension it would also refer to the state of being of "pure content-less consciousness," to quote Larson's translation of the *bhāṣya* or commentary to verse 1.3 of the Yoga Sūtra.[44]

While the Pātañjalan interpretation of *svarūpa* is probably lurking in the background, I do not believe it fully accounts for Sabhapati's frequent usage of the term, and its technical definition appears tangential at best when considering the literature of Sabhapati. For example, Sabhapati also applies this term to divine bodies or forms (e.g., *liṅgasvarūpa*, "the inherent nature of [Shiva's] *liṅga*"), as is commonly the case in Tantric, philosophical, and devotional Hindu literature (e.g., *brahmasvarūpa*, and less frequently *devīsvarūpa*, and the *svarūpa* of Krishna). His hagiographical account (the Ur-account, see Chapter 1) even quotes Mahādeva as saying the following: "Consider the Lingam [*liṅga*] to be nothing more than my Universal Infinite Spiritual circle or Brahmasaroopa [*brahmasvarūpa*] itself. He who thinks so receives Brahmagiyana [*brahmajñāna*]."[45] Throughout both VRY1 and CPSPS he also mentions a wide variety of *svarūpas*, including *śivaliṅgasvarūpa* ("the inherent nature of Shiva's phallus"), *śuddhacaitanyākāśasvarūpa* ("the inherent nature of the ether of pure consciousness"), *jñānasvarūpa* ("the inherent nature of gnosis"), *jñānākāśasvarūpa* ("the inherent nature of gnostic ether"), *brahmānandasvarūpa* ("the inherent nature of the bliss of Brahman"), *saccidānandasvarūpa* ("the inherent nature of being, consciousness, and bliss"), and many others. His "Four Brightnesses" of Brahman (see Chapter 3) also possess *svarūpas*, such as *sākṣisvarūpa*, "the inherent nature of the eyewitness."

Sabhapati's general usage for the most part seems to be an idealized "thing-in-itself," similar to the Kantian *Ding an sich*. Sabhapati's Bengali translator and interpreter Ambikacharan Bandyopadhyay certainly interpreted it in such a way, and related it to a cosmic substance that lies beyond the multiplicity of forms (translation my own from original Bangla):

> That which we call "things" or "categories" in this universe, therefore, are only the fabricated shapes [*racita ākār*] of qualities [*guṇ*] and powers [*śakti*]. The substance, however, which becomes constrained under the influence of the powers of the qualities of these forms [*rūpas*], becomes manifest in the transformation of forms, and we are not able to understand anything about what this inherent nature [*svarūp*, < Skt. *svarūpa*] of substance is. The actual nature of this substance has become completely covered due the influence of these powers of the qualities, and we only have the perception of its disfigured nature. However, they who are knowers of the principles (*tattvajñānīgaṇ*) have determined that, if there is a break [*birām*] in the continuity of the powers of the qualities, the left-over thing that remains is constant essence [*bastu*, = *vastu*].[46]

However, the term *svarūpa* also had an additional salience in Tantra that also informs its usage in Sabhapati's literature, not just as a Bengali phenomenon but also an idea that also has roots in Tantra more widely (including Buddhist Tantra). Upendranath Bhattacharya, in his well-known compendium of Bāul songs, noted the following (translation my own from the original Bengali/Bangla):

> To speak of "form" [*rūp*], one understands that there is an external shape. One calls this form, resorting to that which has its own individual existence within this form, the "inherent nature" [*svarūp*]. We find mention of this *rūp/svarūp* in many Bāul songs. At its core their practice [*sādhanā*] is a crossing over from form to inherent nature—having converted a material body into an immaterial one, there is a perception of the highest principle

[*param-tattva*] within the body. Having made the body the central principle, there is a mystery that is inherent in their practice of converting form into inherent form. It can generally be said that *this* is the Indian practice of Tantra [*tāntrik-sādhanā*]. This is the cornerstone [*bhitti-prastar*] of Hindu Tantric practice, Buddhist Tantric practice, Buddhist-Sahajiyā practice, Vaiṣṇava-Sahajiyā practice, Bāul practice, and the practices of the Nāth Siddhas.[47]

As we have seen, Sabhapati in his own literature describes a *sādhana* of refuting and canceling the Tantric cakras and the multiplicity of forms that they encompass, an action that was predicated on the idea that, as Upendranath Bhattacharya noted, one can cross over from illusionary form (*rūpa*), or the *nāmarūpa* of the Buddhists, to the inherent nature (*svarūpa*) of Shiva or Brahman.

Sabhapati describes this in his own terminology of the tattvas as follows, notably also using *rūpa* (in compound with *nāmarūpa*, making its connotation clear):

Tattwas or *maya tatva*, *nishchaya*, *nam arupa*, *sthula sarira Uttpatti sthapitum*,[48] by the intervention of *aggayanam* [< Skt. *ajñāna*, "ignorance"];—which established the separate existence of the finite spirit called *jivatmeegum* [Mpvl. *jīvātmīkam*, "individual self"]. Thus it hath fallen from its original truth into twelve sorts of spiritual reflections; by passing through twelve stages or *dwadasha tattwa utpatti* [< Skt. *dvādaśatattvotpatti*, "the emergence of the twelve tattvas"]. From these twelve came forth *shahasra thatwa Uttpatti* [< Skt. *sahasratattvotpatti*, "the emergence of the one thousand principles," i.e., the multiplicity of forms].[49]

I would argue therefore that Sabhapati's visual diagrams, predicated on the sense capacity of sight (*rūpa*), are similarly designed to lead the viewer to a realization of inherent forms that lie beyond name and form, which these diagrams are limited by but nevertheless attempt to transcend. Diamond explains this as follows:

If we understand the work of representation as the attempt to make something visible, the representation of yogic insight is a paradoxical challenge. Beyond the comprehension of ordinary individuals, ultimate reality can be perceived only by advanced adepts . . . artists rose to this challenge when they represented masters of yoga embodying the universe.[50]

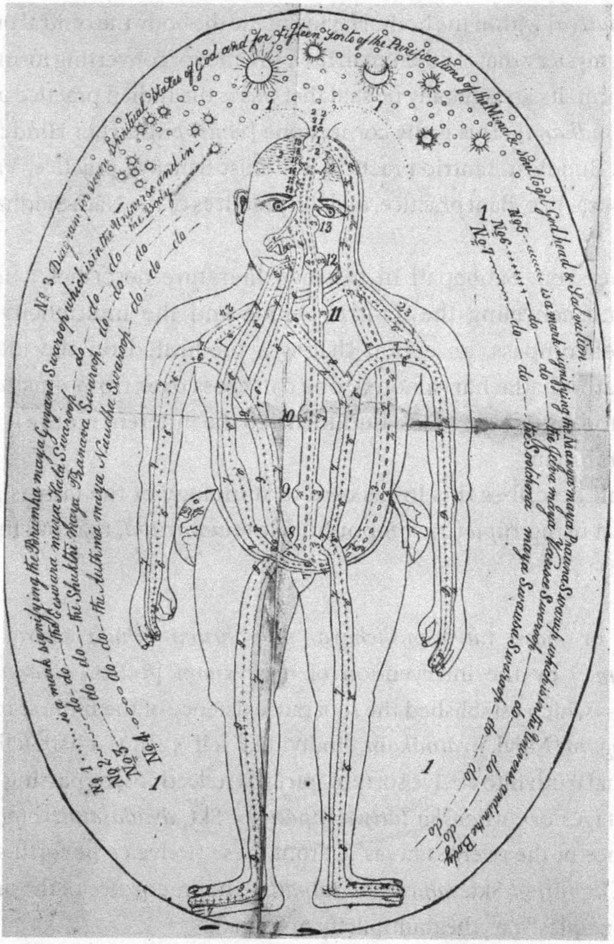

Figure 5.9 A diagram published in CPSPS, Second Book (1890), entitled "No. 3 Diagram for Seven Spiritual States of God [*svarūpa*s] and for fifteen sorts of the Purifications of the Mind & Soul to get Godhead and Salvation." Photo by the author at the Adyar Library and Research Centre.

While in Sabhapati's case most of the diagrams are not idealized representations of masters of yoga but pedagogical in scope, I would posit that the same paradigm applies to his work.

Apart from his more general usage of *svarūpa*, Sabhapati also developed a technical formulation of specific *svarūpa*s that were depicted diagrammatically (see Figure 5.9). These seven *svarūpa*s, which he calls the "seven spiritual states of God," are as follows:

1. *brahmamayajñānasvarūpa* in the universe and the "centre seat of the skull."
2. *īśvaramayakalāsvarūpa* in the "brain."
3. *śaktimayapraṇavasvarūpa*, which "runs downwards from the Kundali [*kuṇḍali*] up to the Brain."
4. *ātmamayanādasvarūpa*, which "runs upwards from the Kundali [*kuṇḍali*] up to the Brain."
5. *māyāmayaprāṇasvarūpa*, which "runs from the Brain to the centre seat of the Nose."
6. *jīvamayavāsisvarūpa*, "which runs from the centre seat of the Nose downwards up to the end of the middle fingers of the hands and toes of the legs."
7. *sūkṣmamayaśvāsasvarūpa*, which "runs from the end of the middle fingers of the hands and from the toes of the legs upwards to the centre seat of the nose."[51]

To these could be added an eighth *svarūpa*, the *sthūla* or physical *svarūpa* that represents the physical world, for which see Chapter 6. The yogi is instructed to formulate meditations in the mind through processes of *bhāvanā* (Mpvl. *pāvaṉā*), which Sabhapati translates as "Formation," more literally a kind of "cultivation," here used in a technical sense as the meditative assumption of a specific form to the exclusion of anything else. The meditations of these *svarūpas* are as follows (first Sabhapati's own translation, followed by Sanskrit and Hindi [corrected in some places from CPSPS], then Maṇipravāla, and then a more literal translation):

1. On being exclusively the "Infinite Spiritual Vision" (Skt. *brahma jñānadṛṣṭi mātra dhyāna*, Mpvl. *pirammakñāṉa tiruṣṭṭimāttira tiyāṉam*, lit. "meditation on the vision of the gnosis of Brahman only")
2. On being "Sights and Lights" (Skt. *nānadṛṣṭi prakāśākāra jñānadṛṣṭi dhyāna*, Mpvl. *nāṉātiruṣṭṭi pirakācākāra kñāṉatiruṣṭṭi tiyāṉam*, lit. "meditation on the vision of gnosis in the shape of the expression of many sights")
3. On being the "sound of letters only" (Skt. *akṣarākāra jñānadṛṣṭi dhyāna*, Mpvl. *aṭkṣarākārakñāṉatiruṣṭṭi tiyāṉam*, lit. "meditation on the sight of gnosis in the shape of phonemes")
4. On being the "sound of Words or Mantras of two or more letters" (Skt. *bījamantrākāra jñānadṛṣṭi dhyāna*, Mpvl. *pījamanttirākārakñāṉatiruṣṭṭi*

tiyāṉam, lit. "meditation on the sight of gnosis in the shape of seed-syllable mantras")

5. On being "Dhavatha Roopa [*devatā rūpa*] appearances and thoughts and powers" (Skt. *devatābhāvanākāra, saṃkalpastutimānasapūjākāras arvasiddhi bhāvanākāra, sarva tattva bhāvanākāra jñānadṛṣṭi dhyāna*, Mpvl. *tēvatā pāvaṉākāra caṅkalpastutimāṉasa pūjākāra carvacitti pāvaṉākāra carvatatva pāvaṉākārakñāṉatiruṣṭṭi tiyāṉam*, lit. "meditation on the sight of gnosis through cultivating shapes of deities, cultivating all the powers in mental worship through hymns and intentional thought, and cultivating all the principles")
6. On being the "absorption of the Mind in the Infinite Spirit" (Skt. and Hi. *brahmajñānadṛṣṭimeṅ manolayabodhānandākārabhāvanā jñānadṛṣṭidhyāna*, Mpvl. *pirammakñāṉa tiruṣṭṭiyil maṉōlayapōta āṉantākārapāvaṉākñāṉatiruṣṭṭi tiyāṉam*, lit. "meditation on the sight of gnosis through cultivating the form of bliss in the mental awakening of absorption in the sight of the gnosis of Brahman")
7. On being "the absorption of the Breath in the Infinite Spirit" (Skt. and Hi. *brahmajñānadṛṣṭimeṅ śvāsalayabodhānandākārabhāvanā jñānadṛṣṭidhyāna*, Mpvl. *pirammakñāṉatiruṣṭṭiyil cuvācalayapōta āṉantākārapāvaṉākñāṉatiruṣṭṭi tiyāṉam*, lit. "meditation on the sight of gnosis through cultivating the form of bliss as the breath's awakening of absorption in the sight of the gnosis of Brahman")[52]

These are then related to the "Fifteen Sorts of the Purifications of the Mind & Soul," which are also described in his Hindi work RYB. It is clear that the intended purpose of meditating on these *svarūpa*s, which run the gamut of phenomenological existence, is precisely to move the yogi beyond the *rūpa* or *nāmarūpa* of the tattvas so as to experience the nature of these tattvas as mere emanations of the *liṅgasvarūpa* or *brahmasvarūpa* (used synonymously), the source of which is beyond ordinary comprehension. As I demonstrate in Chapter 6, these *svarūpa*s were also engaged by Sabhapati in his Tamil work CTCSPV where they were correlated with English terminology pertaining to the Victorian naturalist worldview.

In concluding this section, I hope that I have clearly demonstrated that the use of diagrams to depict Śivarājayoga, either directly or tangentially, underscores the pedagogical and practical nature of Sabhapati's diagrams when considered more broadly. While on the one hand they certainly illuminate Sabhapati's literature and make it more aesthetically appealing, on the other hand they were clearly designed as guides of sorts to assist the yogi in cultivating various embodied forms until such cultivation was ultimately no longer necessary. In a contemporary world of saturated visual images reaching us from every angle and screen imaginable, the intended depth of such visual depictions and the obvious care in their preparation warrants further reflection and analysis.

Notes

1. Interview with Narayanaswamy Raju (Nārāyaṇacuvāmi Rāju) by Keith Cantú and Vinayagam at Sabhapathy Swamy Koil, audio and video recording, March 4, 2020.
2. One of this composition's full titles (in Tamil) is *śrīkailācaterisaṉakālattil capāpati yōkīsvaracuvāmikaḷ aruḷiya yōkaparipāṣācivāparaṇālaṅkāra kayilācavāca civastutimālā*, "Garland of Praise for Śiva who Resides on Kailāsa."
3. For a published collection of the songs of the Siddhas, see Aru. Rāmanātaṉ, ed., *Cittar pāṭalkaḷ*, 18th ed. (1959; Chennai: Pirēmā Piracuram [Prema Pirasuram], 2017).
4. For the first dedicated English translation of Maṇikkavācakar's compositions, see G. U. Pope, *The Tiruvāçagam, or "Sacred Utterances" of the Tamil Poet, Saint, and Sage Māṇikka-Vāçagar* (Oxford: Clarendon Press, 1900). For his hagiography (in Tamil) see Ci. Marutapiḷḷai Āciriyar, ed., *Tiruvātavūraṭikaḷ Purāṇam* (Cuḻipuram: Pajaṉaiccapai, Vaḻakkamparai, 1982). For a selection of scholarly treatments on his life and works see Kamil Zvelebil, *Lexicon of Tamil Literature* (Leiden: Brill, 1995); David Shulman, *Tamil Temple Myths: Sacrifice and Divine Marriage in the South Indian Śaiva Tradition* (Princeton, NJ: Princeton University Press, 1980); Vedachalam Pillai and R. S. Nagapattinam, *Māṇikkavācakar Vāḻārum Kālamum: St. Manickavachakar His Life and Times* (Madras: South India Saiva Siddhanta Works Publishing Society, 1957); C. V. Narayana Ayyar, *Origin and Early History of Śaivism in South India* (Madras: University of Madras, 1974); Deborah Louise Waldock, "Text, Interpretation and Ritual Usage of Tamil Śaiva Poems" (PhD dissertation, McMaster University, 1995); and for his worship in contemporary bhakti contexts see C. J. Fuller, *The Camphor Flame: Popular Hinduism and Society in India*, rev. ed. (Princeton, NJ: Princeton University Press, 2018). I am grateful to the Oxford Bibliography on Māṇikkavācakar compiled by Leah Comeau (https://www.oxfordbibliographies.com/view/document/obo-9780195399318/obo-9780195399318-0159.xml) for helping to compile some of these sources; see the bibliography entry for many more publications that deal with this important figure in Tamil Śaivism.
5. For some useful performative and musicological considerations of Tamil poetry see Indira Viswanathan Peterson, *Poems to Śiva: The Hymns of the Tamil Saints* (Princeton, NJ: Princeton University Press, 2014), 59–67; 76–82.
6. Interview with Narayanaswamy Raju. The Tamil text and English translation of this composition is found in Pope, *The Tiruvāçagam*, 1–7.

7. Peterson, *Poems to Śiva*, 3.
8. Ibid., 59–62.
9. Ibid., 59.
10. CTCSPV, v.
11. CPSPS, 33–35.
12. CPSPS, 33.
13. CTCSPV.
14. This is attested by Narayanaswamy Raju in our interview.
15. Alexis Sanderson, "The Śaiva Literature," *Journal of Indological Studies* 24–25 (2012–2013, 2014): 89 n. 366.
16. Interview with Narayanaswamy Raju.
17. Makoto Kitada and Śārṅgadeva, *The Body of the Musician: An Annotated Translation and Study of the Piṇḍotpatti-Prakaraṇa of Śārṅgadeva's Saṅgītaratnakara* (Bern, Switzerland: Peter Lang, 2012). I am grateful to Mark Singleton for pointing out this possible connection to me during a personal meeting.
18. CPSPS, Second Book, 155–56.
19. CPSPS, First Book, 53–54.
20. CPSPS, First Book, 54.
21. For a useful translation of Tamil verses pertaining to these syllables, see Pope, *The Tiruvāçagam*, xxxix–xlii. For more analysis of the mantra in Tamil Śaiva-specific contexts see Mary Elizabeth Winch, "The Theology of Grace in Saiva Siddhanta, in the Light of Umapati Sivacharya's Tiruarutpayan" (PhD dissertation, McMaster University, 1975), 72–75.
22. CPSPS, Second Book, 157.
23. See Carol Salomon, *City of Mirrors: Songs of Lālan Sãi*, ed. Keith Cantú and Saymon Zakaria (New York: Oxford University Press, 2017), 86–92; Carola Erika Lorea, "Pregnant Males, Barren Mothers, and Religious Transvestism: Transcending Gender in the Songs and Practices of 'Heterodox' Bengali Lineages," *Asian Ethnology* 77, nos. 1–2 (2018): 169–213; Barbara A. Holdrege, *Bhakti and Embodiment: Fashioning Divine Bodies and Devotional Bodies in Kṛṣṇa Bhakti* (New York: Routledge, 2015).
24. André Padoux, *Vāc: The Concept of the Word in Selected Hindu Tantras* (Albany: State University of New York Press, 1990), x.
25. CPSPS, Second Book, 158.
26. See, for example, Debra Diamond, ed., *Yoga: The Art of Transformation* (Washington, DC: Arthur M. Sackler Gallery, Smithsonian Institution, 2013); Robert N. Linrothe, Debra Diamond, and Rubin Museum of Art, eds., *Holy Madness: Portraits of Tantric Siddhas* (New York: Chicago: Rubin Museum of Art, Serindia Publications, 2006).
27. Diamond, *Yoga*, 160–71.
28. Ibid., 166.
29. Tony George Jacob, "History of Teaching Anatomy in India: From Ancient to Modern Times," *Anatomical Sciences Education* 6, no. 5 (September 2013): 353–54.
30. Ibid, 354.
31. W. Mortimer, *A Manual of Anatomy with The Elements of Physiology and Pathology; Compiled for the Use of the Students of the Subordinate Branch of the Medical Service*

Attending the Medical School (Madras: E. Marsden at the Male Asylum Press, 1842), 139–56.

32. Barbara Obrist, "Visualization in Medieval Alchemy," *Hyle: International Journal for Philosophy of Chemistry* 9, no. 2 (2003): 131.
33. The missing text (added in brackets) can be filled in thanks to VRY3.
34. Francesca Orsini, *The History of the Book in South Asia* (New York: Routledge, 2016).
35. CPSPS, First Book, 24–25.
36. Pt. Vrajavallabh Dwivedi, ed., *Netratantram, with the Commentary Udyota of Kṣemarājācārya* (Delhi: Parimal Publications, 1985), 57; Gavin Flood, Bjarne Wernicke-Olesen, and Rajan Khatiwoda, eds., *The Lord of Immortality: An Introduction, Critical Edition, and Translation of the Netra Tantra, Vol. I, Chapters 1–8* (London: Routledge, forthcoming); see also Diamond, *Yoga*, 166–67.
37. Arthur Seymour Jennings, *Paint & Colour Mixing: A Practical Handbook* (London: E. & F.N. Spon, 1921), 138–42.
38. Diamond, *Yoga*, 180–202.
39. See Patañjali and Philipp André Maas, *Samādhipāda: Das erste Kapitel des Pātañjalayogaśāstra zum ersten Mal kritisch ediert* (Aachen: Shaker, 2006), 4–7, for a critical edition of the Sanskrit text and commentary of the first *pada* only; and David Gordon White, *The Yoga Sutra of Patanjali: A Biography* (Princeton, NJ: Princeton University Press, 2014), 10–15, for the various ways this verse has been interpreted and translated by scholars. See also Gerald Larson, *Classical Yoga Philosophy and the Legacy of Samkhya* (Delhi: Motilal Banarsidass, 2018).
40. Patañjali and Maas, *Samādhipāda*, 7–8. I am indebted to Seth Powell for pointing out the direct relevance of this early reference to *svarūpa* in Pātañjalayoga.
41. *svarūpapratiṣṭhā tadānīṃ cicchaktir, yathā kaivalye. vyutthānacitte tu sati tathāpi bhavantī na tathā*. Loose translation: "At that time, just as mental power [*citśakti*] in isolation is established in its inherent nature [*svarūpa*], so, however, when the mind has emerged [from samādhi] it is not present."
42. The term *rūpa* ("form") alone, however, does occur numerous times, perhaps most notably in verse 63, which treats of *prakṛti*'s seven forms (*buddhi* or *mahat* "intelligence," *ahaṅkāra* "ego," and the five *tanmātras*, "subtle elements").
43. Gerald Larson, *Classical Samkhya: An Interpretation of Its History and Meaning* (Delhi: Motilal Banarsidass, 1969), 265.
44. Gerald James Larson and Ram Shankar Bhattacharya, "Yoga: India's Philosophy of Meditation," in *Encyclopedia of Indian Philosophies*, ed. Gerald James Larson and Ram Shankar Bhattacharya (Delhi: Motilal Banarsidass, 2011), 77.
45. VRY1, ii.
46. BRY, 6–7. Original Bengali: সুতরাং এই ব্রহ্মাণ্ড মধ্যে আমরা যাহা কিছু পদার্থ বলিয়া দেখিতেছি তাহা কেবল গুণ ও শক্তির রচিত আকার মাত্র। কিন্তু এইরূপ {৭} গুণ-শক্তির প্রভাবে যে দ্রব্য নিয়তই রূপ হইতে রূপান্তরে প্রতিভাত হইতেছে, সেই দ্রব্যের স্বরূপ কি তাহা আমরা কিছু বুঝিতে পারি না। গুণ-শক্তির প্রভাবে দ্রব্যের প্রকৃত ভাব সমাচ্ছাদিত রহিয়াছে, তাহার বিকৃত ভাবেই কেবল আমাদিগের উপলব্ধি হইতেছে। অতএব তত্ত্ব-জ্ঞানীগণ এইরূপ সিদ্ধান্ত করিয়াছেন যে গুণ-শক্তির নিঃশেষে বিরাম হইলে যাহা কিছু অবশিষ্ট থাকে তাহাই নিত্য বস্তু (*sutarāṃ ei brahmāṇḍa madhye āmrā yāhā kichu padārtha baliẏā dekhitechi tāhā kebal guṇ o śaktir racita ākār mātra. kintu eirūp guṇ-śaktir prabhābe ye drabya niẏata-i rūp haite rūpāntare pratibhāt haiteche, sei*

drabyer svarūp ki tāhā āmrā kichu bujhite pāri nā. guṇ-śaktir prabhābe drabyer prakṛta bhāb samācchādita rahiẏāche, tāhār bikṛta bhābei kebal āmādiger upalabdhi haiteche. ataeba tattva-jñānīgaṇ eirūp siddhānta kariẏāchen ye guṇ-śaktir niḥśeṣe birām haile yāhā kichu abaśiṣṭa thāke tāhāi nitya bastu).

47. Upendranāth Bhaṭṭācārya, *Bāṅglār bāul o bāul gān* (Calcutta: Orient Book Company, 1981), 357–58. Original Bengali: "*'rūp' balite bāhirer ekṭā ākār bujhāẏ, ār ei rūpke āśraẏ kariẏā ei rūper abhyantare uhār ye nijasva baiśiṣṭya bartamān, tāhāke 'svarūp' balā yāẏ. bahu bāulgāne āmrā ei rūp-svarūper ullekh dekhi. mūlataḥ tāhāder sādhanā haiteche rūp haite svarūpe uttīrṇa haoẏā—prakṛta dehake aprākṛte pariṇata kariẏā deher madhyei paramatattver upalabdhi karā.*"

48. Skt. *māyātattvaniścayanāmarūpasthūlaśarīrotpannasthāpita*, lit. "the establishment of the emergence of the principle of illusion's [*māyatattva*] resolve, name and form [*nāmarūpa*], and the material body [*sthūlaśarīra*]. The corresponding passage in CPSPS is "the Creations of *Twelve faculties*," Tam. *māyātatvaniscaya nāmarūpacarvacarīravutpannastāpitam*.

49. VRY1, 33.

50. Diamond, *Yoga*, 160.

51. CPSPS, First Book, 213–17.

52. CPSPS, Second Book, 216–17.

6

Dissecting the Nature of Śivarājayoga

> சொரூபவிர்த்தி ஏகமய அதிகாரத்தால் உண்டாக்கப்பட்டதாயும் அவ்விர்த்தியில் தனது உற்பத்தியைக் கொண்டதாயும் விளங்குவது. இந்த ஏழாவது ரூபசொரூபங் காணவும் ஸ்பரிசிக்கக் கூடியதுவுமானது அந்த ஆறுவகை அரூபசொரூபங்களும் அறிவுக்கண்ணாலன்றி மற்ற புறக்கண்ணால் காணவும், கையால் ஸ்பரிசிக்கவுங் கூடாதது.
>
> It is possible for one to touch and perceive this seventh inherent nature, endowed with form. However, it is not possible to touch with the hands or perceive those [other] six kinds of inherent natures, which are formless, with the outer eye, except for with the eye of knowledge.
>
> —CTCSPV, 27

> পাশ্চাত্য পণ্ডিতগণ এই ভাব ধারণা করিতে সমর্থ হন নাই, তাঁহারা ইচ্ছা-শক্তির প্রভাবে প্রমাতা ও প্রমেয় ভাবকে সহসা বর্জ্জন পূর্ব্বক অন্তরে অনুভব করিতে প্রবৃত্ত হইলে, প্রমাতা প্রমেয়ের ভাব বর্জ্জিত হইল বটে.
>
> The Western pandits have not been capable of concentrating on these conditions. If they were to suddenly give up their aforementioned [inquiry] and become engaged in internally experiencing, under the influence of willpower, the conditions of the prover and that which is proven, then certainly the prover and that which is proven would become devoid of conditions.
>
> —BRY, 28

The previous chapters have foregrounded the historical, philosophical, technical, and artistic aspects of Sabhapati Swami's system of Śivarājayoga, but little attention has been paid to how the system was believed to have functioned, or even the question of whether it was meant by its author to work at all. By "work" I mean whether there is any theoretical justification

Like a Tree Universally Spread. Keith Edward Cantú, Oxford University Press. © Oxford University Press 2023.
DOI: 10.1093/oso/9780197665473.003.0007

that a yogi (Skt. *yogī*, < stem *yogin*), by following out the instructions in these manuals, could even partially experience the many sensations and effects that are outlined throughout Sabhapati's literature of yoga. One does not need to be a mahatma to realize that closing the eyes, assuming certain postures, and breathing in a controlled way can bring calm and provoke certain physiological changes; otherwise Modern Postural Yoga would not be a billion-dollar global industry. However, what of Sabhapati's seemingly extravagant claim that the successful practice of Śivarājayoga will grant you "one eye to the universe . . . embracing the sun, moon, stars, the earth, and all their creations within the universal circle of your Linga Sorup [*liṅgasvarūpa*]," of which the illusionary body is the mere pedestal or literally "seat" (*gaurīpīṭha*, Tam. *āvuṭaiyār*)?[1] Soteriological claims and promises of special powers (*siddhi*s) or experiences (*anubhava*s) like this, however, are commonplace in Indian yogic literature, and Sabhapati's literature is no exception.[2] Yet their extravagance would lead many people even in Sabhapati's own day to doubt the validity of these promises, as did Henry Olcott when confronted with his claim that he flew to Mount Kailāsa (see Chapter 1). At the other end of the spectrum, the Indological scholar Max Müller was simply content to consider Sabhapati's flight as an unverifiable "miracle" and say little more.[3]

Adequately addressing the yogis' soteriological truth claims and doubts on a rational, often Lockean basis would itself necessitate a separate book-length treatment on the ontological basis of yoga, not to mention religion more broadly, and in any case would also necessitate careful forays into the uncomfortable and controversy-generating realms—from an academic standpoint, at least—of apologetics and ahistoricity. At the same time, it is impossible to ignore that Sabhapati Swami's literature emerged at a time in which theories of "Western pandits" (*pāścātya paṇḍitgaṇ*) had been sweeping through the colonial urban centers of India, not just Madras but also Calcutta and Bombay, and that Sabhapati and his own students understandably reacted to and engaged, to a lesser or greater extent, these theories, especially those that dealt with questions of sense perception and physics; it would have indeed been odd at that time for them *not* to react to these strange, new ideas in some way.

The scientific authors that Sabhapati and his interpreters engaged for the most part participate in what Asprem has usefully framed as the "Victorian naturalist" worldview.[4] Subsequent discursive responses to and critiques of these authors led to a wide range of implications for a variety of fields such as biology and evolutionary psychology, although much if not all of their work is of course in the ancient past as far as science goes and is disproven or superseded today. The point is that the Victorian naturalist worldview ought to be contextualized as a historical movement not only in Europe but also within India itself at a certain time, just as one can historically contextualize Vedānta or Vīraśaivism. While its origin was foreign and its outgrowth made possible by aggressive colonial-era knowledge structures that largely marginalized or minimized traditional Indian modes of knowledge, it nevertheless provoked a wide-ranging discourse on "scientism" (i.e., that "science" which is deprecated or would not be considered as such today) that authors or inheritors of these traditional modes of knowledge felt comfortable accessing and responding to in compelling and creative ways. At the same time, Sabhapati was also entering this discourse with his own presuppositions based on the history of Indian perspectives on the "positive sciences," in this case theoretical analysis based on observation, which is also important to consider.[5] I would argue that this engagement is important for academics to record and acknowledge, especially as yoga is concerned, and that examples in Sabhapati's literature are some of the oldest records available in extant publications on yoga as expressed by Indian yogis or their followers.[6]

In this chapter I therefore wish to suspend argument on the epistemological verifiability or falsifiability of Sabhapati's yogic system to focus on what I consider to be a much more interesting question from an academic perspective, namely how Sabhapati and his Bengali interpreter Ambikacharan Bandyopadhyay engaged the Western "science" of Victorian naturalism and framed theories on "ether" (*ākāśa*). This question warrants a thematic analysis of Sabhapati's literature and of the perspective of one of his main interpreters, and thus is historical in scope. To answer it I will dissect Sabhapati's views on cosmology and discourse on "pure ether" or *śuddhākāśa*, and also analyze Ambikacharan's engagement with the Victorian naturalist worldview. These questions of cosmology relate to what Sabhapati calls a "divine pilgrimage in the universe of your body,"[7] the latter of which also bears historical relevance to parallel and later occult interpretations of his work (see Chapter 7).[8] For Sabhapati Swami this pilgrimage was a central part of his theory of "pure ether"; it was to be embarked upon in order to find out how the "gnostic ether of Brahman as pure consciousness" (Skt. *śuddhacaitanyab rahmajñānākāśamaya*) descends to the "organ of throwing urine" at the base of the spine (*kuṇḍali*) through the central channel (*suṣumnā*) and ascends up to the fontanelle (*brahmarandhra*) through the spine (*khumbaka-nāḍī*), the descent and ascent of which maintains the "whole creation of your body" until the "time of death" (see Appendix 3).

As a humanities scholar, this discussion of "science" in the context of Sabhapati's Śivarājayoga is not intended to make any claim as to whether his system of yoga is "true" or "false" from a scientific or epistemological point of view. Instead, I wish to make his theories more accessible, on the one hand, to historians of either yoga or physical sciences who may be interested in analyzing how Victorian "scientific" material was interpreted in primary sources on yoga, and on the other hand to cognitive scientists and psychologists who may be interested in evaluating how a yogi in the nineteenth century framed questions of the limits of sense perception and human experience.

Spiritual and Physical Phenomena

As treated in Chapter 3, Sabhapati Swami and some of his early "Admirers" expressed a negative attitude toward what they called "the Atheism," and by extension so-called "western" scientific materialism, which is a discourse that doesn't emerge in his literature until 1884 with the publication of the First Book of CPSPS. However, the reason for this attitude should be contextualized. First, Sabhapati was not anti-Western, since, as noted in Chapter 2 (also see Chapter 7), he was profusely complimentary of Helena Petrovna Blavatsky and the Theosophical Society despite never joining, and he also engaged in conversation with Indian domiciled authors such as John Campbell Oman. Western-educated Indians like Shrish Chandra Basu also flocked to him, and his views (at least initially) turned them into enthusiastic "Admirers." Nor can he be said to have been entirely antiscience, since his main critique of science was inextricable from his criticism of "atheism," namely that the perspective only acknowledged the reality of physical phenomena. To some extent this was a valid critique on account of the Victorian period's obsession with mechanistic theories of the universe and rejection of subjective differences in perception; if sciences of the mind or brain (e.g., psychology, neuroscience) or sciences of what Sabhapati would have considered to be subtle energy (e.g., quantum physics) had been invented, his view might have been very different. It appears that Sabhapati nevertheless came to advocate what could fairly be called a "traditionalist" outlook on yoga compared to the relative openness of Vivekananda, in that the former believed that the views of the Indian yogis, specifically those of Agastya's Hermitage (see Chapter 1), were superior to anything that the atheism or scientific materialism of the modern world had to offer.[9]

Sabhapati's literature does, however, reflect some limited engagement with the scientific views of his day, most explicitly in his cosmology. As mentioned in Chapter 3, his main critique of "the Atheism," whether his own caricature or based on interactions he had with students, was predicated on their refusal to look beyond the "twelfth kingdom" of the elements or physical world as situated in the *mūlādhāra cakra* or lotus of the *kuṇḍali*. Sabhapati simply could not fathom an atheistic rejection of such a vast world that to him undeniably existed beyond the material elements, not only in the inner recesses of the mind but also in what ostensibly lies beyond mind or thought (*manas* and *citta*).

While his apologetic engagement with atheism was predicated on the perceived limitations of its materialism, Sabhapati did nevertheless allow for a terminological harmony between the English terms that Victorian scientists and philosophers were familiar with and the Hindu terms of his own Tamil- and Sanskrit-based cosmology. In his Tamil work CTCSPV, for example, he expressed a much more open perspective on the relativization of terminology and noted that "the companions of the world's other religion[s] (*aṉṉiyamatam*) are united in the language of those religions with the companions of the Hindu religion (*intumatam*)."[10] He then went on to outline the following points, worth quoting in full (English words as present in the original text are underlined):

> Oh! Listen, oh my students of the highest trifold divine image [*trimūrtti*]! The expansion of the cosmos [*pirapañcam*, < Skt. *prapañca*] is of seven types. First: Infinite Spiritual Phenomena, or the pure expansion in the shape of the knowledge of the happiness and bliss of unity that is absolutely interwoven [*carvāṉucūtam*, < Skt. *sarvānusyūta*]; this is Spirit or Space, and is "brilliance" [*caitaṉṉiyam*, < Skt. *caitanya*]. Within this is the emergence of (2nd) Spirit or Spiritual Phenomena, or the absolute intimate expansion of the pure Absolute in the shape of the fragmented powers of the bliss of wishful thinking. This is Presence and Atoms, which is "divine presence" [*caṉṉitāṉam*]. Within this is the emergence of (3rd) Finite Spiritual Phenomena, or the expansion of the absolute pervading pure Shakti [*cakti*] in the form of the syllable Om [*piraṇavākāram*, < Skt. *praṇavākāra*], which is the bliss of the imagination. This is Power, which is "power" [*catti*, < *śakti*].

> Within this is the emergence of (4th) Conscious Spiritual Phenomena, or the expansion of the absolute witness (*carvacākṣi*, < Skt. *sarvasākṣin*) as the soul [*āṉmā*, < Skt. *ātman*] in the shape of the cosmic sound [*nātam*, < Skt. *nāda*], which is the bliss of absolute awakening. This is Essence, which is "existence" [*cattu*, < Skt. *sat*].[11] Within this is the emergence of (5th) Mental Spiritual Phenomena, or the expansion of the absolute pervader [*carvaviyāpakam*, < Skt. *sarvavyāpaka*] of absolute ignorance [*aññāṉam*, < Skt. *ajñāna*], which is the individual [*jīvam*, < Skt. *jīvan*] consisting of the illusion [*māyā* = Skt.) of the shape of the syllable Om. This is Force and Motion, which is "strength and speed" [*valivum vicaiyum*, < Skt. *bala* and root *vij*]. Within this is the emergence of (6th) Sensual Spiritual Phenomena, or the subtle expansion [*cūṭcumappirapañcam*, < Skt. *sūkṣmaprapañca*] of the absolute void [*carvacūṉṉiyam*, < Skt. *sarvaśūnya*], which is in the shape of the subtle channel [Mpvl. *vāci*] of absolute misconceptualization of self [*apimāṉam*, < Skt. *abhimāna*]. This is Action and Creation, which is "motion and production" [*acaivum ceykaiyum*]. Within this is the emergence of (7th) Elemental Physical Phenomena or Material Phenomena, or the quintuple elemental expansion of the absolute appearance [*carvatōṟṟam*], which is the appearance in the shape of breath [*cuvāsam*, < Skt. *śvāsa*] of the absolute binding of the noose of desire [*ācāpācapantam*, < Skt. *āśāpāśabandha*], the attached fruits of action and virtue [*tontakuṇakarma*], birth [*jeṉmam*, < Skt. *janma*], and sorrow [*tukkam*, < Skt. *duḥkha*]. This is Visible Show, which is "appearance" [*tōṟṟam*]. Elemental Physical Phenomena is consequently like the expansion of the five elements in the sequence of creation [*ciruṣṭikiramam*, < Skt. *sṛṣṭikrama*]. It is the seventh as well as what are beyond it, since within its cause is the growth of the [other] six kinds of inherent natures [*corūpam*, < Skt. *svarūpa*] that are united as one and have been created by authority—in its growth it is expressed as its own emergence. It is possible for one to touch and perceive this seventh inherent nature, endowed with form [*rūpacorūpam*]. However, it is not possible to touch with the hands or perceive those [other] six kinds of inherent natures, which are formless [*arūpacorūpaṅkaḷ*], with the outer eye [*puṟakkaṇ*], except for with the eye of knowledge [*aṟivukkaṇ*]. Two types of nature [*iyaṟkai*] are Oxygen, which is a formless [*arūpa*] cosmic expansion of the five elements, and Nitrogen, which is a cosmic expansion of the five elements that has a uniting form [*cērkkairūpa*].[12]

While this sequence of philosophical gobbledygook may be obscure, some interesting information can nevertheless be gleaned from it. First, the seven types of "Phenomena" are consistent with Sabhapati's doctrines on the seven *svarūpa*s that I have treated in the context of visual diagrams in the previous chapter (Chapter 5). This further confirms that Sabhapati's theory of the seven *svarūpa*s, as reflected visually and published a year later in the Second Book of CPSPS, was fully intended to be a theory of cosmogonic emanation that would have complemented his system of the thirty-two tattvas (see Chapter 3). These *svarūpa*s culminated in the seventh *svarūpa* of the "Visible Show," his translation of Tam. *tōṟṟam*, literally "appearance," which Sabhapati held to be the world perceptible to the senses. While this seventh *svarūpa* is technically labeled *sūkṣmamayaśvāsasvarūpa*, or the "inherent nature of the breath that consists of the subtle," Sabhapati also had this *svarūpa* encompass the material world as "Puncha Bhuthathmakum" (*pañcabhūtātmaka*, "having the nature of the five elements").[13] In some places these are separated into eight distinct *svarūpa*s or sixteen faculties (= twelve lotuses + four superseding faculties), but retain the same general order and structure throughout CPSPS, CTCSPV, and even RYB (see Chapter 3).[14]

Notably, however, Sabhapati ascribes "Presence and Atoms" not to this seventh *svarūpa* but to the second highest *svarūpa* (see Table 6.1), which indicates that atoms, though held by the Victorian physicists of his day to be physical and mechanistic, were interpreted by Sabhapati as being subtle or idealized particles that were beyond the materiality of the five material elements. This bears some resonance with the Nyāya-Vaiśeṣika theory that atoms are "eternal, ultimate, indivisible, and infinitesimal," which may be the (unstated) philosophical ground for Sabhapati's perspective.[15] While Democritus had theorized the presence of atoms as early as the fifth century BCE, the theory of their presence as usually understood today was formulated by John Dalton (1766–1844), who died less than fifty years before Sabhapati's works were published and on a different continent entirely; Western theories on the "atom" were accordingly still on the cutting edge of Indian thought, even in cities. Sabhapati's idealized interpretation of the "atom" also accords with his cosmological placement of the *āṇavamala* or "filth of materiality" (Skt. *āṇava*, < *aṇu*, a kind of "particle" also usually translated "atom" today). As we have seen (Chapter 3), Sabhapati attributed the three *mala*s, including *āṇavamala*, to the seventh or *ājñā* cakra, far above the *kuṇḍali* that represents the material elements—this representation is made clear in Sabhapati's critique of atheism. While Sabhapati does not elaborate on this distinction, this all provides evidence that he made a distinction between the "materiality" of an "atom" (*aṇu*) and the "materiality" of the physical elements,

Table 6.1 Each of the "Phenomena" compared with the principles from the "Other Religion"

	"Phenomena" (CTCSPV and CPSPS)	"Other Religion" (CTCSPV)	Translation in Tamil	Associated *svarūpa* (CPSPS, Second Book)	Associated faculty of the yogic body (CPSPS, Second Book)
1	Infinite Spiritual Phenomena	Spirit or Space	*caitanniyam*	*brahmamaya-jñānasvarūpa*	*parātparātmaka*
2	Spirit or Spiritual Phenomena	Presence and Atoms	*caṉṉitāṉam*	*īśvaramayakalā-svarūpa*	*parātmaka*
3	Finite Spiritual Phenomena	Power	*catti*	*śaktimayapraṇa-vasvarūpa*	*kalātmaka*
4	Conscious Spiritual Phenomena	Essence	*cattu*	*ātmamayanāda-svarūpa*	*nādātmaka*
5	Mental Spiritual Phenomena	Force and Motion	*vali* and *vicai*	*māyāmayaprāṇa-svarūpa*	*trimalātmaka triguṇātmaka*
6	"	"	"	*jīvamayavāśi-svarūpa*	*caturantaḥkaraṇ-ātmakam*, etc.
7	Sensual Spiritual Phenomena	Action and Creation	*acai* and *ceykai*	*sūkṣmamaya-śvāsasvarūpa*	*daśendriyātmakāni*
8	Elemental Physical Phenomena or Material Phenomena	Visible Show (including Oxygen and Nitrogen)	*tōṟṟam*	[not separate from *sūkṣmamaya-śvāsasvarūpa*]	*pañcabhūtātmakāni*

Note: By "Other Religion" Sabhapati means materialistic philosophy as expressed in English, along with equivalents in Tamil and their associated *svarūpas* suitable for meditative cultivation (*bhāvanā*) and yogic faculties in CPSPS.

and that perhaps in his literature "materiality" is not even a good translation for *āṇava*, but rather something like "particularity," as in coalescing into "particles." In other words, the *aṇu* of the *āṇavamala*, like the "atom" of Democritus and later premodern philosophers, could be conceived as a more spiritual substance apart from the five elements on account of the fact that no one in medieval to early modern India (or Europe for that matter) could at that time have claimed to have physically seen or perceived one. As stated in the quotation above, an element of "physical phenomena" was physical precisely because it could be perceived by the senses and possessed form (*rūpa*), while the higher "phenomena," or *svarūpas*, were formless (*arūpa*). Since "atoms" in Sabhapati's time were only just beginning to be perceived by physical instruments such as the microscope, a fact possibly unknown to Sabhapati, they could still be relegated to the position of a spiritualized and formless substance that they had had in earlier systems of Indian philosophy prior to their interaction with the physical elements.[16]

At the same time, Sabhapati's explicit mention in English of oxygen and nitrogen (see also Figure 6.1) reflects the fact that earlier distinctions between "form" (*rūpa*) and "formless" (*arūpa*), as mapped onto the "physical" versus "subtle" dichotomy, were beginning to break down and be challenged by the discovery of substances that were not possible to see or feel, but which were beginning to be perceived by technological advancements in scientific instruments. Oxygen was independently discovered by both Joseph Priestly (1733–1804) and Carl Wilhelm Scheele (1742–1786) around 1774, and nitrogen was discovered by Daniel Rutherford (1749–1819) two years earlier, in

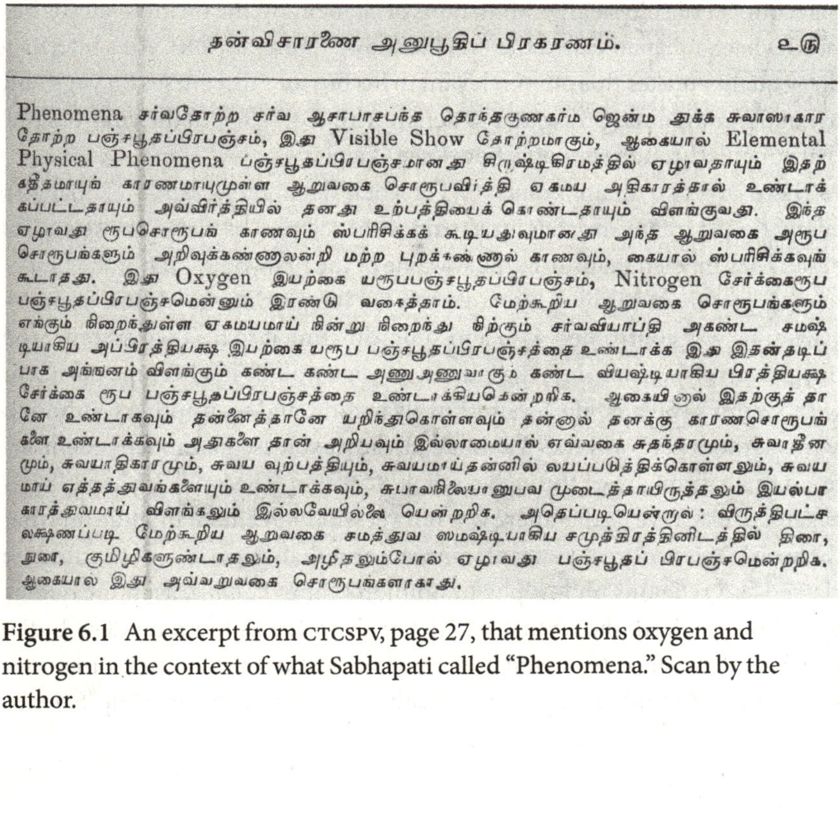

தன்விசாரணை அனுபூதிப் பிரகரணம். உரு

Phenomena சர்வதோற்ற சர்வ ஆசாபாசபந்த தொந்தகுணகர்ம ஜென்ம துக்க சுவாஸாகார தோற்ற பஞ்சபூதப்பிரபஞ்சம், இது Visible Show தோற்றமாகும், ஆகையால் Elemental Physical Phenomena பஞ்சபூதப்பிரபஞ்சமானது சிருஷ்டிகிரமத்தில் ஏழாவதாயும் இதற்கதீதமாயுங் காரணமாயுமுள்ள ஆறுவகை சொரூபவிர்த்தி ஏகமய அதிகாரத்தால் உண்டாக்கப்பட்டதாயும் அவ்விர்த்தியில் தனது உற்பத்தியைக் கொண்டதாயும் விளங்குவது. இந்த ஏழாவது ரூபசொரூபங் காணவும் ஸ்பரிசிக்கக் கூடியதுமானது அந்த ஆறுவகை அரூப சொரூபங்களும் அறிவுக்கண்ணாலன்றி மற்ற புறக்கண்ணால் காணவும், கையால் ஸ்பரிசிக்கவுங் கூடாதது. இது Oxygen இயற்கை யரூபபஞ்சபூதப்பிரபஞ்சம், Nitrogen சேர்க்கைரூப பஞ்சபூதப்பிரபஞ்சமென்னும் இரண்டு வகைத்தாம். மேற்கூறிய ஆறுவகை சொரூபங்களும் எங்கும் நிறைந்துள்ள ஏகமயமாய் நின்று நிறைந்து நிற்கும் சர்வவியாப்தி அகண்ட சமஷ்டியாகிய அப்பிரத்தியக்ஷ இயற்கை யரூப பஞ்சபூதப்பிரபஞ்சத்தை உண்டாக்க இது இதன்தடிப்பாக அங்ஙனம் விளங்கும் கண்ட கண்ட அணு அணுவாகும் கண்ட வியஷ்டியாகிய பிரத்தியக்ஷ சேர்க்கை ரூப பஞ்சபூதப்பிரபஞ்சத்தை உண்டாக்கியதென்றறிக. ஆகையினால் இதற்குத் தானே உண்டாகவும் தன்னைத்தானே யறிந்துகொள்ளவும் தன்னால் தனக்கு காரணசொரூபங்களை உண்டாக்கவும் அதுகளை தான் அறியவும் இல்லாமையால் எவ்வகை சுதந்தரமும், சுவாதீனமும், சுவயாதிகாரமும், சுவய வுற்பத்தியும், சுவயமாய்தன்னில் லயப்படுத்திக்கொள்ளலும், சுவயமாய் எத்தத்துவங்களையும் உண்டாக்கவும், சுபாவநிலையானுபவ முடைத்தாயிருத்தலும் இயல்பாகாரத்துவமாய் விளங்கலும் இல்லவேயில்லை யென்றறிக. அதெப்படியென்றால்: விருத்திபட்ச லக்ஷணப்படி மேற்கூறிய ஆறுவகை சமத்துவ ஸமஷ்டியாகிய சமுத்திரத்தினிடத்தில் திரை, நுரை, குமிழிகளுண்டாதலும், அழிதலும்போல் ஏழாவது பஞ்சபூதப் பிரபஞ்சமென்றறிக. ஆகையால் இது அவ்வறுவகை சொரூபங்களாகாது.

Figure 6.1 An excerpt from CTCSPV, page 27, that mentions oxygen and nitrogen in the context of what Sabhapati called "Phenomena." Scan by the author.

1772, so the presence of these chemical elements had already been pervading the discourse on "air" for about a hundred years prior to Sabhapati's literature. Indeed, Sabhapati wasn't the first author on yoga to engage the findings of chemistry in his writings, as the compound carbon dioxide (CO_2) also figured into the discourse of the Bengali physicist N. C., or Nobin Chander, Paul (Nabīn Candra Pāl), who had written about it in the context of *prāṇāyāma* three decades earlier.[17] However, Sabhapati may have been the first yogi to include consideration of these elements in a practical work, and this was almost certainly their first mention in an Indic vernacular work on yoga. The context of the quotation indicates that he felt compelled to address such exceptional cases; oxygen and nitrogen were formless (*arūpa*) but still had to be classified as physical phenomena since they did not evidently possess any spiritual qualities. It appears that "air" was somewhat of a special case even in the Nyāya-Vaiśeṣika discourse, which is likely salient to Sabhapati's perspective on oxygen; while atoms could not exist in an "uncombined state in creation," the structure of air was nevertheless believed to be "monatomic in structure, *i.e.* to consist of masses of atoms in a loose uncombined state." In other words, air—and in this context also oxygen and nitrogen—has qualities that connect the physical combinations of elements to the formless atoms beyond what Sabhapati called the "visible show" (Tam. *tōṟṟam*). Air's intermediary quality makes this point relevant to his broader discourses on yoga and use of the compound *prāṇākāśa* to denote a kind of "ether of the vital-breath" that courses through the yogi's body (see Chapter 4).

There are two main points to consider here. First, while Sabhapati's emanationist framework has little to do with "science" as viewed by scientists either now or even in his time, he was one of the first yogis—if not the first—to even gesture in his own literature toward integrating the Victorian materialism he was confronted with and subordinating it to his own system. The integration of "science" into discourses on yoga would later become the norm with Swami Vivekananda, Swami Kuvalyananda, and many others, although some authors such as N. C. Paul had already expressed an independent interest in analyzing yoga through a scientific frame.[18] Second, Sabhapati's engagement also reveals that there was not yet wide agreement in India on what the word "science" really meant, anyway, and that scientific ideas could be classed as a religious philosophy or opinion (Tam. *matam*), as in the quotation above. Indeed, the textual vehicle for the sciences in premodern India, which were mostly categorized under various *śāstra*s or *śruti*s, are sometimes synonymous in Sabhapati's literature with science itself; "Science" or "Science and Philosophy" are translations of *śāstra* (Mpvl. *sāstiram*), and "science" is also used to translate the first *śruti* (Mpvl. *sruti*) that Sabhapati was said to have published in Tamil.[19]

Additionally, strategies of subordination and of supersession are a staple feature of many South Asian cosmological systems (including, perhaps most notably, the way Śaiva cosmologers subordinated Sāṃkhya itself), and this shows that similar strategies were initially salient to a Tamil Śaiva encounter with Victorian physical science. I would posit that the benefit to more deeply analyzing Sabhapati's integration of these terms into his Tamil system, which were printed in English, is not only the excavation of a kind of obscure colonial-era philosophical syncretism at work. The integration of these terms also furthers our ability to interpret what precisely was meant by Sabhapati's sometimes difficult Tamil and Sanskrit complex concepts that were in wider circulation during his lifetime. The history of Western philosophical and scientific concepts (e.g., "atoms" and "oxygen" as expressed in English) has been treated much more comprehensively in scholarship than these Sanskrit and Tamil cosmological concepts to date. As a result, Sabhapati's allowance for these subordinate analogies makes it possible to map his more difficult Tamil and Sanskrit terms onto terms with more stable meanings, such as "oxygen," which has a much more limited connotative value than, say, *vāyu* or *prāṇa*. While these terms are not directly comparable or possible to equate, the general use of analogies accordingly helps clarify his own theoretical rationales (whether logical or not) for Śivarājayoga and its emanationist cosmology as it was expressed in Sanskrit and local, vernacular languages such as Tamil, Hindi, and Bengali.

The Pure Ethers

The remarks on cosmological levels in the previous section could naturally lead one to further question the nature of the higher six phenomena that Sabhapati postulates, and more specifically the theoretical substance (if any) that informed his belief in them. As noted in Chapter 4, Sabhapati often invoked the quintessential element *ākāśa*, "space," "sky," "spirit," which he himself (and possibly inspired by his editor Shrish Chandra Basu) often translated into English as "ether." This is the most obvious substance that informs his theory of levels of reality beyond the "Visible Show" (Tam. *tōṟṟam*), while at the same time his idea of *ākāśa* is multilayered and warrants further analysis. In this section I shall first note the possible logic for his translation and then distinguish between at least three different kinds of *ākāśa* in Sabhapati's literature, the analysis of which will show that two of these kinds are genealogically distinct from the deprecated scientific theory of ether.

Several scholars have noted that Theosophical authors and Swami Vivekananda would draw connections at the end of the nineteenth century between the idea of *ākāśa* and the now-deprecated luminiferous ether of Western scientists.[20] However, as noted throughout this book, Vivekananda's most famous works were first published over fifteen years after Sabhapati's lectures, and Sabhapati's own links with the Theosophical Society were historical but tenuous at best since he himself never joined and was initially rejected at least partially on account of an unbelievable flight (see chapter 1). An influence cannot be entirely ruled out, as there is evidence for earlier engagement with *ākāśa* as ether in Theosophical literature, however, and the most obvious connection is Sabhapati's editor Shrish Chandra Basu. At the same time, Shrish Chandra did not join the Theosophical Society until a year after meeting Sabhapati and publishing the first edition of his lectures. However, even in Theosophical contexts not all yogis or pandits agreed on the nature of this substance. For example, Sabhapati's contemporary Rama Prasad Kashyap (Rāma Prasāda Kaśyapa), an Indian Theosophist who was president of a Theosophical branch in Meerut, explicitly and strongly differentiated the "ether" (*ākāśa*) of Indian metaphysics and the "ether" of the Western scientists as early as 1890. He wrote, speaking of the *mahābhūta* or great element of *ākāśa*:

> The word *âkâśa* is generally translated into English by the word ether. Unfortunately, however, to modern English Science sound is not known to be the distinguishing quality of ether. Some few might also have the idea that the modern medium of light is the same as *âkâśa*. This, I believe, is a mistake. The luminiferous ether is the subtle *taijas tatwa* [*taijas tattva*, "the principle of fire," related to the sense capacity of sight], and not the *âkâśa*. All the five subtle *tatwas* might no doubt be called ethers, but to use it for the word *âkâśa*, without any distinguishing epithet, is misleading. We might call *âkâśa* the sonoriferous ether, the *vayu* the tangiferous ether, *apas* the gustiferous ether, and *prithivi* the odoriferous ether. . . . The luminiferous ether is supposed by Modern Science to be Matter in a most refined state. It is the vibrations of this element that are said to constitute light.[21]

Rama Prasad curiously does not reject the Western idea of ether as a salient idea, but only notes that *ākāśa* is specific to "sound" in Indian metaphysics, whereas the Western theory of ether is dependent on light, a quality of sight.[22] As a result, he argued that to use the idea "without any distinguishing epithet" is misleading.

Sabhapati's literature, however, appears to be somewhat removed from these discourses since he also had a distinct view of *ākāśa* that did not neatly map onto the ether of the Western scientists at the time, nor in his writings did he attempt to draw such a correlation. Even Sabhapati's brief treatment of Western cosmology in CTCSPV (see previous subsection) makes no mention of such a connection. He did posit "ether" as a translation for *ākāśa* in VRY1, but then again Shrish Chandra Basu also referenced Socrates, Plato, Plotinus, and Proclus in an appended section of Sabhapati's work in the second edition (VRY2),[23] and ostensibly was also familiar with Aristotle from his education in Lahore. As a result, there is no reason to believe that Sabhapati's translation of "ether" could not also have derived from the works of Greek philosophers whom Shrish Chandra knew of in translation, philosophers who also posited ether (Greek *aithēr*) as a quintessential element. At the very least the classical idea of the element "ether" should also be considered part of Sabhapati's or Shrish Chandra's logic of translating *ākāśa* as ether, with the modern scientific discourses also lurking in the background and likely providing additional encouragement for Sabhapati and Shrish Chandra to do so.

Regardless of whether "ether" as a translation was inspired by the science of the times, Greek philosophical literature in translation, or a combination of both, however, Sabhapati's use of *ākāśa* contains its own logic that warrants analysis on its own terms. Sabhapati's earliest lectures in 1880 mention "ether" five times and "æther" nine times, always in the explicit context of a translation of the term "akas" and plural "akashes" (i.e. *ākāśa*), and this would become a standard translation in all his subsequent reprints and editions of his literature in English. Despite a one-to-one translation of "æther" or "ether" for *ākāśa*, it is critical to keep in mind that not all Sabhapati's contextual usages of *ākāśa* imply the same meanings. In his earliest lectures, for example, at least three different contextual meanings of *ākāśa* can be distinguished:

1. The physical or gross element (*bhūta*) of *ākāśa* as operative in the physical body (*sthūlaśarīra*); this is ultimately linked to the idea of the element *ākāśa* in Sāṃkhya cosmology as mediated by Tamil Śaivism, and

which gives "care and arrogiam [*arogya*, immunity from disease] to [the] body."[24]

2. The subtle element (*tanmātra*) of *ākāśa*, related to the sense capacity of sound and the subtle body (*sūkṣmaśarīra*), also linked to Sāṃkhya cosmology as mediated by Tamil Śaivism.[25]
3. A spiritual principle called "pure ether" (*śuddhākāśa*) that courses in the subtle channels of the body of causation (*kāraṇaśarīra*), which he variously refers to alone and in compound as *prāṇākāśa* (lit. "ether of the vital breath"), *ātmaprāṇākāśa* (lit. "ether of the self's vital breath"), *jīvātmaprāṇākāśa* (lit. "ether of the individual self's vital-breath"), *jñānākāśa* ("ether as gnosis"), or simply *jñāna* ("gnosis").[26]

These distinctions are based on Sabhapati's own delineation in some of his works of a threefold hierarchy of *ākāśa*s that ranges from the most physical to the most subtle, and by extension from the most impure to the purest. For example, in VRY1 these three different *ākāśa*s are outlined as follows, this time from purest to most impure:

> mahakash [*mahākāśa*] of karana sareer [*kāraṇaśarīra*] (the essential, spiritual faculties); ghatakash [*ghaṭākāśa*] of sukshma sareer [*sūkṣmaśarīra*] or (the subtle mental faculties); and mathakasha [*maṭhākāśa*] of sthoolasareer [*sthūlaśarīra*] (or gross material corporeal faculties).[27]

As is evident, the first and purest *ākāśa* is the *mahākāśa* of *kāraṇaśarīra*, or "the great ether of the body of causation." The term *mahākāśa* appears in the Gauḍapāda's *kārikā* or "concise statement" on the *Māṇḍūkyopaniṣat* and its commentary attributed to Śaṅkara (Shankaracharya) (III. 3–5), where it refers to the *akāśa* that exists outside the "pot" (Skt. *ghaṭa*) of the human body.[28] Sabhapati's classification attributes this *ākāśa* to the *kāraṇaśarīra*, which in Vedānta was viewed as an "embryo or source" of the body that exists with Brahman.[29] The second and third editions of VRY (VRY1 and VRY2) also include the following passage alluding to this notion of the body as a "pot" as derived from an excerpted translation of the *Mahānirvāṇa Tantra*: "As the *akas* (ether) is outside and inside of every object, similarly this self-existing, all-witnessing spirit dwells inside and outside of all."[30] This inclusion of portions of the *Mahānirvāṇa Tantra*, however, was undoubtedly added later by Shrish Chandra Basu or another editor and could be seen as tangential or ancillary to the main uses above in Sabhapati's work, so will not be further considered here.

The second kind of *ākāśa* mentioned is the *ghāṭākāśa* of the *sūkṣmaśarīra*, or "the potted-ether of the subtle body." In the aforementioned commentary to the *Māṇḍūkyopaniṣat* this refers to the ether in the pot (Skt. *ghaṭākāśa*) of the human body; when the body is destroyed, it merges with the "great ether" (*mahākāśa*) outside. Sabhapati uses *sūkṣmaśarīra* synonymously with *liṅgaśarīra* (see the caption to Sabhapati's main diagram in BRY), the "mark(ed) body" that transmigrates upon the physical body's death, and which Sabhapati also says can be cultivated prior to death through the practice of Śivarājayoga (see Chapters 3 and 4). For Sabhapati this *ākāśa* would refer to the so-called *sūkṣmabhūtas*, or "classes of subtile matter," that are related to the sense capacities as *tanmātras*.[31]

The third kind of *ākāśa* is the *maṭhākāśa* of *sthūlaśarīra*, or "the domiciled (or hut-like home-like) ether of the material body."[32] References to this *ākāśa* in these terms are not as common as the above two, although it makes sense following the analogy of the pot (*ghaṭa*). While there can be an *ākāśa* both inside and outside the pot, the pot nevertheless must be made out of something or located physically within some sort of domestic sphere. For Sabhapati this *ākāśa* refers to its role in the combinations of the gross elements (*mahābhūtas*), in which it manifests sound.[33]

While the meanings of Sabhapati's *sthūla* and *sūkṣma* attributions of *ākāśa* are well documented in scholarship both on Sāṃkhya and on Vedānta, in Sabhapati's case the nature of the third or "pure *ākāśa*" is also salient to the "hydraulics" of haṭha yoga (Skt. *haṭhayoga*) and the vital breath (*prāṇa*), not as a physical air but as a spiritual principle (*prāṇākāśa*). This principle courses both inside and outside the body in a nonphysical, subtle form, somewhat akin to the *bindu* of the Tantric Buddhists (see Chapter 4).[34] These "pure ethers" preside over six subtle "streams" (Tam. *vāci*, synonymous with *nāḍī*), which preside over "three different functions of our body, spirit, and mind" and the "three qualities" (*sattva*, *rajas*, and *tamas*):

> The Shuddha Akases [*śuddhākāśa*] running through the three divisions of the Sukhmana [*sukhmanā* = *suṣumnā*], preside over three different functions of our body, spirit, and mind. The first presides over our sensations and has the name of *Adhomukh Idakala Vasi Kamyamala antarmukh mano Dhrishti*;[35] the third presides over five elements of nature and receives the name of *Adomukh Pingla Vasi Anavamal antarmukh buddhi Dhrishti*,[36] the second presides over notions and is called the Adhomukh *Sukhmana Vasi Maya mal anter mukh chitta dhrishti*.[37] . . . (a.) The fourth presides over

> *intellects* and is called *Urdhmukh Rechak Chandrakala Vasi Antermukh tamo guna dhrishti*,[38] (b.) the fifth presides over *consciousness* and is called *Urdh mukh Kumbhak agni kala vasi antermukh Satwa guna dhrishti*,[39] the sixth is termed *Urdh mukh Purak Surya, Kala vasi antar mukh Raja guna Dhrishti*[40] and presides over ideas. Therefore my *Shuddha Akash Sarup* [*śuddhākāśasvarūpa*] descends and ascends in two forms. First the direct downward *Triune Divine Presence* of always acting, as creating, preserving, and destroying, i.e., *Adhomukh trijiva Tri pranatmak Vritti akash of Shrishti, Shthiti and Sanghar*.[41] The second *Direct Triune Divine Presence* of always non-acting as blessing, embracing, and becoming or *Urdh mukh Trijiva Tripranatmaklaya akash of Trorpan, Anugrahum yaikyam*.[42]

The principal distinction to be made is that the physical element (*mahābhūta*) *ākāśa* is not conceived as a spiritual or subtle substance, while *ākāśa* as both the "subtle element" (*tanmātra*) and the "pure ethers" (*śuddhākāśas*), consolidated as an "inherent nature of pure ether" (*śuddhākāśasvarūpa*) in the quotation above, are undoubtedly subtle and beyond as causative principles (i.e., linked to *kāraṇaśarīra*). However, I have already demonstrated in my analysis of Sabhapati's cosmology (see Chapter 3) that the subtle element (*tanmātra*) and physical element (*bhūta*) of *ākāśa* are limited to the lower eleventh and twelfth cakras (< Skt. *cakra*, "wheel"), respectively, and there is no indication of them circulating around the body as the pure *ākāśa*s do, as evident from the quotation above. This distinction is likely behind Sabhapati's use of the clarifying adjective *śuddha*, "pure," for his third kind of *ākāśa*, which logically implies there must also be impure ethers (*aśuddhākāśas*).[43]

Sabhapati's third use of *ākāśa* probably derived from an as-yet-unknown source on Tantric metaphysics or was his own innovation based on a combination of sources, both oral and textual. As pointed out in Chapter 4, in contrast to some other Tantric systems, for Sabhapati—as well as for some medieval Buddhists—it is not *kuṇḍalinī* that rises as the cakras are canceled; his use of the word *kuṇḍali* "ring" only refers to the *mūlādhāra cakra* or associated bodily organs, which is where Sabhapati locates the physical elements or faculties (including "gross" or physical ether or *ākāśa*).[44] Instead, what rises is this *jñānākāśa*, *ātmaprāṇākāśa*, or simply *jñāna*—a kind of "gnostic ether" or "vital ether" that is linked to the breath but converted into something more subtle on account of the breath's entrance into the *nāḍīs* or subtle channels. Sabhapati does refer in CPSPS to the flow of *ākāśa* as rising like a "serpent" in such a way as to make his conception consistent with the idea of *kuṇḍalinī* conceived more generally, but the distinction is nevertheless striking when compared to the general conception of *kuṇḍalinī* itself rising, not as any kind of "pure ether" or *śuddhākāśa*.[45] In any event, Sabhapati's descriptions of *śuddhākāśa* take the definition of ether far outside of any comparable theories circulating in Western science during that time, and also are to be contrasted with the treatment of it by Swami Vivekananda and the Theosophical Society (although inspiration the other way around, i.e., of Sabhapati's literature on Vivekananda, Henry Olcott, and H. P. Blavatsky, cannot be entirely ruled out).

A Naturalistic Cosmology of Yoga

As noted in the previous section, Sabhapati's limited engagement with Western viewpoints was first published in 1889 (CTCSPV), with a few minor references in 1884 and to greater extent 1890 (CPSPS, First and Second Book). There was no substantial engagement with science or Western viewpoints in his first lectures, published in 1880 (VRY1), although he does translation *ākāśa* as "ether" and there was some limited comparative philosophical engagement with Vedānta-inspired themes in an appended section to the second and third editions of VRY, first published in 1883 (VRY2), and likely authored or at least heavily edited by Shrish Chandra Basu; this, however, does not extend in any significant way to science. The exception to this trend is the Bengali translation of Sabhapati's lectures (BRY), published in 1885 and also sponsored by Shrish Chandra (see Figure 6.2). Shrish Chandra did not translate this work himself, but assigned it to one Ambikacharan Bandyopadhyay, a Bengali Theosophical author with a demonstrated knowledge of poetry, about whom unfortunately very little is still known at the time of writing. In this edition Ambikacharan included a Bengali prologue (Bng. *abataraṇikā*) in which he strikes a discursive balance between what he called the "modern Western theoretical pandits" (Bng. *ādhunik pāścātya tattvabiśārad paṇḍitgaṇ*) on the one hand, and on the other hand the "noble rishis" (Bng. *aryaṛṣigaṇ*), synonymous with yogis and knowers of the principles (*tattvajñānins*), who had discovered the experiential secrets of what the Western pandits only had intellectual knowledge of.[46]

Ambikacharan's prologue to BRY opens by comparing fluctuations in religious duty (*dharma*) among human societies to waves of water, noting that the profound teachings on the *brahmajñāna* of rāja yoga (<Skt. *rājayoga*) have

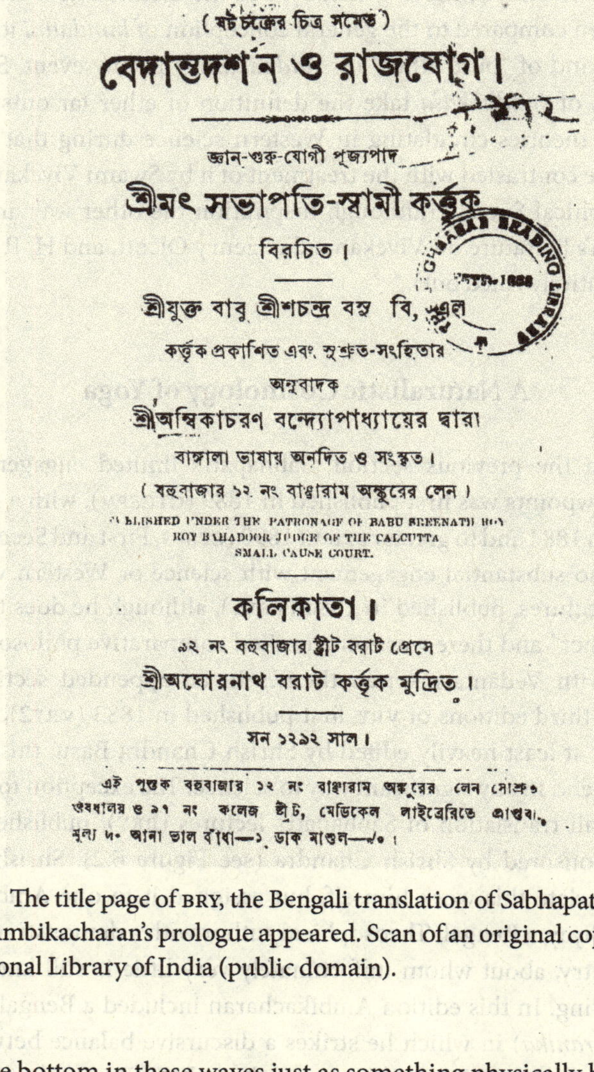

(ষট্‌চক্রের চিত্র সমেত)

বেদান্তদর্শন ও রাজযোগ।

জ্ঞান-গুরু-যোগী পূজ্যপাদ

শ্রীমৎ সভাপতি-স্বামী কর্ত্তৃক

বিরচিত।

শ্রীযুক্ত বাবু শ্রীশচন্দ্র বসু বি, এল

কর্ত্তৃক প্রকাশিত এবং সুশ্রুত-সংহিতার

অনুবাদক

শ্রীঅম্বিকাচরণ বন্দ্যোপাধ্যায়ের দ্বারা

বাঙ্গালা ভাষায় অনূদিত ও সংস্কৃত।

(বহুবাজার ১২ নং বাঞ্ছারাম অক্রুরের লেন)

PUBLISHED UNDER THE PATRONAGE OF BABU SREENATH ROY
ROY BAHADOOR JUDGE OF THE CALCUTTA
SMALL CAUSE COURT.

কলিকাতা।

৯২ নং বহুবাজার ষ্ট্রীট বরাট প্রেসে

শ্রীঅঘোরনাথ বরাট কর্ত্তৃক মুদ্রিত।

সন ১২৯২ সাল।

এই পুস্তক বহুবাজার ১২ নং বাঞ্ছারাম অক্রুরের লেন সোক্স
ঔষধালয় ও ৯৭ নং কলেজ ষ্ট্রীট, মেডিকেল লাইব্রেরিতে প্রাপ্তব্য।
মূল্য ৸৹ আনা ভাল বাঁধা—১ ডাক মাশুল—৵৹।

Figure 6.2 The title page of BRY, the Bengali translation of Sabhapati's lectures in which Ambikacharan's prologue appeared. Scan of an original copy consulted at the National Library of India (public domain).

sunk to the bottom in these waves just as something physically heavy would sink to the bottom while something light could float and survive. Notably, he recognizes that no book of its kind has circulated in vernacular languages to date and that studying it will "allow one to practice and understand what yoga is even without the instruction of a guru."[47] He also anticipates a skeptical response on the part of his educated Bengali audience, noting that rāja yoga has been clearly expressed in the book but that "many doubts may arise for communities of readers (*pāṭhak maṇḍalī*) on this topic of the highest religion of humanity."[48] He then goes on to analyze the etymology of *dharma* and explain the motivation of the noble rishis in cultivating the arts and prescribing methods of yoga for humanity.

Ambikacharan next describes four kinds of yoga in succession: (1) the "yoga of gnosis" (*jñānyog*, < Skt. *jñānayoga*), 92), the "yoga of meditation" (*dhyānyog*, < Skt. *dhyānayoga*), (3) the "yoga of devotion" (*bhaktiyog*, < Skt. *bhaktiyoga*), and (4) the "yoga of action" (*karmayog*, < Skt. *karmayoga*). While each has its own specific quality, Ambikacharan's entire prologue is really predicated on information that he supplies first in the section on *jñānyog* and continues to develop throughout his exposition. These four yogas are comparable to Swami Vivekananda's well-known tetrad of *jñānayoga*, *karmayoga*, *bhaktiyoga*, and *rājayoga* that he would formulate a decade later, although notably Vivekananda would employ *rājayoga* while Ambikacharan used *dhyānyog*. De Michelis in her survey argues that Vivekananda derived his system, which she points out later became a "core teaching of Modern Yoga," from Keshubchandra (also Keshub Chandra) Sen's fourfold classification of devotees: the "Yogi" (*yogī*), the "Bhakta" (*bhakta*), the "Jnani" (*jñānī*), and the "Sebak" (*sebak*, < Skt. *sevaka*).[49] While this influence is certainly likely, it still does not account for Vivekananda's adoption of *rājayoga* in place of simply *yoga* (or *dhyānayoga* for that matter, which as Bng. *dhyānyog* had more salience in Bengali vernacular milieus); the former may have been adopted from either Manilal Nabhubhai Dvivedi's translation of the *Aparokṣānubhūti* (see Chapter 4) or inspired from Ambikacharan's own interpretation of rāja yoga in BRY.[50] Further evidence that Vivekananda engaged Ambikacharan's translation is offered by the fact that he had stayed at Sabhapati's editor Shrish Chandra Basu's house prior to his American lecture tour,[51] and, given his interest in rāja yoga and work in Calcutta, Shrish Chandra or one of his Bengali followers would almost certainly have made him aware of this translation.[52] As we shall see in subsequent parts of this section A Naturalistic Cosmology of Yoga, Ambikacharan's prologue also brings Patañjali's emphasis on yoga as the stilling of the turnings of the mind to the forefront, whereas Patañjali is virtually absent from Sabhapati's early lectures, which could also be yet another thread that points to Vivekananda's willingness to treat rāja yoga largely as a Pātañjalan mental science of stilling the mind.[53]

In any event, Ambikacharan in his treatment of *jñānyog* draws a contrast between the outer world or the universe (*bāhya-jagat bā birāṭ-deha*] and the inner world or the human body (*antarjagat bā mānab-deha*]. It is here that he then outlines a cosmological theory that he will later compare with the

Western pandits, and one worth quoting in full for the sake of clarity on his position when engaging his later integration of their theories:

> It is acknowledged by all that all of creation exists by means of substance [*drabya*, < Skt. *dravya*], qualities [*guṇ*, < Skt. *guṇa*], and actions [*kriyā*], and the yogis who are the knowers of the principles have these kinds of teachings. Among them the principle of substance is permanent, that is, that substance is present when nonexistence is absent. Qualities stay absorbed in substance, and only when they come to be expressed does the power of action [*kriyā-śakti*] arise within them. Substance is singular, beyond the intelligence, situated indivisibly amid a continuous interval. The three kinds of qualities are *sattva*, *rajas*, and *tamas*. Power [*śakti*] moves by means of them. There are two kinds of power: "activity" [*prabṛtti*, < Skt. *pravṛtti*] and "cessation" [*nibṛtti*, < Skt. *nivṛtti*]. If, by the influence of the powers of the qualities, the flowing of the momentum of activity starts, these two types of the power of action [*kriyāśakti*] emerge. The powers of the qualities [*guṇ-śakti*], becoming constantly possessed of being while in the nature of substance and while being driven by means of internal qualities, have developed, thanks to these two powers of action, into many different shapes with the aim of accomplishing different powers. Creation, maintenance, and change in this whole universe consist of gross, subtle, and eternal shapes by means of all these powers. All actions are also performed. Atoms [*paramāṇu*], being ejected under the influence of a power's momentum, are all brought together on one side by the concealing power [*ābaraṇ śakti*, < Skt. *āvaraṇaśakti*], and then assume a form or shape. Atoms on the other side, after they all are separated by the power of casting forth [*bikṣepa śakti*, < Skt. *vikṣepaśakti*], develop into a multitude of forms. These [atoms], becoming newly united yet again, acquire their manifestation in the shape of other substances [*padārtha*]. That which we call "things" or "categories" in this universe, therefore, are only the fabricated shapes [*racita ākār*] of qualities [*guṇ*] and powers [*śakti*]. The substance, however, which becomes constrained under the influence of the powers of the qualities of these forms, becomes manifest in the transformation of forms, and we are not able to understand anything about what this inherent nature [*svarūp*, < Skt. *svarūpa*] of substance is. The actual nature of this substance has become completely covered due the influence of these powers of the qualities, and we only have the perception of its degenerated nature.[54]

The above assertions can be summarized in a point that Ambikacharan continually makes recourse to in his prologue, namely that essential substance cannot be perceived on account of the motion of qualities (*guṇ*) and powers (*śakti*). This is not only salient to the external world but also to the "I" (Bng. *āmi*, Skt. *aham*) of the human body, since "those qualities in the universe are all situated in the body" (Skt. *brahmāṇḍe ye guṇāḥ sarve śarīreṣu vyavasthitāḥ*), especially since the body's link with the external universe is nutrition (*anna*) as well as the physical substances of semen and menstrual blood (*śukra śoni*).[55] Ambikacharan claims that this notion is summarized by the modern knowers of the principles (*ādhunik tattva-jñānī gaṇ*) as "Internal is the typical of the external."[56]

The crux of the connection between the internal and external is perception, the understanding of which is the work of *jñānyog*. After noting how knowledge pervades the physical and subtle bodies during various states of waking (*jāgradabasthā*), dreaming (*svapnābasthā*), and deep, dreamless sleep (*gabhīr niḥsvapna-nidrākāl*, i.e., Skt. *suṣuptyavasthā*), Ambikacharan outlines a second postulate that he will return to in his engagement with the Western pandits:

> It can be said that the entirety of the intelligence, memory, thought, and the knowledge of the ego, are the instrument of the internal organ [*antaḥkaraṇ-yantra*). And the eyes, ears, nose, tongue, skin, and so on are called the instrument of the sense capacities of knowledge [*jñānendriẏa-yantra*]. When knowledge is situated in the instrument of the internal organ and remains to think concentratedly, then the instrument of the sense capacities of knowledge, despite being in the knowledge of external substance [i.e., cognizing the outside world], does not receive expression, or the nature of its expression becomes diminished. When it [knowledge] is attached concentratedly to the external world by means of the instrument of the sense capacities of knowledge, then the actions of the instrument of the internal organ are not expressed, or rather its power of action [*kriẏā-śakti*] becomes diminished. Knowledge, therefore, becomes contracted and expanded as it is kept controlled or bound amid the internal organ of knowledge and the external sense capacities of knowledge.[57]

Ambikacharan's treatment of the sense capacities, which in his case correspond to those outlined in Sāṃkhya, is predicated on the idea of a tripartite distinction between the actor, that which is to be enacted, and the object of the action, which is a theme that Sabhapati himself also returns to and one that was also salient to Tamil discourses on Śivayoga and Śivarājayoga (see Chapter 3). Ambikacharan declares that even the notion of the ego or "I" is only a feeling (*bhāb*, < Skt. *bhāva*), since it varies according to perceived distinctions between "self" and "other."

The next yoga that Ambikacharan treats is *dhyānyog*, or the "yoga of meditation," which continues this discourse on "knowledge" (*jñāna*) in the previous section on *jñānyog* but expands it to speak of its role as a "link" or "connection" (*saṃyog*, < Skt. *saṃyoga*) by means of which the sense capacities (*indriẏa*) can express their sense objects (*biṣaẏ*, < Skt. *viṣaya*). He then argues, however, that knowledge also has a power latent in and of itself that can only be accessed when it is not joined, that is, focused on, these sense capacities with their cosmic motion of qualities (*guṇ*) and powers (*śakti*). Ambikacharan then offers a critical discursive move by weaving his cosmological theory with Pātañjalayoga and linking it with Sabhapati's Śivarājayoga as expressed in his lectures, which is a step that Sabhapati himself did not take in his earliest work:

> The power of knowledge is "thought" [*cintā*]. The turnings of thought [*citta-bṛtti*, < Skt. *cittavṛtti*] is called thinking [*cintā*]. "Thinking" is a special state of knowledge [*jñāna*]. If "thinking," therefore, or the turnings of thought, can be completely removed, then knowledge also becomes deprived of its power. The knowers of the principles call the removal of this turning of thinking or turning of thought "yoga." "Yoga is said to be free from thinking, or the abandonment of all thinking."[58] [Also] within that book: "Yoga is the cessation of the turnings of thought."[59] . . . The royal yoga [*rājayog*] has the inherent nature of the art of becoming free from the influence of the qualities and powers, and the necessary yogic auxiliaries are especially described in this book. The ultimate fruit of this practice of yoga is composure [*samādhi*].[60]

Ambikacharan goes on to explain the nature of this samādhi as a knowledge that consists purely of a consciousness (*cetan*) in which the qualities (*guṇ*) and powers (*śakti*) are absent. Notably, he compares it also to the "nothing" or "void" (*śūnya*) of the Buddhists, in a clear nod to those in his educated Bengali audience who would have likely been aware of the Tantric Buddhist legacy in Bengal.[61] In closing his treatment of *dhyānyog* Ambikacharan quotes both the *Muṇḍaka Upaniṣad* 2.2.8 and Bhagavad Gita 6.22 in Sanskrit (in Bengali script), highlighting his remarkable ability to weave Sanskrit passages into his cosmological engagement.

Ambikacharan's next section, on *bhaktiyog*, is striking for its initial absence on the surface of what is usually thought in contemporary terms to be bhakti, or devotion. Instead, he simply continues the logical progression of his last two sections, reiterating his perspective that "the human body or human instrument is an imitation of the cosmic body [*birāṭ-deha*] or cosmic instrument [*birāṭ-yantra*]."[62] On the one hand, the cosmos could be said to "wake up" at the time of creation (*sṛṣṭi kāl*), just as a human being wakes during the relevant state (*jagradabasthā*, < Skt. *jagratavasthā*), an awakening in which knowledge expresses the body "with consciousness up to the tip of the fingernails."[63] On the other hand, when all the cosmic powers of nature are withdrawn, then the universe could be said to be in a state of sleep (*nidrābasthā* or *suṣuptikāl*), absorbed in its own nature just as when a person sleeps. It is here that Ambikacharan begins to explicitly integrate the theories of the Western pandits, noting that the "activity" of awakening and the "cessation" of sleeping is what the "modern scientists" (*ādhunik baijñānikerā*) call "contraction and expansion" (Ambikacharan uses the English words and also offers the Bengali equivalents *saṃkoc* and *prasāraṇ*).[64]

Ambikacharan then applies the same logic of microcosm and macrocosm to other scientific concepts such as "space" and "time," and by extension a philosophical idea of "will" or "volition." When the microcosmic body awakes and the knowledge of the ego is expressed to the consciousness, then memory arises and is internally expressed by the "Conception of Space" (given in English, correlated with *sthānrūp*) and the power of expansion is called and perceived as the "Conception of time" (also given in English, correlated with *kāl*). Ambikacharan leaves little to the imagination in terms of his sources, and even provides the following two quotations in note to these concepts, one by the German philosopher Immanuel Kant (1724–1804) and one by the British naturalist Herbert Spencer (1820–1903), the latter of whom he will continue to cite throughout the rest of the prologue:

> [Kant] says that Time and space are "a priori laws or conditions of the conscious mind." Mr. Spencer says, "Our conception of space (and time) are [*sic*] produced by some mode of the unknowable; complete unchangeableness of our conception of it, simply implies a complete uniformity in the effect, wrought by this mode of the unknowable upon us."[65]

Following the rise of memory, both desire and an orientation toward action arise, the motion of which is called "will" or "wish" (*icchā*). Ambikacharan also applies these concepts to macrocosmic terms, noting that when the universe awakes from its state of dissolution (*pralaya*), then "the memory of she who has the form of the world's germ [*jagater aṅkur-rūpiṇī*] arises in that womb which has the form of ego-knowledge."[66] This knowledge expands into the form of a circle (*maṇḍalākār*), which is expressed in the cosmic body in the form of a vacuum (*abakāś*) called "Space" (given in English).[67] As this cosmic memory expands, then "Time" (given in English, with correlate *kāl*) is given expression, and Ambikacharan here proceeds to provide a note referencing Spencer's *First Principles* to the effect that both time and space are "relative realities." At this point the macrocosmic "desire" is expressed in terms of a variety of Bengali synonyms, each with different shades of meaning: desire (*bāsanā*),[68] volition (*saṅkalpa*), or longing (*ākāṅkṣār*), and when these are stimulated, then the motion gives rise to "will" (*icchā*).[69] Under this desire and volition "billions of types of powers who take their form at will" are manifested in Space, including as "the actions of creation, maintenance, upholding, the processes of change (*paribarttita karaṇ*), and so on."[70] Ambikacharan then makes his critical pivot toward a rationale for bhakti, noting that "all these powers are what have been described in the scriptures of the nobles as local gods (*debatā*, < Skt. *devatā*)."[71] In other words, Ambikacharan espouses the strikingly contemporary perspective that religious devotion for local deities, in this case as present in the Hindu scriptures, at least partially if not entirely developed out of a reverence for the powers of nature (e.g., worship of personifications of the wind, fire, rain, and so on).[72]

Ambikacharan in the final part of his section on *bhaktiyog* outlines the mechanistic quality of yogic devotion, noting that the yogis, who understood both the human body's states and powers as well as those that unite within this cosmic instrument of the Lord (*īśvar*), "turned to the form of scripture, mantras, and sacrifices to carry out the stimulation of all the powers."[73] He then defines this androgynous Lord as "the individual's father (*pitā*), mother (*mātā*), support (*dhātā*), master (*bhartā*), motion (*gati*), and seed (*bīj*)," quoting the Bhagavad Gita in a footnote.[74] Devotion (*bhakti*) is the "link" (*saṃyog* again) between individual consciousness (*jīb-cetan*) and divine consciousness (*īśvar-cetan*), and operates by means of "favor" (*anugraha*) or "affection" (*sneha*). While this may appear imprecise to a contemporary reader, it is important to keep in mind that for Ambikacharan this is not simply a vague emotional state but rather a mechanistic process tied to the laws of nature; bhakti "is a special activity or motion of feeling" that is endowed with "velocity" (*beg*, < Skt. *vega*) in a given direction toward a part or whole of the macrocosmic Īśvara. In a normal individual this velocity is restrained or blocked by competing emotions that possess their own velocities, although if this devotion were to somehow be unrestrained, then it would be so strong that it could even destabilize the entirety of nature. For this reason Ambikacharan instructs the reader to train the entirety of the sense capacities, which as we have seen are predicated on knowledge (*jñāna*), to continually perceive the "glory of the limitless deity with its cosmic form [*birāṭrūpī anantadeber mahimā*]," which will cause both "the world as the identity of name and form [*nām rūpātmak jagat*)" and the self to be forgotten. As before, the path for this is yoga as framed in Pātañjalan terms, with the addition of "inner longing for the Lord" (*īśvara praṇidhānādvā*).[75] However, Ambikacharan notably departs from the Pātañjalan view of "isolation" (*kaivalya*) in speaking of an "equilibrium" (*sāmyabhāb*) of internal and external knowledge that leads to "release" (*mocan*).[76] His overall idea is that knowledge, if unrestrained in its impartial devotion, facilitates an equilibrium between the individual cosmos and universal cosmos that simultaneously collapses the turnings of the thought in the individual and the motion of the powers and qualities in the external universe.

Ambikacharan's section on the last yoga of his tetrad, or the "yoga of action" (*karmayog*), opens with a reference to the "ninth, tenth, eleventh, and twelfth chapters of that Upaniṣadic scripture called the *Śrīmad Bhagavadgītā*,[77] where it is Sri Krishna (Śrī Kr̥ṣṇa), the knower of the principles, the great Lord of Yoga, who is called the Lord (Īśvara)." Ambikacharan's mention of Krishna, as well as his inclusion of a poem following his prologue that references the circa fifteenth-century reformer Chaitanya Mahaprabhu (Caitānya Mahāprabhu), is significant because the original lectures by Sabhapati Swami do not reference the Bhagavad Gita nor make any recourse to Vaiṣṇava doctrines, not even Tamil ones, much less references specific to Bengali and Gauḍiya Vaiṣṇavism.[78] Sabhapati's later works (especially from 1889 onward), however, do include Vishnu, the Goddess (Devī), and other deities as divine principles who are compatible with the practice of Śivarājayoga, so there was probably no perceived issue for Ambikacharan to integrate these references that would be familiar to his local Bengali audience.

In any event, the section on *karmayog* is considerably shorter than the other sections and references the yogis' prescription of different types of devotion and methods of worship in the Vedas and Tantras (*tantraśāstra*) for those who are not capable of concentrating on Narayana (Nārāyaṇ, an epithet of Vishnu) directly. Using this logic of devotional (and by extension moral) relativity, Ambikacharan claims the following that helps transition to his discourse on the Western pandits directly:

> The yogis who are the knowers of the principles, in thoroughly discussing the nature of this human instrument or cosmic instrument in the perspective of science [*bijñān*], have prescribed all these methods. Their opinions are said to be harmonious with science and therefore they can be called free from confusion [*abhrānta*]. The conduct, behavior, and so on that they have ascertained as well as their methods for society are also conducive to scientific duties [*baijñānik dharma*].[79]

In other words, the noble rishis or yogis had themselves analyzed the "human instrument" (*mānab-yantra*, < Skt. *mānavayantra*) in their own experiments, and the moral conduct that they had prescribed is scientific in the sense that it was based on their understanding of the "nature" (*prakṛti*) of the human being, however limited or dated from a modern perspective. Ambikacharan stops short of explicitly noting what would undoubtedly be a controversial corollary to this line of thought if logically extended, namely that the yogis' traditional prescriptions for conduct and behavior, if they are indeed based on science, could also potentially be deemed irrelevant or outdated when confronted by contemporary and future advancements in the scientific understanding of human nature. While he does not consider this possibility, he does express a karmic theory that repeated actions leads to "habit" (*abhyās*), and that habits lead to "impressions" (*saṃskār*) and that a change in these impressions' "radiance" (*prabhā*) or "self-nature" (*svabhāb*) will lead to a change in one's "condition" (*bhābāntar*).[80]

These descriptions of yoga, apart from a few scattered references to Western theories, are mostly rooted in a blend of Pātañjalan, Vedānta-inspired, and Tantric theories on cosmology and perception. However, they are necessary to consider since they are critical to Ambikacharan's subsequent and final section after treating his tetrad of yogas, in which he transitions to make extensive quotations in English from the "modern Western theoretical pandits" (*ādhunik pāścātya tattvabiśārad paṇḍitgaṇ*), by which he primarily means the philosophical naturalist Herbert Spencer and authors quoted in Spencer's book *First Principles*, first published in 1862.

Ambikacharan's engagement with these Western pandits begins with a consideration of the importance of both "religion" (which he translates with the Bengali word *dharma* according to standard Bengali usage even today) and "science" (which he translates into *bijñān*, another common translation in Bengali). The following engagement provides a good example Ambikacharan's engagement in general, which is often based on a quotation in English, either followed or preceded by a summary of it in Bengali, and an interpretation of its meaning in the light of his yogic understanding of *jñāna* as expressed in the preceding sections (words given in English underlined to distinguish my own translation into English from Bengali):

> H. Spencer says that religion [*dharma*] and science [*bijñān*] should remain consistent with each other. When science surpasses [its limits], religion can no longer remain. His opinion on this subject is like this: "Thus the consciousness of an inscrutable power manifested to us through all phenomena, has been growing ever clearer; and must eventually be freed from its imperfections. The certainty that on the one hand such a power exists, while on the other hand its nature transcends intuition and is beyond imagination, is the certainty towards which intelligence has from the first been progressing. At this conclusion science inevitably arrives as it reaches its confines; while to this conclusion Religion is irresistably driven by criticism."[81] The meaning being expressed by this saying is that the inconceivable power that manifests the world is unexplainable and, since it is determined that it is unexplainable, both religion [*dharma*] and science [*bijñān*] are to be practiced. Later, in another place, he says, "Is it not just possible that there is a mode of Being transcending Intelligence and will, as these transcend mechanical motion? It is true that we are totally unable to conceive any such higher mode of being, but this is not a reason for questioning its existence, it is rather the reverse. Have we not seen how utterly incompetent our minds are to form even an approach to a conception of that which underlies all phenomena? Is it not proved that this incompetency is the incompetency of the conditioned to grasp the unconditioned?"[82] Here the meaning being expressed is that the essence which is beyond the intellect, and which is the constituent-mattter [*upādāna*] of the world-substance distinguished by name and form, is beyond all states; therefore our (limited) disposition toward knowledge-power [*jñānśakti*] is unable to grasp it.[83]

In other words, Ambikacharan takes Spencer's somewhat agnostic position to imply that the Absolute cannot be grasped by means of the current conditioned state of our knowledge. He then provides a similar perspective from a different thinker, Henry Longueville Mansel (1820–1871), as quoted in Spencer's work:

> Mr. Mansel states this in the following way, in relation to determining the inherent nature of this constituent-matter of the world and the inherent nature of the eternal substance, which is beyond all states: "The absolute and infinite are thus like the inconceivable and imperceptible, names indicating, not an object of thought or consciousness at all, but mere absence of the conditions under which consciousness is possible."[84] Here the meaning being expressed is that the names "absolute" [*svayaṃ pūrṇa*][85] and "infinite" [*ananta*) [indicate] that which is beyond knowledge or thought. If conditioned by states or conditioned by existence, the action of the power of knowledge is merely the absence of a state or a condition.[86]

These passages are lengthy but critical to Ambikacharan's sustained argument, which is predicated on the idea of an "absence" of a state, which as shown at the end of his prologue he equates with what in the Western method (*upāẏ*) is called the "negation of thought."[87] To this end he also quotes an assertion by Sir William Hamilton, 9th Baronet (1788–1856), namely that "the absolute is conceived by a negation of conceivability."[88]

Ambikacharan's engagement is not limited to questions on the existence of the Absolute or an absolute substance, however, as he appears more concerned with the implications on an idea of "negation" for the function of consciousness itself from both a Western and yogic perspective, as inspired by both Sabhapati Swami's work that follows the prologue as well as Patañjali. His prologue is possibly the first publication in Bengali (or in any Indian vernacular language) in which Western views on consciousness were treated to any substantial extent in a comparative frame with yogic views on thought (Bng. *cintā*, Skt. *citta*). The substance of his engagement on this topic will therefore be given below in full as follows:

> Mr. Spencer says, "our consciousness, of the unconditioned, being literally the unconditioned consciousness, or raw material of thought, to which in thinking we give definite forms, it follows that an ever present sense of real existence is the very basis of our intelligence."[89]

> The meaning of this is that knowledge, if it is devoid of all existence and that which is conditioned by states, can be called the knowledge of the essence (*bastu*) that is beyond existence. Secondly, in this place the meaning of the word "consciousness" has been rendered in such a way to mean knowledge-in-itself (*svayaṃ-jñān*) or the constituent-matter of thought (*cintār upādān*), that is, that which we develop into special forms at the time of thinking. By this it is ascertained that the perception (*anubhūti*) of the power of knowledge's actual being [*sattā*] is constantly present internally.
>
> It was already demonstrated how the celebrated Spencer says that "to which in thinking we give definite forms,"[90] that is, at the time of thinking we grant distinct shapes to it (knowledge). The word "we" signifies the condition of an ego [*ahaṃ bhāb*]. If what was said earlier is acknowledged about the condition of the ego being the conductor [*paricālak*] of knowledge, then it must be acknowledged that it [i.e., the condition of the ego] must be something that consists of a being that is separate from knowledge. However, Mr. Spencer and Mr. Mansel and many others acknowledge in unison that knowledge has a distinct state or existence because the condition of the ego is expressed within knowledge. What has been said above is inconsistent [with their ideas] as a result.[91] They say this only on account of an absence of stability in perception.[92]

The last sentence on the "absence of stability in perception" is the most critical for our understanding of Ambikacharan's view and critique. One of his key points is that Spencer and Mansel and the other modern Western pandits who are "investigators into the principles of the self" (*ātmatattvānusandhyāẏī*) provide factual information yet are nevertheless unable to experience some things clearly on account of a "fault of perception" (*anubhūtir doṣ*).

The fault of perception is related to subject and object, and Ambikacharan does recognize that both Spencer and Mansel gesture to this problem and try their best to express it. He quotes Spencer's assertion as follows: "clearly a true cognition of self implies a state in which the knowing and known are one, in which subject and object are identified; and this Mr. Mansel rightly holds to be the annihilation of both."[93] He also notes that both Spencer and Mansel have "spoken in agreement with the noble knowers of the principles, in that, if the self is to be known, then the existence of both knowledge [*jñān*] and the knower [*jñātā*], and the proven [*prameẏa*] and the prover [*pramātā*] is destroyed,"[94] although he does note that Mansel has not addressed whether or not anything remains following the destruction of both knowledge and knower or proof and prover.[95] This leads Ambikacharan to make his own intervention into this discourse, citing the existence of a third state between subject and object:

> By means of power itself, the knowledge of the three states [*tin bhāb*] is expressed: the prover [*pramātā*], that which is proven [*prameẏa*], and proof [*pramāṇ*]; or the knower [*jñātā*], that which is known [*jñeẏa*], and knowledge [*jñān*]; or the actor [*karttā*], that which is enacted [*karmma*], and action [*kriẏā*].[96] "Proof" can be called that by which the prover is expressed in the prover's inherent nature [*svarūp*] in connection [*sambandhe*] to what is proven; and that by which what is proven is expressed in the inherent nature of that which is proven in connection to the one who proves. In other words, it is not only the existence of both the knower and that which is known that is expressed through knowledge. The connecting thread [*sambandha-sūtra*], by which are connected the knower and that which is known, is also a connecting thread that consists of a form of an action as expressed in knowledge, such as when the essence of that which is known becomes a sense object of sight. If this happens then knowledge, having concentrated on the existence of the act of seeing, expresses the essence of that which is known in connection with the knower. If the sense object is one of hearing then knowledge, having concentrated on the existence of the act of hearing, also expresses the essence of that which is known.[97]

While this discussion of agency may appear confusing or technical, Ambikacharan's general point is the need for more focus on the processes of perception (*anubhūti*) that inform various actions and the claims on reality that result from the limitations of one's existence of the ego or "nature of 'I'" (*ahaṃ-bhāb*). This includes a recognition of the dependence of proof upon the person who is proving (the "prover") and that which is proven, the dependence of knowledge upon the knower and that which can be known, and the dependence of sound upon the hearer and that which can be heard.[98] Ambikacharan argues in the first case that "proof" of the reality or existence of anything will always to some degree be conditioned by the inherent nature (*svarūp*) of the person who is doing the act of proving, which is also to some degree connected to what is able to be proven—no object of perception can be completely considered in isolation from the person who is perceiving. The logic of this is not merely intended to invite the reader to appreciate the entire scope of the spectrum of reality and our perception of it, but to go a step further and collapse the individual's conditioned distinction between subject and object. This is made clear in Ambikacharan's following claim:

> The Western pandits have not been capable of concentrating [*dhāraṇā karā*] on these conditions. If they were to suddenly give up their aforementioned [inquiry] and become engaged in internally experiencing, under the influence of willpower [*icchā-śakti*], the conditions of the prover and that which is proven, then certainly the prover and that which is proven would become devoid of conditions. However, they instead focus on the condition of that knowledge which is impelled by means of power, and the velocity of this power does not stop even once.[99]

In other words, Ambikacharan's critique is that Spencer, Mansel, and the rest are only focusing on the effects of conditions (*bhāb*), namely the "qualities" and "powers" by which the cosmos is continually maintained and enlivened; in his view they should devote more time to analyzing the problems of perception and the cause behind knowledge (*jñāna*) being conditioned in the individual. This is then reconciled with his understanding of the purity of knowledge when considered beyond the active motion of the cosmos, an understanding that itself is predicated upon a harmonization between Sabhapati's discourse on the "gnosis (or knowledge) of Brahman" (*brahmajñāna*) and Patañjali's doctrine of stilling the turnings of the mind. He closes his prologue with the following statement:

> The regulated state of knowledge is the binding of the individual [*jīber bandhan*]. If one is able to even once stop the velocity of power, and release knowledge from this restrained state, then that existence which is free from impurity [*nirmal*], unmoving [*niścal*], and perpetual [*nitya*] will yet emerge in knowledge. The Western pandits have mentioned their method [*upāẏ*] as the negation of thought, that is, the nonexistence of the turnings of thought [*cintā bṛttir abhāb*], and the noble knowers of the principles have also given instruction on this aim as the cessation of the turnings of thought [*cittabṛtti nirodha*]. However, this cannot happen all at once—practice and skill are needed. This skill is yoga. Only the noble ones, they who know the principles, know it.[100]

In other words, the process of yoga for Ambikacharan is not only a spiritual quest but also a scientific one as a process that can reduce limitations on knowledge and reconcile problems of perception. The claim that its origin is specific to the "noble rishis" seems to prefigure contemporary nationalist discourses on yoga, with a notable twist: here the Western pandits and Bengali readers alike are invited to experiment with the practice on their own by reading Sabhapati's teachings and to attempt to discover what, if anything, lies beyond these turnings of thought. As is explored further in the next chapter, occultists following the founding of the Theosophical Society, referenced by Ambikacharan himself in the prologue, often welcomed these kinds of invitations and were interested in engaging in—and sometimes challenging—similar discourses on science to promote their own teachings on yoga and occultism.[101] I suggest therefore that Ambikacharan's writing not only be considered in the context of political appropriations of science to grant authority to yoga, but also be viewed as part of an emerging South Asian perspective on a broader synthesis of science and spiritual experimentation emerging in urban centers across Europe and North America. It is notable that Sabhapati's system of Śivarājayoga provided an impetus for authors like Ambikacharan to engage in this kind of interpretive discourse, and it speaks to the chord that Sabhapati's teaching struck in some intellectual circles.

Notes

1. VRY1, 27.
2. Somadeva Vasudeva, "Powers and Identities: Yoga Powers and the Tantric Śaiva Traditions," in *Yoga Powers: Extraordinary Capacities Attained Through Meditation and Concentration*, ed. Knut A. Jacobsen (Leiden: Brill, 2012), 264–302; David Gordon White, *Sinister Yogis* (Chicago: University of Chicago Press, 2009).
3. F. Max Müller, *The Six Systems of Indian Philosophy* (New York: Longmans, Green, 1899), 462–64.
4. Egil Asprem, *The Problem of Disenchantment: Scientific Naturalism and Esoteric Discourse, 1900–1939* (Albany: State University of New York Press, 2018).
5. See Brajendranath Seal, *The Positive Sciences of the Ancient Hindus* (London: Longmans, Green, 1915).
6. For other engagement on this theme see Joseph S. Alter, *Yoga in Modern India: The Body between Science and Philosophy* (Princeton, NJ: Princeton University Press, 2004); Magdalena Kraler, "Tracing Vivekananda's Prāṇa and Ākāśa: The Yogavāsiṣṭha and Rama Prasad's Occult Science of Breath," in *The Occult Nineteenth Century: Roots, Developments, and Impact on the Modern World*, ed. Lukas Pokorny and Franz Winter (London: Palgrave Macmillan, forthcoming). Neither of these sources analyzes "science" in the works of Sabhapati Swami, however.

7. VRY1, 38.
8. A similar model of pilgrimage is attested in Kubjikā sources; see Mark S. G. Dyczkowski, *A Journey in the World of Tantras* (Varanasi: Indica Books, 2004), 93–175.
9. A modern trend among yogis toward "traditionalism" in India remains an interesting and largely unexplored subject. For traditionalism in the "West" and also in the writings of the Sri Lankan Tamil art historian A. K. Coomaraswamy, see Mark J. Sedgwick, *Against the Modern World: Traditionalism and the Secret Intellectual History of the Twentieth Century* (New York: Oxford University Press, 2004). For a survey of Vivekananda's own response to scientific theories of evolution, see D. H. Killingley, "Yoga-Sūtra IV, 2–3 and Vivekānanda's Interpretation of Evolution," *Journal of Indian Philosophy* 18, no. 2 (June 1, 1990): 151–79; and for the Theosophical relationship to these views in terms of reincarnation, see Julie Chajes, *Recycled Lives: A History of Reincarnation in Blavatsky's Theosophy* (New York: Oxford University Press, 2019).
10. Tam. *ulakattiṉ aṉṉiyamatat tōḻarkaḷum ammatapāṣaiyaikkaṟkum intumatat tōḻarkaḷum*. CTCSPV, 24.
11. This is reminiscent of existentialist philosophy with its equation of existence and essence, although most strands of European existentialist thought, with a notable exception being George Berkeley (1685–1753), would not necessarily admit the phenomenal world as illusionary or at least immaterial at its core, as Sabhapati does.
12. CTCSPV, 24–25. Tam.: "*o! eṉatu uttama tirimūrtti ciṣiyarkaḷē kēḷuṅkaḷ—pirapañcam ēḻuvakaittākum: mutalāvatu.*—Infinite Spiritual Phenomena *carvāṉucūta ēkacukānanta ñāṉākāra cuttappirapañcam, itu* Spirit or Space *caitaṉṉiyamākum, itil utayam; (2-vatu)* Spirit or Spiritual Phenomena *carva antaryāmitva caṅkalpāṉanta kalākāra cuttēsvara pirapañcam, itu* Presence and Atoms *caṉṉitāṉamākum itil utayam; (3-vatu)* Finite Spiritual Phenomena *carvaviyāpti kalpitāṉanta piraṇavākāra cuttacaktippirapañcam, itu* Power *cattiyākum, itil utayam; (4-vatu)* Conscious Spiritual Phenomena *carvacākṣi carvapōtāṉanta nātākāra āṉmappirapañcam,* Essence *cattākum, itil utayam; (5-vatu)* Mental Spiritual Phenomena *carvaviyāpaka carva aññāṉa piraṇavākāramāyāmaya jīvappirapañcam, itu* Force and Motion *valivum, vicaiyumākum, itil utayam; (6-vatu)* Sensual Spiritual Phenomena *carvacūṉṉiya carva apimāṉa vāciyākāra cūṭcumappirapañcam itu* Action and Creation *acaivum ceykaiyumākum, itil utayam; (7-vatu)* Elemental Physical Phenomena or Material {25} Phenomena *carvatōṟṟa carva ācāpācapanta tontakuṇakarma jeṉma tukka cuvāsākāra tōṟṟa pañcapūtappirapañcam, itu* Visible Show *tōṟṟamākum, ākaiyāl* Elemental Physical Phenomena *pañcapūtappirapañcamāṉatu ciruṣṭikiramattil ēḻāvatāyum itaṟ katītamāyuṅ kāraṇamāyumuḷḷa āṟuvakai corūpavirtti ēkamaya atikārattāl uṇṭākkappaṭṭatāyum avvirttiyil taṉatu uṟpattiyaik koṇṭatāyum viḷaṅkuvatu. inta ēḻāvatu rūpacorūpaṅ kāṇavum sparicikkak kūṭiyatuvumāṉatu anta āṟuvakai arūpacorūpaṅkaḷum aṟivukkaṇṇālaṉṟi maṟṟa puṟakkaṇṇāl kāṇavum, kaiyāl sparicikkavuṅ kūṭātatu. itu* Oxygen *iyaṟkai yarūpapañcapūtappirapañcam,* Nitrogen *cērkkairūpa pañcapūtappirapañcameṉṉum iraṇṭu vakaittām.*
13. CPSPS, Second Book, 216.
14. The treatment on related faculties in RYB is located in the second chapter, pages 21–32.

15. See Seal, *Positive Sciences*, 99. For a broader survey of the Nyāya-Vaiśeṣika school, see Amita Chatterjee, "Nyāya-Vaiśeṣika Philosophy," in *The Oxford Handbook of World Philosophy*, ed. William Edelglass and Jay L. Garfield (Online, 2011).
16. Seal, *Positive Sciences*, 98–103, 117–21.
17. N. C. Paul, *A Treatise on the Yoga Philosophy* (1851; Benares: E.J. Lazarus, 1882). See also treatment of N. C. Paul in Magdalena Kraler, "The Prāṇāyāma Grid—Defining the Place of Yogic Breath Cultivation within Discourses of Modern Yoga," *Journal of Yoga Studies*, forthcoming.
18. Alter, *Yoga in Modern India*; see also Kraler, "Tracing Vivekananda's Prāṇa and Ākāśa."
19. CPSPS, First Book, 4, 30.
20. David Gordon White, *The Yoga Sutra of Patanjali: A Biography* (Princeton, NJ: Princeton University Press, 2014), 129–30; Anna Pokazanyeva, "Mind within Matter: Science, the Occult, and the (Meta)Physics of Ether and Akasha," *Zygon: Journal of Religion & Science* 51, no. 2 (June 2016): 318–46; Kraler, "Tracing Vivekananda's Prāṇa and Ākāśa."
21. Ráma Prasád, *The Science of Breath and the Philosophy of the Tatwas: Nature's Finer Forces* (New York: Theosophical Publishing Society, 1890), 1–2.
22. Ibid.
23. VRY2, 77–78.
24. VRY1, 17–18.
25. VRY1, 15. The term *ākāśa* is there not mentioned but rather the "sense of hearing or *Shabda Indriyam* [*śabdendriya*]," which we know is linked to *ākāśa* in classical Sāṃkhya. See Gerald James Larson, *Classical Sāṃkhya: An Interpretation of Its History and Meaning* (Delhi: Motilal Banarsidass, 1979).
26. VRY1, 10.
27. VRY1, 41.
28. See Swāmi Nikhilānanda, trans., *The Māndūkyopanishad with Gaudapāda's Kārikā and Śankara's Commentary* (Mysore: Sri Ramakrishna Ashrama, 1949), 149–52
29. M. Monier-Williams, *A Sanskrit-English Dictionary: Etymologically and Philologically Arranged with Special Reference to Cognate Indo-European Languages* (Oxford: Clarendon Press, 1899), s.v. *kāraṇaśarīra*.
30. VRY2, 75. Shrish Chandra Basu nowhere states the authorship of the section where this verse is found, entitled "Search after Knowledge of Spirit," which would lead one to think it was composed by Sabhapati Swami and translated later by Shrisha Chandra for this edition. The section is, however, not composed by Sabhapati Swami but is a direct translation from the *Mahānirvāna Tantra*, chapter 14, comprising verses 107 to 140 in the ubiquitous translation by Arthur Avalon (the collaboration between John Woodroffe and other Indian scholars). See Chapter 2 for the place of this section in the textual corpus of the editions of VRY.
31. Seal, *Positive Sciences*, 86.
32. See James Thomas Molesworth, *A Dictionary, Marathi and English*, 2nd ed. (Bombay: Bombay Education Society's Press, 1857), s.v. *mahākāśa*.
33. Seal, *Positive Sciences*, 87.

34. For the "hydraulics" of haṭha yoga in the context of Indian alchemy, see David Gordon White, *The Alchemical Body: Siddha Traditions in Medieval India* (Chicago: University of Chicago Press, 1996). See also James Mallinson and Mark Singleton, eds., *Roots of Yoga* (London: Penguin Books, 2017).
35. Skt. *adhomukheḍākalāvāṃśikāmyamalāntarmukhamanodṛṣṭi*, lit. "the downward vital channel of the fragmented power of Iḍā, the impurity of desire [*kāmyamala*], which is the mental sight that sees within itself." These references to the functions of the subtle body can be translated and interpreted in multiple ways. Sabhapati is attributing the three principal channels of the subtle body to the three "impurities" or "filths" (Skt. *mala*) of Śaiva Siddhānta and to the "mind" (Skt. *manas*), the "intellect" (*buddhi*), and "thought" (*citta*), here idiosyncratically glossed as mind, body, and spirit.
36. Skt. *adhomukhapiṅgalavāṃśyāṇavamalāntarmukhabuddhidṛṣṭi*, lit. "the downward-facing vital channel of Piṅgalā, the filth of material particles [*āṇavamala*], which is the sight of the intellect that absorbs in itself."
37. Skt. *adhomukhapiṅgalavāṃśyāṇavamalāntarmukhabuddhidṛṣṭi*, lit. "the downward vital channel of Suṣumnā, the impurity of desire [*kāmyamala*], which is the sight of thought that becomes within itself."
38. Skt. *ūrdhvamukharecakacandrakalāvāṃśyantarmukhatamoguṇadṛṣṭi*, lit. "the upward-facing vital channel of the fragmented power of Iḍā in inhalation, which is the vision within of the quality [*guṇa*] of darkness [*tamas*]."
39. Skt. *ūrdhvamukhakumbhakāgnikalāvāṃśyantarmukhasattvaguṇadṛṣṭi*, lit. "the upward vital channel of the fragmented power of fire in breath-retention, which is the vision within of the quality [*guṇa*] of goodness [*sattva*]."
40. Skt. *ūrdhvamukhapūrakasūryakalāvāṃśyantarmukharajoguṇadṛṣṭi*, lit. "the upward vital channel of the fragmented power of the sun in exhalation, which is the vision within of the quality [*guṇa*] of activity [*rajas*]."
41. Skt. *adhomukhatrijīvatriprāṇātmakavṛddhyākāśa* of *sṛṣṭisthitisaṃhāra*, lit. "the downward expanding ether, which is the three spirits of the vital air of the three individual spirits, of creation, maintenance and destruction."
42. Skt. *ūrdhvamukhatrijīvatriprāṇātmakalayākāśa* of *tirobhāvānugrahaikya*, lit. "the upward dissolving ether, which is the three spirits of the vital air of the three individual spirits, of concealment, bestowing favor, and unity."
43. This bears some relevance to the way in which the pure and impure worlds were separated in Śaiva Saiddhāntika discourses by five or six *kañcukas*, or "sheaths"; see Chapter 3 and White, *The Alchemical Body*, 214; Dominic Goodall and Harunaga Isaacson, "How the Tattvas of Tantric Śaivism Came to Be 36: The Evidence of the Niśvāsatattvasaṃhitā," in *Tantric Studies: Fruits of a Franco-German Collaboration on Early Tantra*, ed. Dominic Goodall and Harunaga Isaacson (Pondicherry: École française d'Extrême-Orient, 2016).
44. See David Gordon White, *Kiss of the Yoginī: "Tantric Sex" in Its South Asian Contexts* (Chicago: University of Chicago Press, 2006), 230–33.
45. For an interpretation and comparison of Sabhapati's teachings on *kuṇḍalinī* with those of the Arthur Avalon collaboration, see Arjan Dass Malik, *Kundalini and Meditation* (Delhi: Motilal Banarsidass; Borehamwood: Motilal, 2002).

46. The full translation of this prologue and original Bengali will be found in the forthcoming first volume of the collected works of Sabhapati Swami, and was also included in the dissertation upon which this book is based. For the discourse around the term "noble" in the Arya Samāj see Kenneth W. Jones, *Arya Dharm: Hindu Consciousness in 19th-Century Punjab* (Berkeley: University of California Press, 1976). It was a term also salient to Shrish Chandra Basu's writings for the *Arya* journal published in Lahore, which may have been where Ambikacharan encountered it.
47. BRY, 2. Bng.: ইহা পাঠ করিলে গুরূপদেশ ব্যতিরেকেও যোগ যে কি তাহা বুঝিতে ও করিতে পারা যায় (*ihā pāṭh karile gurupadeś byatirekeo yog ye ki tāhā bujhite o karite para yaẏ*).
48. BRY, 2. Bng.: কিন্তু ইহাই যে মানবের উচ্চতম ধর্ম্মে, তদ্বিষয়ে পাঠক মণ্ডলীর মধ্যে অনেকেরই সংশয় জন্মিতে পারে (*kintu ihāi ye mānaber uccatam dharmme, tadviṣaẏe pāṭhak maṇḍalīr madhye anekeri saṃśaẏ janmite pāre*).
49. Elizabeth De Michelis, *A History of Modern Yoga: Patañjali and Western Esotericism* (reprint, London: Continuum, 2008), 87. I am grateful to Magdalena Kraler for pointing this claim out to me.
50. The compound *dhyānyog* in Bengali is diffused in folk songs, such as in a song attributed to Lālan Fakir (although it may not be authentic) *tumi eso he prabhu nirañjan* "Come thou, oh Stainless Lord." The second *antarā* of this song is *dhyānyoge tomāke dekhi / tumi sakhā āmi sakhī / mama hṛdaẏ o mandire thāki / dāo oi arūp darśan*, "I see you in the yoga of meditation / you are the male and I the female companion / I remain here in my heart and the temple / Grant me the formless vision." The compound *rājayoga*, however, is much less used in Bengali vernacular sources (if present at all).
51. Phanindranath Bose, *Life of Sris Chandra Basu* (Calcutta: R. Chatterjee, 1932), 134.
52. We know that Swami Vivekananda privately circulated Shrish Chandra Basu's translation of the *Śivasaṃhitā* (his earlier, unexpurgated translation) to advanced disciples, so was familiar with his work in general; see Leigh Eric Schmidt, *Heaven's Bride: The Unprintable Life of Ida C. Craddock, American Mystic, Scholar, Sexologist, Martyr, and Madwoman* (New York: Basic Books, 2010), 126–27. I am grateful to Karl Baier for sharing this source with me.
53. De Michelis, *History of Modern Yoga*; Jason Birch, "Rājayoga: The Reincarnations of the King of All Yogas," *International Journal of Hindu Studies* 17, no. 3 (2013): 399–442.
54. BRY, 6. Bng.: দ্রব্য গুণ ও ক্রিয়া দ্বারাই যে সমুদয় সৃষ্টি ইহা সকলেই স্বীকার করেন, এবং তত্ত্বজ্ঞানী যোগিদিগেরও এইরূপ উপদেশ। ইহাদিগের মধ্যে দ্রব্যতত্ত্ব নিত্য, অর্থাৎ যাহার কখন অভাব হয় না তাহাই দ্রব্য। গুণ সেই দ্রব্যে লীন হইয়া থাকে, যখন তাহা হইতে প্রকাশ পায়, তখনই তাহাতে ক্রিয়া-শক্তির আবির্ভাব হয়। দ্রব্য একমাত্র, বুদ্ধির অতীত, অনন্ত অবকাশ-মধ্যে অপরিচ্ছিন্ন ভাবে অবস্থিত। গুণ তিন প্রকার সত্ব রজঃ এবং তমঃ। ইহাদিগের দ্বারা শক্তি চালিত হয়। শক্তির দুই প্রকার গতি — প্রবৃত্তি ও নিবৃত্তি। গুণ-শক্তির প্রভাবে প্রবৃত্তি বেগ প্রবাহিত হইতে আরম্ভ হইলে, আবরণ বিক্ষেপ এই দুই প্রকার ক্রিয়াশক্তি সমুদ্ভুত হয়। গুণ-শক্তি, দ্রব্যের নিত্য সত্তায় সত্তবতী হইয়া এবং আভ্যন্তরিক গুণের দ্বারা চালিত হইয়া এই দুই ক্রিয়া-শক্তি সহকারে ভিন্ন ভিন্ন ক্রিয়া সম্পাদনার্থে বহুবিধ আকারে পরিণত হইয়াছে। সেই সকল শক্তির দ্বারা স্থূল সুক্ষ্ম অনন্ত আকার বিশিষ্ট এই বিশ্ব সংসারে সৃজন পোষণ পরিবর্ত্তন। প্রভৃতি সকল ক্রিয়া সম্পাদিত হইতেছে। শক্তির বেগ-প্রভাবে নিঃসৃত পরমাণু সকল একদিকে আবরণ শক্তির দ্বারা সংশ্লিষ্ট হইয়া রূপ বা আকার ধারণ করিতেছে। অপর দিকে বিক্ষেপ শক্তির প্রভাবে পরমাণু সকল বিশ্লিষ্ট হইয়া রূপান্তরে পরিণত হইতেছে। তাহারা পুনর্ব্বার নুতন ভাবে সংশ্লিষ্ট হইয়া অন্য পদার্থের আকারে প্রকাশ পাইতেছে। সুতরাং এই ব্রহ্মাণ্ড মধ্যে আমরা যাহা কিছু পদার্থ বলিয়া দেখিতেছি তাহা কেবল গুণ ও শক্তির রচিত আকার মাত্র। কিন্তু এইরূপ {৭} গুণ-শক্তির প্রভাবে যে দ্রব্য নিয়তই রূপ হইতে রূপান্তরে প্রতিভাত হইতেছে, সেই দ্রব্যের

স্বরূপ কি তাহা আমরা কিছু বুঝিতে পারি না । গুণ-শক্তির প্রভাবে দ্রব্যের প্রকৃত ভাব সমাচ্ছাদিত রহিয়াছে, তাহার বিকৃত ভাবেই কেবল আমাদিগের উপলব্ধি হইতেছে (*drabya guṇ o kriẏā dvārāi ye samudaẏ sṛṣṭi ihā sakalei svīkār karen, ebaṃ tattvajñānī yogidigero eirūp upadeś. ihādiger madhye drabyatattva nitya, arthāt yāhār kakhan abhāb haẏ nā tāhāi drabya. guṇ sei drabye līn haiẏā thāke, yakhan tāhā haite prakāś pāẏ, takhan-i tāhāte kriẏā-śaktir ābirbhāb haẏ. drabya ekmātra, buddhir atīta, ananta abakāś-madhye aparicchinna bhābe abasthita. guṇ tin prakār satva rajaḥ ebaṃ tamaḥ. ihādiger dvārā śakti cālita haẏ. śaktir dui prakār gati—prabṛtti o nibṛtti. guṇ-śaktir prabhābe prabṛtti beg prabāhita haite ārambha haile, ābaraṇ bikṣep ei dui prakār kriẏāśakti samudbhūta haẏ. guṇ-śakti, drabyer nitya sattāẏ sattabatī haiẏā ebaṃ ābhyantarik guṇer dvārā cālita haiẏā ei dui kriẏā-śakti sahakāre bhinna bhinna kriẏā sampādanārthe bahubidh ākāre pariṇata haiẏāche. sei sakal śaktir dvārā sthūl sūkṣma ananta ākār biśiṣṭa ei biśva saṃsāre sṛjan poṣaṇ paribarttan. prabhṛti sakal kriẏā sampādita haiteche. śaktir beg-prabhābe niḥsṛta paramāṇu sakal ekdike ābaraṇ śaktir dvārā saṃśliṣṭa haiẏā rūp bā ākār dhāraṇ kariteche. apar dike bikṣep śaktir prabhābe paramāṇu sakal biśliṣṭa haiẏā rūpāntare pariṇata haiteche. tāhārā punarbbār nūtan bhābe saṃśliṣṭa haiẏā anya padārther ākāre prakāś pāiteche. sutarāṃ ei brahmāṇḍa madhye āmrā yāhā kichu padārtha baliẏā dekhitechi tāhā kebal guṇ o śaktir racita ākār mātra. kintu eirūp guṇ-śaktir prabhābe ye drabya niẏat-i rūp haite rūpāntare pratibhāt haiteche, sei drabyer svarūp ki tāhā āmrā kichu bujhite pāri nā. guṇ-śaktir prabhābe drabyer prakṛta bhāb samācchādita rahiẏāche, tāhār bikṛta bhābei kebal āmādiger upalabdhi haiteche*).

55. BRY, 8.: This is also related to a similar saying among the Bāul fakirs of Bengal: যা আছে ব্রহ্মাণ্ডে তাই আছে এই দেহ ভাণ্ডে (*ya āche brahmāṇḍe tāi āche ei deha bhāṇde*), "whatever is in the universe is in the receptacle of the body," also sometimes framed in negation ("whatever is *not* in the universe is *not* in the body," etc.); see Keith Cantú, "Islamic Esotericism in the Bengali Bāul Songs of Lālan Fakir," *Correspondences* 7, no. 1 (2019): 140–41.

56. BRY, 8. This phrase would occur six years later in Kaviraj Russick Lall Gupta, *Science of Sphygmica or Sage Kanàd on Pulse, An English Translation with Sanskrit Passages* (Calcutta: S.C. Addy, 1891), 47. Here it is mentioned in connection with the "great Rishi-physician Susruta," providing further evidence that the author of this prologue was the same Ambikacharan as the translator of the Bengali edition of *Suśrutasaṃhitā*.

57. BRY, 9–10. Bng.: বুদ্ধি, স্মৃতি, চিত্ত, অহংজ্ঞান ইহাদিগের সমষ্টিকে অন্তঃকরণ-যন্ত্র বলা যায়। এবং চক্ষু, কর্ণ, নাসিকা, জিহবা, ত্বক ইহাদিগকে জ্ঞানেন্দ্রিয়-যন্ত্র বলে। জ্ঞান, যখন অন্তঃকরণ-যন্ত্রে অবস্থিত হইয়া একাগ্রভাবে চিন্তা করিতে থাকে, তখন জ্ঞানেন্দ্রিয়-যন্ত্র সত্ত্বেও বাহ্য পদার্থ জ্ঞানেতে প্রকাশ পায় না, অথবা {১০} প্রকাশ-ভাবের হ্রাস হয়। যখন জ্ঞানেন্দ্রিয়-যন্ত্রের দ্বারা বাহ্য জগতে একাগ্রভাবে সংযোজিত হয়, তখন অন্তঃকরণ যন্ত্রের ক্রিয়া প্রকাশ পায় না, অথবা তাহার ক্রিয়া-শক্তি হ্রাস হইয়া যায়। অতএব জ্ঞান অন্তঃকরণ-যন্ত্রের ও বাহ্য-জ্ঞানেন্দ্রিয়-যন্ত্রের মধ্যে যন্ত্রিত বা বদ্ধ থাকিয়া আকুঞ্চিত ও প্রসারিত হইতেছে (*buddhi, smṛti, citta, ahaṃjñān ihādiger samṣṭike antaḥkaraṇ-yantra balā yāẏ. ebaṃ cakṣu, karṇa, nāsikā, jihbā, tvak ihādigake jñānendriẏa-yantra bale. jñān, yakhan antaḥkaraṇ-yantre abasthita haiẏā ekāgrabhābe cintā karite thāke, takhan jñānendriẏa-yantra sattveo bāhya padārtha jñānete prakāś pāẏ nā, athabā prakāś-bhāber hrās haẏ. yakhan jñānendrīẏa-yantrer dvārā bāhya jagate ekāgrabhābe saṃyojita haẏ, takhan antaḥkaraṇ yantrer kriẏā prakāś pāẏ nā, athabā tāhār*

kriyā-śakti hrās haiẏā yāẏ. ataeba jñān antaḥkaraṇ-yantrer o bāhya-jñānendriẏa-yantrer madhye yantrita bā baddha thākiẏā ākuñcita o prasārita haiteche).

58. This is a Sanskrit verse idiosyncratically rendered in Bengali script: *sarva cintā parityāgānniścinto yoga ucyate*. A double consonant is added after a muted *r* according to traditional orthography (e.g., *sarvva* for *sarva*), which I have mostly omitted from the transliteration.

59. This is also a Bengali rendering of Sanskrit: *yogaścitta-vṛtti nirodhaḥ*, a well-known verse from the second verse of the first *pāda* (*samādhipāda*) of the Pātañjalayogaśāstra; see Patañjali and Philipp André Maas, *Samādhipāda: Das erste Kapitel des Pātañjalayogaśāstra zum ersten Mal kritisch ediert* (Aachen: Shaker, 2006), 4–7 for a critical edition of the Sanskrit text and commentary; and White, *Yoga Sutra of Patanjali*, 10–15, for the various ways this verse has been interpreted and translated.

60. BRY, 13–14. Bng.: জ্ঞানের শক্তি—চিন্তা। চিত্ত-বৃত্তিকেও চিন্তা বলে। চিত্ত, জ্ঞানের একটি অবস্থা বিশেষ। সুতরাং চিন্তা বা চিত্ত-বৃত্তিকে নিঃশেষে বর্জ্জিত করিতে পারিলেই জ্ঞান, শক্তি-বর্জ্জিত হইল। এই চিন্তা বৃত্তি বা চিত্ত-বৃত্তির বর্জ্জনকেই তত্ত্ব-জ্ঞানীরা যোগ বলেন। "সর্ব্ব চিন্তা পরিত্যাগান্নিশ্চিন্তো যোগ উচ্চতে।" গ্রন্থান্তরে "যোগশ্চিত্ত-বৃত্তি নিরোধঃ।" পূর্ব্বে বলা হইয়াছে যে ক্রোধ, মোহ, সুখ, দুঃখ প্রভৃতি অন্তঃকরণের ভাব সমস্ত জ্ঞান-শক্তির বা চিন্তার পরিচালক, এবং ভাব সমূহের পরিচালক, গুণ। শম, দম, উপরতি, তিতিক্ষা, সমাধান এই কয়েকটি যোগাঙ্গ {১৪} অভ্যাসেই অন্তঃকরণের ভাব সমস্ত তিরোহিত হয়। ভাব সমস্ত তিরোহিত হইলে, অভ্যাসের বলে গুণেরও প্রভাব তিরোহিত হইয়া যায়। গুণ-শক্তির প্রভাব রহিতের কৌশল-স্বরূপ রাজযোগ, প্রয়োজনীয় যোগাঙ্গ সমেত এই গ্রন্থে বিশেষ রূপে বর্ণিত হইয়াছে। এই যোগাভ্যাসের চরম ফল সমাধি (*jñāner śakti—cintā. citta-bṛttikeo cintā bale. citta, jñāner ekṭi abasthā biśeṣ. sutarāṃ cintā bā citta-bṛttike niḥśeṣe barjjita karite pārilei jñān, śakti-barjjita haila. ei cintā bṛtti bā citta-bṛttir barjjanke-i tattva-jñānīrā yog balen. 'sarbba cintā parityāgānniścinto yoga ucyate.' granthāntare 'yogaścitta-bṛtti nirodhaḥ.' . . . guṇ-śaktir prabhāb rahiter kauśal-svarūp rājyog, praẏojanīẏa yogāṅga sameta ei granthe biśeṣ rūpe barṇita haiẏāche. ei yogābhyāser caram phal samādhi*).

61. One of the earliest cosmological accounts extant in Bengali is the medieval text *Śūnya Purāṇa*, attributed to one Rāmāi Paṇḍit, which in some of its recensions also included Islamic references.

62. BRY, 15. Bng.: জগৎকে বিরাট্-দেহ বা বিরাট্-যন্ত্র বলা যায়, মানব দেহ বা মানবযন্ত্র তাহার অনুকরণ (*jagatke birāṭ-deha bā birāṭ-yantra balā yāẏ, mānab deha bā mānabyantra tāhār anukaraṇ*).

63. BRY, 15. Bng.: আনখাগ্র দেহকে সচেতন ভাবে প্রকাশ করে (*ānakhāgra dehake sacetan bhābe prakāś kare*).

64. BRY, 16. Bng.: আধুনিক বৈজ্ঞানিকেরা ইহাকে সংকোচ ও প্রসারণ (Contraction and expansion) বলিয়া থাকেন (*ādhunik baijñānikerā ihāke saṃkoc o prasāraṇ* (Contraction and expansion) *baliẏā thāken*).

65. The first quotation refers to a theory of mind developed by Immanuel Kant (1724–1804), for which see Andrew Brook, Julian Wuerth, and Edward N. Zalta, "Kant's View of the Mind and Consciousness of Self," in *The Stanford Encyclopedia of Philosophy*, ed. Edward N. Zalta, Winter 2020 ed., https://plato.stanford.edu/archives/win2020/entries/kant-mind/. The second quotation, by Herbert Spencer (1820–1903), is taken from his *First Principles* (London: Williams and Norgate, 1862), 231.

66. BRY, 17. Bng.: প্রকৃতি-যন্ত্রে অহং-জ্ঞান প্রকাশ হইবামাত্র, সেই অহং-জ্ঞানরূপ গর্ভে জগতের অঙ্কুর-রূপিণী স্মৃতির উদয় হয় (*prakṛti-yantre ahaṃ-jñān prakāś haibāmātra, sei ahaṃ-jñānrūp garbhe jagater aṅkur-rūpiṇī smṛtir. udaẏ haẏ*). On the awakening from *yoganidrā* see

also White, *The Alchemical Body*, 215–16; David Gordon White, "The Yoga of the Mahāyogin: Reflections on Madeleine Biardeau's 'Cosmogonies Purāṇiques,'" unpublished paper.

67. BRY, 17–18.
68. The semantic range of *bāsanā* is broader than erotic "desire" (*kām*). In the songs of Ambikacharan's contemporary Lālan Fakir and among contemporary Bāul fakirs, the term more often connotes what in English would be called the "heart's desire" or "heartfelt purpose" (e.g., *maner bāsanā*).
69. BRY, 18.
70. BRY, 18. Bng.: কোটি কোটি প্রকার ইচ্ছা-রূপিণী শক্তি . . . সৃজন, পোষণ, ধারণ এবং পরিবর্ত্তিত করণ প্রভৃতি ক্রিয়ার দ্বারা এই বিশ্ব-সংসারের ব্যাপার সমস্ত সম্পাদন করিতেছে (*koṭi koṭi prakār icchā-rūpiṇī śakti . . . sṛjan, poṣaṇ, dhāraṇ ebaṃ paribarttita karaṇ prabhṛti kriẏār dvārā ei biśva-saṃsārer byāpār samasta sampādan kariteche*).
71. BRY, 18. Bng.: সেই সকল শক্তি আর্য্যশাস্ত্রে দেবতা বলিয়া বর্ণিত হইয়াছে (*sei sakal śakti āryyaśāstre debatā baliẏā barṇita haiẏāche*).
72. This idea also bears relevance to the idea of "daemons" as shared by a wide variety of cultures, both independently originated and spread via myths and legends, for which see David Gordon White, *Daemons Are Forever: Contacts and Exchanges in the Eurasian Pandemonium* (Chicago: University of Chicago Press, 2021).
73. BRY, 18–19.
74. The verse Sabhapati quotes is 9.17–18 (90–3) in the edition of Franklin Edgerton, which has the following translation:
   I am the father of this world,
   The mother, the establisher, the grandsire,
   The object of knowledge, the purifier, the sacred syllable *om*,
   The verse of praise, the chant, and the sacrificial formula;
   The goal, supporter, lord, witness,
   The dwelling-place, refuge, friend,
   The origin, dissolution, and maintenance,
   The treasure-house, the imperishable seed.

   Transliteration from BRY: "*pitāhamasya jagato mātā dhātā pitāmahaḥ / vedyaṃ pavitra moṅkāra ṛk sāma yajurevaca // gati vartā prabhuḥ sākṣī nivāsaḥ śaraṇaṃ suhṛt / prabhavaḥ pralayaḥ sthānaṃ nidhānaṃ bīja mavyayaṃ.*"
75. This is a Bengali rendering of Sanskrit: *īśvarapraṇidhānād vā*. This is from the twenty-third verse of the first *pāda* (*samādhipāda*) of the Pātañjalayogaśāstra; see Patañjali and Maas, *Samādhipāda*, 34–35. The term *praṇidhāna* can also mean "abstract contemplation" or "great effort" (here for Īśvara), but I have here favored the mention of *abhidhyāna* in the commentary attributed to Vyāsa (which may be Patañjali himself), which refers to a kind of meditative or inner longing.
76. Ambikacharan writes the following (BRY, 21): "If the thought becomes deposited [*praṇihita*, past participle of Skt. *praṇidhāna*] in the Lord, then the thought becomes composed in that self which consists of the knowledge of the cosmos. Yet when the work [*kārya*] of one, namely the inner, has commenced, afterwards there is an equilibrium [*sāmyabhāb*] of external and internal knowledge. When the work of the

other, the external, has commenced, then afterwards one will, either gradually or in another life, receive an equilibrium of internal and external knowledge." Bng.: ঈশ্বরে চিত্ত প্রণিহিত হইলে, বিরাটের জ্ঞানময় আত্মাতে চিত্ত সমাহিত হয়। তবে একটির কার্য্য অন্তরে আরব্ধ হইয়া পরে বাহ্য ও অন্তরে জ্ঞানের সাম্যভাব হয়। অপরটির কার্য্য বাহিরে আরব্ধ হইয়া ক্রমশঃ বা জন্মান্তরে অন্তরে ও বাহ্যে জ্ঞান সাম্যভাব প্রাপ্ত হয় (*īśvare citta praṇihita haile, birāṭer jñānmaẏ ātmāte citta samāhita haẏ. tabe ekṭir kāryya antare ārabdha haiẏā pare bāhya o antare jñāner sāmyabhāb haẏ. aparṭir kāryya bāhire ārabdha haiẏā kramaśaḥ bā janmāntare antare o bāhye jñān sāmyabhāb prāpta haẏ*).

77. The Bhagavad Gita is technically not an Upanishad, but here is probably referred to as one on account of its religious and philosophical importance, or perceived resemblance thereto. The Bhagavad Gita forms part of the Mahabharata epic, although scholars do continue to debate whether it was composed contemporaneously with the rest of the epic or added later.
78. For the latter see Barbara A. Holdrege, *Bhakti and Embodiment: Fashioning Divine Bodies and Devotional Bodies in Kṛṣṇa Bhakti* (New York: Routledge, 2015).
79. BRY, 21. Bng.: তত্ত্বজ্ঞানী যোগীগণ মানব-যন্ত্র ও বিরাট যন্ত্রের প্রকৃতি বিজ্ঞান-দৃষ্টিতে পর্য্যালোচনা করিয়া সেই সকল প্রণালী অবধারণ করিয়াছেন। বলিয়াই তাঁহাদিগের মত বিজ্ঞান সঙ্গত সুতরাং অভ্রান্ত বলা যায়। এবং তাঁহাদিগের নির্ণীত আচার ব্যবহার প্রভৃতি সমাজ প্রণালীও সেই বৈজ্ঞানিক ধর্ম্মের অনুকূল (*tattvajñānī yogīgaṇ mānab-yantra o birāṭ yantrer prakṛti bijñān-dṛṣṭite paryyālocanā kariẏā sei sakal praṇālī abadhāraṇ kariẏāchen. baliẏāi tãhādiger mat bijñān saṅgata sutarāṃ abhrānta balā yāẏ. ebaṃ tãhādiger nirṇīta ācār byabahār prabhṛti samāj praṇālīo sei baijñānik dharmmer anukūl*).
80. BRY, 22.
81. This quotation is in Spencer, *First Principles*, 108.
82. This quote is in ibid., 109.
83. BRY, 22–23. English and Bng.: "H. Spencer মহাশয় বলেন যে ধর্ম্ম ও বিজ্ঞান সামঞ্জস্যভাবে থাকা উচিত। বিজ্ঞান অতিক্রম করিয়া ধর্ম্ম থাকিতে পারে না। তদ্বিষয়ে তাঁহার মত এইরূপ (H. Spencer *mahāśaẏ balen ye dharmma o bijñān sāmañjasyabhābe thākā ucit. bijñān atikram kariẏā dharmma thākite pāre nā. tadviṣaẏe tãhār mat eirūp*)—Thus the consciousness of an inscrutable power manifested to us through all phenomena, has been growing ever clearer; and must eventually be freed from its imperfections. The certainty that on the one hand such a power exists, while on the other hand its nature transcends intuition and is beyond imagination, is the certainty toward which intelligence has from the first been progressing. At this conclusion science inevitably arrives as it reaches its confines; while to this conclusion Religion is irresistably driven by criticism. এই উক্তির দ্বারা এই অভিপ্রায় প্রকাশ পাইতেছে যে জগৎ প্রকাশক অচিন্ত্য-শক্তি দুর্জ্ঞেয়, ইহাকে দুর্জ্ঞেয় বলিয়া সিদ্ধান্ত করা, ধর্ম্ম এবং বিজ্ঞান উভয়েরই কর্ত্তব্য। পরে অন্যত্র বলিয়াছেন (*ei uktir dvārā ei abhiprāẏ prakāś pāiteche ye jagat prakāśak acintya-śakti durjñeẏa, ihāke durjñeẏa baliẏā siddhānta karā, dharmma ebaṃ bijñāna ubhaẏer-i karttabya pare anyatra baliẏāchen*), Is it not just possible that there is a mode of Being transcending Intelligence and will, as these transcend mechanical motion? It is true that we are totally unable to conceive any such higher mode of being, but this is not a reason for questioning its existence, it is rather the reverse. Have we not seen how utterly incompetent our minds are to form even an approach to a conception of that which underlies all phenomena? Is it not proved that this incompetency is the incompetency of the conditioned to grasp the unconditioned? এস্থলে

এই অভিপ্রায় প্রকাশ পাইতেছে যে, যে বুদ্ধির অতীত বস্তু নামরূপ-বিশিষ্ট জগৎ পদার্থের উপাদান হইয়াছেন তিনি সর্ব্বাবস্থার অতীত বলিয়া আমাদিগের (যন্ত্রিত) অবস্থাপন্ন জ্ঞানশক্তি তাঁহাকে ধারণা করিতে পারে না (*esthale ei abhiprāẏ prakāś pāiteche ye, ye buddhir atīta bastu nāmrūp-biśiṣṭa jagat padārther upādān haiẏāchen tini sarbbābasthār atīta baliẏā āmādiger (yantrita) abasthāpanna jñānśakti tãhāke dhāraṇā karite pāre nā*).

84. This quotation, attributed to Henry Longueville Mansel (1820–1871), was referenced in Spencer, *First Principles*, 87, which is likely where Ambikacharan read it. It was published in Henry Longueville Mansel, *The Limits of Religious Thought Examined in Eight Lectures, Preached before the University of Oxford, in the Year M.DCCC.LVIII*, 4th ed. (London: John Murray, 1859), 63 (in Lecture III).
85. The phrase *svayaṃ pūrṇa* can also be translated as "complete-in-itself."
86. BRY, 24. English and Bng.: সর্ব্বাবস্থার অতীত, জগতের উপাদান স্বরূপ সেই নিত্য বস্তুর, স্বরূপ নির্ণয় সম্বন্ধে Mr. Mansel এইরূপ বলিয়াছেন (*sarbbābasthār atīta, jater upādān svarūp sei nitya bastur, svarūp nirṇaẏ sambandhe* Mr. Mansel *eirūp baliẏāchen*)—"The absolute and infinite are thus like the inconceivable and imperceptible, names indicating, not an object of thought or consciousness at all, but mere absence of the conditions under which consciousness is possible." ইহাতে এইরূপ অভিপ্রায় প্রকাশ করিতেছেন যে স্বয়ং পুর্ণ অনন্ত, এই নামই জ্ঞান বা চিন্তার অতীত। কেবল যেরূপ অবস্থাপন্ন বা ভাবাপন্ন হইলে জ্ঞান শক্তির ক্রিয়া হয়, সেই অবস্থার বা ভাবের অভাব মাত্র (*ihāte eirūp abhiprāẏ prakāś karitechen ye svaẏaṃ pūrṇa ananta, ei nām-i jñān bā cintār atīta. kebal yerūp abasthāpanna bā bhābāpanna haile jñān śaktir kriẏā haẏ, sei abasthār bā bhāber abhāb mātra*).
87. BRY, 29.
88. This quote, attributed to Hamilton, was referenced in Spencer, *First Principles*, 75, 87, and 91–92, which is also likely where Ambikacharan read it. The ideas are found expressed in his "Refutation of the Various Doctrines of the Unconditioned, Especially of Cousin's Doctrine of the Infinito-Absolute," first published in the *Edinburg Review* for October 1829; see O. W. Wight, *Philosophy of Sir William Hamilton, Bart*, 3rd ed. (New York: D. Appleton, 1855), 441–83.
89. This quotation is in Spencer, *First Principles*, 96.
90. Ibid.
91. This passage presents some ambiguity in translation. What Ambikacharan appears to be saying is that both he and Western scientists agree that knowledge can be distinguished from the state of the ego, but that the difference is *how* it is distinct; Ambikacharan views the ego as the conductor (*paricālak*) of knowledge and therefore separate, while (in his view) Spencer and Mansel would see the state of the ego as separate on account of its emergence concurrently within the thought processes of knowledge itself.
92. BRY, 24–25. English and Bng. "Mr. Spencer বলেন [*balen*, Bng. "says"] our consciousness, of the unconditioned, being literally the unconditioned consciousness, or raw material of thought, to which in thinking we give definite forms, it follows that an ever present sense of real existence is the very basis of our intelligence.

    অভিপ্রায় এই যে, জ্ঞান, সকল ভাব বর্জ্জিত হইলে যে অবস্থাপন্ন হয় তাহাই ভাবাতীত বস্তুর জ্ঞান বলা যায়। এস্থলে দ্বিতীয় consciousness শব্দের এইরূপ অর্থ করা হইয়াছে যথা — স্বয়ং-জ্ঞান, চিন্তার উপাদান, অর্থাৎ চিন্তা করিবার কালে আমরা যাহাকে বিশেষ বিশেষ আকারে পরিণত করি। ইহাতে সিদ্ধান্ত হইতেছে যে আমাদিগের জ্ঞান-শক্তির অভ্যন্তরে

প্রকৃত সত্তার অনুভুতি নিত্য বর্ত্তমান রহিয়াছে। ইতিপুর্ব্বে প্রদর্শন করা হইয়াছে যে Spencer মহাশয় বলেন যে "to which in thinking we give definite forms" অর্থাৎ চিন্তাকালে আমরা যাহাকে (জ্ঞানকে) বিশেষ আকার প্রদান করি। "আমরা" শব্দটি অহং ভাবের জ্ঞাপক। পুর্ব্বোক্ত উক্তি স্বীকার করিলে অহংভাব জ্ঞানের পরিচালক, সুতরাং জ্ঞান অপেক্ষা ভিন্নসত্তা-বিশিষ্ট কিছু বলিয়া স্বীকার করিতে হয়। কিন্তু Mr. Spencer ও Mr. Mansel প্রভৃতি অনেকেই একবাক্যে স্বীকার করিয়াছেন যে অহংভাব জ্ঞানেতে প্রকাশ পায়, সুতরাং জ্ঞানের অবস্থা বা ভাব বিশেষ। অতএব পুর্ব্বের উক্তিটি অসংলগ্ন হইতেছে। এরূপ উক্তির কারণ কেবল অনুভুতির স্থিরতার অভাব (*abhiprāẏ ei ye, jñān, sakal bhāb barjjita haile ye abasthāpanna haẏ tāhāi bhābātīta bastur jñān balā yāẏ. esthale dvitīẏa* consciousness *śabder eirūp artha karā haiẏāche yathā—svaẏaṃ-jñān, cintār upādān, arthāt cintā karibār kāle āmrā yāhāke biśeṣ biśeṣ ākāre pariṇata kari. ihāte siddhānta haiteche ye āmādiger jñān-śaktir abhyantare prakṛta sattār anubhūti nitya barttamān rahiẏāche. itipūrbbe pradarśan karā haiẏāche ye* Spencer *mahāśaẏ balen ye* "to which in thinking we given definite forms" *arthāt cintākāle āmrā yāhāke (jñānke) biśeṣ ākār pradān kari, "āmrā" śabdaṭi ahaṃ bhāber jñāpak. pūrbbokta ukti svīkār karile ahaṃbhāb jñāner paricālak, sutarāṃ jñān apekṣā bhinnasattā-biśiṣṭa kichu baliẏā svīkār karite haẏ. kintu* Mr. Spencer *o* Mr. Mansel *prabhṛti anekei ekbākye svīkār kariẏāchen ye ahaṃbhāb jñānete prakāś pāẏ, sutarāṃ jñāner abasthā bā bhāb biśeṣ. ataeba pūrbber uktiṭi asaṃlagna haiteche. erūp uktir kāraṇ kebal anubhūtir sthiratār abhāb*).

93. This quotation is in Spencer, *First Principles*, 65–66.
94. BRY, 26. Bng. "*ubhaẏei āryya-tattvajñān-sammata prakṛta kathāi balilen, ye ātmāke jānite gele jñān o jñātā, pramātā o prameẏa, ei ubhaẏ bhāb-i dhvaṃsa haẏ.*"
95. BRY, 26.
96. This is related to what Merleau-Ponty called a "phenomenology of perception"; see Maurice Merleau-Ponty, *Phénoménologie de la perception* (Paris: Librairie Gallimard, 1945).
97. BRY, 27. Bng.: শক্তির দ্বারা হইয়াই প্রমাতা প্রমেয় প্রমাণ, বা জ্ঞাতা জ্ঞেয় জ্ঞান, বা কর্ত্তা কর্ম্ম ও ক্রিয়া, জ্ঞান এই তিন ভাবে প্রকাশ পায়। যদ্দ্বারা প্রমাতা প্রমেয়-সম্বন্ধে প্রমাতা-স্বরূপে প্রকাশ পায়, এবং যদ্দ্বারা প্রমেয় প্রমাতা-সম্বন্ধে প্রমেয়-স্বরূপে প্রকাশ পায়, তাহাকে প্রমাণ বলা যায়। অর্থাৎ জ্ঞাতা এবং জ্ঞেয় এই দুইটি মাত্র ভাবই যে জ্ঞানে প্রকাশ পায় এমত নহে। জ্ঞাতা এবং জ্ঞেয় যে সম্বন্ধ-সুত্রে পরস্পর গ্রথিত, সেই ক্রিয়ারূপ সম্বন্ধ-সুত্রও জ্ঞানে প্রকাশ পায় অর্থাৎ জ্ঞেয় বস্তু যদি দর্শনের বিষয় হয়। তাহা হইলে জ্ঞান দর্শন-ক্রিয়ার ভাব ধারণ করিয়া জ্ঞেয় বস্তুকে জ্ঞাতার সম্বন্ধে প্রকাশ করে। যদি শ্রবণের বিষয় হয়, তবে জ্ঞান শ্রবণ-ক্রিয়ার ভাব ধারণ করিয়া জ্ঞেয় বস্তুকে প্রকাশ করে (*śaktir dvārā haiẏāi pramātā prameẏa pramāṇ, bā jñātā jñeẏa jñān, bā karttā karmma o kriẏā jñān ei tin bhābe prakāś pāẏ. yaddvārā pramātā prameẏa-sambandhe prāmātā-svarūpe prakāś pāẏ, ebaṃ yaddvārā prameẏa pramātā-sambandhe prameẏa-svarūpe prakāś pāẏ, tāhāke pramāṇ balā yāẏ. arthāt jñātā ebaṃ jñeẏa ei duiṭi mātra bhāb-i ye jñāne prakāś pāẏ emata nahe. jñātā ebaṃ jñeẏa ye sambandha-sūtre paraspar grathita, sei kriẏārūp sambandha-sūtra-o jñāne prakāś pāẏ arthāt jñeẏa bastu yadi darśaner biṣaẏ haẏ. tāhā haile jñān darśan-kriẏār bhāb dhāraṇ kariẏā jñeẏa bastuke jñātār sambandhe prakāś kare. yadi śrabaṇer biṣaẏ haẏ, tabe jñān śrabaṇ-kriẏār bhāb dhāraṇ kariẏā jñeẏa bastuke prakāś kare*).
98. These are also categories salient in Tamil discourses on Śaiva Siddhānta and present in the main body Sabhapati Swami's work (see Chapter 3).
99. BRY, 28. Bng.: পাশ্চাত্য পণ্ডিতগণ এই ভাব ধারণা করিতে সমর্থ হন নাই। তাঁহারা ইচ্ছা-শক্তির প্রভাবে প্রমাতা ও প্রমেয় ভাবকে সহসা বর্জ্জন পুর্ব্বক অন্তরে অনুভব করিতে প্রবৃত্ত হইলে, প্রমাতা প্রমেয়ের ভাব বর্জ্জিত হইল বটে, কিন্তু যে শক্তি-দ্বারা চালিত হইয়া জ্ঞান এই ভাব ধারণ করে, সেই শক্তির বেগ এক কালে নিবৃত্ত হইল না (*pāścātya paṇḍitgaṇ*

ei bhāb dhāraṇā karite samartha han nāi. tāhārā icchā-śaktir prabhābe pramātā o prameẏa bhābke sahasā barjjan pūrbbak antare anubhab karite prabṛtta haile, pramātā prameẏer bhāb barjjita haila baṭe, kintu ye śakti-dvārā cālita haiẏā jñān ei bhāb dhāraṇ kare, sei śaktir beg ek kāle nibṛtta haila nā).

100. BRY, 28. Bng.: জ্ঞানের যন্ত্রিত অবস্থাই জীবের বন্ধন। শক্তির বেগ এক কালে নিবৃত্ত করিয়া জ্ঞানকে যন্ত্রিত অবস্থা হইতে মোচন করিতে {২৯} পারিলে, তবে সেই জ্ঞানে নির্ম্মল নিশ্চল নিত্য ভাবের উদয় হয়। পাশ্চাত্য পণ্ডিতগণ যে negation of thought অর্থাৎ চিন্তা বৃত্তির অভাবই তাহার উপায় বলিয়া উল্লেখ করিয়াছেন, আর্য্যতত্ত্বজ্ঞানীগণও সেই অভিপ্রায়ে চিত্তবৃত্তি নিরোধের উপদেশ দিয়েছেন। কিন্তু তাহা সহসা হইতে পারে না — অভ্যাস ও কৌশল প্রয়োজন। সেই কৌশল — যোগ। তাহা কেবল আর্য্যতত্ত্ব জ্ঞানিরাই জানেন (*jñāner yantrita abasthāi jīber bandhan. śaktir beg ek kāle nibṛtta kariẏā jñānke yantrita abasthā haite mocan karite pārile, tabe sei jñāne nirmmal niścal nitya bhāber udaẏ haẏ. pāścātya paṇḍitgaṇ ye* negation of thought *arthāt cintā bṛttir abhāb-i tāhār upāẏ baliẏā ullekh kariẏāchen, āryyatattvajñānīgaṇ-o sei abhiprāẏe cittabṛtti nirodher upadeś diẏechen. kintu tāhā sahasā haite pāre nā—abhyās o kauśal praẏojan. sei kauśal—yog. tāhā kebal āryyatattva jñānirāi jānen*).

101. On the Theosophical reception of science see Chajes, *Recycled Lives*; For Crowley see Egil Asprem, "Magic Naturalized? Negotiating Science and Occult Experience in Aleister Crowley's Scientific Illuminism," *Aries* 8 (2008): 139–65.

7
Magical Fruits of Occult Yoga

I happened to pay a visit to Madame Blavatsky and Colonel Olcott. I remained with them from 8 A. M. to 4 P. M. of the 8th November 1880. I had a long conversation with them on the theory and practice of ancient occult sciences (*Sarva Sidhoo Shastras*), and on the *Vedantic Giyana Yog Shastras i.e.*, the science of holding communion with one's Self Impersonal God—The Infinite Spirit.

—Sabhapaty Swamy, *The Amrita Bazar Patrika*, November 16, 1880

Now let a current of light, deep azure flecked with scarlet, pass up and down the spine, striking as it were upon thyself that art coiled at the base as a serpent.

—Aleister Crowley, "SSS" in *Liber HHH* (1911)

The tree of Śivarājayoga, to continue the metaphor, started to bear strange kinds of fruit as it spread to occult mediators who, for a variety of reasons, became fascinated with Sabhapati Swami's techniques of yoga. In this final chapter I summarize how Sabhapati's works were interpreted in these milieus of modern occultism and related currents at the turn of the twentieth century.[1] As I have already treated in the first chapter, Sabhapati met with Helena P. Blavatsky (1831–1891) and Henry S. Olcott (1832–1907), the founding members of the Theosophical Society, during his lifetime, although there is no evidence that Sabhapati himself joined the society. Other occultists, the most notable of which are Franz Hartmann (1838–1912), Aleister Crowley (1875–1947), and the mental healer and charlatan William Estep (1896–1967) a generation later, do not appear to have met Sabhapati physically yet continued to engage his work both during his lifetime and in subsequent decades.[2] In a strange case of circularity, Sabhapati's own student Om Prakash Swamigal even joined the Latent Light Culture, an Indian occult society known for integrating Aleister Crowley's teachings on Thelema, the organizational structure of Freemasonry, and methods of New Thought. In this chapter I treat these engagements in turn so as to stress the specificity of each

Like a Tree Universally Spread. Keith Edward Cantú, Oxford University Press. © Oxford University Press 2023.
DOI: 10.1093/oso/9780197665473.003.0008

interaction; though all of these figures had ties to occultism as construed generally, their motivations and the way they approached Sabhapati's literature were all quite different.

Lingering in the background behind this discussion is the specter of Orientalism, or in this context the exoticization of various aspects of Indian teachings, including yoga, ultimately for the political purposes of paving the way for colonial rule and expansion. As I have already treated in a separate chapter and also emphasize in the sections that follow, however, the reception history of Sabhapati Swami's literature is somewhat complicated by the fact that a primary intent of some occult authors—at least as explicitly stated—was to learn and disseminate techniques that were deemed objectively efficacious, and not to intentionally exoticize or inscribe difference.[3] This is perhaps most exemplified by the negative attitude toward "Oriental" fascination with yoga in Crowley's *Eight Lectures on Yoga*, who humorously stated the following:

> There is more nonsense talked and written about Yoga than about anything else in the world. Most of this nonsense, which is fostered by charlatans, is based upon the idea that there is something mysterious and Oriental about it. There isn't. Do not look to me for obelisks and odalisques, rahat loucoum, bul-buls, or any other tinsel imagery of the Yoga-mongers. I am neat but not gaudy. There is nothing mysterious or Oriental about anything, as everybody knows who has spent a little time intelligently in the continents of Asia and Africa. I propose to invoke the most remote and elusive of all Gods to throw clear light upon the subject—the light of common sense.[4]

Statements like this one by Crowley demonstrate that not all authors on yoga partook in the same Orientalist project—if they partook in Orientalism at all. Perhaps it is therefore more useful to speak of several "Orientalisms," not all of which are necessarily negative, thus discursively distinguishing: the political "Orientalism" of Edward Said from the mystical pole-star "Orientalism" of Henry Corbin;[5] the "Orientalism" of Indologists as examined by David Smith;[6] "Theosophical Orientalism" as analyzed by Karl Baier, Wouter Hanegraaf, and Christopher Partridge;[7] and perhaps even a thelemic "Orientalism" that also partakes in a kind of period-specific "anti-Orientalism" (as evident by Crowley's comments). As a result of these wide and often discordant valences of the term Orientalism, an alternative approach that I favor is to see the integration and appropriation of Sabhapati's teachings by occultists as part of a broader and more context-specific phenomenon of "translocalization" (see introduction).

Sabhapati and Theosophy

The Theosophical "founders" Blavatsky and Olcott, along with other prominent supporters such as William Quan Judge (1851–1896), held a public meeting to establish the Theosophical Society at Blavatsky's New York apartment in 1875. Both Blavatsky and Olcott arrived in Bombay (today Mumbai) a few years later, on February 16, 1879.[8] As I have already treated in Chapter 1, Olcott recorded that he and Blavatsky met Sri Sabhapati Swami on November 8, 1880, in Lahore after each one individually had delivered an address to the same crowd the previous day, on the occasion of the third anniversary of the Arya Samaj in Lahore, a branch of the reformist society founded by Dayananda Saraswati (Dayānanda Sarasvatī, 1824–1883).[9] However, soon after Olcott and Blavatsky met Sabhapati they had a falling out over his description of a vision, first mentioned in the Ur-account, of flying to visit Mahādeva on Mount Kailāsa. While there is no evidence that he himself joined the Theosophical Society, Sabhapati by all indications retained positive feelings for Blavatsky and Olcott and even published a letter in the newspaper *Amrita Bazar Patrika* that spoke highly of the meeting and of Blavatsky in particular. He also later appeared as a significant figure in early Theosophy via a translation into German by the occult author Franz Hartmann (see the following section), and to a much lesser extent via a translation of portions of his biographical account into French by the president of Le Disciple Branch of the Theosophical Society in Paris, Paul Gillard (d. 1901).[10]

Olcott at least initially engaged Sabhapati's work positively, and it is notable that the only surviving copy of the first edition of Sabhapati's published lectures (VRY1) was Olcott's personal copy and bears his signature. He appears to have been especially interested in Sabhapati's diagram of the *liṅgaśarīra* (see Chapter 5), and perhaps most notably makes the explicit connection between this visual diagram and the Theosophical interest in the astral "projection of the double":

> Look, if you please, at this engraving. It is from a little work published two years ago at Lahore by Sabhapathy Swami. It represents the system of psychic

development, by *Raj Yoga*. Here is traced a series of lines and circles upon the naked body of a man sitting in the posture of *Padmásan*, and practicing *Yoga*. The triple line passes down the front of the head and body, making the circles at certain points—*viz.*, over the *vomer*, or nasal cavity, the mouth, the root of the throat, the heart, the umbilicus and the spleen. The artist, to bring the whole system into one view, traces for us the parts of the line and circles that would be out of sight, such as that over the lower end of the spinal column, the line of the spine, and over the cerebellum and cerebrum, until it unites with the front line. This is the line travelled by the will of the *Yogi* in his process of psychic development. He, as it were, visits each of the centres of vital force in turn, and subjugates them to dependence upon the will. The circles are the *chakras*, or centres of forces, and when he has traversed the entire circuit of his corporeal kingdom, he will have perfectly evolved his inner self—disengaged it from its natural state of commixture with the outer shell, or physical self. His next step is to project this "double" outside the body, transferring to it his complete consciousness, and then, having passed the threshold of his carnal prison-house, into the world of psychic freedom, his powers of sight, hearing, and other senses are indefinitely increased, and his movements no longer trammelled by the obstacles which impede those of the external man. Do not understand me as saying that this is the only method of psychic evolution; there are others than Patanjali's, and some better ones.[11]

While Olcott seems to conflate Sabhapati's method of yoga with Pātañjalayoga (see Chapter 4 for notable differences), it is important that he brings up the idea of projecting a "double" outside the body. We know that the cultivation of such techniques was a main priority of the early Theosophical Society, and as we shall see the author Franz Hartmann also engaged this question.[12]

Despite this interest in Sabhapati's subtle physiology and techniques of "divine pilgrimage," he remained skeptical, and a response to Olcott's rejection of Sabhapati can be traced in later editions of Sabhapati's works. As mentioned in chapter 1, reprints of his 1880 work adds the following editorial note, presumably written by Basu, in the part of Sabhapati's account that mentions this vision:

> This need not have been in the *physical* body of the Rishis; they might have flown towards the holy mountain in their *Mayavi Rupa Kama Rupa* [*sic*] (astral body), which to our author (who certainly is not an Adept in the sense the Theosophists use the word) must have been as real as if he had travelled through air in his physical body.[13]

A second note also adjusts the identities of the Rishies (Skt. *ṛṣi*), who are changed from sages of the Mahabharata epic to "Brothers of the Theosophical Society."[14] The Bengali translation of the account of Sabhapati's vision (BRY) appears to emphasize that Sabhapati was describing a state of samādhi and not a physical flight.

This commotion over his vision did not daunt Sabhapati, who appeared content to continue his work with new networks of students (as stated previously) outside the aegis of the Theosophical Society. At the same time, he also continued for at least a decade to "persuade all his disciples to join the Theosophical Society,"[15] despite the fact, as previously mentioned, that there is no record of Sabhapati himself ever joining. Olcott for his part continued to maintain a skeptical distance from Sabhapati for the remainder of his life and discouraged people from "running after Yogis, Gurus, and Hermetic Brotherhoods of sorts," also noting that "while it is kind of [Sabhapati] to advise people to join the Theosophical Society, I should like to see his credentials before undertaking to believe that he ever went into or came out of Agasthya's Ashrum."[16] The invoking of "Hermetic Brotherhoods" by Olcott in connection with Sabhapati is intriguing since that is language that Sabhapati never himself used to describe his "meditation halls," or his networks of yogis (Skt. *yogīs*, < stem *yogin*). Olcott was likely referencing his awareness of the fact that Sabhapati's work was also starting to circulate among the leadership of the Hermetic Brotherhood of Luxor.[17]

Sabhapati largely disappeared from subsequent Theosophical discourse in the twentieth century, and there is no record of popular later authors such as Annie Besant (1847–1933) and C. W. Leadbeater (1854–1934) engaging his work to any significant extent, although Besant did refer to Agastya, which may have been inspired by Sabhapati's reverence for the same (see Chapter 1). Despite this absence from most of Theosophy's subsequent history, his work today continues to be engaged by contemporary Theosophists on account of its teachings on the cakras (< Skt. *cakra*, "wheel") and relevance to discourses on the aforementioned phenomenon of "astral projection."[18]

Franz Hartmann and Sabhapati in German Translation

Despite Sabhapati's disappearance from the mainstream of Theosophical literature, he did appear as a significant figure in German-speaking Theosophical circles via a translation by the Bavarian occult author and

"Wild West" doctor Franz Hartmann (1838–1912), an enigmatic author who translated most of VRY2 into German (FH1, FH2) and published it near the end of his life.[19] Hartmann led a colorful life and traveled widely, from Mexico to Texas and Colorado, from Germany and Austria to Adyar, Chennai in India. Hartmann's work is also one of the first to partake in a broader trend during this period of perceiving an identity between yoga and ritual magic, and he published widely on both topics.[20] Specifically, one of his views was an equation respectively between rāja yoga (German *Radscha Yoga*), haṭha yoga, and Tantra on the one hand and German terms for "white magic" (*weiße Magie*), "black magic" (*schwarze Magie*) and "sorcery" (*Hexerei*) on the other hand.[21]

There are at least two notable features of Hartmann's engagement with Sabhapati, whom he does not appear to have met, but whose works he probably first encountered during his stay in Adyar or by reading *The Theosophist*. First is his willingness to translate what we have seen (see Chapter 5) in the caption of Sabhapati's first diagram (*liṅgaśarīra*, lit "mark(ed) body") as *Astralkörper*, "the Astral Body" (see Figure 7.1). As I have previously mentioned, this reflects an early priority among members of the Theosophical Society—including Henry Olcott himself—to see comparable techniques of astral projection in Indian methods of yoga.[22] As we see from subsequent reprints of Hartmann's translation by the Theosophical Society, however, a curious note was added to clarify that this must have been Hartmann's guarded interpretation, omitting the fact that Olcott also made a similar assertion. The note reads as follows: "Franz Hartmann in some places intentionally confused the terms 'Etheric' and 'Astral Body' since he had qualms about publishing the mystery of the Etheric Body too early."[23] Assumed differences between the "Etheric" and "Astral" bodies would continue to be formulated in later Theosophical discourses on the subtle body in the Esoteric Section, which could have been what the note refers to.

A second interesting point of engagement is Franz Hartmann's own notes that he interspersed throughout Sabhapati's text, which provide a window into how Hartmann as a reader engaged Sabhapati's ideas and literature. For example, he cites authorities as varied as H. P. Blavatsky,[24] the Bhagavad Gita,[25] the Upanishads,[26] the biblical gospels of John,[27] Matthew,[28] Luke,[29] the *Tattvabodha*,[30] the Christian mystic Meister Eckhart,[31] Jakob Böhme,[32] and Swami Vivekananda.[33] The diversity of Hartmann's references speaks to his interpretive frame and also the ability of occultists to connect disparate ideas to a certain trajectory that was intended to overcome polarization into

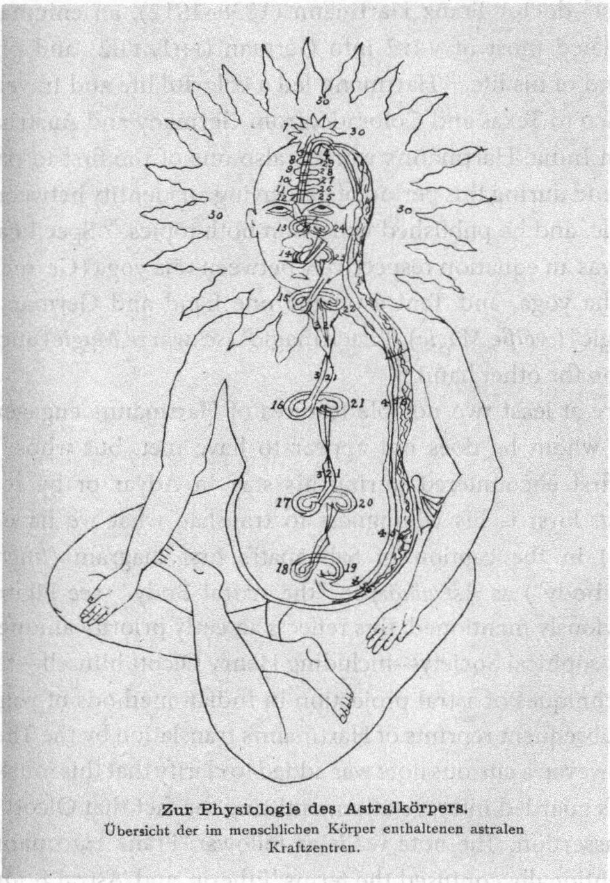

Figure 7.1 "Zur Physiologie des Astralkörpers," published in the first edition of Franz Hartmann's work (FH1) and prompting a later note by Theosophical publishers to stress a distinction between the "etheric" and "astral" bodies. Scan by the author.

one religion or another; this was and still is, after all, one of the main projects of the Theosophical Society.

Sabhapati and Thelemic "Magick"

The continuing practice of certain aspects of Sabhapati's yoga has perhaps most tangibly survived in another occult current that is historically related but nevertheless distinct from that of Theosophy and the works of Franz Hartmann, however. This current is Thelema, a modern religio-philosophical tradition inseparable from its founding "prophet," prolific occult author, and polymath Aleister Crowley (see Figure 7.2).[34] Crowley's engagement of Sabhapati's works has been ignored to date apart from what I have summarized in a recent chapter containing some of the information

Figure 7.2 A portrait of Aleister Crowley published in *The Rites of Eleusis* (1910), likely depicting a *yoni* on account of Crowley being framed by a "vesica piscis," a shape he consciously employed and wrote about in his works. Photo by the author of a copy held in the Adyar Library and Research Centre.

that follows in expanded form.[35] Like Hartmann, Crowley also was an instrumental figure in promoting a perceived identity between yoga and ceremonial or ritual magic.[36] His views were additionally an important turning point for European and North American discourses on the so-called "subtle body" subsequent to Theosophy.[37]

Deeply invested in the idea of the *liṅga* as a cosmic phallus and *yoni* as a cosmic "kteis" (understood as the female "phallus"), Crowley attracted controversy by experimenting with their interplay—both mentally and physically, depending on the context—in the ritual meditations and experimental ceremonies he helped to craft. These ceremonies and ritual meditations combined a variety of sources outside of yoga, including Greek, Egyptian, and Latin medieval and early modern magic, and some were optionally to be engaged in while experimenting with alcohol or mind-altering drugs.[38] At least two of Crowley's meditations (including the third chapter in *Liber HHH*, entitled "SSS") were directly inspired by Sabhapati Swami, but as will be shown, these meditations included additional content that cannot be fully understood by recourse to yogic teachings alone.

The reverse is also true, however, and Sabhapati's teachings on the *liṅga* form an integrated part of Crowley's broader theory of magical practice. For example, Crowley's more advanced magical techniques included a ritual construction of a pyramid, in some places identified with the phallus (i.e., *liṅga*), around the directional quarters of the magician's place of working. This idea is present in several ritual contexts, including an illustrated initiatory ritual entitled *Liber DCLXXI vel Pyramidos*, subtitled *A Ritual of Self-Initiation based upon the Formula of the Neophyte* (cf. this ritual's mention at the bottom of Figure 7.3).[39] Another place where this construction of a pyramid is alluded to is his annotations to the preliminary invocation of *Goetia*, itself part of the *Lemegeton*, a text of Solomonic magic containing five books and dating from at least the seventeenth century CE.[40] Crowley's own preliminary invocation was not however from *The Goetia* but from a creative adaptation of a Greco-Egyptian exorcism rite entitled "The Stele of Jeu the hieroglyphist in his letter" (Betz's translation).[41] While on a historical level this is all far afield from Sabhapati Swami's yoga, a central connection is Crowley's linking of the pyramid with the erect phallus, or *liṅga*.[42] In other words, the ritual construction of the pyramid, which itself forms part of one method of invoking one's personal daimon or Holy Guardian Angel as derived from a ritual operation in the *Book of Abramelin* that was later expanded upon by Crowley, is also connected to the practice

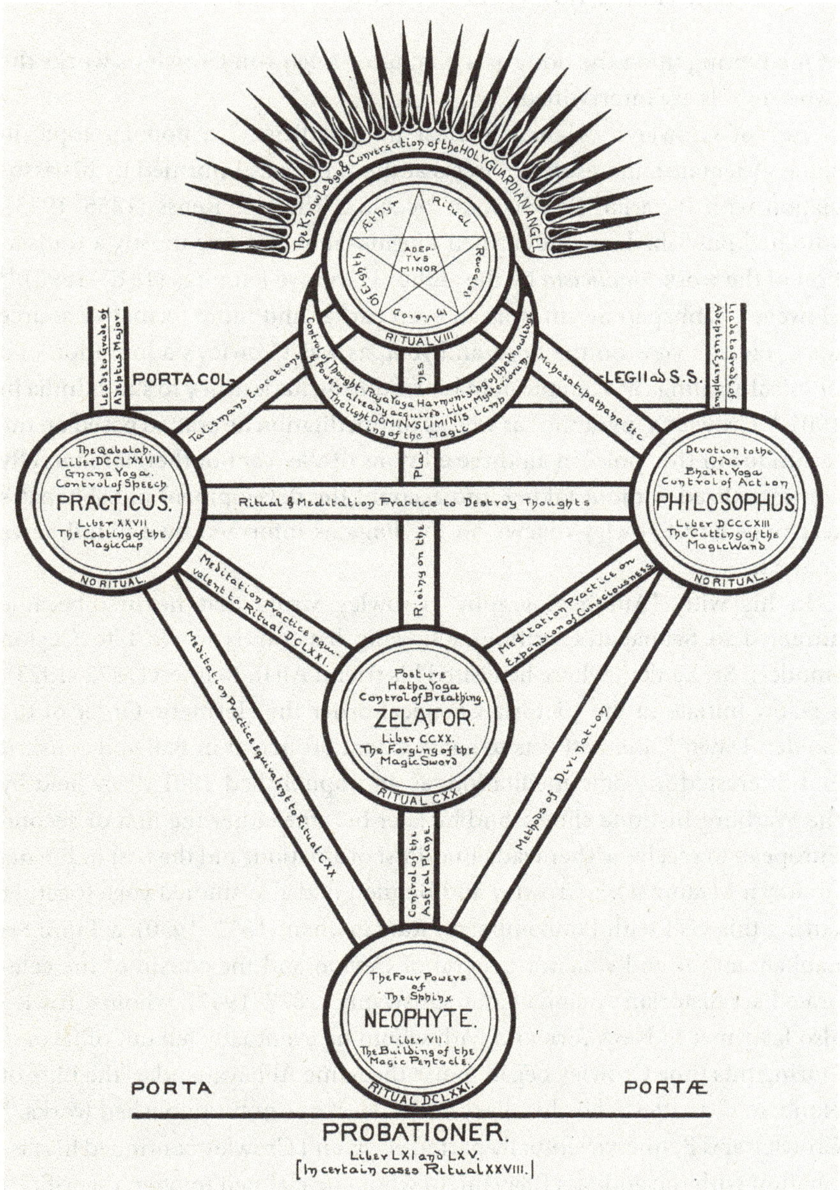

Figure 7.3 A diagram from "Liber XIII" (1910) in *The Equinox* that includes the lower degrees of A.·.A.·., which culminate in the "Knowledge and Conversation of the Holy Guardian Angel." One of two meditations related to Sabhapati's Śivarājayoga (*Liber HHH, SSS*) is part of the task of the Zelator, the *sefira* also attributed to haṭha yoga and the "Forging of the Magic Sword." Several of the other yoga categories appear to derive from Crowley's engagement with Swami Vivekananda's work. From a high-definition scan uploaded by Scott Wilde (used with permission, image in public domain).

of meditating upon the body as a phallus or *liṅga*—in Crowley's works the two symbols are intertwined.[43]

Part of Crowley's original interest in "phallicism," a popular topic in some Orientalist and esoteric circles at the time, was informed by his association with Bavarian Freemasonic occultist Theodor Reuss (1855–1923), who had published a work entitled *Lingam-Yoni* that was mostly a translation of the work *Phallicism* by the author Hargrave Jennings (1817–1890).[44] However, Sabhapati Swami was an even earlier and more formative source for Crowley's view on the *liṅga* and *yoni*, as was Crowley's admiration of a physical Śivaliṅga at a temple in Madurai during his journey to south India in 1901.[45] Crowley's "pyramid" as well as the meditation he crafted based on the technique of the "pole" in all three editions of VRY cannot therefore be fully contextualized without taking into account the development of Sabhapati's teachings and Crowley's views on the *liṅga* as informed by a Tamil Śaiva context.

In his witty "Autohagiography" Crowley wrote that he first became attracted to Sabhapati's writings following his travels in 1901 to Ceylon (modern Sri Lanka), where he visited his friend Allan Bennett (1872–1923), a fellow initiate in the Victorian magical order the Hermetic Order of the Golden Dawn.[46] Bennett was to some extent proficient in Pali and Sanskrit and interested in yogic meditation, as an unpublished 1901 diary held by the Warburg Institute shows, and he later became either the first or second European to receive a Theravada Buddhist ordination, and the first in Burma (modern Myanmar).[47] Crowley and Bennett had also studied yoga together during this visit with Ponnambalam Ramanathan (1851–1930), a Tamil Sri Lankan author and solicitor-general of Ceylon and the cousin of the celebrated art historian Ananda Coomaraswamy (1877–1947), whom Crowley also later met in New York and with whom he eventually fell out of favor.[48] During this time Crowley began to use the name Abhāvānanda, "the Bliss of Nonbeing," as attested by his diary and at least one of his published works.[49] Crowley and Bennett eventually parted ways, and Crowley continued his fascination with the goddess Bhavānī, to whom he claimed to offer a sacrificial goat in a temple in Madurai after discreetly obtaining entrance, citing inspiration from Richard Burton's illicit entry into the Kaaba at Mecca.[50]

The information given in Crowley's *Confessions* and diary entries is corroborated by the writings of Gerald Yorke (1901–1983), who wrote that in "southern India he studied Vedanta and Raja Yoga with 'the Mahatma Jnana Guru Yogi Sabhapaty Swami' "[51] and in his marginal notes to his copy of Kenneth Grant's *Aleister Crowley and the Hidden God* that Crowley told him he "did get Tantrik knowledge from Subhapati Swami [*sic*] in Madras."[52] While Sabhapati's yoga could certainly be considered to be a kind of Tantric yoga,[53] there is nevertheless no further proof that Crowley himself ever personally considered Sabhapati's knowledge as "Tantric," or that they physically met in Madras or elsewhere.[54] Instead, Crowley elsewhere stated that he was exposed to the "writings" of Sabhapati Swami during his aforementioned journeys in Madurai through a man who "spoke English well and was himself a great authority on Yoga."[55] This is verified in a letter from Crowley to David Curwen (dated September 11, 1945), in which he recounts that he "was only at Madura for three days and was nobody's pupil."[56] Despite Crowley's denial of receiving any instruction in his letter to Curwen, he elsewhere does indicate that he received a teaching on yogic meditation at Madurai, but does not mention Madras. In his commentary to H. P. Blavatsky's *The Voice of the Silence* (1899) he writes that he got a "certain point in the body suitable for meditation" from his "*guru* in Madura [Madurai]."[57] The identity of this guru has unfortunately not been possible to determine at present, but he may have been the same person who introduced him to the literature of Sabhapati Swami.[58] In any event, in the same commentary Crowley also counts Sabhapati's name among teachers "who know their subject from experience"—high praise coming from Crowley, who was often quick to disparage or roast religious authors whom he disliked.[59]

A good indication of Crowley's engagement with the practical teachings of Sri Sabhapati Swami can be gleaned through an examination of references to Sabhapati throughout his published works and diary entries. Most of these references are in the context of instructions of A.·.A.·. (also called "Order of the Silver Star"), a thelemic magical teaching order that Crowley cofounded in 1907 with George Cecil Jones (1873–1960), and which is still extant today.[60] This order consists "of Eleven Grades or Degrees" that have been mapped onto a system of correspondences related to the Kabbalah of Jewish mysticism, specifically the so-called *sefirot* of the "Tree of Life" as outlined in a published lists of tables called "Book 777," which also includes the symbolism of Daoism, Egyptian deities, and many other religions (see Figure 7.3).[61] Various of these grades include experimental instructions that allude to Sabhapati's teachings alongside teachings from Crowley's other sources for Hinduism and yoga. These include the Pātañjalayogaśāstra,[62] the works of Swami Vivekananda,[63] the aforementioned oral teachings he and Bennett received from Ponnambalam Ramanathan, teachings on the tattvas as derived from the Hermetic Order of the Golden Dawn and the translation by Rama Prasad (Rāma Prasād Kaśyapa) of the medieval text *Śivasvarodaya*,[64] and colonial-era translations on haṭha yoga texts such as the *Haṭhapradīpikā* and Shrish Chandra Basu's earlier translation of the *Śiva Saṃhitā*, to name a few of the most prominent sources.[65] The widely disseminated instruction "Liber O vel Manus et Sagittae," attributed to the grade of Neophyte, refers in a note to the methods of Sabhapati Swami alongside mention of "progress by slaying the Cakkrâms," teachings that evidently were later published in the second and third "methods" of a separate instruction entitled "Liber Yod [originally Liber Tav]."[66] Sabhapati's *Om* (i.e., VRY1) is also mentioned in conjunction with the physical longevity of yogis in "The Temple of Solomon the King" (see Figure 7.4), a serialized essay authored by the British military strategist John Frederick Charles Fuller (1878–1966), one of the original "aspirants" to the A.·.A.·. alongside Crowley.[67] Fuller also published his own modified version of the yogic teachings in "The Temple of Solomon the King," in which the same reference to Sabhapati is given, after he and Crowley had a falling out.[68]

One of Crowley's most direct engagements with Sabhapati's work, however, is found in a typescript to Crowley's March–April 1905 diary, which Hymenaeus Beta (Bill Breeze) published as a note in the second revised edition to Crowley's *Magick: Book Four*.[69] In the diary entry, Crowley summarizes a passage from VRY1 that was reprinted in all subsequent English editions of this work. The passage reflects a practical and explicit instruction on the method of Sabhapati's Śivarājayoga:

> Draw the light of your two eyes internally to *kuṇḍali* by *iḍā* and *piṅgalā* respectively. Imagine the mind as a straight pole *brahmarandhra-kuṇḍali* and the consciousness at the bottom of this pole. Take hold of the consciousness by the two keennesses of your eyes and pull it slowly up. . . . Keep consciousness in *brahmarandhra* for 20 min. more. Then drop and lift it through *suṣumnā* so fast that it takes less than 1 sec.[70]

Crowley incorporated these notes, adding references to thelemic metaphysics derived from the text of *The Book of the Law* (1904), and synthesized them into the instruction entitled "SSS," which forms the third chapter of a small book of meditations called *Liber HHH*, first published in 1911.[71] The title of this instruction is at once cleverly esoteric and exoteric: "SSS" refers to a repetition of the Hebrew letter *shin*, here denoting the element fire, as well as most probably to <u>S</u>ri <u>S</u>abhapati <u>S</u>wami. *Liber HHH* was prescribed

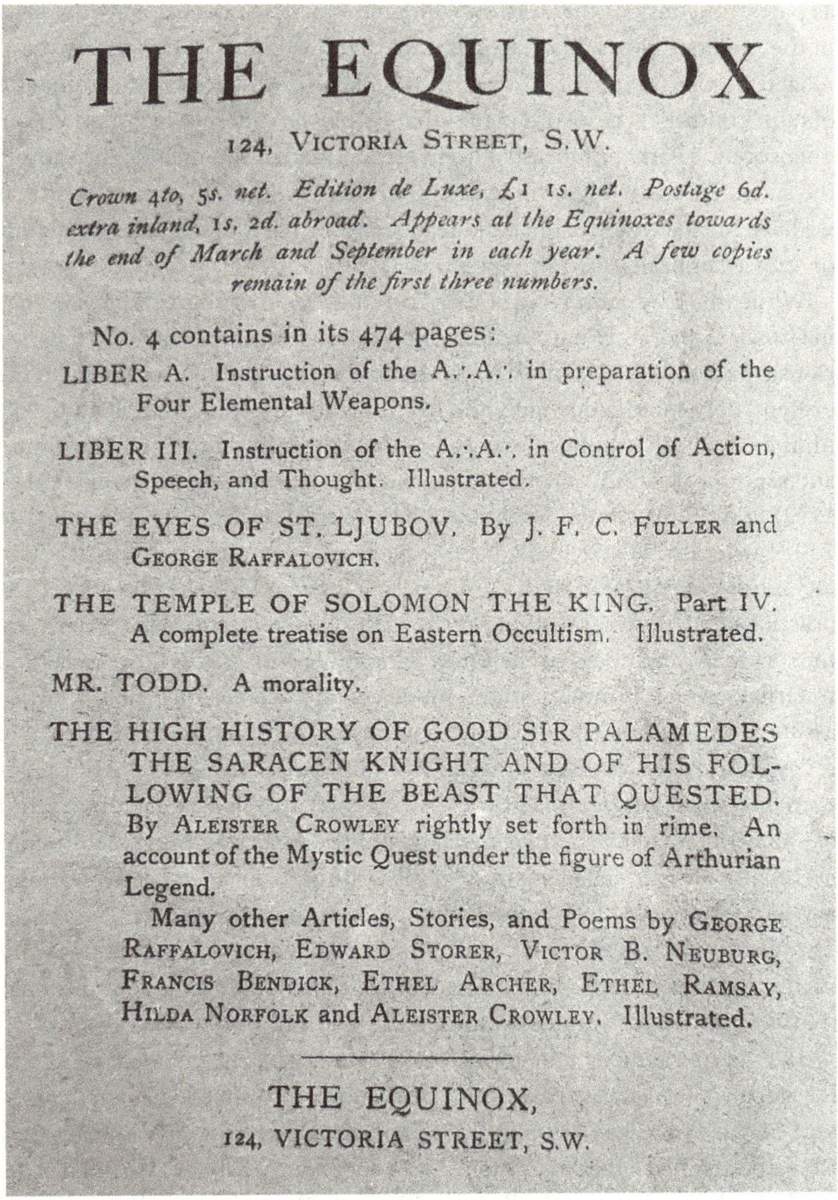

THE EQUINOX

124, VICTORIA STREET, S.W.

Crown 4to, 5s. net. Edition de Luxe, £1 1s. net. Postage 6d. extra inland, 1s. 2d. abroad. Appears at the Equinoxes towards the end of March and September in each year. A few copies remain of the first three numbers.

No. 4 contains in its 474 pages:

LIBER A. Instruction of the A.·.A.·. in preparation of the Four Elemental Weapons.

LIBER III. Instruction of the A.·.A.·. in Control of Action, Speech, and Thought. Illustrated.

THE EYES OF ST. LJUBOV. By J. F. C. FULLER and GEORGE RAFFALOVICH.

THE TEMPLE OF SOLOMON THE KING. Part IV. A complete treatise on Eastern Occultism. Illustrated.

MR. TODD. A morality.

THE HIGH HISTORY OF GOOD SIR PALAMEDES THE SARACEN KNIGHT AND OF HIS FOLLOWING OF THE BEAST THAT QUESTED. By ALEISTER CROWLEY rightly set forth in rime. An account of the Mystic Quest under the figure of Arthurian Legend.

Many other Articles, Stories, and Poems by GEORGE RAFFALOVICH, EDWARD STORER, VICTOR B. NEUBURG, FRANCIS BENDICK, ETHEL ARCHER, ETHEL RAMSAY, HILDA NORFOLK and ALEISTER CROWLEY. Illustrated.

THE EQUINOX,

124, VICTORIA STREET, S.W.

Figure 7.4 An advertisement for *The Equinox* that includes the serialized essay "The Temple of Solomon the King" in which Sabhapati Swami's VRY1 is cited, and other instructions on ceremonial "Magick" specific to Crowley's order A.·.A.·.. Photo by the author of a copy held in the Adyar Library and Research Centre.

as part of the task of the Zelator, while the Practicus was expected to "pass in the meditation practice S.S.S., in Liber HHH."[72] Part of this practice was related to a technique of "Rising on the Planes," which was a technique to obtain "control of the Astral plane" that employed different techniques than Theosophy.[73] Perhaps most strikingly, the SSS meditation includes imagining the spinal cord as a *liṅga*, while the *yoni* is the "cavity of the brain," which as we have seen is where Sabhapati locates various parts of the *brahmarandha*, or "crevice of Brahman" (see Appendix 3).

While this meditation and "Liber Yod" may seem obscure, their presence in Crowley's literature have striking implications: any aspirants who have seriously pursued the system of A.·.A.·. from the early twentieth century to the present, both male and female, and from a wide variety of countries and cultural contexts all around the world, and even relatively famous Thelemites and aspirants to A.·.A.·., like the Caltech rocket scientist Jack Parsons (1914–1952) and the Australian musician Leila Waddell (1880–1932) (see Figure 7.5),[74] would have eventually been expected to demonstrate proficiency in techniques of yoga that derive from passages given in the text of VRY1. The practice of these ritual meditations is not exclusive to the order A.·.A.·., either, as many members of the Ordo Templi Orientis (O.T.O.), a social and fraternal "research organization" modeled on Freemasonry that Crowley assumed the leadership of in 1912, have also historically been (and are still today) intimately familiar with Crowley's literature. Those in the O.T.O. or even unaffiliated readers of Crowley's works who are interested in the practice of "Thelemic Magick" more generally would come across these meditations eventually in their engagement with his writings or in social conversations, and as a result could feel compelled to practice them on an individual basis. This also includes celebrities with known connections to Crowley's work such as the filmmaker Kenneth Anger (1927–2023), the guitarist Jimmy Page (b. 1944), and the drummer Danny Carey (b. 1963)

The Tamil author and former accountant-general of Madras, T. K. Rajagopalam (also Rajagopalan), also independently commented upon this passage in the 1940s, just prior to Indian independence (see also Chapter 2).[75] Rajagopalam linked the passage to "Tāraka Yoga," or the "Yoga of the Pupil of the Eye," as a phase of "Amanaska Yoga,"[76] citing a similar technique given in part of the first and second *brāhmaṇams* (1.2–2.4) of the *Maṇḍalabrāhmaṇopaniṣad*, one of the so-called "Yoga Upanishads."[77] Another author named Arjan Dass Malik (1938–2006), a former civil servant in the north Indian state of Haryana, was also enamored of the technical dynamics at play in the above passage, noting

Figure 7.5 A portrait of Leila Waddell published in *The Rites of Eleusis* (1910). Her seated posture and A.·.A.·. hood forms a notable contrast to Crowley's portrait in the same publication. Photo by the author of a copy held in the Adyar Library and Research Centre.

that Sabhapati's inclusion of both upward and downward flows of "consciousness" is significant. More specifically, Malik asserted that Sabhapati "correctly mentions that the Kundalini having reached the top of the brain first descends to the *Ajña* [i.e., the *ājñā cakra*] and later on ascends from the *Ajña* to the top of the brain."[78]

It is important to keep in mind that Crowley's legacy is not merely limited to occultism in Europe, North America, and Australia, but also informed teachings in India itself. In Chapter 1 we examined the life of one of Sabhapati's main students, Om Prakash Swamigal, who headed a meditation hall in the Kandal area of Udhagamandalam (Ooty). As mentioned previously, Om Prakash Swamigal became a member of Latent Light Culture, a still-extant occult society originally based in Tinnevelly (modern Tirunelveli, Tamil Nadu), India that in its early days engaged Crowley's writings.[79] While many of Om Prakash Swamigal's teachings in Tamil reflect engagement with techniques on haṭha yoga that derive from his gurus and not the Latent Light Culture, there is some limited evidence that he did incorporate these techniques into his work. For instance, in his book *Śrīsatsampāṣiṇi* he alludes to "Mesmerism, Hypnotism, Magnetism . . . Personal Magnetism, Will Force . . . [and] Mirror Practice."[80] Latent Light Culture also preserved at least one typescript of Sabhapati Swami's reprinted lectures (see Chapter 2).

William Estep and "Super Mind Science"

Almost two decades after Crowley published his interpretive meditation on Sabhapati's technique of Śivarājayoga, Sabhapati's work CPSPS was separately reprinted in two volumes by another author named William Estep (1896–1967). The work was entitled *Esoteric Cosmic Yogi Science, or Works of the World Teacher* (WE) and was published out of Excelsior Springs, Missouri, in 1929 by his own society, "The Super Mind Science Publications," which can be situated in the American movements known as "New Thought" or "mental healing."[81] As treated in Chapter 2, the volumes contain the full English text of CPSPS and its diagrams (though shrunk to size), although they are stripped of any contents in Tamil and Devanagari scripts. Estep also placed his own photo in the opening pages of the book and otherwise made it challenging for the reader to easily determine whether the books were Estep's own work or whether they were Sabhapati's (see Figure 7.6). He claimed to be a direct disciple of Sabhapati Swami, although there is no validation of this claim in Sabhapati's own published writings.

In fact, an analysis of Estep's life reveals a checkered history of misrepresenting products and legal troubles, and it is therefore possible that he merely sought to profit from Sabhapati's teachings on yoga without any actual philosophical interest or substantial engagement with his techniques or

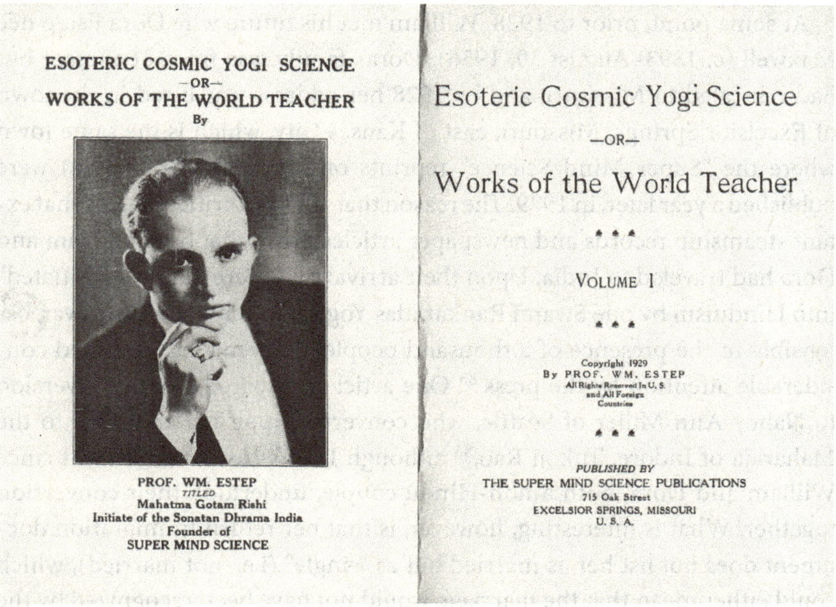

Figure 7.6 A portrait of William Estep in the frontispiece and the title page of his reprint of Sabhapati's work CPSPS (WE), published with its subtitle "Esoteric Cosmic Yogi Science." Scan courtesy of Michael Kolson.

method, unlike what we previously saw with Hartmann and Crowley. While it was indeed commonplace for modern occultists to lead relatively marginal or checkered lives and market esoteric teachings in the form of books or lectures to support their livelihoods in the absence of conventional employment, by the end of his life Estep had crossed a line beyond mere innocuous entrepreneurial tendencies to the point of being imprisoned for criminal manipulation.

William Estep was born in Virginia to Edmond Osborn Estep (July 1856–1936) and Violet Estep née Fauber (April 1860–1942), who were married in 1883.[82] His father Edmond was a day laborer from Virginia, who by the time of William's birth had relocated to rural Cabin Creek, a district southeast of Charleston in Kanawha County, West Virginia.[83] William was the third-oldest child and had two older brothers, one younger sister and one younger brother.[84] To my knowledge nothing has been published on Estep's early life (or personal life at all) to date, but extant records do enable one to piece together a bit of his later history.

At some point, prior to 1928, William met his future wife Dora Estep née Maxwell (c. 1893–August 30, 1956). Dora's family was from Tennessee but had relocated to Missouri, and by 1928 her address was listed in the town of Excelsior Springs, Missouri, east of Kansas City, which is the same town where the "Super Mind Science" reprints of Sabhapati's book (WE) were published a year later, in 1929. The reason that 1928 is a critical year is that extant steamship records and newspaper articles prove that both William and Dora had traveled to India. Upon their arrival they were publicly "initiated" into Hinduism by one Swami Rankaradas Yogiraj in Kankhal, Haridwar, ostensibly in the presence of a thousand people, an event that attracted considerable attention by the press.[85] One article compared Dora's conversion to Nancy Ann Miller of Seattle, who converted upon her marriage to the Maharaja of Indore, Tukoji Rao,[86] although Dora's case was different since William and Dora, both a non-Hindu couple, undertook their conversion together. What is interesting, however, is that her return immigration document does not list her as married but as "single" (i.e., not married), which could either mean that the marriage would not have been recognized by the immigration authorities or even that the entire marriage and conversion was a publicity stunt to begin with.[87] Articles on their marriage also confirms the source for Estep's alias "Mahatma Gotam Rishi" (also awkwardly spelled Mahatma Gantama), a title he uses to represent himself in WE. Dora for her part took the name "Sadhvi Ahalyabai" and "planned to start a missionary society in Western Europe and America for the propagation of Hinduism."[88]

Either concurrent with or prior to this journey to India, William's parents and possibly some of his siblings too had moved from West Virginia to the Columbia City neighborhood of Seattle, where their house still stands on Hudson Street; his father Edmond was listed as a landscape gardener.[89] At the same time, William had established Super Mind Science with an address not in Seattle but in Excelsior Springs, Missouri, the location associated with his wife Dora on a steamship record.[90] It is clear that both William and Dora used the Super Mind Science imprint together to market an occult correspondence course of instruction, and his publications included a variety of works such as *The Path of Light*, *Mysteries of God and Man*, *Threads of Wisdom*, and *The White Prophecy*, and three years later (in 1932) he would publish *Eternal Wisdom & Health*, a work of over seven hundred pages on mental healing that also included an exegesis of certain books of the Bible and claimed to present "Super Mind Science" as the "restored message of Jesus Christ."[91] Curiously, none of these later publications seem to focus at all on Sabhapati Swami's teachings in CPSPS and reprinted in WE, and as a result the latter seems to be somewhat of an anomalous outlier. There is evidence that the American yogi Deva Ram Sukul tried to publish Sabhapati's work as well around this period but to no avail; it is possible that the impulse behind both publications came from a similar motivation and that Deva Ram Sukul abandoned the publication once Estep's efforts were successful.[92]

William Estep continued to lecture and promote his lectures on success and health in association with Super Mind Science, and at one point even called his institution a "Super-Mind Science Church" and established "chapels" in various cities. In 1949, he had to respond to court "adverse questioning" for using a "wistful looking chimpanzee" named Mona and Billie Brian to demonstrate his theories in "supermind science" in Chicago in 1930; Estep had claimed he taught the chimpanzee "half of all the 800 words included in basic English.[93] By the 1950s he had moved to Texas, where a dark side to his New Thought prosperity gospel was exposed; William Estep the "Confidence Man" was convicted in Abilene of mail fraud and income tax evasion in Austin.[94] Estep died in 1967, and throughout this later period up to the end of his life there does not appear to be any further engagement with the literature or yogic practice of Sabhapati Swami, although his publications remain an interesting record of American receptivity to yogic teachings in the 1920s and 1930s.

Notes

1. For more on the contours of the phrase "modern occultism" see "Occult/Occultism," in *Dictionary of Gnosis & Western Esotericism*, ed. Wouter J. Hanegraaff (Leiden: Brill, 2006), 884–89; and Henrik Bogdan and Gordan Djurdjevic, eds., *Occultism in a Global Perspective* (London: Routledge, 2013). For the broader context of India-specific exchanges happening during this time see Gordan Djurdjevic, *India and the Occult: The Influence of South Asian Spirituality on Modern Western Occultism* (New York: Palgrave Macmillan, 2014). Some of the material in this chapter was revised and expanded from Keith Cantú, "Sri Sabhapati Swami: The Forgotten Yogi of Western Esotericism," in *The Occult Nineteenth Century: Roots, Developments, and Impact on the Modern World*, ed. Lukas Pokorny and Franz Winter (London: Palgrave Macmillan, 2021), 347–73, which itself was based on a conference paper delivered at the annual American Academy of Religion meeting in San Antonio in 2016.
2. See Karl Baier, "Theosophical Orientalism and the Structures of Intercultural Transfer: Annotations on the Appropriations of the Cakras in Early Theosophy," in *Theosophical Appropriations: Esotericism, Kabbalah and the Transformation*

of Traditions, ed. Julie Chajes and Boaz Huss (Be'er Sheva, Israel: Ben-Gurion University of the Negev Press, 2016), 309–54; its first mention in academic scholarship was probably Karl Baier, *Meditation und Moderne: Zur Genese eines Kernbereichs moderner Spiritualität in der Wechselwirkung zwischen Westeuropa, Nordamerika und Asien* (Würzburg: Königshausen & Neumann, 2009). Other works analyzing this engagement from the perspective of the cakras include Kurt Leland, *Rainbow Body: A History of the Western Chakra System from Blavatsky to Brennan* (Lake Worth, FL: Ibis Press, 2016); and Phil Hine, *Wheels within Wheels: Chakras Come West* (London: Twisted Trunk, 2018). For a condensed treatment that builds on Baier's work and cites unpublished diary entries and a published letter by Sabhapati referenced in Chapter 1 see Cantú, "Sri Sabhapati Swami."

3. For more on this topic see Cantú, "Sri Sabhapati Swami."
4. Aleister Crowley, *Eight Lectures on Yoga* (1939; Scottsdale, AZ: O.T.O. in association with New Falcon Publications, 1985).
5. Edward W. Said, *Orientalism* (New York: Vintage Books, 1979); Henry Eugène Corbin and Nancy Pearson, *The Man of Light in Iranian Sufism* (New Lebanon, NY: Omega Publications, 1994).
6. David Smith, *Hinduism and Modernity* (Malden, MA: Blackwell, 2003).
7. Baier, "Theosophical Orientalism"; Wouter Hanegraaff, "Western Esotericism and the Orient in the First Theosophical Society," in *Theosophy across Boundaries: Transcultural and Interdisciplinary Perspectives on a Modern Esoteric Movement*, ed. Hans Martin Krämer and Julian Strube (Albany: State University of New York Press, 2020), 29–65; Christopher Partridge, "Lost Horizon: H.P. Blavatsky and Theosophical Orientalism," in *Handbook of the Theosophical Current*, ed. Olav Hammer and Mikael Rothstein (Boston: Brill, 2013), 309–33.
8. Joscelyn Godwin, "Blavatsky and the First Generation of Theosophy," in *Handbook of the Theosophical Current*, ed. Olav Hammer and Mikael Rothstein (Leiden; Boston: Brill, 2013), 15–31; Joscelyn Godwin, *The Theosophical Enlightenment* (Albany: State University of New York Press, 1994), 307–31. For more on Blavatsky's engagement with India, specifically in the context of reincarnation, see Julie Chajes, *Recycled Lives: A History of Reincarnation in Blavatsky's Theosophy* (New York: Oxford University Press, 2019).
9. For sources specific to this region that treat on the Arya Samaj, Dayananda Saraswati, and their relation to modern Hindu reformist movements see Kenneth W. Jones, *Arya Dharm: Hindu Consciousness in 19th-Century Punjab* (Berkeley: University of California Press, 1976); also J. Barton Scott, *Spiritual Despots: Modern Hinduism and the Genealogies of Self-Rule* (Chicago: University of Chicago Press, 2016).
10. Paul Gillard, "Le pas décisif," *Le Lotus Bleu: Revue Theosophique Mensuelle* 8, no. 1 (1897): 20–24. I am grateful to Julian Strube for sharing with me some sources on Paul Gillard and his connection to French fin de siècle esoteric milieus.
11. Henry S. Olcott, *Theosophy: Religion and Occult Science* (London: George Redway, 1885), 151–53.
12. For an overview of astral projection in Theosophy see John Patrick Deveney, *Theosophical History Occasional Papers*, vol. 6, *Astral Projection or Liberation of the*

Double and the Work of the Early Theosophical Society (Fullerton, CA: Theosophical History, 1997).

13. VRY3, iv; VRY2, 15.
14. VRY3, iv; VRY2, 15.
15. M. Muncherjee Shroff, "The Work in Bombay," supplement to *The Theosophist: A Magazine of Oriental Philosophy, Art, Literature and Occultism* 11 (April 1890): cxxiv.
16. Ibid.
17. Patrick D. Bowen, "'The Real Pure Yog': Yoga in the Early Theosophical Society and the Hermetic Brotherhood of Luxor," in *Imagining the East: The Early Theosophical Society*, ed. Tim Rudbøg and Erik Reenberg Sand (New York: Oxford University Press, 2020), 143–65. For more on this society see Joscelyn Godwin, Christian Chanel, and John P. Deveney, eds., *The Hermetic Brotherhood of Luxor: Initiatic and Historical Documents of an Order of Practical Occultism* (York Beach, ME: S. Weiser, 1995).
18. Leland, *Rainbow Body*.
19. I am grateful to Bill Breeze for sharing the first edition of Hartmann's translation with me. For more on Hartmann and his sojourn in the United States, Mexico, and India see Richard Kaczynski, *Forgotten Templars: The Untold Origins of Ordo Templi Orientis* (n.p.: Published for the author, 2012); Sven Eek, *Damodar and the Pioneers of the Theosophical Movement* (Adyar, Madras: Vasanta Press, 1978).
20. For more on this phenomenon see Suzanne Newcombe, "Magic and Yoga: The Role of Subcultures in Transcultural Exchange," in *Yoga Traveling: Bodily Practice in Transcultural Perspective*, ed. Beatrix Hauser (New York: Springer, 2013), 57–79; Mark Singleton, *Yoga Body: The Origins of Modern Posture Practice* (New York: Oxford University Press, 2010), 64–70; for the contours of "modern ritual magic" see Egil Asprem, "Contemporary Ritual Magic," in *The Occult World*, ed. Christopher Partridge (Abingdon, UK: Routledge, 2014).
21. Franz Hartmann, *Radscha Yoga Hatha Yoga und Tantrika oder Weiße und schwarze Magie und Hexerei*, ed. Johannes Fährmann (Buenos Aires, Argentina: Bücher der Schatzkammer, 1990); for Hartmann's best-known work on magic, see Franz Hartmann, *Magic: White and Black; The Science of Finite and Infinite Life, Containing Practical Hints for Students of Occultism* (Boston: by the Author, 1885). For some of the first examples of yoga being equated with magic (although in a stigmatizing way) see Keith Cantú, "Haṭhayoga as 'Black Magic' in Early Theosophy and Beyond," in *Proceedings of the ESSWE6 Conference on Esotericism and Deviance*, ed. Tim Rudbøg and Manon Hedenborg White (Leiden: Brill, forthcoming).
22. One important and apparently non-Indic source for the astral body in occult literatures was the concept of a "Scin Laeca" or "shining body" that also appeared in Edward Bulwer-Lytton's popular occult novel *A Strange Story* (1862).
23. "Franz Hartmann hat ab und zu mit Absicht die Begriff: Äther- und Astralkörper verwechselt, weil er Bedenken hatte, die Geheimnisse des Ätherkörpers zu früh zu veröffentlichen."
24. FH2, 16n, 21n (including a reference to her work *The Voice in the Silence*).
25. FH2, 18–19n, 27n, 33n, 52n.
26. FH2, 33n.

27. FH2, 19n, 23n, 43n.
28. FH2, 28n, 33n.
29. FH2, 34n.
30. FH2, 54n, 57n, 63.
31. FH2, 59–60n, 82.
32. FH2, 60n.
33. FH2, 75–76n.
34. For a few examples of both etic and emic scholarly sources that in various ways record the historical continuity of Thelema and the Ordo Templi Orientis from Crowley's death into the present day, see Henrik Bogdan and Martin P. Starr, eds., *Aleister Crowley and Western Esotericism* (New York: Oxford University Press, 2012); the articles in Manon Hedenborg White, ed., "Special Issue: Rethinking Aleister Crowley and Thelema," *Aries* 21, no. 1 (2021); Richard Kaczynski, Frater Iskandar, and Frater Taos, eds., *Success Is Your Proof: One Hundred Years of O.T.O. in North America, a Festschrift in Honor of Hymenaeus Beta, Celebrating Thirty Years of Leadership* (New York: Sekmet Books, 2015); Martin P. Starr, *The Unknown God: W.T. Smith and the Thelemites* (Bolingbrook, IL: Teitan Press, 2003); Manon Hedenborg White, *The Eloquent Blood: The Goddess Babalon and the Construction of Femininities in Western Esotericism* (New York: Oxford University Press, 2020); Hymenaeus Beta, ed., *The Equinox. The Review of Scientific Illuminism: The Official Organ of the O.T.O.*, vol. 3, no. 10 (New York: 93 Publishing, by special arrangement with Samuel Weiser, 1990); J. Gordon Melton, "Thelemic Magick in America," in *Alternatives to American Mainline Churches*, ed. Joseph Henry Fichter and William Sims Bainbridge (New York: Unification Theological Seminary, 1983), 67–87; Israel Regardie, *The Eye in the Triangle: An Interpretation of Aleister Crowley* (1970; Phoenix, AZ: Falcon Press, 1986).
35. Cantú, "Sri Sabhapati Swami." Henrik Bogdan had earlier alluded to this connection in Aleister Crowley, David Curwen, and Henrik Bogdan, *Brother Curwen, Brother Crowley: A Correspondence* (York Beach, ME: Teitan Press, 2010).
36. Aleister Crowley, "Postcards to Probationers," in *The Equinox: The Official Organ of the A.·.A.·. the Review of Scientific Illuminism*, vol. 1, no. 2 (London: Simpkin, Marshall, Hamilton, Kent, 1909), 196–200; see also Singleton, *Yoga Body*, 65–66.
37. Simon Paul Cox, *The Subtle Body: A Genealogy*, New York: Oxford University Press, 2022), 137–59.
38. For contemporary forms of ritual magic see Asprem, "Contemporary Ritual Magic"; and Egil Asprem, "Magic Naturalized? Negotiating Science and Occult Experience in Aleister Crowley's Scientific Illuminism," *Aries* 8 (2008): 139–65.
39. Aleister Crowley et al., *Commentaries on the Holy Books and Other Papers: The Equinox*, vol. 4, no. 1 (York Beach, ME: S. Weiser, 1996), 59–72.
40. For an edition of this text see Joseph H. Peterson, *The Lesser Key of Solomon: Lemegeton Clavicula Salomonis* (York Beach, ME: Weiser Books, 2001). For its context see Claire Fanger, ed., *Conjuring Spirits: Texts and Traditions of Medieval Ritual Magic* (University Park: Penn State Press, 1998); and Richard Kieckhefer, *Forbidden Rites: A Necromancer's Manual of the Fifteenth Century* (University Park: Pennsylvania State University Press, 1998).

41. For Crowley's annotated edition of this invocation see S. L. MacGregor Mathers, Aleister Crowley, and Hymenaeus Beta, eds., *The Goetia: The Lesser Key of Solomon the King: Lemegeton—Clavicula Salomonis Regis, Book One* (York Beach, ME: Samuel Weiser, 1995). For a critical edition of the invocation used (PGM V. 96–172), see Hans Dieter Betz, ed., *The Greek Magical Papyri in Translation, Including the Demotic Spells* (Chicago: University of Chicago Press, 1986), 103.
42. See for example Mathers et al., *The Goetia*, 9 n. 28.
43. The notion of the "Holy Guardian Angel" was originally based on a translation of a ca. sixteenth- to seventeenth-century German text known as the *Buch Abramelin*, attributed to a Jew named Abraham von Worms. By Crowley's time three of its four parts had been translated into an incomplete French version and from the French into English by Mathers. For a contemporary edition of this text edited by Georg Dehn see Abraham ben Simeon et al., *The Book of Abramelin: A New Translation* (Lake Worth, FL: Ibis Press, 2006). For a review that covers discrepancies between these several editions and Crowley's use of the "Holy Guardian Angel" concept outside of the *Book of Abramelin* see my review of this book in *Correspondences: Journal for the Study of Esotericism* 4 (2016): 129–54. See also the editor's preface in Mathers et al., *The Goetia*, xiii–xxvi.
44. Theodor Reuss, *Lingam-Yoni oder die Mysterien des Geschlechts-Kultus als die Basis der Religionen aller Kulturvölker des Altertums und des Marienkultus in der christlichen Kirche sowie Ursprung des Kreuzes und des Crux Ansata* (Berlin: Wilsson, 1906); and Hargrave Jennings, *Phallicism, Celestial and Terrestrial, Heathen and Christian, Its Connection with the Rosicrucians and the Gnostics and Its Foundation in Buddhism, with an Essay on Mystic Anatomy* (London: George Redway, 1884). For criticism of these figures from a post-Orientalist perspective see Hugh B. Urban, *Magia Sexualis: Sex, Magic, and Liberation in Modern Western Esotericism* (Berkeley: University of California Press, 2006); and for their historical intersection with Theosophy see Godwin, *The Theosophical Enlightenment*. Neither author however mentions Sabhapati Swami as a potential South Asian source for Orientalist interest in phallicism during this period.
45. Aleister Crowley, *The Confessions of Aleister Crowley: An Autohagiography*, ed. John Symonds and Kenneth Grant (New York: Hill and Wang, 1970), 256.
46. Crowley, *Confessions*, 252–58; Richard Kaczynski, *Perdurabo: The Life of Aleister Crowley*, rev. ed. (Berkeley, CA: North Atlantic Books, 2010), 93–97; Marco Pasi, *Aleister Crowley and the Temptation of Politics* (Durham, UK: Acumen, 2014), 12; Djurdjevic, *India and the Occult*, 37. For more on the innovative nature and history of the Hermetic Order of the Golden Dawn see Alison Butler, *Victorian Occultism and the Making of Modern Magic: Invoking Tradition* (New York: Palgrave Macmillan, 2011); Ellic Howe, *The Magicians of the Golden Dawn: A Documentary History of a Magical Order, 1887–1923* (New York: S. Weiser, 1978).
47. Following the schism of the Hermetic Order of the Golden Dawn, Bennett took orders as a Theravada Buddhist monk and relocated first to Ceylon and later Akyab in Burma (modern Sittwe, Myanmar). For more on Bennett's acceptance of Theravada Buddhism, see John L. Crow, "Allan Bennett & the Emergence of Buddhism in the West," *Insight: The Journal of the Theosophical Society in England* 49, no. 3 (Autumn 2008): 30–33 and his

forthcoming publication coauthored with Elizabeth Harris *The Life of Allan Bennett, Bhikkhu Ananda Metteyya*; Godwin, *The Theosophical Enlightenment*, 369–75. A 1901 diary proves that Bennett (and possibly Crowley) experimented with writing Sanskrit using Devanagari script. While there is no evidence that Crowley ever learned more than a basic knowledge of Sanskrit, he did confess that he picked up conversational Hindustani (a precursor to modern Hindi and Urdu) during his Himalayan mountain-climbing expeditions; Crowley, *Confessions*, 260.

48. See Pasi, *Aleister Crowley*, 135–36; Kaczynski, *Perdurabo*, 298–301. Ananda Coomaraswamy and Aleister Crowley's falling out was apparently over a consensually arranged romantic affair between Crowley and Coomaraswamy's wife, the musician Ratan Devi (Alice Ethel Richardson, 1889–1958), which later turned sour after Ratan Devi's artistic career developed and Coomaraswamy wanted her back. This prompted Crowley in some unpublished contexts to refer to Coomaraswamy using racially charged slurs about his mixed ancestry. The use of such language is despicable, even for that period, but it must be noted that it was also in the context of a broken relationship. Given Crowley's heartfelt reverence for other South Asian teachers like Swami Vivekananda, Poonambalam Ramanathan, and Sabhapati Swami, Crowley's use of slurs seems more reflective of the anger of a dirty lover taking the low road when faced with frustration at a partner's miscarriage and a love affair gone horribly wrong. His critical attitude toward Jiddu Krishnamurti (1895–1986), with whom he tried to compete for the theosophical title of World Teacher (see Pasi, *Aleister Crowley*, 17–18), seems to have similarly arisen out of a kind of temporary and contextual frustration at not getting his way. In any case, there is no evidence in Crowley's writings to support the idea that he had any kind of categorical racism against people of mixed ancestry or of South Asian descent.
49. For more on this historical figure see M. Vythilingam, *The Life of Sir Ponnambalam Ramanathan*, 2 vols. (Colombo: Ramanathan Commemoration Society, 1971).
50. Crowley, *Confessions*, 255–60; Crowley et al., *Brother Curwen, Brother Crowley*. For a comprehensive treatment of Crowley's wider travels in India see Tobias Churton, *Aleister Crowley in India: The Secret Influence of Eastern Mysticism on Magic and the Occult* (Rochester, VT: Inner Traditions, 2019). Animal sacrifices, while today rarer, were once more common in many of India's temples, especially to Tantric deities such as forms of Kali.
51. N∴ [Gerald Yorke], "Editorial Preface" in *777* [revised] (Publisher and date unknown, ca. 1950s), viii. This was reprinted in 1973 in a compilation edited by Israel Regardie (1907–1985) and reprinted as Aleister Crowley, "777," in *777 and Other Qabalistic Writings of Aleister Crowley: Including Gematria & Sepher Sephiroth*, ed. Israel Regardie (York Beach, ME: S. Weiser, 1983), vii–viii.
52. Crowley et al., *Brother Curwen, Brother Crowley*, xxxiv. For more on Yorke's relationship to Crowley and turn toward Buddhism see Gerald Yorke et al., *Aleister Crowley, the Golden Dawn and Buddhism: Reminiscences and Writings of Gerald Yorke* (York Beach, ME: Teitan Press, 2011). For Yorke's later relationship with B. K. S. Iyengar and the British yoga scene, see Suzanne Newcombe, *Yoga in Britain: Stretching Spirituality and Educating Yogis* (Bristol: Equinox Publishing, 2019), 28–38.

53. For some contours of what constitutes Tantric yoga, see Mallinson and Singleton, *Roots of Yoga*; and André Padoux, *Comprendre le tantrisme: Les sources hindoues* (Paris: Albin Michel, 2010) and its shortened English translation André Padoux, *The Hindu Tantric World: An Overview* (Chicago: University of Chicago Press, 2017).
54. It is probably Kenneth Grant (1924–2011) who most helped transform Crowley's image into a *tāntrika*, albeit one who in Grant's view (correctly or incorrectly) did not fully realize the importance of female sexual fluids, which he called "kalas" (< Skt. *kalā*, lit. "(lunar) digit," "fragmented power"); see Manon Hedenborg White, "The Other Woman: Babalon and the Scarlet Woman in Kenneth Grant's Typhonian Trilogies," in *Servants of the Star & the Snake: Essays in Honour of Kenneth & Steffi Grant*, ed. Henrik Bogdan (London: Starfire Publishing, 2018); and Hedenborg White, *The Eloquent Blood*, 157–93.
55. Crowley, *Confessions*, 255.
56. Crowley et al., *Brother Curwen, Brother Crowley*, 49.
57. Crowley et al., *Commentaries*, 301.
58. It is possible though not conclusive that both the man who "spoke English well" and Crowley's "guru"-who-is-not-a-guru was one Karunananda Swami, who collaborated with the Latent Light Culture and commented upon Crowley's commentary on Blavatsky's "The Voice of the Silence" as advertised in *The Kalpaka*, although more research would be needed to determine this. I am grateful to Henrik Bogdan and Munish Kumar for sharing with me various aspects of this possibility.
59. Crowley et al., *Commentaries*, 291.
60. For a historical summary of this order and its relationship with Crowley's student Karl Germer and the Brazilian occultist Marcelo Motta see Keith Readdy, *One Truth and One Spirit: Aleister Crowley's Spiritual Legacy* (Lake Worth, FL: Ibis Press, 2018); and for the late twentieth century James Wasserman, *In the Center of the Fire: A Memoir of the Occult, 1966–1989* (Lake Worth, FL: Ibis Press, 2012). The two most important recent publications of the A.·.A.·. or "Order of the Silver Star" have been J. Daniel Gunther, *Initiation in the Aeon of the Child: The Inward Journey* (Lake Worth, FL: Ibis Press, 2009) and J. Daniel Gunther, *The Angel and the Abyss: Comprising The Angel and the Abyss and The Hieroglyphic Triad, Being Books II & III of The Inward Journey* (Lake Worth: Ibis Press, 2014). There are other claimants to A.·.A.·. (especially in the United States) who do not recognize Gunther's writings, such as a group affiliated by the College of Thelema and promoted by the author David Shoemaker. The order as outlined by Readdy, however, is the only so-called "chain" officially recognized as such by Ordo Templi Orientis and has been the most proactive with publishing Crowley's literature. Their publication Aleister Crowley et al., *Magick: Liber ABA, Book Four, Parts I–V*, 2nd ed. (York Beach, ME: Samuel Weiser, 1997) contains the only known emic engagement with Sabhapati's teachings in recent decades.
61. Crowley et al., *Commentaries*, 9. This "Book 777" is an occult "dictionary" of comparative attributions modeled on the alphabetical paths of the *Sefer Yeṣira* and the ten *sefiroth* of the Tree of Life; see Anonymous [Aleister Crowley], *777 vel Prolegomena Symbolica ad Systemam Sceptico-Mysticae Viae Explicandae, Fundamentum Hieroglyphicum Sanctissimorum Scientiae Summae* (London: Walter Scott Publishing,

1909). For the innovative engagement of Jewish and Christian Kabbalah among occultists see Liz Greene, *Magi and Maggidim: The Kabbalah in British Occultism, 1860–1940* (Ceredigion, Wales: Sophia Centre Press, 2012); for the medieval context specific to Juḍaism see Elliot R. Wolfson, *Through a Speculum That Shines: Vision and Imagination in Medieval Jewish Mysticism* (Princeton, NJ: Princeton University Press, 1997).

62. The *Pātañjalayogaśāstra* is a term used by scholars to refer to the ca. fourth- early fifth-century CE Yoga Sūtras of Patañjali along with their commentary, or *bhāṣya*, attributed to Vyāsa, which Philipp Maas has argued is a pseudonym for Patañjali himself (see also Chapter 4). In Crowley's day, and indeed prior to the twenty-first century, however, they were usually considered to be separate authors. For a critical edition of the first *pāda* of Patañjali's work see Patañjali and Philipp André Maas, *Samādhipāda: Das erste Kapitel des Pātañjalayogaśāstra zum ersten Mal kritisch ediert* (Aachen: Shaker, 2006); for a biography of the text see David Gordon White, *The Yoga Sutra of Patanjali: A Biography* (Princeton, NJ: Princeton University Press, 2019). For prominent examples of Crowley's engagement with Patañjali in a syncretic frame that also included Jewish Kabbalah and Daoism see the first part of Crowley et al., *Magick*; and Crowley, *Eight Lectures on Yoga*.

63. The most notable work engaged by Crowley was Swami Vivekananda, *Yoga Philosophy: Râja Yoga or Conquering the Internal Nature*. (London: Longmans, Green, 1896). Crowley especially adopted Vivekananda's typology of the four types of yoga, "Karma Yoga" (*karmayoga*), "Bhakti Yoga" (*bhaktiyoga*), "Raja Yoga" (*rājayoga*], and "Gnana Yoga" (*jñānayoga*), and attributed these to the lower grades in the A.∴A.∴ system, significantly also adding haṭha yoga; cf. Aleister Crowley, ed., "Liber XIII vel Graduum Montis Abiegni: A Syllabus of the Steps upon the Path," in *The Equinox*, vol. 1, no. 3 (London: Simpkin, Marshall, Hamilton, Kent, 1910), 3–8. For the roots of this fourfold typology as interpreted by Vivekananda see Elizabeth De Michelis, *A History of Modern Yoga: Patañjali and Western Esotericism* (London: Continuum, 2008), 123–25. A similar typology of four yogas that may have inspired Swami Vivekananda's own usage was also used a decade earlier in Ambikacharan's Bengali introduction to BRY (see Chapter 6).

64. For more on this figure and text see Cantú, "Haṭhayoga as 'Black Magic'"; Magdalena Kraler, "Tracing Vivekananda's Prāṇa and Ākāśa: The Yogavāsiṣṭha and Rama Prasad's Occult Science of Breath," in *The Occult Nineteenth Century: Roots, Developments, and Impact on the Modern World*, ed. Lukas Pokorny and Franz Winter (London: Palgrave Macmillan, 2021); see also Egil Asprem, "Explaining the Esoteric Imagination: Towards a Theory of Kataphatic Practice," *Aries* 17, no. 1 (2017): 17–50.

65. For a summary of these sources see Cantú, "Haṭhayoga as 'Black Magic.'" For the engagement of these translations by Carl Kellner see Karl Baier, "Yoga within Viennese Occultism: Carl Kellner and Co.," in *Yoga in Transformation: Historical and Contemporary Perspectives*, ed. Karl Baier, Philipp A. Maas, and Karin Preisendanz (Vienna: Vienna University Press, 2018), 183–222; for Theodor Reuss see my forthcoming article "The 'Mystic Anatomy' of Theodor Reuss," based on a paper presented at the Ascona conference hosted by Academia OTO.

66. Aleister Crowley, ed., "Liber Tav [Yod] svb figvrâ DCCCXXXI," in *The Equinox*, vol. 1, no. 7 (London: Wieland & Co., 1912), 93–100.
67. A few years earlier Fuller had also written a book on the spiritual interpretation of Crowley's poetry that was included as part of the A.·.A.·. curriculum: Capt. J. F. C. Fuller, *The Star in the West: A Critical Interpretation upon the Works of Aleister Crowley* (London: Walter Scott Publishing, 1907). For Fuller's contributions to military history and for his controversial authoritarian and fascist sympathies during World War II see Brian Holden Reid, *J. F. C. Fuller: Military Thinker* (reprint, Basingstoke: Macmillan, 1990).
68. Kaczynski, *Perdurabo*, 234; J. F. C. Fuller, *Yoga: A Study of the Mystical Philosophy of the Brahmins and Buddhists* (London: William Rider & Son, 1925), 69 n. 2.
69. Crowley et al., *Magick*, 780.
70. The original passage Crowley commented on is found in VRY1, 35–36; cf. also CPSPS, First Book, 112–14.
71. Aleister Crowley, ed., "Liber HHH svb figvrâ CCCXLI," in *The Equinox*, vol. 1, no. 5, 5–14. For an analysis of this ritual see Djurdjevic, *India and the Occult*, 49–52.
72. Aleister Crowley, ed., *Liber Collegii Sanctii sub figurâ CLXXV, Being the Tasks of the Grades, and Their Oaths, Proper to Liber XIII, the Publications of the A.·.A.·. in Class D from B to G* (1910); these were later published in Crowley et al., *Commentaries*.
73. For an analysis of this technique in Crowley's literature and its precedents in a practice in the Hermetic Order of the Golden Dawn of scrying the tattvas, see Asprem, "Explaining the Esoteric Imagination."
74. For more on Leila Waddell and other female Thelemites see the results of "The Thelemic Women's History Project" headed by Manon Hedenborg White and the forthcoming book *Women of Thelema: Selected Essays*, edited by Manon Hedenborg White and Christian Giudice (Kamuret Press, forthcoming). For Jack Parsons and his connection to L. Ron Hubbard, the founder of Scientology, see Henrik Bogdan, "The Babalon Working 1946: L. Ron Hubbard, John Whiteside Parsons, and the Practice of Enochian Magic," *Numen: International Review for the History of Religions* 63, no. 1 (2016): 12–32; for a popular source on Parsons see John Carter and Robert Anton Wilson, *Sex and Rockets: The Occult World of Jack Parsons* (Los Angeles, CA: Feral House, 2005).
75. T. K. Rajagopalan, *Hidden Treasures of Yoga: Revealing Certain Ancient and Secret Methods of Practical Mysticism* (1945; Delhi: Oriental Book Centre, 2005), 76–80.
76. For an evaluation of the contours of Amanaska see Jason Birch, "The Amaraughaprabodha: New Evidence on the Manuscript Transmission of an Early Work on Haṭha- and Rājayoga," *Journal of Indian Philosophy*, no. 47 (2019): 947–77; and Jason Birch, "Rājayoga: The Reincarnations of the King of All Yogas," *International Journal of Hindu Studies* 17, no. 3 (2013): 399–442; see also David Gordon White, *The Alchemical Body: Siddha Traditions in Medieval India* (Chicago: University of Chicago Press, 1996), 316–17; and *Amanaskayoga* 1.50–98.
77. For an analysis of the later date of many of these so-called Upanishads see Christian Bouy, *Les Nātha-yogin et les Upaniṣads* (Paris: Diffusion de Boccard, 1994).
78. Malik, *Kundalini and Meditation*, 43.

79. Henrik Bogdan, "Reception of Occultism in India: The Case of the Holy Order of Krishna," in Bogdan and Djurdjevic, *Occultism*, 177–201; Śrī Ti. Ku Piḷḷai, *Nīlakiri, utakamanṭalam, tirukkāntal Śrī Takṣiṇāmūrtti Maṭam Lōkōpakāra Vityātāṉa Capai stāpakar acalapīṭam Śrīmat Ompirakāsa Cuvāmikaḷ carittirac curukkam* (Tirupparāytturai: Śrīmat Citpavānanta Cuvāmikaḷatu muṉṉuraiyuṭaṉ kūṭiyatu, 1957), 31.
80. Ōm Pirakāca Cuvāmikaḷ, *Śrīsatsampāṣiṇi* (Nīlakiri: Śrī Carasvati Ācramam, 1915), 72.
81. For more on New Thought see Wouter J. Hanegraaff, "New Thought Movement," in *Dictionary of Gnosis & Western Esotericism*, ed. Wouter J. Hanegraaff (Leiden: Brill, 2006), 861–65; Catherine L. Albanese, *A Republic of Mind and Spirit: A Cultural History of American Metaphysical Religion* (New Haven, CT: Yale University Press, 2008), 394–97; Charles Braden, *Spirits in Rebellion: The Rise and Development of New Thought* (Dallas: Southern Methodist University Press, 1963).
82. The information that follows was obtained by creating a family tree for William Estep on Ancestry.com and discovering the salient details, which are well recorded, and supplemented by investigation into newspaper archives that also mention his and his wife's names. I am grateful to Philip Deslippe for encouraging me to use this method to learn more about his life and to the user Marc Demarest for uploading many details about Estep's life to Ancestry.com.
83. "Twelfth Census of the United States" (1900), West Virginia, Kanawha County, Cabin Creek District.
84. Ibid.
85. On July 29, 1928, the Esteps arrived in Cardiff, England, from New York City on the steamship *George Washington*. See also (as a select few among many similar articles) "All Around the World," *Minneapolis Journal*, October 30, 1928; "American Hindoo Converts Would Spread Religion Here," *Indiana Gazette*, November 21, 1928; "American Pair Hindu Converts," *Boston Globe*, October 31, 1928. Other proof of their arrival is found in "List of United States Citizens (for the Immigration Authorities), S.S. Île de France Sailing from Le Havre, November 28th, 1928, Arriving at the Port of New York, December 4th, 1928," in *New York, U.S., Arriving Passenger and Crew Lists (including Castle Garden and Ellis Island), 1820–1957* [database online] (Lehi, UT: Ancestry.com Operations, Inc., 2010).
86. "Daughter Is Born to 'Maharanee'; Former Nancy Miller and Husband, Ex-Maharajah of Indore, Are at Chateau Near Paris," *New York Times*, January 29, 1929.
87. "List of United States Citizens," 1928.
88. "American Pair Hindu Converts," *Boston Globe*, October 31, 1928.
89. His parents are listed at this address in Seattle, Washington, City Directory 1928, 629, in Ancestry.com, *U.S. City Directories, 1822–1995* [database on-line], Provo, UT: Ancestry.com Operations, 2011. The same address is attached to William Estep's name in a steamship record, proving that he associated it with his residence too.
90. "List of United States Citizens," 1928.
91. Professor WM. Estep, *Eternal Wisdom and Health with Light on the Scriptures* (Excelsior Springs, MO: Super Mind Science Publications, 1932), 10.

92. I am grateful to Philip Deslippe for sharing with me helpful information and a document that shows Deva Ram Sukul was proposing to publish Sabhapati's works. Sukul instead published a work *Seven Class Lessons on Raja Yoga and Vedanta Philosophy* (New York: Yoga Institute of America, 1936).
93. " 'Old Doc' Estep Admits Ape was Stock in Trade," *Chicago Daily Tribune*, Part 2, p. 6, October 6, 1949.
94. "Confidence Man Back into Prison," *Abilene Reporter News*, January 31, 1962. His fraud allegedly ran even deeper than mere tax evasion, however, and the *San Antonio Express* newspaper ran a three-part series in January 1954 that exposed this "Healer's" fraudulent activities in connection to his new venture, the Atomotor Manufacturing Company, Inc., which marketed a "fuelless engine" that was capable of curing cancer; see Charles Ross, "S.A. 'Healer's' Activities Exposed," *San Antonio Express*, January 26, 1954, front page.

Epilogue

Parts of a Universal Tree

The "universal tree" of Sri Sabhapati Swami's literature and teachings on Śivarājayoga beckons us to take a closer look at its many parts, from its translocal leaves down to its local roots. His literature remained quietly relegated to local Tamil religious spheres and diffused in translocal occult milieus for almost a century and a half, as our journey from the first chapter to the seventh has demonstrated. While it did not have the widespread success that Sabhapati had perhaps initially envisaged, engaging his body of work now has unique advantages from a scholarly point of view. First, its history at both the translocal and local levels remains discrete and trackable relative to many other modern traditions of yoga that became "globalized," so to speak, in the middle to late twentieth century. The contents of Sabhapati's literature and visual diagrams, like a time capsule of sorts gathering dust in library archives and private bookcases, offers much additional perspective on the intersection between social and religious concerns as well as on how yoga fit into daily life and discourses. Their detailed descriptions also afford scholars and interested readers in South Asia and beyond an unprecedented opportunity to better access and understand the religious history of a vast and understudied network of locations and places (e.g., Velachery, Sathuragiri, Courtallam, Papanasam, Pothigai Malai, among many others) that were considered important sacred sites prior to the colonial period and up to the present day. In other words, further examination of the life and teachings of this yogi (or Jñānaguru Yogī, to use one of his titles) continues to reveal so much more even outside of just this single figure, including an interconnected web of personal relationships and publication history, translocal flows and interactions with occultists and other known personalities, sacred places and temples, and philosophical, religious, and scientific engagement. If this book has focused on Śivarājayoga as the main connecting thread given its importance to Sabhapati himself, it is by no means the only aspect of this yogi worthy of further research. In concluding, however, I will cite two overarching scholarly assumptions among many that this research at once complicates and enriches.

Like a Tree Universally Spread. Keith Edward Cantú, Oxford University Press. © Oxford University Press 2023.
DOI: 10.1093/oso/9780197665473.003.0009

On the global or translocal end of the spectrum, Sabhapati's techniques and works lived on in the writings of certain authors on yoga with ties to modern occultism, some of whom, like Helena Blavatsky, Henry Olcott, and Aleister Crowley, are undoubtedly quite famous (or infamous, depending on the character). However, while Sabhapati is a key figure in these writings, or in what I would call "Modern Occult Yoga," his name is strikingly nowhere to be found in the vast majority of books on either the Theosophical Society or the Thelema of Aleister Crowley, much less on the New Age or New Thought. Likewise, Sabhapati appears to have never been picked up as a major figure in the translocalized postural yoga (or "Modern Postural Yoga" as coined by De Michelis) that most would readily recognize as yoga today outside of these niche occultist circles, and this despite the fame he enjoyed as a yogi in South Asia during his lifetime (see the introduction). The fact of Sabhapati's omission in most scholarship on esotericism and yoga raises even deeper questions about the nature of fame, and about selection bias among scholars and popular authors as they choose who is worth remembering and writing biographies and histories about.

In spite of Sabhapati's ultra-niche persistence in global marketplaces of occultism and yoga, one possible complication is to consider the dissemination of his Śivarājayoga among occultists as a secondary diffusion in and of itself, meaning that aspects of his works have trickled into popular culture without much knowledge of Sabhapati as a personality per se. For example, while Crowley acknowledged Sabhapati by name in several instances, subsequent readers of Crowley after his death (e.g., Kenneth Grant, John Symonds (1914–2006), and Gerald Yorke, all of whom personally knew Crowley and helped manage his literary estate) were much less inclined to research this personality and were more concerned with other meditative and/or Tantric practices that may be linked to Sabhapati's system but only indirectly. This has led to what Leland in the Theosophical context has called "source amnesia," in which a practice lives on without much idea of where it originally came from, or from whom.[1] This is where a history-of-religions approach can contribute to a much deeper understanding of some of the sources for teachings that would have been more immediately known to, say, Crowley, Hartmann, Blavatsky, and Estep but gradually forgotten by their readers and by people who follow or historically followed their prescribed practices. It also invites a more serious and rigorous historical examination of many other such sources on yoga that occultists consulted, many of which were once widespread but continue to be neglected by scholars on account of modern occultists' perceived inauthenticity, lack of cultural relevance, or potential to generate controversy, or as a result of circulating—and almost always uncritical—popular media and literary misrepresentations of their teachings as "black magic."[2] Correcting such neglect and misrepresentation is especially warranted given that Modern Occult Yoga, as an inherently marginal space for practice, is also often also populated by women, LGBTQ people, and people of color, and as a result this space has the potential to broaden our scholarly understanding of how yoga is reinterpreted as global communities continue to access it in diverse ways.

At the other end of the spectrum, the local contexts in which Sabhapati lived and operated continued to change and evolve but never disappeared. In these contexts, however, Sabhapati's published works were mostly forgotten, while his identity as a great saint (Tam. *periya mahāṉ*) of a prominent *paramparā* continues to be remembered and revered. Examples of such contexts include the remnants of Konnur Meditation Hall (see Chapter 1; today called Sri Sabhapathy Lingeshwarar Koil) and Om Prakash Swamigal's own extant meditation hall and library in the Kandal village outside Udhagamandalam (Ooty), which also includes a primary school bearing his name. In the former case, part of the lack of further engagement with Sabhapati's publications may be due to thieves breaking into Sabhapathy Lingeshwarar Koil and stealing valuable property during land disputes following Aanandha Aanandha Swamigal's death in 1983 (see Chapter 1). In the latter case, Sabhapati Swami himself is for the most part not remembered by the custodians of Om Prakash Swamigal's meditation hall, although he was mentioned in Om Prakash Swamigal's biographical account published in the mid-twentieth century, a text that remains accessible and of which dozens of copies survive. In both these cases, Sabhapati's decline in prominence seems to coincide directly with the ascent of another yogi who could more effectively satisfy the global demand at that period with more direct recourse to prevailing discourses of the day. Swami Vivekananda's subsequent fame swept through south India in 1893 following his visit, and the first Ramakrishna Mission in Tamil Nadu was established in Madras in 1897.

The impact of these developments is more directly felt in the literature of Sabhapati's students, and seems to have been initially harmonious and compatible; an author who offered a dedication to Om Prakash Swamigal's biography signed his affiliation with the Ramakrishna Mission and lent his support to Om Prakash Swamigal's efforts. At the same time, however, the subordinating and eclipsing tendency continued in subsequent decades, and today most scholars of Hinduism are expected to know about the

Ramakrishna Mission, while Om Prakash's ashram has been mostly forgotten outside Tamil Nadu. The Dravidian language movement in the early twentieth century, with its emphasis on a return to "pure Tamil" (Tam. *centamiḻ*) as devoid as possible of Sanskrit, also would have rendered Sabhapati's heavily Sanskritized works outdated and archaic.

Despite these changes in the Tamil religious landscape, Sabhapati will likely continue to be remembered as one of the first "modern gurus" who, similar to some others both during and after his lifetime, such as Chidambaram Ramalinga Swamigal (1823–1874), created a Hindu consensus of sorts that united teachings from disparate Śaiva, Vaiṣṇava, and Śākta temple traditions. Such a trend continued in south India with later figures like Ramana Maharshi (1879–1950) and perhaps still continues at present with celebrity gurus like Sadhguru (Jagadish Vasudev, b. 1957). At the same time, no single figure since Sabhapati Swami has managed to both unite disparate local Hindu traditions in south India *and* generate such an enduring interest among global occultists and esoteric practitioners who continued to practice various aspects of Śivarājayoga, even if they did not always remember Sabhapati's name or where it came from. Sabhapati Swami's relative openness to manipulating and cancelling subtle physiology and his depictions of esoteric transfers of energy between teachers and students as expressed in his diagrams, as well as the sheer amount of technical Sanskrit terms he expected his students to internalize, also seems contrary to the popularizing trend of many modern gurus.

This book's findings at what I call the "mesolocal," or pan-South Asian, level, however, may very well add the most striking complexity to contemporary research on yoga. On account of the advent of railroads and printing technology, a method of Śivarājayoga that had been relegated to relatively obscure Tamil Vīraśaiva lineages of gurus prior to the nineteenth century exploded across India in a matter of decades, and in languages as diverse as Hindi, Bengali, Telugu, English, and many others. In other words, Sabhapati's system of Śivarājayoga, as cultivated and developed in south India, was at the forefront of a pan-Indian translation enterprise decades prior to subsequent modern yogis from the south like Tirumalai Krishnamacharya (1888–1989) and Seetharaman Sundaram (1901–1994).[3] It cannot be doubted, of course, that Sabhapati was also inspired and influenced by his journeys in Lahore and beyond, as well as by his interlocutors and supporters across north India as well as abroad. These interactions as well as the ways in which his literature was regionalized to fit various linguistic and local religious paradigms provide meaningful data that has the potential to vastly expand our understanding of how yoga was perceived in the colonial period as well as its subsequent developments post-Independence. If the past is any indication of the present, similar developments in the world of yoga may just be continuing to happen before our very eyes, that is, if we are willing to climb our trees and take a look.

Notes

1. Kurt Leland, *Rainbow Body: A History of the Western Chakra System from Blavatsky to Brennan* (Lake Worth, FL: Ibis Press, 2016).
2. For more on yoga and the question of authenticity see Keith Cantú, "'Don't Take Any Wooden Nickels': Western Esotericism, Yoga, and the Discourse of Authenticity," in *New Approaches to the Study of Esotericism*, ed. Egil Asprem and Julian Strube (Leiden: Brill, 2020), 109–26.
3. For Krishnamarcharya see Mark Singleton, *Yoga Body: The Origins of Modern Posture Practice* (New York: Oxford University Press, 2010), 175–210; David Gordon White, *The Yoga Sutra of Patanjali: A Biography* (Princeton, NJ: Princeton University Press, 2014), 197–223; and many others. For Sundaram see Singleton, *Yoga Body*, 125–29 and the doctoral dissertation of Magdalena Kraler.

APPENDIX 1

A Translation of T2 (in MCVTS)

Excerpt of T2 (English Translation)

Om, reverence to Shiva and Hari [*civahari*, < Skt. *śivahari*], and Śakti [*cakti*, < *śakti*].
An account of the blessed incarnation of the Yogi Guru of Gnosis [*kñāṉakuruyōki*, < *jñānaguruyogī*], Guru Father Rishi, Sabhapati Swami who is the author of this book on the Collected Instructions of the Scriptures composed by his student **Shiva Jnana Prakasha Yogishwara,** being one who has received the isolated state [*kaivalliyam*] from experience in the practice of all the instructions of this aforementioned guru swami.[1]

Sacred Song for the Sacred Avatar of Guru Father Rishi

The great Guru Father Rishi, having incarnated for much time by the favor of God, is one who has forced open the bond of illusion [*pācam*, < Skt. *pāśa*], seeking beast [*pacu*, < *paśu*] and lord [*pati*], uniting with the supreme [*paraṉ*, < *parama*].

He has received the favor of the Lord [*īcaṉ*, < *īśa*] and in that place is like a servant, even as one who says, "I submit humbly."

He has come close by taking commands, through the expressions of love [*nēcam*], singing poems of all the sacred places, together with songs for the Guru.

Making a cave for his dwelling, as a capable man in the dedication [*cātanai*, < *sādhanā*] to austerity, he is called the fervent devotee [*tācaṉ*, < *dāsa*], one who is strong in his service, and one who has received all experience [*aṉupavam*, < *anubhava*].

As one who has his dwelling in the gnosis of Brahman [*prammakñāṉam*, < *brahmajñāna*], he is one who is preeminent in his ripeness.

Listen directly, from his [own] mouth, to the one who was even the servant, disciple, and son of the godlike rishi Śivajñānabodha.

He today protects all the people on the earth, going to each country, and the people of these countries, bestowing with affection instruction that sets one on a straight path.

As the form of speech, he is creating and writing the experience of all practice [*carvacātaṉāṉupavam*, < *sarvasādhanānubhava*], protecting the illusory world that arises by the favor of the supreme Guru.

By means of your mercy, as speech you flow forth like a rain-shower, as does your dedication.

Crossing to the other shore in the gnosis of the compiled scriptures [*caṅkiravētañāṉam*, < *saṃgrahavedajñāna*], you are supreme among gurus, O powerful Guru Father Rishi.

Reverence to Brahman as the Guru.

[Song] by the Learned Student Thiruvenkitasamy Pillai of the Nilgiris

I have adorned his head, having worshiped his feet,
being the blossom lifted up as the golden awakening,[2]
the good awakening that Guru Father Rishi begins,
and the self-awakening that is lost when the bliss of Shiva strikes.
Be favorable after you cause these three awakenings.

[Song] by Ramalinga Swamigal, the Yogi Guru of Gnosis Appointed as the Meditation Hall Chief for Guru Father Rishi's Meditation Hall

Being omniscient, he has the fullness of knowledge,
the learned sage, praised as one who has compassion.
He who is adored as the supreme guru,
he who has cut off attachments,
and he who has salvific tapas,
the good Guru Father Rishi is he.

{3} The creator of this work *Compiled Instructions*, the Yogi Guru of Gnosis, Guru Father Rishi, Sabhapati Swami, was incarnated at the place of Natesamurthy Shivakami Amman Metalworks in Vedashreni within the southern part of India, in Tondayan Chakravartin's [Toṇṭayāṉ Cakkiravartti] city of Tondama [Toṇṭamā Nakaram], in the city of Chennai, to a father named Gurunatha Baktar [Kurunāta Pakttar], from an illustrious family of gurus who mark their foreheads, who worked in [*paṇi*] and was trained as one of the best restorers [*jīrṇōttāraṇam*, < Skt. *jīrnoddhara*] of divine temples, and to his wife named Punyavati [Puṇṇiyavati]. The directions of Gurunatha Baktar's guru Vedashreni Chidambara Swamigal [Vētacirēṇi Citampara Svāmikaḷ], author of *The Truth of Instruction* [*Upatēca Uṇmai*], were carried out by Gurunatha Baktar along with Kumbalinga Acharya of Mylapore [Tirumayilai Kumpaliṅka Ācāriyai] at the location of the auspicious Vedashreni. The year was 1828, the month of Markazhi [December–January], the lunar mansion of Thiruvathirai, at the time of a celestial great moment [*tivya mahāmukūrttam*, < Skt. *divya mahāmuhūrta*], on an auspicious day of Mars. At the time there were six planetary bodies in the Elevated Position [*uccastāṉam*, < Skt. *uccasthāna*], two planetary bodies in the Position of Speech [*vākkustāṉam*, < Skt. **vāksthāna*], and one planetary body in the Position of Happy Heat [Mpvl. *sukatapastāṉam*, < Skt. **sukhatapasthāna*].

In childhood he was renowned as being foremost in good virtue, devotion, benevolence to creatures, kindness to living beings, perception and intelligence, service to sadhus, charity, helpfulness to others, purity of speech, engagement in the Puranas and scriptures, the knowledge of six languages, pilgrimage, nonattachment toward all, and in every ascetic practice of dispassion. By age twenty he was fully competent in English, {4} had read the whole Bible, and had examined the truth of the Christian religion. Up to age twenty-five he had a great job. Afterward, quitting this and leaving for Rangoon, he investigated the truth of the Buddhist religion while carrying on a large business, through spiritual companionship [< Skt. *satsaṅga*] with exquisite Burmese monks and by using the Pali language. Realizing that the Buddhist religion, Hindu religion, and Vedānta are one and the same, he was disenchanted with this business and renounced it as illusory.

Leaving that business and returning to Chennai, he sustained himself by his ancestral property and special goods and, becoming the student of Vedashreni Chidambara Swami, the author of the guru-sayings called *The Truth of Instruction*, obtained through him the knowledge of the principles of all scriptures. He desired after this unity to understand the truth of Muhammad, and for this visited the tumulus [< Skt. *samādhi*] of Nagur Mira Sayappu Andavar [Nākūr Mīrā Cāyappu Āṇṭavar]. There, in spiritual company with the people of the Islamic religion, he learned the truths of Muhammad and the Quran. Again returning to the city of Chennai, he performed the worship of the Lord of the Dance as the Lord of the Universe in mental meditation, together with severe asceticism [*akōra tapam*, < Skt. *aghora tapas*]. After obtaining the knowledge of the Four Vedas, the Seven Scriptures, the Sixty-Four Arts, and the knowledge of all the Upanishads and the Gita, he considered the world's Christian religion, Buddhist religion, and Islamic religion and moreover these religions' entire mysteries, truths, discourses, rites, and exercises to be pieces of the Hindu religion. He therefore felt that evidently the Hindu religion is the father-religion of the world, and the Sanskrit language of the Hindu Vedas is the mother tongue of the world.

Up to his twenty-eighth year it was as follows: [He thought,] "I have been able to engage in the knowledge and examination of all scriptures, yet I have not obtained the gnosis of experience through this knowledge and examination. What will I do? If I do not even know what not beyond the range of sight [< Skt. *aparokṣa*], what is the use of this knowledge of what *is* beyond the range of sight [< Skt. *parokṣa*]?

Even though I have received analytical knowledge by means of Sāṃkhya's knowledge of what is beyond sight, and have obtained analytical knowledge through a guru on the knowledge of teaching, the knowledge of clarity, the knowledge of time, and the knowledge of dispassion, I have not obtained that gnosis through experience and ritual that is permanent knowledge, being the experience of what is not beyond sight. What will I do? I therefore desire to become liberated while alive [< Skt. *jīvanmukta*], as the highest gnosis of Brahman."

He was like someone whose reflection is afflicted and who is sorrowful, and like someone who has a singular concern alongside faith, devotion, and detachment. He was at the feet of him whose three impurities are perfected and, desiring liberation, he was praying with all his soul toward, and meditating upon, the Lord of All [Carvēcuvarar, < Skt. *sarveśvara*].

At the age of thirty, one day at midnight the Lord of All appeared in his dream and said: "O crest-jewel among devotees, since I have called you out as my messenger, I will give you the name Azhaitthat Kondamurtthy [*aḻaittāṭkoṇṭamūrtti*]. I honor your adherence to devotion [< Skt. *bhakti*]. {5} You, becoming free, will receive liberation [< Skt.

mukti] on the southern Kailāsa mountain called Agastyachala ["Agastya's Mountain"], through the discipline of an experienced guru. Go." Having said this, he whose sacred mouth blossomed with grace disappeared. [Sabhapati's] sleep being broken, he woke up. Forgetting himself and the world, and resting his mind upon Shiva, he felt that this had happened by the favor of Shiva, and composed a song of praise [called the "Song of Dedication in Praise" (Tam. *stottiyārppaṇappā*)] . . .

Having reached the fullness of gnosis through learning [< Skt. *vidyā*], gnosis through inqury [< Skt. *vicāraṇa*], and gnosis through experience while near Vedashreni Chidambara Swamigal, he was always in samādhi [< Skt. *samādhi* "communion," "composure"]. His vision of engaging the Lord in a dream was expressed to his mother Punyavathi as he was paying respects to her. That mother, being submerged in composure and the bliss of Brahman by means of the gnosis of Brahman, said: "O my son, from the day you were incarnated in my womb, you were highly fortunate to not want illusion [< Skt. *māyā*] to ensnare you. Today, receiving renunciation [< Skt. *saṃnyāsatva*], as one who is liberated by the gnosis of Brahman and as one who is the path to receiving liberation, your soul [*ātman*] is the same as my own soul, by virtue of becoming the gnosis of Brahman. Take your leave from me and go to your guru. We will see each other there."

Upon acknowledging that order, he reached Chidambara Swamigal at the midnight watch, and he solemnly put on red ocher clothes and a tied forelap [*laṅkōṭu*] after coming from the worship rites [*pūjai*, < Skt. *pūjā*]. After that he came to the sacred site of Vedashreni, which was his family clan's [*kulam*, < Skt. *kula*] and his own divine, sacred place [*teyvastalam*, < Skt. *divyasthala*]. In that sacred place's locale of Taṇṭapāṇīsvara [< Skt. Daṇḍapāṇīśvara, "The Lord in whose Hand is a Staff"], over three days, during both the day and night, he remained in meditation [*tiyāṉam*, < Skt. *dhyāna*]. On the third day at night, a splendor of radiance [*cōtippirakācam*, < Skt. *jyotiḥprakāśa*] appeared at the place of the phallic stone [*liṅkam*, < Skt. *liṅga*]. "We are called out for truth. What is this? Recite your composition of a "Garland as a Hymn of Mercy" at all sacred places, and afterward go to the place of the guru." Upon hearing that, he uttered the "Garland of Mercy" [Tam. *kirupāstippāmālai*] while full of bliss and ecstasy. {6} . . .

{7} After this he went to all the sacred places in the lands of the Toṇṭa, Cōḻa, Koṅku, Pāṇṭiyan, and Cēra, and here and there recited his five-stanza and ten-stanza "Garland Hymn of Mercy." While ascending Agastya's Mountain, which is the mountain of southern Kailasa situated between the Nilgiris and Mahendragiri, he desired to break through the jungle, a place frequented by animals that surrounded the mountain. Not knowing the path, and eating only fruits and edible roots, he didn't know where the guru was. After tottering with fatigue, he lay down at the base of a tree. At that time Shivajnana Bodha Rishi [Civakñāṉapō:taruṣi, < Skt. *śivajñānabodha ṛṣi*],[3] Agastya Rishi's righteous student on Agastya's Mountain and the twenty-fourth Guru Father [< Skt. *guru pitā*], was in a state of samādhi. He perceived the Lord of All as communicating the following in the vision of his gnosis: "Oh servant of mine, your devotee Azhaitthat Kondamurtthy has come. Make him to be your own student." After knowing everything, he called and sent out for his principal student Chitthanai, the Supreme Guru Yogi [Paramakuruyōkicit:ta:ṉai]. After he arrived and his fatigue was treated, he took him along to the place of the guru. After paying obeisance to that Shivajnanabodha Rishi, [Sabhapati] sung this "Servant's Hymn" [*aṭumai stuti*]. . . .

He expressed this hymn as a servant, and Shivajnana Bodha Rishi became his guru. Shivajnanabodha gave to his student the name "Yogi who is the Guru of Gnosis" [Ñānakuruyōki, < Skt. *jñānaguruyogī*]. He went on to spend twelve years with that guru.

While in a cave, and while eating bulbs, roots, and so on, he received all the instructions [*upatēcaṅkaḷ*, < Skt. *upadeśa*], experienced all the rites [*cātaṉaikaḷ*, < Skt. *sādhana*], and obtained every experience [*aṉupavam*, < Skt. *anubhava*]. He obtained the fullness of experience in mantra, concentration [*tāraṇā*, < Skt. *dhāraṇā*] of vigor [*vayam*, < Skt. *vayas*], and the yogas of devotion [*paktiyōkaṅkaḷ*, < Skt. *bhaktiyoga*]. He obtained the power [*citti*, < Skt. *siddhi*] and experience of all yogas by means of the binding [*pantaṉam*, < Skt. *bandhana*] of the exhalation [*rēcakam*, < Skt. *recaka*], inhalation [*pūrakam*, as Skt.], and retention [*kumpakam*, < Skt. *kumbhaka*], and by the arresting [*stampanam*, < Skt. *stambhana*], fixing [*stāpaṉam*, < Skt. *sthāpana*], and the six acts [*ṣaṭkiriyaikaḷ*, < Skt. *ṣaṭkriyā*] of the foremost yogas of the breath [*cuvācam*, < Skt. *śvāsa*] and vital channel [*vāci*, < Skt. *vāṃśi*], the life-breath [*pirāṇam*, < Skt. *prāṇa*], the drop [*vintu*, < Skt. *vindu*], the sound [*nātam*, < Skt. *nāda*], the syllable Om [*piraṇavam*, < Skt. *praṇava*], and the digit [*kalā* = Skt.]. He experienced a vision of all the principles [*tattuva taricaṉam*, < Skt. *tattvadarśana*], the divine natures of visible appearance, splendor, the womb, and power and energy [*kākṣi, mākṣi, yākṣi, kukṣi, citti cakti*]. Having refuted all of these through his guidance, [his] isolated nondual self was united to Brahman by the experience of the steadfast communion with Brahman [*pirammaniṣaṭai camātiyaṉupavam*, Skt. *brahmaniṣṭhā samādhyanubhava*], which is the Yoga of Kings for Shiva as Brahman [*civapiramma rājayōka*]. While being in the most excellent and {8} fully developed, unwavering, and superior samādhi, he said, "I am neither the gnosis of thinking nor the gnosis of happiness. I possess every nature and am Brahman itself." One day his guru, Shivajnana Bodha Rishi, was remaining in his unwavering samadhi [*nirvikalpa camāti*, < Skt. *nirvikalpa samādhi*] while facing outward toward the door of his cave. While he was sitting on the banks of the Thamirabarani River [Tāmpiraparaṇi Nati], his first student, Paramaguruyogi Siddhijnani [Paramakuruyōki Cittikñāṉi], and his second student, Jnanaguruyogi Sujnani [Kñāṉakuruyōki Cukñāṉi], were remaining opposite to him, and he was facing these two people. His command was as follows: "Oh students and sons, this friend dwelling on our mountain in the wilderness in a cave has understood all ascetic practice [*tapam*, < Skt. *tapas*]. After receiving the grace of the Lord, the grace of every energy [*cakti*, < Skt. *śakti*], and the favorable glance of the guru, he has obtained every energy, power, and divine nature. We have brought him to liberation as a person who has gnosis of Brahman and who is liberated while alive.

The Lord by his benevolence is protecting the world, and from the day this person came near to us his dharma has been attaining to these things—he is one of us. They who are like us are as mahatmas, and we therefore wish to protect their souls through compassion [*kāruṇya* = Skt.] for the sentient beings of the world. As we attain we wish to become a guide for them to attain. It is therefore our duty out of this supreme desire [*parāmārttīkam*, < Skt. *paramārthika*] to assume the forms of gurus to help others [*parōpakāram*, < Skt. *paropakāra*]. For 438 years I, being seated majestically as the disciple of Agastya who is the Lord of the Great Rishis [Akastiya Mahārṣīśvara], have generated compassion in my heart for sentient beings, compassion to help others, for the protection of every soul, and the protection of the soul of the universe.

You, becoming a Guru Yogi of Gnosis, have obtained from me the fullness of all inquiry and practical experience [*cātaṉāṉupavam*, < Skt. *sādhanānubhava*], and you have obtained the production of new sacred writings [*cāstiraṅkaḷ*, < Skt. *śāstra*] and sacred writings yet to be carried out. In this manner it has all been like something you have experienced, but in what manner have you obtained it? You obtained all this experience even during your interactions [*viyavahāram*, < Skt. *vyavahāra*], from your horoscope [*ārūṭam*, < Skt. *ārūḍha*], ordinary life [*cahajam*, < Skt. *sahaja*], journeying [*cañcāram*, < Skt.

saṃcāra], conceptualizing, and so on, and while you were always in a state of samādhi free from conceptuality, or in the samādhi of the experience of your own Brahman. Count me, then, as someone worthy to praise you. It is you who are competent to express the expression of Agastya who is the Lord of the Great Rishis, and you are "Isanazhaitthatkondanar" [Īcaṉaḻaittāṭkoṇṭaṉar], the sign of Invoking the Protector of the Soul of the Universe. You know six languages. I command you therefore to complete this work of helping others. However, you must not reveal our utmost secrets, the foremost among them being alchemy [*vātam*, < Skt. *vāda*], mercury [*kavuṉam*], medical arts [*kalpam*, < Skt. *kalpa*], entering into other bodies [*parakāyappiravēcam*, < Skt. *parakāyapraveśa*], the magical ointment [*añcaṉam*, < Skt. *añjana*], powers [*sitti*, < Skt. *siddhi*], energy [*cakti*, < Skt. *śakti*], theurgy [*mūrttikaram*, < Skt. *_mūrtikara_],[4] increasing the life force [*āyurvirutti*, < Skt. *āyurvṛddhi*], the power of the eight acts [*aṣṭakkiriyācitti*], and the eight powers [*aṣṭacitti*], to the people of the world. Instead, [you should reveal] the forms of teaching on exercises [*aṉupavaṅkaḷ*, < Skt. *anubhava*] of devotion [*pakti*, < Skt. *bhakti*], meditation [*tiyāṉam*, < Skt. *dhyāna*], gnosis [*ñāṉam*, < Skt. *jñāna*], and practice [*cātaṉam*, < Skt. *sādhana*], which are for the benefit of the soul, for reaching the desires of now and the hereafter, and for desirelessness. After making a new sacred text with a sequence of instructions [*upatēcakkiramam*, < Skt. *upadeśakrama*] and a path of initiation [*tīkṣāmārkkam*, < Skt. *dīkṣāmārga*], and displaying every inquiry, ritual, and all exercises in the form of pictures, you should send it to be printed. Worship [*pūjai*, < Skt. *pūjā*] is to be performed in the same way by people of every caste [*carvavarṇastarkaḷ*, < Skt. *_sarvavarṇastha_]. It is your duty to go and assist the people in this way and then return to me. {9} However, if there is arguing, then you must not do a given work, because people always receive curses out of ignorance. In such a way may everything come to pass for your growth and let the earth be fruitful." This Yogi who is the Guru of Gnosis, Sabhapati Swami, then left that hermitage and visited the Malayali, Tamil, Telugu, Kannada, Marathi, Gujarati, Hindustani, Bengali, Nepali, Punjabi, Rajputhani, Kashmiri, Sindhi, Multani, and Himachali lands. He composed stanzas of praise [*patikam*, < Skt. *padika* = *pada*] about every sacred site and brought forth his "Kirupā Stauttiyamālai" after obtaining sight of the deity at sacred sites [*stalataricaṉaṅkaḷ*, < Skt. *sthaladarśana*], bathing in rivers [*natisṉāṉam*, < Skt. *nadisnāna*], and going on pilgrimage to sacred sites [*stalatīrttayāttirai*, < Skt. *sthalatīrthayātra*] in various places.

In each respective country and language, and also in the English language, he expressed the wisdom of the sacred scriptures [*cāstirapōtaṉai*, < Skt. *_śāstrabodhana_] on the nature of reality [*tattuvam*, < Skt. *tattva*] in the form of lectures [*piracaṅkaṅkaḷ*, < Skt. *prasaṅga*] and in images about the nature of reality [*tattuvapaṭaṅkaḷ*, < Skt. *tattva* + Tam. *paṭam*, "picture"].

He revealed the experiences of practicing the rites [*cātaṉāppiyācāṉupavaṅkaḷ*, < Skt. *_sādhanābhyāsānubhava_] of the steadfast composure in the gnosis of Brahman [*pirammaññāṉaniṣṭai camāti*, < Skt. *_brahmajñānaniṣṭhāsamādhi_] by means of print, primarily in the languages of Sanskrit, Urdu, Hindustani, Bengali, Telugu, Marathi, Dravidian Tamil, and English, as well as in images that depict the experience of these rites, which include actions, inquiries, and acts of worship [*kiriyāṉucantāṉapūjaikaḷ*, < Skt. *_kriyānusaṃdhānapūjā_] toward all the gods and goddesses [*carvatēvatātēvikaḷ*, < Skt. *sarvadevatādevī*], and for the performance of daily ceremonies [*nittiyakarmāṉuṣṭāṉaṅkaḷ*, < Skt. *_nityakarmānuṣṭhāna_] by means of a sequence of instructions [*upatēcakkiramam*, < Skt. *upadeśakrama*]. This knowledge about the natures of all things [*carvatattuvañāṉaṅkaḷ*, < Skt. *_sarvatattvajñāna_], devotion [*pakti*, < Skt. *bhakti*], yoga [*yōkam*], and gnoses [*ñāṉaṅkaḷ*, < Skt. *jñāna*] are to be engaged in [*aṉukkirahittu*, < Skt. *anugrahīta*] by people of any of the four castes [**catur varṇastarkaḷ*, < Skt. **caturvarṇasthā*] as well as by both men and women. He [Sabhapati] established 464 meditation societies [*tiyāṉa capaikaḷ*, < Skt. *dhyāna sabhā*] in various places of India [*hintutēcam*] for his students to carry out the practice of the rites.

He afterward met with his childhood friend, the composer of the *Tiruvaruṭpā*, the gracious [Chidambaram] Ramalinga Swami [Irāmaliṅka Svāmi], full of ascetic worship, in Vadalur [Vaṭalūr].

After again returning to the northern part [of India] and departing for the northern side of the Himalayas [Himāñcal], he bathed in Manasarovar, that body of water which is the source of the Indus River and the Brahmaputra River. With the help of three rishis he obtained a vision of the holy Kailasa. He set forth the "Garland of the Praise of Mercy" [*kirupāstauttiyamālā*, < Skt. *kṛpāstutyamālā*] in 108 verses [*slōkam*, < Skt. *śloka*] in the form of an homage [*arccaṉārūpam*, < Skt. *arcan*] in Sanskrit terminology [*paripāṣai*, < Skt. *paribhāṣā*] to the Lord of Kailasa [Kailācēsvarar, < Skt. Kailāśeśvara] both "with shape" [*cākāram*, < Skt. *sākāra*] and as "shapeless" [*nirākāram* = Skt.]. . . . {10}

After paying respects to these three rishis and standing before them, they asked, "Oh Guru Yogi of Gnosis! What do you want?"

He said, "I don't want anything—I only want the liberation of unity [*aikya mukti* = Skt.]."

Praising him as free from desire [*niṣkāmmiyam*, < Skt. *niṣkāmya*], they said, "You have been elevated by your guru into the liberation of unity. You have been elevated as a "Guru Father Rishi" [Kurupitā Ruṣī] by those of your hermitage [*ācīrmam*, < Skt. *āśrama*] who are those Beloved by the Guru." After speaking, they vanished as they entered the sky [*kaka:ṉam*, < Skt. *gagana*].

He afterward went into the southern region of the Himalayas, specifically to catch sight of places and to bathe in rivers at Pasupatinath, Kedarnath, Bhadrinath, Jwalamukhi, Triloknath, Bhutanath, the source of the Ganges, the source of the Yamuna, Amarnath, and Manikaran. While he was in Kashmir his guru Shivajnana Bodha Rishi was at Agastya's Hermitage, and Agastya who is the Lord of the Great Rishis was going to come to his hermitage, as he does once in every fifty years, to grant the Beloved Students of the Guru a brief period to have a vision of him. The Guru Yogi of Gnosis [Sabhapati Swami] realized this by means of his sequence of initiation [*tīkṣākiramam*, < Skt. *dīkṣākrama*] into the sight of the gnosis of Brahman [*pirammañāṉa tiruṣṭi*, < Skt. *brahmajñānadṛṣṭi*], in his formulated sight of gnosis, and through the sight of gnosis. Both merged with each other, and he perceived the connection. Agastya Rishi came within his vision and said, "You must come and join us at our hermitage." Bewildered by this command [*ākñā*, < Skt. *ājñā*], he came from his place to the three banks [along the Ganges] of Rishikesh, Haridwar, and then Vindhyachal. After coming to Vedashreni via Kishkindha and Srisailam, he worshiped with a poem of praise [for Vedashreni]. . . . {11} Afterward, arriving in Chidambaram, he expressed a song of praise. . . .

After that, he visited Thirukkadaiyur, Tirupperunturai, Rameswaram, Madurai, and Courtallam and then came to the mountain called "Agastya's Mountain," which is his guru's hermitage and the Kailāsa of the South. Having worshiped his teacher's feet, he composed the "Poem of Keeping the Teacher's Command" ["Kurākñaparipālaṉappā"]. . . .

In this way he was with [his] teacher in the composure that is free from conception in the year 1880 on the day of the full moon in the asterism of Chaitra [April–May, i.e., Chitra Pournami], when the planets and lunar nodes, the polestar, and the houses were in their highest positions. Then the most auspicious Agastya who is the Lord of the Great Rishis had entered his soul, filled with Brahman, in his pure and formulated body [*cuttakalpa carīram*, < Skt. **śuddhakalpaśarīra*]. He understood in his interior vision at the time of his coming that the Gnostics [Ñāṉikaḷ, < Skt. *jñānin*], the Hearers [Ruṣikaḷ, < Skt. *ṛṣi*], the Accomplished Ones [Cittarkaḷ, < Skt. *siddha*], and the Yoked Ones [Yōkikaḷ, < Skt. *yogin*] had gathered together on Agastya's Mountain. They came by means of flight [lit. "entering the sky"] and in many other ways from the ascetic hermitages of the eleven mountain ranges, namely the Himalayas [Himāñcalam], Kush Mountain [Kuṣācalam], Mount Abu [Apā:calam], Vindhya Mountain [Vintācalam], Kishkindha Mountain [Kiṣkintācalam], the Holy Kailasa Mountain [Śrī Kailācam], Bala Mountain [Pā:lācalam], Udhaga Mountain [Utakācalam] and Velliangiri [Veḷḷiyaṅ:ri] in the Nilgiris [Nīlakiri], Mahendragiri, and Kandy Mountain of the mountains on Lanka. These mahatmas of asceticism had been desiring a vision of Agastya, and the rest of the people of the world were also deprived of a vision.

In the year 1880, on the day of the full moon in the asterism of Chitra, at the time of sunrise, just as with [Sabhapati's] vision before his very eyes of Shiva on holy Kailasa, the twenty-four mahatmas who are the Guru's Beloved, with their students encircling them at their side and performing the sixteen acts of reverence [*cōṭacōpacāram*, < Skt. *ṣoḍaśopacāra*], came within and beneath him. They were continually reciting praises and the collections of the Vedas, and their students were making the sounds of the conch and the lion's roar [*ciṅkunātañcaṅkunātam*, < Skt. **siṃhanādaśaṅkhanāda*]. The Goddesses of Power [*caktitēvikaḷ*, < Skt. *śaktidevī*] were waving their chowries [*kṣamaram*, < Skt. *chāmara*] and fans [*viciri*, possibly < Skt. √*vij*] to the great rishi Agastya, the undivided Whirler of the Teacher's Wheel [*kurucakkiravartti*, < Skt. **gurucakravartin*], accompanied by his retinue [*āravāram*, < Skt. *ārava*], with his threefold mark [*tiripuṇṭaram*, < Skt. *tripuṇḍra*] and his mark on the lower neck [*kantatilakam*, < Skt. **skandhatilaka*]. He was ornamented by a necklace of rudraksha seeds [*ruttirākṣaciramālā*, < Skt. *rudrākṣamālā*], a collar [*kaṇḍamālā*, < Skt. *kaṇṭhamālā*], an armlet [*pujamālā*, < Skt. *bhujamālā*], and a bracelet [*kaṅkaṇamālā* = *Skt.], {12} and was wearing red ocher and golden robes, a girdle of ascetics, and had a crown of dreadlocks [*jaṭāmakuṭam*, < Skt. *jaṭāmakuṭa* or *jaṭāmukuṭa*] with matted hair [*kapirṇam*, possibly < Skt. *kapardin*] falling upon his feet. He was holding in his hands a wand [*cukkumāntaṭi*], a yogic staff [*yōkataṇṭu*, < Skt. *yogadaṇḍa*], a water vessel [*kamaṇṭalam*, < Skt. *kamaṇḍalu*], a bag [*jōlṇā*, < Hi. and Bng. *jholā*, likely < Skt. *jyaulikā*], and a pouch filled with the ashes of cow dung [*viputicañci*, < Skt. **vibhūticañca*], and he was wearing a yoga strap [*yōkappaṭṭai*, < Skt. *yogapaṭṭa*]. He came to the entryway of his cave, and then was at the base of the tree of sixteen qualities [*cōṭcakalāviruk̩ṣam*, < Skt. *ṣoḍaśakalāvṛkṣa*] that he himself had created, which is his same size, and which comprises sixteen kinds of branches, leaves, blossoms, and fruits. He was lying on a tiger skin [*viyākirācaṉam*, < Skt. *vyāghrāsana*], a dark sheet [*kiruṣṇācaṉam*, < Skt. *kṛṣṇāsana*], a thick blanket of jewels [*rattiṉajamakkāḷācaṉam*, < Skt. *ratna* + a compound of Hi. *jama* + Skt. *kālāsana*], a skin of musk deer [*kastūri mirukācaṉam*, < Skt. **kastūrimṛgāsana*], a mat made from tree bark [*mara uriyāl tiṇṭu*], and a sheet made from golden fabric [*pītāmparattāl mettai*, < Skt. *pītāmbara* + Tam. *mettai*]. He then rose and sat upon the lion throne [*cimahācaṉam*, < Skt. *siṃhāsana*] of the Whirler of the Teacher's Wheel.

After the first day of this vision was finished, the students who are the Beloved of the Guru of his hermitage discussed welfare and prosperity, and after discussing their welfare with the mahatmas of the [above] hermitages, a blessing was given to everyone who was there. Then they who reside at his hermitage came and the mahatmas composed a hymn of praise. At that time this Guru Father Rishi also made a hymn of praise [called "A Song of Praise at the Time of Seeing Agastya, by Guru Father Rishi" (Tam. *kurupitāruṣiyāl akastiyar taricaṉakālastauttiyam*)] . . .

On the second day, everyone's doubts concerning all the sacred scriptures were removed. On the third day, the benefit of new instruction was conferred upon all. On the fourth day the Wish-Granting Cow [*kāmatēṉu*, < Skt. *kāmadhenu*], all the Goddesses of Power, and the enjoyment of the offering to the guru [*kuruppiracātam*, < Skt. *guruprasāda*], which is the consumption of the nectar of the immortality of the gods, were graciously granted to his students and to the mahatmas who had come. On the fifth day he entered the cave and, while retaining his own body [*carīram*, < Skt. *śarīra*], became the undivided soul of the Infinite Spirit [*akaṇṭātma pirammam*, < Skt. **akhaṇḍātmabrahma*]. All the mahatmas took their leave from the {13} Guru's Beloved Ones, and each of them returned to their respective hermitage.

One day at an auspicious time this Guru Yogi of Gnosis, after having his vision of Agastya, was in the company of his guru and twenty-four of the Guru's Beloved Ones of this hermitage. He was atop the mountain where there is a confluence of the Thamirabirani River, the Siddhi River, and the Amrita River. Having reached this triple-braided confluence of liberation [*mukti tirivēṇi caṅkam*, < Skt. *mukti triveṇī saṅga*], he bathed there. After concluding his mantra recitation [*jepam*, < Skt. *japa*] and austerities [*tapam*, < Skt. *tapas*], exercising his devotion [*niṣṭai*, < Skt. *niṣṭhā*], and begging, they all agreed that the title of the sacred name "Guru Father Rishi" [Kurupitāruṣi] should be bestowed upon this Guru Yogi of Gnosis.

In this manner he dwelt for a period of two years in the hermitage's cave, and afterward at his guru's command again set out for the Nilgiris for a few days before descending and embarking on a pilgrimage to all the sacred sites in the northern regions. He showed favor there to the people of all places, and printed his sacred writings in various languages. He then approached the city of Chennai and came to Holy Konnur in Villivakkam. In ancient times [here was] established a pilgrimage bathing site for Agastya and a temple for Agastya at a forest of bael trees [*vilvavaṉam*, < Skt. *bilvavana*] where Agastya slew the asuras Vatapi and Ilvala. [Sabhapati] established a large pool, called the Offering Pool [Yākakuṇṭam, < Skt. *yajñakuṇḍa*], and made an offering [*yākam*, < Skt. *yajña*] upon coming to Holy Konnur. He approached the large pool, and was in his gnostic vision of the past, present, and future [*tirikāla ñāṉatiruṣṭi*, < Skt. *trikālajñānadṛṣṭi*] while on the ground in steadfast devotion. By means of his steadfast devotion he also established a hermitage and meditation hall [*maṭālayam*, < Skt. **maṭhālaya*] after a short time. He dwelt there in that place and made offerings at the great lake called the Offering Pool. On the ground at the north side of this Pool of Offering was where the Lord of All [Carvēsvara, < Skt. Sarveśvara] had given a vision of his dance [*naṭaṉam*, < Skt. *naṭana*] of five activities [*pañcakiruttiyam*, < Skt. *pañcakṛtya*] to Agastya, and where his disciples had gone to perform worship rites to 1,008 lingas and 108 shaligrams.

In Konnur, which arose as Great Vishnu [Mahāviṣṇu] gave his disk to the Sun [Sūryaṉ], [Sabhapati] established this Guru Father Rishi Meditation Hall for Agastya. He facilitated the establishment of 1,008 lingas and the establishment of 108 shaligrams there, and then went to Sri Kashi [Varanasi] and resolved to perform the same rites at the Temple of the Lord of All and the Lady of All [Carvēsvari, < Skt. Sarveśvarī], where the Lord of All has made an established custom of performing the dance of his five activities on every full moon [*paurṇimai*, < Skt. *pūrṇimā*]. He created an instructive scripture, recollected teaching, and sacred writing in the Dravidian language of Tamil, and in it he showed the performance of acts, the gnosis of yoga, and all kinds of austerities, practices of the rites, exercises, and knowledge of all the principles of being, and all this through forty diagrams on the principles of being and through diagrams on meditation [*tiyāṉapaṭaṅkaḷ*]. This was given the name *Collected Instructions of the Vedas: Every Discourse and Ritual Exercise* [*carva vicāraṇā cātaṉāṉupava caṅkiraha vētōpatēcam*, < Skt. *sarva vicāraṇā sādhanānubhava saṅgraha vedopadeśa*] and published by the Guru's Beloved Ones who stayed at his hermitage, and all those mahatmas, joining together, gave him the title "Guru of Indivisible Gnosis who is the Whirler of the Wheel" [*akaṇṭa kñāṉakuru cakkiravartti*, < Skt. *akhaṇḍa jñānaguru cakravartī*].

He then resolved to create the meditation hall called Guru Father Rishi's Meditation Hall, a pilgrims' bathing site [*tirttam*, < Skt. *tīrtha*] for an abode of the gods, for an abode of the Lord of All, and a pilgrims' bathing site for giving liberation. At the foundation of the place was to be five phallic stones, namely the Phallic Stone that has the Nature of Brahman [Birammapā:valiṅkam, < Skt. Brahmabhāvaliṅga], the Phallic Stone that has the Nature of the Lord of All [Carvēsvarapā:valiṅkam, < Skt. Sarveśvarabhāvaliṅga], {14} the Phallic Stone that has the Nature of the Lady of All [Carvēsvaripā:valiṅkam, < Skt. Sarveśvarībhāvaliṅga], the Phallic Stone that has the Nature of the Guru [Kurupā:valiṅkam, < Skt. Gurubhāvaliṅga], and the Phallic Stone that has the Nature of Vishnu [Viṣṇupā:valiṅkam, < Skt. Viṣṇubhāvaliṅga]. The mahatma rishis in his guru hermitages established halls in towns or mountains for the Lord of All, and gave sacred names to these sacred sites, such as the Quinary Celestial Phallic Stone that is the Highest Embodiment of the Radiance of the Universe as the Five Deities, the Five Faces in the Form of One, who is the Lord of the Dance of the Five Activities; and for the Highest Goddess who is the Radiance of the Universe, being the Quinary Goddess with the Five Faces in the Form of One, who is the Lady of the Dance of the Five Activities. . . .

He spent a little time in each place also, including this Holy Konnur Meditation Hall and Hermitage of Austerities, the Nilgiri Hermitage of Austerities, and the Hermitage of Austerities of the mountain and cave on Mount Agastya, realizing the steadfast devotion of experiencing the nonconceptual composure of the gnosis of Brahman. In the various lands of this India [Tam. *hintudēcam*] he has been given the following names and titles by his students: (1) Guru of the Gnosis of the Universe [Jakatñāṉakuru, < Skt. Jagatjñānaguru], (2) Guru of the Meditation for Liberation [Muktitiyāṉakuru, < Skt. Muktidhyānaguru], (3) Composer of the Revelation of Practices for the Gnosis of Devotion [Paktiñāṉa Cātaṉai Curutikarttā, < Skt. Bhaktijñāna Sādhanā Śrutikartā], and (4) The Guru who has Descended for the Elevation of Religion [Matōttāraṇa Avutārakuru, < Skt. Matoddhāraṇāvatāraguru]. He obtained great renown as he received these sacred names.

Excerpt of T2 (Original Tamil)

ஓம் சிவஹரி சக்தி பிரம்மணேநம:

இந்த சாஸ்திரோபதேச சங்கிரஹ வேதசாஸ்திர கர்த்தாவாகிய
க்ஞானகுருயோகி, குருபிதாருஷி சபாபதி சுவாமிகளது
திரு அவுதார சரித்திரம்.
இஃதை ஷை குருசுவாமிகளின் சர்வோபதேச சாதனானுபவ
கைவல்லியம்பெற்ற
சிவக்ஞானப்பிரகாசயோகீஸ்வர
சிஷ்யராலியற்றியது.

குருபிதாருஷி திருவவுதாரத்திருப்பா.

ஈசனருளாலவதரித்தனனீடிற்குருபிதாருஷிமஹான்,
பாசத்தைநீக்கிதன்பசுபதியைநாடிப்பரனைக்கூடி
ஈசனருள்பெற்றவரீங்கடுமைக்கொள்ளயடியேனாகி,
நேசத்தோடாக்ஞாபித்தவாறேநேர்ந்துஸ்தலமெலாம்பாடி,
வீசன்நியமித்தகுருபாதஞ்சேர்ந்திசைந்தவருடன்றான்,
வாசங்குஹையிற்செய்துவல்லவனாய்த்தபச்சாதனையிற்
றாசனெனுமடுமையாற்றான்னனுபவமெலாம்பெற்றங்கு
வாசமாய்ப்ரம்மக்ஞானததிலிருக்கும்வரிஷ்ட்டபக்குவத்தி
லிசன்நிகர்சிவக்ஞானபோதருஷியிவர்முகம்நோக்கிகேளுந்,
தாசசிஷ்யபுத்திரனே தரணியிலுள்ளாரைகாக்கநீரின்றே.
தேசங்கட்டோருஞ்சென்றுதேசங்களுளாரியாவர்க்கும்நீர்,
நேசம்வைத்துபோரதித்துபதேசித்துநேரேயாவருமறிந்துய்ய,
{3} வாசகரூபமாய்ச்சர்வசாதனானுபவம்வறைந்தச்சிட்டிந்து,
பாசவுலகைக்காக்குகவென்றுபரமகுருயருளினதேற்று,
வாசகமாய்கிருபையாற்பொழிந்தனர்மாரிபோற்சாதனையாவும்
வரைகடந்தசங்கிரவேதஞானமும்வல்லகுருபிதாருஷிகுருபரனே.
குருப்பிரம்மணேநம:

நீலகிரி திருவேங்கிடசாமி பிள்ளை வித்வசிஷ்யரால்

தற் போத மீடழிய தாக்குஞ் சிவானந்த
நற் போத மாக்குங் குருபிதாரிஷி-தூக்குமலர்
பொற் போத மாகுமடி போற்றி சிரசணிந்தேன்
சிற் போத மாக்கியருள் செய்.

குருபிதாருஷியின் மடத்திற்கு மடாதிபதியாய் நியமிக்கப்பட்ட ஞானகுருயோகி,
இராமலிங்கசுவாமிகளால்

முற்றுமுணர்ந்தமூழுஞானியாகுவான்
கற்றவரேத்துங்கருணையாளனாகுவான்
பற்றற்றவர்பரவும்பரமகுருவாகுவான்
நற்றவமுடையான்நற்குருபிதாருஷியே.

இந்துதேச தட்சண காண்டத்தில், தொண்டயான் சக்கிரவர்த்தியின் தொண்டமா நகரத்தில், சென்னைபுரியில், தனத்தில், தேவாலய ஜீர்ணோத்தாரண பணியில், கல்வியில், சிரேஷ்டராய் விளங்கிய குருகுல திலகராகிய குருநாத பக்த்தர்ராம் பதி:க்கும், புண்ணியவதி என்னும் சதி:க்கும் குருநாத பக்த்தரால் திருவேத சிரேணி க்ஷேத்திரத்திற்காக, திருமயிலை கும்பலிங்க ஆசாரியைக் கொண்டு, குருநாத பக்த்தரின் குருவாகிய (உபதேசவுண்மை) சாஸ்த்திரகர்த்தா வேதசிரேணி சிதம்பர ஸ்வாமிகளின் ஆக்ஞாபிரகாரம். நடேசமூர்த்தி சிவகாமியம்மன் வார்ப்படம் வேதஸ்ரேணியில் செய்தருளிய ஆறுக்கிரகம் உச்சஸ்தானத்தில், இரண்டு கிரகம் வாக்குஸ்தானத்தில், ஒரு கிரகம் சுகதபஸ்தானத்திலுள்ள காலமாகிய 1828 வருஷம் மார்கழி மாதம் திருவாதிரை நட்சத்திர திவ்ய மஹாமுகூர்த்தகால மங்கள் சுபதினத்தில் இந்த சங்கரகவேதோபதேச, சாஸ்திர கர்த்தாவாகிய ஞானகுருயோகி குருபிதாருஷி சபாபதி சுவாமிகள் திருவவதாரஞ் செய்தனர்.

இவர் பாலபக்குவத்திலேயே, சத்குணத்தில், பக்தியில், பூததயாளத்தில், ஜீவகாருண்யத்தில் புத்திகோசரத்தில், சாதுசேவையில், தர்மகுணத்தில், பரோபகாரத்தில் சுத்தமான வாக்குக் கிரியையில், சாஸ்திரபுராண சிரவணத்தில்

ஆறு பாஷா வித்தையில், யாத்திரையில், சர்வவிராகத்தில், சர்வதபோவைராக்கிய சாதனையில், மகா சிரேஷ்டராய் விளங்காநின்று (20) வயதுக்குள் இங்கிலிஷில் {4} புரோபசராய், பைபில் முழுதும் வாசித்து கிருஸ்துமதவுண்மை ஆராய்ந்தும் (25) வயது வரையிலும் பெரிய உத்தியோகத்திலிருந்தும். பின்பு அதை விட்டு விட்டு ரங்கோனுக்கும் போய் பாரியவர்த்தகஞ்செய் துக்கொண்டும் பவுத்தமத உண்மையை யரிய பர்மாதேச பொங்கிகள் சத்சங்கத்தால் பாலிபாஷையினால் ஆராய்ந்து பவுத்தமதமும் இந்துமத வேதாந்தமும் ஒன்றெனத்தெரிந்துக்கொண்டும், இந்த வர்தகம் மாயையில் விரத்திசெய்கின்றதென்று வெருத்து. அவ்வர்த்தகத்தை நீக்கி சென்னைபுரிக்கு வந்து தன் பிதுரார்ஜித விசேஷ சொத்தால் ஜீவித்துக் கொண்டும் தன் குருவாகிய உபதேசவுண்மை சாஸ்திர கர்த்தாவேதஸ் சிரேணி சிதம்பர ஸ்வாமிகளுக்கு சிஷ்யராய் அவரிடம் சர்வ சாஸ்திர ததுவகிஞானமடைந்து அவர் ஐக்கியமான பிறகு மகமத் உண்மையை அறியவேண்துமென்று நாகூர் மீரா சாயப்பு ஆண்டவர் சமாதிக்குச்சென்று அங்கு மகுமத் மதஸ்தான்களோடு சத்சங்கம் செய்து மகமத் குரான் உண்மைகளை அறிந்து பின்னும் சென்னை புரிக்கு வந்து சர்வேஸ்வரராகிய நடேசர் உபாசனை மானசீக தியானத்தில் அகோர தபம் செய்துகொண்டும், சதுர்வேத, ஷட் சாஸ்திர 64 கலைக்கிஞான சர்வ உபநிஷதம் கீதைகளின் கிஞானமடைந்து, இந்த உலகத்தின் கிருஸ்த்துமதம் பவுத்த மதம், மகமத் மதங்களாகிய இந்த மதங்களுக்கு மேலாக சகல ரஹஸ்யங்களையும், உண்மைகளையும் விசாரணைகளையும் சாதனைகளையும் அனுபவங்களையும் உடையது இந்த இந்துமதம் ஆகையால் இந்துமதம் ஜெகத் பிதா மதமாயும் இந்துவேத சமுஸ்கிருத பாஷை ஜெகத் மாதா பாஷையாயும் விளங்குகின்றதென்று உணர்ந்தனர்.

இந்த தனது (28-வது) வயது வரையிலும் சர்வ சாஸ்திர விசாரணை கிஞானத்தில் வல்லனாயினேனே யன்றி அந்தந்த விசாரணைக்கியானங்களுக்குரிய அனுபவக்கிஞானம் அடைந்திலேனே, என் செய்வேன் அபரோக்ஷக்கிஞானியானவனல்லேனே என்ன பிரயோஜனம் இந்த பரோக்ஷக்ஞானம். நான் அடைந்த விசாரணக்கிஞானமாகிய சாங்கிய பரோக்ஷக்கிஞானத்தால் குருவிநிடம் விசாரணைக்கியானம் கிரஹிதக்யானம், தெளிவுக்கியானம், யுகக்கியானம் நிஷ்சமிஸ்சியக்கியானம் யடைந்தேனேயன்றி அனுபவ அபரோக்ஷ ஸ்திரக்கியானமாகிய சாதனா அனுபவ கிஞானம் யடைந்திலேனே என் செய்வேன் எவ்வண்ணமுசுப்பிரம்மக்கியானியாய் ஜீவன் முக்தன் ஆகவேண்டுமென்றும் வியாகூல விசார விசனத்தோடும் கவலை யேக்கத்தோடும் சிரத்தா பச்தி வைராக்கியத்தோடும் இருவினயொப்பு, மூம்மல பரிபாகசத்தினி பாதமும்: மூம்க்ஷுத்வபக்குலத்தோடும், தன் யாத்மார்ந்த சர்வஸ்வரரை ப்ராத்தனை செய்துத் தியானித்துக்கொண்டிருக்கும், தன் (30-வது வயதாகிய ஓர் தின் இராத்திரி உச்சிகாலத்தில் தன் சொற்பனத்தில் சர்வேசுவரர் தோன்றி ஒ பக்த சிரோன்மணியே உன்னை யழைத்தாட்கொள்ள வந்தபடியால் உனக்கு (யழைத்தாட்கொண்டமூர்த்தி) என்னும் நாமமிட்டேன், உன் பத்திக் {5} கிரக்கமுள்ளேன், நீ முக்தனாகி முக்திபெற அகஸ்தியாசல தக்ஷணகைலாஸ பர்வதத்தில் உனக்கனுபவ குருவை நியமித்தேனவரிடஞ் செல்லெனத் திருவாய் மலர்ந்தருளி மறைந்தனர் அப்பொழுதே சொற்பனாவஸ்தைபோய் ஜாக்கிராவஸ்தையடைந்து சாவப்ரக. ஹையற்று தன்னையும் உலகத்தையும் மறந்து தன் சித்ததைச் சிவன்பால்வைத்து இவ்வனுக்கிரஹஞ் சிவஞ்செயலென உணர்ந்து ஸ்துதித்தனர் . . .

என்று ஸ்துதித்து-வேதஸ்சிரேணி சிதம்பர சுவாமிகளிடம் பூர்ணவித்தியா க்ஞானத்தையும்[emended]; விசாரணை க்ஞானத்தையும்; அனுபவக்ஞானத்தையுமடைந்து சதா சமாதியிலிருக்கும், தன் மாதாவாகிய

புண்ணியவதியை நமஸ்கரித்து தன் சொற்பனத்திலீசுவரனனுக்கிரஹித்த காக்ஷியைத் தெரிவிக்க அந்த மாதா பிர்ம்ம க்ஞானியாகையால் ப்ரஹமானந்த பரவசத்தில் மூழ்கி ஒ புத்திரா நீ அவதரித்த என்கெ:ர்ப்பமின்றே கிருதார்த்தமாயிற்று நீ மாயையிற் சிக்கவேண்டாம், இன்றே சன்நியாசித்துவம்பெற்று ப்ரஹம்மக்ஞானி முக்தனாய் முக்திபெறக்கடவாய், உன்னாத்மமு மென்னாத்மமும் ஒரே பிரம்மக்ஞானமாகையால், அங்கிருவருந்தரி சித்துக்கொள்வோம் நீ என்னிடத்து விடைபெற்று கு:ருவிடஞ் செல்லென, அவ்வாக்ஞையை சிரசிற்கொண்டு அர்த்தஜாமத்தில் சிதம்பர ஸ்வாமிகளிடம் பெற்று பூஜைபிலிருந்த காவிவஸ்திரம், லங்கோடு கபீ:ர்ணமணிந்து, அத்துடனே தன் குலத்திர்க்கு ஆத்மார்த்ததெய்வஸ்தலமாகிய திருவேதசிரேணி க்ஷேத்திரத்திற்கு வந்து யந்தஸ்தல தண்டபாணீஸ்வரருக்கெதிரில் மூன்றுதினம் இராத்திரி பகல் ஒரே தியானத்திலிருந்துவிட்டார் மூன்றாம் நாளிராத்திரி அந்த லிங்கத்தினிடம் சோதிப்பிரகாசம் தோன்றி அசரீரவாக்காய், (நாம் உம்மையழைத்தாட்கொண்டோம்) ஏன் ஸ்தலங்கள்தோரும் கிருபாஸ்துதி கருத்து நடைப்பா மாலைச்சாற்றி பின்னர் குருவிடம் போகுக) என்றதைத்தான் கேட்டு யானந்த பரவசனாய் (கிருபாஸ்திப்பாமாலை) சாற்றினர் . . . {6}

{7} அதின் பிறகு தொண்டநாட்டின் சோழநாட்டின் கொங்குநாட்டின் பாண்டியநாட்டின் சேரநாட்டின் ஸ்தலங்கள்தோருஞ்சென்று ஆங்காங்கு பஞ்சபதிக, பத்தும்பதிக: கிருபாஸ்துதிப்பாமலை, சாற்றிவிட்டு நீலகிரிக்கும் மஹேந்திரகிரிக்கும் மத்தியிலுள்ள இகஸ்தியாசல தக்ஷணகைலாச பர்வதமேறிச்செல்லுங்காலத்தில் அப்பர்வதம் அடர்ந்த காடும் மிருகசஞ்சாரமுமுடையதாகையால் மார்க்கம் தெரியாமல் கனிகளையும் கிழங்குகளையும் புசித்தலைந்து குருவிருக்குமிடந்தெரியாது ஓர் மரத்தடியில் ஆயாசத்:தாடு படுத்திருந்தனர் அப்பொழுது அகஸ்திய ருஷியின் நேர் சிஷ்யராகிய அகஸ்தியாசல பர்வதத்தில் (24 வது குருபீடமாகிய (சிவக்ஞானபோ:தருஷியின் சமாதி லக்ஷியத்தில் நானடுமைகொண்ட (அழைத்தாட்கொண்டமூர்த்தி) வருகிறான் அவனை சிஷ்யராக்கிக்கொள் யென்று சர்வேஸ்வரன் தெரிவிக்க தன் க்ஞானதிருஷ்டியில் யாவும் தெரிந்துகொண்டு தன் பிரதம சிஷியனாகிய (பரமகுருயோகிசித்:த:னை) யிவரை யழைத்துவரயனுப்ப, யவர் வந்து யிவர் யாயாசத்தை தீர்த்து யிட்டுக்கொண்டுபோய் குருவிடம் விட்டனர் அச்சிவக்ஞானபோத ருஷியை நமஸ்கரித்து (அடுமை ஸ்துதி பாடினர்.) . . .

இவ்வித ஸ்தௌத்தியத்தோடு யடுமைப்பட்டவுடனே குருவானவராம் ஞானபோதரிஷி யானவர் இந்த சிஷ்யருக்கு ஞானகுருயோகி என்னுந்திருநாமமிட்டனர், பின்பு அந்த குருவோடு (12) வருஷ காலம், அவர் குஹையிலேயே, கந்தமூலாதி பக்ஷக்ஷணை செய்துகொண்டு சர்வ உபதேசங்களைப்பெற்று சர்வ சாதனைகளையுற்று, சர்வானுபவமடைந்து, மந்திர, வய, தாரணா, பக்தியோகங்களில் பூர்ணானுபவப்பெற்று சுவாசம் வாசி, பிராணம், விந்து, நாதம், பிரணவம், கலா முதலிய யோகங்களின் ரேசக, பூரக கும்பக பந்தன, ஸ்தம்பன ஸ்தாபன ஷட்கிரியைகளால் சர்வ யோகானுபவ சித்தியடைந்து சர்வ தத்துவ தரிசனம் காக்ஷி, மாக்ஷி, யாக்ஷி, குக்ஷி, சித்தி சக்தி மூர்த்தீகரங்களையனுபவித்து நயதியால் நிவாரணஞ் செய்து கேவவாத் துவைத ஆத்ம பிரம்ம ஐக்ய சிவபிரம்ம ராஜயோக பிரம்மநிஷடை சமாதியனுபவத்தால் சித்துக்ஞானியல்லாதசுக்ஞானியாய நாஹஞ்சர்வம் எத்பிரகாரமயம் அஹஞ்சுவப்பிரம்மம்) என்னும் சுவானுபவ வரிஷ்ட்ட {8} பக்குவ நிர்விகல்ப காஷ்ட்ட சமாதியிலிருக்கும் சமயத்தில், ஓர் தினந், தன்குருவான, சிவக்ஞானபோத ருஷியானவர், தன் நிர்விகல்ப சமாதியில் நின்று ப:ஹிர் முகபபட்டு, தன் குஹை வாசலிலிருக்கும், தாம்பிரபரணி

நதிதீரத்திலுட்கார்ந்து கொண்டிருக்கும்பொழுது பிரதமசிஷ்யர் (பரமகுருயோகி சித்திக்ஞானியும்) துவிதிய சிஷ்யர் (க்ஞானகுருயோகி சுக்ஞானியும்) அவரெதிரில் நின்றுக்கொண்டிருக்கும்பொழுது இவ்விருவரையும் நோக்கி ஓ சிஷ்யபுத்திரர்களே கேளீர் நாம் யிம்மலைவாச வனாந்திரமத்தில் குஹை வாசத்தில் சர்வதபம் புரிந்து, ஈசுவரனருளையும் சர்வ சக்தியினருளையும், குரு கடாக்ஷத்தையும் பெற்று சர்வ சக்தி சித்தி மூர்த்திகரமடைந்து, பிரம்மக்ஞானியாய், ஜீவன் மூக்தராய் முக்திக்காளானோம்.

நாம் ஒருவரே நம்மடுக்கும் இதுகளையடைவது தர்மமமன்று, ஈசுவரன் தன்னருளாலுலகத்தை ரக்ஷிக்கின்றனர், மஹாத்மக்களாகிய நம்போலியர்கள், ஜீவ காருண்ணியத்தாலுலகத்தவர்களுக்கு ஆத்மரக்ஷகஞ் செய்யவேண்டுமாகையால், நாமடைந்தவாறுயவர்களுமடையச் செய்யவேண்டும், யிந்த பராமார்த்தீக, பரோபகாரம் குருமூர்த்தங்களாகிய நம்முடைய கடமையாகையால். இந்த ஜீவகாருண்யபரோபகார காருண்ய சர்வாத்மரக்ஷக ஜகத்தாத்ம ரக்ஷக உத்தாரணம் என் மனதில் நான் அகஸ்திய மஹா ருஷீஸ்வருக்கு சிஷ்யறாகிய இந்த (438) வருஷகாலமாய் வீற்றிருக்கின்றது, ஆகையால் (க்ஞானகுருயோகி [emended]) யாகிய நீ என்னிடஞ் சர்வ விசாரணை, சாதனானுபவம், பூர்ணமாயடைந்துவிட்டாய், நூதன சாஸ்திரோத்பத்தி சாஸ்திர கர்த்தவ்வியமுமடைந்தாய், இங்ஙனம் யனுபவிப்பதுபோல் எங்ஙனமும், வியவஹார, ஆரூட, சஹஜ, சஞ்சார, சவ்விகல்ப[5] முதலிய காலத்திலும் சதா நிற்விகல்ப சமாதியில் சதா சுவப்பிரம்மானுபவ சமாதியிலிருக்கும் அனுபவ முமடைத்தாய், ஆகையால் என் எண்ண முடிக்கதக்கவனும், அகஸ்திய மஹாருஷீஸ்வரரின் பிரகாசத்தை பிரகாசிக்கச்[6] செய்யுமதிகாரி நீயே, உன்னை ஜகதா:த்மரக்ஷக உத்:த:ரண நிமித்தியம் (ஈசனழைத்தாட்கொண்டனர்) நீ ஆறு பாஷை தெர்ந்தவன் ஆகையால் நான் ஆஞ்ஞாபிக்கும் இந்த பரோபகார கிரியை முடிக்குக, ஆனுலும் நம்முடைய யதிரஹஸ்யங்களாகிய, வாதம், க:வுனம், கல்பம், பரகாயப்பிரவேசம், அஞ்சனம், சித்தி, சக்தி, மூர்த்திகரம், ஆயுர்விருத்தி அஷ்டடக்கிரியாசித்தி அஷ்டசித்தி முதலியதுகளை உலகத்தவர்களுக்குத் தெரிவிக்காமல், ஆத்ம லாபத்திற்கும், இஹபரகாம்ய நிஷ்காம்யத்திற்குமுறிய பக்தி தியான ஞான சாதனானுபவங்களை போதனாரூபமாயும், உபதேசக்கிரமமாயும், தீக்ஷாமார்க்கமாயும் இந்த சர்வ விசாரணை, சாதனை, யனுபவங்களை, படங்களில் காட்டி நூதன சாஸ்திரஞ்செய்து அச்சிபடுக்கொடுப்பதாயும், சர்வவர்ணஸ்தர்களுஞ் சமமாய் பூஜை செய்வதுமாகிய இந்த பரோபகாரத்தைசெய்துகொண்டும் என்னிடம் வந்து கொண்டும் போய்க்கொண்டுமிருக்கக்கடவாயென்று ஆக்ஞா பித்தபிரகாரம். {9} ஆயினும் வாதத்தினால் எந்த காரியமுஞ் செய்யொண்ணாது யேனெனில் சர்வத்திராள் சாபங்கள் பெற்றிருக்கின்றமையரல், யதினாலெதுவும் விருத்திக்கு வாராவாம். பலனைத்தராவாம்.

(இஞ்ஞானகுருயோகி சபாபதி சுவாமியானவர்) அவ்வாசிர்மமலையைவிட்டு மலையாளம், தமிழ், தெலுங்கு, கன்னடி, மஹாராஷ்ட்டி, குஜராட்டி ஹிந்துஸ்தாணி, பெங்காலி, நேபாளம், பஞ்சாப், ரஜபுட்டானா, காஷ்மியர், சிந்து, முல்டான் ஹிமாஞ்சலம், முதலியதேசங்களுக்குச்சென்று ஆங்காங்கு ஸ்தலதரிசனம், நதிஸ்னானம், ஸ்தல தீர்த்தயாத்திரை செய்துகொண்டே அந்தந்த ஸ்தலங்கள் பேரில் பதிகங்கள்பாடி (கிருபா ஸ்தௌத்தியமாலை) காற்றிக்கொண்டே அந்தந்த வூரிலும் அந்தந்த பாஷையிலும் இங்கிலீஷ் பாஷையிலும் பிரசங்க ரூபமாய் தத்துவபடங்களில்காட்டி தத்துவ சாஸ்திரபோதனை செய்துகொண்டும், நித்தியகர்மானுஷ்டானங்களின் சர்வதேவதாதேவிகளின் கிரியானுசந்தானபூஜைகளின் பிரம்மஞானனிஷ்டை

சமாதியின் சாதனாப்பியாசானுபவங்களை உபதேசக்கிரமமாய் சதுர் வர்ணஸ்தர்களுக்குள் ஸ்திரீபுருஷர்களுக்கும் அனுக்கிரஹித்து சர்வதத்துவஞானங்களையும், பக்தி, யோக, ஞானங்களையும் விசாரணை, சாதனை அனுபவரூபமாய் படங்களோடு சமஸ்கிருதம், உருது, ஹிந்துஸ்தானி, பெங்காலி, தெலுங்கு, மஹராஷ்டி, திராவிட தமிழ், இங்கிலீஷ் முதலிய பாஷைகளில் செய்து அச்சிட்டு வெளிப்படுத்தியும், ஹிந்துதேசத்திற்குள் தன் சிஷ்யர்கள் அப்பியாச சாதனைசெய்ய (464) தியான சபைகளை ஆங்காங்கு ஸ்தாபித்தனர். பின்பு திருவருட்பாசெய்தருளிய தன் பாலயிஷ்டரும் தபத்தொழருமான இராமலிங்க ஸ்வாமியை வடலூரில் சந்தித்தனர் பின்பு உத்திரகாண்டம் மறுபடியுஞ்சென்று ஹிமாஞ்சல் வடபாரிசதிபட்டுக்குப்போய் சிந்து நதிக்கும், பர்மபுத்திரா நதிக்கும் உத்பத்திதடாகமாம் மானசராவர தடாகத்தில் ஸ்னானஞ்செய்து, மூன்று ருஷிகள் உதவியினால் பூ:கைலாசதரிசனம்செய்து கைலாசேஸ்வரர் பேரில் சமஸ்கிருத பரிபாஷையால் சாகார, நிராகார, அர்ச்சனாரூப (108) ஸ்லோகத்தால் (கிருபாஸ்தௌத்தியமாலா காற்றினர். . . .

{10} அந்த மூன்று ருஷியை நமஸ்கரித்து எதிர்நிற்க ஒ ஞானகுருயோகியே உனக்கு என்னவேண்டும் கேளென்ன எனக்கு ஒன்றும் வேண்டாம் ஐக்ய முக்தியொன்றே வேண்டுமென்ன இவர் நிஷ்காம்மியத்தை மெச்சி உன் குருவால் நீ ஐக்கிய முக்திக்காளாய்விட்டாய் உன் ஆசீர்ம குருபீடிகளால் உன்னை குருபிதா ருஷீயாக்குவரென்ரியம்பி கக:னப்பிரவேசமாய் மரைந்தனர். பிறகு யிவர் ஹிமாஞ்சல் தக்ஷணபாரிசத்திலுள்ள, பசுபதிநாத், கேதாரநாத், பத்திரிநாத், ஜுவாலாமுகி திரிலோகநாத், பூதநாத் கெங்கோத்பத்தி, யமுனோத்பத்தி, அமர்நாத், மனிகர்ணிகா முதலிய க்ஷேத்திர திரிசனம், நதிஸ்நானம் செய்து காஷ்மீரத்திலிருக்கும் பொழுது அகஸ்தியராஸ்ரமத்திலிருக்குந் தன் குருவாகிய சிவஞானபோதருஷியானவர் (50) வருஷத்திற்கு ஒருவிசை, அகஸ்திய மஹாருஷீஸ்வரர், தன் ஆஸ்ரம சிஷ்ய குருபீடஸ்தர்களுக்கு வந்து தரிசனங்கொடுக்குஞ்சமயம் வந்துவிட்டமையால், தன் பிரம்மஞான திருஷ்டி தீக்ஷாகிரமத்தால் அவர் ஞான திருஷ்டியை இந்த ஞானகுருயோகி ஞானதிருஷ்டியில் கலப்பித்ததை யிவரறிந்து இருவருங்கலந்தவுடன் அகஸ்தியருஷி தரிசனந்தரவருஞ்சங்கதியை தெரிவித்து நீ வுடனே நம்மாஸ்ரமம் வந்துசேரக்கடவாயென்று ஆக்ஞாபித்தவுடனே தன்னிடத்திலிருந்த மூன்று கரைக்குடுகையக்கொண்டு ருஷிகேசம் ஹரத்துவாரம் விந்தாசலம் வந்து பின்பு கிஷ்கிந்தா, ஸ்ரீ சைலம் வேதசிரேணி வந்து ஒரு ஸ்தௌத்தியப்பாவாலர்ச்சித்தனர். . . .

{11} பிரகு, திருக்கடையூ, திருப்பெருந்துரை, ராமேஸ்வரம், மதுரை, குற்றாலம், பாபநாசம் தரிசித்து தன்னுடைய குருவீனாஸ்ரமமாகிய தக்ஷணகைலாசமாகிய அகஸ்தியாசலபர்வதத்திற்கு வந்து தன் குருபாதம் வணங்கி குராக்ஞபரிபாலனப்பா செய்தனர். . . .

இவ்வண்ணம் குருவோடு தான் நிர்விகல்ப சமாதியிலிருந்துகொண்டிருக்குஞ்சமயத்தில் 1880 வருஷம் சித்திராபௌர்ணமி தினம் நவக்கிரகங்கள், துர்வம், வாஸ்த்து, சுக உச்சகாலத்தில் ஸ்ரீலஸ்ரீ அகஸ்தியமஹாருஷீஸ்வரர் தன் பிரம்மயாத்மாவை தன் சுத்தகல்ப சரீரத்தில் பிரவேசிக்கச்செய்து தரிசனந்தர வருங்காலமறிந்து, ஞானிகள், ருஷிகள், சித்தர்கள், யோகிகள் ஹிமாஞ்சலம், குஷாசலம், அபா:சலம் விந்தாசலம், கிஷ்கிந்தாசலம், ஸ்ரீ கைலாசம், பா:லாசலம் நீலகிரி, உதகாசலம், வெள்ளியங்:ரி, மஹேந்திரகிரி, லங்காசலகண்டிகிரி யென்னு ஏகாதச பர்வத தபாசீர்மங்களிலிருந்து தக்ஷணகைலாச அகஸ்தியாசல பர்வதத்திற்கு க:க:னப்பிரவேசமாயும், மற்றயனேகவிதமாயும், வந்துசேர்ந்தனர்கள் (இந்த அகஸ்தியர் தரிசனம் தபோமஹாத்மாக்களுக்கன்றி, மற்ற உலகத்தவர்களுக்கு கிடைப்பதில்லை.)

1880 வருஷத்தில் சித்திரா பௌர்ணமி தினத்தில் சூர்யோதயகாலத்தில் சாக்ஷாத் ஸ்ரீகைலையில் சிவதரிசனம்போன்று தன்கீழுள்ள (24) குருபீடிகளும் யவர்சிஷ்யவர்க்கங்களும் புடைசூழ்ந்து சோடசோபசாரஞ்செய்யவும், வந்த மஹாத்மாக்கள், வேத:கோ:ஷம், ஸ்தௌத்தியஞ்செய்துவர, இவர்களின் சிஷ்யவர்க்கங்கள் சிங்குநாதஞ்சங்குநாதஞ்செய்ய, சக்திதேவிகள் க்ஷமரம் விசிரிபோட அகண்ட குருசக்கிரவர்த்தியாம் ஸ்ரீ அகஸ்திய மஹா ருஷிஸ்வரர் ஆரவாரத்துடன், திரிபுண்டரம், கந்ததிலகம், ருத்திராக்ஷசிரமாலா, கண்டமாலா, புஜமாலா, கங்கணமாலா {12} தரித்தும் காவிகாபீதாம்பரம் சிரசிலணிந்தும் லங்கோடு கபிர்ணத்தோடும் ஜடா மகுடத்தோடும் பாதரக்ஷையின்பேரில், சுக்குமாந்தடி, யோகதண்டு கமண்டலம் ஜோல்ணா. விபூதிசஞ்சி கையிலேந்தி யோகப்பட்டை மாரிலிணைந்து வந்து தன் குஹை வாசலில் தன்னால் சிருஷ்டிக்கப்பட்ட ஒரே திம்மை, பதினாறுவித கிளைகள், இலைகள், புஷ்பங்கள், கனிகள் உடைய சோட்சகலாவிருக்ஷத்தடியில் வியாகிராசனம் கிருஷ்ணாசனம் ரத்தினஜமக்காளாசனம், கஸ்தூரி மிருகாசனம், மர உரியால் திண்டு பட்டுபீதாம்பரத்தால் மெத்தை முதலியதுகளாலமைத்த உயர்ந்த குருசக்கிரவர்த்தி சிமஹாசனத்தின் பேரிலுட்கார்ந்தனர்.

தான் தரிசனந்தந்த அந்த முதல் தினத்தில் தன்னாசிர்ம குருபீடிகள், சிஷ்யவர்க்கங்கள் க்ஷேமங்களை விசாரித்துபின்பு மற்றயாசிர்மங்களின் மஹாத்மாக்களின் க்ஷெமங்களை விசாரித்து, சர்வத்திறாள்களையும் ஆசீர்வாதஞ்செய்தனர் அப்பொழுது அந்த யாசீர்மஸ்தர்களும், வந்த மஹான்களும் ஸ்துதித்தனர் அந்த காலத்தில் இந்த குருபிதாருஷியும் ஸ்துதித்தனர்....

இரண்டாம் நாளில் சர்வத்திறாள் சர்வ சாஸ்திர சம்சய நிவாரணஞ்செய்து, மூன்றாம் நாள் சர்வத்திராளுக்கும் நூதன உபதேசானுக்கிரஹஞ்செய்து, நான்காம் நாள், காமதேனுவைக்கொண்டு சர்வசக்திதேவிகளைக்கொண்டு தேவாமிருத போஜ:ன குருப்பிரசாத பிக்ஷையை தன் சிஷ்யர்களுக்கும், வந்த மஹான்களுக்குஞ்செய்தருளிவித்து ஐந்தாப் நாள் குஹைப்பிரவேசமாகி, சரீரத்தை வைத்துவிட்டு அகண்டாத்ம பிரம்மமாயினர், வந்த மஹான்கனெல்லோரும் இவ்வாசீர்ம குரு {13} பிடிகளிடத்தில் விடைபெற்று, அவாளவாளாசீர்மத்திற்குச் சென்றனர்.

இந்த ஞானகுருயோகி அகஸ்த்தியர் தரிசனஞ்செய்து குரு சங்கத்திலிருக்கு[ம்]பொழுது ஓர் தின புண்யகாலத்தில் இந்த யாசீர்ம (24) குருபீடிகளும், இப்பர்வத:த்தின்பேரில், தாம்பிரபரணிநதி, அமிருதநதி, சித்திநதி சங்கமமாகி முக்தி திரிவேணி சங்கத்தில் கூடி ஸ்நானஞ்செய்து, ஜெபதபமுடித்து நிஷ்டை புரிந்து பி:க்ஷைசெய்தபின் யவர்களொருங்கச் சம்மதித்து இந்த ஞானகுருயோகிக்கு குருபிதாருஷி என்னும் திருநாம பட்டங்கொடுத்தனர், இவ்வாறு இரண்டுவருஷ காலமவ்வாசீர்ம கு:ஹாவாசியாயிருந்த பின்னர் குராக்ஞையால், மறுபடியும் புரப்பட்டு நீலகிரியில் கொஞ்சநாளிருந்து கீழிரங்கி உத்திரகாண்ட சர்வஸ்தல்யாத்திரை செய்து சர்வத்திறாளுக்கும் யனுக்கிரஹித்து, அந்தந்த பாஷைகளில் சாஸ்திரமச்சிட்டும், சென்னைபுரிக்கடுத்த வில்லிவாக்க திருக்கொண்ணூராம் வில்வவனத்தில் ஆதியில் அகஸ்த்தியர் வாதாபி, வில்வாபியசுராளைக்கொன்று அகஸ்த்தியாரலயமும், அகஸ்த்திய தீர்த்தமும் ஸ்தாபித்து இப்பெரேரி யெ:ன்பதில் யாககுண்டம் எர்படுத்தி யாகஞ்செய்துபோன திருக்கொண்ணூரிற்குவந்து பேரேரிக்கு யடுத்த நிலத்தில் நிஷ்டையிலிருக்கும்பொழுது தன் திரிகால ஞானதிருஷ்டியில், தான் நிஷ்டையிலிருக்குமிடம் அகஸ்த்தியருஷி கொஞ்சகாலம் மடாலயயாசீர்மம் எற்படுத்தி, வசித்துபோனயிடமாயும், பேரேரி அவர் யாகஞ்செய்தயாக குண்டமாயும் இந்த யாககுண்டவடபுறநிலத்தில் அகஸ்தியருக்கு சர்வேஸ்வரர்

தன் பஞ்சகிருத்திய நடன தரிசனம் கொடுத்ததாயும், 1008 லிங்கங்களை 108 சாலிக்கிராமங்களை தன் சிஷ்யர்கள் பூஜித்து போனதாயும்.

மஹாவிஷ்ணு சூர்யனுக்கு சக்கிரங்கொடுத்ததாயும் தோன்றயக்கொண்ணூரில் அகஸ்தியவர்க்க குருபிதாருஷி மடாலயம் ஸ்தாபித்து யதில் (1008) லிங்கப்பிரதிஷ்டைசெய்ய (108) சாலிக்கிராமபிரதிஷ்டைசெய்ய சதுர்வர்ணஸ்தர்களும் ஸ்ரீகாசியைப்போன்று சமமாய் பூஜிக்க சர்வேஸ்வர சர்வேஸ்வரியாலய நிற்ணயஞ் செய்தனர். சர்வேஸ்வரர் பிரதி பௌர்ணிமையில் பஞ்சக்கிருத்தியனடனஞ்செய்யும் ஏற்பாடுஞ்செய்தனர், கர்மக்கிரியா யோகக்ஞான சர்வவித தபங்களையும், சாதனாப்பியாசங்களையும், அனுபவங்களையும், தத்துவக்ஞானங்களையும் (40) தத்துவபடங்களில், தியானபடங்களில் காட்டி உபதேசானுக்கிரஹமாய் தமிழ் திராவிட பாஷையில் சுருதி ஸ்மிருதி சாஸ்திரஞ்செய்தருளி (சர்வ விசாரணா சாதனானுபவ சங்கிரஹ வேதோபதேசம்) என்னும் சாஸ்திர நாமந்தன்னாசீர்ம குருபீடஸ்தர்களால் தரப்பட்ட நாமத்தோடு அச்சிடப்பட்டிருக்கின்றது இதுவுந்தவிர அந்த மஹாத்மாக்களனைவரும் ஒருங்கே சேர்ந்து இவருக்கு (அகண்ட க்ஞானகுரு சக்கிரவர்த்தி) என்னும் பட்டமும் கொடுத்தனர்.

இவர் நிர்ண்ணயஞ்செய்த மடாலயத்திற்கு குருபிதாருஷி மடாலயம், தேவாலயத்திற்கு சர்வேசுவாரலயம் தீர்த்தத்திற்கு மோக்ஷத:யக:தீர்த்தம், மூலஸ்தான {14} பஞ்சலிங்கங்களாகிய பிரம்மபா:வலிங்கம், சர்வேஸ்வரபா:வலிங்கம், சர்வேஸ்வரிபா:வலிங்கம். குருபா:வலிங்கம் விஷ்ணுபா:வலிங்கங்களுக்கு பஞ்சபரத்துவலிங்கம், உச்சவமூர்த்திக்கு விஸ்வவிராட் பஞ்சதேவதா பஞ்சமுக ஏகரூப பஞ்சகிருத்திய நடேஸ்வரர், உச்சவதேவிக்கு விஸ்வவிராட் பஞ்சதேவி பஞ்சமுக ஏகரூப பஞ்சகிருத்திய நடேஸ்வரி, இந்த யாலய[நி]ர்ணயஸ்தலத்திற்கு சர்வேஸ்வரகிரிபுரி, என்னுந்திருநாமங்களை தன் குராஸ்ரமங்களிலுள்ள மஹாத்மருஷிகள் கொடுத்தனர்கள். . . .

இவரும் இந்த திருக்கொண்ணூர் மடாலய தபாசீர்மத்திலும் நீலகிரி தபாசீர்மத்திலும் தன் குருவின் அகஸ்த்தியாசல பர்வத குஹை தபாசீர்மத்திலும் கொஞ்சம் கொஞ்சங்காலமாங்காங்கு பிரம்மக்ஞான நிர்விகல்ப சமாதி நிஷ்டை புரிந்து வருகின்றனர். இதன்றியும் இந்த ஹிந்துதேச சிஷ்யர்களால், ஆங்காங்கு கொடுக்கப்பட்ட நாமங்களாகிய 1. ஜகத்ஞானகுரு, 2. முக்திதியானகுரு, 3. பக்திஞான சாதனை சுருதிகர்த்தா, 4. மதோத்தாரண அவுதாரகுரு என்னும் திருநாமங்களையும் பெற்றுவிளங்குகின்றார்.

Notes

1. I have translated this material from T2, a Tamil hagiographical account of Sabhapati's life prefaced to the longer version of MCVTS, published in 1913 (see Chapter 2). The account was written by one Shiva Jnana Prakasha Yogishwara (Civakñāṉappirakāca Yōkīsvara), a student of Sabhapati's about whom nothing is known at the time of writing. I have included several "prose poems" by Sabhapati's students and admirers found at the beginning of this account, and I am grateful to Ilona Kędzia and members of the Cultures of Patronage project at the Jagiellonian University for reading through some of these poems with me and offering helpful suggestions.

At present I have omitted the remaining poems, some of which are short excerpts from Sabhapati's other works, to preserve space and to focus on the narrative of Sabhapati's life. I plan to include annotated translations of these remaining poems and compositions in a forthcoming translation of MCVTS as part of Sabhapati's collected works.

2. The compound *pōṟpōtam* (*pōṉ + pōtam*), here translated as "golden awakening," also appears in the first *tantiram* of the Tirumantiram, verse 141 in most editions, and may also have a technical meaning here.
3. Sabhapati and this hagiography's author sometimes irregularly use a colon (:) in their printed text to break up syllables, which I have retained for this translation and in the original.
4. Some Sanskrit/Maṇipravāla compounds that are uncommon or have a technical Tamil significance that is unique to the yogic contexts of Sabhapati's work are given an asterisk (*).
5. சவ்விகல்ப] em. சவ்விரல்ப.
6. பிரகாசிக்க] em. இரகாசிக்க.

APPENDIX 2

Lexicon of Common Terms and Variants

Sanskrit nominal form	Devanagari	VRY (archaic roman transliteration)	CPSPS (Tamil transliteration)	CPSPS (Tamil script)
agni	अग्नि	agni	akṉi	அக்னி
atīta	अतीत	ateeta, ateetam	atītam	அதீதம்
adhomukha	अधोमुख	Adhomukh	atōmukam	அதோமுகம்
anubhava	अनुभव	Anbhawam, anubhavam	aṉupavam	அனுபவம்
antaḥkaraṇa	अन्तःकरण	antakarna, antakarana	antakaraṇam	அந்தகரணம்
antaḥkaraṇaśuddhi	अन्तःकरणशुद्धि	antakarana Shuddhi	antakaraṇacutti	அந்தகரணசுத்தி
abhimāna	अभिमान	Abhimanam	apimāṉam	அபிமானம்
amṛta	अमृत	Amritum	amirtam	அமிர்தம்
aṣṭamāsiddhi	अष्टमासिद्धी	Ashtama Siddhis	aṣṭamā sitti	அஷ்டமா ஸித்தி
ahaṃkāra	अहंकार	Ahankar	akaṅkaram	அகங்கரம்
ākāśa	आकाश	Akash	ākācam	ஆகாசம்
ātmaka	आत्मक	atmak	ātmakam	ஆத்மகம்
ātmaprāṇākāśa	आत्मप्राणाकाश	Atma Pran akas	ātmapirāṇākācam	ஆத்மபிராணாகாசம்
ātman	आत्मन	atma	ātmā	ஆத்மா
ānanda	आनन्द	anunda, anundum, anandam	āṉantam	ஆனந்தம்

Sanskrit nominal form	Devanagari	VRY (archaic roman transliteration)	CPSPS (Tamil transliteration)	CPSPS (Tamil script)
ānandātīta	आनन्दातीत	Ánundateetum	āṉantātītam	ஆனந்தாதீதம்
āpa	आप	apa, uppa	appu	அப்பு
āvaraṇa	आवरण	Avarna	āvaraṇam	ஆவரணம்
āvaraṇaśakti	आवरणशक्ति	Avarna Sakti	āvaraṇacakti	ஆவரணசக்தி
āśrama	आश्रम	Ashrum, Ashram	ācramam	ஆச்ரமம்
indriya	इन्द्रिय	indriyam	intiriyam	இந்திரியம்
indriyaśuddhi	इन्द्रियशुद्धि	Indriya Shuddhi	intiriyacutti	இந்திரியசுத்தி
īśvara	ईश्वर	Eshwara, Eeshwara	īsvara	ஈஸ்வர
upāsana	उपासन	upasna, upasana	upācaṉam	உபாசனம்
ūrdhvamukha	ऊर्ध्वमुख	Urdh mukh, urdhmukh	ūrtamukam	ஊர்தமுகம்
kamala	कमल	kamalam, Kamalum, etc.	kamalam	கமலம்
karma	कर्म	karma, karmas	karmam	கர்மம்
kalā	कला	calá, cala, kala	kalā	க்லா
kalpanā	कल्पना	kalpana, kulpana, etc.	kalpaṉā; kaṟpaṉai	கல்பனா; கற்பனை
kuṇḍalī	कुण्डली	koondli, kundlee, etc.	kuṇṭali	குண்டலி
kumbhaka	कुम्भक	kumbhak, koombhak	kumpakam	கும்பகம்
guru	गुरु	guru, guroo	kuru	குரு
gṛhastin	गृहस्तिन्	Grihastee, grihusti	kirahastarkaḷ	கிரஹஸ்தர்கள்
cittaśuddhi	चित्तशुद्धि	chitta shuddhi	cittasutti	சித்தஸுத்தி
japa	जप	jap, japa	jepam	ஜெபம்
jivatman	जिवात्मन्	jivatma	jīvātmā	ஜீவாத்மா

jīvanmukti	जीवन्मुक्ति	Jivanmookti	jīvaṉmukti	ஜீவன்முக்தி
jñāna	ज्ञान	giyan, giyana, giana	kñāṉam	க்ஞானம்
jñānaśāstra	ज्ञानशास्त्र	Giyan Shastras	ñāṉacāstiraṅkaḷ	ஞானசாஸ்திரங்கள்
jñānākāśa	ज्ञानाकाश	giyanakasha, giana akasha, etc.	ñāṉākācam	ஞானாகாசம்
tattva	तत्त्व	tattwa, tatwam, tatva	tattuvam	தத்துவம்
tattvaśāstra	तत्त्वशास्त्र	Tatwa Shastras	tatvasāstiram	தத்வஸாஸ்திரம்
darśana (1)	दर्शन	Darshanas	taricaṉaṅkaḷ	தரிசனங்கள்
darśana (2)	दर्शन	darshonum	taricaṉam, tericaṉam	தரிசனம், தெரிசனம்
dvādaśānta	द्वादशान्त	Twatasantum	tuvātasāntam	துவாதஸாந்தம்
dhyāna	ध्यान	dhyanm, dhyan, dhyana	tyāṉam, tiyāṉam	த்யானம், தியானம்
nāḍī	नाडी	nadee	nāṭi	நாடி
paramaguruyogī ṛṣi	परमगुरुयोगीऋषि	Param Guroo Yogi Rishi	paramakuruyōki riṣi	பரமகுருயோகி ரிஷி
paramabrahman	परमब्रह्मन्	Param Brahma	parappirammam	பரப்பிரம்மம்
brahmacaitanya	ब्रह्मचैतन्य	brahmachaithunnium, etc.	pirummacaitaṉṉiyam	பிரும்மசைதன்னியம்
brahmajñāna	ब्रह्मज्ञान	brahmagiyana, brahma giana	pirmakkiñāṉa	பிரும்மகியானம்
brahmajñānī	ब्रह्मज्ञानी	brahmagiyani, brahmagiyanis	pirummakkiyāṉi	பிரும்மக்கியானி
brahman	ब्रह्मन्	brahman, bramhum, etc.	pirammam	பிர்ம்மம்
brahmarandhra	ब्रह्मरन्ध्र	brahmarantar, brahma rantar	pirummarantaram	பிரும்மரந்தரம்
bhakti	भक्ति	bhakti, bhukti	pakti	பக்தி
bhaktiśāstra	भक्तिशास्त्र	Bhakti Shastras	paktisāstiram	பக்திஸாஸ்திரம்
bhrānti	भ्रान्ति	bhranti, bhranty	pirānti	பிராந்தி
manas	मनस्	mano, manas	maṉō	மனோ
mumukṣu	मुमुक्षु	Moomookhshoo	mumukṣu	மும்முக்ஷு

Sanskrit nominal form	Devanagari	VRY (archaic roman transliteration)	CPSPS (Tamil transliteration)	CPSPS (Tamil script)
mūrti	मूर्ति	Murti	mūrtti	மூர்த்தி
mokṣa	मोक्ष	moksh	mōkṣam; mōṭcam	மோக்ஷம்; மோட்சம்
maunātīta	मौनातीत	(only present in CPSPS)	mauṉātītam	மௌனாதீதம்
sattvaguṇabhojana	सत्त्वगुणभोजन	Satwa guni Bhojan	mitasatvakuṇa-pōjaṉam	மிதஸத்வகுண-போஜனம்
samādhi	समाधि	samadhi, Smâdhi	camāti	சமாதி
sākṣyātīta	साक्ष्यातीत	Sakshiateetum	cāṭkṣiyātītam	சாட்க்ஷியாதீதம்
suṣumnā	सुशुम्ना	sushoomana, sushoomna, etc.	suṣumuṉā	ஸுஷுமுனா
svarūpa	स्वरूप	saroop, sarup, sorup, soroop	corūpam	சொரூபம்
śāntātīta	शान्तातीत	Shantateetum	cāntātītam	சாந்தாதீதம்
śāstra	शास्त्र	Shastras	sāstiram/sāstiraṅkaḷ	ஸாஸ்திரம்
śivadarśana	शिवदर्शन	darshonum of Mahadeva	civataricaṉam	சிவதரிசனம்
śivarājayoga	शिवराजयोग	Shiva Yoga, Shiva Raja Yoga	civaññāṉa rājayōkam	சிவஞான ராஜயோகம்
śivamaya	शिवमय	Shivmayam	civamayam	சிவமயம்
śivasāyujya	शिवसायुज्य	(only present in CPSPS)	civacāyujjiyam	சிவசாயுஜ்ஜியம்
śūnyātīta	शून्यातीत	Soonneateetum	cuṉṉiyātītam	சுன்னியாதீதம்
śruti	श्रुति	Shruti; Soorooti	sruti	ஸ்ருதி
yoga	योग	Yoge, Yogue	yōkam	யோகம்
yogin	योगिन्	Yogee, Yogis	yōki	யோகி
liṅga	लिङ्ग	lingam, lingum	liṅkam	லிங்கம்
liṅgaśarīra	लिङ्गशरीर	lingasarir	liṅkacarīram	லிங்கசரீரம்
liṅgasvarūpa	लिङ्गस्वरूप	linga sorup, linga soroop	liṅkacorūpam	லிங்கசொரூபம்
veda	वेद	veda, Vedas	vētam	வேதம்

APPENDIX 3

A Passage from VRY1 on the "Pole" of Śivarājayoga

Search after the Infinite Spirit, and its powers which seem to descend and ascend in circle or NISHKAMYA BRAHMAGGIYANA BHAVANA, UPASANA SHIVA RAJAYOGA SADHANA,[1] *or* PAROKHSHA GIANANOOBHAVUM[2] AND PAROKHSHA GIANA YOGA ANOBHAVUM.[3]

(*Caution.*—before you enter in this practice is it absolutely necessary that you discard shame and pride which prevent you from going to Gianees and Yogees;[4] also you must have full faith and belief in the practice and allow no doubts to enter your mind; as the success in samadhi will show you the truth of this doctrine.)[5]

Sit for ten minutes steadily in a posture that may be the least inconvenient that is in the sukhasanum,[6] and the squatting is the best one; and if it be not very difficult at the outset the beginner might commence at once to habituate himself to sit in the posture represented in the diagram, or in Padmasanum.[7] Then imagine*[8] that you throw, or draw within the real and actual light of your two eyes internally to Koondali,[9] which will appear the acute and keen divine sight; here the *sushoomana* vessel joins the *lingam* and ascends upwards through the backbone. The sight must be thrown in such a way that the keenness of these two sights or the imaginary giyanam or consciousness of these two eyes should descend through the right and left side holes of the *sushoomana* to the lowest point of kundalee. By the keenness of sight is meant that indescribable something that seems to proceed from the eyes when you steadily gaze at a distant object with half shut eyes.[10]

Now imagine the mind to be a straight pole whose top is in the middle of the Brahmarantar,[11] and whose bottom is in the kundlee.[12] Moreover consider the mental vision of consciousness[13] to be lodged in the bottom of this pole.

Now take hold of this mental vision by the keenness or imaginary *giyana akasha saroopam*[14] of the two eyes; and lift it up gradually and {36} slowly by the two keenness serving as tongs, to the Brahmarantar. The time taken in this pulling up of the mental consciousness must not be less than twenty minutes.[15]

Now stop this imaginary mental consciousness in the Brahmarantar for twenty minutes more.[16] Then drop and draw it up, so fast that within a second it must descend to the kundlee, and reascend to the Brahmarantar; running straight up and down through the middle vessel of the large *sushoomana* which we have considered to be the mental pole.[17]

After practicing this for a few minutes make your mind to stand upon the pole steady and straight as if it was fixed to a firm rocky pole. There let it stand immovable and without descending again. Make it to be in dead and calm silence, void and without motion, and free from all thoughts and fickleness.

After succeeding in making the pole of your mind (or eternal Divine conscious sight) straight and steady by the foregoing process, join the Giyana conscious sight of the two eyes with the top of the mind in the Brahmarantar. Thus it forms a triangle whose vertex is the mind, and the two keenness[18] that proceed from the eyes to join the former, the two sides.[19]

Having got success in this practice imagine strongly that your head is removed and off course with it eyes, ears, nose, mouth and every thing pertaining to the head. Instead of it consider that the whole space is filled up by the universal *Giyanakasha* consciousness which now becomes the holy *akash* itself.[20]

Brahma Giyanakasha.[21] This *akasha* is perfect giyana voidness and nothingness or *sarva sunya giyanakasha matram*.[22] This is neither[23] the *akasha* of darkness or *andhakaramayam*,[24] nor of brightness or *prakasha mayam*.[25] It is without any color or resemblance, but full and all pervading consciousness and pure wisdom; or *sarva giyana vyapaka matram*.[26] It is the only spiritual divine witness or *shuddha giyana sakshi matram*.[27] It is like the clear light of the candle, which is itself (1) *giyanakasha saroop*,[28] because it is perfectly permeating in its own space; (2) it is *sunya saroopa*[29] or vacuum, because nothing can be seen *in* it, nothing can be got *from* it, and nothing can be placed *on* it; (3) it is itself *giyana vyapakasaroop*,[30] because it sheds its light on every direction and every where; (4) it is itself *sakshi saroop*,[31] because the light spreads over everything, and reveals and discovers that which is in that space and that which is not; still it is the only *sakshi matra*[32] to the place, knowing what is passed, passing and going to come.*[33]

{37} Consider the holy *akash*[34] in these four aspects,[35] and think these four to be the very holy akash,[36] without making any distinction; consider that this holy Giana *akasha* or *shuddha chaitannya giyanakasha saroop*[37] will be these four giyana.[38]

This *Rahasyam*[39] is everywhere pervading all in one soroop.[40] If you introduce creations by Bhranti[41] it will be pervading them too, and if you cancel creations by non-*Bhranti*[42] still it will be every where in itself.[43] Do not therefore consider that this holy Giana *akash* is limited;[44] but endless, stretching to infinity in the right, in the left, in the up in the down, in the front and in the back sides.[45] Instead therefore limiting this Giana *akash* in the sphere of the head, consider it to be a universally pervading orb of consciousness or *giyana saroop*.[46] Do not imagine it to be a hollow sphere whose, surface is in the infinity, but consider it to be filled by *giyanakash* thus solidifying it.[47]

Now consider by your wisdom or consciousness (or *sakshi sarwa giyanakash saroop*)[48] that the earth floats a little below the centre of this universal infinite *giyanakasha* sphere,[49] with all its created beings[50] upon it. A little above the centre of the sphere consider the sun to be in the right, and the moon in the left, and the stars and planets at the top.[51]

Then expand your universally diffused holy *giyanakasha saroop* of *sakshi*, of *ananda*, of *vyapaka* and of *sunya matram*,[52] in such a way that it may penetrate in full through all the planets, sun, moon, stars, earth &c. and even all the created being of them, leaving no space whether within and without these, empty of its presence.[53] By this practice you will get success in becoming the *andapinda charachara sarvasunya giyana maya akasha saroop*,[54] and *sarvagiyana ananta maya saroop*,[55] *sarvagiyana vyapaka maya saroop*,[56] and *sarwagiyana sakshi maya saroop*[57] and survageana Anunda maya saroop[58] [and] consider that this *suddha chaitanya giyanakasha saroop*[59] is the self-diffused and the universal infinite spirit comprehending the sun, moon, stars, planets[60] &c. within the infinity of its own self. In this practice you must consider it to be the *Brahma giyananu bhawam*.[61] *This giana akash*[62] is the holy *akash* or the *suddha chaitanya akash*;[63] not any of those *akashas* that have colors and seem dark or luminous.[64] Cancel the latter as untrue while the former is only true.[65] In fact *giyanakash*[66] has no color [and] is neither dark nor bright, but perfect vacuum.[67]

But in cancelling those false akashes[68] do not cancel your *giyanakash* too,[69] for if you take the latter to be one of those untrue akashes, you will never get *Brahmagiyanam*; you must bear in mind that this *sarva suddha chaitanya giyanakhasha saroop*[70] whom you must not cancel differs from others in being: (1) *sarva sunnya giyana mayam*;[71] (2) *sarva giyana vyapaka mayam*;[72] (3) *sarva saktchi giyana mayam*;[73] (4) *sarva giyana ananda mayam*.[74] Therefore they are all the *layabodha Brahma giyana shiva mayam*.[75] Consider all other akashas except this, to be as {38} *maya vikara akasha saroopam*[76] that deceive owing to your impurities and sins. Therefore cancel these all saying "you are not my true *Brahma giyana akasha saroopam*."[77]

To recapitulate: sitting in a secluded place—

1*st*. Shut your eyes and throw the keenness of the two sights to the kundlee.[78]
2*nd*. Imagine the mind to be a pole, and the mental consciousness placed in the koondli.[79]
3*rd*. Draw up this mind by the two sights to the Brahmarantara, and drop and draw it again and again.[80]
4*th*. Fix it in the Brahmarantara and make the mental pole straight and steady.[81]
5*th*. Fix also the two keenness on the mind seated in the Brahmarantar.[82]
6*th*. Imagine the head to be removed and its place occupied by the *giyanakash* or spiritual consciousness.[83]
7*th*. Make this universally spread imagining the sun, moon, stars, planets and earth floating in it; and this pervading through all.[84]

Practice this for a few days and when you have got success in it you would become *Bhawana Brahmagiyani Brahmachari*.[85]

Divine Pilgrimage—Next consider that this *Bhawana Brahma giyan*[86] is within the *Brahma rantar*. Now you should make a divine pilgrimage in the universe of your body in order to find out how the *suddha chaitannya Brahma giyanakasha mayam*[87] descends to the kundli through the *sushoomana*[88] and ascends up to Brahmarantar through *khumbak*.[89] By this descent and ascent the whole creation of your body is maintained till the time of death. This practice will much help you in the Yogue which is to be for ever immerged and absorbed in the *suddha chaitannya Brahma giyanakash*[90] through *laya bodham*.[91]

Therefore consider the *Brahma chaitanya giyanakasha saroop*[92] to run[93] through *Sukhmana*—a hollow pipe containing three smaller pipes[94] within it, which descends from the centre of the skull through the middle of the brain down to Kundli. The *giyana akasha* runs through all the three subdivisions of the *sushoomana*,[95] viz:—

(1) Through the left pipe of the sushoomana called Idakala (No. 7 in the diagram).[96] The one-third of the *giyanakash*[97] flowing through it gets the name of *Pranava Ugra giyanakasha chandrakala vasi*[98] or *Brahma chaitanya suddha sampurna suyam prakasha drishti*[99] or the divine light as spirit or ether.
(2) Through the middle pipe called susoomana (No. 2). The one-third of the *giyanakash*[100] running through it is called *Nirakara Yayikia* {39} *Agni Kala Vasi*[101] or *Brahma chaitanya suddha giyanakasha sarvingitwa sarva giyana drishti*[102] or the divine sight of spirit—
(3) Through the right hand pipe of the sushoomna called *pingala*[103] (No. 3). The one-third of the giyanakash flowing through it is called *Omkara kripa surya kala Vasi*[104] or the *Brahma chaitnanya suddha giyanakasha sarva yayike sarva sunnya drishti*,[105] or spiritual vision.

Consider now the Giyanakash[106] to descend from the centre of the skull one-eighth of an inch, and rest on the top of the brain. This space between the skull and the brain is a perfect vacuum and is called Brahmarantar. From the top of the brain one-eighth of an inch to the middle of the brain, from the middle of the brain, one-eighth of an inch it descends to the bottom of the brain. Again it descends one eighth of an inch from the bottom of the brain and settles in the centre of the forehead; from this it descends one-eighth of an inch and settles in the centre of the eye-brows. Wherefrom the Súshoomna separates into three parts, the left vessel[107] going to the left eye, the right vessel going to the right eye; and the middle vessel going straight down and settles in the centre of the tip of the nose.[108] Here the vessels that had entered the eyes[109] come and join the third, and become one. Descending one inch from the centre of the tip of the nose, it settles in the centre of the tongue.[110] From this place it enters behind the gullet and runs along the alimentary canal into which it also sends a branch.[111] From the centre of the tongue it descends two inches and settles in the throat; from here it descends six inches and settles in the centre of the heart; from this heart it again descends six inches, and settles in the internal centre of the navel; from the navel it descends five inches and settles in the kúndli, where it joins with the lingam and bends downward to ascend upwards. Therefore this place is called Kundli. Now it rises up through Kumbhak Nadi, which is the upward prolongation of the sushoomna through the three vessels of the same. Here the natures of the Gyánákásh while running downward is totally changed. The Idakala Nadee here becomes *Kundlee stambhana laya purana Vyapekagiyana kalá mayam Irechak Nadee*[112] **(No. 4** in the diagram) or *Bramha chaitanya súddha santha kasha sarva anda pinda charachara sarva shrishti antar Vyapaka drishti*[113] or the infinite consciousness.

The Súshoomna nadee becomes the *kúndali trikala nittya sumpurna ananda kala maya kumbhaka Nadee*[114] **(No. 5)** or *Brahma Chaitanya suddha shanta sadakasha sarva laya bodha pari purnanandam*[115] or the infinite bliss.

The Pingala Nadee becomes *kundlee kumbitha bodha purna sakshi kalamaya Puraka Nadee*[116] **(No. 6)** or *Brahma chaitannya suddha shanta akasha sarvasthana, sarvagiyana sarva sakshi drishti,*[117] or the perfect infinite witness.

{40} Consider that these three rise together with great speed to Brahmarantar and become absorbed there; then again descend and again ascend. Practice this for a few days till you get success in it. Then you will be called *Bhawana Brahmagiyana Bramachari in Raja Yoga*[118] or *Brahmagiyana Shiva yoga yathree*[119] *or the divine pilgrim.*

Consider by the *chinmudra*[120] of your left hand fingers, that your Giyanakash is descending; and by the chinmudra of the right hand fingers, that it is ascending; and by the chinmudra formed by the junction of the two keenness of the sights with the mind in Brahmarantara that is absorbed in the infinite spirit. This process may be continued in sitting in *Sukshasana*[121] or easy posture.

As you descend from the Brahmarantara make your Giyanakash to pronounce by the tongue of its mowna giyana drishti matrum*[122] the following divine mantras: *Shivhá, shiva, shiva, shiva, shiva shiva, shiva, shivohum, Brahmohum, Giyanohum, Akashohum, Shunnyohum, Shakshiyohum, Vyapakohum, Anandohum;*[123] and as you ascend pronounce in the same way the following divine mantras. Layohum Bodhohum, Shantohum, Shúddhohum, Nittyohum, Pranavohum, Onkarohum, Nirakarohum, Oogrohum, Kripakarum, Ayiakium, Arohum, Sthumbhanum, Koombhithum, Paramanoobavum, Sumpoornum Agum Brahmahum.[124]

Having gained success in this practice you must now become Tatwa Giyani[125] or *Utpattidarshana Grishasti;*[126] that is you must examine the *Maya Bhranti, kalpana Sankalpa tatwa Grahashrumum,*[127] and after examining them and finding them useless and injurious to renounce them and become the *Sannyasi mawnagiyani,*[128] which will make you true Brahma-Giyanee,[129] whom Maya[130] will never assail.

Notes

1. "nishkamya Brahmaggiyana bhavana, upasana shiva Rajayoga sadhana" < Skt. *niṣkāmyabrahmajñānabhāvanopāsana śivarājayogasādhanā* निष्काम्यब्रह्मज्ञानभावनोपासन शिवराजयोगसाधना; lit. "the cultivation (*bhāvana*), the contemplative worship (*upāsana*), and the practice (*sādhanā*) of the royal yoga for Shiva, which is the gnosis of Brahman that is free from self-interest." "*The First Practical Instruction in Sitting Posture of Ecstasy of attaining the Godhead of being the Infinite Spirit and its Infinite Spiritual Divine Vision or Holy Sight as Actively with powers descending and as Passively without Powers ascending in circular Form*," Tam. *niṣkkāmmiya pirmañāṉapāvaṉōpāsaṉacivarājayōkasātaṉā* நிஷ்க்காம்மிய பிர்மஞானபாவனோபாஸன-சிவராஜயோகஸாதனா CPSPS.
2. "Parokhsha giananoobhavum"] < Skt. *parokṣajñānānubhava* परोक्षज्ञानानुभव; lit. "the experience of the gnosis that is beyond sight." This and the next phrase are subsumed into the quotation given in the previous note.
3. "parokhsha giana yoga anobhavum"] < Skt. *parokṣajñānayogānubhava* परोक्षज्ञानयोगानुभव; lit. "the experience of the yoga of gnosis that is beyond sight."
4. "*Gianees and Yogees*"] "*Gnyanís* and *Yógís*" in CPSPS.
5. CPSPS here adds a much longer note of "Caution" that includes much more social and political commentary, including a brief nod to H. P. Blavatsky and Henry Olcott and a discourse on the importance of preserving Indian teachings. It then adds additional processes and practical instructions, including a consideration of the place of practice.
6. "sukhasanum"] < Skt. *sukhāsana* सुखासन; lit. "the posture of happiness." "*Sugasanum*," Tam. *cukāsaṉam* சுகாஸனம் CPSPS. Normally this is considered to be any pose that is easy to adopt, but CPSPS specifies, as the text in VRY1 also suggests, that this is the "*Squatting posture* of any kind," to be adopted in case one's assumption of *padmāsana* is unsuccessful.
7. "Padmasanum"] < Skt. *padmāsana* पद्मासन; lit. "the posture of the lotus." "Pathmásanum," Tam. *patmāsaṉam* பத்மாஸனம் CPSPS. Almost a full page of additional text is here inserted in CPSPS.
8. [Note from VRY1, omitted in CPSPS:] * Here imagine or consider means a positive assertion which will end in the practical success and truth.
9. "Koondali"] < Skt. *kuṇḍali* कुण्डलि or *kuṇḍalī* कुण्डली, lit. "ring." Transliteration of Sanskrit terms was not widely standardized when Sabhapati published his instructions, and other variants in the editions of VRY include "koondli," "kundlee," "kundalee," and "kundli," among others.
10. This and the following paragraphs are greatly expanded into a lengthier treatment in CPSPS that provides a wealth of additional instructions, definitions, and other additions that are not present in the editions of VRY. Only few of the many differences are indicated in the notes that follow, and the reader is invited to consult subsequent volumes for Sabhapati's full presentation of these techniques.

11. "Brahmarantar"] < Skt. *brahmarandhra* ब्रह्मरन्ध्र, lit. "crevice of Brahman," or the fontanelle. Other variants between the editions of VRY and CPSPS include "brahma rantar," "Brummaranthra," "Brummarunthra," and a few others.
12. "kundlee"] "in the middle of the Urine Organ" CPSPS.
13. "consciousness"] "of seeing the truths of Internal faculties, external things, and much more the whole Universal things; both internally and externally penetrating" + CPSPS.
14. "*giyana akasha saroopam*"] < Skt. *jñānākāśasvarūpa* ज्ञानाकाशस्वरूप; lit. "inherent nature (*svarūpa*) of the gnostic ether (*jñānākāśa*)." "Consciousness," Tam. *pāvaṉāñāṉam* பாவனாஞானம் CPSPS.
15. "not be less than twenty minutes"] "not be less than 48 minutes" CPSPS. CPSPS then delineates a period of two minutes for raising the "consciousness" (*bhāvanājñāna*) through each lotus.
16. "Now stop . . . twenty minutes more"] "Now stop this imaginary mental Consciousness in the Brummaranthra or Centre of the Brain for 2 minutes more steadily and quietly all in a deep solemn and silent meditation" CPSPS.
17. "Then drop . . . mental pole"] "Then drop it down to *Kundali* and draw it up to *Brummaranthra* by devotional meditation [Tam. *pāvaṉō pāsaṉattiyāṉam*, < Skt. *bhāvanopāsanadhyāna*] so fast that within a second it must descend to *Kundali* and re-ascend to *Brummarunthra*, running straight up and down through the middle Vessel of large *Sushumumna*, filling that Vessel or Organ as solid as possible by this Spiritual mental vision, having the absorbing Self Intoxication [Tam. *svayalayō yayikkiya stampaṉapōtā*, < Skt. *svayalayo aikyastambhanabodhā*] from each seat of faculties; this Sushumuna Nadi is the Mental pole which fixes its bottom in Kundali, and its top in Brummaranthra, standing straight perpendicular, looking at the Zenith internally" + CPSPS.
18. "keenness"] em. "keeness" VRY.
19. "Thus it forms . . . two sides"] "Thus it forms a triangle whose vertex is the Mind, and the two keenness, that proceed from the eyes to join the former, are the two sides" CPSPS. "Now drop these three Visions jointly as one Vision of conscious witnessing blissfullness [*sic*] to Kúndali and make itself rise like a serpent through Spinal Cord or backebone [*sic*] meeting it again in Brimharuntra" + CPSPS.
20. "Instead of . . . *akash* itself"] "Instead of it, consider that the whole space is filled up by the *Universal Circle of solidly pervaded Conscious Witnessing Blissful Infinite Spirit* [Tam. *sarvaviyāpitacarvaviyāpaka sākṣiyāṉanta yantaryāmittuvāṉusūtapirmañāṉa cakkirākirutavaṭṭa tiruṣaṭimayam*] which now becomes the holy Sphere or Orb-like Divine Æther [Tam. *maṇṭalākāra cakkirākirutavaṭṭa cuttapirmmākāsam*] or Infinite Spiritual Æther [Tam. *sarvastāṉaviyāpitacakkirākirutavaṭṭa pirmañāṉākāsam*] itself" CPSPS. The text then adds several pages of instruction in the form of a "Special note" and subsequent sections that are absent from all editions of VRY; the text that follows what is given here in VRY1 resumes on CPSPS, First Book, 119.
21. "Brahma Giyanakasha"] < Skt. *brahajñānākāśa* ब्रहज्ञानाकाश; lit. "gnostic ether of Brahman." This is the "Infinite Spiritual Æther" mentioned in the longer quotation found in CPSPS (see previous note), and likely was supposed to form part of the previous paragraph.

22. "*sarva . . . matram*"] < Skt. *sarvaśūnyajñānākāśamātra* सर्वशून्यज्ञानाकाशमात्र; lit. "the gnostic ether (*jñānākāśa*) of the absolute void (*sarvaśūnya*) itself." "perfect Spiritual Voidness and Nothingness," Tam. *carvacūṉṉiya ñāṉākāsā māttiram* சர்வசூன்னிய ஞானாகாஸா மாத்திரம் CPSPS.
23. "neither"] em. "niether" VRY1.
24. "*andhakaramayam*"] < Skt. *andhakāramaya* अन्धकारमय; lit. "that which consists of darkness." "Æther of darkness," Tam. *antākārākāsamayam* அந்தாகாராகாஸமயம் CPSPS.
25. "*prakasha mayam*"] < Skt. *prakāśamaya* प्रकाशमय; lit. "that which consists of brightness." "Æther of brightness," Tam. *pirakāsākāsamayam* பிரகாஸாகாஸமயம் CPSPS.
26. "*sarva . . . matram*"] < Skt. *sarvajñānavyāpakamātra* सर्वज्ञानव्यापकमात्र; lit. "the pervader of absolute gnosis itself." "all pervading Spiritual Consciousness and pure Wisdom," Tam. *sarvañāṉa viyāpakamāttiram* ஸர்வஞான வியாபகமாத்திரம் CPSPS.
27. "*shuddha giyana sakshi matram*"] < Skt. *śuddhajñānasākṣimātra* शुद्धज्ञानसाक्षिमात्र; lit. "the eyewitness of absolute gnosis itself," "the only Spiritual Divine Witness," Tam. *suttañāṉacākṣimāttiram* ஸுத்தஞானசாக்ஷிமாத்திரம் CPSPS. "and it is the only Holy Eternal Bliss [Tam. *sarvaparicuttapirmmañāṉāṉantāmāttiram*]. Remember that there is no four separate sorts of Spirits but one Sort of Infinite Spirit with four sorts of *Brightness* in that one at the same Unity" + CPSPS.
28. "*giyanakasha saroop*"] < Skt. *jñānākāśasvarūpa* ज्ञानाकाशस्वरूप; lit. "the inherent nature of gnostic ether." "*Pure, Holy and Divine Spiritual Sight-like Nature*" CPSPS.
29. "*sunya saroopa*"] < Skt. *śūnyasvarūpa* शून्यस्वरूप; lit. "the inherent nature of the void." "A perfect Vacuum and Void with nothingness, as only a Holy Divine Infinite Spiritual Universal Vision or Sight-like state," Tam. *aṇṭapiṇṭamaṇṭalākāra carvacūṉṉiyāmaya cuttasvayañāṉa tiruṣṭi pirakācāmāttiram* அண்டபிண்டமண்டலாகார சர்வசூன்னியாமய சுத்தஸ்வயஞான திருஷ்டி பிரகாசாமாத்திரம் CPSPS.
30. "*giyana vyapakasaroop*"] < Skt. *jñānavyāpakasvarūpa* ज्ञानव्यापकस्वरूप; lit. "the inherent nature of the pervader (*vyāpaka*) of gnosis (*jñāna*)." "Universally pervading Consciousness," Tam. *aṇṭapiṇṭacarācara carvamaṇṭalākāraṉucūta carva viyāpakāmāttiram* அண்டபிண்டசராசர சர்வமண்டலாகாரனுசூத சர்வ வியாபகாமாத்திரம் CPSPS.
31. "*sakshi saroop*"] < Skt. *sākṣisvarūpa* साक्षिस्वरूप; lit. "the inherent nature of the eyewitness." "Universally pervading and permeating in solid as a Witness," Tam. *carva aṇṭapiṇṭacarācaramaṇṭalākārāṉucūtacarvacāṭcimāttiram* சர்வ அண்டபிண்டசராசர-மண்டலாகாரானுசூதசர்வசாட்சிமாத்திரம் CPSPS.
32. "*sakshi matra*"] < Skt. *sākṣimātra* साक्षिमात्र; lit. "the witness itself." "only a Witness" CPSPS.
33. [Original footnote from VRY1:] * "It is also *Anandamatram* [< Skt. *ānandamātra* आनन्दमात्र, "the bliss itself"], as it is pleasant to behold, and its rays are cool and charming because it is the U[niversal], I[nfinite], spirit or Brahm." CPSPS revises the original paragraph and adds further details on the "Bliss" as an aspect of Brahman that were absent in VRY1.
34. "Consider . . . *akash*"] "Consider therefore this Holy and Divine Infinite Spiritual Æther," Tam. *pirmañāṉākāsam* பிர்மஞானாகாஸம் CPSPS.
35. "four aspects,"] "5 aspects" CPSPS. In a paragraph given above these are the void, the pervader, the eyewitness, and the bliss, in addition to that which is strung together or

connected without interruption (Tam. *aṉucūtam*, < Skt. *anusyūta*, pfx. *anu* + a past participle of √ *siv*, cognate with English "sew").

36. "the very holy akash"] "the only unanimously mingled Holy Infinite Spirit" CPSPS.
37. "*shuddha . . . saroop*"] < Skt. *śuddhacaitanyajñānākāśasvarūpa* शुद्धचैतन्यज्ञानाकाशस्वरूप; lit. "the inherent nature (*svarūpa*) of the gnostic ether (*jñānākāśa*) of pure brilliance." Om. CPSPS.
38. "consider . . . giyana"]. ". . . among themselves neither do they stand separately from one another."
39. "*Rahasyam*"] < Skt. *rahasya* रहस्य; lit. "mystery." "secrecy," Tam. *rahasyam* ரஹஸ்யம் CPSPS.
40. "soroop"] "appearance" CPSPS.
41. "creations by Bhranti"] "creations of delusions," Tam. *carvamāyā ciruṣṭi tericaṉaṅkaḷ* சர்வமாயா சிருஷ்டி தெரிசனங்கள் CPSPS.
42. "cancel . . . *non-Bhranti*"] "exclude delusions" CPSPS.
43. "still . . . itself"] "still it will be pervading everywhere by *Itself*" CPSPS.
44. "Do not . . . limited"] "Do not consider therefore that the Holy and Divine Infinite Spirit or Infinite Spiritual Vision [Tam. *pirummañāṉa pirakāsa tiruṣṭi* பிரும்மஞான பிரகாஸ திருஷ்டி (< Skt. *brahmajñānaprakāśadṛṣṭi*)] is limited one." CPSPS.
45. "back sides"] "everywhere embracing in its bosom and permeating too, all the things if there be any such thing as creations, Sun, Moon, Stars, Planets, World, Clouds, Air, Fire, Water and created Beings &c" CPSPS.
46. "*giyana saroop*"] < Skt. *jñānasvarūpa* ज्ञानस्वरूप; "the inherent nature of gnosis." "void Conscious Witnessing Blissful Infinite Spirit" CPSPS.
47. "Instead . . . solidifying it"] These sentences are expanded and modified in CPSPS.
48. "*sakshi . . . saroop*"] < Skt. *sākṣisarvajñānākāśasvarūpa* साक्षिसर्वज्ञानाकाशस्वरूप; lit. "the witness (*sākṣī*) who is the inherent nature (*svarūpa*) of all gnostic ether (*sarva jñānākāśa*)." "Spiritual Wisdom or Consciousness," Tam. *cāṭcicorūpa pirmmañāṉa-pāvaṉāmayam* சாட்சிசொரூப பிர்ம்மஞானபாவனாமயம் CPSPS.
49. "that the earth . . . sphere"] "that the earth floats a little below the centre of the Universal Infinite Spiritual *Orb* or *Sphere* or *Circle* [Tam. *pirmñāṉāṉucūta arivākāramaṇṭala cakkirākirutavaṭṭākāsamayaliṅkākāramattiya jekat ihapūlōkam* பிர்ம்ஞானானுசூத அரிவாகாரமண்டல சக்கிராகிருதவட்டாகாஸமயலிங்காகாரமத்திய ஜெகத் இஹபூலோகம்]" CPSPS.
50. "beings"] "being" CPSPS.
51. "A little . . . top"] "A little above the centre of this Universal Infinite Spiritual Sphere consider the Sun to be in the right of the sky and the Moon in the left of the sky and the Stars and Planets at the top of the sky, of this Universal Spiritual Sky or Orb" CPSPS.
52. "*giyanakasha . . . matram*"] < Skt. *jñānākāśa svarūpa* of *sākṣī*, of *ānanda*, of *vyāpaka*, and of *śūnyamātra* ज्ञानाकाश स्वरूप of साक्षी, of आनन्द, of व्यापक, and of शून्यमात्र; lit. "the inherent nature of the gnostic ether who is the eyewitness (*sākṣī*), bliss (*ānanda*), pervader (*vyāpaka*), and the void (*śūnya*) itself." "Then expand your Universally diffused Holy and Divine Infinite Spirit of witnessing and blissful consciousness" (Tam. *carvāṉucūtacarvaviyāpaka cāṭciyāṉanta pirmmañāṉamayam* சர்வானுசூதசர்வவியாபக சாட்சியானந்த பிர்ம்மஞானமயம்) CPSPS.

53. "in such a way . . . presence"] "in such a way that it may permeate and penetrate entirely and in full through all the planets, Stars, Sun, Moon, Earth, and all creations &c., so solidly with its presence, so as not to leave even the tip of a point-like space in the Universe whether within and without or externally and internally empty of its presence" CPSPS.
54. "*andapinda . . . saroop*"] < Skt. *aṇḍapiṇḍacarācarasarvaśūnyajñānamayākāśasvarūpa* अण्डपिण्डचराचरसर्वशून्यज्ञानमयाकाशस्वरूप; lit. "the inherent nature of the ether that consists of the absolute void (*sarvaśūnya*), which is the cosmic motion (*carācara*) of the egg and embryo (*aṇḍapiṇḍa*)." The term *piṇḍa* can also refer to a kind of ball of rice that is offered to dead ancestors, representative of a human being. CPSPS: "the all Void the Universally pervading Wisdom or Conscious Witnessing Blissfulness the *Self*; having no end but Eternal everlasting, the only all Witnessing Bliss" (Tam. *catā cuttanittiya carvvacūṉṉiya viyāpaka cāṭci yāṉanta pirmmañāṉākāra akaṇṭamayam* சதா சுத்தநித்திய சர்வ்வசூன்னிய வியாபக சாட்சி யானந்த பிர்ம்மஞானாகார அகண்டமயம்) CPSPS. The passage in CPSPS appears to encompass the next four *svarūpa*s that follow.
55. "*sarvagiyana . . . saroop*"] < Skt. *sarvajñānānandamayasvarūpa* सर्वज्ञानानन्दमयस्वरूप; lit. "the inherent nature that consists of the bliss of the absolute gnosis." Om. CPSPS VRY2.
56. "*sarvagiyana . . . saroop*"] < Skt. *sarvajñānavyāpakamayasvarūpa* सर्वज्ञानव्यापकमयस्वरूप; lit. "the inherent nature that consists of the pervader of the absolute gnosis." Om. CPSPS VRY2.
57. "*sarwagiyana . . . saroop*"] < Skt. *sarvajñānasākṣimayasvarūpa* सर्वज्ञानसाक्षिमयस्वरूप; lit. "the inherent nature that consists of the eyewitness of the absolute gnosis" Om. CPSPS VRY2.
58. "survageana . . . saroop"] < Skt. *sarvajñānānandamayasvarūpa* सर्वज्ञानानन्दमयस्वरूप; lit. "the inherent nature that consists of the bliss of the absolute gnosis." Om. CPSPS VRY2.
59. "*suddha . . . saroop*"] < Skt. *śuddhacaitanyajñānākāśasvarūpa* शुद्धचैतन्यज्ञानाकाशस्वरूप; lit. "the inherent nature of the gnostic ether of pure brilliance. "Holy Spirt [*sic*]," Tam. *pirummañāṉatiruṣṭimayam* பிரும்மஞானதிருஷ்டிமயம் CPSPS.
60. "planets"] "and Creations" + CPSPS.
61. "*Brahma . . . bhawam*"] < Skt. *brahmajñānānubhava* ब्रह्मज्ञानानुभव; lit. "the experience of the gnosis of Brahman." "imagining Infinite Spirit," Tam. *pirummañāṉapāvaṉā* பிரும்மஞானபாவனா CPSPS.
62. "*giana akash*"] "Holy Infinite Spiritual Æther" (Tam. *cuttapirmmañāṉākāsam* சுத்தபிர்ம்மஞானாகாஸம்) CPSPS.
63. "*suddha . . . akash*"] < Skt. *śuddhacaitanyākāśa* शुद्धचैतन्याकाश; lit. "the ether of pure brilliance."
64. "luminous"] "and that have various changes and brightness of Sun, Moon, Fire, Light, Lightning &c., with differing colours, as suddenly appearing and suddenly disappearing, as different sorts of clouds and different appearance of Sky, Heaven or Air, but it is a perfect void like Æther, all conscious, all witnessing, all Blissful Infinite Spiritual Vision or Sight fully and Universally and in all Creations pervaded" + CPSPS.
65. "while the former is only true"] "cancel the latter untrue false Æther-like Spirits and become the former the only Infinite Spiritual Æther" CPSPS.

66. "*giyanakash*"] "Spiritual Æther" (Tam. *pirmmañāṉākāsam* பிர்ம்மஞானாகாஸம், < Skt. *brahmajñānākāśa*) CPSPS.
67. "vacuum"] "or void with the nothingness of the above things" + CPSPS.
68. "these false akashes"] "the above false Æther," Tam. *pirāntimāyākāsam* பிராந்திமாயாகாஸம் CPSPS.
69. "your *giyanakash* too"] "the Spiritual Æther," Tam. *pirmmañāṉākāsam* பிர்ம்மஞானாகாஸம் CPSPS.
70. "*sarva . . . saroop*"] < Skt. *sarvaśuddhacaitanyajñānākāśasvarūpa* सर्वशुद्धचैतन्यज्ञानाकाशस्वरूप; lit. "the inherent nature of the gnostic ether of the absolute pure brilliance." Om. CPSPS.
71. "*sarva . . . mayam*"] < Skt. *sarvaśūnyajñānamaya* सर्वशून्यज्ञानमय; lit. "that which consists of the gnosis of the absolute void."
72. "*sarva . . . mayam*"] < Skt. *sarvajñānavyāpakamaya* सर्वज्ञानव्यापकमय; lit. "that which consists of the pervader of the absolute gnosis."
73. "*sarva . . . mayam*"] < Skt. *sarvasākṣijñānamaya* सर्वसाक्षिज्ञानमय; lit. "that which consists of the gnosis of the absolute eyewitness."
74. "*sarva . . . mayam*"] < Skt. *sarvajñānānandamaya* सर्वज्ञानानन्दमय; lit. "that which consists of the bliss of the absolute gnosis."
75. "*layabodha Brahma giyana shiva mayam*"] < Skt. *layabodhabrahmajñānaśivamaya* लयबोधब्रह्मज्ञानशिवमय; lit. "that which consists of Shiva as the gnosis of Brahman, which is the awakening of absorption (*layabodha*)." Om. CPSPS.
76. "*maya . . . saroopam*"] < Skt. *māyāvikārākāśasvarūpa* मायाविकाराकाशस्वरूप; lit. "the inherent nature of ether as the fluctuation (*vikāra*) of illusion (*māyā*)." Om. CPSPS.
77. "*Brahma giyana akasha saroopam*"] < Skt. *brahmajñānākāśasvarūpa* ब्रह्मज्ञानाकाशस्वरूप; lit. "the inherent nature of ether as the gnosis of Brahman." Om. CPSPS.

    "Consider . . . *saroopam*"] "Consider all the false *Æthers* except *This One* to be as the delusive appearances as false Æthers to deceive you owing to your Impurities, Sins, and Vices; but the Infinite Spiritual Æther . . . is as follows" CPSPS. The "First Book" of CPSPS ends here. The Second Book begins with instructions, abbreviated in VRY, on "removing the different sorts of ætherial spiritual visions" (Tam. *ṉāṉākñāṉākāca tiruṣṭi pētanivartti* னானாக்ஞானாகாச திருஷ்டி பேதநிவர்த்தி, < Skt. *nānājñānākāśadṛṣṭibhedanivṛtti*) and on "the Purifications and Preparations for Gyanamayam" (Tam. *pirmmakñāṉa carvacuttattuvacarvātikārattuvacātaṉāppiyāca upatēṣam* பிர்ம்மக்ஞான சர்வசுத்தத்துவசர்வாதிகாரத்துவசாதனாப்பியாச உபதேஷம், < Skt. *brahmajñānasarvaśuddhatvasarvādhikāratvasādhanābhyāsopadeśa*).
78. "Shut . . . kundlee"] "Shut your eyes, and throw the above-like I[nfinite]. spiritual keen sights of the two sights (No. 1-3) to the Kundalee. (No. 18-19)" CPSPS. These and the following instructions were adapted by Aleister Crowley for his meditation "S.S.S." in *Liber HHH* as evident by his diary; see Aleister Crowley et al., *Magick: Liber ABA, Book Four, Parts I–IV*, 2nd ed. (York Beach, ME: Samuel Weiser, 1997) and Chapter 7. These instructions were also independently engaged by Arjan Dass Malik (2002) and T. K. Rajagopalan (2005 [1945]).

79. "Imagine . . . koondli"] "Imagine the mind as the above I[nfinite] spiritual conscious state to be a pole of the mental spiritual consciousness (No. 2) having the bottom in Kundalee (No. 18-19) and the top in the Brimharunthra or skull (No. 7-30) filling the pole from head to foot by conscious Sight [Tam. *kñāṉa tiruṣṭṭi* க்ஞான திருஷ்ட்டி, < Skt. *jñānadṛṣṭi*]" CPSPS.
80. "Draw . . . again"] "Draw up this Mind by the I[nfinite] spiritual conscious visions of the two sights (No. 1-3) up to the Brahmarunthram through the middle part (No. 2) and drop and draw it again and again in circle through Soosoomuna organ and Kumbaca organ i.e. starting downwards from Brahmarunthram touching Kundali, going round through backbone to Brahmarunthram over and over as the conscious spiritual state or as the Infinite mantraic mum spiritual state of (Om Ahum)" CPSPS.
81. "Fix . . . steady"] "Fix it in the Brahmarunthram and make the mental pole straight and steady" CPSPS.
82. "Fix . . . Brahmarantar"] "Fix also the two keennesses of the sights of that pole to be seated in the Brahmarunthram" CPSPS.
83. "Imagine . . . consciousness"] "Imagine the head to be removed and its place occupied by the universally and in-all-creations pervading I[nfinite] spiritual void witnessing and blissful consciousness (Tam. *carvāṉucūtayantaryāmittuva pirmakñāṉākāsa corūpam* சர்வானுசூதயந்தர்யாமித்துவ பிர்மக்ஞானாகாஸ சொரூபம், < Skt. *sarvānusyūtāntaryāmitatva brahmajñānākāśasvarūpa*)" CPSPS.
84. "Make . . . all"] "Make this to be as the universally spread, imagining the sun, moon, stars, planets and earth floating in it; and this pervades in them all" CPSPS.
85. "*Bhawana . . . Brahmachari*"] < Skt. *bhāvanā brahmajñānī brahmacārī* भावना ब्रह्मज्ञानी ब्रह्मचारी; lit. "Student-ascetic and gnostic of Brahman in (meditative) cultivation." "Bachelor of Practising I. spiritual ecstasy by deeply meditating Yogue [Tam. *pāvaṉā pirmmakñāṉapirmmaccāri* பாவனா பிர்ம்மக்ஞானபிர்ம்மச்சாரி < Skt. *bhāvanā brahmajñānabrahmacārī*] the divine spiritual Bachelor in the spiritual Pilgrimage" CPSPS. "Secondly consider that this deeply meditating spiritual ecstasy [Tam. *pāvaṉā pirmmakñāṉam* பாவனா பிர்ம்மக்ஞானம், < Skt. *bhāvanā brahmajñāna*] is within the centre of brain and skull [Tam. *pirmmarantiram* பிர்ம்மரந்திரம், < Skt. *brahmarandhra*]." The Sanskrit word *brahmacārī* (from stem *brahmacārin*), "follower of Brahman," is a synonym for *brahmacarya*, the first of four traditional "stages" (*āśramas*) of life as codified in the Dharmaśāstras, ancient Indian texts on society and ḍuty. Sabhapati in this section uses three of these four stages to describe titles of yogic attainment rather than referring literally to their social, economic, and political functions.
86. "*Bhawana Brahma giyan*"] < Skt. *bhāvanābrahmajñāna* भावनाब्रह्मज्ञान; lit. "the gnosis of Brahman through (meditative) cultivation."
87. "*suddha . . . mayam*"] < Skt. *śuddhacaitanyabrahmajñānākāśamaya* शुद्धचैतन्यब्रह्मज्ञानाकाशमय; lit. "that which consists of the gnostic ether of Brahman as pure consciousness." "Infinite Spirit" CPSPS.
88. "*sushoomana*"] "Sushoomna Nadi or spiritual nerve" CPSPS. The latter part may have read "I[nfinite]. spiritual nerve" on account of a mark in the text.

89. "*khumbak*"] "Kumbaka-Nadi or spinal cord" CPSPS.

90. "*suddha…giyanakash*"] < Skt. *śuddhacaitanyabrahmajñānākāśa* शुद्धचैतन्यब्रह्मज्ञानाकाश; lit. "the gnostic ether (*jñānākāśa*) of Brahman that is pure brilliance (*śuddhacaitanya*)." "I[nfinite]. Spirit," Tam. *cuttapirmma* சுத்தபிர்மம, < Skt. *śuddhabrahman* CPSPS.

91. "*laya bodham*"] < Skt. *layabodha* लयबोध; lit. "awakening of absorption." "Absorption and everlasting spiritual intoxication," Tam. *pirammakñāṉamayalīṉalayayaikkiya pōtam* பிரம்மக்ஞானமயலீனலயயைக்கிய போதம் CPSPS.

92. "*Brahma chaitanya giyanakasha saroop*"] < Skt. *brahmacaitanyajñānākāśasvarūpa* ब्रह्मचैतन्यज्ञानाकाशस्वरूप; lit. "the inherent nature of the gnostic ether that is the brilliance of Brahman." "I[nfinite]. spiritual vision," Tam. *pirammamaya ñāṉākācatiruṣṭṭi* பிரம்மமய ஞானாகாசதிருஷ்ட்டி CPSPS.

93. "run"] "runs and fills" CPSPS.

94. "three smaller pipes"] "three parallel sights" CPSPS.

95. "*sushoomana*"] + "as thin as hair" CPSPS.

96. "No. 7 in the diagram"] "No. 1 in the diagram" CPSPS.

97. "*giyanakash*"] "I. Spiritual void æther-like blissful consciousness of witness," Tam. *pirmmakñāṉāṟivumayam* பிர்ம்மக்ஞானாறிவுமயம் CPSPS.

98. "*Pranava . . . vasi*"] < Skt. with Tam. *praṇavograjñānākāśacandrakalāvāṃśī* प्रणवोग्र-ज्ञानाकाशचन्द्रकलावांशी; lit. "the channel (*vāṃśī*, < Tam. *vāci*) of the fragmented power of the moon (*candrakalā*) that is the gnostic ether of the ferocity of the syllable Om (*praṇava*)." "The un-sounding spiritual divine word-like state as (Om) in the form of the consciousness of calmness and coolness," Tam. *piraṇavavukrañāṉākāsa cantirakalāvāci* பிரணவவுக்ரஞானாகாஸ சந்திரகலாவாசி CPSPS.

99. "*Brahma . . . drishti*"] < Skt. *brahmacaitanyaśuddha sampūrṇasvayamprakāśadṛṣṭi* ब्रह्मचैतन्यशुद्ध सम्पूर्णस्वयम्प्रकाशदृष्टि; lit. "the sight [*dṛṣṭi*] of one's pure and complete self-manifestation as the brilliance of Brahman." "The conscious sight of spirit of mildness," Tam. *pirma caitaṉṉiya cutta campūrṇacuyampirakāsa tiruṣṭṭi* பிர்ம சைதன்னிய சுத்த சம்பூர்ணசுயம்பிரகாஸ திருஷ்ட்டி CPSPS.

100. "*giyanakash*"] "I[nfinite]. Spirit," Tam. *ñāṉamayam* ஞானமயம் CPSPS.

101. "*Nirakara . . . Vasi*"] < Skt. and Tam. *nirākāraikyāgnikalāvāṃśi* निराकारैक्याग्निकलावांशि; lit. "the channel (*vāṃśi* = Tam. *vāci*, loosely synonymous with *nāḍī*) of the fragmented power of fire (*agnikalā*) as the unity of the formless (*nirākāraikya*)." "The all absorbed void conscious sight-like Holy I. Spirit as spiritual sight, of being as (Ahum) in the form of the consciousness of soundlessness and silence," Tam. *nirākāra aikkiya kñāṉākkiṉi kalāvāci* நிராகார ஐக்கிய க்ஞானாக்கினி கலாவாசி CPSPS.

102. "*Brahma . . . drishti*"] < Skt. *brahmacaitanyaśuddhajñānākāśasarvajñatva-sarvajñānadṛṣṭi* ब्रह्मचैतन्यशुद्धज्ञानाकाशसर्वज्ञत्वसर्वज्ञानदृष्टि; lit. "the sight [*dṛṣṭi*] of all intelligence and all knowledge [*sarvajñāna*] in the pure gnostic ether of the brilliance of Brahman." Conscious sight of spirit," Tam. *pirmacaitaṉṉiya cuttañāṉākāsa carvaññattuvacarvakñāṉa tiruṣṭi* பிர்மசைதன்னிய சுத்தஞானாகாஸ சர்வஞ்ஞுத்துவசர்வக்ஞான திருஷ்டி CPSPS.

103. "*pingala*"] "Pingala organ," Tam. *piṅkalāṭi* பிங்கலாடி CPSPS.

104. "*Omkara . . . Vasi*"] < Skt. with Tam. *oṃkārakṛpāsūryakalāvāṃśī* ॐ-कारकृपासूर्यकलावांशी; "the channel of the fragmented power of the sun [*sūryakalā*],

which is the mercy [*kṛpā*] of the syllable Om [*oṃkāra*]." "the unsounding spiritual word-like state as (Brumho) in the form of the consciousness of heat and excitement," Tam. *oṅkārakirupācūriyakalāvācī* ஒங்காரகிருபாசூரியகலாவாசீ CPSPS.

105. "*Brahma chaitnanya suddha giyanakasha sarva yayike sarva sunnya drishti*"] < Skt. *brahmacaitanyaśuddhajñānākāśasarvaikyasarvaśūnyadṛṣṭi* ब्रह्मचैतन्यशुद्धज्ञानाकाशसर्वैक्यसर्वशून्यदृष्टि; "the sight [*dṛṣṭi*] of the absolute unity [*sarva aikya*] and the absolute void (*sarvaśūnya*) as the pure gnostic ether (*śuddhajñānākāśa*), which is the brilliance of Brahman [*brahmacaitanya*]." "Spiritual vision," Tam. *pirmacaitanṉiyacutta kñāṉākāsacarva aikkiya carvaccūṉṉiyatiruṣṭi* பிர்மசைதன்னியசுத்தக்ஞானாகாஸசர்வ ஐக்கிய சர்வச்சூன்னியதிருஷ்டி CPSPS.

106. "*Giyanakash*"] "I[nfinite]. Spirit as divine ether in the Sushumna nerve," Tam. *pirmakñāṉamayam* பிர்மக்ஞானமயம் CPSPS.

107. "vessel".] CPSPS reads "hollow nerve" or "hollow nerves" for "vessel" throughout this passage.

108. "settles . . . nose"] "settles in the centre seat of the nose giving a branch to it" CPSPS.

109. "eyes"] "from eyebrow" + CPSPS.

110. "descending . . . tongue"] " . . . descending one inch further down from the centre of the nose, settle in the centre seat of the tongue" CPSPS. CPSPS also pluralizes the rest of this passage that describes the motion of the "vessels" or "hollow nerves."

111. "From . . . branch"] Om. CPSPS.

112. "*Kundlee . . . Nadee*"] < Skt. *kuṇḍalīstambhanalayapūrṇavyāpakajñānakalāmayarecakanāḍī* कुण्डलीस्तम्भनलयपूर्णव्यापकज्ञानकलामयरेचकनाडी; "the channel of exhalation [*recakanāḍī*] that consists of the fragmented power [*kalā*] of the gnosis of the pervader [*vyāpakajñāna*], which is entirely dissolved [*layapūrṇa*] in the arresting [*stambhana*] of the ring [*kuṇḍalī*, here the *mūlādhāra* lotus]." "The steadily Starting 'Seeing state' as the Holy Divine I[nfinite]. Spiritual Vision of graceful Wisdom of Void Consciousness," Tam. *stampaṉalayapūrṇaviyāpaka kñāṉāṉantakalāmaya irēcakavāci* ஸ்தம்பனலயபூர்ணவியாபக க்ஞானானந்தகலாமய இரேசகவாசி CPSPS.

113. "*Bramha . . . drishti*"] < Skt. *brahmacaitanyaśuddhaśāntākāśasarvāṇḍapiṇḍacarācarasarvasṛṣṭyantarvyāpakadṛṣṭi* ब्रह्मचैतन्यशुद्धशान्ताकाशसर्वाण्डपिण्डचराचरसर्वसृष्ट्यन्तर्व्यापकदृष्टि; "the sight of the inner pervader that is the entirety of the cosmic motion [*carācara*] of egg and embryo [*aṇḍapiṇḍa*], and the entirety of creation, which is the pure and tranquil ether of the brilliance of Brahman." "Perfect spiritual Infinite conscious Void," Tam. *pirmmacaitanṉiyacutta cāntākāsacarva aṇṭa piṇṭacarācaracarvacirṣṭi yantiralayaviyāpaka āṉantakiyāṉatiruṣṭi* பிர்ம்மசைதன்னியசுத்த சாந்தாகாஸசர்வ அண்ட பிண்டசராசரசர்வசிர்ஷ்டி யந்திரலயவியாபக ஆனந்தகியானதிருஷ்டி CPSPS.

114. "*kúndali . . . Nadee*"] < Skt. *kuṇḍalitrikālanityasampūrṇānandakalāmayakumbhakanāḍī* कुण्डलित्रिकालनित्यसम्पूर्णानन्दकलामयकुम्भकनाडी; "the channel of breath-retention [*kumbhakanāḍī*, here the spinal cord] that consists of the fragmented power of the ring's [*kuṇḍalī*] constant and full bliss throughout the three times (i.e., past, present, and future)." "The steadily Fixing and Mingling. 'Becoming State' as the Holy I[nfinite].

Spiritual Vision of Graceful Wisdom of Bliss," Tam. *kumpita pōtacampūraṇapirm-āṉantakalāmayakumpakavāci* கும்பித போதசம்பூரணபிர்மானந்தகலாமயகும்ப கவாசி CPSPS.

115. "*Brahma . . . purnanandam*"] < Skt. *brahmacaitanyaśuddhaśāntasad-ākāśasarvalayabodhaparipūrṇānanda* ब्रह्मचैतन्यशुद्धशान्तसदाकाशसर्वलयबोधपरिपूर्णानन्द; "the fulfilling bliss [*paripūrṇānanda*] in the absolute awakening of absorption in the pure, tranquil, and true ether, which is the brilliance of Brahman [*brahmacaitanya*]." "The perfect Spiritual Infinite conscious Bliss," Tam. *pirmacaitaṉṉiyacutta cāntacarvastāṉacarvaññāṉa aikkiyacarvapirmāṉantaññāṉa-tiruṣṭi* பிர்மசைதன்னியசுத்த சாந்தசர்வஸ்தானசர்வஞான ஐக்கியசர்வபிர்மா னந்தஞானதிருஷ்டி CPSPS.

116. "*kundlee . . . Nadee*"] < Skt. *kuṇḍalikumbhitabodhapūrṇasākṣikalāmayapūraka-nāḍī* कुण्डलिकुम्भितबोधपूर्णसाक्षिकलामयपूरकनाडी; "the channel of inhalation [*pūrakanāḍī*] that consists of the fragmented power of the eyewitness [*sākṣikalā*], which is the fullness of the retained awakening of the ring [*kuṇḍalī*]. CPSPS gloss: "the steadily Going 'Absorbing state' as the Holy Divine I[nfinite]. Spiritual Vision of Graceful Wisdom of Witness," Tam. *pantaṉa aikkiyapūraṇacāṭciyāṉantatirikālakñāṉa kalāmaya pūrakavāci* பந்தன ஐக்கியபூரணசாட்சியான்ந்ததிரிகாலக்ஞான கலாமய பூரகவாசி CPSPS. CPSPS switches "binding" (*bandhana*) and "retained" (*kumbhita*) between the channel of *kumbhaka* and the *pūraka*. These processes are somewhat described in Sabhapati's short instructions on haṭha yoga in CPSPS but are not elaborated on in VRY.

117. "*Brahma . . . drishti*"] < Skt. *brahmacaitanyaśuddhaśāntākāśasarvasthānasarva-jñānasarvasākṣidṛṣṭi* ब्रह्मचैतन्यशुद्धशान्ताकाशसर्वस्थानसर्वज्ञानसर्वसाक्षिदृष्टि; "the sight of the absolute eyewitness [*sarvasākṣī*], which is omnipresent [*sarvasthāna*] and omniscient [*sarvajñāna*] in the pure and tranquil ether, which is the brilliance of Brahman." "The perfect spiritual Infinite Witness," Tam. *pirmacaitaṉṉiyacutta cāntacitākāscarv-apōtaparipūraṇāṉantacāṭkñāṉa tiruṣṭi* பிர்மசைதன்னியசுத்த சாந்தசிதாகாஸ்சர் வபோதபரிபூரணானந்தசாட்க்ஞான திருஷ்டி CPSPS.

118. "*Bhawana . . . Raja Yoga*"] < Skt. *bhāvanābrahmajñānabrāhmacārī* in *rājayoga* भावनाब्रह्मज्ञानब्राह्मचारी in राजयोग; lit. "a student- ascetic of the gnosis of Brahman in the royal yoga (Rājayoga)." "Practical Professor in Spiritual Ecstasy," Tam. *pāvaṉāpir makñāṉapirmacārirājayōka appiyāci* பாவனாபிர்மக்ஞானபிர்மசாரிராஜயோக அப்பியாசி CPSPS.

119. "*Brahmagiyana Shiva yoga yathree*"] < Skt. *brahmajñānaśivayogayātrī* ब्रह्मज्ञानशिवयोगयात्री; lit. "a pilgrim (*yātrī*) in the yoga for Shiva, which is the gnosis of Brahman." "Pilgrim in the Divine Kingdom of Infinite spirit's Ecstasy," Tam. *civarājayōka pirmmakñāṉayāttiri* சிவராஜ்யோக பிர்ம்மக்ஞானயாத்திரி CPSPS.

120. "*chinmudra*"] *cinmudrā* चिन्मुद्रा; lit. "seal (*mudrā*) of thought (*cit*)." "The steady sign," Tam. *ciṉmuttirā* சின்முத்திரா CPSPS. The *cinmudrā* is a well-known *mudrā* (here a hand-gesture) often formed by making a loop with the index finger and the thumb.

121. "*Sukshasana*"] *sukhāsana* सुखासन; lit. "posture of happiness." "easy posture," Tam. *cukāsaṉam* சுகாஸனம் CPSPS. "or by lying" (i.e., lying down) + CPSPS.

122. "mowna . . . matrum"] < Skt. *maunajñānadṛṣṭimātra* मौनज्ञानदृष्टिमात्र; lit. "the sight of the gnosis in silence itself." "Divine name-like spiritual state without sound of any kind," Tam. *nirākārayasapta mauṉamayapiraṇava aikkiyākārap pirmamaya svarūpam* நிராகாரயஸப்த மௌனமயபிரணவ ஐக்கியாகாரப் பிர்மமய ஸ்வரூபம் CPSPS. [Footnote in the original publication:] * "Or by the tongue of the dumbness of consciousness."

123. "*Shivhá . . . Anandohum*"] < Skt. *śivā, śiva, śiva, śiva, śiva, śiva, śiva, śivo 'ham, brahmo 'ham, jñāno 'ham, ākāśo 'ham, śūnyo 'ham, sākṣyaham, vyāpako 'ham, ānando 'ham* शिवा, शिव, शिव, शिव, शिव, शिव, शिव, शिवो ऽहम्, ब्रह्मो ऽहम्, ज्ञानो ऽहम्, आकाशो ऽहम्, शून्यो ऽहम्, साक्ष्यहम्, व्यापको ऽहम्, आनन्दो ऽहम्; lit. "Shiva, Shiva, Shiva, Shiva, Shiva, Shiva, Shiva, I am Shiva, I am Brahman, I am gnosis, I am ether, I am the void, I am the eyewitness, I am the pervader, I am bliss." "Siva, Siva, Siva, Siva, Siva, Siva, Siva. Siva, Sivum, Brumum, Gnyanum, Akasham, Survasunnium, Survasatchi, Survaviapakum, Surva Aunandum," Tam. *civā, civa, civa, civa, civā, civa, civa, civa, civam, pirmamam, ñāṉam, ākācam, carvacūṉṉiyam, carvacāṭcī, carvaviyāpakam, carva āṉantam* [*sic*]. சிவா, சிவ, சிவ, சிவ, சிவா, சிவ, சிவ, சிவ, சிவம், பிர்மமம், ஞானம், ஆகாசம், சர்வசூன்னியம், சர்வசாட்சீ, சர்வவியாபகம், சர்வ ஆனந்தம் CPSPS. "Stay at Kundalee after descending in the deep meditation of its spiritual state for a few minutes." + CPSPS. CPSPS removes the first person pronoun *aham* that seems inherent to other mantras in VRY, like *śivo 'ham*, so the reading may be mere recitation of the above names rather than "I am . . ."

124. "Layohum . . . Brahmahum"] < Skt. *layo 'ham, bodho 'ham, śānto 'ham, ugro 'ham, kṛpākāra, aikya, āroham, sthambhanam, kumbhitam, paramānubhavam, saṃpūrṇam, ekam, brahmo 'ham* लयो ऽहम्, बोधो ऽहम्, शान्तो ऽहम्, उग्रो ऽहम्, कृपाकार, ऐक्य, आरोहम्, स्थम्भनम्, कुम्भितम्, परमानुभवम्, संपूर्णम्, एकम्, ब्रह्मो ऽहम्; one possible reading is "I am dissolution, I am awakening, I am peaceful, I am ferocious, I am the giver of mercy, I am the unity, I am the one who ascends, the fixer, the retainer, the highest experience, the completion, the one, I am Brahman." "Hahum Surva Layum, Bodum, Sandum, Suddum, Nittium, Pranavam, Onkaram, Nirakarum, Oogram, Kripakarum, Ayikiam, Arohum, Sthumbanum, Kumbithum, Bunthanaum, Anatham, Paramamsum, Survanusuthum, Akakrithum, Thathakarum, Paramanubavum, Sumpurnum; Akum, Brummum, Thuthbrammum, Thathobrammum, Anusuthabrammum Swayabrunam, Anthryamibrammum," Tam. *ahañcarvalayam, pōtam, cāntam, cuttam, nittiyam, piraṇavam, oṅkāram, nirākāram, ukram, kirupākaram, ayikkiyam, āṉantam, stampaṉam, kumpitam, pantaṉam, aṉātam, parmāmcam, carvāṉucūtam, carvō ēkamayam, ēkākirītam, tatātkāram, paramāṉupavam, campūraṇam, ēkam, pirmmam, tatpirmam, tatōpirmam, aṉucūtapirmmam, antaryāmi pirmmam, cuvayampirmam* அஹஞ்சர்வலயம், போதம், சாந்தம், சுத்தம், நித்தியம், பிரணவம், ஓங்காரம், நிராகாரம், உக்ரம், கிருபாகரம், அயிக்கியம், ஆனந்தம், ஸ்தம்பனம், கும்பிதம், பந்தனம், அனாதம், பர்மாம்சம், சர்வானுசூதம், சர்வோ ஏகமயம், ஏகாகிரீதம், ததாத்காரம், பரமானுபவம், சம்பூரணம், ஏகம், பிர்ம்மம், தத்பிர்மம், ததோபிர்மம், அனுசூதபிர்ம்மம், அந்தர்யாமி பிர்ம்மம், சுவயம்பிர்மம் CPSPS. As before, CPSPS removes the first-person pronoun *aham* that

seems inherent to other mantras in VRY1, like *śivo 'ham*, so an alternate reading of some of the above terms may omit "I am . . ."

125. "Tatwa Giyani"] < Skt. *tattvajñānī* तत्त्वज्ञानी; lit. "knower (*jñānī*, < stem *jñānin*) of the principles (*tattva*)." "Thatwa Gnyani" CPSPS.

126. "*Utpattidarshana Grishasti*"] < Skt. *utpattidarśanagṛhasthin* उत्पत्तिदर्शनगृहस्थिन्; lit. "a householder in whom discernment (*darśana*) arises." "The family-man of the knowledge of Truth or the Soul in the perfection of piety on, prayer of, devotion on, meditation upon, seeing only, absorbing in, becoming off, and being as, the only Infinite Spirit," Tam. *pirmmasvarūpam* i.e. *carvāṇupūti nirantaraniraṅcaṉacamakaivalliyakñāṉōkirahastaṉ* பிர்ம்மஸ்வரூபம் i.e. சர்வானுபூதி நிரந்தரநிரஞ்சனசமகைவல்லியக்ஞானோகிரஹஸ்தன் CPSPS.

127. "*Maya . . . Grahashrumum*"] < Skt. *māyābhrāntikalpanāsaṃkalpatattvagṛhāśrama* मायाभ्रान्तिकल्पनासंकल्पतत्त्वगृहाश्रम; lit. "the householder stage (*gṛhāśrama*) of [knowing] the principles (*tattva*) to be an illusion, confusion, fabricated thought, and wishful thinking." "You must examine further the delusion of false deceipt [*sic*], false show, false dreams of faculties, happiness and worldly enjoyments," Tam. *māyāpirānticaṅk alppakalpaṉātattuvacukatukkam* மாயாபிராந்திசங்கல்ப்பகல்பனாதத்துவசுகதுக்கம் CPSPS.

128. "*Sannyasi mawnagiyani*"] < Skt. *sāṃnyāsī manojñānī* सांन्यासी मनोज्ञानी; lit. "a renunciate (*sāṃnyāsī*, < stem *saṃnyāsin*) who has the gnosis of mind." "'Sanniasi Mowna Gnyana' in heart or the sacrificer of delusions" CPSPS.

129. "Brahma- Giyanee"] *brahmajñānī* ब्रह्मज्ञानी; lit. "one who has gnosis of Brahman." "Brumma Gnyani or spiritual man" CPSPS.

130. "Maya"] "or delusions" + CPSPS.

References

I have retained the original romanizations and vernacular diacritics (where applicable) of Sabhapati's name on all books he authored on account of wide variation in library catalogs and archives. Some of the sources in this list may also be considered secondary sources in some contexts but were considered primary for the purposes of this book.

Primary

Admirer, An. "The Madras Yogi Sabhapaty Swami." *The Theosophist: A Monthly Journal Devoted to Oriental Philosophy, Art, Literature and Occultism: Embracing Mesmerism, Spiritualism, and Other Secret Sciences* 1, no. 6 (March 1880): 145–47.

"All Around the World." *Minneapolis Journal*. October 30, 1928.

"American Hindoo Converts Would Spread Religion Here." *Indiana Gazette*. November 21, 1928, 10.

"American Pair Hindu Converts." *Boston Globe*. October 31, 1928, 11.

Anonymous. *The Secret of Longevity and Verses by Yogi Sabhapathy Swami*. Coimbatore: K.N. Easwariah at the Literary Sun Press, 1895.

Anonymous [Aleister Crowley]. *777 vel Prolegomena Symbolica ad Systemam Sceptico-Mysticae Viae Explicandae, Fundamentum Hieroglyphicum Sanctissimorum Scientiae Summae*. London: Walter Scott Publishing, 1909.

Another Hindu Theosophist. "Do the Rishis Exist?" *The Theosophist: A Magazine of Oriental Philosophy, Art, Literature and Occultism* 4 (May 1883): 203.

Āpṭe, Hari Nārāyaṇa, trans. *Pātañjalayogasūtrāṇi*. Pune: Ānandāśramamudraṇālayā, 1919.

Avalon, Arthur. *The Serpent Power, Being the Shat-Chakra-Nirūpana and Pāduka-Panchakā*. 1919; Madras: Ganesh, 1950.

Bary, R. C. *The Prayer Book of the Aryans, Being a Translation in English of Sandhia and Gayutree, with Original Mantras in Sanscrit, as Well as Rules for Their Observance, with Scientific Explanation*. Lahore: R.C. Bary, printed at the "Arya Press," 1883.

Beta, Hymenaeus, ed. *The Equinox. The Review of Scientific Illuminism: The Official Organ of the O.T.O.* Vol. 3, no. 10. New York: 93 Publishing, 1989.

Blavatsky, H. P. "A Hindu Professor's Views on Indian Yoga." *The Theosophist: A Magazine of Oriental Philosophy, Art, Literature and Occultism* 2, no. 7 (April 1881): 158–59.

Blavatsky, Helena, and Henry Olcott, eds. "The 'Trieste [*sic*] on Vedantic Raj Yoga.'" *The Theosophist: A Magazine of Oriental Philosophy, Art, Literature and Occultism* 1, no. 7 (April 1880): 190.

Bose, Phanindranath. *Life of Sris Chandra Basu*. Calcutta: R. Chatterjee, 1932.

Braidwood, Rev. John. *True Yoke-Fellows in the Mission Field: The Life and Labours of the Rev. John Anderson and the Rev. Robert Johnston, Traced in the Rise and Development of the Madras Free Church Mission*. London: James Nisbet, 1862.

Caldwell, Robert. *A Comparative Grammar of the Dravidian or South-Indian Family of Languages*. 2nd ed. London: Trübner, Ludgate Hill, 1875.

Caldwell, Robert. *A Political and General History of the District of Tinnevelly, in the Presidency of Madras, from the Earliest Period to Its Cession to the English Government in A.D. 1801*. Madras: E. Keys, at the Government Press, 1881.

Ceṭṭiyār, V. Cuppiramaṉiya. Interview by Keith Cantú and Vinayagam. Audio recording, August 17, 2019.

Chandru, Justice K. "Thiru Sabanatha Oli Sivachariyar v/s The Commissioner, H.R. & C.E. Department & Others." Chennai: Madras High Court, March 24, 2010.

Cīkāḻic Ciṟṟampalanāṭikaḷ. *Tukaḷaṟu pōtam*. Paruttitturai (Point Pedro), Sri Lanka: Kalānitiyantiracālai, 1950.

Civāṉantapōtam. Chennai: Manoṉmaṇivilācam Accukkūṭam, 1897.

"Confidence Man Back into Prison." *Abilene Reporter News*. January 31, 1962.

Crowley, Aleister. "777," in *777 and Other Qabalistic Writings of Aleister Crowley: Including Gematria & Sepher Sephiroth*, edited by Israel Regardie. 1973. York Beach, ME: S. Weiser, 1983.

Crowley, Aleister. *The Confessions of Aleister Crowley: An Autohagiography*. Edited by John Symonds and Kenneth Grant. New York: Hill and Wang, 1970.

Crowley, Aleister. *Eight Lectures on Yoga*. 1939; Scottsdale, AZ: O.T.O. in association with New Falcon Publications, 1985.

Crowley, Aleister, ed. "Liber HHH sub figvrâ CCCXLI." In *The Equinox*, vol. 1, no. 5, 5–14. London: Self-published, 1911.

Crowley, Aleister, ed. "Liber Tav [Yod] svb figvrâ DCCCXXXI." In *The Equinox*, vol. 1, no. 7, 93–100. London: Wieland, 1912.

Crowley, Aleister, ed. "Liber XIII vel Graduum Montis Abiegni: A Syllabus of the Steps upon the Path." In *The Equinox*, vol. 1, no. 3, 3–8. London: Simpkin, Marshall, Hamilton, Kent, 1910.

Crowley, Aleister, ed. "Postcards to Probationers." In *The Equinox*, vol. 1, no. 2, 196–200. London: Simpkin, Marshall, Hamilton, Kent, 1909.

Crowley, Aleister, H. P. Blavatsky, J. F. C. Fuller, and Charles Stansfeld Jones. *Commentaries on the Holy Books and Other Papers: The Equinox*. Vol. 4, no. 1. Edited by A.∴A.∴ [*sic*]. York Beach, ME: S. Weiser, 1996.

Crowley, Aleister, David Curwen, and Henrik Bogdan. *Brother Curwen, Brother Crowley: A Correspondence*. York Beach, ME: Teitan Press, 2010.

Crowley, Aleister, Mary Desti, Leila Waddell, and Hymenaeus Beta. *Magick: Liber ABA, Book Four, Parts I–IV*. 2nd ed. York Beach, ME: S. Weiser, 1997.

Cuvāmikaḷ, Capāpati. *Carva māṉaca nittiya karmānuṣṭāṉa, carva tēvatātēvi māṉaca pūjāttiyāṉa, pirammakñāṉa rājayōka niṣṭai camāti, carva tīkṣākkramattiyāṉa, cātaṉā appiyāca kiramāṉucantāṉa, caṅkiraha vēta tiyāṉōpatēca smiruti*. Tiruccirāppaḷḷi: Ṣaṇmukavilās Piras, 1913.

Cuvāmikaḷ, Citampara. *Upatēcavuṇmaiyum*. Edited by Ciṅkāravēlu Piḷḷai. Koṉṉūr: Māṇikkamutaḷiyār's Maṉōṉmaṇivilācavaccukkūṭam, 1881.

Cuvāmikaḷ, Citampara Periya. *Upatēca uṇmai, viḷakka uraiyuṭaṉ*. Vēḷaccēri, Chennai: Vēḷaccēri Makāṉ Patippakam, 2014.

Cuvāmikaḷ, Hariharaṉ. Interview by Keith Cantú and Sivasakthi at Aruḷmiku Śrī Capāpati Liṅkēsvar Jīvacamāti Ālayam. Audio recording, July 2018.

Cuvāmikaḷ, Hariharaṉ. Interview by Sivasakthi, Beulah, and Mathan Raj at Aruḷmiku Śrī Capāpati Liṅkēsvar Jīvacamāti Ālayam. Audio recording, August 12, 2018.

Cuvāmikaḷ, Ñāṉakuruyōki Capāpati. *Carvōpatēsa tatvañāṉa civarājayōka svayap pirammañāṉāṉupūti vētapōtam*. Madras: Empress of India Piras [Press], 1889.
Cuvāmikaḷ, Vētacirēṇi Citampara. *Upatēcavuṇmaiyum upatēcavuṇmaikkaṭṭaḷaiyum tōttiramālaiyum aṭaṅkiyirukkiṉṟatu*. Edited by Tirumayilai Vaitiliṅkatēcikar. Chennai: Cakalakalānilaiyaccukkūṭam, 1881.
Cuvāmikaḷ, Ōm Pirakāca. *Śrī satsampāṣiṇi*. Madras: Eveready Press, 1939.
Cuvāmikaḷ, Ōm Pirakāca. *Śrīsatsampāṣiṇi*. Nīlakiri: Śrī Carasvati Ācramam, 1915.
"Daughter Is Born to 'Maharanee'; Former Nancy Miller and Husband, Ex-Maharajah of Indore, Are at Chateau Near Paris." *New York Times*. January 29, 1929.
Dvivedi, Manilal Nabhubhai. *Rája Yoga, or the Practical Metaphysics of the Vedánta, Being a Translation of the Vákyasudhá or Drigdrishyaviveka of Bháratitirtha, and the Aparokshánubhuti of Shri Shankarácharya, with an Introduction, Appendix Containing the Sanskrit Text and Commentary of the Vákyasudhá, and Notes Explanatory and Critical*. Bombay: "Subodha-Prakasha" Printing Press, 1885.
Dwivedi, Pt. Vrajavallabh, ed. *Netratantram, with the Commentary Udyota of Kṣemarājācārya*. Delhi: Parimal Publications, 1985.
Estep, WM. *Eternal Wisdom and Health with Light on the Scriptures*. Excelsior Springs, MO: Super Mind Science Publications, 1932.
Fuller, Capt. J. F. C. *The Star in the West: A Critical Interpretation upon the Works of Aleister Crowley*. London: Walter Scott Publishing, 1907.
Fuller, Capt. J. F. C. *Yoga: A Study of the Mystical Philosophy of the Brahmins and Buddhists*. London: William Rider & Son, 1925.
Gillard, Paul. "Le Pas Décisif." *Le Lotus Bleu: Revue Theosophique Mensuelle* 8, no. 1 (1897): 20–24.
Gunther, J. Daniel. *The Angel and the Abyss: Comprising The Angel and the Abyss and The Hieroglyphic Triad, Being Books II & III of The Inward Journey*. Lake Worth, FL: Ibis Press, 2014.
Gunther, J. Daniel. *Initiation in the Aeon of the Child: The Inward Journey*. Lake Worth, FL: Ibis Press, 2009.
Gupta, Kaviraj Russick Lall. *Science of Sphygmica or Sage Kanàd on Pulse, an English Translation with Sanskrit Passages*. Calcutta: S.C. Addy, 1891.
Hariharaṉ, Cuvāmi Pi. Pi. Ār. *Aruḷmiku Śrī Capāpati Liṅkēsvar Jīvacamāti Ālayamstala varalāṟu*. Maṇavūr: Kaviñar Murukāṉantam Accakam, 2017.
Hartmann, Franz, trans. "Aus dem Leben des indischen Mahātmā Jñāna Guru Yogī Sabhapatti Svāmī." In *Neue Lotusblüten*, 1:259–70. Leipzig: Jaeger'sche Verlagsbuchhandlung, 1908.
Hartmann, Franz. *Die Philosophie und Wissenschaft des Vedanta und Rāja-Yoga oder Das Eingehen in Gottheit von Mahātma Jnāna Guru Yogi Sabhapatti Svāmī aus dem Englischen übersetzt von Franz Hartmann*. Leipzig: Jaeger, 1909.
Hartmann, Franz. *Magic: White and Black; The Science of Finite and Infinite Life, Containing Practical Hints for Students of Occultism*. Boston: by the Author, 1885.
Hartmann, Franz. *Radscha Yoga Hatha Yoga und Tantrika oder Weiße und schwarze Magie und Hexerei*. Edited by Johannes Fährmann. Buenos Aires: Bücher der Schatzkammer, 1990.
Hunt, Miss Chandos Leigh. *Private Instructions on the Science and Art of Organic Magnetism*. 3rd ed. London: Printed for the authoress by G. Wilson, 1885.
Jennings, Hargrave. *Phallicism, Celestial and Terrestrial, Heathen and Christian, Its connection with the Rosicrucians and the Gnostics and its Foundation in Buddhism, with an Essay on Mystic Anatomy*. London: George Redway, 1884.

Kailaṣnāt, Yōki. *Caṟkurunāta yōkam: Śrīcaṟkurunāta Svāmikaḷ aruḷiya sivarāja yōkam, taṉarāja yōkam, yōkarāja yōkam, oṭṭirāja yōkam, tavarāja yōkam (mūlamum - uraiyum)*. Chennai: Kaṟpakam Puttakālayam, 2012.

Kailaṣnāt, Yōki. *Cittar kaḷañciyam*. Chennai: Kaṟpakam Puttakālayam, 2017.

Kailaṣnāt, Yōki. *Virutācalattil Śrīperiyanāyakiyār varapiracātiyāy eḻuntaruḷiyirunta cāttirakkōvai*. Edited by Āṟumuka Mutaliyār and Koṉṉūr Māṇikka Mutaliyār. Cheṉṉai: Parappiramamuttirākṣaracālai, 1871.

Kasyapa, Pandit Rama Prasad. *Occult Science, the Science of Breath*. 2nd ed. Lahore: R.C. Bary & Sons, Printed at the "New Lyall Press," 1892.

Kumāratēvar, Śrī. *Tiruvāymalarntaruḷiya cāstirakkōvai*. Edited by Caccitānantacuvāmikaḷ and Āṟumukamutaliyār. Chennai: Manōṉmaṇivilāca Acciyantiracālai, 1908.

"List of United States Citizens (for the Immigration Authorities), S.S. Ile de France Sailing from Le Havre, November 28th, 1928, Arriving at the Port of New York, December 4th, 1928." N.d.

Madras Record Office. *Classified Catalogue of Books Registered from 1890–1900 at the Office of the Registrar of Books*. Madras: Controller of Stationery and Printing, Madras, on Behalf of the Government of Madras, 1962.

Madras Record Office. *Classified Catalogue of Books Registered from 1911–1915 at the Office of the Registrar of Books*. Madras: Controller of Stationery and Printing, Madras, on Behalf of the Government of Madras, 1965.

Malik, Arjan Dass. *Kundalini and Meditation*. Delhi: Motilal Banarsidass; Borehamwood: Motilal, 2002.

Mansel, Henry Longueville. *The Limits of Religious Thought Examined in Eight Lectures, Preached before the University of Oxford, in the Year M.DCCC.LVIII*. 4th ed. London: John Murray, 1859.

Marutapiḷḷai Āciriyar, Ci., ed. *Tiruvātavūraṭikaḷ purāṇam*. Cuḻipuram: Pajaṉaiccapai, Vaḻakkamparai, 1982.

Mathers, S. L. MacGregor, Aleister Crowley, and Hymenaeus Beta, eds. *The Goetia: The Lesser Key of Solomon the King. Lemegeton—Clavicula Salomonis Regis, Book One*. York Beach, ME: Samuel Weiser, 1995.

Mavalankar, D. K. "The Philosophy and Science of Vedantic Raja Yoga." Edited by Helena Blavatsky and Henry Olcott. *The Theosophist: A Magazine of Oriental Philosophy, Art, Literature and Occultism* 5, no. 6 (March 1884): 146.

Mitra, Vihari Lala, trans. *The Yoga Vaśishtha Mahārāmāyana of Valmiki*. Vol. 2. Calcutta: Kahinoor Press, 1893.

Müller, F. Max. *The Six Systems of Indian Philosophy*. London: Longmans, Green, 1899.

Muthalali, Koshi. "Proceedings of the Tahsildar of Saidapet Taluk, Ref: Transfer of Registry-Saidapet Taluk 71, Konnur Village Patta Nos. 54 and 68." Unpublished legal document, 1936.

N∴ [Yorke, Gerald]. "Editorial Preface." *In 777* [revised], vii–viii. Publisher and date unknown, ca. 1950s.

Nambiar, P. K., and N. Krishnamurthy. *Census of India 1961*. Vol. 9, *Madras, Part XI-D: Temples of Madras State, 1. Chingleput District and Madras City*. Delhi: Manager of Publications, 1965.

Narayanaswamy Raju [Nārāyaṇacuvāmi Rāju]. Interview by Keith Cantú and Vinayagam. Audio and video recording, March 4, 2020.

Nāzir, Ghulām 'Abdu'l-Qādir. *Bahār-i-a'zam jāhī*. Translated by S. Muhammad Husayn. Madras: University of Madras, 1950.

Nikhilānanda, Swāmi, trans. *The Māndūkyopanishad with Gaudapāda's Kārikā and Śankara's Commentary*. Mysore: Sri Ramakrishna Ashrama, 1949.

Olcott, Henry S. "The Fourth Anniversary Address." In *A Collection of Lectures on Theosophy and Archaic Religions, Delivered in India and Ceylon by Colonel H.S. Olcott, President of the Theosophical Society*, edited by A. Theyaga Rajier, 18–25. Madras: A. Theyaga Rajier, 1883.

Olcott, Henry S. *Old Diary Leaves: Second Series 1878–83*. London: Theosophical Publishing Society and Theosophist Office, 1900.

"'Old Doc' Estep Admits Ape Was Stock in Trade." *Chicago Daily Tribune*, Part 2, p. 6, October 6, 1949.

Oman, John Campbell. *Cults, Customs and Superstitions of India, Being a Revised and Enlarged Edition of "Indian Life, Religious and Social," Comprising Studies and Sketches of Interesting Peculiarities in the Beliefs, Festivals and Domestic Life of the Indian People; Also of Witchcraft and Demoniacal Possession, as Known amongst Them*. London: T. Fisher Unwin, 1908.

Oman, John Campbell. *The Mystics, Ascetics, and Saints of India: A Study of Sadhuism, with an Account of the Yogis, Sanyasis, Bairagis, and Other Strange Hindu Sectarians*. London: T. Fisher Unwin, 1905.

Oman, John Campbell. *Indian Life, Religious and Social*. London: T. Fisher Unwin, 1889.

Pāṇini. *The Ashtadhyayi*. Translated by Srisa Chandra Vasu. Benares: Published by Sindhu Charan Bose, at the Panini Office, 1897.

Pargiter, F. Eden, trans. *The Mārkaṇḍeya Purāṇa*. Calcutta: Asiatic Society, 1904.

Patañjali and Philipp André Maas. *Samādhipāda: Das erste Kapitel des Pātañjalayogaśāstra zum ersten Mal kritisch ediert*. Aachen: Shaker, 2006.

Paul, N. C. *A Treatise on the Yoga Philosophy*. Benares: E.J. Lazarus, 1882.

Pillai, J. M. Nallaswami, trans. *Sivagnana Botham of Meikanda Deva*. Tinnevelly: South Indian Saiva Siddhanta Works Publishing Society, 1984.

Pillai, J. M. *Śivajñāna Siddhiyār of Aruṇandi Śivāchārya*. Madras: Meykandan Press, 1913.

Piḷḷai, Nā. Katiraivēṟ. *Tāyumāṉa Cuvāmi pāṭalkaḷ: mūlamum uraiyum*. 1937; Chennai: Cantiyā Patippakam, 2010.

Piḷḷai, Śrī Ti. Ku. *Nīlakiri, utakamaṇṭalam, tirukkāntal Śrī Takṣiṇāmūrtti Maṭam Lōkōpakāra Vityātāṉa Capai stāpakar acalapīṭam Śrīmat Ompirakāsa Cuvāmikaḷ carittirac curukkam*. Tirupparāytturai: Śrīmat Citpavānanta Cuvāmikaḷatu muṉṉuraiyuṭaṉ kūṭiyatu, 1957.

Pope, G. U. *The Tiruvāçagam, or "Sacred Utterances" of the Tamil Poet, Saint, and Sage Māṇikka-Vāçagar*. Oxford: Clarendon Press, 1900.

Prasád, Ráma. *The Science of Breath and the Philosophy of the Tatwas: Nature's Finer Forces*. London: Theosophical Publishing Society, 1890.

Probsthain & Co. *Probsthain's Oriental Catalogue, No. XXVIII. Indian Literature: Art and Religion*. London: Probsthain, 1913.

Rajagopalan, T. K. *Hidden Treasures of Yoga: Revealing Certain Ancient and Secret Methods of Practical Mysticism*. 1945; Delhi: Oriental Book Centre, 2005.

Rāmanātaṉ, Aru., ed. *Cittar pāṭalkaḷ*. 18th ed. Chennai: Pirēmā Piracuram (Prema Pirasuram), 2017.

Reuss, Theodor. *Lingam-Yoni oder die Mysterien des Geschlechts-Kultus als die Basis der Religionen aller Kulturvölker des Altertums und des Marienkultus in der christlichen Kirche sowie Ursprung des Kreuzes und des Crux Ansata*. Berlin: Wilsson, 1906.

Ross, Charles. "S.A. 'Healer's' Activities Exposed." *San Antonio Express*. No. 26, 89th year. January 26, 1954, 1.

Sadāśivayogīśvara. *Śivayogadīpikā*. Edited by Hari Nārāyaṇa Āpṭe. Ānandāśrama: Pune, 1907.

"Sadhu Srila Srikrishnaveni Amma vs the State Rep. By Its Secretary." Legal document, March 18, 2015. Madurai: Madras High Court. https://indiankanoon.org/doc/181195509/, accessed January 31, 2023.

Sharīf, Ja'far. *Islam in India or the Qānūn-i-Islām*. Translated by G. A. Herklots. London: Oxford University Press, 1921.

Shroff, M. Muncherjee. "The Work in Bombay." *Supplement to The Theosophist: A Magazine of Oriental Philosophy, Art, Literature and Occultism* 11 (April 1890): cxxiii–cxxiv.

Sivananda, Swami, and Swami Venkatesananda. *Sivananda's Lectures: All-India Tour*. Rishikesh: Sivananda Publication League, 1951.

Spencer, Herbert. *First Principles*. London: Williams and Norgate, 1862.

Sūda, Haramohana Lāl. *Bhāratendu maṇḍal ke samānāntara aur āpūrak Murādābād maṇḍal*. New Delhi: Vāṇī Prakāśan, 1986.

Sukul, Deva Ram. *Seven Class Lessons on Raja Yoga and Vedanta Philosophy*. New York: Yoga Institute of America, 1936.

Superintendent, The. *A Manual of Instructions for Conducting Resettlements in the Madras Presidency (under the Simplified System)*. Madras: The Superintendent, Government Press, 1937.

Svāmī, Mahātmā Jñānaguruyogī Sabhāpati. *Rājayoga brahmajñānānubhūti saṅgraha veda*. Mumbai: Tattvavivecaka Chāpakhānemem Chāpe, 1892.

Svami, Sabhapatti. *Die Philosophie und Wissenschaft des Vedānta und Rāja-Yoga oder das Eingehen in Gott*. Translated by Franz Hartmann. Leipzig: Theosophisches Verlagshaus, 1926.

Svāmī, Sabhāpati. *Yogī Sabhāpati Svāmīke hālāt*. Bareilly [Barelī]: Rohilkhand Theosophical Society, 1883.

Svāmī, Śrīmat Sabhāpati. *Bedāntadarśan o rājayog*. Translated by Śrī Ambikācaraṇ Bandyopādhyāy. Kalikātā: Śrī Aghoranāth Barāṭ, Bengali year 1292 [1885].

Svāmikaḷ, Ñāṉakuru Yōkisvara Capāpati. *Koṇṇūr kñāṉa kurumaṭālaya tapācīrmattiṉuṭaiya Ñāṉakuru Yōkīsvara Capāpati Svāmikaḷ aṉukkirakitta cātaṉāppiyāsāṉupava upatēcam*. Vellore: Natasun & Co.—V.N. Press, 1898.

Svātmārāma. *Haṭhapradīpikā of Svātmārāma*. Edited by Swami Digambarji and Raghunatha Shastri Kokaje. 3rd ed. Lonavla: Kaivalyadhama, 2016.

Swami, Maahtma [*sic*] Giana Guroo Yogi Sabhapaty. *Vedantic Raj Yoga: Ancient Tantra Yoga of Rishies*. New Delhi: Pankaj Publications, 1977.

Swami, Mahatma Giana Guroo Yogi Sabhapaty. *Om. A Treatise on Vedantic Raj Yoga Philosophy*. Edited by Siris Chandra Basu. Lahore: "Civil and Military Gazette" Press, 1880.

Swami, Mahatma Jnana Guru Yogi Sabhapaty. *Om. The Philosophy & Science of Vedanta and Raja Yoga*. Edited by Srish Chandra Vasu. 3rd ed. Lahore: R.C. Bary & Sons, 1895.

Swami, The Mahatma Jnana Guru Yogi Sabhapaty. *The Philosophy & Science of Vedanta and Raja Yoga*. 2nd ed. Lahore: R.C. Bary at the "Arya Press" by Ram Das, 1883.

Swamy, Sabhapaty. "The Madras Yogi Sabhapaty Swamy, Madame Blavatsky and Colonel Olcott at Lahore." *Amrita Bazar Patrika*. November 16, 1880.

Swami, Sabhapaty. *The Philosophy and Science of Vedanta and Raja Yoga*. Edited by Siris Chandra Vasu. 2nd ed. Reprint, Bombay: C.P. Mandali, 1950.

Swami, Sabhapaty, and Wm. Estep. *Esoteric Cosmic Yogi Science, or, Works of the World Teacher*. Excelsior Springs, MO: Super Mind Science Publications, 1929.

Tāsar, Aruṭkavī Śrī Tēvī Karumārī. *Vilvāraṇyat tala purāṇac curukkam*. Villivākkam, Chennai: Iḷaiñar Aruṭpaṇi Maṉṟam, 2000.

Tatya, Tookaram. *A Compendium of the Raja Yoga Philosophy, Comprising the Principal Treatises of Shrimat Sankaracharya and Other Renowned Authors*. Theosophical Publication Fund. Bombay: Subodha-Prakash Press, 1888.

Tirumular. *Tirumantiram: A Tamil Scriptural Classic*. Translated by B. Natarajan and N. Mahalingam. Madras: Sri Ramakrishna Math, 1991.

Tirumūlar. *The Tirumandiram*. Translated by T. N. Ganapathy, T. V. Venkataraman, T. N. Ramachandran, K. R. Arumugam, P. S. Somasundaram, and S. N. Kandaswamy. 10 vols. Eastman, Quebec, Canada: Babaji's Kriya Yoga and Publications, 2013.

Tirumūlar. *Tirumūlar Tirumantiram: mūlamum—viḷakka uraiyum*. Edited by Ñā. Māṇikkavācakaṉ. Pattām Patippu. Chennai: Umā Patippakam, 2016.

Theosophist [Anonymous]. "Un Yogui." *Le Lotus Bleu: Revue Theosophique Mensuelle* 8, no. 1 (1897): 18–20.

Vandyke Survey Office. "No. 71, Konnur, Saidapet Taluk, Chingleput District, Traced from the Original Map of 1906." Madras: Vandyke Survey Office, 1938.

Vandyke Survey Office. "No. 73, Villivakkam, Saidapet Taluk, Chingleput District, Traced from the Original Map of 1906." Madras: Vandyke Survey Office, 1938.

Vivekananda, Swami. *Yoga Philosophy: Râja Yoga or Conquering the Internal Nature*. London: Longmans, Green, 1896.

Wight, O. W. *Philosophy of Sir William Hamilton, Bart*. 3rd ed. New York: D. Appleton, 1855.

Yogi, G. Sabhapathi. *Aṭukkunilai pōtam*. Publisher unknown, 1894.

Yogindra, Sadasiva. "Sivayogadipika." *The Brahmavâdin* 8, no. 12 (December 1903): 681–91.

Yogiswer, The Mahathma Brumha Gnyana Mavuna Guru Sabhapathy Swamy. *Om. The Cosmic Psychological Spiritual Philosophy and Science of Communion with and Absorption in the Infinite Spirit, or Vedhantha Siva Raja Yoga Samadhi Brumha Gnyana Anubuthi, First Book*. Madras: Hindu Press, 1884.

Yogiswer, The Mahathma Brumha Gnyana Mavuna Guru Sabhapathy Swamy. *Om. The Cosmic Psychological Spiritual Philosophy and Science of Communion with and Absorption in the Infinite Spirit, or Vedhantha Siva Raja Yoga Samadhi Brumha Gnyana Anubuthi, Second Book*. Bombay: Karnatak Press, 1890.

Yōkīsvarar, Ñāṉakuru Capāpati. *Amcumati cūriyamūrttikkup pōtitta cakalākama tiraṭṭu. itil civālayamātapūjai, viṉāyakacaturtti, caṅkaṭacaturtti, . . . tira āṭaṅkiyirukkiṉraṉa*. Part I. Madras: Printed by N. Kupusawmy Chettiar at the Duke of Edinburgh Press, 1894.

Yōkīsvarar, Ñāṉakuru Capāpati. *Amcumati cūriyamūrttikkup pōtitta cakalākama tiraṭṭu. itil caṅkirāntti, tiruvūcaluṟcavam, tīpāvali (naraka caturttaci) aṭaṅkiyirukkiṉraṉa*. Part I-A. Madras: Printed by N. Kupusawmy Chettiar at the Duke of Edinburgh Press, 1894.

Yōkīsvarar, Ñāṉakuru Capāpati. *Amcumati cūriyamūrttikkup pōtitta cakalākama tiraṭṭu. itil tēppōṟcavam, navarāttiri viratam, parācatti ānanta taricaṉap pūjai āṭaṅkiyirukkiṉraṉa*. Part I-C. Madras: Printed by C. Murugesa Mudalyar at the Hindu Theological Press, 1894.

Yōkīsvarar, Ñāṉakuru Capāpati. *amcumati cūriyamūrttikkup pōtitta cakalākama tiraṭṭu. itil vināyakar, cuppiramaṇiyar, cukkiravāram, caṣṭi, aṅkārakacaturtti, tiruvātirai viratam mutaliyavai āṭaṅkiyirukkiṉraṉa*. Part I-D. Madras: Printed by C. Murugesa Mudalyar at the Hindu Theological Press, 1894.

Yorke, Gerald, Keith Richmond, Timothy D'Arch Smith, Clive Harper, David Tibet, and Aleister Crowley. *Aleister Crowley, the Golden Dawn and Buddhism: Reminiscences and Writings of Gerald Yorke*. York Beach, ME: Teitan Press, 2011.

Secondary

Advaita Ashrama. *Reminiscences of Swami Vivekananda*. New ed. Kolkata: The Adhyaksha, Advaita Ashrama, 2018.

Aiyar, A. V. Subramania. *The Poetry and the Philosophy of the Tamil Siddhars: An Essay in Criticism*. Chidambaram: Manivasakar Noolakam, 1969.

Albanese, Catherine L. *A Republic of Mind and Spirit: A Cultural History of American Metaphysical Religion*. New Haven, CT: Yale University Press, 2008.

Almond, Philip C. *The British Discovery of Buddhism*. Cambridge: Cambridge University Press, 1988.

Alter, Joseph S. *Yoga in Modern India: The Body between Science and Philosophy*. Princeton, NJ: Princeton University Press, 2004.

Anonymous. *Who Was Who*. Vol. 1, *1897–1915: A Companion to Who's Who Containing the Biographies of Those Who Died during the Period 1897–1915*. 7th ed. London: A. & C. Black, 2014.

Asprem, Egil. "Contemporary Ritual Magic." In *The Occult World*, edited by Christopher Partridge, 382–95. Abingdon, UK: Routledge, 2014.

Asprem, Egil. "Explaining the Esoteric Imagination: Towards a Theory of Kataphatic Practice." *Aries* 17, no. 1 (2017): 17–50.

Asprem, Egil. "Magic Naturalized? Negotiating Science and Occult Experience in Aleister Crowley's Scientific Illuminism." *Aries* 8 (2008): 139–65.

Asprem, Egil. *The Problem of Disenchantment: Scientific Naturalism and Esoteric Discourse, 1900–1939*. Albany: State University of New York Press, 2018.

Baier, Karl. *Meditation und Moderne: Zur Genese eines Kernbereichs moderner Spiritualität in der Wechselwirkung zwischen Westeuropa, Nordamerika und Asien*. Würzburg: Königshausen & Neumann, 2009.

Baier, Karl. "Mesmeric Yoga and the Development of Meditation within the Theosophical Society." *Theosophical History* 16, nos. 3–4 (October 2012): 151–61.

Baier, Karl. "Theosophical Orientalism and the Structures of Intercultural Transfer: Annotations on the Appropriations of the Cakras in Early Theosophy." In *Theosophical Appropriations: Esotericism, Kabbalah and the Transformation of Traditions*, edited by Julie Chajes and Boaz Huss, 309–54. Beersheba, Israel: Ben-Gurion University of the Negev Press, 2016.

Baier, Karl. "Yoga within Viennese Occultism: Carl Kellner and Co." In *Yoga in Transformation: Historical and Contemporary Perspectives*, edited by Karl Baier, Philipp A. Maas, and Karin Preisendanz, 183–222. Vienna: Vienna University Press, 2018.

Bakshi, Rohini. "The Vedānta of the Vīraśaivas." *Sanskrit Reading Room* (blog post), May 23, 2018.

Bayly, Susan. *Saints, Goddesses and Kings: Muslims and Christians in South Indian Society 1700–1900*. Cambridge: Cambridge University Press, 1989.

Ben-Herut, Gil. *Śiva's Saints: The Origins of Devotion in Kannada according to Harihara's Ragaḷegaḷu*. New York: Oxford University Press, 2018.

Betz, Hans Dieter, ed. *The Greek Magical Papyri in Translation, Including the Demotic Spells*. Chicago: University of Chicago Press, 1986.

Bevilacqua, Daniela. "Let the Sādhus Talk. Ascetic Understanding of Haṭha Yoga and Yogāsanas." *Religions of South Asia* 11, nos. 2–3 (2017): 182–206.

Bharati, Agehananda. "The Hindu Renaissance and Its Apologetic Patterns." *Journal of Asian Studies* 29, no. 2 (February 1970): 267–87.

Bhaṭṭācārya, Upendranāth. *Bāṅglār bāul o bāul gān*. Calcutta: Orient Book Company, 1981.

Biardeau, Madeleine, and Charles Malamoud. *Le sacrifice dans l'Inde ancienne*. Paris: Presses Universitaires de France, 1976.

Bingenheimer, Marcus. *Island of Guanyin: Mount Putuo and Its Gazetteers*. New York: Oxford University Press, 2016.

Birch, Jason. "The Amaraughaprabodha: New Evidence on the Manuscript Transmission of an Early Work on Haṭha- and Rājayoga." *Journal of Indian Philosophy* 47 (2019): 947–77.

Birch, Jason. "Haṭhayoga's Floruit on the Eve of Colonialism." In *Śaivism and the Tantric Traditions: Essays in Honour of Alexis G.J.S. Sanderson*, edited by Dominic Goodall, Shaman Hatley, Harunaga Isaacson, and Srilata Raman, 451–79. Leiden: Brill, 2020.

Birch, Jason. "Rājayoga: The Reincarnations of the King of All Yogas." *International Journal of Hindu Studies* 17, no. 3 (2013): 399–442.

Birch, Jason, and Jacqueline Hargreaves. "The Yamas and Niyamas: Patanjali's View." *Yoga Scotland*, January 2016.

Bogdan, Henrik. "The Babalon Working 1946: L. Ron Hubbard, John Whiteside Parsons, and the Practice of Enochian Magic." *Numen: International Review for the History of Religions* 63, no. 1 (2016): 12–32.

Bogdan, Henrik. "Reception of Occultism in India: The Case of the Holy Order of Krishna." In *Occultism in a Global Perspective*, edited by Henrik Bogdan and Gordan Djurdjevic, 177–203. London: Routledge, 2013.

Bogdan, Henrik, and Gordan Djurdjevic, eds. *Occultism in a Global Perspective*. London: Routledge, 2013.

Bogdan, Henrik, and Martin P. Starr, eds. *Aleister Crowley and Western Esotericism*. New York: Oxford University Press, 2012.

Böhtlingk, Otto. *Sanskrit-Wörterbuch in kürzerer Fassung*. Part 3. St. Petersburg: Buchdruckerei der Kaiserlichen Akademie der Wissenschaften, 1882.

Bouthillette, Karl-Stéphan. *Dialogue and Doxography in Indian Philosophy: Points of View in Buddhist, Jaina, and Advaita Vedānta Traditions*. Abingdon, Oxon: Routledge, 2020.

Bouy, Christian. *Les Nātha-yogin et les Upaniṣads*. Paris: Diffusion de Boccard, 1994.

Bowen, Patrick D. "'The Real Pure Yog': Yoga in the Early Theosophical Society and the Hermetic Brotherhood of Luxor." In *Imagining the East: The Early Theosophical Society*, edited by Tim Rudbøg and Erik Reenberg Sand, 143–65. New York: Oxford University Press, 2020.

Braden, Charles. *Spirits in Rebellion: The Rise and Development of New Thought*. Dallas: Southern Methodist University Press, 1963.

Bradlaugh, Charles. *A Plea for Atheism*. London: Freethought Publishing Company, 1883.

Briggs, George Weston. *The Religious Life of India: Gorakhnāth and the Kānphaṭa Yogīs*. Calcutta: Y.M.C.A. Publishing House, 1938.

Brook, Andrew, Julian Wuerth, and Edward N. Zalta. "Kant's View of the Mind and Consciousness of Self." In *The Stanford Encyclopedia of Philosophy*, edited by Edward N. Zalta, Winter 2020 ed. https://plato.stanford.edu/archives/win2020/entries/kant-mind/, accessed January 31, 2023.

Brooke, Christopher. "How the Stoics Became Atheists." *Historical Journal* 49, no. 2 (2006): 387–402.

Brunner, Hélène. "The Sexual Aspect of the Liṅga Cult according to the Saiddhāntika Scriptures." In *Studies in Hinduism*, vol. 2, *Miscellanea to the Phenomenon of Tantras*, edited by Gerhard Oberhammer, 87–103. Vienna: Verlag der Osterreichischen Akademie der Wissenschaften, 1998.

Brunner-Lachaux, Hélène, Gerhard Oberhammer, and André Padoux, eds. *Tāntrikābhidhānakośa: Dictionnaire des termes techniques de la littérature hindoue tantrique = A Dictionary of Technical Terms from Hindu Tantric Literature = Wörterbuch zur Terminologie hinduistischer Tantren*. Vienna: Verlag der Österreichischen Akademie der Wissenschaften, 2000.

Butler, Alison. *Victorian Occultism and the Making of Modern Magic: Invoking Tradition*. New York: Palgrave Macmillan, 2011.

Cantú, Keith Edward. "'Don't Take Any Wooden Nickels': Western Esotericism, Yoga, and the Discourse of Authenticity." In *New Approaches to the Study of Esotericism*, edited by Egil Asprem and Julian Strube, 109–26. Leiden: Brill, 2020.

Cantú, Keith Edward. "Haṭhayoga as 'Black Magic' in Early Theosophy and Beyond." In *Proceedings of the ESSWE6 Conference on Esotericism and Deviance*, edited by Tim Rudbøg and Manon Hedenborg White. Leiden: Brill, forthcoming.

Cantú, Keith Edward. "Islamic Esotericism in the Bengali Bāul Songs of Lālan Fakir." *Correspondences* 7, no. 1 (2019): 109–65.

Cantú, Keith Edward. "Review of Book of Abramelin: A New Translation by Georg Dehn." *Correspondences* 4 (2016): 129–54.

Cantú, Keith Edward. "Shrish Chandra Basu and Modern Occult Yoga." In *Occult South Asia*, edited by Karl Baier and Mriganka Mukhopadhyay, forthcoming.

Cantú, Keith Edward. "Sri Sabhapati Swami: The Forgotten Yogi of Western Esotericism." In *The Occult Nineteenth Century: Roots, Developments, and Impact on the Modern World*, edited by Lukas Pokorny and Franz Winter, 347–73. London: Palgrave Macmillan, 2021.

Cantú, Keith Edward. "Translating Esotericism: Tamil." In "Translating Esotericism," edited by Wouter Hanegraaff and Mriganka Mukhopadhyay. *Correspondences*, forthcoming.

Carter, John, and Robert Anton Wilson. *Sex and Rockets: The Occult World of Jack Parsons*. Los Angeles, CA: Feral House, 2005.

Caṭṭopādhaẏ, Śrīrāmānanda. "Bāmandās Basu." *Prabāsī* 30, 2nd khaṇḍa, 3 (January 1339 [1932]): 400–408.

Chajes, Julie. *Recycled Lives: A History of Reincarnation in Blavatsky's Theosophy*. New York: Oxford University Press, 2019.

Chatterjee, Amita. "Nyāya-Vaiśeṣika Philosophy." In *The Oxford Handbook of World Philosophy*, edited by William Edelglass and Jay L. Garfield. Online, 2011.

Chevillard, Jean-Luc. "The Pantheon of Tamil Grammarians: A Short History of the Myth of Agastya's Twelve Disciples." In *Écrire et transmettre en Inde classique*, edited by Colas Gérard and Gerdi Gerschheimer, 243–68. Paris: École française d'Extrême-Orient, 2009.

Churton, Tobias. *Aleister Crowley in India: The Secret Influence of Eastern Mysticism on Magic and the Occult*. Rochester, VT: Inner Traditions, 2019.

Civañāṉam, Ma. Po. *The Universal Vision of Saint Ramalinga: Vallalar Kanda Orumaippadu*. Translated by R. Ganapathy. Annamalainagar: Annamalai University, 1987.

Collins, Randall. *The Micro-sociology of Religion: Religious Practices, Collective and Individual*. State College: Association of Religion Data Archives at the Pennsylvania State University, 2011.

Comeau, Leah. "Māṇikkavācakar." Oxford Bibliographies in Hinduism, 2016. doi: 10.1093/obo/9780195399318-0159, accessed January 31, 2023.

Corbin, Henry Eugène, and Nancy Pearson. *The Man of Light in Iranian Sufism*. New Lebanon, NY: Omega Publications, 1994.

Cox, Simon Paul. *The Subtle Body: A Genealogy*. New York: Oxford University Press, 2022.

Cox, Whitney. "Making a Tantra in Medieval South India: The Mahārthamañjarī and the Textual Culture of Cōḻa Cidambaram: Volume I." PhD dissertation, University of Chicago, 2006.

Crow, John L. "Allan Bennett & the Emergence of Buddhism in the West." *Insight: The Journal of the Theosophical Society in England* 49, no. 3 (Autumn 2008): 30–33.

Crow, John L., and Elizabeth J. Harris, eds. *The Life of Allan Bennett, Bhikkhu Ananda Metteyya*. Volume 1 of *Allan Bennett, Bhikkhu Ananda Metteyya: Biography and Collected Writings*. Sheffield, UK: Equinox Publishing, forthcoming.

Cuvāminātaṉ, Pi. *Caturakiri yāttirai / Sadhuragiri yaththirai*. Chennai: Vikaṭaṉ Piracuram, 2014.

Dabral, Shivaprasad. *Shri Uttarakhand Yatra Darshan*. Narayankoti: publisher unknown, 1960.

Das, Rahul Peter. "Problematic Aspects of the Sexual Rituals of the Bāuls of Bengal." *Journal of the American Oriental Society* 112, no. 3 (1992): 388–432.

Dās, Śrījñānendramohan. *Baṅger bāhire bāṅgālī (uttar bhārat)*. Kalikātā: Śrī Anāthanāth Mukhopādhyāẏ, Bengali year 1322 [1915].

Das Gupta, Shashi Bhusan. *Obscure Religious Cults*. 3rd ed. Calcutta: Firma K.L. Mukhopadhyay, 1969.

Dash, Trilochan. *The Story of the Deities and the Temples in Southern Indian Peninsula*. Bhubaneswar: Soudamini Dash, 2010.

De Michelis, Elizabeth. *A History of Modern Yoga: Patañjali and Western Esotericism*. London: Continuum, 2008.

Deslippe, Philip. "From Maharaj to Mahan Tantric: The Construction of Yogi Bhajan's Kundalini Yoga." *Sikh Formations* 8, no. 3 (2012): 369–87.

Deveney, John Patrick. *Paschal Beverly Randolph: A Nineteenth-Century Black American Spiritualist, Rosicrucian, and Sex Magician*. Albany: State University of New York Press, 1997.

Deveney, John Patrick. *Theosophical History Occasional Papers*. Vol. 6, *Astral Projection or Liberation of the Double and the Work of the Early Theosophical Society*. Fullerton, CA: Theosophical History, 1997.

Diamond, Debra, ed. *Yoga: The Art of Transformation*. Washington, DC: Arthur M. Sackler Gallery, Smithsonian Institution, 2013.

Djurdjevic, Gordan. *India and the Occult: The Influence of South Asian Spirituality on Modern Western Occultism*. New York: Palgrave Macmillan, 2014.

Djurdjevic, Gordan, and Shukdev Singh, trans. *Sayings of Gorakhnāth: Annotated Translation of the Gorakh Bānī*. New York: Oxford University Press, 2019.

Doniger O'Flaherty, Wendy. *Dreams, Illusion, and Other Realities*. Chicago: University of Chicago Press, 1984.

Duquette, Jonathan. "Is Śivādvaita Vedānta a Saiddhāntika School? Pariṇāmavāda in the Brahmamīmāṃsābhāṣya." *Journal of Hindu Studies* 8 (2015): 16–43.

Dyczkowski, Mark S. G. *The Doctrine of Vibration: An Analysis of the Doctrines and Practices of Kashmir Shaivism*. Delhi: Motilal Banarsidass, 1989.

Dyczkowski, Mark S. G. *A Journey in the World of Tantras*. Varanasi: Indica Books, 2004.

Edgerton, Franklin. *The Bhagavad Gītā*. Cambridge, MA: Harvard University Press, 1952.

Eek, Sven. *Damodar and the Pioneers of the Theosophical Movement*. Adyar, Madras: Vasanta Press, 1978.

Eliade, Mircea. *Yoga: Immortality and Freedom*. Translated by Willard Trask. New York: Routledge & Kegan Paul, 1958.

Ernst, Carl. "The Islamization of Yoga in the Amṛtakuṇḍa Translations." *Journal of the Royal Asiatic Society of Great Britain & Ireland* 13, no. 2 (2003): 199–226.

Ernst, Carl. "Situating Sufism and Yoga." *Journal of the Royal Asiatic Society*, 3rd series 15, no. 1 (April 2005): 15–33.

Ezhilraman, R. "Siddha Cult in Tamiḻnādu: Its History and Historical Continuity." PhD dissertation, Pondicherry University, 2015.

Fabricius, Johann Philipp. *J. P. Fabricius's Tamil and English Dictionary*. 4th ed. Tranquebar, Tamil Nadu: Evangelical Lutheran Mission Pub. House, 1972.

Faivre, Antoine. *Access to Western Esotericism*. Albany: State University of New York Press, 1994.

Fanger, Claire, ed. *Conjuring Spirits: Texts and Traditions of Medieval Ritual Magic*. University Park: Pennsylvania State University Press, 1998.

Fisher, Elaine M. "A New Public Theology: Sanskrit and Society in Seventeenth-Century South India." PhD dissertation, Columbia University, 2013.

Fisher, Elaine M. "Remaking South Indian Śaivism: Greater Śaiva Advaita and the Legacy of the Śaktiviśiṣṭādvaita Vīraśaiva Tradition." *International Journal of Hindu Studies* 21, no. 3 (December 2017): 319–44.

Fisher, Elaine M. "The Tangled Roots of Vīraśaivism: On the Vīramāheśvara Textual Culture of Srisailam." *History of Religions* 59, no. 1 (2019): 1–37.

Flood, Gavin D. *The Tantric Body: The Secret Tradition of Hindu Religion*. London: I.B. Tauris; distributed in the U.S. by Palgrave Macmillan, 2006.

Flood, Gavin D., Bjarne Wernicke-Olesen, and Rajan Khatiwoda, eds. *The Lord of Immortality: An Introduction, Critical Edition, and Translation of the Netra Tantra, Vol. I, Chapters 1–8*. London: Routledge, forthcoming.

Foxen, Anya P. *Biography of a Yogi: Paramahansa Yogananda and the Origins of Modern Yoga*. New York: Oxford University Press, 2017.

Foxen, Anya P. *Inhaling Spirit: Harmonialism, Orientalism, and the Western Roots of Modern Yoga*. New York: Oxford University Press, 2020.

Fuller, C. J. *The Camphor Flame: Popular Hinduism and Society in India*. Rev. ed. Princeton, NJ: Princeton University Press, 2018.

Fuller, C. J., and Haripriya Narasimhan. *Tamil Brahmans: The Making of a Middle-Class Caste*. Chicago: University of Chicago Press, 2014.

Garrett, H. L. O., ed. *A History of Government College, Lahore, 1864–1914*. Lahore: "Civil and Military Gazette" Press, 1914.

Gharote, M. L., V. K. Jha, Parimal Devnath, and S. B. Sakhalkar, eds. *Encyclopedia of Traditional Asanas*. Lonavla: Lonavla Institute, 2006.

Glover, William J. *Making Lahore Modern: Constructing and Imagining a Colonial City*. Minneapolis: University of Minnesota Press, 2008.

Godwin, Joscelyn. "Blavatsky and the First Generation of Theosophy." In *Handbook of the Theosophical Current*, edited by Olav Hammer and Mikael Rothstein, 15–31. Leiden: Brill, 2013.

Godwin, Joscelyn. *The Theosophical Enlightenment*. Albany: State University of New York Press, 1994.

Godwin, Joscelyn, Christian Chanel, and John P. Deveney, eds. *The Hermetic Brotherhood of Luxor: Initiatic and Historical Documents of an Order of Practical Occultism*. York Beach, ME: S. Weiser, 1995.

Goodall, Dominic, ed. *The Niśvāsatattvasaṃhitā: The Earliest Surviving Śaiva Tantra*. Pondicherry: Institut Français de Pondichéry and École française d'Extrême-Orient, 2015.

Goodall, Dominic, and Harunaga Isaacson. "How the Tattvas of Tantric Śaivism Came to Be 36: The Evidence of the Niśvāsatattvasaṃhitā." In *Tantric Studies: Fruits of a Franco-German Collaboration on Early Tantra*, edited by Dominic Goodall and Harunaga Isaacson, 77–112. Pondicherry: Institut Français de Pondichéry and École française d'Extrême-Orient, 2016.

Greene, Liz. *Magi and Maggidim: The Kabbalah in British Occultism, 1860–1940*. Ceredigion, Wales: Sophia Centre Press, 2012.

Guenzi, Caterina. *Le Discours du destin: La pratique de l'astrologie à Bénarès*. Paris: CNRS Editions / Bibliothèque de l'Anthropologie, 2013.

Halbfass, Wilhelm. *India and Europe: An Essay in Philosophical Understanding*. Delhi: Motilal Banarsidass, 1990.

Hanegraaff, Wouter J. "New Thought Movement." In *Dictionary of Gnosis & Western Esotericism*, edited by Wouter J. Hanegraaff, 861–65. Leiden: Brill, 2006.

Hanegraaff, Wouter J. "Occult/Occultism." In *Dictionary of Gnosis & Western Esotericism*, edited by Wouter J. Hanegraaff, 884–89. Leiden: Brill, 2006.

Hanegraaff, Wouter J. "Western Esotericism and the Orient in the First Theosophical Society." In *Theosophy across Boundaries: Transcultural and Interdisciplinary Perspectives on a Modern Esoteric Movement*, edited by Hans Martin Krämer and Julian Strube, 29–65. Albany: State University of New York Press, 2020.

Harder, Hans. *Sufism and Saint Veneration in Contemporary Bangladesh: The Maijbhandaris of Chittagong*. Hoboken, NJ: Taylor & Francis, 2011.

Hardy, Friedhelm. *Viraha-Bhakti: The Early History of Kṛṣṇa Devotion in South India*. Delhi: Oxford University Press, 1983.

Hayes, Glen. "The Necklace of Immortality: A Seventeenth-Century Vaiṣṇava-Sahajiyā Text." In *Tantra in Practice*, edited by David Gordon White, 308–26. Princeton, NJ: Princeton University Press, 2000.

Hedenborg White, Manon. *The Eloquent Blood: The Goddess Babalon and the Construction of Femininities in Western Esotericism*. New York: Oxford University Press, 2020.

Hedenborg White, Manon. "The Other Woman: Babalon and the Scarlet Woman in Kenneth Grant's Typhonian Trilogies." In *Servants of the Star & the Snake: Essays in Honour of Kenneth & Steffi Grant*, edited by Henrik Bogdan. London: Starfire Publishing, 2018.

Hedenborg White, Manon, ed. "Special Issue: Rethinking Aleister Crowley and Thelema." *Aries: Journal for the Study of Western Esotericism* 21, no. 1 (2021).

Hedenborg White, Manon, and Christian Giudice, eds. *Women of Thelema: Selected Essays*. n.p.: Kamuret Press, forthcoming.

Hikosaka, Shu. "The Potiyil Mountain in Tamil Nadu and the Origin of the Avalokiteśvara Cult." In *Buddhism in Tamil Nadu: Collected Papers*, 119–41. Chennai: Institute of Asian Studies, 1998.

Hine, Phil. *Wheels within Wheels: Chakras Come West*. London: Twisted Trunk, 2018.

Holdrege, Barbara A. *Bhakti and Embodiment: Fashioning Divine Bodies and Devotional Bodies in Kṛṣṇa Bhakti*. London: Routledge, 2015.

Howe, Ellic. *The Magicians of the Golden Dawn: A Documentary History of a Magical Order, 1887–1923*. New York: S. Weiser, 1978.

Humbach, Helmut. "Mithra in India and the Hinduized Magi." In *Études Mithriaques: Actes du 2e Congrès International Téhéran, du 1er au 8 Septembre 1975*, edited by Jacques Duchesne-Guillemin, 230–52. Leiden: Brill, 1978.

Hussain, Syed Sultan Mahmood. *50 Years of Government College Lahore (1864–1913)*. Lahore: Izhar Research Institute of Pakistan, 2005.

Inden, Ronald B. *Imagining India*. Bloomington: Indiana University Press, 2000.

Irājakōpālaṉ, Em. *Vēḷaccēri tiruttalam*. Chennai: A4 (Āṉant), 2003.

Jacob, Tony George. "History of Teaching Anatomy in India: From Ancient to Modern Times." *Anatomical Sciences Education* 6, no. 5 (September 2013): 351–58.

Jain, Andrea R. *Selling Yoga: From Counterculture to Pop Culture*. New York: Oxford University Press, 2015.

Jennings, Arthur Seymour. *Paint & Colour Mixing: A Practical Handbook*. London: E. & F.N. Spon, 1921.

Jones, Kenneth W. *Arya Dharm: Hindu Consciousness in 19th-Century Punjab*. Berkeley: University of California Press, 1976.

Kaczynski, Richard. *Forgotten Templars: The Untold Origins of Ordo Templi Orientis*. N.p.: Published for the author, 2012.

Kaczynski, Richard. *Perdurabo: The Life of Aleister Crowley*. Rev ed. Berkeley, CA: North Atlantic Books, 2010.

Kaczynski, Richard, Frater Iskandar, and Frater Taos, eds. *Success Is Your Proof: One Hundred Years of O.T.O. in North America, a Festschrift in Honor of Hymenaeus Beta, Celebrating Thirty Years of Leadership*. New York: Sekmet Books, 2015.

Kieckhefer, Richard. *Forbidden Rites: A Necromancer's Manual of the Fifteenth Century*. University Park: Pennsylvania State University Press, 1998.

Killingley, D. H. "Yoga-Sūtra IV, 2–3 and Vivekānanda's Interpretation of Evolution." *Journal of Indian Philosophy* 18, no. 2 (June 1, 1990): 151–79.

Kitada, Makoto, and Śārṅgadeva. *The Body of the Musician: An Annotated Translation and Study of the Piṇḍotpatti-Prakaraṇa of Śārṅgadeva's Saṅgītaratnākara*. Bern, Switzerland: Peter Lang, 2012.

Kraler, Magdalena. "The Prāṇāyāma Grid—Defining the Place of Yogic Breath Cultivation within Discourses of Modern Yoga." *Journal of Yoga Studies*, forthcoming.

Kraler, Magdalena. "Tracing Vivekananda's Prāṇa and Ākāśa: The Yogavāsiṣṭha and Rama Prasad's Occult Science of Breath." In *The Occult Nineteenth Century: Roots, Developments, and Impact on the Modern World*, edited by Lukas Pokorny and Franz Winter, 373–99. London: Palgrave Macmillan, 2021.

Krämer, Hans Martin, and Julian Strube, eds. *Theosophy across Boundaries: Transcultural and Interdisciplinary Perspectives on a Modern Esoteric Movement*. Albany: State University of New York Press, 2020.

Kṛṣṇadāsa Kavirāja, Edward Cameron Dimock, and Tony Kevin Stewart. *Caitanya Caritāmṛta of Kṛṣṇadāsa Kavirāja: A Translation and Commentary*. Cambridge, MA: Harvard University Press, 1999.

Larson, Gerald James. *Classical Sāṃkhya: An Interpretation of Its History and Meaning*. Delhi: Motilal Banarsidass, 1979.

Larson, Gerald James. *Classical Yoga Philosophy and the Legacy of Samkhya*. Delhi: Motilal Banarsidass, 2018.

Larson, Gerald James, and Ram Shankar Bhattacharya. "Philosophy of Sāṃkhya." In *Encyclopedia of Indian Philosophies*, vol. 4, *Sāṃkhya: A Dualist Tradition in Indian Philosophy*, edited by Gerald James Larson and Ram Shankar Bhattacharya, 43–103. Delhi: Motilal Banarsidass, 1987.

Larson, Gerald James, and Ram Shankar Bhattacharya. "Yoga: India's Philosophy of Meditation." In *Encyclopedia of Indian Philosophies*, vol. 12, edited by Ram Shankar Bhattacharya, Karl H. Potter, and Gerald James Larson. Delhi: Motilal Banarsidass, 2011.

LeBuffe, Michael. "Paul-Henri Thiry (Baron) d'Holbach." In *The Stanford Encyclopedia of Philosophy*, edited by Edward N. Zalta, Spring 2020 ed. https://plato.stanford.edu/archives/spr2020/entries/holbach/.

Leland, Kurt. *Rainbow Body: A History of the Western Chakra System from Blavatsky to Brennan*. Lake Worth, FL: Ibis Press, 2016.

Linrothe, Robert N., Debra Diamond, and Rubin Museum of Art, eds. *Holy Madness: Portraits of Tantric Siddhas*. New York: Rubin Museum of Art and Chicago: Serindia Publications, 2006.

Lorea, Carola Erika. "Playing the Football of Love on the Field of the Body: The Contemporary Repertoire of Baul Songs." *Religion and the Arts* 17, no. 4 (2013): 416–51.

Lorea, Carola Erika. "Pregnant Males, Barren Mothers, and Religious Transvestism: Transcending Gender in the Songs and Practices of 'Heterodox' Bengali Lineages." *Asian Ethnology* 77, nos. 1–2 (2018): 169–213.

Lorenzen, David N, and Adrián Muñoz. *Yogi Heroes and Poets: Histories and Legends of the Nāths*. Albany: State University of New York Press, 2011.

Lucia, Amanda J. *White Utopias: The Religious Exoticism of Transformational Festivals*. Oakland: University of California Press, 2020.

Maas, Philipp. "A Concise Historiography of Classical Yoga Philosophy." In *Periodization and Historiography of Indian Philosophy*, edited by Eli Franco, 53–90. Vienna: Sammlung de Nobili, Institut für Südasien-, Tibet- und Buddhismuskunde der Universität Wien, 2013.

Madaio, James. "Rethinking Neo-Vedānta: Swami Vivekananda and the Selective Historiography of Advaita Vedānta." *Religions* 8, no. 101 (2017): 1–12.

Madaio, James. "Transformative Dialogue in the Yogavāsiṣṭha." In *In Dialogue with Classical Indian Traditions: Encounter, Transformation and Interpretation*, edited by Brian Black and Ram-Prasad Chakravarthi, 107–29. London: Routledge, 2019.

Mahmood, Saba. *Politics of Piety: The Islamic Revival and the Feminist Subject*. Princeton, NJ: Princeton University Press, 2005.

Makdisi, Saree. *Making England Western: Occidentalism, Race, and Imperial Culture*. Chicago: University of Chicago Press, 2014.

Malinar, Angelika. "Something Like Liberation: Prakṛtilaya (Absorption in the Cause/s of Creation) in Yoga and Sāṃkhya." In *Release from Life—Release in Life: Indian Perspectives on Individual Liberation*, edited by Andreas Biggar, Rita Krajnc, Annemarie Mertens, Markus Shüpbach, and Heinz Werner Wessler, 129–56. Bern: Peter Lang, 2010.

Mallinson, James. "The Amṛtasiddhi: Haṭhayoga's Tantric Buddhist Source Text." In *Śaivism and the Tantric Traditions: Essays in Honour of Alexis G.J.S. Sanderson*, edited by Dominic Goodall, Shaman Hatley, Harunaga Isaacson, and Srilata Raman, 409–25. Leiden: Brill, 2020.

Mallinson, James. "Kālavañcana in the Konkan: How a Vajrayāna Haṭhayoga Tradition Cheated Buddhism's Death in India." *Religions* 10, no. 4 (2019): 1–33.

Mallinson, James. *The Khecarīvidyā of Ādinātha: A Critical Edition and Annotated Translation of an Early Text of Haṭhayoga*. New York: Routledge, 2007.

Mallinson, James. "The Nāth Saṃpradāya." *Brill Encyclopedia of Hinduism* 3 (2011): 407–28.

Mallinson, James, and Mark Singleton, eds. *Roots of Yoga*. London: Penguin Books, 2017.

Masuzawa, Tomoko. *The Invention of World Religions, or, How European Universalism Was Preserved in the Language of Pluralism*. Chicago: University of Chicago Press, 2005.

Melton, J. Gordon. "Thelemic Magick in America." In *Alternatives to American Mainline Churches*, edited by Joseph Henry Fichter and William Sims Bainbridge, 67–87. New York: Unification Theological Seminary, 1983.

Merleau-Ponty, Maurice. *Phénoménologie de la perception*. Paris: Librairie Gallimard, 1945.

Michael, R. Blake. *The Origins of Vīraśaiva Sects: A Typological Analysis of Ritual and Associational Patterns in the Śūnyasaṃpādane*. Delhi: Motilal Banarsidass, 1992.

Mitterwallner, Gritli v. "Evolution of the Liṅga." In *Discourses on Śiva: Proceedings of a Symposium on the Nature of Religious Imagery*, edited by Michael W. Meister, 12–37. Philadelphia: University of Philadelphia Press, 1984.

Molesworth, James Thomas. *A Dictionary, Marathi and English*. 2nd ed. Bombay: Bombay Education Society's Press, 1857.

Monier-Williams, M. *A Sanskrit-English Dictionary: Etymologically and Philologically Arranged with Special Reference to Cognate Indo-European Languages*. Oxford: Clarendon Press, 1899.

Mortimer, W. *A Manual of Anatomy with The Elements of Physiology and Pathology; Compiled for the Use of the Students of the Subordinate Branch of the Medical Service Attending the Medical School*. Madras: E. Marsden at the Male Asylum Press, 1842.

Muller-Ortega, Paul. "On the Seal of Śambhu: A Poem by Abhinavagupta." In *Tantra in Practice*, edited by David Gordon White, 573–86. Princeton, NJ: Princeton University Press, 2000.

Nambiar, P. K., and N. Krishnamurthy. *Census of India 1961*. Vol. 9, *Madras, Part XI-D: Temples of Madras State, 1. Chingleput District and Madras City*. Delhi: Manager of Publications, 1965.

Nambiar, P. K., and K. C. Narayana Kurup. *Census of India 1961*. Vol. 9, *Madras, Part XI-D: Temples of Madras State, v Kanyakumari & Tirunelveli*. Delhi: Manager of Publications, 1968.

Nambiar, Sita Krishna, ed. *Prabodhacandrodaya of Kṛṣṇa Miśra*. Delhi: Motilal Banarsidass, 1971.

Narayana Ayyar, C. V. *Origin and Early History of Śaivism in South India*. Madras: University of Madras, 1974.

Narayanan, Vasudha. "Religious Vows at the Shrine of Shahul Hamid." In *Dealing with Deities: The Ritual Vow in South Asia*, edited by William P. Harman and Selva J. Raj, 65–85. Albany: State University of New York Press, 2006.

Newcombe, Suzanne. "Magic and Yoga: The Role of Subcultures in Transcultural Exchange." In *Yoga Traveling: Bodily Practice in Transcultural Perspective*, edited by Beatrix Hauser, 57–79. New York: Springer, 2013.

Newcombe, Suzanne. *Yoga in Britain: Stretching Spirituality and Educating Yogis*. Bristol: Equinox Publishing, 2019.

Obrist, Barbara. "Visualization in Medieval Alchemy." *Hyle* 9, no. 2 (2003): 131–70.

Olivelle, Patrick. *The Early Upaniṣads*. New York: Oxford University Press, 1998.

Openshaw, Jeanne. *Seeking Bāuls of Bengal*. Cambridge: Cambridge University Press, 2002.

Orsini, Francesca. *The History of the Book in South Asia*. New York: Routledge, 2016.

Osborne, Samuel. "Woman Becomes First in India to Climb Sacred Mountain Agasthyakoodam after Ban on Females Lifted." *Independent*. January 16, 2019. https://www.independent.co.uk/news/world/asia/agasthyakoodam-climb-mountain-woman-first-india-sacred-dhanya-senal-kerala-a8731146.html, accessed January 31, 2023.

Padoux, André. *Comprendre le tantrisme: Les sources hindoues*. Paris: Albin Michel, 2010.

Padoux, André. *The Hindu Tantric World: An Overview*. Chicago: University of Chicago Press, 2017.

Padoux, André. *Vāc: The Concept of the Word in Selected Hindu Tantras*. Albany: State University of New York Press, 1990.

Pālacuppiramaṇiyaṉ, Ci. *Tamiḻ ilakkiya varalāṟu*. Chennai: Maṇamalarp patippakam, 1998.

Partridge, Christopher. "Lost Horizon: H.P. Blavatsky and Theosophical Orientalism." In *Handbook of the Theosophical Current*, edited by Olav Hammer and Mikael Rothstein, 309–33. Leiden: Brill, 2013.

Pasi, Marco. *Aleister Crowley and the Temptation of Politics*. Durham, UK: Acumen, 2014.

Peterson, Indira Viswanathan, ed. *Poems to Śiva: The Hymns of the Tamil Saints*. Princeton, NJ: Princeton University Press, 1989.

Peterson, Joseph H. *The Lesser Key of Solomon: Lemegeton clavicula Salomonis*. York Beach, ME: Weiser Books, 2001.

Pillai, Vedachalam, and R. S. Nagapattinam. *Māṇikkavācakar vāḻārum kālamum: St. Manickavachakar His Life and Times*. Madras: South India Saiva Siddhanta Works Publishing Society, 1957.

Pokazanyeva, Anna. "Mind within Matter: Science, the Occult, and the (Meta)Physics of Ether and Akasha." *Zygon* 51, no. 2 (June 2016): 318–46.

Powell, Seth. "Advice on Āsana in the Śivayogapradīpikā." *The Luminescent* (blog), June 30, 2017. https://www.theluminescent.org/2017/06/advice-on-asana-in-sivayogapradipika.html.

Powell, Seth. "A Lamp on Śiva's Yoga: The Unification of Yoga, Ritual, and Devotion in the Fifteenth-Century Śivayogapradīpikā." PhD dissertation, Harvard University, forthcoming.

Powell, Seth. "A Lamp on Śiva's Yoga: The Unification of Yoga, Ritual, and Devotion in the Fifteenth-Century Śivayogapradīpikā." PhD prospectus, Harvard University, 2018.

Raman, Srilata. *The Transformation of Tamil Religion: Ramalinga Swamigal (1823–1874) and Modern Dravidian Sainthood*. New York: Routledge, 2022.

Ramaṇaṉ, Pā. Cu. *Cittarkaḷ vāḻvil*. Vol. 2. Amazon: Digital Publication, Kindle ed. 2018.

Rao, Velcheru Narayana, and Gene H. Roghair. *Siva's Warriors: The Basava Purana of Palkuriki Somanatha*. 1990; Princeton, NJ: Princeton University Press, 2016.

Readdy, Keith. *One Truth and One Spirit: Aleister Crowley's Spiritual Legacy*. Lake Worth, FL: Ibis Press, an imprint of Nicolas-Hays, 2018.

Reddy, Prabhavati C. *Hindu Pilgrimage: Shifting Patterns of Worldview of Srisailam in South India*. New York: Routledge, 2014.

Regardie, Israel. *The Eye in the Triangle: An Interpretation of Aleister Crowley*. 1970 Phoenix, AZ: Falcon Press, 1986.

Reid, Brian Holden. *J. F. C. Fuller: Military Thinker*. Basingstoke: Macmillan, 1990.

Ros, Alejandra. "Translocalization." In *Encyclopedia of Global Religion*, edited by Mark Juergensmeyer and Wade Clark Roof, 1:1301–2. Thousand Oaks, CA: Sage Publications, 2012.

Roy, Asim. *The Islamic Syncretistic Tradition in Bengal*. New Delhi: Sterling Publishers, 1983.

Said, Edward W. *Orientalism*. New York: Vintage Books, 1979.

Salomon, Carol. "Bāul Songs." In *Religions in India in Practice*, edited by Donald Lopez, 187–208. Princeton, NJ: Princeton University Press, 1995.

Salomon, Carol. *City of Mirrors: Songs of Lālan Sãi*. Edited by Keith Cantú and Saymon Zakaria. New York: Oxford University Press, 2017.

Sand, Erik, and Tim Rudbøg, eds. *Imagining the East: The Early Theosophical Society*. Oxford: Oxford University Press, 2019.

Sanderson, Alexis. "The Śaiva Age—the Rise and Dominance of Śaivism during the Early Medieval Period." In *Genesis and Development of Tantrism*, edited by Shingo Einoo, 41–351. Tokyo: Institute of Oriental Culture, University of Tokyo, 2009.

Sanderson, Alexis. "The Śaiva Literature." *Journal of Indological Studies* 24 and 25 (2012 and 2013, 2014): 1–113.

Śarīph, Ahmad. *Bāul tattva*. Dhaka: Bangla Academy, 1973.

Sastry, P. V. Parabrahma. *Srisailam, Its History and Cult*. Guntur: Lakshmi Mallikarjunna Press, 1985.

Schmidt, Leigh Eric. *Heaven's Bride: The Unprintable Life of Ida C. Craddock, American Mystic, Scholar, Sexologist, Martyr, and Madwoman*. New York: Basic Books, 2010.

Scott, J. Barton. *Spiritual Despots: Modern Hinduism and the Genealogies of Self-Rule*. Chicago: University of Chicago Press, 2016.

Seal, Brajendranath. *The Positive Sciences of the Ancient Hindus*. London: Longmans, Green, 1915.

Sedgwick, Mark. *Against the Modern World: Traditionalism and the Secret Intellectual History of the Twentieth Century*. New York: Oxford University Press, 2009.

Shearer, Alistair. *The Story of Yoga from Ancient India to the Modern West*. London: C. Hurst, 2020.

Shulman, David Dean. *Tamil: A Biography*. Cambridge, MA: Belknap Press of Harvard University Press, 2016.

Shulman, David Dean. *Tamil Temple Myths: Sacrifice and Divine Marriage in the South Indian Śaiva Tradition*. Princeton, NJ: Princeton University Press, 1980.

Silburn, Lilian. *Le Vijñāna Bhairava*. Paris: Éditions E. de Boccard, 1961.

Singh, Mohan. *Gorakhnath and Mediaeval Hindu Mysticism*. Lahore: Dr. Mohan Singh, Oriental College, Lahore, 1936.

Singleton, Mark. *Yoga Body: The Origins of Modern Posture Practice*. New York: Oxford University Press, 2010.

Singleton, Mark, and Ellen Goldberg, eds. *Gurus of Modern Yoga*. New York: Oxford University Press, 2014.

Smith, David. *Hinduism and Modernity*. Malden, MA: Blackwell, 2003.

Sørensen, Søren. *An Index to the Names in the Mahābhārata*. London: Williams and Norgate, 1904.
Sperber, Dan. "Intuitive and Reflective Beliefs." *Mind & Language* 12, no. 1 (March 1997): 67–83.
Starr, Martin P. *The Unknown God: W.T. Smith and the Thelemites*. Bolingbrook, IL: Teitan Press, 2003.
Stausberg, Michael, and Yuhan Sohrab-Dinshaw Vevaina, eds. *The Wiley Blackwell Companion to Zoroastrianism*. Chicester, West Sussex: John Wiley & Sons, 2015.
Steinschneider, Eric. "Beyond the Warring Sects: Universalism, Dissent, and Canon in Tamil Śaivism, ca. 1675–1994." PhD dissertation, University of Toronto, 2016.
Steinschneider, Eric. "Subversion, Authenticity, and Religious Creativity in Late-Medieval South India: Kaṇṇuṭaiya Vaḷḷal's Oḻiviloṭukkam." *Journal of Hindu Studies* 10, no. 2 (August 2017): 241–71.
Strube, Julian. *Global Tantra: Religion, Science, and Nationalism in Colonial Modernity*. New York: Oxford University Press, 2022.
Strube, Julian. "Yoga and Meditation in Modern Esoteric Traditions." In *Routledge Handbook of Yoga and Meditation Studies*, edited by Suzanne Newcombe and Karen O'Brien-Kop, 130–46. Routledge: London, 2021.
Sukthankar, Vishnu S. *The Āraṇyakaparvan (Part 1), Being the Third Book of the Mahābhārata the Great Epic of India*. Bhandarkar Oriental Research Institute: Poona, 1942.
Supreme Court of India. *Courts of India: Past to Present*. Delhi: Supreme Court of India, 2017.
Talbot, Ian. *Punjab and the Raj, 1849–1947*. New Delhi: Manohar Publications, 1988.
Thayanithy, Maithili. "The Concept of Living Liberation in the Tirumantiram." PhD dissertation, University of Toronto, 2010.
Topsfield, Andrew. "The Indian Game of Snakes and Ladders." *Artibus Asiae* 46, no. 3 (1985): 203–26.
Torella, Raffaele. "The Kañcukas in the Śaiva and Vaiṣṇava Tantric Tradition: A Few Considerations between Theology and Grammar." In *Studies in Hinduism*, vol. 2, *Miscellanea to the Phenomenon of Tantras*, edited by Gerhard Oberhammer, 55–86. Vienna: Der Österreichischen Akademie der Wissenschaften, 1998.
Trento, Margherita. "Translating the Dharma of Śiva in Sixteenth-Century Chidambaram: Maṟaiñāṉa Campantar's Civatarumōttaram." In *Śivadharmāmṛta: Essays on the Śivadharma and Its Network*, edited by Florinda De Simini and Csaba Kiss, 101–45. Naples: UniorPress, 2022.
Urban, Hugh B. *Magia Sexualis: Sex, Magic, and Liberation in Modern Western Esotericism*. Berkeley: University of California Press, 2006.
Urban, Hugh B. "The Yoga of Sex: Tantra, Orientalism, and Sex Magic in the Ordo Templi Orientis." In *Hidden Intercourse: Eros and Sexuality in the History of Western Esotericism*, edited by Wouter J. Hanegraaff and Jeffrey J. Kripal, 401–43. Leiden: Brill, 2008.
Vasudeva, Somadeva. "Powers and Identities: Yoga Powers and the Tantric Śaiva Traditions." In *Yoga Powers: Extraordinary Capacities Attained through Meditation and Concentration*, edited by Knut A. Jacobsen, 264–302. Leiden: Brill, 2012.
Vasudeva, Somadeva, ed. *The Yoga of Mālinīvijayottaratantra: Chapters 1–4, 7–11, 11–17*. Pondicherry: Institut Français de Pondichéry and École Française d'Èxtrême-Orient, 2004.

Venkatraman, Ramaswamy. *A History of the Tamil Siddha Cult*. Madurai: Ennes Publications, 1990.

Vythilingam, M. *The Life of Sir Ponnambalam Ramanathan*. 2 vols. Colombo: Ramanathan Commemoration Society, 1971.

Waldock, Deborah Louise. "Text, Interpretation and Ritual Usage of Tamil Śaiva Poems." PhD dissertation, McMaster University, 1995.

Wallace, Vesna A. *The Inner Kālacakratantra: A Buddhist Tantric View of the Individual*. New York: Oxford University Press, 2001.

Wallace, Vesna A. "The Six-Phased Yoga of the *Abbreviated Wheel of Time Tantra* (*Laghukālacakratantra*) According to Vajrapāṇi." In *Yoga in Practice*, edited by David Gordon White, 204–22. Princeton, NJ: Princeton University Press, 2012.

Wasserman, James. *In the Center of the Fire: A Memoir of the Occult, 1966–1989*. Lake Worth, FL: Ibis Press, 2012.

Weiss, Richard S. *The Emergence of Modern Hinduism: Religion on the Margins of Colonialism*. Oakland: University of California Press, 2017.

Weiss, Richard S. *Recipes for Immortality: Medicine, Religion, and Community in South India*. New York: Oxford University Press, 2009.

White, David Gordon. *The Alchemical Body: Siddha Traditions in Medieval India*. Chicago: University of Chicago Press, 1996.

White, David Gordon. *Daemons Are Forever: Contacts and Exchanges in the Eurasian Pandemonium*. Chicago: University of Chicago Press, 2021.

White, David Gordon. *Kiss of the Yoginī: "Tantric Sex" in Its South Asian Contexts*. Chicago: University of Chicago Press, 2006.

White, David Gordon. *Sinister Yogis*. Chicago: University of Chicago Press, 2009.

White, David Gordon. "The Yoga of the Mahāyogin: Reflections on Madeleine Biardeau's 'Cosmogonies Purāṇiques.'" Unpublished paper, n.d.

White, David Gordon. *The Yoga Sutra of Patanjali: A Biography*. Princeton, NJ: Princeton University Press, 2014.

Winch, Mary Elizabeth. "The Theology of Grace in Saiva Siddhanta, in the Light of Umapati Sivacharya's Tiruarutpayan." PhD dissertation, McMaster University, 1975.

Wolfson, Elliot R. *Through a Speculum That Shines: Vision and Imagination in Medieval Jewish Mysticism*. Princeton, NJ: Princeton University Press, 1997.

Wujastyk, Dagmar. "Acts of Improvement: On the Use of Tonics and Elixirs in Sanskrit Medical and Alchemical Literature." *History of Science in South Asia* 5, no. 2 (2017): 1–35.

Zoehrer, Dominic S. "From Fluidum to Prāṇa: Reading Mesmerism through Orientalist Lenses." In *The Occult Nineteenth Century: Roots, Developments, and Impact on the Modern World*, edited by Lukas Pokorny and Franz Winter, 85–111. New York: Palgrave Macmillan, 2021.

Zvelebil, Kamil Veith. *Companion Studies to the History of Tamil Literature*. Leiden: Brill, 1992.

Zvelebil, Kamil Veith. *Lexicon of Tamil Literature*. Leiden: Brill, 1995.

Zvelebil, Kamil Veith. *The Poets of the Powers*. London: Rider, 1973.

Zvelebil, Kamil Veith. *The Siddha Quest for Immortality*. Oxford: Mandrake, 1996.

Index

For the benefit of digital users, indexed terms that span two pages (e.g., 52–53) may, on occasion, appear on only one of those pages

Tables, figures, and boxes are indicated by *t*, *f*, and *b* following the page number

A.'.A.'. (thelemic order), 365*f*, 367–70, 369*f*
Liber DCLXII vel Pyramidos, 364–66
"Liber HHH: SSS," 364, 368–70
"Liber O vel Manus et Sagittae," 367–68
"Liber Yod," 367–68
"Temple of Solomon the King," 367–68
See also Crowley, Aleister
Abhāvānanda. *See* Crowley, Aleister
Abhinavagupta, 170
Active Principle, 172–75, 185, 204–5, 211–12, 218–19, 241
"Adhikari," six truths of, 202–3, 211–12
Admirers, the, 6–7, 69, 201–2, 316–17
Advaita Vedānta, 10–11, 20–21, 48, 119–20, 155, 171, 257–58
advertisements, 141–42, 147
Adyar, 360–61
Adyar Library and Research Centre, 21, 57, 90, 117–18, 136–38, 144–47
Agastya (Akastiyar அகஸ்தியர்), 10–11, 21–22, 40, 41–50, 66–76, 81–83, 84, 142, 394–96, 397–98
Aṭukkunilai pōtam (ANB), 142
as Avalokiteśvara, 39
and bael forest, 72–74
digestion of Ilvala and Vātāpi, 72–74
as grammarian, 40
hermitage (*āśrama*) of, 36, 38–40, 45–50, 66–71, 85, 133–34, 142, 316–17
and Konnur Meditation Hall, 72–76, 86–87, 399–400
as Siddha, 40
vision of every 50 years, 66–71, 397–99
waterfalls of, 41
Agastya Mala (Agastyachala, "Mount Agastya"), 36, 39–44, 50–51, 66–71, 81–82, 85, 142, 393–94, 397, 400
See also Pothigai Malai
agni (अग्नि fire), 181, 209–10, 327–28
agnihotra (अग्निहोत्र), 209–10, 267–68
Agnihotri, Shiv Narayan, 55–56
Ahalyabai, Sadhvi. *See* Estep, Dora
ahaṃkāra (अहंकार ego-making faculty), 181, 192, 199–200, 255–56
aikyavāda (ऐक्यवाद doctrine of unity), 197–98
Aiyar, A.V. Subramania, 164–66
ājñā (आज्ञा). *See* cakras
ākāśa (आकाश, আকাশ ether, space), 181–82, 217, 237, 250–51, 303–4, 315–16, 323–29
ghaṭākāśa, 327
and Greek *aithēr*, 325
jñānakāśa, 180, 237, 251, 261, 268–70, 326, 328–29
mahākāśa, 326
maṭhākāśa, 327
prāṇākāśa, 180, 237, 251, 258–60, 268, 321–22, 326, 328–29
and science, 315–16, 324–25
as sonoriferous, 324
as subtle element (*tanmātra*), 326
śuddhākāśa (pure ethers), 315–16, 323–29
three meanings of, 323–29
alchemy, 41, 47–49, 164–67, 251, 292, 299–301
diagrams of, 292–301, 395–96
Allahabad High Court, 64
Amanaska Yoga, 370–71
See also yoga
Amaraughaprabodha. *See* Sanskrit texts
Amarnath, 51, 397
Amma, Srila Srikrishnaveni, 44–45
Ammani, Shrimati Ratnam, 80
Amrita River, 42–43, 399

Amrita Bazar Patrika, 51, 62–63, 358
Amṛtakuṇḍa. *See* Sanskrit texts
Amṛtasiddhi. *See* Sanskrit texts
anāhata (अनाहत). *See* cakras
ānanda (आनन्द bliss), 142, 173*f*, 174, 191, 202, 223–24, 242*t*, 244, 308
of absorption
of all gnosis, 223–24
with being and consciousness, 303–4
beyond bliss, 183–84
bliss of Brahman, 303–4
"blissful state" (*svarūpa*), 242*t*
as Infinite Spirit, 173*f*, 174, 202
of inherent nature, 142
of nonbeing (name of Aleister Crowley), 366
power of happy bliss, 191
in samādhi, 245
during sex (momentary), 251–52
of Shiva, 79
spiritual (everlasting), 253
anātman (अनात्मन्), 203–4
anatomy (medical), 291–92
āṇavamala (आणवमल filth of materiality), 191, 197–98, 319–21, 327–28
See also *malas*
Anderson, John (missionary), 26–28
Anger, Kenneth (film director), 370
animals (embodied), 192–93, 199
antaḥkaraṇa (अन्तःकरण internal instrument), 176, 198–200
See also *caturantaḥkaraṇa*
anti-Orientalism, 357–58
anubhava (अनुभव experience, exercise), 34, 46–47, 313–14, 391
anubhūti (अनुभूति perception), 48, 120–21, 124, 129, 130–31, 134, 142, 254–56, 263, 341–43
fault of, 341
ap (अप् water), 181, 289–90
aparokṣajñāna (अपरोक्षज्ञान unmediated gnosis), 34
Aparokṣānubhūti (अपरोक्षानुभूति), 254–56, 331
arcana (अर्चन praising deities), 284–85
Aristotle, 325
Arthur Avalon collaboration, 182–83, 268–70
Arulmigu Agatheeswarar Temple, 73–74
See also Agastya
Arya, The (periodical), 58–59
Arya Press, 118
Arya Samaj (आर्य समाज), 9, 55–56, 58–59, 60, 63–64, 118, 201–2, 211–14, 215–16, 358
and Bombay, 60
Lahore Arya Samaj, 55–56, 58–60, 118, 358
principles of, 60
ārya (आर्य "Noble"), 214
"ancestral Aryans," 215
"Aryan dress," 50
"Aryans of yore," 209, 211–12
as members of any caste, 215
and Parsis, 209
reviving beliefs of, 215
subsequent racist appropriation of, 235n.178
as teachers to foreigners, 215
āsana (आसन posture, seat), 88–89, 244, 245–48, 398
Sabhapati's ten sorts of, 244, 246–48, 247*t*
in ŚYP and Haṭhapradīpikā, 247*t*
See also Pātañjalayoga
āśrama (आश्रम hermitage), 39, 50–51, 66, 74–75, 209, 395–400
See also *maṭālayam*; Agastya
āśramas (आश्रम life stages)
of yoga, 261–62
Aṣṭādhyāyī. *See* Sanskrit texts
aṣṭamāsiddhi (अष्टमासिद्धि). See *aṣṭasiddhi*
aṣṭāṅgayoga (अष्टाङ्गयोग)
See also Pātañjalayoga
aṣṭasiddhi (अष्टसिद्धि eight powers), 47, 50, 262–63
See also *siddhi*
astral body, 60–61, 186–87, 361
"astral bodily deities," 186–87
Astralkörper, 361
astral projection, 358–59, 360–61
confusion with etheric body, 361
projection of the double, 358–59
Rising on the Planes, 368–70
"Scin Laeca," 377n.22
astrology, 76
horoscope of Sabhapati, 23

atheism, 86, 121, 155, 167, 172, 174–75, 197–98, 201–2, 203, 211–12, 217–24, 316–21
critique of materialism, 218–20, 316–21
atīta (अतीत beyond), 183–84, 196–97, 253–54
beyond intelligence and states, 339–40
ātman (आत्मन् soul, self), 4–5, 36, 125–26, 191, 317–18
See also *jīvātman*; *paramātman*
atoms, 220, 317–23, 332
as *aṇu* अणु, 319–21, 332
Australia, 372
Austria, 105n.139, 360–61
Avalon, Arthur (collaborative authors), 182–83, 268–70, 346n.30
avasthā (अवस्था state), 176, 199, 333
four or five, 253–54
in Pātañjalayoga, 303
sleeping and dreaming, 253–54, 333, 335
Avesta. *See* Zoroastrianism
Azam Jah Walajah IV (A'zam Jāh Wālājāh IV), 32
Azhaitthat Kondamurtthy. *See* Swami, Sabhapati

Badrinath (or Five Badris), 51
Bael Forest, the, 72–74, 399
Baḥr al-ḥayāt (Ocean of Life), 32
Bain, Alexander, 117–18
Baktar, Gurunatha (Sabhapati's father), 25, 392
Banaji, Framji Cowasji, 71
Banatheertham, 41
Bandyopadhyay, Ambikacharan, 126–27, 220–21, 291–92, 304, 315–16, 329–44
Bangladesh, 53, 194
Maijbhandaris of, 194
Satkhira District, 53
Bary, Ruttun Chund, 58–59, 61, 63, 118, 120
Sandhyāpaddhati, 118
Basava, 257–58
Basu, Bamandas, 53, 54*f*
Basu, Shrish Chandra, 1–2, 4–5, 19–21, 34–35, 51–64, 54*f*, 69, 117–20, 126–27, 200, 211, 214–15, 220–21, 238–39, 316–17, 323–25, 326
and *ākāśa* as ether, 323–25
and Aleister Crowley, 367–68
as author of Ur-account, 20–21, 51–53
and Bengali BRY, 86, 126–27, 329
and Hegelian language, 227n.41
later life, 64
leader of "Students' Rebellion," 60
and Max Müller, 57
and a Nāth Yogī, 54–55
nationalist yoga poem of, 58
and Pātañjalayoga, 238–39, 243, 245–46
publications on yoga and tantras, 55–56, 105n.139
as Sabhapati's editor, 34–35, 57, 61, 117–18, 243, 245–46, 323–24, 329
and societies, 55–56, 211
student of J.C. Oman, 65
and Swami Vivekananda, 331
and theosophy, 58–60, 63–64, 214–15, 324
translation of *Mahānirvāṇa Tantra* excerpt, 326, 346n.30
See also *Śiva Saṃhitā*
Basu, Shyama Charan, 53
Batra, Bhavani Das, 63
Bāul fakirs of Bengal, 194–95, 251–52, 289, 349n.55, 351n.68
Bengal. *See* lands of India *and* Bangladesh
Bennett, Allan (monk), 366–68, 379–80n.47
Besant, Annie (theosophist), 360
Bhagavad Gita (*Bhagavadgītā*). *See* Sanskrit texts
Bhagavan, Dev Guru. *See* Shiv Narayan Agnihotri
Bhāgavata Purāṇa. *See* Sanskrit texts
bhakti (भक्ति), 36, 47, 81–82, 207, 214, 244, 257–58, 279–80, 283–85, 335–37, 393–94, 395, 396–97
bhaktiyoga (भक्तियोग), 331, 335–37, 350n.63, 394–95
feminine role in, 289
bhāvana (भावन cultivation), 134–36, 261–62, 266–67, 307–8, 320*t*
bhrānti (भ्रान्ति delusion), 123–24, 149n.37, 178
Bhringi (Bhṛṅgi), 50
Bible, the. 26, 33, 127–28, 206–7, 374–75, 393
See also Christianity

bījamantra (बीजमन्त्र seed-syllable mantras), 285, 289–90, 307–8
bindu (बिन्दु, also *vindu*, drop or generative fluid), 46, 193–94, 199, 248, 251–176, 254, 395
bindusthāna. *See* cakras
Black authors, 5–6
black magic, 240–41, 360–61, 387–88
Blavatsky, Helena Petrovna, 5–6, 52–53, 58–64, 127–28, 187–88, 206, 214–15, 220–21, 316–17, 328–29, 356–58, 361–62, 366–67, 387–88
  having *siddhis*, 62–63
  Isis Unveiled, 187–88, 206
  meeting with Sabhapati, 58–61
  The Secret Doctrine, 187–88
  The Voice of the Silence, 366–67
bliss. See *ānanda*
body. See *deha*
Böhme, Jakob (philosopher), 361–62
Bombay. *See* cities and towns, India
"Book 777," 357
  and Jewish Kabbalah, 381–82n.61
Book of the Law, The, 368–70
Book of Abramelin, 364–66, 379n.43
Bose, Phanindranath (biographer), 52–53, 54–55
Bradlaugh, Charles (atheist thinker), 218
brahmajñāna (ब्रह्मज्ञान gnosis of Brahman), 32–33, 38, 48, 50–51, 66–67, 69–70, 81–82, 85, 114, 145–46, 174, 238, 391, 393, 394, 396–97, 400
  fourth state as, 253–54
  initiation into, 81–82
  liberation of, 263
  perception (*anubhūti*) of, 120–21, 129, 134
  as practice of yoga, 266–67
  samādhi of, 85, 238
  sight (*dṛṣṭi*) of, 174, 262–63, 308
  soul of in cakras, 178
  as "Spirituality," 32–33
  See also "Eye to the Universe"; *jñāna*; *jñānākāśa*; *jñānayoga*; *jñānīs*
Brahmā Sūtra. *See* Sanskrit texts
Brahmo Samaj (ब्रह्म समाज)
Brahman (ब्रह्मन्), 46, 125–26, 168–69, 190*f*, 202, 206–7, 212, 223, 240, 255–56, 260–61, 305, 326, 397–98
  bliss of, 36, 394
  and Christian trinity, 202, 206–7
  crevice of (see *brahmarandhra*)
  division into Paraśiva and Śakti, 185
  four brightnesses of, 303–4
  gnosis of,
  gnostic ether of, 315–16
  as Guru, 392
  identity with, 265*t*, 287–89
  inherent form (*svarūpa*) of, 38
  knower of (*brahmajñānī*), 261–62
  nerve of, 270–71
  phallic stone of, 400
  as Sarveśvara, 36, 122, 168–69, 241
  separation from, 260–61
  as Shiva, 46, 122, 168–69, 185, 241
  and Śivarājayoga, 240, 265*t*, 394–95
  in sixteen tattvas of RYB, 180
  translated Infinite Spirit, 36, 122, 168–69, 171, 239, 286–87
  as Universal Infinite Spirit, 172, 204–5, 241
  and Universal Spirit (Shiva), 260–61
  universe/egg of (*brahmāṇḍa*), 333
brahmarandhra (ब्रह्मरन्ध्र cranial cavity, fontanelle), 172, 179*t*, 218–19, 223, 252, 261, 268–70, 315–16, 368–70
  in Aleister Crowley diary, 368–70
  and divine pilgrimage, 261
  as *yoni*, 368–70
Brahmins (caste), 25–26, 215, 263
  and missionaries, 27–28
  and Sabhapati, 23, 25–26
  sacred thread (*pūṇūl*) of, 88–89
brain, 172, 179*t*, 218–20, 222, 223–24, 245
  abode of Universal Spirit 172
  anatomy of, 291–96
  bodily region of (*kapāla*), 223–24
  "Brain of Knowledge" (*tatparasthāna*), 173*f*, 176, 179*t*
  "Brain of Prudence" (*kalāsthāna*), 173*f*, 176, 179*t*
  "Brain of wit and intelligence" (*parasthāna*), 173*f*, 175, 179*t*
  center seat of, 202
  critique of atheist views on, 222
  and *dhyāna*, 245
  and "fixing bliss" during sex, 252

and *kuṇḍalinī*, 370–71
and psychology, 219–20, 316–17
and spiritual "fixing bliss," 253
and *svarūpa*, 307
and thought-creation, 223–24
three parts of, 179*t*
and unconscious movement, 218–19, 222
visual depictions of, 295*f*, 298*f*
yoni as cavity of, 368–70
See also cakras
breath. *See prāṇa*
Breeze, Bill (Hymenaeus Beta), 368
British East India Company, 23
British Library, 21, 72, 76, 86–87, 118, 120, 139–41, 145–47
British Raj, 22, 64–65
"bubbles" of mantras, 289–90
See also cakras
Buddha, Gautama, 20–21, 202, 203–4
See also Buddhism
buddhi (बुद्धि intellect, will)
in Sāṃkhya, 181
as a serpentess, 190*f*, 192
buddhīndriyas (बुद्धीन्द्रिय sense capacities), 181
Buddhism, 5–6, 29, 33, 203–4
Agastya as Avalokiteśvara, 39
and Allan Bennett, 366–68, 379–80n.47
in Burma, 28–29, 227n.47, 379–80n.47
Mahayana, 233n.143
among occultists, 5–6, 33, 58
as one with Hinduism and Vedānta, 29
"Poongees" (monks), 28–29
in Sri Lanka, 99n.47
Tantric Buddhism, 194–95, 203–4, 233n.143
and Theosophical Founders, 58
Theravada, 366, 379–80n.47
in yogic texts, 10–11, 233n.143
Bulwer-Lytton, Edward (novelist), 65–66
and "Scin Laeca," 377n.22
burial
of yogis, 89–90, 94–95
Burma, 28–29, 203–4, 366, 379–80n.47

caitanya (चैतन्य consciousness, brilliance), 261, 270, 303–4, 315–16, 317–18
cakra (चक्र *cakra*)
"6+1" enumeration, 182–83
as 12 Spiritual Lights, 174–75
as Cakkrâms, 367–68
as Kingdoms. 174–75
as tattvas, 305
12. *mūlādhāra*, 173*f*, 176, 179*t*, 184–85, 193*t*, 218–19, 223, 261–62, 265*t*, 270–71, 289–90, 317, 328–29
11. *svādhiṣṭhāna*, 173*f*, 176–78, 179*t*, 193*t*, 265*t*
10. *maṇipūraka*, 173*f*, 176, 178, 179*t*, 193*t*, 199, 265*t*
9. *anāhata*, 173*f*, 176, 178, 179*t*, 193*t*, 193, 199, 265*t*
8. *viśuddhi*, 173*f*, 176, 179*t*, 193*t*, 265*t*
7. *ājñā*, 173*f*, 176, 179*t*, 193*t*, 197–98, 265*t*, 319–21, 370–71
6. *bindusthāna*, 173*f*, 176, 179*t*, 193–94, 265*t*, 286–87, 327
5. *nādasthāna*, 173*f*, 176, 178, 179*t*, 265*t*
4. *kalāsthāna*, 173*f*, 176, 178, 179*t*, 265*t*
3. *tatparasthāna*, 173*f*, 176, 179*t*, 265*t*
2. *parasthāna*, 173*f*, 175, 179*t*, 265*t*
1. *parātpara-pīṭha* or *dvādaśānta*, 173*f*, 175, 179*t*, 265*t*
praṇavasthāna, 178, 179*t*, 265*t*
brahmajñānātmakasthāna, 178, 179*t*
sahasrāra (*sahasttirakamalam*), 179*t*, 183
twelve in *Netra Tantra*, 296
Calcutta. *See* cities and towns, India
Caldwell, Robert (missionary), 39–40, 41
canceling. See *śuddhi*
caṉmārkkam (right path சன்மார்க்கம்), 158
carbon dioxide, 321–22
Carey, Danny (drummer), 370
Carnatic music, 130–31, 283–84
Cārvāka (materialism), 217
Carvēsvarar (சர்வேஸ்வரர்). *See* Sarveśvara
Carvēsvari (சர்வேஸ்வரி). *See* Shakti
caste. See *varṇa*
Catholicism. *See* Christianity
caturantaḥkaraṇa (चतुरन्तःकरण fourfold internal instrument), 195–96, 198–200, 320*t*

Central Survey Office (Chepauk), 22–23, 91–93, 92*f*
Ceylon (Sri Lanka), 58, 366, 379–80n.47
  Kandy Mountain, 68, 397–98
Chaitanya Mahaprabhu, 7–8, 9–10, 337
Chaitanya, Swami Krishna, 119
Chaitanya Prabha Mandali, 119
chanting, 279–80, 285–90
Chennai. *See* cities and towns, India
Chettiar, V. Subramaniya, 87, 94–95
Chicago, University of, 129, 136–38
Chinese, 180–81
Chitra Pournami (சித்ரா பௌர்ணமி), 68–69, 397–98
Christianity, 4–6, 26–28, 33, 201–2, 203, 204–7
  and *arūpa bhakti*, 207
  and English education, 26
  Catholicism, 27–28
  Church of Scotland, 26–27, 53
  Disruption of 1843, 26–27
  and idolatry, 27–28
  Jesus Christ, 128, 204–5, 207, 374–75
  Judgment Day, 204–5
  Princeton Theological Seminary, 53
  Protestantism, 27–28, 204–5
  Purgatory, 204–5
  Scottish "Free Church," 26–27
  Trinity of, 206
  See also Bible, the
Christian Science, 220–21
Ciṟṟampalanāṭikaḷ, Cikāḻi, 183–84
  See also Tamil texts
cities and towns, Bangladesh
  Khulna, 53
  Tengra-Bhavanipur, 53
cities and towns, India
  Adyar (in Madras), 360–61
  Ahmedabad, 62
  Allahabad (Prayagraj), 42–43, 64
  Badami, 73–74
  Bangalore (Bengaluru), 80–81
  Bareilly, 64
  Baroda (Vadodara), 136–38
  Benares (Varanasi), 66
  Bhadraw (Bhadra), 136–38
  "Black Town" (in Madras), 26–27, 73
  Bombay (Mumbai), 58–59, 60, 70–72, 80, 116, 119, 120–21, 128, 134, 136–38, 187–88, 212–13, 214, 217, 254, 290–91, 296, 314, 358
Calcutta (Kolkata), 26, 53–54, 57, 64–65, 116, 126–27, 182–83, 212–13, 217, 291–92, 314, 331
  Chidambaram, 66–67
  Chingleput, 22–23
  Courtallam (Kutralam), 40–41, 66–67, 386, 397
  Delhi/New Delhi, 116, 117–18, 120, 227n.41
  Fort St. George (in Madras), 23, 73
  Hampi, 73–74
  Haridwar, 66–67, 374, 397
  Jelander (Jalandhar), 66
  Kangra, 44*f*, 51–52
  Kishkindha, 66–67, 397
  Konnur, 72–77, 84–94, 116–17, 129–30, 138–43, 263–64, 267–68, 279–80, 299–301, 388, 399–400
  Madras (Chennai), 22–23, 26–28, 29, 32–33, 35, 66, 68–71, 72–73, 74–75, 76–77, 90–91, 93, 116, 119, 120–21, 129–30, 132–33, 138–41, 145–46, 158–59, 212–13, 217, 290–92, 294–96, 314, 366–67, 370–71, 388
  Madura (Madurai), 66–67, 87–88, 263–64, 366–67, 397
  Meerut, 64, 69, 324
  Moradabad, 72, 134
  Murugambakkam, 87, 90*f*, 93–94
  Mylapore (in Madras), 25, 30–31, 69–70, 72, 120–21, 134–36, 141–42, 160–62, 162*f*, 163*f*, 392
  Mysore (Mysuru), 22, 80–82, 83–84, 262–63
  Nagapatam (Nagapattinam), 31–33, 194–95, 207–8
  North Poigainallur, 194–95
  Ooty (Udhagamandalam and Kandal), 21–22, 76–77, 80–84, 85, 133, 136–38, 144, 250, 299, 372, 388
  Papanashan (Papanasam), 40–41, 43–44, 85, 386
  Rameswaram, 66–67

Rishikesh, 66–67
Royapettah (in Madras), 80
Royapuram (in Madras), 79
Soorooli (Suruli), 40
Srinagar, 57, 293–94
Srisailam, 66–67, 73–74, 164–66, 194–95, 397
Thirukkadaiyur, 66–67
Thiruporur (Tiruppōrūr), 79–80
Thiruttani (Tiruttaṇi), 79–80
Thiruvanmiyur, 168–69
Tinnevelly (Tirunelveli), 22–23, 83–84, 372
Tirupperunturai, 66–67
Trichy (Tiruchirappalli), 76–77, 145–46
Vadalur, 49, 397
Velachery (Vedashreni), 20–22, 23–25, 30–31, 34–39, 41, 49, 81, 158–59, 168–69, 263–64, 386
Villivakkam, 21–23, 72–74, 86–87, 91–93, 94–95, 263–64, 399
Vindhyachal, 66–67
cities and towns, Nepal
Pashupatinath (in Kathmandu), 51
cities and towns, Pakistan
Lahore, 20–22, 47, 51–66, 68–69, 116, 117–18, 129–32, 208, 211, 212–13, 291–92, 293–94, 296, 325, 358–59, 389–90
Multan, 48–49
cities and towns, United States
Austin, 375
Chicago, 201–2, 375
Excelsior Springs, 116, 128, 372–75
New York City, 58, 214, 384n.85
Seattle, 374–75
citta (चित्त thought), 190*f*, 192, 198–200, 255–56, 317, 334, 336–37, 340–44, 347n.35
negation of, 340, 343
cittarkaḷ. *See* Siddhas
"Cittarkaṇam" (of Tāyumāṉavar). *See* Tamil texts
Civācāriyār, Aruḷnanti (Arunandhi Sivachariyar), 158
civam (சிவம் godhead, supreme Shiva), 172, 183–84, 196–97, 260–61, 289
"Civil and Military Gazette" Press, 57, 117–18
colonial period
and periodization of yoga, 2–4
South Asian agency, 3, 6–7
yoga and occultism during, 5–6
colorization (of diagrams), 290–91, 296–99
communion. *See* samādhi
composure. *See* samādhi
Confessions (of Aleister Crowley), 366–67
Conscience, Tongue of, 173*f*, 176
consciousness, 125–26, 174, 261, 270, 303–4, 329
in Aleister Crowley's diary, 368
ascent and descent of, 370–71
beyond deep sleep, 253–54
as *cetan*, 334–37
ego-consciousness, 183–84, 196–97
of eleven faculties, 222
and projection of astral double, 358–59
pure consciousness, 315–16
puruṣa as, 181, 192, 303–4
self consciousness, 223–24
unconditioned, 220–21
"Western" views on, 340
See also *vyāpaka*
conscious sleeping, 253–54
Coomaraswamy, Ananda (art historian), 366, 380n.48
Corbin, Henry (author), 357–58
Courtallam. *See* cities and towns, India
Crowley, Aleister, 1–2, 5–6, 220–21, 356–58, 362–72
cultural influence of, 370
exposure to Sabhapati, 366–67
Liber Yod, 367–68
and phallicism, 364–66
"SSS" in *Liber HHH*, 368–70
and yoga in A∴A∴ instructions, 367–68
Curwen, David, 366–67
Cuttacātakam of Kumara Devar. *See* Tamil works
cuvāmikaḷ (சுவாமிகள்). *See* Swamigal

Dalton, John (scientist), 319–21
Dandeeswarar Vedashreni Temple, 37–38, 37*f*, 168–69
Daoism, 5–6, 367–68

darśana (दर्शन vision, viewing deities), 38, 46, 48–49, 67, 68, 287–89
śivadarśana as one of ten acts, 229n.85
Dass, Sain (Arya Samaj secretary), 58–59
Dayal, Lala Shiv (classmate of Shrish Chandra), 55–56
death
mysteries of life after, 56
of Sabhapati Swami, 94–95
deha (देह body), 169
cosmic body (*birāṭ-deha*), 335
dehatattva (body's truth), 188–95
division into Shiva/Shakti, 186
as *ghaṭa* (pot), 327
as instrument (*yantra*), 335
as *maṭha* (home), 327
Delhi. *See* cities and towns, India
Democritus (pre-Socratic), 319–21
Desai, Sriyuth Manilal, 119
Desikar, Shri Ekambara (yogi), 80
Devanagari, 20–21, 50–51, 57, 72, 116, 120–21, 124, 130–32, 138, 145, 168–69, 245, 263
omission of, 128, 372
devatā (देवता local deity), 145–46, 186–87, 210, 336
portion (*aṃśa*) of, 289–90
See also Hindu deities and forms
Devi, Bhubaneshwari (mother of Shrish Chandra), 53
Devi, Ratan (musician) 380n.48
devotion. See *bhakti*
Dev Samaj (देव समाज), 55–56
dharma (धर्म, श्धर्म duty), 329–31, 338, 395
as religion, 339
Dharmaśāstras, 261–62
d'Holbach, Baron (thinker), 218
dhyāna (ध्यान, श्यान meditation), 38, 47, 68, 143, 245
for Hindus and Parsis, 210
in silent mantra-recitation, 289–90
societies, 49
on *svarūpas*, 307–8
See also Pātañjalayoga; yoga
dhyānayoga (ध्यानयोग yoga of meditation). *See* yoga
diagrams, 290–309
dīkṣā (initiation), 47, 66–67, 81–83, 158–59, 166–67
as mesmerism, 63, 74
divine pilgrimage, 257–58, 261, 268–70, 315–16, 359
divine words, 178, 289–90
See also *bījamantra*
Diwali, 74–75
Dravidian Tamil, 48–49, 76, 388–89
"Dravid language,"
See also languages, Indic
dreams
blessing in, 83
dreamless sleep (*suṣupti*), 253–54
initiation through, 81–83
Sabhapati's vision in, 35–36
dṛṣṭānta (illustration), 171
drugs, 364
dualism, 48, 155, 197–98
of Śaiva Siddhānta, 157–58, 172
Duff, Alexander (missionary), 26
Dvivedi, Manilal (writer), 254–55

Eckhart, Meister (mystic), 127–28
Eddy, Mary Baker (author), 220–21
Egyptian deities, 367–68
elements (*bhūtas*), 142, 181
combinations of, 221–23
conquest of, 170
as five vitals, 218–19
man of five, 193
Eliade, Mircea (author), 34–35, 186
Elk Hill, 81–82
Empress of India Press, 132–33
England, 53, 64–65, 384n.85
English, 1–5, 7–10, 8*f*, 26, 82–83
Esoteric Cosmic Yogi Science (WE), 128
esotericism, 2–3, 5–6, 12–13, 203
See also occultism
Esoteric Section. *See* Theosophical Society
Estep, Dora, 374
Estep, William, 128, 372–75
Eternal Wisdom & Health, 128
"eternal return," 186
ether. See *ākāśa*
evolution
and atheism, 218–19
and Christianity, 206–7

Darwinian, 220–21
psychic, 359
as transmigration, 186–88
Eweler, Maria (mother of J.C. Oman), 64–65
"Eye-Brows of Muse," 173*f*, 176
See also cakras
"Eye to the Universe" (*brahmajñānadṛṣṭi*), 174, 219–20, 262–63, 313–14
See also *brahmajñāna*

faculties. *See* tattva
fakirs, 31–32, 207–8, 251–52, 289
"fakir-yogi," 64–65
malang order of, 32
female devotees, depiction of, 263
female workers (in the body), 192–93
feminine role (in devotion), 289
Finite Spirit. See *jīvātman*
fire. See *agni*
five-syllabled mantra (*pañcākṣaramantra*), 287
fontanelle. See *brahmarandhra*
force (physical) 220, 221–22, 252, 313, 317–18
"Forehead of Memory," 173*f*, 176
See also cakras
foreigners, 60–61
spiritual education of 215
Forman, Charles William (missionary), 53
Fort St. George. *See* cities and towns, India
Four Brightnesses (of Infinite Spirit), 173*f*, 260–61
1. Bliss (*sarvānanda*), 174
2. Witness (*sarvasākṣin*), 174, 317–18
3. Consciousness (*sarvavyāpaka*), 174, 223–24, 317–18
4. Void (*sarvaśūnya*), 174, 317–18
fourth state (*turīya*), 253–54
beyond the fourth (*turīyātīta*), 253–54
See also *avasthā*
Framjee Cowasjee Institute, 71
Free Church Mission School, 26, 204–5
See also Christianity
Freemasonry, 356–57
French, 9, 34–35, 218
translation of Ur-account, 20–21, 358
Freud, Sigmund (psychologist), 219–20
Fuller, J.F.C. (author), 367–68
gamut of the Vedas, 283, 284, 287
Ganesh. *See* Hindu deities and forms
Ganges (river), 42–43, 51, 66–67, 397
Gauḍapāda (philosopher), 326
Gauḍiya Vaiṣṇava, 289, 337
Gāyatrī (mantra), 118, 143, 179*t*
General Assembly's Institution (Calcutta), 53
General Assembly's School (Madras), 26–27
"Generative Fluid". See *bindu*
German, 1–2, 9
text *Buch Abramelin*, 379n.43
translation of VRY2 or VRY3, 20–21, 57, 116, 127–28, 358, 360–62
translation of yoga and tantra, 360–61
Germany, 116–17, 360–61
Bavaria (Bayern), 360–61, 366
Leipzig, 116
Gilani, Abdul Qadir (ʿAbd al- Qādir Gīlānī), 31–32
Gillard, Paul (theosophist), 20–21, 358
glazing (art), 296–99
gnosis. See *jñāna*
gnostic ether. See *jñānākāśa*
Gnostics. See *jñānīs*
God, 34, 62, 68–69, 125–26, 172, 185, 204–5, 206–7, 210, 212, 213–14, 216, 218–20, 222, 223, 262–63, 264–66, 285–86, 306–7, 306*f*
Goddess (Devī). *See* Hindu deities and forms
gods, 76, 79–80, 155, 204–6, 210, 218, 357
and deities, 48–49, 367–68
as elements, 222
mother of the, 289
See also Hindu deities and forms
Goga (Sufi *pīr*), 207–8
Gorakhnath (Gorakhnāth), 55
as Kōrakkar, 194–95
Gorakṣanātha. *See* Gorakhnath
Gospels, the, 205–6, 361–62
Grant, Kenneth (author), 120, 366–67
and Crowley's image, 381n.54
granthi (knots), 296
Greco-Egyptian rites, 5–6, 356, 364
guṇas (qualities), 176, 187, 190*f*, 193, 320*t*, 327–28, 332–33
and worldly divisions, 187

gurus, 6–7, 25, 36, 389–90
of any caste, 215
Gorakhnath as, 55
Guru-Yogis and theosophy, 71, 360
limits of, 34
longevity of, 20–21
remote communication with, 66–67
of Sabhapati, 19–25, 29–31, 36, 38–39, 42–47, 68–69, 157–67, 195–96, 201–2
See also *dīkṣā*
Gwaliyari, Muhammad Ghaus (Muḥammad Ghawth Gwāliyārī), 32
gyān chaupar (Board of Knowledge), 188

Ḥamilton, William (metaphysician), 220–21, 340
Hartmann, Franz (author), 1–2, 20–21, 57, 356–57, 358, 360–62
and astral body, 359, 361
and German translations of Sabhapati, 127–28, 360–62
Haṭhapradīpikā. *See* Sanskrit texts
Haṭha Rājayoga. *See* yoga
haṭha yoga (yoga for force). *See* yoga
"Heart of Passions," 173*f*, 176
See also cakras
Hegelian philosophy, 168–69, 227n.41
Hermetic Brotherhood of Luxor, 71–72
Hermetic Order of the Golden Dawn, 71–72, 366
and the tattvas, 367–68
hermitage. See *āśrama*
Himalayas, 50–51, 68, 203–4, 397
other side of, 203–4
Hindi. *See* languages, Indic
Hindu deities and forms
Bhavānī, 366
Brahma (Brahmā), 206–7
Dhandapani (Daṇḍapāṇi, Taṇṭapāṇi), 38, 79–80, 394
Ganesh (Gaṇapati, Vināyakar), 74–75, 79, 141
Gaurī, 186, 294
Goddess (Devī), 76, 183–84, 196–97, 303–4, 337
Goddesses of Power (*caktitēvikaḷ*), 398–99
Hari, 391
Īśvara, 174, 180, 182, 185, 203–5, 206–7, 244, 245, 273n.20, 287–89, 336–37
Kartikeya (Skanda), 79–80
Krishna (Kṛṣṇa), 303–4, 337
local deities (*devatā*), 145–46, 186–87, 210, 336
Mahadeva (Mahādeva), 19, 38, 42, 50, 60–61, 168–69, 279, 303–4, 358
Mahavishnu (Mahāviṣṇu), 399–400
Maheśvara, 265*t*
Murugan (Murukaṉ), 79–80
Narayana (Nārāyaṇ), 337–38
Naṭēcar/Naṭēcamūrtti (Lord of the Dance), 32–33
Paramaśiva, 172
Paraśiva, 185
Parvatī, 186
Perumal, 73, 77–78, 91
Rudra, 265*t*, 273n.20
Sadāśiva, 172, 182
Sarpeśvara (Carppēcuvarar), 168–69
Sarveśvara (Carvēsvarar), 36, 72–73, 122, 168–69, 241
Sarveśvarī (Carvēsvari), 399–400
Shakti (Śakti), 155, 180, 182, 185–86, 191, 204–5, 206–7, 242–43, 289, 317–18, 391
Shiva (Śiva), 20–21, 34–36, 46, 86–87, 122, 155, 168–69, 172, 182, 185–86, 191–92, 197–99, 241–43, 257–58, 260–63, 286, 391, 392, 393–95, 398
Skanda (Kartikeya), 79–80
Trika goddess forms, 183–84, 196–97, 229–30n.86
Trimūrti, 206–7
Vāc, 289
Vishnu (Viṣṇu), 41, 155, 206–7, 337–38, 399–400
Yama (Yamaṉ), 79
See also Brahman; *liṅga*
Hinduism, 29, 388–89
Aleister Crowley and, 366–68
and other religions, 201–24
Esteps and, 374
Sabhapati and, 32–33
Srish Chandra Basu and, 55
subtle body in, 182
See also Hindu deities and forms

Hindu Press, 120–21
Hindustani. *See* languages, Indic
Holy Ghost (Holy Spirit).
  See Christianity
Holy Guardian Angel, the, 364–66, 365*f*, 379n.43
Holy Order of Krishna. *See* Latent Light Culture
Huxley, Thomas Henry (biologist), 220–21

iḍā (nerve). See *nāḍī*
idols (statues), 30–31, 79–80, 165*f*
illusion. See *māyā*
Ilvala (daemon), 72–74, 399
  See also Agastya
imagination. See *kalpanā*
India, 1–11
  See lands of India
Indian Institute of Technology, 37, 158–59
Indian Mirror (periodical), 58
indriyas (इन्द्रिय sense-faculties), 176–78, 181–82, 190*f*, 192–93, 243, 334
  control of (*indriyasaṃyama*), 250–51
  purification of (*indriyaśuddhi*), 265*t*
Infinite Spirit. *See* Brahman
inherent form. See *svarūpa*
initiation. See *dīkṣā*
intellect. See *buddhi*
Irāmatēvar, 165*f*
  See also Siddhas
Iran, 209–10
Islam, 4–5, 31–32, 33, 194, 201–2, 207–8, 393
  Burton and the Kaaba, 366
  maraikkāyar (kings of the boat), 31–32
  Muhammad, the Prophet, 32, 202, 207–8, 393
  Qadiriyya Sufi order of, 31–32
  al-Quran, 32
  Sabhapati's views on, 207–8
  Shaṭṭārī order of, 32
  Sufism, 31–32, 194
  See also Nagore Dargah; Naguri, Shah al-Hamid; fakirs
Īśvara (Lord). *See* Hindu deities and forms
Īśvarakṛṣṇa, 180–81, 303

Jainism, 201–2
Janaka (king), 209
Jesus Christ. *See* Christianity
jīvanmukti (जीवन्मुक्ति liberated in life), 34, 124, 263–64, 393
**jīvasamādhi* (jeeva samadhi, tumulus), 94–95, 98n.29, 263–66
  of Chidambara Swamigal, 23–25, 30–31, 165*f*
  of Konnur Ramalinga Swamigal, 87
  of Kōrakkar, 194–95
  of Kuzhandaivel Swamigal, 160–62, 162*f*, 163*f*
  of Saangu Nayanar, 81
  of Sabhapati Swami, 87–88, 91–95, 95*f*, 264–66
  samādhi of Sayappu Andavar (al-Hamid Naguri), 393
jīvātman (जीवात्मन् Finite Spirit), 123–24, 149n.30, 169, 186, 189–91, 190*f*, 199, 203–4, 212, 251–52, 260–61, 270–71, 286–87
  as feminine, 289
  longing for liberation, 169
  six truths of Adhikari, 202
  as twelve kingdoms, 256–57, 286–87
  and vital breath, 326
  See also *ātman*
Jnana Guru Yogi. *See* Swami, Sabhapati
jñāna (ज्ञान gnosis/knowledge), 47, 237, 255–57, 326, 334
  of absolute void (Haṭha Yoga)
  of bliss, 223–24
  of dissolution of mind (Haṭha Rājayoga, 239–40
  in introduction of BRY, 329–44
  lack of (*ajñāna*), 305, 317–18
  as pure ether, 326, 328–29
  of self, 191
  of Shiva, 255–56
  Shiva's power of, 189–91
  as stage in *Tirumantiram*, 34–35
  subjugation of (Śivarājayoga), 240, 255–60, 266–67, 267*f*, 270–71, 302
  of tattvas (*tattvajñāna*), 69–70, 123, 287–89
  of three times (*trikāla*), 72–73
  in Vedānta and Siddhānta, 197
  See also *brahmajñāna*; *jñānayoga*; *jñānākāśa*; *jñānīs*

jñānākāśa (ज्ञानाकाश gnostic ether), 180, 237, 251, 268–70, 314–15, 328–29
jñānayoga (ज्ञानयोग yoga of gnosis), 81–82, 130–31, 202, 212, 213–14, 223
 in grades of A∴A∴, 382n.63
 in introduction of BRY, 331, 334
 as Śivarājayoga, 256–57, 266–67, 267*f*, 302
 of Vivekananda, 331
*jñānī*s (Ñāṉikaḷ, gnostics), 68, 209–10, 331, 397–98
John, St., 204–5
 See also Christianity
Johnston, Robert (missionary), 26
Jones, George Cecil, 367–68
Judaism, 201–2
 kabbalah, 5–6, 367–68, 382n.62
Jung, Carl, 219–20
Jwalamukhi (Jvālāmukhī), 51, 397

Kaaba, 366
 See also Islam
Kabbalah. *See* Judaism
Kailāsa, 19, 36, 397
 Agastya Mala as southern Kailāsa, 43*f*, 44*f*, 66–67, 68, 393–94
 Sabhapati's flight to, 50–51, 61–62, 119, 313–14, 358, 397
 See also Agastyamalai
kaivalya (कैवल्य isolation), 48, 124, 181–82
 in Pātañjalayoga, 303, 337
kalā (कला fragmented power), 46, 288*t*, 317–18
kalāsthāna. *See* cakras
kalpa (day of Brahmā)
kalpanā (कल्पना imagination), 171, 190*f*, 191, 286–87, 317–18, 339
Kalyana Theertham, 41
kañcukas (कञ्चुक), 182
Kandal. *See* cities and towns, India
Kandy Mountain. *See* Ceylon
Kannada. *See* languages, Indic
Kanphata (Kāṇphaṭa). See *Nāth Yogī*s
Kant, Immanuel, 220–21
kapāla (कपाल brain), 172, 188–89
Kapaleeshwarar Temple, 69
kāraṇaśarīra (Finite Spiritual Body), 184–85, 326–28
kāraṇa vāyu (कारण वायु wind of causation), 242–43, 242*t*, 248
karma, 191
Karma Yoga, 238–39, 331, 337–38, 382n.63
Karnatak Press, 120–21
Kashmir. *See* lands of India
Kashyap, Rama Prasad, 63, 108n.194, 118, 120, 324–25, 367–68
Kāyasiddhas, 166
 See also Siddhas
Kedarnath, 51, 104n.127, 397
Khoth, Vithal Hari (professor), 128
Kingdoms (in the body). *See* cakras
knowledge. See *jñāna*
Kolkata. *See* cities and towns, India
Konnur Meditation Hall, 72–77, 84–94, 116–17, 129–30, 138–43, 263–64, 267–68, 279–80, 299–301, 388, 399–400
Kōrakkar (Siddha), 194–95
 See also Gorakhnath
*kośa*s (कोश sheaths), 176, 190*f*, 193
Krishna. *See* Hindu deities and forms
Krishnamacharya, Tirumalai, 82–83, 389–90
Krishnamurti, Jiddu, 380n.48
kteis (κτείς female phallus), 364
Kumar, Munish, 120
Kumara Devar (Kumāratēvar), 30–31, 53, 158–64, 163*f*, 164*f*, 195–96, 258
 Attuvitavuṇmai (அத்துவிதவுண்மை), 159–60
 Cāstirakkōvai (சாஸ்திரக்கோவை), 159–62, 161*f*
 Cuttacātakam (சுத்த சாதகம்), 159–60
 Makārājātuṟavu (மகாராஜாதுறவு), 159–60
 See also Tamil texts
kumbhaka. See *prāṇāyāma*
kumbhaka-nāḍī (कुम्भक-नाडी spinal cord), 261
 prolonged as *suṣumnā*, 270–71
kuṇḍali (कुण्डलि ring), 173*f*, 175, 176, 218–19, 223, 239–40, 241, 252, 253, 261–62, 268–71, 317, 319–21, 328–29
 and Aleister Crowley, 368
 contrast with *kuṇḍalinī*, 268–70, 328–29

as elements, 176, 289–90
explanation for name, 228n.63
as organ of throwing urine, 315–16
and *svarūpas*, 307
See also cakras
kuṇḍalinī (कुण्डलिनी she who is coiled), 178, 179*t*, 268–71, 328–29, 370–71
as *kuṇḍalinīśakti*, 182–83
and T.K. Rajagopalan, 370–71
Kush Mountains (Kuśācala), 68, 397–98
Kutralanathaswamy Temple, 41
Kuvalyananda, Swami, 322–23

La Martiniere Institution, 64–65
Lady of All. *See* Shakti.
Lahore. *See* cities, Pakistan
Lahore Government College, 53–54
Lal, Bishan (theosophist), 64
Lal, Chandra, 63
lands of India (including ethnicity)
Andhra Pradesh, 164–66
Baroda (Vadodara), 136–38
Bengal (Bengal Presidency, incl. modern Bangladesh), 1–2, 11, 19, 48–49, 52–53, 58, 127, 194–95, 251–52, 289, 304, 315–16, 322–23, 329–44
Deccan (Dakkan), 25–26, 194–95, 262–63
Gujarat, 48–49, 62, 136–38, 137*f*
Haryana, 370–71
Himachal, 48–49, 51–52, 395–96
Karnataka, 10–11, 48–49, 73–74, 80–81, 167
Kashmir, 48–49, 51, 57, 66–67, 170, 183–84, 185, 196–97, 224n.2, 229–30n.86, 293–94, 395–96, 397
Kerala (Malayalam), 40, 43–44, 48–49, 78–79, 86–87, 88–89
Madras Presidency (Tamil Nadu), 22–23, 66, 73, 76–77, 90–91, 138
Marathi (Bombay Presidency, Maharashtra), 48–49, 71–72
North-Western Provinces, 64
Punjab Province (Punjab), 1–2, 48–49, 51–55, 58–59, 207–8
Rajputhani, 48–49
Telangana, 164–66
Telugu, 25–26, 48–49
Travancore State (Kerala), 78–79
See also cities and towns, India
lands of Pakistan
Multan, 48–49
Punjab Province (Punjab), 1–2, 48–49, 51–55, 58–59, 207–8
Sindh, 48–49
landscapes (of yoga), 291–92, 299, 301*f*
languages, Indic
Bengali, 6–10, 8*f*, 11–12, 20–21, 48–49, 54*f*, 57, 64, 115–16, 126–27, 132, 188–89, 193–95, 200, 220–21, 270–71, 292–94, 304, 323, 329–44, 330*f*, 389–90
"Dravidian" Tamil, 48–49, 76, 129–30, 388–89
Gujarati, 129–30, 138
Hindi, 9–10, 20–21, 55, 72, 129, 134, 379–80n.47
Hindustani, 48–49, 129, 379–80n.47
Kannada (Kanarese), 126, 157–58, 167, 191, 257–58
language of the North (*vaṭamoḻi*), 134
Malayali (Malayalam), 115–16, 126
Maṇipravāla, 21–22, 115–16, 132, 210, 245, 307
Marathi (Maharashtrian), 7–8, 8*f*, 25–26, 48–49, 72, 129–31, 134, 138, 266–67
Pali, 29, 366
Punjabi (Panjabi), 55, 126
Sanskrit (Sanscrit), 1, 3–6, 8*f*, 9–11, 20–22, 32–33, 48–49, 50, 52–55, 57, 64, 72, 74, 115–16, 119–22, 126, 128–32, 133–34, 143–44, 147, 169, 174, 176–78, 182, 183–86, 192–93, 194, 196, 200, 209, 240–41, 251, 257–61, 265*t*, 268–70, 280–81, 283–84, 285, 294, 307, 317, 323, 334–35, 366, 379–80n.47
Tamil, 1, 4–5, 7–11, 8*f*, 21–22, 25–26, 39–40, 48–49, 57, 64, 69–70, 73–74, 75–94, 77*f*, 115–18, 126, 129–34, 138–47, 158–60, 164–67, 168–69, 182, 183–84, 188–200, 203, 239–40, 257–60, 267–68, 280–85, 289, 292–93, 299, 316–23, 372, 388–89

languages, Indic (*cont.*)
Telugu, 7–9, 23, 25–26, 48–49, 57, 116, 125*f*, 126, 132, 134–36, 143–45, 157–58, 200, 292–93, 299, 389–90
Urdu, 20–21, 48–49, 120, 129, 134, 379–80n.47
Latent Light Culture, 83–84, 120, 356–57, 372
laya (लय dissolution, absorption), 124, 210, 250–51, 261, 286, 297*f*, 308
of breath and mind, 239–40
in seven sounds, 287
svarūpa of, 242*t*
Layayoga. *See* yoga
Leadbeater, C.W., 127–28, 360
Leitner, Gottlieb Wilhelm (educator), 53, 59–60
Lemegeton, 364–66
"Liber HHH: SSS". *See* A.·.A.·.
Liber DCLXII vel Pyramidos. *See* A.·.A.·.
"Liber O vel Manus et Sagittae". *See* A.·.A.·.
"Liber Yod". *See* A.·.A.·.
Lindsay, Charles Richard (Justice), 59–60
liṅga (लिङ्ग Śaiva phallic stone), 38–39, 94–95, 95*f*, 185–86, 197–98, 263–66, 366
1,008 in Konnur, 72–74
Aleister Crowley's interest in, 364–66
diagrams of, 257–58, 294, 358–59
disappearance into, 263–66
as human body, 185, 364–66
as infinite circle, 38
and *liṅgeśvara*, 264–66
naturally arising (*svayambhū*), 41, 263–64
and phallicism, 366
and *pīṭha* of Gaurī, 186, 313–14
and pyramid, 366
as spinal cord, 368–70
of Sri Sabhapathy Lingeshwarar Koil, 95*f*
state of union with, 10–11, 197–98
svarūpa of, 185, 262–63, 294, 303–4, 308, 313–14
as tumuli, 94–95, 263–66
two forms of, 68–69
in Vedashreni, 37–38
and Vishnu, 41
See also *jīvasamādhi*; Hindu deities and forms
liṅgaikyabhāva. See *liṅga*
Lingam-Yoni (book), 366
liṅgaśarīra (mark[ed] body), 126–27, 270–71, 293–94
as astral body, 361
diagram of, 358, 361
as subtle body (*sūkṣmaśarīra*), 127, 182, 270–71, 327
liṅgasvarūpa. See *liṅga*
lotuses (*kamala*). *See* cakras

Madras. *See* cities and towns, India
Madras General Assembly's School. *See* Free Church Mission School
Madras Medical School, 291–92
Madras Presidency. *See* lands of India
Madras Record Office, 21, 74–75, 76, 145–47
Madura (Madurai). *See* cities and towns, India
magic, 1–2, 240–41, 362–72
black magic (*schwarze Magie*), 360–61
ceremonial, 364
Forging of the Magic Sword, 365*f*
haṭha yoga stigmatized as, 240–41
and mantra, 284–85
ointment, 47
and science, 221
Solomonic, 364–66
sorcery (*Hexerei*), 360–61
as thelemic "Magick," 362–72
of *vaśya*, 256–57
of waterfalls, 41
white magic (*weiße Magie*), 360–61
and yoga, 1–2, 240–41, 360–61, 362–64
See also A.·.A.·.
magnetic energy, 246–48
Mahabharata (Mahābhārata), 58
Agastya in Āraṇyakaparvan, 73–74
and Parāśara, 209
Sabhapati meets rishis from, 50, 60–61, 62, 360
and *videhamukti*, 263–64
See also Sanskrit texts
mahābhūtas (महाभूत gross elements), 181
ākāśa as, 324, 327, 328
See also *ākāśa*

Mahadeva (Mahādeva). *See* Hindu deities and forms
mahākāraṇaśarīra (Infinite Spiritual Body), 184–85
Mahānirvāṇa Tantra
  partial translation of, 326, 346n.30
Maha Pralayakala (*mahāpralayakāla*), 206–7
Maharshi, Ramana, 389
Mahatmas (Tamil), 45, 395, 397–400
Mahatma Letters, 58
malas (मल impurities), 191, 319–21
  as three (*trimala*) 34–35, 176, 190*f*, 193, 197–98, 265*t*
  See also *āṇavamala*
male workers (in the body), 192–93, 193*t*
Malik, Arjan Dass (author), 370–71
manas (मनस् mind), 199
  absorption of, 308
  dissolution of breath and, 239–40
  full of doubts, 200
  purifications of, 297*f*
  subjugation of, 250–51
  witness of, 189–91
mānasa pūjā (मानस पूजा mental worship), 214, 308
Manasasarovar (lake), 50, 397
Manikaran, 51
Māṇikkavācakar (Manikkavacakar), 280–82, 284–85
  Tiruvācakam (திருவாசகம்), 280–82
  See also Tamil texts
Maṇipravāla (*maṇippiravāḷam*, மணிப்பிரவாளம்). *See* languages, Indic
maṇipūraka. *See* cakras
Mansel, Henry Longueville (philosopher), 220–21, 340–43
mantras, 21, 46, 75, 76, 237, 279–80, 285–90, 307–8, 336–37
  and cosmology, 172
  for each cakra, 265*t*
  as musical syllables, 287–89, 288*t*
  in Sabhapati's works, 118, 134–36, 143, 147, 263
  for silent (*mauna*) recitation, 289–90
  for Śivarājayoga, 261–62
Mantrayoga. *See* yoga
Marathi. *See* languages, Indic
Markandeya (Mārkkaṇṭēyar), 79
mark(ed) body. See *liṅgaśarīra*
Marundeeswarar Temple, 168–69
maṭālayam (மடாலயம் meditation hall), 72–73, 74–75, 94–95, 154–55, 301*f*
materialism, 58, 155, 316–23
  Cārvaka, 217
  critique of, 217–24
  See also atheism
Mavalankar, Damodar, 62
māyā (माया illusion), 36, 123, 171
  as illusion of dualism, 197–98
  as impure water, 289–90
  in *māyāvātam* (Vedānta), 195–96
  power of, 191
  svarūpa of, 288*t*
  as tattva, 180, 182
  yogi as free of, 261–62
meditation. See *dhyāna*
meditation hall. See *maṭālayam*
Meenakshi Amman Temple, 263–64
Meikandadevar (Meykaṇṭatēvar), 45
memory, 171, 333
  See also "Forehead of Memory"
menstrual blood (red *bindu*), 251–52, 333
mental healing, 128, 372, 374–75
mesmerism, 61, 74, 82–83, 246–48, 266, 372
  See also *dīkṣā*
mesolocal, 6–10, 8*f*, 116, 389–90
Mexico, 360–61
Miller, Nancy Ann (convert), 374
miracles, 50, 57, 94–95
mirror stone (*sphaṭika*), 171
Mishra, Jwalaprasad, 9–10, 72, 134
missionaries, 4–5, 26–28, 53–54, 204–5, 215
  Hindu missionaries, 215, 374
Mitra Vilas Press, 56–57, 293–94
Modern Postural Yoga, 3–6, 313–14, 387
mokṣa (मोक्ष liberation), 63, 208
monism, 36, 48, 155–56
Moodelliar, M.S. Mooroogasa, 69, 85
Moodliar, M. Mooragasa, 70, 72, 74
Moodliar, M. Nagaruthanum, 69–70, 72, 134–36
moon, 68–69, 82–83, 262–63, 313–14
  made of green cheese, 67

Mortimer, William, 291–92
Mortimer's Manual of Anatomy, 291–92, 294–96
mountain ranges, eleven, 68
Mudaliar, Sri Sabhapati (Śrī Capāpati Mutaliyār), 80
mudrās (मुद्रा seals), 242–43, 242*t*
Muhammad, the Prophet. *See* Islam
mūlādhāra. *See* cakras
Müller, Friedrich Max, 1–2, 20–21, 57, 313–14
Mulraj, Lalla (Arya Samaj), 59–60
Mumbai. *See* cities and towns, India
music, 26, 127, 130–31, 194–95, 258–60, 266, 279–90, 370
Muslims. *See* Islam
Myanmar. *See* Burma
Mylapore. *See* cities and towns, India
Mysore. *See* cities and towns, India
mysticism, 5–6, 367–68

nāda (नाद sound), 46, 176, 193, 248, 307, 317–18, 320
of Om, 241–42, 288*t*
nāḍīs (नाडी channel), 182–83, 239–40, 241–43, 242*t*
iḍā, 182–83, 270–71, 368
piṅgalā, 182–83, 270–71, 368
suṣumnā, 180, 182–83, 239–40, 242, 261, 268–71, 315–16, 368
as *vāci*, 180
See also *kumbhaka-nāḍī*
Nagapattinam. *See* cities and towns, India.
Nagore Dargah, 31–33, 194–95, 207–8
See also Islam
Naguri, Shah al-Hamid (Shāh al-Ḥamīd Nagurī), 31–32, 207–8
See also Islam
Nair, Kasul (theosophist), 63
Nair, Raman. *See* Swamigal, Aanandha Aanandha
Ñāṉikaḷ (Gnostics). See *jñānīs*
Naṭēcamūrtti. *See* Shiva
Nāth Yogīs, 54–55, 194–95
Navaratri, 74–75
Nawab of the Deccan, story of, 262–63
Nayager, Mayilai Munisami, 74–75
Nayanar, Saangu S.S., 81
Nayanars (Nāyaṉmārkaḷ), 37, 283
negation (of thought), 340
Nepal, 48–49, 51
Neue Lotusbluthen (journal), 127–28
New Thought, 1–2, 128, 356–57, 372–75
New York City. *See* cities and towns, United States
Nilgiri (Blue Mountains), 40, 68, 70, 76–78, 80–81, 85–86, 392
niṣṭhā (steadfast). See samādhi
nitrogen, 220, 317–18, 320*t*, 321–22, 321*f*
"Nose of Ideas," 173*f*, 176
See also cakras
nyāsa (न्यास depositing mantras), 143, 283–84
Nyāya-Vaiśeṣika (philosophy), 319–22

Occidentalism(s), 2–3
occultism, 1, 5–6, 83–84, 121, 343–44, 356–57, 372, 387–88
See also magic
Olcott, Henry Steel (theosophist), 5–6, 23, 51–53, 57–64, 117–18, 136–38, 187–88, 214–158, 313–14, 356–57, 358–60, 361
and Sabhapati's diagram, 358
Oman, John Campbell (author), 64–66
citing Sabhapati, 65
and *séances*, 65
Om (syllable), 46, 178, 199, 248, 287–89, 288*t*, 317–18
Ooty. *See* cities and towns, India
Ordo Templi Orientis (O.T.O.), 370
orientalism(s), 33, 357–58
oxygen, 220, 317–18, 320*t*, 321–22, 321*f*

Page, Jimmy, 370
Pakistan, 51–52
Palestine, 207–8
paṇ (பண் musical mode), 284
Pandya 39
Papanasam. *See* cities and towns, India
Papavinasar Temple, 41
parables, 203
parai (பறை supreme), 183–84, 185, 196–97
paramātman (परमात्मन् Universal Spirit), 189–91, 190*f*, 203–4
See also *atman*; *jivātman*
paramparā (परम्परा line), 10–11, 21–22, 43*f*, 155–58, 163–67, 196–98, 258, 388

Parashara (Parāśara), 209–10
parasthāna. *See* cakras
parātpara-pīṭha. *See* cakras
Parliament of the World's Religions, 201–2, 215
parokṣajñāna (परोक्षज्ञान mediated gnosis), 34
Parsi. *See* Zoroastrianism
Parsons, Jack (rocket scientist), 370
Pashupatinath, 51
Pātañjalayoga, 34–35, 122, 241, 243, 246, 250–51, 263–64
  auxiliaries (*aṅga*) of, 243–45, 254
  and *svarūpa*, 303
Patañjali. *See* Pātañjalayoga
Patel, Jamsetjee Pestonjee (Sabhapati's address), 72
Patel, Jashabhai Bhailal Bhai (student of Om Prakash), 136–38
Paul, Nobin Chander (Nabīn Candra Pal), 321–22
perception. See *anubhūti*
phallicism, 366
phallic stone. See *liṅga*
picture poems (*cittirakkavi*), 80
"pipes". See *nāḍī*
pīṭha (पीठ seat), 175–76, 186
pizza effect, 6
Plato, 325
Plotinus, 325
"Poongees" (*poṅkikaḷ*). *See* Buddhism
post-Orientalism, 6–7
posture. See *āsana*
Pothigai Malai (Pothigai Hills). *See* Agastya Mala
pradoṣa (*piratōṣam*), 74–75
prakṛti (प्रकृति primal materiality), 181–82
prāṇa (प्राण vital breath), 46, 197, 242, 261–62, 270–71, 323, 327
prāṇākāśa, 180, 237, 258–60, 268, 321–22, 326, 327
prāṇāyāma (प्राणायाम control of vital breath), 239–40, 241, 245, 246–50, 251, 270–71, 321–22
  exhalation (*recaka*), 46, 241–42, 245, 270–71
  inhalation (*pūraka*), 46, 241–42, 245, 270–71
  retention (*kumbhaka*), 46, 245, 270–71
  seven kinds of, 248–50
  and six-phased yoga, 250
  three types of, 248
  See also yoga
Prarthana Samaj, 201–2
Pratyabhijñā school, 185
prayer, 118, 123, 212, 286–87
Priestly, Joseph (chemist), 321–22
principles. *See* tattva
Proclus, 325
Protestantism. *See* Christianity
pṛthivī (पृथिवी earth), 181
Psalms, 205–6
"Psychic Powers". See *siddhis*
psychology, 219–20
pūjā (पूजा worship rites), 38, 47, 79–80, 88–89, 284–85
  See also *mānasa pūjā*
pūjārī (पूजारी ritual specialist), 284–85
Pulastya Rishi, 142
Punjab University College, 59
Punyavathi (Sabhapati's mother), 25, 392
pūraka (inhalation). See *prāṇāyāma*
Puranas (*purāṇa*), 10–11
  sthala purāṇa 73–74
pure ethers. See *ākāśa*
pure Tamil (*centamiḻ*), 388–89
puruṣa (consciousness), 181–82
pyramid, 364

Quran, the. *See* Islam

raga. *See* Carnatic music
rāgadveṣa (passion/aversion), 265*t*
railway lines, 22–23, 24*f*, 73, 90–91, 389–90
Rajagopalam, T.K. (author), 119, 370–71
rāja yoga (royal yoga). *See* yoga
Raju, Narayanaswamy (singer), 279–81, 284–85
Ram, Lala Jhinda, 120
Ram, Pandit Mukund, 57, 293–94
Ramakrishna Mission, 84, 388
Ramanathan, Ponnambalam (solicitor-general), 366
Rangoon (Yangon), 203–4
Rao, Tukoji, 374

R.C. Bary & Sons (publisher), 61, 118, 120
recaka (exhalation). See *prāṇāyāma*
Reuss, Theodor (occultist), 366
rishi. See *ṛṣis*
Rishi, Mahatma Gotam. *See* Estep, William
Rishi, Shivajnana Bodha. *See* Yogishwarar, S. Shivajnana Bodha
ritual specialist (temples). See *pūjārī*
rocky pole, 263
Royal yoga for Śiva. *See* yoga
ṛṣis (ऋषि seers), 40, 42, 50–51, 62, 67–68, 142, 209, 329
Rutherford, Daniel, 321–22

"Sacred Books of the Hindus," 52–53
Sadāśiva. *See* Hindu deities and forms
sādhanā (साधना practice, also *sādhana*), 46, 143–46, 194–95, 260–61, 304–5
  Patañjali's *sādhanapāda*, 245
  of purification, 266–67
  singing after, 263
  of "six-phased yoga," 250
  and *svarūpa*, 304–5
Sadhguru (Jagadish Vasudev), 389
"Sadhuism," 64–66
sadhus, 43–44
  saṃnyāsī sādhus, 213
  service to, 393
sahasrāra. *See* cakras
Sahib, Kunangudi Masthan (Cākipu), 79
Śaiva Age, 155–58, 195–96
Śaivāgamas, 45
  and Shivajnana Bodha, 45
  thirty-six tattvas in, 169–70
  See also Śaiva Siddhānta
Śaiva Siddhānta, 20–21, 129, 155, 195–96, 209
  dualism of, 10–11, 157–58
  "equal flavor" with Vedānta, 129, 197
  in Sabhapati's works, 48, 129, 155
  states (*avasthā*) in, 253–54
  tattvas as "reality levels" in, 170
  as "Theism," 206–7
  "Vedanticization of," 197
sākṣin (साक्षिन् witness), 174, 202
  as brother and sister, 189–91, 190*f*
  of mind and sound, 189–91
  See also Four Brightnessess
Śākta (Goddess tradition), 20–21, 76, 168–69, 389
  and *dehatattva*, 194–95
  in Sabhapati's works, 263
  views in *Tirumantiram*, 168–69
Śakti. *See* Hindu deities and forms
śaktibhāg (शक्तिभाग division of Shakti), 186
samādhi (समाधि composure, communion, ecstasy), 4–5, 34–35, 42, 50, 87–88, 122, 154–55, 167, 238–39, 254–55
  and absorption (*laya*), 206, 286, 334
  as absence of qualities or powers, 334–35
  and *āsana*, 244
  attained by canceling cakras, 237–38
  as auxiliary of Pātañjalayoga, 245, 250–51
  Buddha alive in, 203–4
  as death (without dying), 84, 90*f*, 264–66
  female student depicted in, 282
  as flight, 360
  male student depicted in, 283
  and mantra, 289–90
  nirvikalpa, 202, 263, 394–95
  niṣṭhā (steadfast composure), 143, 145–46, 255–56, 267–68
  rāja yoga without, 254–55
  samādhipāda of Pātañjalayogaśāstra, 350n.59, 351n.75, 367–68
  in Sabhapati's diagrams, 127, 175*f*, 293–96, 295*f*
  as Śivarājayoga, 124, 240
  "Solemn State" of, 51–52
  and states (*avasthā*), 253–54
  as tree universally spread, 203, 260–61
  See also *jīvasamādhi*; *Pātañjalayoga*; yoga
samājīs (समाजी members of societies), 211–14
samarasa ("equal flavor"), 129, 197
saṃnyāsa (संन्यास renunciation), 36, 55–56
  of Sabhapati, 36, 213
  sannyasi sadhus, 213
Sanjivi, T.R. (occultist), 83–84

Sāṅkhya (Sāṃkhya, philosophy), 155, 180–83, 393
ākāśa (ether) in, 325–26, 327
and Puruṣa, 303
Sāṅkhyakārikā, 303
sense capacities in, 333–34
subordination of, 170, 323
and *svarūpa*, 303
tanmātras of, 184
tattvas of, 169–70, 180–82, 192, 194, 303
tripartite internal instrument in, 198–99
See also Pātañjalayoga; Śaiva Siddhānta; tattvas
Sanskrit. *See* languages, Indic
Sanskrit texts
Amaraughaprabodha (अमरौघप्रबोध), 238
**Amṛtakuṇḍa* (अमृतकुण्ड), 32
Amṛtasiddhi (अमृतसिद्धि), 240–41, 251
Aṣṭādhyāyī (अष्टाध्यायी), 52–53, 57
Bhagavadgītā (भगवद्गीता), 127–28, 334–35, 336–37, 352n.77, 361–62
Bhāgavata Purāṇa (भागवत पुराण), 39, 182, 194
Brahmasūtra (ब्रह्मसूत्र), 238
Dattatreyayogaśāstra (दत्तत्रेययोगशास्त्र), 240–41
Gorakṣaśataka (गोरक्षशतक), 182
Haṭhapradīpikā (हठप्रदीपिका), prev. *Haṭha Yoga Pradīpikā*, 246, 247*t*, 367–68
Kubjikāmatatantra (कुब्जिकामततन्त्र), 182
Mālinīvijayottaratantra (मालिनीविजयोत्तरतन्त्र), 170
Netratrantra (नेत्रत्रन्त्र), 296
Niśvāsatattvasaṃhitā (निश्वासतत्त्वसंहिता), 170, 182
Saṅgītaratnākara (संगीतरत्नाकर), 285
Sāṅkhyakārikā (सांख्यकारिका), 303
Sārdhatriśatikālottara (सार्धत्रिशतिकालोत्तर), 182
Sekoddeśaṭīkā (सेकोद्देशटीका), 250
Siddhasiddhāntapaddhati (सिद्धसिद्धान्तपद्धति), 182
Śivasaṃhitā (*Śiva Saṃhitā* शिवसंहिता), 55–56, 182, 367–68
Śivasvarodaya (शिवस्वरोदय), 120, 367–68
Śivayogapradīpikā (शिवयोगप्रदीपिका ŚYP), 196–98, 238, 243, 247*t*
Tattvabodha (तत्त्वबोध), 127–28, 361–62
Yogabīja (योगबीज), 182
Yogavāsiṣṭha (योगवासिष्ठ), 171
See also Dharmaśāstras; Mahābhārata; Upanishads
Saraswati, Dayananda (reformer), 52–53, 55–56, 63–64, 211, 214, 358
Sarveśvarī. *See* Hindu deities and forms
śāstra (शास्त्र scripture, "science"), 67
as science or philosophy, 322–23
Sathuragiri, 40, 386
and Siddhas, 41, 194–95
Scheele, Carl Wilhelm (chemist), 321–22
scholars and authors, contemporary
Baier, Karl, 6, 56, 357–58
Bharati, Agehananda, 6
Bhattacharya, Upendranath, 304–5
Birch, Jason, 10–11
Bouthillette, Karl-Stéphan, 201–2
Chajes, Julie, 220–21
De Michelis, Elizabeth, 3–6, 254, 331
Deveney, Patrick, 216
Djurdjevic, Gordan, 5–6
Ezhilraman, R., 164–66
Fisher, Elaine, 10–11
Halbfass, Wilhelm, 201–2
Harder, Hans 194
Leland, Kurt, 387–88
Malinar, Angelika, 263–64
Obrist, Barbara, 292
Padoux, André, 178, 185
Powell, Seth, 247*t*
Raman, Srilata, 10–11, 158, 257–58
Ros, Alejandra, 7
Sanderson, Alexis, 155–56, 195–96, 284–85
Shearer, Alistair, 4–5
Singleton, Mark, 52–53
Steinschneider, Eric, 10–11, 157–60, 183–84, 196–97
Urban, Hugh, 6
Venkatraman, R., 164–66, 258
Weiss, Richard, 164–66
White, David Gordon, 67–68, 164–66
Zvelebil, Kamil, 164–66

science, 48, 120, 167, 314–23
  Cosmic Yogi, 128
  J.C. Oman and, 64–65
  occult, 62, 118
  and phenomena, 316–23
  of samādhi, 356
  spiritual, 62–63
  Super Mind, 372–75
  and yoga, 329–44
  See also "Western pandits"
seed-syllables (*bīja*). *See* mantra
semen (white *bindu*), 251–52, 333
  of females, 251–52
Sen, Babu Narendra Nath (journalist), 58
Sen, Kehubchandra (reformer), 331
sense faculties. See *indriyas*
serpent, 168–69, 268–71, 328–29, 356
  ākāśa rising like a, 268–70, 328–29
  buddhi as serpentess, 190*f*, 192, 199
  See also *kuṇḍalinī*
Serpent Power, The, 182–83, 268–70
sex
  as interplay of *liṅga* and *yoni*, 364
  sexual rites, 166–67
  temporary bliss of, 251–53
Shakti (Śakti). *See* Hindu deities and forms
shaligram (fossil sacred to Vishnu), 72–73, 74
Shankaracharya (Śaṅkarācārya), 20–21, 119, 127–28, 254
  and *ākāśa*, 326
Shanmuga Vilasa Press, 145–46
Shastras. See *śāstra*
Shishyanath (Ciṣṣiyanāt), 69–70
Shiva (Śiva). *See* Hindu deities and forms
Shivanath (Nāth Yogī), 54–55, 56
Shivaratri (*civarāttiri*), 141, 284–85
Shroff, Muncherjee M (librarian), 71
Shuka (Śuka, rishi), 50
Siddhan, Paramaguruyogi, 42, 394–95
Siddhānta. *See* Śaiva Siddhānta
Siddhas (Cittarkaḷ), 10–11, 30–31, 40, 44–45, 68, 86–87, 154–55, 163–67, 257–58, 304–5
  Agastya as guru of, 81–82, 142–43, 163–64
  disappearance into *liṅga*, 263–64
  and Māṇikkavācakar, 280–81
  nature assocated with, 41
  Om Prakash and, 83–84
  Sabhapati's connection to, 156–57, 163–67
  Shivajnana Bodha and, 163–67
  and Śivarājayoga, 257–60
  songs of, 79, 280–81
  Thayumanavar and, 10
  troops of (*cittarkaṇam*), 81–82, 167
  visual depiction of, 290–91
Siddhi River, 42–43
siddhis (special powers), 46, 47–48, 50, 262–63
  Blavatsky having, 62–63
  claims of, 313–14
  connected to Śivarājayoga, 257
  and haṭha yoga, 240–41
  mental cultivation of, 308
  See also *aṣṭasiddhi*
silent mantra-recitation (*maunajapadhyāna*), 289–90
singing, 81–82, 266, 280–81, 283–85
  and mantra, 285–87
  at Sabhapati's meditation hall, 283–85
  See also music
Sinnett, Alfred Percy, 58
Śiva Saṃhitā. *See* Sanskrit texts
śivabhāg (शिवभाग division of Shiva), 186
śivamaya (शिवमय consisting of Shiva), 172, 206–7
  and Christianity, 206
  as both masculine and feminine, 289
  similar to *civam*, 196–97, 289
Sivananda, Swami, 119
Sivarahasyam Press P.T., 145–46
Śivayoga. *See* yoga
Śivayogapradīpikā (ŚYP), 196–98
  āsanas shared with Sabhapati, 247*t*
  and non-dual unity with Shiva's *liṅga*, 196–98
  and Pātañjalayoga, 243
  tetrad of yogas in, 238
  See also Śaiva Siddhānta; Sanskrit texts; Siddhas; Vedānta
six-phased yoga, 250
  See also *prāṇāyāma*
six stages (*ṣaṭsthala*), 257–58
  See also Vīraśaivism
Sixteen Rays (*ṣoḍaśa īśvarakalāṃśa*), 173*f*, 174

skull, 133–34, 172, 179*t*, 223
as magnet, 241
being penetrated by *kāraṇa vāyu*, 242
See also *brahmarandhra*; See also *kāraṇa vāyu*
Socrates, 325
sorcery (*Hexerei*), 360–61
See also magic
soteriology, Śaiva, 156–58, 257–58
soul. See *ātman*
source amnesia, 84
space. See *ākāśa*
Spencer, Herbert, 127, 220–21, 335
First Principles, 338
spine, 260–61, 356
kuṇḍali at base of, 315–16
in "Liber HHH," 356
physical and spiritual, 270–71
and "psychic development," 358–59
spirits
of higher faculties (cakras) creating elements, 221
as parts of deities (*devatāṃśa*), 289–90
spiritualism, 61
Oman and *séances*, 65
as opposite of materialism, 155
Spirituality. See *brahmajñāna*
Sri Lanka. *See* Ceylon
Sri Sabhapathy Lingeshwarar Koil, 91, 92*f*, 93–95
liṅga of, 94–95, 95*f*, 264–66
Śrīsatsampāṣiṇi. *See* Swamigal, Om Prakash
śruti (श्रुति listening, sacred knowledge), 322–23
as "science," 48
stambhana (स्तम्भन fixing, arresting), 46, 242–43, 242*t*
See also *prāṇāyāma*
Stele of Jeu, the, 364–66
See also magic
stemmas (of Sabhapati's works)
alpha (English-Sanskrit), 117–28
beta (Hindustani), 130–32, 134–38
gamma (Tamil), 132–34, 138–47
sthūlaśarīra (स्थूलशरीर physical body), 184–85, 294
ākāśa in, 325–26
maṭhākāśa in, 326, 327
Strange Story, A, 65–66
substance (*dravya*), 332
subtle body. See *liṅgaśarīra*
śuddhākāśa (pure ethers). *See ākāśa*
śuddhi (शुद्धि purification), 134–36, 265*t*, 297*f*
as cancelation of cakras, 263
of internal organ, 199
mantras for, 265*t*
and Śivarājayoga, 266–67
Sufism. *See* Islam
Sukul, Deva Ram, 374–75
sūkṣmaśarīra (सूक्ष्मशरीर subtle body), 126–27, 182, 184–85, 270–71
in Bengali, 126–27, 294
and *gaṭākāśa*, 326–27
and subtle *ākāśa*, 326
sūkṣma vāyu, 241–42
See also *liṅgaśarīra*; *svarūpa*
sun, 139–41
embracing in *liṅgasvarūpa*, 262–63, 313–14
Infinite Spirit as, 171
piercing the orb of the, 209
Sundaram, Seetharaman, 389–90
Super Mind Science, 128, 372–75
See also Estep, William
suṣumnā. See *nāḍī*
svādhiṣṭhāna. *See* cakras
svaras (स्वर tones), 284, 285–89
of Om, 287, 288*t*
vedasvara, 284
See also music; singing
svarūpa (inherent form), 59, 177*f*, 302–9
and absolute *siddhi* of yoga, 257
in Bengali Tantra, 304–5
and *bhāvanā*, 307–8
as bliss (*svarūpānanda*), 142
of Brahman, 38, 213
in BRY, 304
of deities, 303–4
and devotion (*bhakti*), 214
and elemental expansion, 220
and fifteen purifications, 308
of the *liṅga*, 185, 262–63, 264–66, 294, 303–4
and *nāmarūpa*, 305
in Pātañjalayoga, 303
of physical and subtle *vāyu*, 241–42
of the self, 213

svarūpa (inherent form) (*cont.*)
  seven or eight spiritual states, 176–78, 220, 306–7, 306*f*
  sounds and syllables of, 287, 288*t*
  and the syllable Om, 287–89
  in the three channels, 242–43, 242*t*
  of "12 Spiritual Lights," 174
  of unity, 213–14
  See also Pātañjalayoga
śvāsa (श्वास breath), 46, 250
  and absorption, 308
  binding of, 239
  dissolution of mind and, 239–40
  prāṇāyāma for, 251
  shape of appearance, 317–18
  svarūpa of subtle, 307, 318–19, 320*t*
  See also *prāṇāẏāma*; prāṇā
svayambhū mahāliṅga (स्वयम्भू महालिङ्ग self-manifesting great phallus), 41, 263–64
Swami, Murugesa (of Konnur), 85–86, 92–93, 141–42
Swami, Satyananda. *See* Shiv Narayan Agnihotri
Swami, Sri Muthukrishna, 260
Swami, Sri Sabhapati
  and Franz Hartmann, 360–62
  and Aleister Crowley, 362–72
  and Shrish Chandra Basu, 52–64
  and William Estep, 372–75
  as Arootpa Moorti (அருட்பா மூர்த்தி), 26
  as Guru Father Rishi (குருபிதா ருஷி), 43*f*, 50–51
  as Guru Yogi of Gnosis (ஞானகுரு யோகீஸ்வர), 50
  at Agastya's hermitage, 39–47
  birth, 23
  Brahmin heritage, 25–26
  death, 94–95
  dream-vision in Velachery, 34–39
  flight to Kailāsa, 50–51
  "Garland Hymn of Mercy," 39
  "Garland of Praise for Shiva," 280
  in Bombay, 71–72
  Konnur Meditation Hall, 72–76
  meeting Blavatsky and Olcott, 60–63
  parents, 25
  renunciation, 36–37
  T1, 21
  T2, 21–22
  Ur-account, 20–21
  vision of Agaysta, 66–71
Swami, Sri Sabhapati (published works), 116–17, 117*f*
  Aṭukkunilai pōtam (அடுக்குநிலை போதம் AP), 74–75, 142–43
  Bedāntadarśan o rājayog (বেদান্তদর্শন ও রাজযোগ BRY), 126–27
  Cakālākama tiraṭṭu (சகாலாகம திரட்டு CĀT), 74–75, 139–42
  Carvōpatēsa…vētapōtam (சர்வோபதேச…வேதபோதம் CTCSPV), 132–34
  Cātana…upatēcam (சாதன…உபதேசம் CU), 75
  Cosmic…Science (CPSPS), 120–22, 130–32
  Esoteric Cosmic Yogi Science (WE), 128
  Die Philosophie … Rāja-Yoga (FH1, FH2, FH3)
  Mantira…smiruti (மந்திர…ஸ்மிருதி MCVTS), 145–46
  Rājayoga…veda (राजयोग…वेद RYB), 134–38
  Sarva…anubhava (SVSAA), 143–44
  Secret of Longevity and Verses, 58
  Om… Vedantic Raj Yoga (VRY1), 117–20
  The Philosophy…Raja Yoga (VRY2), 118–20
  Om: The Philosophy…Raja Yoga (VRY3), 120
Swamigals, from Siddhas to, 250
Swamigal, Aanandha Aanandha (Konnur Ramalinga's student), 22–23, 86–87, 91–92, 94–95
Swamigal, Chidambara Periya. *See* Swamigal, Vedashreni Chidambara
Swamigal, Chidambara Ramalinga, 49, 389
  meeting with Sabhapati, 397
Swamigal, P.P.R. Hariharan (Aanandha Aanandha's student), 86–87
Swamigal, Konnur Ramalinga (Sabhapati's student), 19, 21–23, 84–94, 89*f*, 90*f*

Swamigal, Kuvalattu, 160
Swamigal, Mylapore Kuzhandaivel (Kuḻantaivēl Cuvāmikaḷ), 30–31, 158–62, 163*f*
Swamigal, Muttaiya, 160, 163*f*
Swamigal, Om Prakash (Sabhapati's student), 22, 77–84, 388–89
  author of *Śrīsatsampāṣiṇi*, 22, 372
  hermitage of, 21, 84, 85, 133, 136–38, 144, 159–60, 296–99, 388
  member of Latent Light Culture, 356–57
  practitioner of haṭha yoga, 250
  and Sargurunathar Swamigal, 260
Swamigal, Pazhani, 160
Swamigal, Perur Santhalinga (Pērūr Cāntaliṅka Cuvāmikaḷ), 30–31, 83–84, 158–60
  author of *Vairākya Catakam* and *Vairākya Tīpam*, 159–60
  books read by Sabhapati's student, 159–60
Swamigal, Puliyur, 160
Swamigal, Retty Chidambara, 160
Swamigal, Sri Sabhapati. *See* Swami, Sri Sabhapati
Swamigal, Sadhu. *See* Swamigal, Om Prakash
Swamigal, Sargurunathar (Caṟkurunāta Cuvāmikaḷ), 260
Swamigal, Sri Suparna, 83
Swamigal, Thiruporur Chidambara (Tiruppōrūr Citambara Cuāmikaḷ), 30–31
  confusion with Vedashreni Chidambara, 158–59
Swamigal, Thuraiyur Sivaprakasa, 160
Swamigal, Vedashreni Chidambara (Vētacirēṇi Citambara Cuvāmikaḷ), 19, 21–22, 23–26, 29–31, 30*f*, 36, 37–39, 158–62, 164*f*, 204–5
  author of *Upatēca uṇmai*, 158–60, 393
  confusion with Thiruporur Swamigal, 158–59
  death of, 30–31, 94
  engagement with *tanmātra*s, 184
  in *paramparā* of Kumara Devar, 159–60
  and Pātañjalayoga, 243
student of Kuzhandaivel Swamigal, 158–59
  as Swamigal, 258
  as Veeraswamy Swamigal, 158–59
  Vīraśaiva leanings of, 82–83
Swamigal, Veeraswamy. *See* Swamigal, Vedashreni Chidambara
Swamigal, Vinayagam (son of Hariharan), 87–89, 91–92, 264–66
Symonds, John (author), 387–88

taca kāriyam. *See* Ten Acts
Tamil. *See* languages, Indic
Tamil Nadu. *See* lands of India
Tamil Nadu Archives, 21, 22–23, 92–93, 139–41, 142–43, 147
Tamil texts
  Attuvitavuṉmai (அத்துவிதவுண்மை), 159–60
  Cāstirakkōvai (சாஸ்திரக்கோவை), 159–62, 161*f*
  "Cittarkaṇam" (of Tāyumāṉavar), 167
  Civañāṉacittiyār (சிவஞானசித்தியார்), 158
  Civañāṉapōtam (சிவஞா்னபோதம்), 45
  Civāṉantapōtam (சிவானந்தபோதம்), 79
  "Civapurāṇam" (சிவபுராணம்), 280–81
  Cuttacātakam (சுத்த சாதகம்), 159–60
  Makārājātuṟavu (மகாராஜாதுறவு), 159–60
  Oḻiviloṭukkam (ஒழிவிலொடுக்கம்), 195–97
Tirumantiram (திருமந்திரம்) 35, 142–43, 155–57, 163–64, 166, 168–69, 182, 184–85)
  Tiruvācakam (திருவாசகம்), 280–81
  Tukaḷaṟupōtam (துகளறுபோதம்), 183–84
  Uṇmaineṟiviḷakkam (உண்மைநெறிவிளக்கம்), 183–84
  Vairākya Catakam (வைராகிய சதகம்), 83–84, 159–60
  Vairākya Tīpam (வைராகிய தீபம்), 83–84, 159–60
*tanmātra*s (तन्मात्र subtle elements), 181, 184, 192
  of *ākāśa*, 326, 327–28
  in Sāṅkhya, 181
Tantras. *See* Sanskrit texts
Tantric Buddhism. *See* Buddhism
Tantric yoga, 182–83, 266–67, 366–67
  See also yoga

tapas (तपस् asceticism, heat), 32–33, 75, 240–41, 244, 245, 392
of Agastya, 163–64
Tāraka Yoga. *See* yoga
tatparasthāna. *See* cakras
tattva (तत्त्व principle, faculty), 142, 155, 167–70, 178, 212, 218–20
as body's truth (*dehatattva*), 188–95
canceling as Śivarājayoga, 263
conquest of principles, (*tattvajaya*), 170
dissolution of, 196–97, 206–7
ether as *taijas*, 323–24
and form (*rūpa*), 305, 308
generative fluid as source of, 251–52
gnosis of principles (*tattvajñāna*), 36, 261–62, 287–89, 304, 329
in Hermetic Order of Golden Dawn, 367–68
highest principle (*param-tattva*), 304–5
including cakras, 180, 237
innovations on, 184
link with vital breath, 261–62
and mantra/music, 286–90
as "reality levels," 170
removing doubts of, 172, 186
Sabhapati's thirty-two, 180, 318–19
in Śaiva Siddhānta, 170, 182
in Sāṅkhya, 169–70, 180–82, 192, 194, 303
of the self, 341
vision of, 46
Western pandits and, xvi
Tattvavicecak Press, 72, 134
Tatya, Tookaram (Tukaram) 254–56
Telugu. *See* languages, Indic
"Temple of Solomon the King," 367–68
See also A.·.A.·.
Ten Acts (*daśakārya*), 183–84
Tengra-Bhavanipur. *See* cities and towns, Bangladesh
Thamirabirani (Tāmiraparaṇi) river, 39–47
Thayumanavar (Tāyumāṉavar), 257–58, 280–81
"Theism," 197–98, 206–7
See also Śaiva Siddhānta
Thelema, 1–2, 5–6, 362–57, 387
global context of, 370
metaphysics of, 368–70
Ordo Templi Orientis, 370
See also A.·.A.·.; Aleister Crowley; magic
Theosophical Society, 1–2, 4–6, 20–22, 56–57, 58–59, 67, 71, 118, 119, 126–27, 201–2, 208, 214–16, 245–46, 324, 356–57, 358–60, 361, 387
and *ākāśa*, 324, 328–29
and astral travel, 216, 358–59
Bombay branch, 71
Esoteric Section of, 361
initiations of Indians into, 63–64
Lahore branch, 64
Le Disciple Branch (Paris), 358
Meerut branch, 324
and mesmerism, 246–48
no record of Sabhapati joining, 9, 33
refashioning modern yoga, 48, 254, 255–56
Rishis as Brothers of, 62
and rival Hermetic Brotherhoods, 71–72
Sabhapati and, 4–5, 9, 63, 214–16, 324
S.C. Basu member of, 52–53, 211, 324
Theosophical World University, 136–38
as translocal network, 9
Youth Lodge in Bombay, 134–36
See also Basu, Shrish Chandra; Blavatsky, Helena Petrovna; Olcott, Henry Steel
Theosophist, The, 20–21, 56–57, 58, 63, 67, 120, 361
Theosophy, 4–7, 8*f*, 63–64, 155, 214–16, 238, 324, 358–60
contemporary Theosophists, 360
Indian Theosophists, 58–59, 61–62, 64, 203, 324
Sabhapati's endorsement of, 58–59, 62–63
and Sabhapati's universalism, 216
Thirugnana Sambandaṛ (Tiruñāṉa Cambantar), 37
"Throat of Intellects," 173*f*, 176
See also cakras
Tiger Hill Cave (புலிக்குகை), 83–84

Tirumantiram (of Tirumūlar), 34–35, 142–43, 155–57, 163–64, 166, 168–69, 182, 184–85
animals in, 192–93
āsana in, 246, 247*t*
association with Śivarājayoga, 258
body as *liṅga* in, 185
four (or five) stages in, 34–35
golden awakening (*pōṟpōtam*) in, 408n.2
and Kashmir, 293–94
Pātañjalayoga in, 243, 245–48
See also Tamil texts
"Tongue of Conscience" (*viśuddhi*), 173*f*, 176. *See also* cakras
trance, 82–83, 121, 223, 251–52, 293–94
See also samādhi
translation, 1–2, 4–5, 10, 20–21, 25–26, 114–53
translocalization, 6–11
transmigration, 186–88, 189*f*
tree (universally spread), 1, 203, 260–61
Trika Śaivism, 183–84
Triloknath, 51
Trinity, the. *See* Christianity
Tulsilinga. *See* Swamigal, Om Prakash
tumulus. See *jīvasamādhi*
Twelve Faculties. *See* cakras
Twelve Kingdoms. *See* cakras
Twelve Spiritual Lights. *See* cakras
twenty-two syllables (of Om), 287–89

Udhagamandalam. *See* cities and towns, India
United States of America
Colorado, 360–61
Kentucky, 53
Missouri, 116, 128, 372
Texas, 360–61, 375
Virginia, 373
Washington State (Seattle), 374–75
West Virginia, 373, 374–75
Universal Church, 216
Universal Spirit. *See śivamaya*
Upanishads (Upaniṣad), 33, 46–47, 155, 168–69, 182, 361–62
Bṛhaddāraṇyaka Upaniṣad (बृहद्दारण्यक उपनिषद्), 182
Kaṭha Upaniṣad (कठ उपनिषद्), 182
Maṇḍalabrāhmaṇopaniṣad (मण्डलब्राह्मणोपनिषद्), 370–71
Māṇḍūkyopaniṣat (माण्डूक्योपनिषत्), 326
"Yoga Upanishads," 155, 238, 370–71
Upatēca uṇmai (Instructive Truth). *See* Swamigal, Vedashreni Chidambara
Ur-account. *See* Swami, Sri Sabhapati
Urdu. *See* languages, Indic

vāci (breath, pipe). See *nāḍī*
Vaiṣṇava, 7–8, 20–21, 39, 76, 91, 143, 157–58, 304–5, 337
Vaḷḷal, Kaṇṇuṭaiya, 183–84
varṇa (वर्ण caste), 25–26, 32
equal worship for every, 47
Vasu, Siris Chandra. *See* Basu, Shrish Chandra
Vātāpi (daemon), 73–74
vāyu (वायु wind), 181, 241–43
kāraṇavāyu, 242–43
ten yogic, 242
Veda Deva Rishee (Vedadevarṣi), 209
Veda Dhatha (Vedadatta), 209
Vedanta (Vedānta), 10–11, 29, 34–35, 48, 84, 129, 154–58, 171, 197–98
Vedashreni (Vētacirēṇi). *See* cities and towns, India
Vedashreni Swayambhu (temple), 37, 37*f*
Vedha Dhesa (Vedadeśa), 209
Velachery. *See* cities and towns, India
vernacular, 1–7
vibhūti (विभूति ash), 94–95
Victorian naturalist worldview, 308, 314–16
videhamukti (विदेहमुक्ति disembodied liberation), 263–64
Videha Purī, 209
Villivakkam. *See* cities and towns, India
Vinayaga Chaturthi, 74–75, 79
Vinayagar. *See* Hindu deities
Vīramaheśvaras. *See* Vīraśaivism
Vīraśaivism, 10–11, 30–31, 34–35, 82–84, 94–95, 154–58, 183–85, 195–200
six stages (*ṣaṭsthala*) in, 257–58
tattvas in Tamil, 183–85
Vishnu (Viṣṇu). *See* Hindu deities and forms

visions. See *darśana*
viśuddhi. *See* cakras
Vivekananda, Swami, 1–2, 5–6, 48, 58, 84, 126–28, 182–83, 215, 217, 220–21, 246–48, 255–56, 316–17
  and *ākāśa*, 324, 328–29
  engaged by Aleister Crowley, 365*f*, 367–68
  engaged by Franz Hartmann, 361–62
  and four yogas, 331
  haṭha and rāja yoga, 254
V.N. Press, 143
void (பாழ் *pāḻ*), 142
vyāpaka (व्यापक pervading "consciousness"), 174, 202, 223–24
  See also Four Brightnesses
Vyasa Rishi (Vyāsa Ṛṣi), 203–4, 209

Waddell, Leila (occultist/musician), 370
Wadiyar IV, Krishna Raja, 80–81
Wadiyar X, Chamarajendra, 80–81
Wallace, Chandos Leigh Hunt, 120
waterfalls, 41, 44–45
Western pandits (পাশ্চাত্য পণ্ডিতগণ), 329, 331–32, 333, 335, 337–38, 339, 341, 343–44
will (philosophy), 335–36, 339
  See also willpower
willpower (*icchāśakti*), 343
winter solstice (சங்கிராந்தி), 74–75
witness, the. See *sākṣin*
women
  performing *sādhan*, 266–67
  in occult movements, 5–6, 387–88
  as students of Sabhapati, 263
  trekking Agastya Mala, 40
Woodroffe, John, 182–83, 268–70
worldly divisions, 187

Yama (god of death). *See* Hindu deities and forms
yama (restraint). *See* Pātañjalayoga
Yamuna (river), 42–43, 51
yoga (union, yoking, samādhi)
  dhyānayoga, 331
  Haṭha Rājayoga (ஹட ராஜயோகம்), 238, 239–40, 250–56
haṭha yoga (yoga of force), 2–3, 10–11, 56, 80, 84, 154, 238–39
  Haṭha Yoga (அடயோகம்), 238, 239, 240–50
  Layayoga, 238, 257–58
  Mantrayoga, 238
  Pātañjalayoga, 243, 246, 250–51
rāja yoga, 1–3, 10–11, 26, 65, 126–27, 238–39, 254–56, 329–31, 360–61, 366–67
  seven methods of Śivarājayoga, 266–67
  Śivarājayoga (சிவராஜயோகம்), 45–46, 238, 240, 256–71
  śivayoga, 240, 257–58
  synonyms for Śivarājayoga, 257
  Tāraka Yoga, 370–71
  tetrad of in ŚYP, 238
  three branches of, 76, 238–40
  Vedāntic Rajayoga, 257–58
  See also *asana*; *Pātañjalayoga*; *prāṇāyāma*; *samādhi*
Yoga Upanishads. *See* Sanskrit texts
Yogi, Shivajnana, 45
"Yogi's Address to His Countrymen," 58
Yoginath, Nagaratna (Sabhapati's student), 69–70
Yoginath, Murugesa (Sabhapati's student), 69–70
Yogindra. *See* Swamigal, Om Prakash
Yogiraj, Swami Rankaradas, 374
Yogishwara, Shivajnanaprakash, 23–25, 39
Yogishwarar, Shivajnana Bodha (Sabhapati's guru), 21–22, 42–43, 43*f*, 45–47, 50–51, 155–56, 163–67, 164*f*, 260, 283–84
yoni (vagina, perineum), 364–66
  as cavity of the brain, 370
  of stone *liṅga*, 186
Yorke, Gerald J., 366–67, 387–88
yuga (युग age), 206–7

Zoroaster, 202, 209
Zoroastrianism ("Parsism"), 201–2, 203, 208–10
  Ahuras/Yazatas, 210
  Avesta (sacred texts), 209
  Daevas as demons in, 210
  Zend (commentaries), 209